# THE BIG CATS

Newly Revised Edition by Herbert S. Zim

illustrations by Dot Barlowe

William Morrow and Company [redacted]
New York 1976

Printed in the United States of America.
1 2 3 4 5 6 7 8 9 10

Library of Congress Cataloging in Publication Data

Zim, Herbert Spencer
The big cats.

1. Felidae—Juvenile literature. I. Barlowe, Dorothea. II. Title.
QL737.C23Z55 1976 599'.74428 76-819
ISBN 0-688-32072-4 lib. bdg.

The author gratefully acknowledges the help of Donald Hoffmeister, Museum of Natural History, University of Illinois, Urbana, Illinois, and Carol Porter McClintock, Division of Biological Sciences, and Betsy Hodgson, both of Cornell University, Ithaca, New York, for obtaining elusive data, checking text and illustrations.

Metric measure, now used the world over, is also used in this book. Lengths and distances are based on the meter (m); 100 centimeters (cm) make one meter and 1000 meters make one kilometer (km). Weights are in kilograms (kg), and temperatures are in degrees Celsius (°C). A meter is just under 40 inches, a kilometer is 0.6 miles, a kilogram equals 2.2 pounds, and 100 degrees Celsius is the same as 212 degrees Fahrenheit.

leopard

Lions, tigers, and other big cats are the most powerful of all hunting animals. Their strength, speed, and cunning assure their success whether they hunt alone or together. Found in snowy mountains, tropical forests, and grasslands, big cats are admired and feared. No wonder that to praise a man we say he has the courage of a lion, he is as tough as a tiger, or he can lick his weight in wildcats.

Because of their reputation, the big cats are a challenge to man. Hunting lions and tigers became a ritual and a sport. A young Masai warrior could prove himself a man by killing a lion single-handedly. Wealthy sportsmen from distant places hunted the same beasts with much less risk. They took trophies back to hang on their walls and amaze their friends.

Lions and tigers have always been a circus attraction. The animal trainer shows his skill and courage by putting them through their paces. Cats are not easy to train, but they learn to sit, jump, and respond to simple commands. Yet a circus is not the place for big cats. They must live in small barred cages that limit their movements. Once the capture of big cats and other animals for the circus or zoo was a standard practice. Now the trade is controlled and sometimes stopped entirely.

Cats belong to a large group of flesh-eating animals—the carnivores. All are strong and active. Their feet have four or five toes with curved claws. The sharp points or edges of their teeth are fine for cutting and tearing. Carnivores include seven families: dogs, cats, bears, raccoons, hyenas, weasels, and civets. Those most closely related to cats seem to be the hyenas and the civets.

CARNIVORE FAMILIES

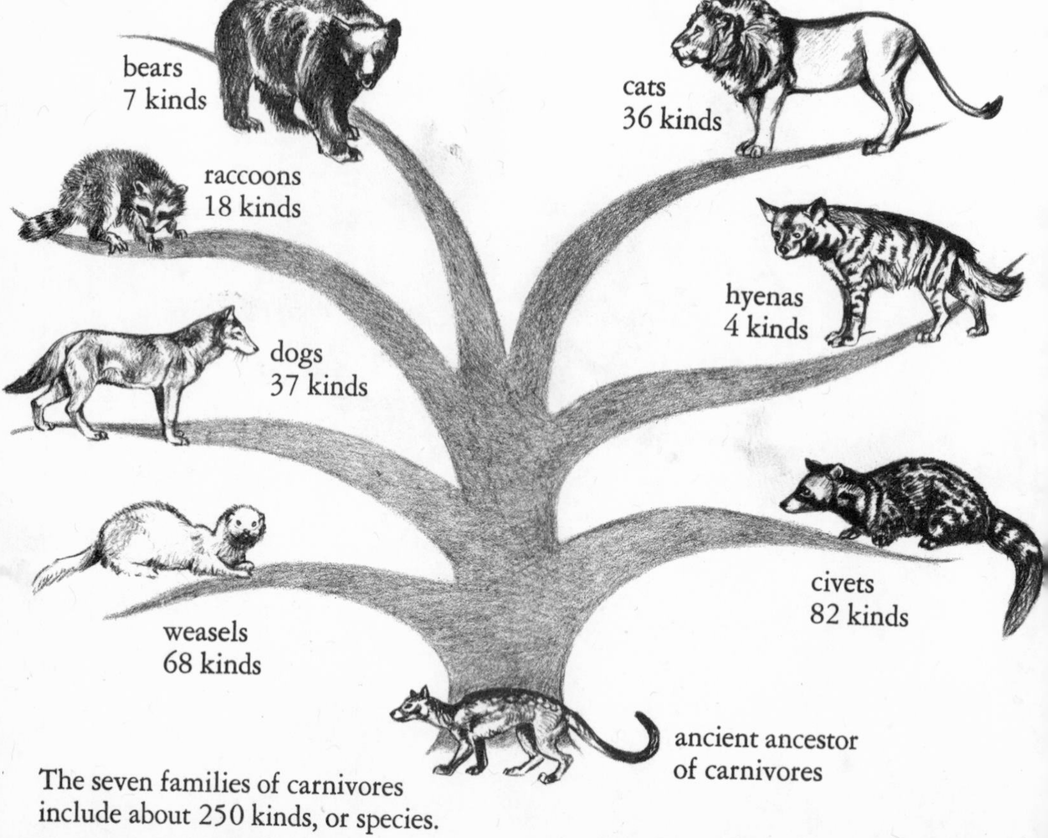


The seven families of carnivores include about 250 kinds, or species.

Not all carnivores are hunters.

Black bears eat berries.

Giant pandas eat bamboo.

Jackals eat dead animals.

Raccoons eat frogs.

In spite of their name, carnivores are not all hunters and flesh eaters. Pandas live only on plant food. A bear's diet includes fruits and berries. The big cats hunt their prey and usually feed on the fresh kill. But even they eat a bit of plant food now and then. No one is sure why. Jackals are flesh eaters too, but they are scavengers, feeding mainly on dead animals.

Cats are not a large family. Only about forty kinds are known. Members of the cat family resemble one another closely. Even the smaller cats have much in common with lions, tigers, and leopards. Other families of backboned animals are much larger and include many more kinds, or species.

THE NUMBER OF SPECIES IN FIVE MAMMAL FAMILIES.

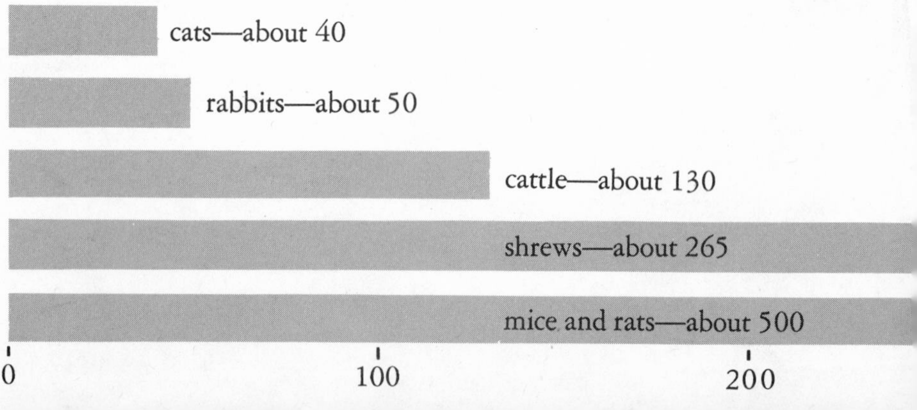

All members of the cat family are very much alike.

The forty or so species of cats fall into three major groups. The first includes lions, tigers, jaguars, and leopards. They are the only ones that can roar. The second is made up of a very singular cat—the cheetah. The third takes in all the other cats, and only one of them, the cougar, is large. What we call big cats are those in the first two groups plus the cougar. How big are big cats? Most weigh from 50 to 200 kilograms.

Among all animals, cats are a small family.

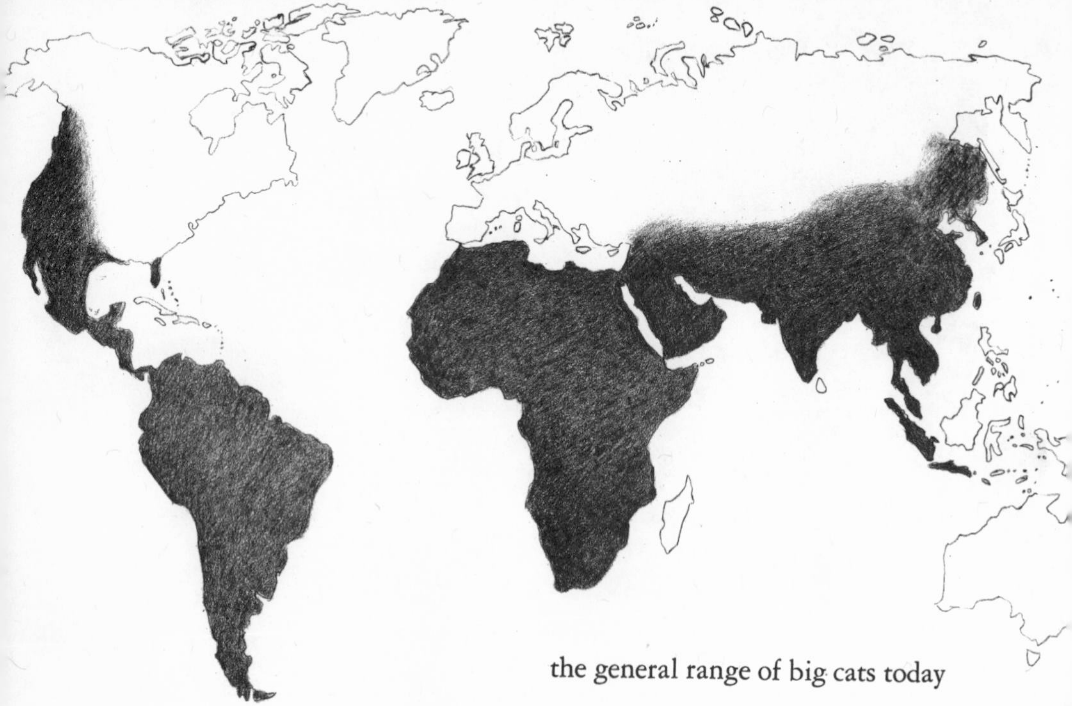

the general range of big cats today

Big cats are found the world over except in Australia, New Zealand, Madagascar, and in the Arctic and Antarctic. They seem to be just as much at home in the snows of Siberia and the Rocky Mountains as in the tropical grasslands of Africa and Asia. More kinds of big cats, and greater numbers of them, live in warmer places. Some are very limited in their range. Others, though widespread, are no longer common anyplace.

The different kinds, or species, of big cats are listed below. Some have local forms or varieties. They are listed also.

| NAME | SCIENTIFIC NAME | WHERE PRESENTLY FOUND | VARIETIES OR FORMS |
|---|---|---|---|
| Lion | *Panthera leo* | Gir, India and Africa from the Sahara to Natal | Two varieties alive today |
| Tiger | *Panthera tigris* | Asia from southern U.S.S.R. through China, Burma, India, Malaya to Java and Sumatra | Six varieties of which the Bengal tiger is best known |
| Jaguar | *Panthera onca* | Southwest U.S.A. through Mexico and Central America to Argentina | One form |
| Leopard | *Panthera pardus* | Africa from Morocco and Egypt southward; Asia minor eastward to southern U.S.S.R.; China, India, and southwest Asia | Six varieties including the widespread common leopard |
| Snow leopard | *Panthera unica* | Mountains of Kashmir, Tibet, and Turkestan, north to U.S.S.R.—Mongolian border | One form |
| Clouded leopard | *Neofelis nebulosa* | Southern China, Burma, Southeast Asia, Sumatra, Taiwan | Two varieties |
| Cougar | *Puma concolor* | Southern Canada through U.S.A. to Central America and on to Argentina | Fifteen varieties in North America and three in South America |
| Cheetah | *Acinonyx jubatus* | Iran and perhaps in other Near East sites; Africa, south of the Sahara | Two varieties and possibly a second species in Rhodesia |

The oldest direct ancestors of the big cats were the first mammals, small warm-blooded animals that appeared while dinosaurs were still common. Later, during some 150 million years, these early mammals developed in several ways. One group became large plant-eating creatures; another group became smaller more active flesh eaters.

Among these creatures that lived some 40 million years ago were the creodonts. In this varied group, several kinds of animals had sharp, cutting teeth, but experts do not think they were ancestors of living carnivores. The creodonts died off and other flesh-eating mammals took their place.

Creodonts were ancient flesh-eating mammals.

Some *Miacids,*
an extinct group,
were catlike carnivores.

One such newer group, the *Miacids,* included catlike carnivores. Some of these animals were larger, heavier, stronger than the others, and they were somewhat like our modern big cats. These hunters developed large, stabbing teeth. But this group too, after some 30 million years, slowly died out and became extinct.

In the same period, through millions of years, another catlike group developed. It is believed to have included the ancestors of both the saber-toothed cats of the Ice Age and the modern cats we know today.

Most famous was *Smilodon,* the saber-toothed tiger that lived less than a million years ago. Tiger-sized, with 20 centimeter daggerlike teeth in its upper jaw, *Smilodon* attacked large, slow animals like sloths and camels. When it hunted animals

trapped in the sticky tar pits of southern California, it too was caught in the tar. Bones preserved there tell the story of this great cat.

*Smilodon* was not the ancestor of our big cats. It became extinct about the time the great ice sheets advanced. Modern big cats developed from another related group. While *Smilodon* became extinct, the ancestors of our modern big cats were doing well and spreading widely over large parts of Europe, Asia, and Africa.

The big cats all hunt large animals, and some kinds have been dangerous to man. What makes them such successful hunters? Scientists find many answers to this question. Claws are one of them. A lot of animals have claws, but those of big cats are perfect weapons—long, curved, and sharp. Cats keep their claws sharp and polished by scraping them on a tree trunk or some other rough surface. This scratching and marking of trees also lets other cats know they have entered an occupied area.

cheetah clawing a tree

detail of claw

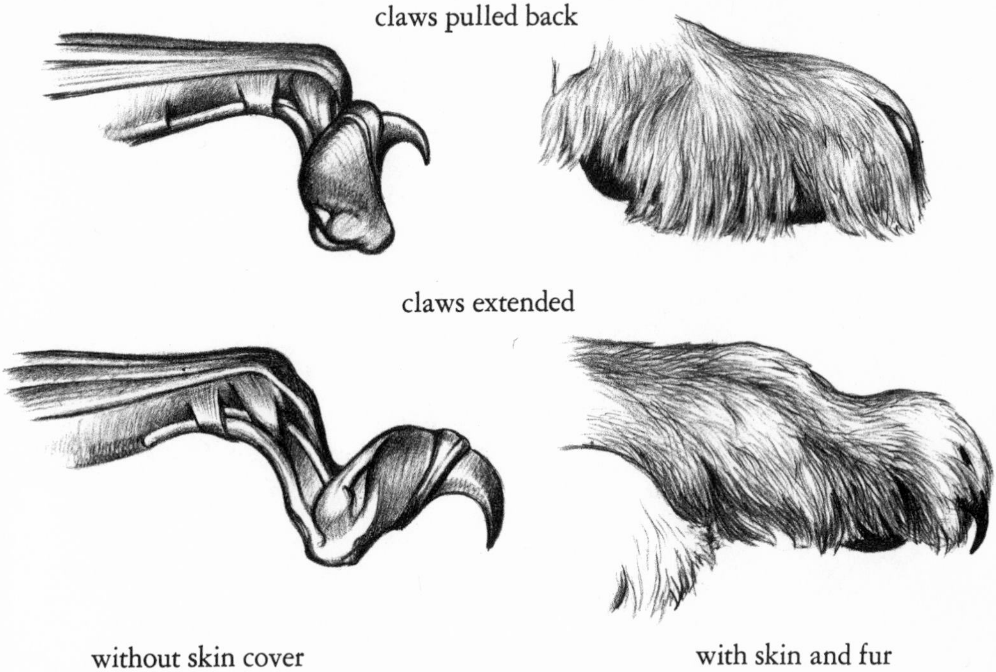


Cats have five toes and claws on their front feet, four on the rear. All eighteen can be pulled back into sheaths at the end of the toes. With claws pulled in, the cat stalks its prey. When it attacks, the claws shoot out. They grip the prey with a hold that is hard to break. Only the cheetah is unable to pull in its claws. They are not as sharp as the claws of other big cats.

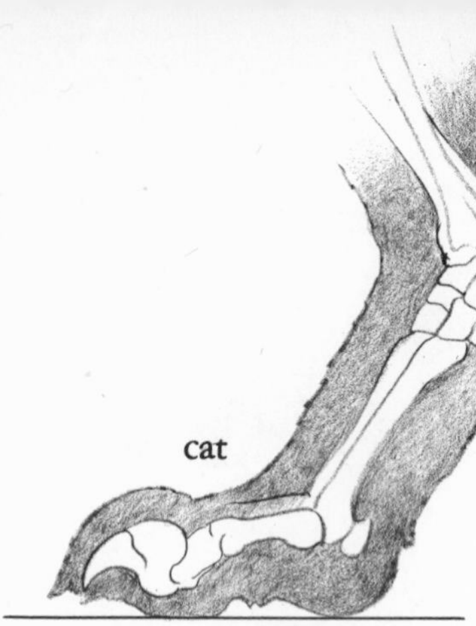


Many animals walk on their entire foot. Cats walk only on their toes.

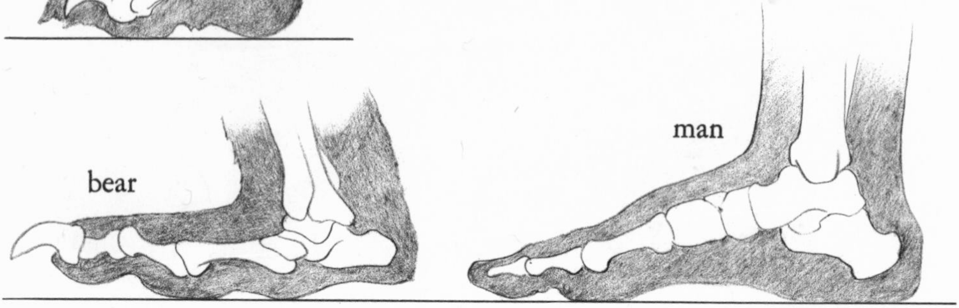


The feet of a cat are perfect for hunting. Thick toes and foot pads ensure quiet stalking. They also cushion the animal's leap. Cats walk on their toes; the heel does not touch the ground. You walk on toes and heels. So does a bear. Not all the toes and pads of a big cat show in a normal footprint.

footprints of a stalking cougar

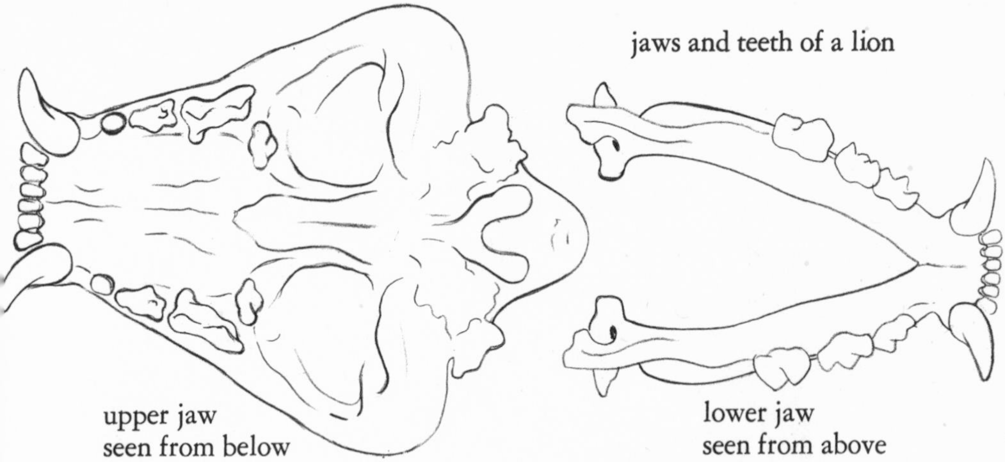

jaws and teeth of a lion

Cats' teeth differ from those of all other animals—even from other carnivores'. All are designed for cutting and tearing. None can be used for grinding, like teeth of cows and horses. Human beings have four types of teeth: incisors, canines, premolars, and molars. So do cats, but only their front teeth, the incisors, are anything like ours. Their pointed canines are long and sharp. Members of the cat family typically have 30 teeth.

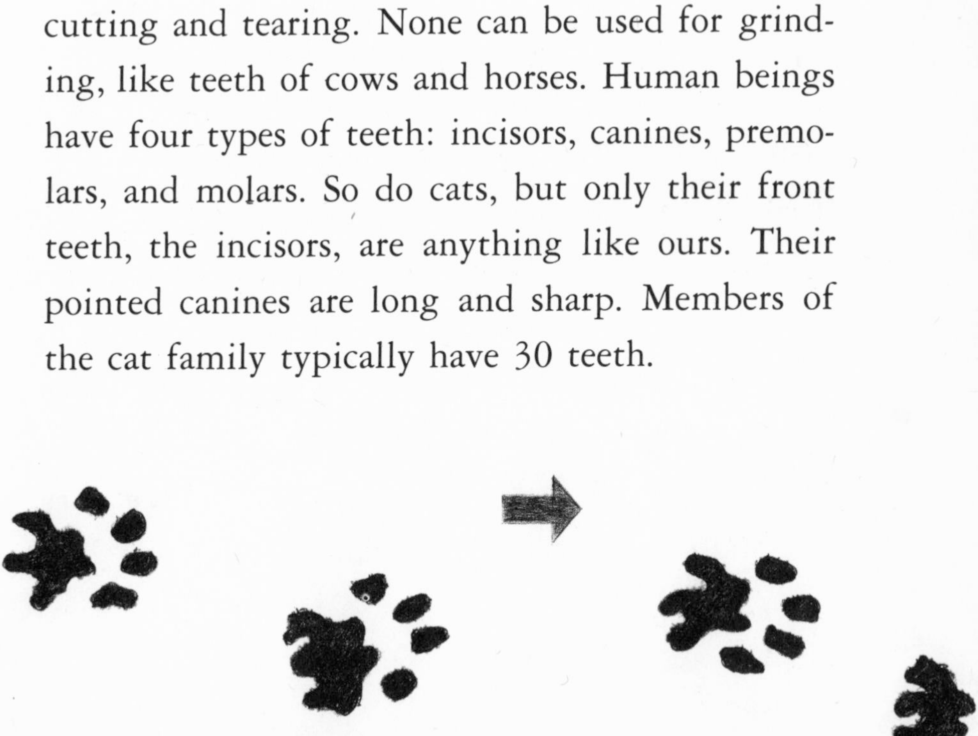

The retina of a cat's eye
has chemicals that reflect light.

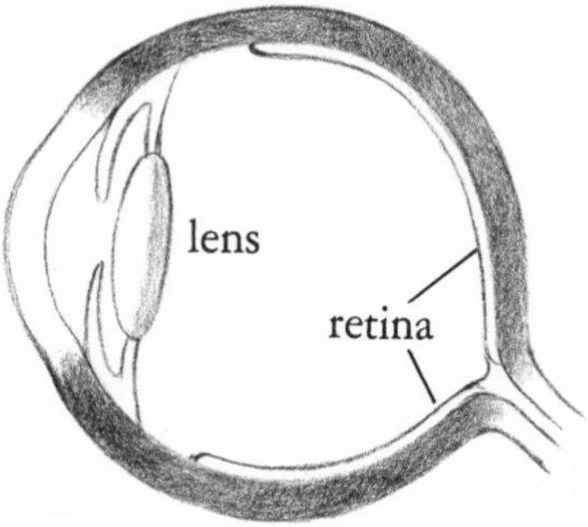


A cat's eyes are quite like our own. But for its body size, a cat's eyes are the largest of all mammals. Size and structure make a cat's eyes much better than ours for seeing in the dark. They contain more of the cells that are especially sensitive to faint light. The retina, which receives light and transmits an image to the brain, also has cells with a chemical that reflects light. When a strong light shines into a cat's eyes at night, they glow like mirrors and can be seen at a distance.

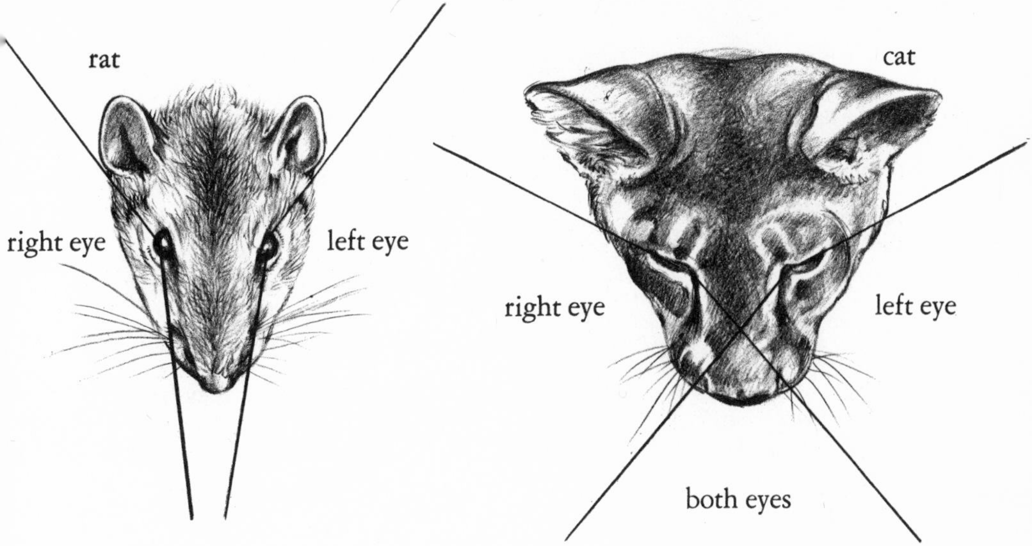

Eyes turned forward give cats better vision.

We do not know whether the eyes of cats are good for seeing colors. If they observe color at all, they may notice very little of it. When tested, cats seem to pay little attention to colors.

A cat's eyes are set in the front of its head, not at the sides like a rat's. Thus, a cat can see a large area in front of itself with both eyes at once (binocular vision). Having binocular vision helps the cat to judge distance, an important hunting aid when it leaps at its prey.

Though most big cats prefer to hunt at night, all can see well by day and some even hunt in the daytime. Those that do have eyes with round pupils. In strong sunlight the eye muscles of many cats narrow the pupil, the opening of the eye, until it is only a slit. In this way the amount of light that enters is cut down. The pupil of a lion, however, closes down to a small circle in strong sunlight, as do the pupils in our eyes.

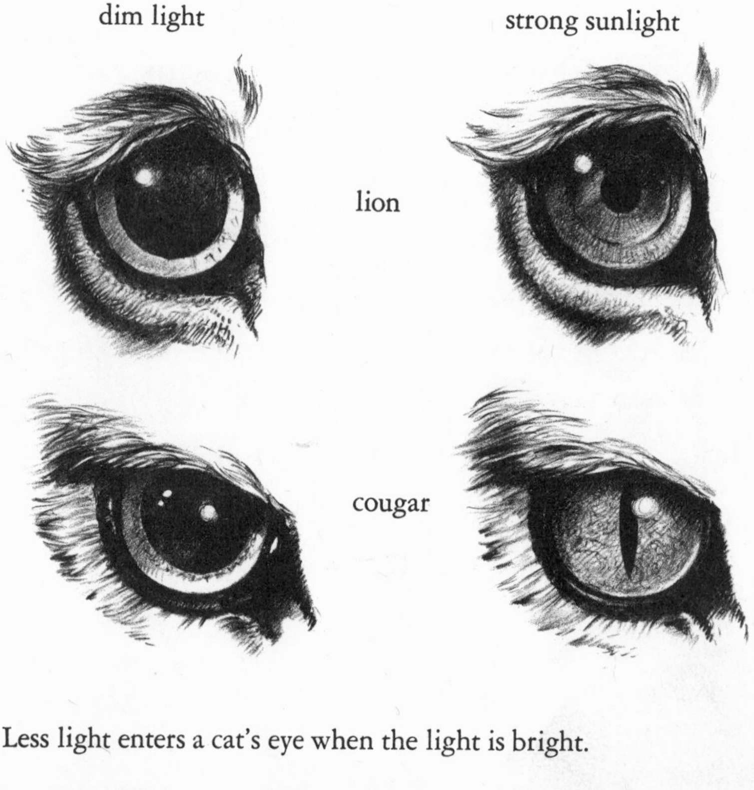


Less light enters a cat's eye when the light is bright.

normal hair covering

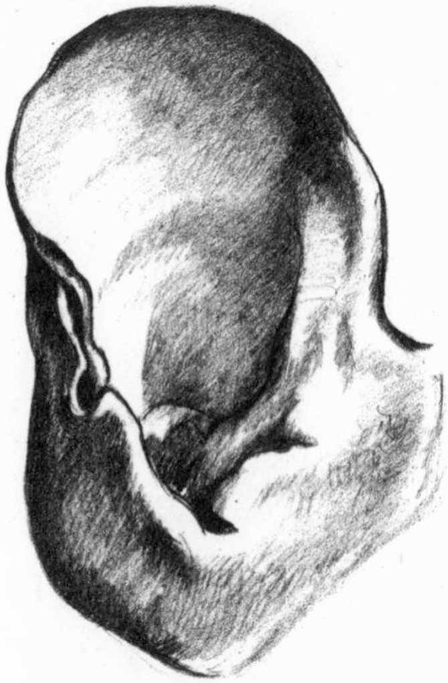

hair removed
to show shape and folds

Hearing is very important for cats, especially for those that hunt at night. Big cats notice and locate very slight sounds, like those made by a gazelle walking through dry grass. Cats can hear sounds that are too shrill or too faint for the human ear. They can move their ears, and this ability may help to locate the direction from which a sound comes. Cats also have long, sensitive hairs on their faces, which aid them in feeling their way.

Scientists studying the bodies of cats are impressed by their muscles. A cat has about 500 voluntary muscles — the kind it can control and use at will. These muscles help make cats the excellent hunters that they are. Jaw muscles put power behind sharp teeth. Foot muscles extend the claws and pull them back again. The cat's strength comes from its big leg and thigh muscles. Those in its chest and abdomen pull the cat's body into a powerful, sleek, streamlined, graceful shape.

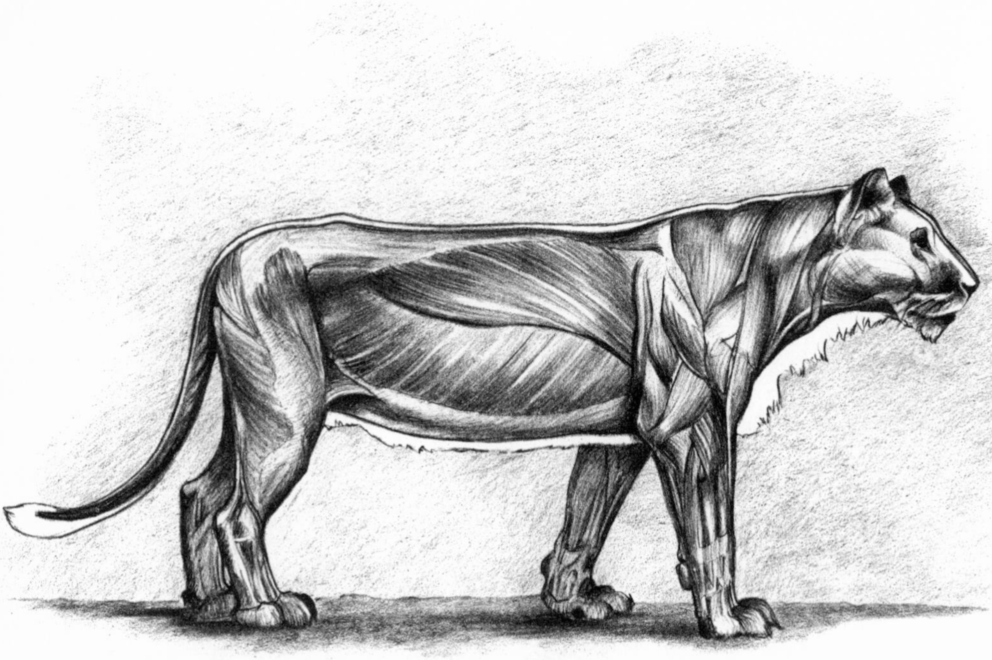

body muscles of a young lion

The color of a full-grown big cat blends with dry grass, dead leaves, and bare rock. This protective coloring makes the cat almost invisible as it crouches motionless, awaiting its prey. Some big cats, like lions, have a tawny color. Tigers are marked with darker stripes. Leopards are spotted and so are jaguars.

cougar spraying a tree
to mark its territory

Cats have a good sense of smell. They use it for finding prey and also to recognize the living areas of other cats. Each big cat has special places that it prefers for hunting, sunning, and living. It marks these areas by scratching trees, by urinating, or by squirting a special scent from anal glands on trees, shrubs, or rocks. This system of a marked territory helps prevent fighting when the living areas of cats overlap.

Cats avoid an area marked by another cat when they see or smell these fresh signs. A strange cat that does enter is usually chased away. If such signals are not fresh, then no other cat is around. So the newcomer can enter safely with little chance of an encounter.

Most big cats hunt alone, but lions and cheetahs often hunt in groups. Sometimes they too are solitary hunters. How a big cat hunts depends on the size and on the behavior of its prey. Sometimes a big cat will seize an animal that crosses its path by accident. More often big cats ambush and surprise their prey as they roam their territory, searching for food.

pride of lions hunting

Once prey has been spotted, the watchful cat, ears alert to catch the slightest sound, edges closer and closer. As it stalks, body low to the ground, it uses every bit of cover to hide. When it is close enough, or when the deer, rabbit, or antelope has made one careless move, the big cat springs.

A big cat can leap 10 meters. With claws spread, it knocks down its prey and bites its throat or the back of its neck. In this way it kills the prey quickly. When the animal is dead, the big cat often drags or carries it to a sheltered spot and then begins to feed.

If the cat should miss, or if its prey breaks loose, the big cat dashes after it. Cats are not built for long-distance running, but they are excellent sprinters. They cover ground with amazing leaps. For short distances, big cats are hard to beat. They not only have speed but fine control as they lunge through brush or dodge around rocks. If the rabbit or antelope is too fast, the cat gives up and continues its search.

cougar stalking sheep

## LIONS

Lions are by far the best known of the big cats. No other cat has the huge mane of the male lion or its bushy-tipped tail. Lions once lived over much of Europe, the open areas of Africa, and in Asia Minor, Iran, and India. Now none roam wild in Europe and very few remain in India. Although not yet an endangered species in Africa, the population of lions has shrunk from about 400,000 to half that number in two decades. Their effective range has also been reduced to about half.

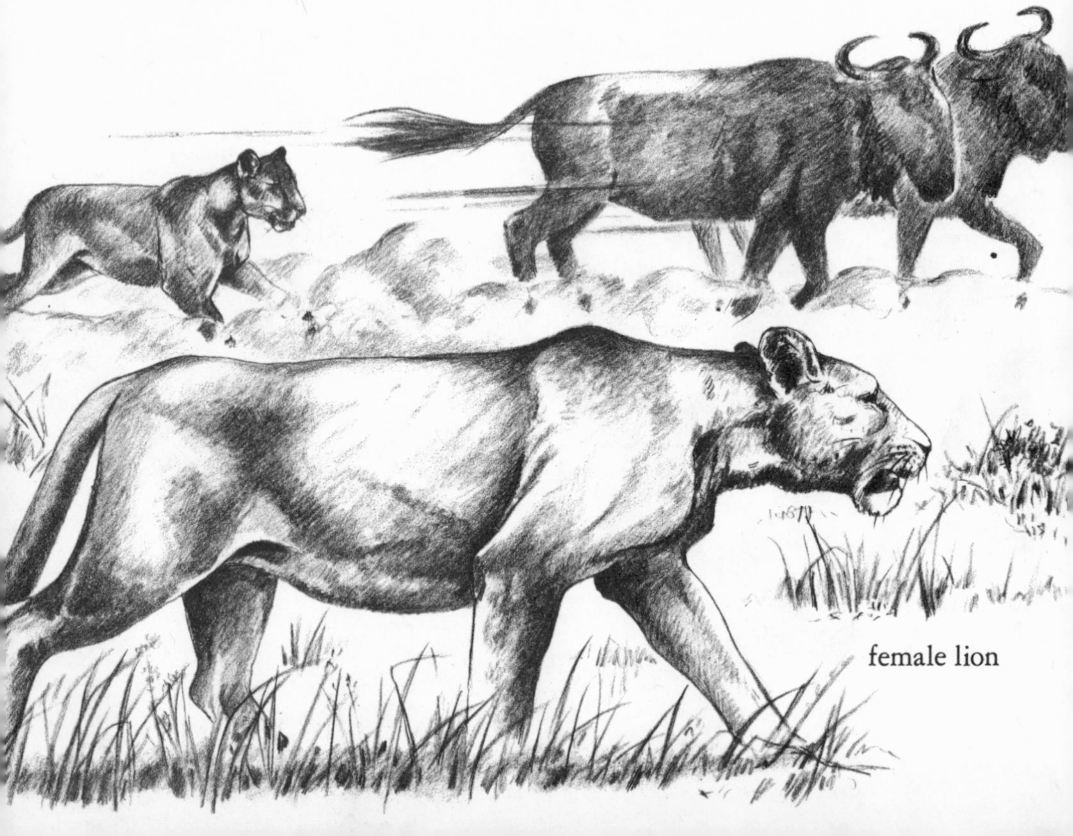

female lion

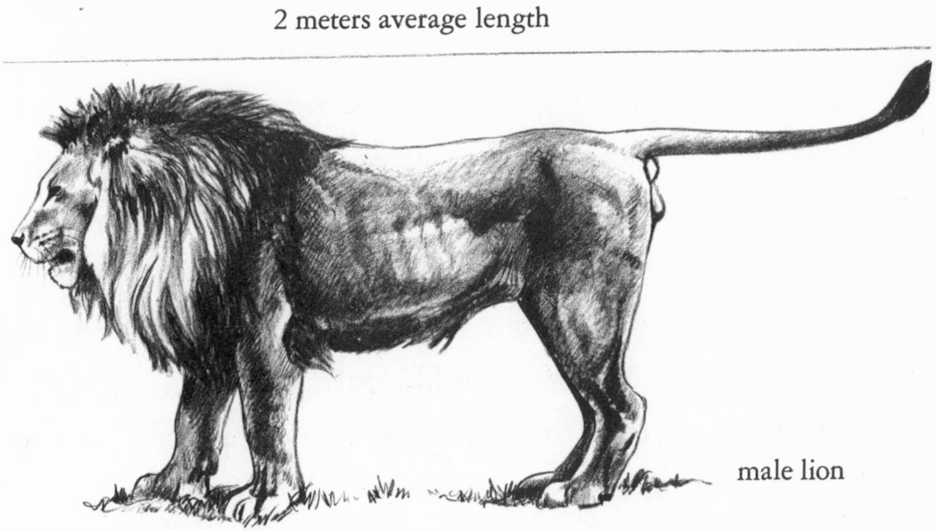


male lion

A full-grown male may measure 3 meters from its nose to the tip of its tail, but 2 meters is more usual. It may weigh up to 225 kilograms. The male's mane of bushy hair spreads over its head, neck, and shoulders. The smaller lioness never has the male's heavy mane. Lions' manes may differ in size and color. Algerian lions, long extinct, had much larger manes than those of any lions still living today.

Lions are the most social of all cats. Nearly all live in groups, or prides, but some live alone. A pride usually consists of several females, their cubs, and a few adult males. Where prey is plentiful, prides may be large, sometimes numbering more than twenty-five lions. Where prey is scarce, and living conditions poor, a pride may have only three or four members. As male cubs grow older, they leave the pride to join or form new prides. Some live alone as nomads.

All adult lions share the work of the pride. Males patrol and scent mark the territory. They chase intruders and protect the young while the females hunt. Female nomads, and prides without

adult males, seem to raise cubs less successfully.

Lions hunt alone or in groups. In the evening, after resting most of the day, the pride moves out in search of food. Females lead the group, and males tag along behind. When prides of lions hunt, they often pursue large prey such as a zebra or a wildebeest. Usually lions stalk or ambush their prey. But sometimes they simply fan out, so that prey flushed by one lion may be caught by another. One or two lions may circle the prey from the far side. The startled prey flees toward the other waiting lions. Sometimes lions rush a herd, separating and confusing the zebras or antelopes till one is seized.

After the females have made the kill, the older males rush in and begin eating. They often allow the cubs to join them before the adult lioness feeds. Lions usually finish the entire carcass before leaving.

Lions hunt wild and domestic animals, preying mainly on the wildebeest, its principal food. The zebra ranks next as a common food of lions. Other animals eaten are African buffalo, warthogs, gazelles, kangoni, and even ostriches.

In addition to her work as a hunter, the female raises the young. About 110 days after mating, two to five blind cubs are born in a den or thicket. In about a week, their eyes open. The young may have faint spots, which often fade during the first year. For a time the mother keeps the cubs separate from the pride. She still goes out to hunt, often leaving the young lions alone. When the cubs are two to four months old, she brings them into the pride where they remain for two or three years.

These are important large prey of African lions.
Smaller animals are also eaten.

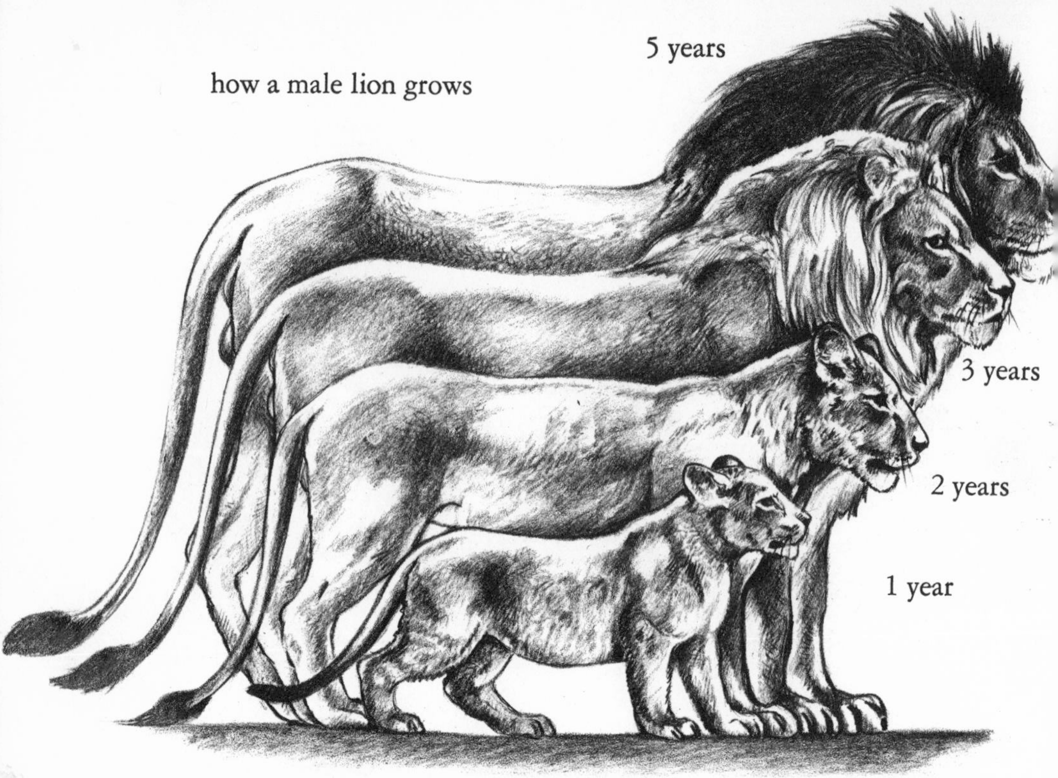


Each lioness in the pride may nurse cubs other than her own, since several females have litters at about the same time. If a mother is killed, another female may raise her cubs. Young lions grow rapidly. In two years they are old enough to mate. A three-year-old male has a growing mane. At five years, lions are in their prime, and they usually live for ten or fifteen years.

Communication is important for social animals like lions that live and work together. Lions communicate in several ways. Their roar may tell of a kill. It may attract a mate or may keep an intruder from entering a home territory. Sometimes a whole pride of lions joins in a ground-shaking roar. Lions also grunt and growl. The females have a special moaning or mewing call that brings their cubs back to them in a hurry.

Gestures of lions express their feelings and signal their actions. During a hunt, changes in posture and movement signal the pride so all the lions work together. Head rubbing is a gesture of friendly greeting between females or females and cubs. Adult males seldom rub heads. An adult mating pair will groom and lick one another as a way of showing affection.

While feeding, an adult male will discourage another (especially a female or cub) by snarling, growling, or hitting out with a forepaw. But serious fighting is rare, even among the males.

leopon, an uncommon cross between a lion and a leopard

In some zoos, lions have been mated with tigers. The young are called "ligers" and "tiglons." A liger is often striped. A male tiglon may have a small mane. Such matings probably do not happen in the wild, but they show how closely these big cats are related. The less common mating of a lion and a leopard produces young with a small mane and typical leopard spots.

## TIGERS

Tigers may grow to be as large as lions—3 meters long, from nose to tip of tail—and may also weigh as much. They can roar like lions, but do so rarely. Tigers are handsome, with tawny coats and black stripes. Some are pale, almost white. This broken pattern makes them hard to see in woods or grasslands. Male and female tigers are much alike, though the female is smaller. Old males have long hair around their necks, but not a real mane.

Tigers live over most of Asia, from the cold mountains of Siberia to the hot plains of India. They live in forests, swamps, and in the marshes and reedbeds of the lowlands. No tigers live in Africa. The Siberian tiger, probably the largest, has been so hunted for its fine, soft fur that it is nearly extinct.

Tigers seem to live alone except for mating pairs or females with their young. Sometimes they come together at kills, but they are never as social as lions.

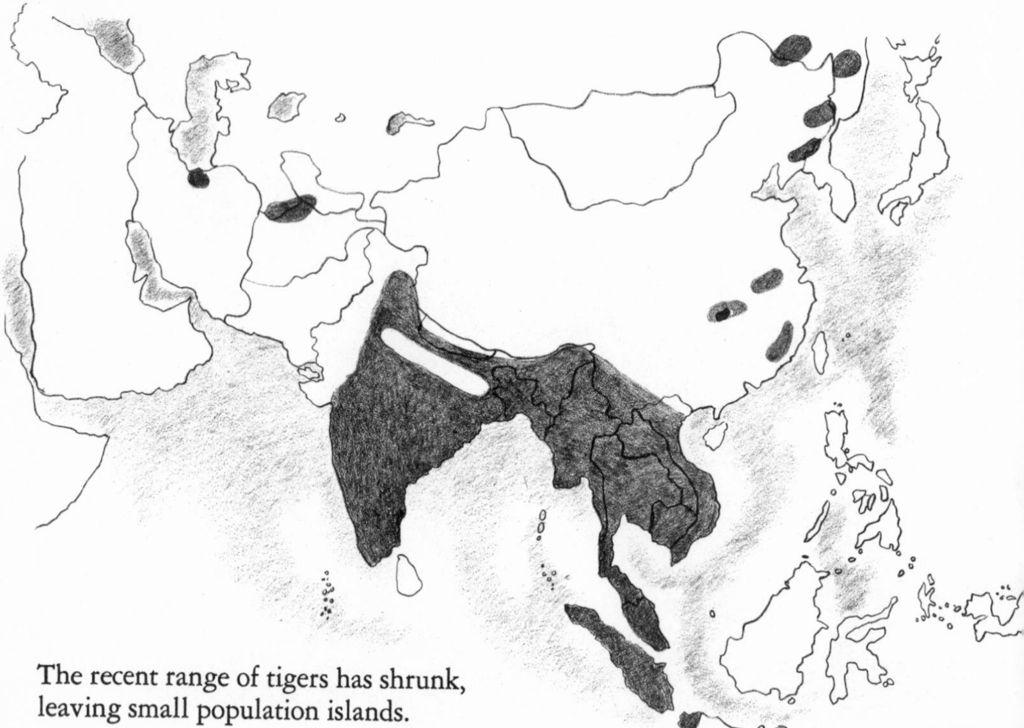

The recent range of tigers has shrunk, leaving small population islands.

mating pair of Siberian tigers

Tigers rest in the shade during the day or soak in a pond when it is hot. With sunset they become active and roam widely in search of prey. They usually hunt alone, but may share their kill with other tigers. To maintain itself, an adult tiger needs to make a kill every three or four days.

Tigers take turns feeding on a kill and so avoid fights. Before they leave the kill, they cover it with dirt and grass to hide it from vultures. Tigers may return several times till the kill is finished. They eat everything but the large bones. Little is left for scavengers.

Tigers attack several kinds of deer, wild boar, wild cattle, and even the Indian bison. When food is scarce, they eat birds, snakes, lizards, frogs, and even grasshoppers. As people move into tiger territory, the cattle, sheep, and goats they bring may become food for tigers too. Man-eating tigers, often reported years ago, are now rare. They may have been wounded, injured, or old tigers.

Few tigers of any kind exist today. From 1800 to 1900, experts estimate that well over 100,000 tigers were killed in India alone. Over 1000 a year were shot till by the 1920's only about 100,000 were left in all Asia. In 1970, when only 5000 remained alive, a great drive began to save tigers from extinction. Money was raised, and reserves were set aside for them. Children all over the world helped too. In the 1980's, we should know how well the plan has worked and if tigers will survive in the wild.

About 105 days after tigers mate, two or more young are born under an overhanging rock or in a den. Only the mother cares for the young. The cubs venture out after about two months and soon go with their mother on hunting trips. They watch their mother and learn how to kill prey. The young may stay with the mother for two years. By that time, the mother may have another litter. Her cubs, now nearly full-grown, are able to take care of themselves.

Tigers, like lions, use sounds and gestures to communicate. They too express friendliness by rubbing faces, necks, and bodies. Tigers make a variety of sounds, including a puffing sound through their nostrils. One, which only tigers make, sounds like *pok-pok-pok.* It warns other animals of their presence and so prevents unexpected meetings.

common leopard

## LEOPARDS

Leopards live in the forests over much of Asia and Africa and in a small area of Europe near the Black Sea. No other Old World big cat has so wide a range. Leopards are smaller but more savage than lions or tigers. Males seldom are more than 2.5 meters long or 90 kilograms in weight. There are three kinds of leopards, each distinct in appearance.

The common leopard has two different color forms. In dry, open country the form commonly seen is light tan to brown, with black spots usually in circles or rosettes. In the forest, especially in India, some may be black or nearly so. These ani-

"black panther"

mals are called "black panthers," although they are only a color variation of the common leopard. Black and spotted cubs are born in the same litter.

High in the mountains of south China, Nepal, and southeast Asia lives the clouded leopard. Smaller and less common, it has lighter fur and

Black and spotted leopard cubs are born in the same litter.

clouded leopard

a different pattern of spots. Higher in the Himalayas and mountains of Tibet, China, and south Russia, the snow leopard (also called the ounce) is found. It has even lighter, soft, thick fur and a dark streak down its back. Little is known about this rare cat.

Leopards hunt mostly at night. They may hide in trees or in the dense brush; then they leap down

snow leopard

or spring out to attack. They feed on baboons, monkeys, small antelopes, the young of large animals, minor game, and even on birds. A leopard often carries its kill up a tree, where it feeds or hides it.

A leopard usually hunts alone, but females may share the same hunting area with males. After mating, the pair remains together awhile, but later the female alone cares for her litter of two or three cubs. They stay with her for almost two years. When the cubs go along to hunt, they watch and follow the female's tail, which she carries upright as a visual signal. At other times the tail hangs down. Leopards have calls, hisses, and grunts, but compared to other cats they are quite silent.

Leopard cubs follow
their mother's tail signal.

## JAGUARS

From Arizona to Argentina, *el tigre* is not the tiger but the jaguar. It is about the size of a leopard and has similar markings. A big one is 2.5 meters long and weighs about 100 kilograms. Females are smaller. Jaguars like thick cover and often take to the trees. They hunt monkeys, birds, deer, wild pigs, alligators, and even fish, which they can scoop out of the water with a quick stroke of a paw.

About three months after mating, the female gives birth to a litter of two to four cubs in a den or rock shelter. The cubs are heavily spotted. Within a month they can follow their mother, and in a year they hunt their own food. Before another year has passed, the young are mature.

leopard

jaguar

fur markings

Jaguars prefer dense woods or swamps, but they may come out into the grasslands. They have large hunting territories, which they patrol by night. Jaguars sometimes attack horses and cattle, and they have been known to attack men.

Both leopards and jaguars have rings or rosettes of dark spots, but the jaguar has a dark spot in the center of each ring. Jaguars snarl, growl, and occasionally roar.

## COUGARS

No other mammal of the Western world has the range of the cougar. It extends from the Canadian Rockies to the southern tip of South America and from the Pacific east to the Atlantic. A century ago the cougar was still common in eastern United States, where it is now almost extinct. This large cat may be 2.5 meters long and weigh 100 kilograms, but most are smaller, especially the females. Known also as the puma, mountain lion, panther, catamount, or painter, the cougar also has many Spanish names.

About a hundred days after mating, the young are born—blind, thickly spotted and weighing only 0.5 kilograms. Their eyes open in two weeks and in two months they are eating meat. Soon they follow their mother on hunts. About that time they weigh some 5 kilograms and six months later their weight is up to 15 to 20 kilograms. They double this weight by the time they are a year old. In another year or so they are adults.

Cougars feed primarily on deer, but they hunt all kinds of small animals from rats to squirrels. They also kill sheep, goats, and even horses. For years cougars have been hunted, trapped, and poisoned till only a few are left. Each marks and protects its territory, which needs to be 40 to 60 square kilometers to enable it to find enough food.

## CHEETAHS

The cheetah, or hunting leopard, is an unusual cat, distinct from all others. It measures about 2 meters long and has solid spots, long fur, a trace of a mane, and claws that do not pull in. Cheetahs hunt antelope and other small game in dry grass and scrubland.

Since the 1950's, cheetahs have been extinct in India. They are still found in nearby Africa but are no longer common there. Cattle graze and men

farm the land where they once hunted. Many of the animals on which they feed are gone. But cheetahs follow the prey that is left and change their territory as they move along.

Cheetahs hunt alone, in pairs, or in small groups. In open country, they use speed instead of cunning. Cheetahs stalk or even walk toward game. Then, with a burst of speed, they chase their prey, knocking it off its feet, and killing it. The cheetah is one of the world's fastest animals. It can run

short distances at speeds up to 100 kilometers per hour. Young cheetahs were once captured in India and trained to hunt for their master.

After the kill, the cubs are called to feed with the adults. Then perhaps a lion will drive the cheetah from its kill, or jackals may snatch a piece. Cheetahs do not hide their kill or return to it. The jackals and vultures take what is left.

Cheetahs purr as they groom one another. They cannot roar because their throats are different from those of other big cats. A chirping cry is used in courtship and for calling their young. Cheetahs communicate with other postures and gestures as well. Still, they are less social than lions.

Two, three, or four young are born in the spring, about three months after the female has mated. Two months later the cubs follow their mother, except when she is chasing prey. The fast-growing cubs mature at an age of 14 to 16 months and may leave their mother at that time.

cheetah cubs

Because people admire big cats (and fear them too) everyone is curious about them. Back in 1720 a lion was first exhibited in Boston, and people flocked to see it. About a hundred years later the emperor of Morocco presented another lion to Andrew Jackson, then president of the United States. Jackson did not know what to do with it and had to ask the advice of Congress. In the end the lion was sold, for in those days there were no zoos in the United States.

Visitors, protected by moat, see lions and antelope in a continuing display.
wall behind lions hidden by rocks
Lions roam on a natural-habitat island.
moat too wide and deep for lions to cross

Modern zoos exhibit big cats in habitat groups.

Since then lions and tigers and other big cats have been captured and exhibited in hundreds of zoos. These fine animals were first kept in small cages without proper attention. Now the zoos give the big cats plenty of room and fine care. Walls and a ditch of water keep the animals separate without cages or bars. People can see the big cats almost as if they were in the wild. The big cats are now healthier and happier in captivity, and in some zoos they even raise litters of young.

Antelope are
in a similiar environment
to lions,
but are separated
from them by a moat.

moat not seen
by visitors

trapped cougar

The big cats still in the wild are those in the most trouble. Few tigers and leopards are left. People have overhunted them for sport or for their fur. With more and more people on earth, more and more land has been cleared for homes, farms, and cattle. In the course of building homes, roads, and towns, people have changed the land so fewer wild animals, including big cats, can survive.

With less and less wild prey, the big cats attack farm animals rather than starve. Farmers do not want their cattle, horses, sheep, or goats killed. So big cats are hunted, trapped, or poisoned, and each year fewer big cats are seen.

Now people have learned that all animals are needed—flesh eaters as well as plant eaters. Both kinds help keep the natural world working smoothly. Big cats developed over millions of years. In only 200 years they have been nearly destroyed.

Can big cats still be saved? Scientists think they can. Hunting has been stopped in many places and so has the sale of their fur. New parks and refuges have been set aside in which they can live safely. Everyone wants to help. Few people like to think of what the twenty-first century would be like without lions, tigers, and other big cats.

## INDEX

**indicates illustration*

# Pitman Research Notes in Mathematics Series



**Submission of proposals for consideration**

Suggestions for publication, in the form of outlines and representative samples, are invited by the Editorial Board for assessment. Intending authors should approach one of the main editors or another member of the Editorial Board, citing the relevant AMS subject classifications. Alternatively, outlines may be sent directly to the publisher's offices. Refereeing is by members of the board and other mathematical authorities in the topic concerned, throughout the world.

**Preparation of accepted manuscripts**

On acceptance of a proposal, the publisher will supply full instructions for the preparation of manuscripts in a form suitable for direct photo-lithographic reproduction. Specially printed grid sheets can be provided and a contribution is offered by the publisher towards the cost of typing. Word processor output, subject to the publisher's approval, is also acceptable.

Illustrations should be prepared by the authors, ready for direct reproduction without further improvement. The use of hand-drawn symbols should be avoided wherever possible, in order to maintain maximum clarity of the text.

The publisher will be pleased to give any guidance necessary during the preparation of a typescript, and will be happy to answer any queries.

**Important note**

In order to avoid later retyping, intending authors are strongly urged not to begin final preparation of a typescript before receiving the publisher's guidelines. In this way it is hoped to preserve the uniform appearance of the series.

**Longman Scientific & Technical**
**Longman House**
**Burnt Mill**
**Harlow, Essex, CM20 2JE**
**UK**
**(Telephone (0279) 426721)**

**Titles in this series. A full list is available on request from the publisher.**

51 Subnormal operators
**J B Conway**
52 Wave propagation in viscoelastic media
**F Mainardi**
53 Nonlinear partial differential equations and their applications: Collège de France Seminar. Volume I
**H Brezis and J L Lions**
54 Geometry of Coxeter groups
**H Hiller**
55 Cusps of Gauss mappings
**T Banchoff, T Gaffney and C McCrory**
56 An approach to algebraic K-theory
**A J Berrick**
57 Convex analysis and optimization
**J-P Aubin and R B Vintner**
58 Convex analysis with applications in the differentiation of convex functions
**J R Giles**
59 Weak and variational methods for moving boundary problems
**C M Elliott and J R Ockendon**
60 Nonlinear partial differential equations and their applications: Collège de France Seminar. Volume II
**H Brezis and J L Lions**
61 Singular Systems of differential equations II
**S L Campbell**
62 Rates of convergence in the central limit theorem
**Peter Hall**
63 Solution of differential equations by means of one-parameter groups
**J M Hill**
64 Hankel operators on Hilbert Space
**S C Power**
65 Schrödinger-type operators with continuous spectra
**M S P Eastham and H Kalf**
66 Recent applications of generalized inverses
**S L Campbell**
67 Riesz and Fredholm theory in Banach algebra
**B A Barnes, G J Murphy, M R F Smyth and T T West**
68 Evolution equations and their applications
**K Kappel and W Schappacher**
69 Generalized solutions of Hamilton–Jacobi equations
**P L Lions**
70 Nonlinear partial differential equations and their applications: Collège de France Seminar. Volume III
**H Brezis and J L Lions**
71 Spectral theory and wave operators for the Schrödinger equation
**A M Berthier**
72 Approximation of Hilbert space operators I
**D A Herrero**
73 Vector valued Nevanlinna theory
**H J W Ziegler**
74 Instability, nonexistence and weighted energy methods in fluid dynamics and related theories
**B Straughan**
75 Local bifurcation and symmetry
**A Vanderbauwhede**
76 Clifford analysis
**F Brackx, R Delanghe and F Sommen**
77 Nonlinear equivalence, reduction of PDEs to ODEs and fast convergent numerical methods
**E E Rosinger**
78 Free boundary problems, theory and applications. Volume I
**A Fasano and M Primicerio**
79 Free boundary problems, theory and applications. Volume II
**A Fasano and M Primicerio**
80 Symplectic geometry
**A Crumeyrolle and J Grifone**
81 An algorithmic analysis of a communication model with retransmission of flawed messages
**D M Lucantoni**
82 Geometric games and their applications
**W H Ruckle**
83 Additive groups of rings
**S Feigelstock**
84 Nonlinear partial differential equations and their applications: Collège de France Seminar. Volume IV
**H Brezis and J L Lions**
85 Multiplicative functionals on topological algebras
**T Husain**
86 Hamilton–Jacobi equations in Hilbert spaces
**V Barbu and G Da Prato**
87 Harmonic maps with symmetry, harmonic morphisms and deformations of metric
**P Baird**
88 Similarity solutions of nonlinear partial differential equations
**L Dresner**
89 Contributions to nonlinear partial differential equations
**C Bardos, A Damlamian, J I Díaz and J Hernández**
90 Banach and Hilbert spaces of vector-valued functions
**J Burbea and P Masani**
91 Control and observation of neutral systems
**D Salamon**
92 Banach bundles, Banach modules and automorphisms of $C^*$-algebras
**M J Dupré and R M Gillette**
93 Nonlinear partial differential equations and their applications: Collège de France Seminar. Volume V
**H Brezis and J L Lions**
94 Computer algebra in applied mathematics: an introduction to MACSYMA
**R H Rand**
95 Advances in nonlinear waves. Volume I
**L Debnath**
96 FC-groups
**M J Tomkinson**
97 Topics in relaxation and ellipsoidal methods
**M Akgül**
98 Analogue of the group algebra for topological semigroups
**H Dzinotyiweyi**
99 Stochastic functional differential equations
**S E A Mohammed**

100 Optimal control of variational inequalities
**V Barbu**
101 Partial differential equations and dynamical systems
**W E Fitzgibbon III**
102 Approximation of Hilbert space operators Volume II
**C Apostol, L A Fialkow, D A Herrero and D Voiculescu**
103 Nondiscrete induction and iterative processes
**V Ptak and F-A Potra**
104 Analytic functions – growth aspects
**O P Juneja and G P Kapoor**
105 Theory of Tikhonov regularization for Fredholm equations of the first kind
**C W Groetsch**
106 Nonlinear partial differential equations and free boundaries. Volume I
**J I Díaz**
107 Tight and taut immersions of manifolds
**T E Cecil and P J Ryan**
108 A layering method for viscous, incompressible $L_p$ flows occupying $R^n$
**A Douglis and E B Fabes**
109 Nonlinear partial differential equations and their applications: Collège de France Seminar. Volume VI
**H Brezis and J L Lions**
110 Finite generalized quadrangles
**S E Payne and J A Thas**
111 Advances in nonlinear waves. Volume II
**L Debnath**
112 Topics in several complex variables
**E Ramírez de Arellano and D Sundararaman**
113 Differential equations, flow invariance and applications
**N H Pavel**
114 Geometrical combinatorics
**F C Holroyd and R J Wilson**
115 Generators of strongly continuous semigroups
**J A van Casteren**
116 Growth of algebras and Gelfand–Kirillov dimension
**G R Krause and T H Lenagan**
117 Theory of bases and cones
**P K Kamthan and M Gupta**
118 Linear groups and permutations
**A R Camina and E A Whelan**
119 General Wiener–Hopf factorization methods
**F-O Speck**
120 Free boundary problems: applications and theory. Volume III
**A Bossavit, A Damlamian and M Fremond**
121 Free boundary problems: applications and theory. Volume IV
**A Bossavit, A Damlamian and M Fremond**
122 Nonlinear partial differential equations and their applications: Collège de France Seminar. Volume VII
**H Brezis and J L Lions**
123 Geometric methods in operator algebras
**H Araki and E G Effros**
124 Infinite dimensional analysis–stochastic processes
**S Albeverio**
125 Ennio de Giorgi Colloquium
**P Krée**
126 Almost-periodic functions in abstract spaces
**S Zaidman**
127 Nonlinear variational problems
**A Marino, L Modica, S Spagnolo and M Degliovanni**
128 Second-order systems of partial differential equations in the plane
**L K Hua, W Lin and C-Q Wu**
129 Asymptotics of high-order ordinary differential equations
**R B Paris and A D Wood**
130 Stochastic differential equations
**R Wu**
131 Differential geometry
**L A Cordero**
132 Nonlinear differential equations
**J K Hale and P Martinez-Amores**
133 Approximation theory and applications
**S P Singh**
134 Near-rings and their links with groups
**J D P Meldrum**
135 Estimating eigenvalues with *a posteriori/a priori* inequalities
**J R Kuttler and V G Sigillito**
136 Regular semigroups as extensions
**F J Pastijn and M Petrich**
137 Representations of rank one Lie groups
**D H Collingwood**
138 Fractional calculus
**G F Roach and A C McBride**
139 Hamilton's principle in continuum mechanics
**A Bedford**
140 Numerical analysis
**D F Griffiths and G A Watson**
141 Semigroups, theory and applications. Volume I
**H Brezis, M G Crandall and F Kappel**
142 Distribution theorems of L-functions
**D Joyner**
143 Recent developments in structured continua
**D De Kee and P Kaloni**
144 Functional analysis and two-point differential operators
**J Locker**
145 Numerical methods for partial differential equations
**S I Hariharan and T H Moulden**
146 Completely bounded maps and dilations
**V I Paulsen**
147 Harmonic analysis on the Heisenberg nilpotent Lie group
**W Schempp**
148 Contributions to modern calculus of variations
**L Cesari**
149 Nonlinear parabolic equations: qualitative properties of solutions
**L Boccardo and A Tesei**
150 From local times to global geometry, control and physics
**K D Elworthy**

151 A stochastic maximum principle for optimal control of diffusions
**U G Haussmann**
152 Semigroups, theory and applications. Volume II
**H Brezis, M G Crandall and F Kappel**
153 A general theory of integration in function spaces
**P Muldowney**
154 Oakland Conference on partial differential equations and applied mathematics
**L R Bragg and J W Dettman**
155 Contributions to nonlinear partial differential equations. Volume II
**J I Díaz and P L Lions**
156 Semigroups of linear operators: an introduction
**A C McBride**
157 Ordinary and partial differential equations
**B D Sleeman and R J Jarvis**
158 Hyperbolic equations
**F Colombini and M K V Murthy**
159 Linear topologies on a ring: an overview
**J S Golan**
160 Dynamical systems and bifurcation theory
**M I Camacho, M J Pacifico and F Takens**
161 Branched coverings and algebraic functions
**M Namba**
162 Perturbation bounds for matrix eigenvalues
**R Bhatia**
163 Defect minimization in operator equations: theory and applications
**R Reemtsen**
164 Multidimensional Brownian excursions and potential theory
**K Burdzy**
165 Viscosity solutions and optimal control
**R J Elliott**
166 Nonlinear partial differential equations and their applications: Collège de France Seminar. Volume VIII
**H Brezis and J L Lions**
167 Theory and applications of inverse problems
**H Haario**
168 Energy stability and convection
**G P Galdi and B Straughan**
169 Additive groups of rings. Volume II
**S Feigelstock**
170 Numerical analysis 1987
**D F Griffiths and G A Watson**
171 Surveys of some recent results in operator theory. Volume I
**J B Conway and B B Morrel**
172 Amenable Banach algebras
**J-P Pier**
173 Pseudo-orbits of contact forms
**A Bahri**
174 Poisson algebras and Poisson manifolds
**K H Bhaskara and K Viswanath**
175 Maximum principles and eigenvalue problems in partial differential equations
**P W Schaefer**
176 Mathematical analysis of nonlinear, dynamic processes
**K U Grusa**
177 Cordes' two-parameter spectral representation theory
**D F McGhee and R H Picard**
178 Equivariant K-theory for proper actions
**N C Phillips**
179 Elliptic operators, topology and asymptotic methods
**J Roe**
180 Nonlinear evolution equations
**J K Engelbrecht, V E Fridman and E N Pelinovski**
181 Nonlinear partial differential equations and their applications: Collège de France Seminar. Volume IX
**H Brezis and J L Lions**
182 Critical points at infinity in some variational problems
**A Bahri**
183 Recent developments in hyperbolic equations
**L Cattabriga, F Colombini, M K V Murthy and S Spagnolo**
184 Optimization and identification of systems governed by evolution equations on Banach space
**N U Ahmed**
185 Free boundary problems: theory and applications. Volume I
**K H Hoffmann and J Sprekels**
186 Free boundary problems: theory and applications. Volume II
**K H Hoffmann and J Sprekels**
187 An introduction to intersection homology theory
**F Kirwan**
188 Derivatives, nuclei and dimensions on the frame of torsion theories
**J S Golan and H Simmons**
189 Theory of reproducing kernels and its applications
**S Saitoh**
190 Volterra integrodifferential equations in Banach spaces and applications
**G Da Prato and M Iannelli**
191 Nest algebras
**K R Davidson**
192 Surveys of some recent results in operator theory. Volume II
**J B Conway and B B Morrel**
193 Nonlinear variational problems. Volume II
**A Marino and M K V Murthy**
194 Stochastic processes with multidimensional parameter
**M E Dozzi**
195 Prestressed bodies
**D Iesan**
196 Hilbert space approach to some classical transforms
**R H Picard**
197 Stochastic calculus in application
**J R Norris**
198 Radical theory
**B J Gardner**
199 The $C^*$-algebras of a class of solvable Lie groups
**X Wang**
200 Stochastic analysis, path integration and dynamics
**K D Elworthy and J C Zambrini**

201 Riemannian geometry and holonomy groups
**S Salamon**
202 Strong asymptotics for extremal errors and polynomials associated with Erdős type weights
**D S Lubinsky**
203 Optimal control of diffusion processes
**V S Borkar**
204 Rings, modules and radicals
**B J Gardner**
205 Two-parameter eigenvalue problems in ordinary differential equations
**M Faierman**
206 Distributions and analytic functions
**R D Carmichael and D Mitrovic**
207 Semicontinuity, relaxation and integral representation in the calculus of variations
**G Buttazzo**
208 Recent advances in nonlinear elliptic and parabolic problems
**P Bénilan, M Chipot, L Evans and M Pierre**
209 Model completions, ring representations and the topology of the Pierce sheaf
**A Carson**
210 Retarded dynamical systems
**G Stepan**
211 Function spaces, differential operators and nonlinear analysis
**L Paivarinta**
212 Analytic function theory of one complex variable
**C C Yang, Y Komatu and K Niino**
213 Elements of stability of visco-elastic fluids
**J Dunwoody**
214 Jordan decomposition of generalized vector measures
**K D Schmidt**
215 A mathematical analysis of bending of plates with transverse shear deformation
**C Constanda**
216 Ordinary and partial differential equations. Volume II
**B D Sleeman and R J Jarvis**
217 Hilbert modules over function algebras
**R G Douglas and V I Paulsen**
218 Graph colourings
**R Wilson and R Nelson**
219 Hardy-type inequalities
**A Kufner and B Opic**
220 Nonlinear partial differential equations and their applications: Collège de France Seminar. Volume X
**H Brezis and J L Lions**
221 Workshop on dynamical systems
**E Shiels and Z Coelho**
222 Geometry and analysis in nonlinear dynamics
**H W Broer and F Takens**
223 Fluid dynamical aspects of combustion theory
**M Onofri and A Tesei**
224 Approximation of Hilbert space operators. Volume I. 2nd edition
**D Herrero**
225 Operator theory: proceedings of the 1988 GPOTS–Wabash conference
**J B Conway and B B Morrel**
226 Local cohomology and localization
**J L Bueso Montero, B Torrecillas Jover and A Verschoren**
227 Nonlinear waves and dissipative effects
**D Fusco and A Jeffrey**
228 Numerical analysis 1989
**D F Griffiths and G A Watson**
229 Recent developments in structured continua. Volume III
**D De Kee and P Kaloni**
230 Boolean methods in interpolation and approximation
**F J Delvos and W Schempp**
231 Further advances in twistor theory. Volume I
**L J Mason and L P Hughston**
232 Further advances in twistor theory. Volume II
**L J Mason and L P Hughston**
233 Geometry in the neighborhood of invariant manifolds of maps and flows and linearization
**U Kirchgraber and K Palmer**
234 Quantales and their applications
**K I Rosenthal**
235 Integral equations and inverse problems
**V Petkov and R Lazarov**
236 Pseudo-differential operators
**S R Simanca**
237 A functional analytic approach to statistical experiments
**I M Bomze**
238 Quantum mechanics, algebras and distributions
**D Dubin and M Hennings**
239 Hamilton flows and evolution semigroups
**J Gzyl**
240 Topics in controlled Markov chains
**V S Borkar**
241 Invariant manifold theory for hydrodynamic transition
**S Sritharan**
242 Lectures on the spectrum of $L^2(\Gamma\backslash G)$
**F L Williams**
243 Progress in variational methods in Hamiltonian systems and elliptic equations
**M Girardi, M Matzeu and F Pacella**
244 Optimization and nonlinear analysis
**A Ioffe, M Marcus and S Reich**
245 Inverse problems and imaging
**G F Roach**
246 Semigroup theory with applications to systems and control
**N U Ahmed**
247 Periodic-parabolic boundary value problems and positivity
**P Hess**
248 Distributions and pseudo-differential operators
**S Zaidman**
249 Progress in partial differential equations: the Metz surveys
**M Chipot and J Saint Jean Paulin**
250 Differential equations and control theory
**V Barbu**

251 Stability of stochastic differential equations with respect to semimartingales
**X Mao**
252 Fixed point theory and applications
**J Baillon and M Théra**
253 Nonlinear hyperbolic equations and field theory
**M K V Murthy and S Spagnolo**
254 Ordinary and partial differential equations. Volume III
**B D Sleeman and R J Jarvis**
255 Harmonic maps into homogeneous spaces
**M Black**
256 Boundary value and initial value problems in complex analysis: studies in complex analysis and its applications to PDEs 1
**R Kühnau and W Tutschke**
257 Geometric function theory and applications of complex analysis in mechanics: studies in complex analysis and its applications to PDEs 2
**R Kühnau and W Tutschke**
258 The development of statistics: recent contributions from China
**X R Chen, K T Fang and C C Yang**
259 Multiplication of distributions and applications to partial differential equations
**M Oberguggenberger**
260 Numerical analysis 1991
**D F Griffiths and G A Watson**
261 Schur's algorithm and several applications
**M Bakonyi and T Constantinescu**

C Bandle
University of Basel, Switzerland

J Bemelmans
University of Saarlandes, Germany

M Chipot
University of Metz, France

M Grüter
University of Saarlandes, Germany

and

J Saint Jean Paulin
University of Metz, France

(Editors)

# Progress in partial differential equations: calculus of variations, applications

Longman Scientific & Technical

Copublished in the United States with
John Wiley & Sons, Inc., New York

**Longman Scientific & Technical**
Longman Group UK Limited
Longman House, Burnt Mill, Harlow
Essex CM20 2JE, England
*and Associated companies throughout the world.*

*Copublished in the United States with*
*John Wiley & Sons Inc., 605 Third Avenue, New York, NY 10158*



First published 1992

AMS Subject Classification: (Main) 35XX, 49XX, 65XX
(Subsidiary) 76XX

ISSN 0269-3674

ISBN 0 582 21014 3

**British Library Cataloguing in Publication Data**

A catalogue record for this book is
available from the British Library

**Library of Congress Cataloging-in-Publication Data**

Progress in partial differential equations. Calculus of variations, applications / C. Bandle ... [et al.] (editors)
p. cm. -- (Pitman research notes in mathematics series ; 267)
Texts of conferences given at Pont-à-Mousson, June 1991 during the First European Conference on Elliptic and Parabolic Problems.
1. Differential equations, Parabolic--Congresses. 2. Differential equations, Elliptic--Congresses. 3. Calculus of variations--Congresses. I. Bandle, Catherine, 1943- . II. Title: Calculus of variations, applications. III. Series.
QA377.P74 1992
515'.353--dc20 92-18954
CIP

Printed and bound in Great Britain
by Biddles Ltd, Guildford and King's Lynn

# Contents

# Preface

This book is a collection of texts from conferences that were given in Pont-à-Mousson in June 1991 during the First European Conference on Elliptic and Parabolic Problems.

The subjects addressed in this volume include Calculus of Variations, Free Boundary Problems, Homogenization, Modelling, Numerical Analysis and various applications in physics, mechanics and engineering.

We would like to thank all the participants to this meeting for their help in making it successful. Special thanks go to the contributors of this volume.

The meeting has been made possible by grants from the "Caisse d'Epargne de Lorraine Nord", the C.N.R.S., the "Région de Lorraine", the Universities of Basel, Metz and Saarbrücken. We express our deep appreciation to them.

Finally, we thank Longman for helping us to publish these proceedings.

C. Bandle, J. Bemelmans, M. Chipot, M. Grüter, J. Saint Jean Paulin

A BENSOUSSAN*, L BOCCARDO† AND F MURAT‡

# Homogenization of a nonlinear partial differential equation with unbounded solution

## Introduction

We consider in this article the following homogenization problem

$$A^\varepsilon u^\varepsilon + g^\varepsilon(x, u^\varepsilon, Du^\varepsilon) = h, \quad u^\varepsilon \in H_0^1(\Omega)$$

where

$$A^\varepsilon u^\varepsilon = -div(a^\varepsilon(x) Du^\varepsilon)$$

$a^\varepsilon(x)$ being a sequence of matrices satisfying the assumptions of $H$-convergence of L. Tartar [6], F. Murat - L. Tartar [5], $g^\varepsilon$ is a nonlinear operator with quadratic growth in $Du^\varepsilon$. In the situation that we consider $h \in H^{-1}(\Omega)$ and the sequence $u^\varepsilon$ is not bounded in $L^\infty(\Omega)$. This creates a specific difficulty. Indeed the case when $u^\varepsilon$ remains bounded ($h$ bounded) has been considered and solved by the authors in a preceding article [1].

For the existence theory of the above equation, an assumption of the form

$$g^\varepsilon(x, s, \xi)s \geq 0$$

is used. We show in this article that it suffices to study the convergence as $\varepsilon \to 0$.

## 1 Statement of the problem

### 1.1 Assumptions and notations

We consider a family of matrices $a^\varepsilon(x)$ satisfying

$$a^\varepsilon(x)\xi.\xi \geq \alpha|\xi|^2, \ \forall \xi \in R^n, \quad \alpha > 0 \tag{1.1}$$

$$(a^\varepsilon(x))^{-1}\xi.\xi \geq \alpha_0|\xi|^2, \ \forall \xi \in R^n, \quad \alpha_0 > 0 \tag{1.2}$$

$$a^\varepsilon(x) \quad \text{measurable} \tag{1.3}$$

*University Paris Dauphine and INRIA
†University of Rome I
‡University of Paris VI and CNRS

We shall say that the family $a^\varepsilon(x)$ belongs to $M(\alpha, \alpha_0)$. Following the theory of abstract homogenization introduced by L. Tartar [6] and F. Murat - L. Tartar [5], we shall assume the following properties. Let $\Omega$ be an open bounded subset of $R^n$. In the sequel $x \in \Omega$. We assume that there exists a sequence of vector functions $v^\varepsilon(x) \in (H^1(\Omega))^n$ such that

$$v^\varepsilon \to x \text{ in } (H^1(\Omega))^n \text{ weakly} \tag{1.4}$$

$$a^\varepsilon(Dv^\varepsilon)^* \to a \text{ in } (L^2(\Omega))^{n\times n} \text{ weakly} \tag{1.5}$$

$$div(a^\varepsilon(Dv^\varepsilon)^*) \to div\ a \text{ in } (H^{-1}(\Omega))^n \text{ strongly.} \tag{1.6}$$

It is classical that the limit matrix $a$ also belongs to $M(\alpha, \alpha_0)$.

We next consider a sequence $g^\varepsilon(x, s, \xi)$ satisfying the assumptions

$$g^\varepsilon(x, s, \xi)s \geq 0 \tag{1.7}$$

$$|g^\varepsilon(x, s, \xi)| \leq b(|s|)(c^\varepsilon(x) + |\xi|^2) \tag{1.8}$$

$b$ increasing function from $R^+$ to $R^+$, $c^\varepsilon \in L^1(\Omega)$, $c^\varepsilon \to c$ in $L^1(\Omega)$ weakly and is equiintegrable, $c^\varepsilon \geq 0$.

### 1.2 The problem

Let $A^\varepsilon$ be the linear operator from $H_0^1(\Omega)$ to $H^{-1}(\Omega)$ defined by

$$A^\varepsilon\varphi = -\ div(a^\varepsilon(x)D\varphi).$$

We consider the following problem

$$A^\varepsilon u^\varepsilon + g^\varepsilon(x, u^\varepsilon, Du^\varepsilon) = h, \quad u^\varepsilon \in H_0^1(\Omega) \tag{1.9}$$

with a right hand side satisfying

$$h \in H^{-1}(\Omega). \tag{1.10}$$

We have proven in a preceding paper [2], that for fixed $\varepsilon$, there exists a solution $u^\varepsilon$ of (1.9) (not necessarily unique).

## 2 A strong convergence result

### 2.1 Preliminaries

Multiplying (1.9) by $u^\varepsilon$ and using (1.7) we immediately deduce

$$\langle A^\varepsilon u^\varepsilon, u^\varepsilon\rangle \leq \langle h, u^\varepsilon\rangle \tag{2.1}$$

and from (1.1), we get

$$\alpha \int |Du^\varepsilon|^2 dx \leq \|h\|\ \|u^\varepsilon\|$$

hence at once

$$\|u^\varepsilon\|_{H_0^1(\Omega)} \leq C. \tag{2.2}$$

Hence we can extract a subsequence still denoted by $u^\varepsilon$, such that

$$u^\varepsilon \to u \text{ in } H_0^1(\Omega) \text{ weakly, and a.e..} \tag{2.3}$$

We shall introduce the function $z^\varepsilon$ solution of

$$A^\varepsilon z^\varepsilon = Au, \quad z^\varepsilon \in H_0^1(\Omega) \tag{2.4}$$

where $A$ is the homogenized operator

$$A\varphi = -\, div(a(x)D\varphi). \tag{2.5}$$

From the classical homogenization theory we have

$$z^\varepsilon \to u \text{ in } H_0^1(\Omega) \text{ weakly and a.e.} \tag{2.6}$$

$$Dz^\varepsilon - (Dv^\varepsilon)^* Du \to 0 \text{ in } (L^1(\Omega))^n \text{ strongly} \tag{2.7}$$

$$a^\varepsilon Dz^\varepsilon \to aDu \text{ in } (L^2(\Omega))^n \text{ weakly} \tag{2.8}$$

$$\int_\Omega a^\varepsilon Dz^\varepsilon Dz^\varepsilon \varphi^\varepsilon dx \to \int_\Omega aDuDu\varphi dx \tag{2.9}$$

whenever $\|\varphi^\varepsilon\|_{L^\infty} \leq c$, $\varphi^\varepsilon \to \varphi$ a.e.

The proof of (2.9) makes use of Meyer's estimate [4], which states that

> there exists $p > 2$, such that $A^\varepsilon$ is an isomorphism from $W_0^{1,p}(\Omega)$ to $W^{-1,p}(\Omega)$. The norm of $A^\varepsilon$ in $L(W_0^{1,p}\,;\,W^{-1,p})$ and of $(A^\varepsilon)^{-1}$ in $L(W^{-1,p}\,;\,W_0^{1,p})$ are bounded in $\varepsilon$ (2.10)

The property (2.10) also allows to assert the equiintegrability

$$\int_\omega |Dz^\varepsilon|^2 dx \to 0, \text{ as meas } \omega \to 0, \text{ uniformly in } \varepsilon. \tag{2.11}$$

Let now $T_k$ be the truncation operator defined by

$$T_k\varphi = \begin{cases} \varphi & \text{if } |\varphi| \leq k \\ k & \text{if } \varphi > k \\ -k & \text{if } \varphi < -k \end{cases} \tag{2.12}$$

Note that

$$|T_k\varphi_1 - T_k\varphi_2| \leq |\varphi_1 - \varphi_2|.$$

## 2.2 The main result

Our objective is to prove the

**Theorem 2.1** *Under the assumptions (1.1) to (1.8) we have*

$$T_k u^\varepsilon - T_k z^\varepsilon \to 0 \text{ in } H_0^1(\Omega). \tag{2.13}$$

■

We begin with the

**Lemma 2.1** *One has the properties*

$$\begin{array}{lll} T_k z^\varepsilon & \to & T_k u \ in\ H_0^1(\Omega)\ weakly \\ DT_k z^\varepsilon - (Dv^\varepsilon)^* DT_k u & \to & 0\ in\ (L^1(\Omega))^n\ strongly \\ a^\varepsilon DT_k z^\varepsilon & \to & aDT_k u\ in\ (L^2(\Omega))^n\ weakly \\ \int_\Omega a^\varepsilon DT_k z^\varepsilon DT_k z^\varepsilon \varphi^\varepsilon dx & \to & \int aDT_k u DT_k u \varphi dx,\ if\ \varphi^\varepsilon \to \varphi\ a.e.\ and\ \|\varphi^\varepsilon\|_{L^\infty} \le C. \end{array} \tag{2.14}$$

**Proof** Since $DT_k z^\varepsilon = Dz^\varepsilon \mathbf{1}_{|z^\varepsilon|\le k}$, $T_k z^\varepsilon$ remains in a bounded subset of $H_0^1(\Omega)$. From (2.6) and the Lipschitz property of $T_k$ we deduce that $T_k z^\varepsilon \to T_k u$ pointwise. Hence the first assertion (2.14). Next

$$\int_\Omega |DT_k z^\varepsilon - (Dv^\varepsilon)^* DT_k u| dx \le \int_\Omega |Dz^\varepsilon - (Dv^\varepsilon)^* Du| dx$$
$$+ \left(\int_\Omega \|Dv^\varepsilon\|^2 dx\right)^{1/2} \left(\int_\Omega |Du|^2 (\mathbf{1}_{|z^\varepsilon|<k} - \mathbf{1}_{|u|<k})^2 dx\right)^{1/2}$$

hence the $2^{nd}$ assertion (2.14), as easily seen.

Writing again

$$a^\varepsilon DT_k z^\varepsilon = a^\varepsilon(DT_k z^\varepsilon - (Dv^\varepsilon)^* DT_k u) + a^\varepsilon (Dv^\varepsilon) DT_k u.$$

We see from the $2^{nd}$ assertion (2.14) that $a^\varepsilon(DT_k z^\varepsilon - (Dv^\varepsilon)^* DT_k u) \to 0$ in $(L^1(\Omega))^n$. Moreover $a^\varepsilon(Dv^\varepsilon)^* DT_k u \to aDT_k u$ in $(L^1(\Omega))^n$ weakly, hence $a^\varepsilon DT_k z^\varepsilon \to aDT_k u$ in $(L^1(\Omega))^n$ weakly. Since $a^\varepsilon DT_k z^\varepsilon$ is bounded in $(L^2(\Omega))^n$, we also have weak convergence in $(L^2(\Omega))^n$.

To prove the last assertion consider a sequence $\varphi_N \in C^\infty(\bar\Omega)$ such that $\varphi_N$ bounded $\varphi_N \to \varphi$ a.e. Let also $u_\mu \in C_0^\infty(\Omega)$, $u_\mu \to u$ in $H_0^1$. Define $z_\mu^\varepsilon$ by

$$A^\varepsilon z_\mu^\varepsilon = Au_\mu.$$

Note that from Meyer's estimate

$$\|z_\mu^\varepsilon\|_{W^{1,p}} \le C_p \|u_\mu\|_{W^{1,p}}$$

with $C_p$ independant of $\varepsilon$, and some convenient $p > 2$. We write

$$\left|\int a^\varepsilon Dz^\varepsilon DT_k z^\varepsilon \varphi^\varepsilon dx - \int aDuDT_k u\varphi dx\right|$$

$$\le \left|\int a^\varepsilon D(z^\varepsilon - z_\mu^\varepsilon) DT_k z^\varepsilon \varphi^\varepsilon dx\right| + \left|\int a^\varepsilon Dz_\mu^\varepsilon DT_k z^\varepsilon (\varphi^\varepsilon - \varphi_N) dx\right|$$

$$+ \left|\int a^\varepsilon D(z_\mu^\varepsilon - z^\varepsilon) DT_k z^\varepsilon \varphi_N dx\right| + \left|\int a^\varepsilon Dz^\varepsilon DT_k z^\varepsilon \varphi_N dx - \int aDuDT_k u\varphi_N dx\right| \tag{2.15}$$

$$+ \left|\int aDuDT_k u(\varphi_N - \varphi) dx\right| \le C\|u_\mu - u\|_{H_0^1} + C_{\mu,p}|\varphi^\varepsilon - \varphi_N|_{L^{2p/p-2}}$$

$$+ \left|\int (a^\varepsilon Dz^\varepsilon DT_k z^\varepsilon - aDuDT_k u)\varphi_N dx\right| + \left|\int aDuDT_k u(\varphi_N - \varphi) dx\right|$$

But

$$\left|\int (a^\varepsilon Dz^\varepsilon DT_k z^\varepsilon - aDuDT_k u)\varphi_N dx\right| \leq \left|\int aDu(DT_k z^\varepsilon - DT_k u)\varphi_N dx\right|$$
$$+ \left|\int aDu.D\varphi_N(T_k z^\varepsilon - T_k u)dx\right| \to 0 \; as \; \varepsilon \to 0$$

hence

$$\overline{\lim_{\varepsilon\to 0}}\left|\int a^\varepsilon Dz^\varepsilon DT_k z^\varepsilon \varphi^\varepsilon dx - \int aDuDT_k u\varphi dx\right|$$
$$\leq C\|u_\mu - u\|_{H_0^1} + C_{\mu,p}|\varphi - \varphi_N|_{L^{2p/p-2}} + \left|\int aDuDT_k u(\varphi_N - \varphi)dx\right|$$

Letting $N$ tend to $\infty$, then $\mu$ tend to $\infty$, the desired result obtains. ■

Let $\theta(s) = s\exp\lambda s^2$, with $\lambda$ a parameter to be selected later. Multiplying (1.9) by $\theta(T_k u^\varepsilon - T_k z^\varepsilon)$ we get

$$\begin{aligned}&\int a^\varepsilon Du^\varepsilon(DT_k u^\varepsilon - DT_k z^\varepsilon)\theta'(T_k u^\varepsilon - T_k z^\varepsilon)dx + \int g^\varepsilon\theta(T_k u^\varepsilon - T_k z^\varepsilon)dx \\ &= \langle h, \theta(T_k u^\varepsilon - T_k z^\varepsilon)\rangle.\end{aligned} \tag{2.16}$$

From (1.7) we deduce

$$\begin{aligned}&\int g^\varepsilon(x, u^\varepsilon, Du^\varepsilon)\theta(T_k u^\varepsilon - T_k z^\varepsilon)dx \geq \int g^\varepsilon(x, T_k u^\varepsilon, DT_k u^\varepsilon)\theta(T_k u^\varepsilon - T_k z^\varepsilon)\mathbf{1}_{|u^\varepsilon|<k}dx \\ &\geq -b(k)\int c^\varepsilon(x)\theta(|T_k u^\varepsilon - T_k z^\varepsilon|)\mathbf{1}_{|u^\varepsilon|<k}dx \\ &-b(k)\int |DT_k u^\varepsilon|^2\theta(|T_k u^\varepsilon - T_k z^\varepsilon|)dx.\end{aligned}$$

From (2.16) it then follows

$$\begin{aligned}&\int a^\varepsilon(DT_k u^\varepsilon - DT_k z^\varepsilon)(DT_k u^\varepsilon - DT_k z^\varepsilon)\theta'(T_k u^\varepsilon - T_k z^\varepsilon)dx \\ &- \int a^\varepsilon Du^\varepsilon DT_k z^\varepsilon \mathbf{1}_{|u^\varepsilon|>k}\theta'(T_k u^\varepsilon - T_k z^\varepsilon)dx \\ &+ \int a^\varepsilon DT_k z^\varepsilon(DT_k u^\varepsilon - DT_k z^\varepsilon)\theta'(T_k u^\varepsilon - T_k z^\varepsilon)dx \leq \langle h, \theta(T_k u^\varepsilon - T_k z^\varepsilon)\rangle \\ &+b(k)\int c^\varepsilon(x)\theta(|T_k u^\varepsilon - T_k z^\varepsilon|)\mathbf{1}_{|u^\varepsilon|<k}dx + b(k)\int |DT_k u^\varepsilon|^2\theta(|T_k u^\varepsilon - T_k z^\varepsilon|)dx\end{aligned} \tag{2.17}$$

hence

$$\begin{aligned}&\frac{\alpha}{2}\int |DT_k u^\varepsilon - DT_k z^\varepsilon|^2\theta'(T_k u^\varepsilon - T_k z^\varepsilon)dx \\ &\leq \alpha_0\|u^\varepsilon\|\left(\int |DT_k z^\varepsilon|^2\theta'^2(T_k u^\varepsilon - T_k z^\varepsilon)dx\right)^{1/2} \\ &+\frac{\alpha_0^2}{2\alpha}\int |DT_k z^\varepsilon|^2\theta'(T_k u^\varepsilon - T_k z^\varepsilon)dx + \langle h, \theta(T_k u^\varepsilon - T_k z^\varepsilon)\rangle \\ &+b(k)\int c^\varepsilon(x)\theta(|T_k u^\varepsilon - T_k z^\varepsilon|)\mathbf{1}_{|u^\varepsilon|<k}dx \\ &+2b(k)\int |DT_k u^\varepsilon - DT_k z^\varepsilon|^2\theta(|T_k u^\varepsilon - T_k z^\varepsilon|)dx \\ &+2b(k)\int |DT_k z^\varepsilon|^2\theta(|T_k u^\varepsilon - T_k z^\varepsilon|)dx\end{aligned}$$

Taking $\lambda$ sufficiently large, depending on $k$, we can derive

$$\begin{aligned}\frac{\alpha}{4}\int |DT_k u^\varepsilon - DT_k z^\varepsilon|^2 dx \le C\Big(\int |DT_k z^\varepsilon|^2 \theta'^2 (T_k u^\varepsilon - T_k z^\varepsilon) dx\Big) \\ + \int |DT_k z^\varepsilon|^2 \left(\frac{\alpha_0^2}{2\alpha}\theta'(T_k u^\varepsilon - T_k z^\varepsilon) + 2b(k)\theta(|T_k u^\varepsilon - T_k z^\varepsilon|)\right) dx \\ + \langle h, \theta(T_k u^\varepsilon - T_k z^\varepsilon)\rangle + b(k)\int c^\varepsilon(x)\theta(|T_k u^\varepsilon - T_k z^\varepsilon|)\mathbf{1}_{|u^\varepsilon|<k} dx.\end{aligned} \tag{2.17)'$$

As $\varepsilon$ tends to 0, the right hand side of (2.17)' tends to 0. For instance we first state

$$\begin{aligned}\Big(\int |DT_k z^\varepsilon|^2 \theta'^2 (T_k u^\varepsilon - T_k z^\varepsilon) dx\Big)^{1/2} \le \sqrt{2}\Big(\int |D(z^\varepsilon - z_\mu^\varepsilon)|^2 \theta'^2 (T_k u^\varepsilon - T_k z^\varepsilon) dx\Big)^{1/2} \\ + \sqrt{2}\Big(\int |Dz_\mu^\varepsilon|^2 \theta'^2 (T_k u^\varepsilon - T_k z^\varepsilon) dx\Big)^{1/2} \\ \le C_k \|u - u_\mu\|_{H_0^1} + C_{\mu,p}\Big(\int \theta'^{2p/p-2}(T_k u^\varepsilon - T_k z^\varepsilon) dx\Big)^{\frac{p-2}{2p}}\end{aligned}$$

hence, letting first $\varepsilon$ tend to 0, then $\mu$ to $\infty$, we see that the first term at the right hand side of (2.17)' tends to 0, as $\varepsilon \to 0$. In a similar way, one proves that the $2^{nd}$ term tends to 0.

Using (1.8), we also see that the last term at the right hand side of (2.17)' tends to 0. Thus the desired result. ■

**Corollary 2.1** *We have*

$$u^\varepsilon - z^\varepsilon \to 0 \text{ in } H_0^1(\Omega). \tag{2.18}$$

**Proof** Write

$$u^\varepsilon - z^\varepsilon = u^\varepsilon - T_k u^\varepsilon + T_k u^\varepsilon - T_k z^\varepsilon + T_k z^\varepsilon - z^\varepsilon.$$

Now

$$\begin{aligned}\alpha\int |D(u^\varepsilon - T_k u^\varepsilon)|^2 dx \le \int a^\varepsilon D(u^\varepsilon - T_k u^\varepsilon).D(u^\varepsilon - T_k u^\varepsilon) dx \\ = \int a^\varepsilon Du^\varepsilon.Du^\varepsilon \mathbf{1}_{|u^\varepsilon|>k} dx = \int a^\varepsilon Du^\varepsilon.D(u^\varepsilon - T_k u^\varepsilon) dx \\ \le \langle h, u^\varepsilon - T_k u^\varepsilon\rangle\end{aligned}$$

hence

$$\overline{\lim_{\varepsilon\to 0}}\|z^\varepsilon - T_k u^\varepsilon\| \le 0_1(k) \quad \text{with } 0_1(k) \to 0 \text{ as } k \to \infty.$$

Similarly

$$\overline{\lim_{\varepsilon\to 0}}\|z^\varepsilon - T_k z^\varepsilon\| \le 0_2(k) \quad \text{with } 0_2(k) \to 0 \text{ as } k \to \infty.$$

These estimates and (2.13) imply the desired result. ■

# 3 The limit problem

## 3.1 Assumptions

Our objective in this section is to identify a limit problem for the limit $u$. It is impossible to go further without additional assumptions of $g^\varepsilon$. We shall assume the following properties

$$\begin{array}{l} |g^\varepsilon(x,s,\xi) - g^\varepsilon(x,s,\xi')| \le b(|s|)(c_1^\varepsilon(x) + |\xi| + |\xi'|)|\xi - \xi'| \\ c_1^\varepsilon \in L^2(\Omega),\ c_1^\varepsilon \to c_1 \text{ in } L^2(\Omega) \text{ weakly, } c_1^\varepsilon \ge 0. \end{array} \tag{3.1}$$

$$\begin{array}{l} \forall k, \text{ and, } s,\ s' \text{ with } |s|,\ |s'| \le k, \\ |g^\varepsilon(x,s,\xi) - g^\varepsilon(x,s',\xi)| \le \omega_k(|s-s'|)(c_2^\varepsilon(x) + |\xi|^2) \\ c_2^\varepsilon \in L^2(\Omega),\ c_2^\varepsilon \to c_2 \text{ in } L^2(\Omega) \text{ weakly, } c_2^\varepsilon \ge 0. \\ \omega_k \text{ continuous on } R^+,\ \omega_k(0) = 0. \end{array} \tag{3.2}$$

$$|g^\varepsilon(x, T_k s, \xi)| \le |g^\varepsilon(x,s,\xi)|. \tag{3.3}$$

In addition, we shall assume

$$\|Dv^\varepsilon\|_{L^\infty} \le K. \tag{3.4}$$

$$\text{The function } c^\varepsilon \text{ in (1.8) is bounded in } L^2. \tag{3.5}$$

These assumptions can be slightly weakned, but the proofs are simplified this way.

## 3.2 Construction of $g(x,s,\xi)$

We follow Boccardo - Murat [3]. We consider the sequence $g^\varepsilon(x,s,(Dv^\varepsilon)^*\xi)$. From (1.8) and (3.4) we deduce

$$|g^\varepsilon(x,s,(Dv^\varepsilon)^*\xi)| \le b(|s|)(c^\varepsilon(x) + K^2|\xi|^2).$$

Let $X$ be a countable dense subset of $R^{n+1}(s,\xi)$. There exists a subsequence such that (thanks to (3.5))

$$g^\varepsilon(x,s,(Dv^\varepsilon)^*\xi) \to g(x,s,\xi) \text{ in } L^2(\Omega) \text{ weakly, } \forall s,\xi \in X. \tag{3.6}$$

We then have the

**Lemma 3.1** *The function $g$ satisfies in the set $X$*

$$\begin{array}{rcl} g(x,s,\xi)s & \ge & 0 \\ |g(s,x,\xi)| & \le & b(|s|)(c(x) + K^2|\xi|^2) \end{array} \tag{3.7}$$

$$\begin{array}{lcl} |g(x,s,\xi) - g(x,s,\xi')| & \le & Kb(|s|)(c_1(x) + K|\xi| + K|\xi'|)|\xi - \xi'| \\ |g(x,s,\xi) - g(x,s',\xi)| & \le & \omega_k(|s-s'|)(c_2(x) + K^2|\xi|^2) \\ \forall s, s' & \textit{with} & |s|, |s'| \le k. \end{array} \tag{3.8}$$

**Proof** Let $\varphi \in C_0^\infty(\Omega)$, $\varphi \geq 0$. Let $(s, \xi) \in X$, $s \geq 0$, one has

$$\int g^\varepsilon(x, s, (Dv^\varepsilon)^* \xi) \varphi(x) dx \geq 0$$

hence $\int g(x, s, \xi) \varphi(x) dx \geq 0$. Since $\varphi$ is arbitrary $g(x, s, \xi) \geq 0$. Similarly $g(x, s, \xi) \leq 0$ whenever $s \leq 0$. The first property (3.7) is proved.

Next we have

$$\begin{aligned} \int g(x, s, \xi) \varphi(x) dx &= \lim \int g^\varepsilon(x, s, (Dv^\varepsilon)^* \xi) \varphi(x) dx \\ &\leq \lim \int b(|s|)(c^\varepsilon(x) + K|\xi|^2) \varphi(x) dx \\ &= \int b(|s|)(c(x) + K|\xi|^2) \varphi(x) dx. \end{aligned}$$

Hence $g(x, s, \xi) \leq b((s))(c(x) + K|\xi|^2)$ a.e. Similarly $g(x, s, \xi) \geq -b((s))(c(x) + K|\xi|^2)$ a.e., hence the second property (3.7).

In the same way

$$\begin{aligned} &\int (g(x, s, \xi) - g(x, s, \xi')) \varphi(x) dx = \lim \int (g^\varepsilon(x, s, (Dv^\varepsilon)^* \xi) \\ &\quad - g^\varepsilon(x, s, (Dv^\varepsilon)^* \xi')) \varphi(x) dx \leq \lim \int K b(|s|)(c_1^\varepsilon + K|\xi| + K|\xi'|)|\xi - \xi'| \varphi(x) dx \\ &\quad = \int K b(|s|)(c_1 + K|\xi| + K|\xi'|)|\xi - \xi'| \varphi(x) dx \end{aligned}$$

hence

$$g(x, s, \xi) - g(x, s, \xi') \leq K b(|s|)(c_1(x) + K|\xi| + K|\xi'|)|\xi - \xi'| \text{ a.e.}$$

Obtaining similarly an opposite inequality, we deduce the first inequality (3.8). The second inequality (3.8) is proved in a similar way. ■

From the estimates (3.8) one can extend the definition of $g$ to any pair $s, \xi$ in $R^{n+1}$ and (3.7), (3.8) are satisfied. Moreover, it is easy to improve (3.6) to

$$g^\varepsilon(x, s, (Dv^\varepsilon)^* \xi) \to g(x, s, \xi) \text{ in } L^2(\Omega) \text{ weakly, } \forall s, \xi \in R^{n+1}. \tag{3.9}$$

We next assert the

**Lemma 3.2** *Let $\varphi \in L^\infty(\Omega)$, and $\Gamma(x) \in (L^2(\Omega))^n$, let $\theta^\varepsilon$ bounded, $\theta^\varepsilon \to \theta$ pointwise, then one has*

$$\int (g^\varepsilon(x, \varphi(x), (Dv^\varepsilon)^* \Gamma(x)) - g(x, \varphi(x), \Gamma(x))) \theta^\varepsilon(x) dx \to 0. \tag{3.10}$$

**Proof** From (3.9) we deduce easily that if $\varphi$ is a step function on $\Omega$ bounded and $\Gamma$ is a step function with values in $R^n$, also bounded, then one has

$$g^\varepsilon(x, \varphi(x), (Dv^\varepsilon)^* \Gamma(x)) \to g(x, \varphi(x), \Gamma(x)) \text{ weakly in } L^2(\Omega). \tag{3.11}$$

Let now $\varphi$ and $\Gamma$ as in the statement of the lemma. We construct a sequence $\varphi_k$, $\Gamma_k$, such that

$$\begin{aligned}\varphi_k &\to \varphi \text{ a.e. and } \|\varphi_k\|_{L^\infty} \leq \beta,\\ \Gamma_k &\to \Gamma \text{ in } (L^2(\Omega))^n \text{ and a.e.}\end{aligned}$$

$\varphi_k$, $\Gamma_k$ being step functions.

We note that

$$\begin{aligned}&|g^\varepsilon(x,\varphi(x),(Dv^\varepsilon)^*\Gamma(x)) - g^\varepsilon(x,\varphi_k(x),(Dv^\varepsilon)^*\Gamma_k(x))|\\ &\quad\leq \omega_\beta(|\varphi_k-\varphi|)(c_2^\varepsilon(x)+K^2\|\Gamma(x)\|^2)+b(\beta)(c_1^\varepsilon+K\|\Gamma(x)\|\\ &\quad +K\|\Gamma_k(x)\|)\|\Gamma(x)-\Gamma_k(x)\|.\end{aligned} \tag{3.12}$$

Next we write

$$\begin{aligned}&\int(g^\varepsilon(x,\varphi(x),(Dv^\varepsilon)^*\Gamma(x)) - g(x,\varphi(x),\Gamma(x)))\theta^\varepsilon(x)dx\\ &\quad= \int(g^\varepsilon(x,\varphi(x),(Dv^\varepsilon)^*\Gamma(x)) - g^\varepsilon(x,\varphi_k(x),(Dv^\varepsilon)^*\Gamma_k(x)))\theta^\varepsilon(x)dx\\ &\quad+\int(g^\varepsilon(x,\varphi_k(x),(Dv^\varepsilon)^*\Gamma_k(x)) - g(x,\varphi_k(x),\Gamma_k(x)))\theta^\varepsilon(x)dx\\ &\quad+\int(g(x,\varphi_k(x),\Gamma_k(x)) - g(x,\varphi(x),\Gamma(x)))\theta^\varepsilon(x)dx = I_k^\varepsilon + II_k^\varepsilon + III_k^\varepsilon.\end{aligned}$$

One has from (3.12)

$$\begin{aligned}\overline{\lim_{\varepsilon\to 0}}|I_k^\varepsilon| &\leq c\int[\omega_\beta(|\varphi_k-\varphi|)(c_2(x)+K^2\|\Gamma(x)\|^2)\\ &+b(\beta)(c_1(x)+K\|\Gamma(x)\|+K\|\Gamma_k(x)\|)\|\Gamma(x)-\Gamma_k(x)\|]|\theta|dx = 0_1(k)\end{aligned}$$

and $0_1(k)\to 0$ as $k\to\infty$.

Similarly

$$\overline{\lim_{\varepsilon\to 0}}|III_k^\varepsilon| \leq 0_3(k)\to 0 \text{ as } k\to\infty.$$

Now in view of (3.11), $\overline{\lim_{\varepsilon\to 0}}|II_k^\varepsilon| = 0$, for fixed $k$. Therefore (3.10) obtains. ■

## 3.3 The main result

We now state the following

**Theorem 3.1** *Assume (1.1) to (1.8) as well as (3.1) to (3.5). Consider a subsequence $u^\varepsilon$ such that (2.3) holds, as well as (3.6). Then the limit $u$ is a solution of*

$$Au + g(x,u,Du) = h, \quad u\in H_0^1(\Omega). \tag{3.13}$$

■

We begin with

**Lemma 3.3** *One has*

$$g^\varepsilon(x,T_ku^\varepsilon,Du^\varepsilon) \to g(x,T_ku,Du) \text{ in } L^1(\Omega) \text{ weakly} \tag{3.14}$$

$$\int g^\varepsilon(x,T_ku^\varepsilon,Du^\varepsilon)T_ku^\varepsilon dx \to \int g(x,T_ku,Du)T_kudx \tag{3.15}$$

**Proof** Let $\varphi \in L^\infty(\Omega)$, then

$$\int |(g^\varepsilon(x, T_k u^\varepsilon, Du^\varepsilon) - g^\varepsilon(x, T_k u, (Dv^\varepsilon)^* Du))\varphi| dx$$
$$\leq \|\varphi\| \int [\omega_k(|T_k u - T_k u^\varepsilon|)(c_2^\varepsilon(x) + K^2\|Du\|^2)$$
$$+ b(k)(c_1^\varepsilon(x) + |Du^\varepsilon| + K|Du|)|(Dv^\varepsilon)^* Du - Du^\varepsilon|]dx.$$

From (2.18) and (2.7) we deduce

$$\overline{\lim_{\varepsilon\to 0}} \left| \int (g^\varepsilon(x, T_k u^\varepsilon, Du^\varepsilon) - g^\varepsilon(x, T_k u, (Dv^\varepsilon)^* Du))\varphi dx \right| = 0 \tag{3.16}$$

On the other hand from lemma 3.2,

$$\lim_{\varepsilon\to 0} \left| \int (g^\varepsilon(x, T_k u, (Dv^\varepsilon)^* Du) - g(x, T_k u, Du))\varphi dx \right| = 0$$

hence(3.14).

To prove (3.15) we proceed similarly using the fact

$$\int (g^\varepsilon(x, T_k u, Du) - g(x, T_k u, Du))T_k u^\varepsilon dx \to 0$$

which follows from (3.10). ■

**Lemma 3.4** *One has*

$$g^\varepsilon(x, u^\varepsilon, Du^\varepsilon) \to g(x, u, Du) \text{ in } L^1(\Omega) \text{ weakly.} \tag{3.17}$$

**Proof** We first notice that from the equation (1.9) one has

$$\int u^\varepsilon g^\varepsilon(x, u^\varepsilon, Du^\varepsilon) dx \leq C. \tag{3.18}$$

Using (3.3) we deduce

$$\begin{aligned} s g^\varepsilon(x, T_k s, \xi) &\leq s g^\varepsilon(x, s, \xi) \\ T_k s g^\varepsilon(x, T_k s, \xi) &\leq s g^\varepsilon(x, s, \xi) \end{aligned}$$

hence also

$$\begin{aligned} \int u^\varepsilon g^\varepsilon(x, T_k u^\varepsilon, Du^\varepsilon) dx &\leq C \\ \int T_k u^\varepsilon g^\varepsilon(x, T_k u^\varepsilon, Du^\varepsilon) dx &\leq C \end{aligned} \tag{3.19}$$

From (3.15) we deduce

$$\int u g(x, T_k u, Du) T_k u dx \leq C$$

and from Fatou's lemma we deduce

$$\int u g(x, u, Du) dx \leq C \tag{3.20}$$

We then write for $\varphi \in L^\infty(\Omega)$,

$$\int (g^\varepsilon(x,u^\varepsilon,Du^\varepsilon) - g(x,u,Du))\varphi dx = \int (g^\varepsilon(x,u^\varepsilon,Du^\varepsilon) - g^\varepsilon(x,T_k u^\varepsilon,Du^\varepsilon))\varphi$$
$$+ \int (g^\varepsilon(x,T_k u^\varepsilon,Du^\varepsilon) - g(x,T_k u,Du))\varphi dx$$
$$+ \int (g(x,T_k u,Du) - g(x,u,Du))\varphi dx = I_k^\varepsilon + II_k^\varepsilon + III_k.$$

But

$$I_k^\varepsilon = \int (g^\varepsilon(x,u^\varepsilon,Du^\varepsilon) - g^\varepsilon(x,T_k u^\varepsilon,Du^\varepsilon))\mathbf{1}_{|u^\varepsilon|>k}\varphi dx$$

hence

$$\begin{aligned} |I_k^\varepsilon| &\le 2\|\varphi\| \int |g^\varepsilon(x,u^\varepsilon,Du^\varepsilon)|\mathbf{1}_{|u^\varepsilon|>k}dx \\ &\le 2\frac{\|\varphi\|}{k}\int u^\varepsilon g^\varepsilon(x,u^\varepsilon,Du^\varepsilon)dx \le \frac{C}{k}. \end{aligned}$$

Similarly

$$|III_k| \le \frac{C}{k}.$$

Using (3.14) one has $II_k^\varepsilon \to 0$ as $\varepsilon \to \infty$, for fixed $k$. The result (3.17) follows immediately. ■

**Proof of Theorem 3.1** It remains to prove (for instance)

$$A^\varepsilon u^\varepsilon \to Au \text{ in } H^{-1}.$$

But

$$\|A^\varepsilon u^\varepsilon - A^\varepsilon z^\varepsilon\|_{H^{-1}} \le c\|u^\varepsilon - z^\varepsilon\|_{H_0^1} \to 0$$

and since $A^\varepsilon z^\varepsilon = Au$, the desired result follows. ■

# References


[1] A. Bensoussan, L. Boccardo, F. Murat, *H-convergence for quasi-linear elliptic equations with quadratic growth*, Univ. Pierre et Marie Curie, Rapports de Recherche, 1989, L.A.N., to be published AMO.

[2] A. Bensoussan, L. Boccardo, F. Murat, *On a nonlinear partial differential equation having natural growth terms and unbounded solution*, Univ. Pierre et Marie Curie, Raports de recherche, 1987, L.A.N.

[3] L. Boccardo, F. Murat, *Homogénéisation de problèmes quasi-linéaires.* Atti del Convegno "Studio di problemi, limite della analisi funzionale"" Bressanone, 7-9 Sett. 1981.

[4] N.G. Meyers, *On $L^p$ estimate for the gradient of solutions of second-order elliptic divergence equations*, Ann. Sc. Norm. Sup. Pisa 17 (1963), 189-206.

[5] *Calcul des variations et homogénisation*, Eyrolles, Paris, 1985, Collect. DER EDF, lectures Notes.

[6] L. Tartar, Cours Peccot, Collège de France.

L E FRAENKEL

# On steady vortex rings with swirl and a Sobolev inequality

## 1. The vortex-ring problem

Let $(X_1, X_2, X_3) = (r\cos\theta,\ r\sin\theta,\ z)$ denote points of $\mathbf{R}^3$, so that $z, r, \theta$ are cylindrical co-ordinates. We are concerned with flows (of an ideal fluid) having velocity components

$$u^z = \frac{1}{r}\psi_r - W, \quad u^r = -\frac{1}{r}\psi_z, \quad u^\theta = \frac{1}{r}\Gamma(\Psi), \tag{1}$$

where $\psi = \psi(z,r)$ is the *stream function due to vorticity*, $u^\theta$ is the *swirl velocity*, and $\Psi := \psi - \frac{1}{2}Wr^2 - k$ is the *total* stream function. The constants $W > 0$ (the velocity at infinity) and $k \geq 0$ (the flux constant), and the swirl circulation function $\Gamma : \mathbf{R} \to [0,\infty)$, are all given.

Denoting any meridional half-plane ($\theta$ = const.) by

$$\Pi := \{(z,r) \mid -\infty < z < \infty, \quad r > 0\},$$

we seek $\psi$ and a bounded open set $A \subset \Pi$, called the *cross-section* of the vortex ring, such that

$$\left.\begin{aligned} L\psi := \psi_{zz} + \psi_{rr} - \frac{1}{r}\psi_r &= \begin{cases} r^2 B'(\Psi) - \Gamma(\Psi)\Gamma'(\Psi) & \text{in } A, \\ 0 & \text{in } \Pi\backslash\bar{A}, \end{cases} \\ \Psi\,|_{\partial A} = 0, \qquad \Psi\,|_{r=0} &= -k; \end{aligned}\right\} \tag{2}$$

also, such that $\psi \in C^1(\bar{\Pi}) \cap C^2(\Pi\backslash\partial A)$ and $|\nabla\psi(z,r)| \to 0$ at infinity in $\bar{\Pi}$. Here $B' : \mathbf{R} \to \mathbf{R}$ is another given function; it is the derivative of the Bernoulli function $B$ (also called the 'total-head pressure').

This problem goes back to Hicks [6], who found a family of explicit solutions (recently and independently re-discovered by H.K. Moffatt [7]) for the particular cases

$$k = 0, \qquad B'(\Psi) = -\lambda_1 \ \ (\lambda_1 \gtrless 0), \qquad \Gamma(\Psi)\Gamma'(\Psi) = \lambda_2\Psi \ \ (\lambda_2 \geq 0),$$

where $\lambda_1$ and $\lambda_2$ are constants. Turkington [10] has adopted a different formulation, in which $\Psi$ and $B'(\Psi)$ are regarded as functions of $\Gamma \equiv ru^\theta$; this seems most appropriate when swirl effects dominate. Note that (2) is still a significant problem when $\Gamma = 0$;

this problem, of steady vortex rings without swirl, has been the subject of many papers in the last twenty years.

In the present paper we indicate that the existence theory in [3] can be extended from the case $\Gamma = 0$ to the full problem (2) with $\Gamma > 0$, subject to the condition $B'(\Psi) \leq 0$. The absence of $r^2$ from the swirl term in (2) makes parts of this extension non-trivial.

The basic tool, for these non-trivial parts of the extension, is an embedding inequality that is believed to be new and may be of interest in its own right. This inequality is presented here; the rest of the existence theory (for the case of swirl) will be the subject of another paper.

Following [2], we also prove uniqueness of those Hicks-Moffatt solutions for which $\lambda_1 \geq 0$ and $\Psi(z,r) > 0$ in $A$; such solutions form a substantial subset of the whole family of Hicks-Moffatt solutions.

## 2. A Sobolev inequality

The Hilbert space $H(\Pi)$ is the completion of the set $C_0^\infty(\Pi)$ (of real-valued, infinitely differentiable functions having compact support in the half-plane $\Pi$) in the norm defined by

$$\|\varphi\|^2 := \iint_\Pi (\varphi_z^2+\varphi_r^2)\, r^{-1}\, dz\, dr,$$

from which the inner product can be inferred. This weighted Sobolev space is relevant not only to stream functions $\varphi$ (equivalently, to vector potentials in $\mathbf{R}^3$ of the form $\varphi(z,r)\, r^{-1}\, \mathbf{e}^\theta$, where $\mathbf{e}^\theta := \nabla\theta/|\nabla\theta|$ and $\|\varphi\|^2$ measures the energy of the corresponding field ), but also to scalar-valued, cylindrically symmetric functions in $\mathbf{R}^N$, $N \geq 4$; see Remark 2 below.

The following lemma is implied by *Hardy's inequality*; in Theorem 327 of [5] choose the exponent to be 2, set $x = r^2$ and finally integrate with respect to $z$. A proof is included here because of what follows.

LEMMA 1. *For all* $\varphi \in H(\Pi)$,

$$\iint_\Pi \varphi^2 r^{-3}\, dz\, dr \leq \|\varphi\|^2; \tag{3}$$

*the constant is the best possible.*

*Proof.* We may suppose that $\varphi \in C_0^\infty(\Pi)$, and shall use the abbreviation (which differs from that used in [3])

$$\iint(\cdot) := \iint_\Pi (\cdot)\, dz\, dr. \tag{4}$$

Integration by parts with respect to $r$, and the Schwarz inequality, give

$$\iint \varphi^2 r^{-3} = \iint \varphi\varphi_r r^{-2} \le \{\iint \varphi^2 r^{-3}\}^{1/2} \{\iint \varphi_r^2 r^{-1}\}^{1/2} ,$$

and we divide through by the first factor on the right.

To construct a sequence $(\varphi_n)$ such that $\iint \varphi_n^2 r^{-3}/\|\varphi_n\|^2 \to 1$ as $n \to \infty$, we begin with the function having values $r^{1-\delta}$ (which is essentially that mentioned in [5]), multiply it by mollifiers that descend smoothly from 1 to 0 in the strips

$$\{0<r<1\},\ \ \{\exp\left(\frac{\log 2}{2\delta}\right) < r < 2\exp\left(\frac{\log 2}{2\delta}\right)\},\ \ \{n < |z| < 2n\},$$

and choose $\delta = 1/\log n$, $\quad n \ge 2$. (The mollifiers decrease in the indicated strips with decreasing $r$, increasing $r$, increasing $|z|$, respectively.)

THEOREM 2. *For each* $p \in [2,\infty)$ *and all* $\varphi \in H(\Pi)$,

$$I_p(\varphi) := \iint_\Pi |\varphi|^p\, r^{-p/2-2}\, dz\, dr \le (A_p \|\varphi\|)^p ; \tag{5}$$

*the value of* $A_p$ *(which depends only on p) is implied by* (10) *and* (11) *below.*

*Proof.* (i) Again we may assume that $\varphi \in C_0^\infty(\Pi)$, and adopt the notation (4). A preliminary step, taken from [8, p.128], is to note that, for any $w \in C_0^\infty(\Pi)$,

$$w(z,r) = \int_{-\infty}^{z} (D_1 w)(z',r) dz' = -\int_z^\infty (D_1 w)(z',r)\, dz',$$

whence

$$2|w(z,r)| \le \int_{-\infty}^{\infty} |(D_1 w)(z',r)|dz';$$

similarly

$$2|w(z,r)| \le \int_0^\infty |(D_2 w)(z,r')|dr'.$$

Multiplication and integration of these two inequalities gives

$$\iint w^2 \le \tfrac14 \{\iint |w_z|\} \{\iint |w_r|\}. \tag{6}$$

(ii) For $p = 2$, the result (5) is that in Lemma 1; we shall use induction after making the transformation

$$\varphi = r^{1/2} u, \qquad I_p(\varphi) = \iint |u|^p\, r^{-2}, \tag{7}$$

$$\|\varphi\|^2 = \iint (u_z^2 + u_r^2 + \tfrac{3}{4} u^2 r^{-2}). \tag{8}$$

(In this last, $uu_r r^{-1}$ has been integrated by parts.) Suppose then that (5) holds for $p = 2m-2$, where $m \in \{2,3,4,\dots\}$; we shall prove it for $p = 2m$ by setting $w = r^{-1}u^m$ in (6). Since

$$w_z = m u^{m-1} u_z r^{-1}, \quad w_r = m u^{m-1} u_r r^{-1} - u^m r^{-2},$$

the Schwarz inequality yields

$$\iint |w_z| \le m \{\iint u^{2m-2} r^{-2}\}^{1/2} A,$$

$$\iint |w_r| \le m \{\iint u^{2m-2} r^{-2}\}^{1/2} (B + \frac{C}{m}),$$

where

$$A := \{\iint u_z^2\}^{1/2}, \quad B := \{\iint u_r^2\}^{1/2}, \quad C := \{\iint u^2 r^{-2}\}^{1/2}.$$

Then (6) shows that

$$\iint u^{2m} r^{-2} \le \tfrac{1}{4} m^2 \{\iint u^{2m-2} r^{-2}\} A(B + \frac{C}{m}). \tag{9}$$

Now, for any $\alpha > 0$ and $\beta > 0$,

$$A(B + \frac{C}{m}) \le \tfrac{1}{2}\{(\alpha + \frac{\beta}{m})A^2 + \frac{1}{\alpha}B^2 + \frac{1}{m\beta}C^2\},$$

and we choose $\alpha = m(m^2 + 4/3)^{-1/2}$, $\beta = 4\alpha/3m$ to obtain

$$A(B + \frac{C}{m}) \le \frac{1}{2m}(m^2 + \frac{4}{3})^{1/2}(A^2 + B^2 + \frac{3}{4}C^2) = \frac{1}{2m}(m^2 + \frac{4}{3})^{1/2}\|\varphi\|^2,$$

in view of (8). It now follows from (7) and (9) that, for $m \in \{2,3,4,\dots\}$,

$$I_{2m}(\varphi) \le \frac{m}{8}(m^2 + \frac{4}{3})^{1/2} I_{2m-2}(\varphi)\|\varphi\|^2; \tag{10a}$$

also,

$$I_2(\varphi) \le \|\varphi\|^2. \tag{10b}$$

(iii) For values of $p$ between even integers, we use (7) and interpolation between the spaces $L_p(\Pi, \mu)$, where $d\mu := r^{-2}\,dz\,dr$ :

$$\left.\begin{aligned} &\text{if} \quad 2 \le a < c \text{ and } \frac{1}{b} = \frac{1-\theta}{a} + \frac{\theta}{c} \quad (0 \le \theta \le 1), \\ &\text{then} \quad I_b(\varphi)^{1/b} \le I_a(\varphi)^{(1-\theta)/a} I_c(\varphi)^{\theta/c}. \end{aligned}\right\} \tag{11}$$

*Remarks.* 1. The inequality fails for $p < 2$; if

$$\varphi(z,r) = r^{1+\delta} e^{-z^2-r^2} \qquad (\delta > 0),$$

then $\varphi \in H(\Pi)$ but, for any fixed $p < 2$ and $\delta$ sufficiently small, $I_p(\varphi)$ does not exist (because of divergence at $r = 0$).

2. We introduce a mapping of $H(\Pi)$ into a space $V(\mathbf{R}^N)$ of cylindrically symmetric functions defined on $\mathbf{R}^N$. First, let

$$z = x_N, \qquad r = (x_1^2 + \ldots + x_{N-1}^2)^{1/2} \qquad (N \geq 2), \tag{12a}$$

so that $\Pi$ is now a meridional half-plane in $\mathbf{R}^N$; then define

$$\mathrm{v}(x) := r^{-(N-1)/2}\varphi(z,r), \qquad x \in \mathbf{R}^N, \quad \varphi \in H(\Pi). \tag{12b}$$

For $N = 2$, this is the transformation used to prove Theorem 2; for $N = 3$, it defines the vector potential $\mathrm{v}\,\mathbf{e}^\theta$ corresponding to a stream function $\varphi$.

For each integer $N \geq 2$, let $C_{0,c}^\infty(\mathbf{R}^N)$ denote the set of cylindrically symmetric functions (depending only on $z$ and $r$) in $C_0^\infty(\mathbf{R}^N)$, and let $V(\mathbf{R}^N)$ be the completion of $C_{0,c}^\infty(\mathbf{R}^N)$ in the norm defined by

$$\|\mathrm{v}\|_V^2 := \frac{1}{\sigma_{N-1}} \int_{\mathbf{R}^N} |\nabla \mathrm{v}|^2 \, dx, \tag{13}$$

where $\sigma_M = 2\pi^{M/2}/\Gamma(M/2)$ denotes the surface area of the [$(M-1)$-dimensional] unit sphere in $\mathbf{R}^M$. The set $C_0^\infty(\Pi)$ is taken by (12) into a proper subset of $C_{0,c}^\infty(\mathbf{R}^N)$; a calculation shows that, after integration by parts of $\varphi\varphi_r r^{-2}$,

$$\|\mathrm{v}\|_V^2 = \|\varphi\|^2 + \tfrac{1}{4}(N-1)(N-5) \iint_\Pi \varphi^2 r^{-3}\, dz\, dr \tag{14}$$

for all $\varphi \in H(\Pi)$. By Lemma 1,

$$\|\mathrm{v}\|_V^2 \leq (1 + k_N)\, \|\varphi\|^2, \tag{15a}$$

where

$$k_N := \max\,\{0, \tfrac{1}{4}(N-1)(N-5)\}. \tag{15b}$$

Thus *the transformation* (12) *defines for each* $N \geq 2$ *a bounded linear operator from* $H(\Pi)$ *into* $V(\mathbf{R}^N)$. For $N = 2$ or 3, this operator is injective (one-to-one) but not surjective (not onto). For $N \geq 4$, one proves the following without difficulty (see [2, p.98] for the case $N = 5$). Let $C_d^\infty(\mathbf{R}^N)$ denote the set of functions in $C_{0,c}^\infty(\mathbf{R}^N)$ that have support disjoint from the $x_N$-axis, and therefore are images under (12) of functions in $C_0^\infty(\Pi)$. Then $C_d^\infty(\mathbf{R}^N)$ is dense in $V(\mathbf{R}^N)$ for $N \geq 4$. In view of (14) and Lemma 1, *the transformation* (12) *defines a linear homeomorphism* (a topological isomorphism) *of* $H(\Pi)$ *onto* $V(\mathbf{R}^N)$ *for* $N \geq 4$. (If $N = 4$, then $\|v\|_V^2 \geq \frac{1}{4}\|\varphi\|^2$.) *When* $N = 5$, *this map is an isometry.*

3. In the context of Theorem 2 the significance of Remark 2 is that, under the transformation (12),

$$I_p(\varphi) = \frac{1}{\sigma_{N-1}} \int_{\mathbf{R}^N} |v|^p \, dx \qquad \text{if} \quad \frac{1}{p} = \frac{1}{2} - \frac{1}{N}, \tag{16}$$

that is, *if p is the critical exponent for the embedding of the Sobolev space* $W_2^1(\mathbf{R}^N)$ *in* $L_p(\mathbf{R}^N)$, $N \geq 3$. In particular, Theorem 2 implies the (known) embedding of $V(\mathbf{R}^N)$ in $L_p(\mathbf{R}^N)$ for $N = 4,5,6,\ldots$ and $p = 4, 10/3, 3, \ldots$ . Of course, the theorem says a good deal more than this about the space $H(\Pi)$.

Conversely, for $p = 6, 4, 10/3, \ldots$ and $N = 3,4,5,\ldots$ one can derive a sharper form of the result in Theorem 2 by means of the inequality

$$\int_{\mathbf{R}^N} |u|^p \, dx \leq C_N^p \, \{ \int_{\mathbf{R}^N} |\nabla u|^2 \, dx \}^{p/2}, \qquad \frac{1}{p} = \frac{1}{2} - \frac{1}{N}, \tag{17}$$

for the embedding of $W_2^1(\mathbf{R}^N)$ in $L_p(\mathbf{R}^N)$. The best constant [9] is

$$C_N = \left\{ \frac{1}{\pi N(N-2)} \right\}^{1/2} \left\{ \frac{\Gamma(N)}{\Gamma(N/2)} \right\}^{1/N}. \tag{18}$$

Although (17) holds for a space much larger than $V(\mathbf{R}^N)$, the function that gives equality in (17) is spherically symmetric (depending only on $|x|^2 = r^2 + z^2$) and hence cylindrically symmetric.

Using (13), (15) and (16), we infer from (17) that, for all $\varphi \in H(\Pi)$,

$$I_p(\varphi) \leq (B_N \|\varphi\|)^p, \qquad \frac{1}{p} = \frac{1}{2} - \frac{1}{N}, \tag{19a}$$

where

$$B_N := C_N \, \sigma_{N-1}^{1/N} \, (1 + k_N)^{1/2} \qquad (N \geq 3). \tag{19b}$$

For $N = 5$ and $p = 10/3$, the identity (14) replaces the inequality (15); then (17) and (19) are exactly equivalent under the transformation (12), so that the constant $B_5$ is the best possible.

A calculation shows that $B_N \to 1$ as $N \to \infty$; since also $p \to 2$, Lemma 1, which has been used in the derivation of (19), is recovered exactly by (19). This property of $C_N$ seems remarkable, because the function giving equality in (17) for finite $N$ is spherically symmetric, whereas we saw in the proof of Lemma 1 that the sequence of functions approaching equality there is obtained by truncating smoothly a function depending only on $r$.

Some values of $A_p$ and $B_N$ are displayed in Table 1.

| $p$ | $N$ | $A_p$ | $B_N$ |
|---|---|---|---|
| 2 | $\infty$ | 1 | 1 |
| 3 | 6 | 0.913 | 0.589 |
| 10/3 | 5 | 0.896 | 0.472 |
| 4 | 4 | 0.872 | 0.588 |
| 6 | 3 | 0.941 | 0.788 |
| 8 | | 1.047 | |
| 10 | | 1.166 | |

TABLE 1. Some values (to three decimal places) of the constants $A_p$ in (5) and $B_N$ in (19). The values of $A_2$, $\lim_{N\to\infty} B_N$ and $B_5$ are the best possible.

## 3. The uniqueness of a set of Hicks-Moffatt solutions

3.1. *Explicit solutions.* As was mentioned in §1, the problem is as follows. We seek a function $\psi \in C^1(\overline{\Pi}) \cap C^2(\Pi \backslash \partial A)$ and a set $A$ in $\Pi$ such that $|\nabla \psi(z,r)| \to 0$ at infinity in $\overline{\Pi}$ and

$$\left.\begin{aligned} L\psi \equiv \psi_{zz} + r\left(\frac{1}{r}\psi_r\right)_r &= \begin{cases} -\lambda_1 r^2 - \lambda_2 \Psi & \text{in } A, \\ 0 & \text{in } \Pi \backslash \overline{A}, \end{cases} \\ \Psi|_{\partial A} = 0, \quad \Psi|_{r=0} &= 0, \end{aligned}\right\} \tag{20}$$

where $\Psi = \psi - \frac{1}{2}Wr^2$, $\lambda_1 \gtrless 0$ and $\lambda_2 \geq 0$. Note that $L\Psi = L\psi$, and that we have a linear equation for $\Psi$ in each of the (initially unknown) sets $A$ and $\Pi \backslash \overline{A}$.

Following M.J.M. Hill's paper of 1894 for the case $\lambda_2 = 0$, Hicks and Moffatt observed that the guess

$$A = \{ (z,r) \in \Pi \mid \rho < a \}, \qquad \text{where} \quad \rho := (z^2+r^2)^{1/2}, \tag{21}$$

still succeeds when $\lambda_2 > 0$, in that all the conditions of the problem can then be satisfied. In terms of the total stream function $\Psi$ and a swirl parameter $\alpha > 0$, the result is

$$\Psi_{HM}(z,r) = \begin{cases} -\frac{3}{2} Wr^2 \{B - C(\alpha\rho)^{-3/2} J_{3/2}(\alpha\rho)\}, & \rho \le a, \\ -\frac{1}{2} Wr^2 (1 - \frac{a^3}{\rho^3}), \quad \rho \ge a, & \end{cases} \tag{22a}$$

where

$$B := \frac{J_{3/2}(\alpha a)}{\alpha a \, J_{5/2}(\alpha a)}, \qquad C := \frac{(\alpha a)^{1/2}}{J_{5/2}(\alpha a)} . \tag{22b}$$

(In equation (57) of [7], the final $J_{5/2}(\alpha a)$ should be $\alpha a J_{5/2}(\alpha a)$.) The spherical radius $a$ and swirl parameter $\alpha$ are related to the data in (20) by

$$\lambda_1 = \frac{3}{2} WB\alpha^2, \qquad \lambda_2 = \alpha^2. \tag{22c}$$

The functions $J_{3/2}$ and $J_{5/2}$ are Bessel functions in the standard notation of Watson [11]; they are also elemementary functions given by

$$J_{3/2}(x) = (\frac{2}{\pi})^{1/2} x^{-3/2} (\sin x - x\cos x),$$

$$J_{5/2}(x) = (\frac{2}{\pi})^{1/2} x^{-5/2} (3 \sin x - 3x\cos x - x^2 \sin x) \qquad (x > 0).$$

For an important discussion of the *helicity* of these flows, and for helpful diagrams of the streamlines and vortex lines, see [7].

In the limit as $\alpha \to 0$, one recovers Hill's solution

$$\Psi_0(z,r) = \frac{3}{4} Wr^2 (1 - \frac{\rho^2}{a^2}), \qquad \rho \le a, \tag{23a}$$

$$\lambda_1 = \frac{15}{2} \frac{W}{a^2}, \qquad \lambda_2 = 0. \tag{23b}$$

(The exterior flow is unchanged.) We regard this solution as the starting point of the solutions (22).

The formulae (22) have been written in accord with our prescription of the velocity at infinity, $W > 0$; this prescription can be criticized because it makes $B$ and $C$ infinite when $\alpha a$ is a positive zero of the function $J_{5/2}$; the first such value is $\alpha a = 5.76\ldots$ . If some other constant is prescribed in place of $W$, then $W$ is zero and the exterior flow vanishes at these values of $\alpha a$. Note also that $\lambda_1$ changes sign when $\alpha a$ is a positive zero of $J_{3/2}$; the first such value is $\alpha a = 4.49\ldots$ . At these values of $\alpha a$, corresponding to $\lambda_1 = 0$, the Bernoulli function $B$ (mentioned in §1) is a constant, which implies that the vorticity curl $\mathbf{u}$ is parallel to the fluid velocity $\mathbf{u}$ wherever both are non-zero, because the momentum equation for an ideal fluid can be written

$$(\mathrm{curl}\,\mathbf{u}) \times \mathbf{u} = -\nabla B,$$

where $\times$ denotes the vector cross product in $\mathbf{R}^3$.

3.2. *The restricted problem.* These last remarks bring us to a basic limitation of the method in [3]. In that paper, in its extension to flows with swirl, and in the uniqueness theorem below, the cross-section $A$ is characterized by

$$A = \{(z,r) \in \Pi \mid \Psi(z,r) > 0\}. \tag{24}$$

This is because the conditions $\Psi|_{\partial A} = 0$ and $\Psi(z,r) \sim -\frac{1}{2}Wr^2 - k$ at infinity (where $W > 0$ and $k \geq 0$), together with the maximum principle, imply that $\Psi < 0$ in $\Pi \backslash \bar{A}$; when the right-hand member of the governing equation $(2)_1$ is non-positive in $A$, the maximum principle also implies that $\Psi > 0$ in $A$. With this approach, based on (24), one can treat only a restricted form of the problem (20) such that $\Psi|_A > 0$, and I do not know how to handle this condition without assuming that $\lambda_1 \geq 0$. The Hicks-Moffatt solutions have $\lambda_1 \geq 0$ for $\alpha a \leq 4.49\ldots$ and $\Psi|_A > 0$ for $\alpha a \leq 5.76\ldots$ (these numbers being the smallest positive zeros of $J_{3/2}$ and $J_{5/2}$, respectively).

The restricted problem will now be specified precisely; in the following definition, $f_H$ denotes the Heaviside function,

$$f_H(t) = 0 \quad \text{if} \quad t \leq 0, \qquad f_H(t) = 1 \quad \text{if} \quad t > 0,$$

and $H(\Pi)$ is the space defined and discussed in §2.

*Definition.* We shall say that $\psi$ is a *weak solution of the restricted Hicks-Moffatt problem* if $\psi \in H(\Pi) \backslash \{0\}$ and if there are constants $\lambda_1 \geq 0$, $\lambda_2 \geq 0$ and $W > 0$ such that, for all $\varphi \in H(\Pi)$,

$$\int_\Pi \frac{1}{r^2}(\varphi_z\psi_z + \varphi_r\psi_r)\,d\tau = \int_\Pi \varphi\{\lambda_1 + \frac{\lambda_2}{r^2}\Psi\}\, f_H(\Psi)d\tau, \tag{25}$$

where $d\tau = r\,dz\,dr$ and $\Psi = \psi - \frac{1}{2}Wr^2$.

In the existence theory claimed in §1 for a restricted form of the problem (2), the data for the present case are either $\|\psi\| > 0$, $W > 0$ and $\lambda_2/\lambda_1 \geq 0$, the parameter $\lambda_1$ being calculated a posteriori, or $\|\psi\| > 0$, $W > 0$ and $\lambda_1/\lambda_2 \geq 0$, the parameter $\lambda_2$ being calculated a posteriori.

3.3. *Symmetry by way of the maximum principle.* Theorem 3 is a slight extension of Theorem 3.9 in [2] and also owes something to Theorem A.3 there. These results are, in turn, slight extensions of parts of the well known paper [4]. (A detailed proof of Theorem 3 has passed the scrutiny of severe colleagues attending my lectures at the University of Bath.)

THEOREM 3. *Assume that a function* $\mathrm{v} : \mathbf{R}^N \to \mathbf{R}$ *has the following properties.*
(a) $\mathrm{v} \in C^1(\mathbf{R}^N)$ *and* $\mathrm{v} > 0$.

(b) $$\int_{\mathbf{R}^N} \{\nabla\Phi\cdot\nabla \mathrm{v} - \Phi f(\mathrm{v})\}\,dx = 0 \quad \text{for all } \Phi \in C_0^\infty(\mathbf{R}^N), \tag{26}$$

*where* $f$ *has a decomposition* $f = f_1 + f_2$ *such that* $f_1 : [0,\infty) \to \mathbf{R}$ *is locally Lipschitz continuous and* $f_2 : [0,\infty) \to \mathbf{R}$ *is non-decreasing.*

(c) *Outside some ball, say for* $\rho := |x| \geq R_{\mathrm{v}}$,

$$\left.\begin{aligned} &\mathrm{v}(x) = a_0\,\rho^{-m} + (a\cdot x)\,\rho^{-m-2} + h(x), && a_0 > 0,\; m > 0,\\ &|h(x)| \leq \text{const.}\ \rho^{-m-2}, && |\nabla h(x)| \leq \text{const.}\ \rho^{-m-3}, \end{aligned}\right\} \tag{27}$$

*where* $a := (a_1,\dots,a_N)$, *and* $a_0, m, a_1,\dots,a_N$ *are constants.*

*Define* $\mathrm{v}_0 : \mathbf{R}^N \to \mathbf{R}$ *by*

$$b := \frac{1}{a_0 m}\,a, \qquad \mathrm{v}_0(x) := \mathrm{v}(x+b). \tag{28}$$

*Then* $\mathrm{v}_0$ *is spherically symmetric (independent of* $x/\rho$*) and* $\dfrac{\partial \mathrm{v}_0}{\partial\rho} < 0$ *for* $\rho > 0$.

3.4. *Uniqueness for the restricted problem.* As for Hill's vortex, the uniqueness theorem rests on the remarkable consequences of the transformation $\psi = r^2 \mathrm{v}$. (Earlier uses of this device by S. Chandrasekhar and by W.-M. Ni are cited in [2]). The transformation is an obvious first step because for the solutions $\psi_{HM}$ (defined by (22) and by $\psi = \Psi + \dfrac{1}{2} W r^2$) the functions $\mathrm{v}_{HM}$ depend only on $\rho$ (and on the parameters). What may be surprising at first sight is the effect of the transformation on equation (25).

THEOREM 4. *If $\psi$ is a weak solution of the restricted Hicks-Moffatt problem, then $\psi(z,r) = \psi_{HM}(z-c,r)$ for some $c \in \mathbf{R}$.*

*Proof.* (i) Using Remark 2 in §2, we apply the transformation (12) with $N = 5$; recall that this is an isometric isomorphism of $H(\Pi)$ onto $V(\mathbf{R}^5)$. In (25), set $\varphi(z,r) =: r^2 u(x)$ and $\psi(z,r) =: r^2 \mathrm{v}(x)$. Then $\|\mathrm{v}\|_V = \|\psi\|$ and, for all $u \in V(\mathbf{R}^5)$,

$$\int_{\mathbf{R}^5} \nabla u \cdot \nabla \mathrm{v} \, dx = \int_{\mathbf{R}^5} u \, \{\lambda_1 + \lambda_2(\mathrm{v} - \tfrac{1}{2}W)\} \, f_H(\mathrm{v} - \tfrac{1}{2}W) \, dx, \tag{29}$$

where we have used the equivalence of the conditions $\Psi > 0$ and $\mathrm{v} > \frac{1}{2}W$ for $r > 0$. (Since the axis $\{r = 0\}$ has measure zero, what happens there is immaterial.) By Remark 3 in §2, the space $V(\mathbf{R}^5)$ is embedded in $L_{10/3}(\mathbf{R}^5)$; hence the (five-dimensional, Lebesgue) measure of the set

$$P(\mathrm{v}) := \{x \in \mathbf{R}^5 \mid \mathrm{v}(x) > \tfrac{1}{2}W\}$$

can be bounded in terms of $\|\mathrm{v}\|_V$ and $W$ [2, p.98].

The next step is to extend (29) to test functions that need not be cylindrically symmetric. Let $E(\mathbf{R}^5)$ denote the completion of $C_0^\infty(\mathbf{R}^5)$ in the norm defined by (13). This Hilbert space has an orthogonal decomposition whereby each $w \in E(\mathbf{R}^5)$ may be written $w = w_0 + w_1$ with $w_0 \in V(\mathbf{R}^5)$. In fact, if $\xi$ denotes points of the unit sphere $S^3$ in $\mathbf{R}^4$, then for smooth functions $w$ in $E(\mathbf{R}^5)$ the value $w_0(z,r)$ is merely the mean value of $w(z,r,\xi)$ over $S^3$; it follows that $w_1(z,r,\xi)$ has mean value zero over $S^3$. For the details, see [2, p.99]. In (29), we may replace $u \in V(\mathbf{R}^5)$ by $w \in E(\mathbf{R}^5)$ because $w_0 \in V(\mathbf{R}^5)$ while $w_1$ contributes zero to each integral there. Therefore we may certainly use test functions in the subset $C_0^\infty(\mathbf{R}^5)$ of $E(\mathbf{R}^5)$ to obtain

$$\int_{\mathbf{R}^5} \nabla \Phi \cdot \nabla \mathrm{v} \, dx = \int_{\mathbf{R}^5} \Phi \, \{\lambda_1 + \lambda_2(\mathrm{v} - \tfrac{1}{2}W)\} \, f_H(\mathrm{v} - \tfrac{1}{2}W) \, dx \tag{30}$$

for all $\Phi \in C_0^\infty(\mathbf{R}^5)$.

(ii) Obviously we intend to apply Theorem 3 to the present function v. Condition (b) of that theorem holds because, if

$$f(t) := \{\lambda_1 + \lambda_2(t - \tfrac{1}{2}W)\}\, f_H(t - \tfrac{1}{2}W), \qquad t \geq 0,$$

then $f$ is non-decreasing.

To prove that $v \in C^1(\mathbf{R}^5)$, we apply the $L_p$ regularity theory of Agmon [1] very much as in [2, p.101]. The additional term $\lambda_2(v - \tfrac{1}{2}W)$ causes no difficulty because $v \in L_{10/3}(\mathbf{R}^5)$ and the measure of $P(v)$ has been bounded. In fact (as in [2]), the regularity theory also shows that $v(x) \to 0$ as $\rho := |x| \to \infty$, so that $P(v)$ is contained in some ball, say $\{\rho < \tfrac{1}{2}R_v\}$.

Again as in [2], we choose the test function $\Phi$ in (30) to be a smooth approximation to the Newtonian kernel for $\mathbf{R}^5$, with fixed field point $x_0$ and varying source point $x$. An integration by parts on the left and a limiting process show that, for all $x_0 \in \mathbf{R}^5$,

$$v(x_0) = \frac{1}{8\pi^2} \int_{P(v)} \frac{\lambda_1 + \lambda_2(v(x) - \tfrac{1}{2}W)}{|x_0 - x|^3}\, dx. \tag{31}$$

If $P(v)$ is empty, or if $\lambda_1 = 0$ and $\lambda_2 = 0$, then $v = 0$, contrary to the hypothesis that $\psi \in H(\Pi)\setminus\{0\}$. Hence $P(v)$ is not empty and at least one of $\lambda_1$ and $\lambda_2$ is positive; since v is continuous, $P(v)$ has positive measure and it follows that $v > 0$ in $\mathbf{R}^5$.

To prove that v satisfies condition (c) of Theorem 3, we recall that $|x| < \tfrac{1}{2}R_v$ in (31), so that for $|x_0| \geq R_v$ we may differentiate under the integral sign and may expand $|x_0 - x|^{-3}$ and its gradient in short Taylor series with remainder. This yields (27) with

$$m = 3, \qquad a_0 = \int_{P(v)} g(y)\, dy, \qquad a_5 = 3\int_{P(v)} g(y)\, y_5\, dy,$$

where

$$g(y) := \frac{1}{8\pi^2}\{\lambda_1 + \lambda_2(v(y) - \tfrac{1}{2}W)\} > 0 \quad \text{on } P(v);$$

also, $a_1 = \ldots = a_4 = 0$ because v and $P(v)$ are cylindrically symmetric.

Accordingly, Theorem 3 can be applied; we contemplate the spherically symmetric function

$$v_0(x) := v(x+b), \quad \text{where } b = (0,\ldots,0,c), \quad c = a_5/3a_0,$$

and wish to prove that $v_0 = v_{HM}$.

(iii) Let $v_1(\rho) := v_0(x)$. By Theorem 3, $v'_1(\rho) < 0$ for $\rho > 0$; since $P(v)$ is not empty, the maximum value $v_1(0) > \frac{1}{2}W$. Hence there exists a unique number $a > 0$ such that $v_1(a) = \frac{1}{2}W$. The result (31) now implies, since in the integral $v \in C^1(\mathbf{R}^5)$, that $v_1$ is a $C^2$ function on $[0,a)$ and on $(a,\infty)$, and that

$$\frac{1}{\rho^4}\frac{d}{d\rho}(\rho^4\frac{d}{d\rho})v_1 = \begin{cases} -\lambda_1 - \lambda_2(v_1 - \frac{1}{2}W) & \text{for } 0 < \rho < a, \\ 0 & \text{for } \rho > a; \end{cases}$$

also

$$v_1(a) = \tfrac{1}{2}W, \qquad v_1(\rho) \to 0 \quad \text{as } \rho \to \infty, \qquad v_1 \in C^1[0,\infty).$$

Then a calculation shows that $v_0 = v_{HM}$.

## References


1. S. AGMON, The $L_p$ approach to the Dirichlet problem. *Ann. Scuola Norm. Sup. Pisa*, (3) 13 (1959), 405-448.
2. C.J. AMICK and L.E. FRAENKEL, The uniqueness of Hill's spherical vortex. *Arch. Rational Mech. Anal.*, 92 (1986), 91-119.
3. L.E. FRAENKEL and M.S. BERGER, A global theory of steady vortex rings in an ideal fluid. *Acta Math.*, 132 (1974), 13-51.
4. B. GIDAS, W.-M. NI and L. NIRENBERG, Symmetry and related properties via the maximum principle. *Comm. Math. Phys.*, 68 (1979), 209-243.
5. G.H. HARDY, J.E. LITTLEWOOD and G. POLYA. *Inequalities*. Cambridge, 1952.
6. W.M. HICKS, Researches in vortex motion. Part III. On spiral or gyrostatic vortex aggregates. *Philos. Trans. Roy. Soc. London*, A 192 (1899), 33-99.
7. H.K. MOFFATT, The degree of knottedness of tangled vortex lines. *J. Fluid Mech.*, 35 (1969), 117-129.
8. L. NIRENBERG, On elliptic partial differential equations. *Ann. Scuola Norm. Sup. Pisa*, (3) 13 (1959), 115-162.
9. G. TALENTI, Best constant in Sobolev inequality. *Ann. Mat. Pura Appl.*, (4a) 110 (1976), 353-372.
10. B. TURKINGTON, Vortex rings with swirl : axisymmetric solutions of the Euler equations with nonzero helicity. *S.I.A.M. J. Math. Anal.*, 20 (1989), 57-73.

11. G.N. WATSON, *The theory of Bessel functions.* Cambridge, 1944.

School of Mathematics,
University of Bath,
Bath BA2 7AY,
England.

M GIAQUINTA, G MODICA AND J SOUČEK*

# Variational problems for the conformally invariant integral $\int |du|^n$

Let $\mathcal{X}$ and $\mathcal{Y}$ be two orientable Riemannian manifolds of dimension respectively $n \geq 2$ and $m \geq 2$. We shall assume that $\mathcal{Y}$ is compact, without boundary, and with torsionless singular homology group $H_n(\mathcal{Y}, \mathbf{Z})$.

Assume for simplicity that also $\mathcal{X}$ is compact and without boundary. As it is well known, every smooth mapping $u : \mathcal{X} \to \mathcal{Y}$ induces a *homology map*, also called *degree mapping*, between the homology groups $H_k(\mathcal{X}, \mathbf{Z})$ and $H_k(\mathcal{Y}, \mathbf{Z})$, $k = 0, 1, \ldots, n$,

$$u_* : H_k(\mathcal{X}, \mathbf{Z}) \to H_k(\mathcal{Y}, \mathbf{Z})$$

In this paper we shall be concerned with the problem of minimizing the conformally invariant integral

$$\mathcal{D}(u, \mathcal{X}) := \frac{1}{n^{n/2}} \int_{\mathcal{X}} |du|^n \, dvol_{\mathcal{X}}$$

among mappings $u : \mathcal{X} \to \mathcal{Y}$ with prescribed degree mapping, up to order $n$,

$$u_* = d_* , \qquad d_* : H_k(\mathcal{X}, \mathbf{Z}) \to H_k(\mathcal{Y}, \mathbf{Z}) , \ k = 0, 1, \ldots, n .$$

Denoting by $\Omega$ a bounded open set of $\mathcal{X}$, we shall also consider the problem of minimizing $\mathcal{D}(u, \Omega)$ among mappings $u : \Omega \to \mathcal{Y}$ with prescribed degree

* This work has been partially supported by the Ministero dell'Università e della Ricerca Scientifica, by C.N.R., and by the European Research project GADGET. It was partially carried out while the first and the third authors were visiting the Mathematisches Institut der Universität Bonn under the support of the Alexander von Humboldt foundation and of the SFB 256.

mapping $d_*$, and with prescribed boundary values $\varphi$ on $\partial\Omega$. Our main goal is to illustrate how ideas and methods introduced in [3] [4] [5] apply to this problem, which may be regarded as the natural generalization of the problem of minimizing the Dirichlet integral among mappings from $S^2$ into $S^2$ with prescribed degree, compare [1], [4] and [9].

One could see that in fact $u_*$ is well defined for all $H^{1,n}$-mappings from $\mathcal{X}$, or $\Omega$, into $\mathcal{Y}$. Thus, trying to apply direct methods, the most natural attempt seems to be the following: Minimize $\mathcal{D}(u)$ in the subclass of $H^{1,n}(\mathcal{X},\mathcal{Y})$, or of $H^{1,n}_{\varphi}(\Omega,\mathcal{Y})$, of functions with prescribed degree mapping. But one soon realizes that, because of the conformal invariance of $\mathcal{D}$, *the degree is not conserved by weak convergence in* $H^{1,n}$. Thus, if we insist in applying direct methods, we need to work with a *stronger notion of convergence* so that the degree be continuous and energy bounded sets be compact, and consequently to work in the class obtained by considering the sequential closure of smooth mappings with respect to such new convergence. This can be achieved if we regard smooth mappings $u$ as "graphs" $G_u$, that is as the *rectifiable currents* integrations of $n$-forms $\omega$ in $\mathcal{X}\times\mathcal{Y}$ over $G_u$

$$[\![G_u]\!](\omega) := \int_{\mathcal{X}} (\mathrm{id}\times u)^{\#}\omega = \int_{G_u} \omega = \int_{G_u} < \xi,\omega > d\mathcal{H}^n$$

where $\xi$ is the tangent $n$-vector to $G_u$, and we work with the weak convergence of currents, with equibounded $\mathcal{D}$-integrals, on $\mathcal{X}\times\mathcal{Y}$, compare [3] [4] [5]. We shall illustrate this in section 1.

By this procedure we are led to work in the so-called class of *cartesian currents* $\mathrm{cart}^n(\mathcal{X},\mathcal{Y})$, and we need to extend *by semicontinuity* the functional $\mathcal{D}$ tothis new class. This is a difficult point. We extend the integrand, by considering its *polyconvex extension*, defined in [3] [4], to all simple $n$-vectors, and we consider the associated integral $\mathcal{D}(T)$ defined for $T\in\mathrm{cart}^n(\mathcal{X},\mathcal{Y})$. The functional $\mathcal{D}(T)$ turns out to be the greatest lower semicontinuous extension of $\mathcal{D}(u)$ in special situations as for instance in the case $\mathcal{Y}=S^n$. But we are not able to prove such a result in general. Its proof seems to depend on the existence of suitable *instantons*, the existence of which we are not able to prove. This will be discussed in section 2 and 3.

# 1 Limits of smooth mappings and cartesian currents.

We denote by $\Omega$ a bounded open set of $\mathcal{X}$ and we allow $\Omega$ to be equal to $\mathcal{X}$ if $\mathcal{X}$ is compact and without boundary. Moreover, we always think of $\mathcal{Y}$ as an oriented submanifold of $\mathbf{R}^N$, and, when dealing with local facts, we think of $\Omega$ as an open set in $\mathbf{R}^n$. For the sake of simplicity, and since this is the most interesting case we shall also assume from now on that the dimension $m$ of $\mathcal{Y}$ is larger or equal to $n$.

We denote by $\mathcal{D}^n(\Omega \times \mathcal{Y})$ the space of all infinitely defferentiable $n$-forms with compact support in the product manifold $\Omega \times \mathcal{Y}$. The product structure of $\Omega \times \mathcal{Y}$ induces the canonical splitting of the exterior differential operator $d$ as $d = d_x + d_y$, and the splitting of $\mathcal{D}^n(\Omega \times \mathcal{Y})$ as direct sum

$$\mathcal{D}^n(\Omega \times \mathcal{Y}) = \bigoplus_{k=0}^{n} \overline{\mathcal{D}}^{n,k}(\Omega \times \mathcal{Y})$$

where $\overline{\mathcal{D}}^{n,k}(\Omega \times \mathcal{Y})$ denotes the $n$-forms in the product $\Omega \times \mathcal{Y}$ with exactly $k$-differentials in $\mathcal{Y}$. A similar splitting we have respectively for $n$-vectors $\xi$ and $n$-covectors $\omega$

$$\xi(x,y) \in \Lambda_n(T_x\Omega \times T_y\mathcal{Y}) = \bigoplus_{k=0}^{n} \Lambda_{n-k}T_x\Omega \otimes \Lambda_k T_y\mathcal{Y}$$

$$\omega(x,y) \in \Lambda^n(T_x\Omega \times T_y\mathcal{Y}) = \bigoplus_{k=0}^{n} \Lambda^{n-k}T_x\Omega \otimes \Lambda^k T_y\mathcal{Y}$$

The dual space of $\mathcal{D}^n(\Omega \times \mathcal{Y})$ will be denoted by $\mathcal{D}_n(\Omega \times \mathcal{Y})$ and referred as to the space of *$n$-currents in $\Omega \times \mathcal{Y}$*. Denoting by $i$ the immersion $i : \mathcal{Y} \to \mathbf{R}^N$, the map

$$(\mathrm{id} \times i)^{\#} : \mathcal{D}^n(\Omega \times \mathbf{R}^N) \to \mathcal{D}^n(\Omega \times \mathcal{Y})$$

is onto. Then, defining the space of *normal* forms to $\Omega \times \mathcal{Y}$ as

$$\mathcal{N}^n(\Omega \times \mathbf{R}^N) := \ker(\mathrm{id} \times i)^{\#} ,$$

one easily sees that $\mathcal{D}_n(\Omega \times \mathcal{Y})$ can be identified with the space of $n$-currents $T$ in $\mathcal{D}_n(\Omega \times \mathbf{R}^N)$ with the property that $T = 0$ on $\mathcal{N}^n(\Omega \times \mathbf{R}^N)$. Such an identification will be from now on understood.

As every form in $\mathcal{D}^n(\Omega \times \mathcal{Y})$ splits as

$$\omega = \sum_{k=0}^{n} \omega^{(k)} ,$$

every $n$-current can be written as

$$T = \sum_{k=0}^{n} T_{(k)} ,$$

where $T_{(k)}(\omega) := T(\omega^{(k)})$. In coordinates, if

$$\omega = \sum_{|\alpha|+|\beta|=n} \omega_{\alpha\beta}(x,y)\, dx^\alpha \wedge dy^\beta$$

we have

$$T_{(k)}(\omega) = \sum_{\substack{|\alpha|+|\beta|=n \\ |\beta|=k}} T^{\alpha\beta}(\omega_{\alpha\beta}) , \qquad T^{\alpha\beta}(\phi(x,y)) := T(\phi(x,y)\, dx^\alpha \wedge dy^\beta) .$$

The Schwartz distributions $T^{\alpha\beta}$ will be referred as to the *components* of the $n$-current $T$. The *mass* of the $n$-current $T$ is defined by

$$\mathbf{M}(T) := \sup\{ T(\omega) \, : \, \omega \in \mathcal{D}^n(\Omega \times \mathcal{Y}), \ \|\omega(x,y)\| \leq 1, \forall (x,y) \in \Omega \times \mathcal{Y} \}$$

where $\|\omega\|$ denotes the *comass* of the $n$-covector $\omega$

$$\|\omega\| := \sup\{ < \omega, \xi >: \xi \text{ simple } n\text{-vector}, |\xi| \leq 1 \} .$$

Recall that an $n$-vector is called *simple* if it can be written as $\xi = v_1 \wedge \ \ldots \ \wedge v_n$. A current $T \in \mathcal{D}_n(\Omega \times \mathcal{Y})$ with finite mass extends naturally as a linear and continuous functional to the space of all compactly supported $n$-forms with continuous coefficients endowed with the sup norm. Consequently, by Riesz's theorem it can be *represented by integration* as

$$T(\omega) = \int < \omega, \vec{T} > d\|T\|$$

where $\|T\|$ is a Radon measure on $\Omega \times \mathcal{Y}$, the total variation of $T$, $\vec{T} := \frac{dT}{d\|T\|}$ is an $n$-vector field with $\|\vec{T}\| = 1$ $\|T\|$-a.e., $\|\xi\|$ denoting the *mass* of the $n$-vector $\xi$

$$\|\xi\| \ := \ \sup\{ < \eta, \xi >: \ \eta \ n\text{-covector}, \|\eta\| \leq 1 \} \ .$$

In the case that

$$\|T\| = \theta(z)\,\mathcal{H}^n(z) \llcorner \mathcal{M} \ , \qquad z = (x,y) \ ,$$

$\mathcal{H}^n$ denoting the $n$-dimensional Hausdorff measure, $\theta(z)$ an $\mathcal{H}^n$-measurable positive and integer valued function called the multiplicity of $T$, $\mathcal{M}$ an $n$-rectifiable set, and

$$\vec{T} \ = \ \xi$$

where $\xi$ is an $\mathcal{H}^n$-measurable unit simple $n$-vector field on $\mathcal{M}$ which for $\mathcal{H}^n$-a.e. $z \in \mathcal{M}$ gives an orientation of the *approximate tangent space* of $\mathcal{M}$ at $z$, that is,

$$T(\omega) \ = \ \int_{\mathcal{M}} < \omega(z), \xi(z) > \theta(z)\, d\mathcal{H}^n(z) \ ,$$

$T$ is called an *integer rectifiable current*, and will be denoted by $\tau(\mathcal{M}, \theta, \xi)$. Every $n$-dimensional oriented smooth submanifold $\mathcal{M}$ with finite area can be regarded as the rectifiable current $[\![\mathcal{M}]\!]$

$$[\![\mathcal{M}]\!](\omega) \ := \ \int_{\mathcal{M}} \omega \ = \ \int_{\mathcal{M}} < \omega(z), \xi(z) > d\mathcal{H}^n(z)$$

where $\xi(z)$ is the $n$-vector orienting the tangent plane $T_z\mathcal{M}$ to $\mathcal{M}$ at $z$.

When $\mathcal{M}$ is the graph of a *smooth* mapping $u : \Omega \to \mathcal{Y} \subset \mathbf{R}^N$, the rectifiable $n$-current integration over the graph $G_u$ of $u$, denoted $[\![G_u]\!]$, is given by

$$[\![G_u]\!](\omega) \ = \ \int_{G_u} \omega = \int_{\Omega} (\mathrm{id} \times u)^{\#} \omega$$

If

$$\omega = \sum_{|\alpha|+|\beta|=n} \omega_{\alpha\beta}\, dx^\alpha \wedge dy^\beta = \sum_{k=0}^{n} \omega^{(k)}, \qquad \omega^{(k)} = \sum_{\substack{|\alpha|+|\beta|=n \\ |\beta|=k}} \omega_{\alpha\beta}(x,y)\, dx^\alpha \wedge dy^\beta$$

we have

$$[\![G_u]\!](\omega) = \sum_{|\alpha|+|\beta|=n} \sigma(\alpha,\bar\alpha) \int_\Omega \omega_{\alpha\beta}(x,u(x))\, M^\beta_{\bar\alpha}(Du(x))\, dx$$

where $M^\beta_{\bar\alpha}(Du(x))$ denotes the (determinant of the) $(\beta,\bar\alpha)$-minor of the $(N\times n)$-matrix $Du(x)$, $M^0_0(Du(x)) := 1$. Here $\bar\alpha$ denotes the complement of the multiindex $\alpha$ in $\{1,2,\ \dots\ ,n\}$ in the natural order and $\sigma(\alpha,\bar\alpha)$ the sign of the permutation which reorders naturally $(\alpha,\bar\alpha)$.

In terms of standard basis $e_1,\ \dots\ ,e_n$ of $\mathbf{R}^n_x$ and $\varepsilon_1,\ \dots\ \varepsilon_N$ of $\mathbf{R}^N_y$ with the identifications $T_x\Omega \simeq \mathbf{R}^n_x$ and $T_y\mathbf{R}^N \simeq \mathbf{R}^N_y$, the simple $n$-vector orienting the tangent plane to $G_u$ is given by

$$\xi := \frac{M(Du)}{|M(Du)|}\ ,$$

where

$$M(Du) = (e_1+v_1)\wedge\ \dots\ \wedge(e_n+v_n)\ , \qquad v_j := \sum_{i=1}^N D_j u^i \varepsilon_i\ ,$$

i.e.

$$[\![G_u]\!](\omega) = \int_{G_u} <\omega,\xi>\, d\mathcal{H}^n = \sum_{k=1}^n \int_\Omega <\omega^{(k)}, M_{(k)}(Du)>\, dx\ .$$

Notice that $[\![G_u]\!]_{(k)}$ are measures with total variation

$$\int_\Omega |M_{(k)}(Du(x))|\, dx$$

and that

$$|M(Du(x))|\, dx = \frac{1}{\xi^{\bar 0 0}(x,u(x))}\, dx\ , \qquad \xi = \sum \xi^{\bar\alpha\beta} e_\alpha \wedge \varepsilon_\beta$$

is the element of area of $G_u$.

Given an $H^{1,n}$-function from $\Omega$ into $\mathcal{Y}\subset\mathbf{R}^N$, by Lusin's theorem for Sobolev functions, there exists a sequence of closed sets $F_k\subset\Omega$ with $\mathcal{H}^n(\Omega\setminus$

$F_k) < 1/k$ and a sequence of functions $u_k \in C^1(\Omega, \mathbf{R}^N)$ with $u_k = u$ and $Du_k = Du$ on $F_k$. Set $\Omega_0 = \cup_{k=1}^{\infty} F_k$ and by induction define

$$H_k = F_k \setminus \bigcup_{i=1}^{k-1} F_i, \quad \mathcal{N}_k := \text{ graph of } u_k \cap \pi^{-1}(H_k)$$

where $\pi : \Omega \times \mathbf{R}^N \to \mathbf{R}^n$ is the linear projection $(x, y) \to x$. Clearly $\mathcal{H}^n(\Omega \setminus \Omega_0) = 0$, $\mathcal{M}_u := \cup_{k=1}^{\infty} \mathcal{N}_k$ is an $n$-rectifiable set. Thus one easily sees that the above formulas and in particular

$$[\![G_u]\!](\omega) := \int_{\mathcal{M}_u} \omega \qquad \omega \in \mathcal{D}^n(\Omega \times \mathcal{Y})$$

allow us to identify functions $u \in H^{1,n}(\Omega, \mathcal{Y})$ with the rectifiable current $\tau(\mathcal{M}_u, 1, \xi)$ that we shall again denote by $[\![G_u]\!]$. Taking into account that by [8] we can approximate strongly in $H^{1,n}$ every map $u \in H^{1,n}(\Omega, \mathcal{Y})$ by $C^\infty$-mappings with values in $\mathcal{Y}$, and that for smooth mappings the *boundary* of $[\![G_u]\!]$ is zero in $\Omega$

$$\partial [\![G_u]\!] = 0 \qquad \text{in } \Omega \,,$$

i.e.,

$$\partial [\![G_u]\!](\omega) := [\![G_u]\!](d\omega) = 0 \qquad \forall \omega \in \mathcal{D}^{n-1}(\Omega \times \mathcal{Y})$$

we can state

**Theorem 1** *Let $u \in H^{1,n}(\Omega, \mathcal{Y})$. Then there exists a sequence of functions in $C^\infty(\Omega, \mathcal{Y})$, which can also be choosen with boundary values $u$ on $\partial\Omega$, such that $[\![G_{u_k}]\!]$ converges weakly to $[\![G_u]\!]$, i.e.,*

$$[\![G_{u_k}]\!](\omega) \;\to\; [\![G_u]\!](\omega) \;\ast\, \forall \omega \in \mathcal{D}^n(\Omega, \mathcal{Y}) \qquad \text{and } u_k \to u \text{ in } H^{1,n} \,.$$

*Moreover, $[\![G_u]\!]$ is an $n$-rectifiable current without boundary in $\Omega$.*

Let $u \in H^{1,n}(\Omega, \mathcal{Y})$ then

$$\|[\![G_u]\!]\|_{\mathcal{D}} := \sup\Big\{ [\![G_u]\!](\omega) \,:\, \omega \in \mathcal{D}^n(\Omega \times \mathcal{Y}),\ \|\omega\|_{\mathcal{D}} \le 1 \Big\} < +\infty$$

where

$$\begin{aligned}\|\omega\|_{\mathcal{D}} := \quad & \max\left\{\sup_{x,y}\frac{|\omega^{(0)}(x,y)|}{1+|y|^n},\ \int(\sup_y\left|\omega^{(1)}(x,y)\right|)^n\,dx,\right.\\ & \int(\sup_y\left|\omega^{(2)}(x,y)\right|)^{n/2}\,dx,\ \ldots,\\ & \left.\int(\sup_y\left|\omega^{(n-1)}(x,y)\right|)^{n/n-1}\,dx,\ \sup_{x,y}\left|\omega^{(n)}(x,y)\right|\right\}.\end{aligned}$$

Moreover, $\|[\![G_u]\!]\|_{\mathcal{D}}$ and $\|u\|_{H^{1,n}}$ are equivalent, and $\mathbf{M}[\![G_u]\!] \le c\,\|[\![G_u]\!]\|_{\mathcal{D}}$. Similarly for every $T \in \mathcal{D}_n(\Omega\times\mathcal{Y})$ we define the *$\mathcal{D}$-norm of $T$* as

$$\|T\|_{\mathcal{D}} := \sup\{\,T(\omega) : \omega\in\mathcal{D}^n(\Omega\times\mathcal{Y}),\ \|\omega\|_{\mathcal{D}}\le 1\,\}.$$

A sequence $\{T_k\}\subset\mathcal{D}_n(\Omega\times\mathcal{Y})$ is said to *converge $\mathcal{D}$-weakly to $T$*, $T_k \overset{\mathcal{D}}{\rightharpoonup} T$, if and only if

$$\sup_k \|T_k\|_{\mathcal{D}} < \infty \quad\text{and}\quad T_k(\omega)\to T(\omega)\quad \forall\omega\in\mathcal{D}^n(\Omega\times\mathcal{Y}).$$

Since $\|.\|_{\mathcal{D}}$ is lower semicontinuous with respect to the weak convergence of $n$-currents, if $T_k \overset{\mathcal{D}}{\rightharpoonup} T$, we obviously have $\|T\|_{\mathcal{D}} < +\infty$.

Let $\{u_k\}$ be a sequence of functions in $C^1(\Omega,\mathcal{Y})$ with equibounded $\mathcal{D}$-norms. Passing to a subsequence, we can assume that

$$G_{u_k} \overset{\mathcal{D}}{\rightharpoonup} T,$$

and that there exists $u_T\in H^{1,n}(\Omega,\mathcal{Y})$ such that

$$u_k \rightharpoonup u_T \text{ in } H^{1,n}(\Omega,\mathcal{Y}),\qquad u_k\to u_T \text{ in } L^2(\Omega,\mathcal{Y}).$$

Moreover $T$ is a rectifiable $n$-current with finite $\mathcal{D}$-norm, by Federer-Fleming closure theorem. One also proves, compare [3] [4], that $T_{(0)}$ is a positive measure which projects onto $\Omega$, $\pi_\# T = [\![\Omega]\!]$, $[\![G_{u_k}]\!]_{(0)} \rightharpoonup [\![G_{u_T}]\!]_{(0)}, \ldots, [\![G_{u_k}]\!]_{(n-1)} \rightharpoonup [\![G_{u_T}]\!]_{(n-1)}$, and, consequently, $T$ can be written as

$$T = [\![G_{u_T}]\!] + S_T$$

where $S_T$ is a *completely vertical*, i.e. $S_{T(i)} = 0$ for $i = 0,\ldots,n-1$, rectifiable current which is in general *not zero*.

More precisely we have (compare with [5])

**Theorem 2** *Let $\{u_k\}$ be a sequence of smooth mappings $u_k : \Omega \to \mathcal{Y}$ with equibounded $\mathcal{D}$-norms and which converges $\mathcal{D}$-weakly to $T$,*

$$[\![G_{u_k}]\!] \overset{\mathcal{D}}{\rightharpoonup} T\,.$$

*Then*

$$T \;=\; [\![G_{u_T}]\!] + S_T$$

*where $u_T$ is the $H^{1,n}$-weak limit of $\{u_k\}$. The $n$-currents $[\![G_{u_T}]\!]$ and $S_T$ are rectifiable and boundaryless in $\Omega \times \mathcal{Y}$. Moreover, on $\mathcal{Z}^n(\Omega \times \mathcal{Y})$*

$$\mathcal{Z}^n(\Omega \times \mathcal{Y}) \;:=\; \left\{\omega \in \mathcal{D}^n(\Omega \times \mathcal{Y}) \;:\; d_y\omega^{(n)} = 0\right\}$$

*$S_T$ is a finite combination of points in $\Omega$ times an integer rectifiable $n$-cycle of type $S^n$, i.e.,*

$$\text{(1)} \qquad S_T \;=\; \sum_{i=1}^{k} [\![x_i]\!] \times C_i \qquad \text{on } \mathcal{Z}^n(\Omega \times \mathcal{Y})$$

*where $C_i$ is a rectifiable cycle, $\partial C_i = 0$, for which there exists a smooth map $\Phi_i : S^n \to \mathcal{Y}$ such that $\Phi_\#[\![S^n]\!]$ is homologous to $C_i$. Finally*

$$\text{(2)} \qquad T \;=\; [\![G_{u_T}]\!] + \sum_{i=1}^{k} [\![x_i]\!] \times C_i + S_{T,sing}\,,$$

*$S_{T,sing}$ being a rectifiable $n$-current in $\Omega \times \mathcal{Y}$ which is completely vertical and with zero periods, i.e.,*

$$S_{T,sing} \llcorner \widehat{\pi}^\# \sigma \;=\; 0$$

*for any closed $n$-form $\sigma$ on $\mathcal{Y}$, $\widehat{\pi}$ being the projection on $\mathcal{Y}$.*

**proof:** We first we observe that for any Borel set $A \subset \Omega$ the current $S_T \llcorner \pi^{-1}(A)$ is boundaryless. We then consider the measure $\mu$ projection of the measure total variation $\|S_T\|$ of $S_T$ and decompose $\mu$ as $\mu = \mu_0 + \overline{\mu}$, where $\mu_0$ is the atomic part, i.e.

$$\mu_0 = \sum_i a_i\, \delta_{x_i}, \qquad x_i \in \Omega, \qquad \sum_i |a_i| < +\infty\,,$$

and $\overline{\mu}(\{x\}) = 0$ for all $x \in \Omega$. Since for $r \to 0$ $\overline{\mu}(B_r(x)) \to \overline{\mu}(\{x\}) = 0$, for any $\varepsilon > 0$ we can find a covering of $\overline{\Omega}$ by (geodesic) balls $B_{r_x}(x)$ such that $\overline{\mu}(B_{r_x}(x)) < \varepsilon$; choosing a finite covering $B_1, B_2, \dots, B_h$ and setting $A_1 = B_1 \cap \overline{\Omega}$, $A_i = (B_i \cap \overline{\Omega}) \setminus (\cup_{j=1}^{i-1} A_j)$, we finally conclude that for every $\varepsilon > 0$ there exists a finite family of disjoint Borel sets $A_i$ such that

$$\overline{\mu}(A_i) < \varepsilon\,, \qquad \bigcup_i A_i = \overline{\Omega}\,,$$

and we can write

$$S = S_0 + \overline{S}$$

where

$$S_0 = \sum_i \{x_i\} \times \tilde{C}_i, \qquad \overline{S} = \sum_i \overline{S}_i, \qquad \overline{S}_i = S_T \llcorner \pi^{-1}(A_i \setminus \cup_j \{x_j\})\,.$$

Observing that $\operatorname{spt} \overline{S}_i \subset \overline{\Omega} \times \mathcal{Y}$ and $\partial \overline{S}_i = 0$, and choosing $\varepsilon$ sufficiently small, since $\mathbf{M}(\overline{S}_i) \le \overline{\mu}(A_i) < \varepsilon$ we conclude from the isoperimetric inequality [2, 4.4.2] that there exist $R_i \in \mathcal{D}_{n+1}(\tilde{\Omega} \times \mathcal{Y})$ , $\tilde{\Omega} \supset\supset \overline{\Omega}$ , such that $\operatorname{spt} \overline{S}_i \subset \overline{\Omega}$ and $\overline{S}_i = \partial R_i$. Therefore we conclude that $\overline{S}_i \llcorner B = 0$ on $\mathcal{Z}^n(\Omega \times \mathcal{Y})$ for any Borel set $B \subset A_i$, consequently $S_T = S_0$ on $\mathcal{Z}^n(\Omega \times \mathcal{Y})$. Finally for all $x_i$ consider now $S_i = S \llcorner \pi^{-1}(x_i)$, obviously $S_0 = \sum_i S_i$. Since, if $\mathbf{M}(S_i)$ is small enough, it follows as previously that $S_i = 0$ on $\mathcal{Z}^n(\Omega \times \mathcal{Y})$, we can finally conclude that $S_0$ is a finite sum of $S_i$, i.e., $S_T = \sum_{i=1}^k [\![x_i]\!] \times \overline{C}_i$. Since $S_T$ is rectifiable and $\partial \overline{C}_i = 0$, we then conclude that (1) holds for suitable rectifiable cycles. It remains to show that the $C_i$'s are cycles of the type $S^n$. This can be done exactly as in the proof of theorem 4.3 of [5], which reminds of the argument in [7]. □

**Remark 1** We can obviously write in (1)

$$S_{T,sing} = \sum_{i=1}^k [\![x_i]\!] \times \tilde{C}_i + S_{T,sing} \llcorner \pi^{-1}(\Omega \setminus \cup_i \{x_i\})$$

where $\tilde{C}_i$ are $n$-cycles which are homologous to zero. Therefore from now on we shall write every $T \in \operatorname{cart}^n(\Omega, S^n)$ as

$$T = [\![G_{u_T}]\!] + \sum_{i=1}^k [\![x_i]\!] \times C_i + S_{T,sing}$$

where $S_{T,sing}$ coincides with $S_{T,sing} \llcorner^{-1}(\Omega \setminus \cup_{i=1}^{k}\{x_i\})$ .

As $C^1$ and $H^{1,n}$-graphs are not $\mathcal{D}$-weakly closed we are then led to introduce the following two classes of *cartesian currents*

$$\mathrm{Cart}^n(\Omega, \mathcal{Y}) := \text{the sequential } \mathcal{D}\text{-closure of the class of } n\text{-currents } [\![G_u]\!] \text{ with finite } \mathcal{D}\text{-norm, where } u \in C^1$$

$$\mathrm{cart}^n(\Omega, \mathcal{Y}) := \{T \in \mathcal{D}^n(\Omega \times \mathcal{Y}) \ : \ \partial T = 0, \quad \|T\|_{\mathcal{D}} < +\infty, \quad T \text{ is of the form (2)}\}$$

Taking into account the arguments in the proof of theorem 2, it is then not difficult to prove the following

**Theorem 3** *The classes* $\mathrm{Cart}^n(\Omega, \mathcal{Y})$ *and* $\mathrm{cart}^n(\Omega, \mathcal{Y})$ *are* $\mathcal{D}$*-weakly closed, and their* $\mathcal{D}$*-bounded sets are* $\mathcal{D}$*-weakly (relatively) compact. Moreover*

$$\mathrm{Cart}^n(\Omega, \mathcal{Y}) \subset \mathrm{cart}^n(\Omega, \mathcal{Y}) \tag{3}$$

In general we do not known whether or not equality holds in (3). Equality does hold if $\mathcal{Y}$ is the $n$-dimensional sphere in $\mathbf{R}^{n+1}$. In this case, as consequence of theorem 2, or directly by means of the constancy theorem, compare [4], we deduce that every $T \in \mathrm{cart}^n(\Omega \times S^n)$ has the form

$$T = [\![G_{u_T}]\!] + \sum_{i=1}^{k} d_i [\![x_i]\!] \times [\![S^n]\!] \, , \qquad d_i \in \mathbf{Z} \tag{4}$$

and we have

**Theorem 4** $\mathrm{Cart}^n(\Omega, S^n) = \mathrm{cart}^n(\Omega, S^n)$. *More precisely, for every* $T \in \mathrm{cart}^n(\Omega, S^n)$ *there exists a sequence of smooth mappings* $\{u_k\}$ *from* $\Omega$ *into* $S^n$ *with equibounded* $H^{1,n}$*-norms such that*

$$[\![G_{u_k}]\!] \overset{\mathcal{D}}{\rightharpoonup} T \, .$$

*Moreover, if* $T$ *has the form (4), then*

$$\frac{1}{n^{n/2}} \int_\Omega |du_k|^n \, dvol_{\mathcal{X}} \ \rightarrow \ \frac{1}{n^{n/2}} \int_\Omega |du_T|^n \, dvol_{\mathcal{X}} + \sum_{i=1}^{k} |d_i| \mathcal{H}^n(S^n) \, . \tag{5}$$

**proof:** First we assume that all $d_i$'s are equal to one and all points $x_i$ are distinct. In this case it suffices to prove (5) assuming also that the set $\{x_i\}$ reduces to a point $x_0$. For the sake of simplicity we now assume that $\Omega$ is a neighbourhood of the origin and that $x_0 = 0$. Let $u_\varepsilon$ be a family of smooth functions converging for $\varepsilon \to 0$ in $H^{1,n}(\Omega, S^n)$ to $u_T$. We can assume

$$\int_{B_{2\varepsilon}} |Du_\varepsilon|^n \, dx \;\to\; 0 \qquad \text{for } \varepsilon \to 0 \, ,$$

thus we find for each $\varepsilon$, a radius $r_\varepsilon$, $\varepsilon < r_\varepsilon < 2\varepsilon$ such that

$$(6) \qquad \int_{S^{n-1}} \left| \frac{\partial u_\varepsilon(r_\varepsilon, \theta)}{\partial \theta} \right|^n d\mathcal{H}^{n-1} \;\to 0 \, .$$

Define now

$$w_\varepsilon \;:=\; \begin{cases} u_\varepsilon & \text{in } \Omega \setminus B_{r_\varepsilon} \\ v_\varepsilon & \text{in } B_\varepsilon \\ \tilde{w}_\varepsilon & \text{in } B_{r_\varepsilon} \setminus B_\varepsilon \end{cases}$$

where $v_\varepsilon$ is the inverse of the stereographic projection $\sigma : S^n \to \mathbf{R}^n$ from the north pole, suitably concentred near the origin, i.e.,

$$v_\varepsilon(x) \;:=\; \sigma^{-1}(\lambda_\varepsilon x)$$

$\lambda_\varepsilon \to +\infty$ as $\varepsilon \to 0$, and $\tilde{w}_\varepsilon$ is a linear transition map of the type

$$\tilde{w}^i_\varepsilon(r, \theta) := A_i(\theta) r + B_i(\theta), \quad i = 1, \, \ldots \, , n-1; \quad \tilde{w}^n_\varepsilon(r, \theta) = \sqrt{1 - \sum (\tilde{v}^i_\varepsilon)^2}$$

determined in such a way to make $w_\varepsilon$ continuous in $\Omega$. Because of (6) one sees that

$$\int_{B_{r_\varepsilon} \setminus B_\varepsilon} |Dw|^n \, dx \;\to\; 0 \, ;$$

choosing suitably $\lambda_\varepsilon$ we see that

$$\frac{1}{n^{n/2}} \int_{B_\varepsilon} |Dw_\varepsilon|^n \, dx \;\to\; \mathcal{H}^n(S^n) \, .$$

Therefore we see that the result follows at once in this case. In the general case we choose, for each $i$, $d_i$ sequences of points $x^j_{i,k}$ converging to $x_i$ for $k \to \infty$, in such a way that all points $x^j_{i,k}$ are distinct. Since

$$[\![G_{u_T}]\!] + \sum_{i,j} [\![x^j_{i.k}]\!] \times [\![S^n]\!] \;\to\; [\![G_{u_T}]\!] + \sum_i d_i [\![x_i]\!] \times [\![S^n]\!]$$

and the $\mathcal{D}$-norms of the elements on the left hand-side are equibounded, the result follows easily by a diagonal procedure. $\square$

**Remark 2** Let $T = \tau(\mathcal{M}_T, \theta, \xi) \in \text{cart}^n(\Omega, S^n)$, $T = [\![G_{u_T}]\!] + S_T$. Using the area formula, compare [3] [4], one shows that

$$\tau(\mathcal{M}_T, \theta, \xi) = \tau(G_{u_T}, 1, \xi) + \tau(\mathcal{M}_{S_T}, \theta_{S_T}, \xi)$$

where $\theta_{S_T}$ is in general larger then one, and that the measures total variations $\|[\![G_{u_T}]\!]\|$ and $\|S_T\|$ are mutually orthogonal, and

$$\|T\| \;=\; \|[\![G_{u_T}]\!]\| + \|S_T\|$$

We conclude this section with a few remarks on the homology map. Let us assume for the sake of simplicity that $\mathcal{X}$ is compact and without boundary, and let $u : \mathcal{X} \to \mathcal{Y}$ be a smooth map. Since $\partial u_\# = u_\# \partial$, the map $u_\#$ which maps any $k$-dimensional integral cycle $C$ in $\mathcal{X}$ into the $k$-dimensional integral cycle $u_\# C$ in $\mathcal{Y}$, defines in fact a map $u_*$ between the real homology groups of degree $k$ of $\mathcal{X}$ and $\mathcal{Y}$

$$u_* : H_k(\mathcal{X}, \mathbf{R}) \;\to\; H_k(\mathcal{Y}, \mathbf{R}), \qquad u_*([C]) = [u_\#(C)]$$

called the *homology (or degree) map*. Assuming that $C$ is a regular cycle, by means of Poincaré duality which associates to $C$ a $(n-k)$-form so that

$$\int_C \eta \;=\; \int_{\mathcal{X}} \omega_C \wedge \eta \qquad \forall \eta \in \mathcal{D}^k(\mathcal{X})$$

we see that

$$u_\#(C)(\eta) = C(u^\# \eta) = \int_{\mathcal{X}} \omega_C \wedge u^\# \eta = \int_{G_u} \pi^\# \omega_C \wedge \hat{\pi}^\# \eta \,.$$

for all $\eta \in \mathcal{D}^k(\mathcal{Y})$. Similarly, for every cartesian current $T \in \text{cart}^n(\mathcal{X}, \mathcal{Y})$ and for every $k \le n$, the matrix of periods

$$T(\pi^\# \omega \wedge \hat{\pi}^\# \eta) \qquad \omega \in \mathcal{Z}^{n-k}(\mathcal{X}),\ \eta \in \mathcal{Z}^k(\mathcal{Y})$$

defines a homology map

$$T_* \; : \; H_k(\mathcal{X}, \mathbf{R}) \; \to \; H_k(\mathcal{Y}, \mathbf{R}) \, .$$

as follows. Consider a $k$-dimensional normal cycle $S$ and its regularization $S_\varepsilon$, $0 < \varepsilon < 1$. The normal current $S_\varepsilon$ is homologous to $S$ [2, 4.1.18] and can be written as

$$S_\varepsilon(\omega) \; = \; \int_{\mathcal{X}} \omega_{S_\varepsilon} \wedge \omega$$

where $\omega_{S_\varepsilon}$ is a smooth closed $(n-k)$-form in $\mathcal{X}$, see [2, 4.1.2]. Thus $T_*$ is given by

$$T_*([S])(\eta) \; := \; T(\pi^\# \omega_{S_\varepsilon} \wedge \hat{\pi}^\# \eta) \qquad \eta \in \mathcal{Z}^k(\mathcal{Y})$$

Actually if the $k$-dimensional singular homology group of $\mathcal{Y}$, $k \leq n$, is torsionless, $T_*$ defines a map between the singular homology groups

$$T_* \; : \; H_k(\mathcal{X}, \mathbf{Z}) \; \to \; H_k(\mathcal{Y}, \mathbf{Z}) \, .$$

In order to see this, we first observe that, if

$$T \; = \; G_{u_T} + \sum_i [\![x_i]\!] \times C_i + S_{T,sing}$$

the map $T_*$ defined above does not depend on $S_{T,sing}$ and by [8] we consider a sequence $\{u_k\} \subset C^1(\mathcal{X}, \mathcal{Y})$ such that

$$u_k \; \to \; u_T \qquad \text{in } H^{1,n}$$

$$[\![G_{u_k}]\!] \rightharpoonup [\![G_{u_T}]\!] \, .$$

Let $S$ be a rectifiable $k$-cycle in $\mathcal{X}$. The real $k$-cycle in $\mathcal{Y}$ $[\![G_{u_k}]\!] \llcorner \omega_S$ is homologous to the integral $k$-cycle $u_{k\#}(S)$. Passing to a subsequence $u_{k\#}(S)$ converge weakly to a rectifiable $k$-cycle $R$ which clearly belongs to the real homology class of $[\![G_{u_T}]\!] \llcorner \omega_S$. Since $H_k(\mathcal{X}, \mathcal{Y})$ is torsionless the singular homology class of $R$ is independent of the approximations $u_k$. If $k < n$, $(\sum [\![x_i]\!] \times C_i) \llcorner \omega_S$ is zero, while if $k = n$ necessarely $S$ is an integer multiple of $\mathcal{X}$, and $S_\varepsilon = S = p\mathcal{X}$, thus $\omega_{S_\varepsilon} = p$, hence we find

$$[T_*(S)] \; = \; [R + p \sum C_i]$$

and this proves that $T_*$ is well defined as a map between the singular homology group of $\mathcal{X}$ and $\mathcal{Y}$.

We notice that if $\{T_k\} \subset \text{cart}^n(\mathcal{X}, \mathcal{Y})$ is a sequence which converges $\mathcal{D}$-weakly to $T$ and all the $T_k$ have the same homology map $\widehat{T}_*$, then also $T_* = \widehat{T}_*$.

We also note that, if $\mathcal{X} = \mathcal{Y} = S^n$, the homology map (of order $n$) of a smooth map $u$ is just described by the degree of $u$. The same is true for any cartesian current $T$ in $\text{cart}^n(\mathcal{X}, \mathcal{Y})$, if we interpret the degree of $T$ as the integer $d$, which exists by the constancy theorem, such that $\widehat{\pi}_\# T = d[\![S^n]\!]$, compare [4].

# 2 The energy in cart$^n$ and the generalized variational problems.

We shall now extend the integral

$$(1) \qquad \mathcal{D}(u) := \frac{1}{n^{n/2}} \int_\Omega |du|^n \, dvol_{\mathcal{X}}$$

to $\text{cart}^n(\Omega, \mathcal{Y})$. In order to do that we extend the integrand $n^{-n/2}|p|^n$ to all simple $n$-vectors with positive first component.

For a fixed $(x, y) \in \Omega \times \mathcal{Y}$ we think of $T_x\Omega \times T_y\mathcal{Y}$ as of a $(n+m)$-subspace of $\mathbf{R}^n_x \times \mathbf{R}^N_y$ and we consider the integrand $n^{-n/2}|p|^n$ as a function on the simple $n$-vectors in

$$\begin{aligned}\Sigma_1 := \Sigma_1(x,y) \ := \ & \{\xi \in \Lambda_n(\mathbf{R}^n_x \times \mathbf{R}^N_y) \ : \ \xi = M(G) \\ & \text{for some } N \times n \text{ matrix } G : \mathbf{R}^n_x \to T_y\mathcal{Y} \subset \mathbf{R}^N\} \ ,\end{aligned}$$

by setting for $\xi = \sum_0^n \xi_{(k)}$

$$f(\xi) := n^{-n/2} |\xi_{(1)}|^n$$

The largest homogeneous one and convex function on $\Lambda_n(\mathbf{R}^n_x \times \mathbf{R}^N_y)$ which stays below $f$ on $\Sigma_1$ is called the *polyconvex extension of* $f$ and denoted by $F(x, y, \xi)$, compare [4],

$$\begin{aligned}F(x,y,\xi) \ := \ & \sup \ \{\phi(\xi) \ : \ \phi \text{ linear}, \ \phi : \Lambda_n \mathbf{R}^{n+N} \to \mathbf{R}, \phi(M(G)) \leq \\ & n^{-n/2}|G|^n, \text{ for all linear map } G : T_x\Omega \to T_y\mathcal{Y}\} \ .\end{aligned}$$

For every $T = \tau(\mathcal{M}, \theta, \overrightarrow{T}) = [\![G_{u_T}]\!] + S_T$ in $\mathrm{cart}^n(\Omega, \mathcal{Y})$ we now define $\mathcal{D}$ on $T$ as

$$\mathcal{D}(T) := \int_{\mathcal{M}} F(x, y, \overrightarrow{T}) \, d\|T\| \tag{2}$$

Since every $T \in \mathrm{cart}^n(\Omega, \mathcal{Y})$ can be written as

$$T = [\![G_{u_T}]\!] + S_{T,hom} + S_{T,sing}$$

with

$$S_{T,hom} = \sum_{i=1}^{k} [\![x_i]\!] \times C_i$$

$$S_{T,sing} = S_{T,sing} \llcorner \pi^{-1}(\Omega \setminus \cup_1^k \{x_i\})$$

we deduce, taking into account remark 2 of section 1, that

$$\begin{aligned} \mathcal{D}(T) \; := \; n^{-n/2} \textstyle\int_\Omega |du_T|^n \, dvol_{\mathcal{X}} \quad &+ \textstyle\int F(x, y, \overrightarrow{S}_{T,hom}) \, d\|S_{T,hom}\| + \\ &\textstyle\int F(x, y, \overrightarrow{S}_{T,sing}) \, d\|S_{T,sing}\| \end{aligned} \tag{3}$$

We now define the *f-comass* of a $n$-covector $\omega \in \bigwedge^n(\mathbf{R}^n \times \mathbf{R}^N)$ by

$$\|\omega\|_f := \sup \left\{ < \omega, M(G) >: \; n^{-n/2} |G|^n \leq 1 \right\}$$

and the *f-mass* of $\xi \in \bigwedge_n(\mathbf{R}^n \times \mathbf{R}^N)$ by

$$\|\xi\|_f := \sup \{ < \omega, \xi >: \; \|\omega\|_f \leq 1 \} .$$

Then, for any $\xi \in \bigwedge_n(T_x\Omega \times T_y\mathcal{Y})$ we have

$$F(x, y, \xi) = \|\xi\|_f$$

**Proposition 1** *Let $\xi$ be the completely vertical simple $n$-vector ($\xi_{(0)} = 0, \; \ldots \; , \xi_{(n-1)} = 0$), orienting the tangent plane of the current $S_{T,hom}$ associated to $T \in \mathrm{cart}^n(\Omega, \mathcal{Y})$. Then*

$$\|\xi\|_f \; = \; \|\xi_{(n)}\| \; .$$

*In particular*

$$(4) \qquad \int F(x,y,\overrightarrow{S}_{T,hom})\, d\|S_{T,hom}\| = \sum_{i=1}^{k} \mathbf{M}(C_i)\ ,$$

*consequently, for every*

$$T = [\![G_{u_T}]\!] + \sum_{i=1}^{k} [\![x_i]\!] \times C_i + S_{T,sing}$$

*we have*

$$(5) \qquad \begin{aligned} \mathcal{D}(T) \ := \quad & n^{-n/2} \textstyle\int_\Omega |du_T|^n \, dvol_{\mathcal{X}} + \sum_{i=1}^{k} \mathbf{M}(C_i) + \\ & \textstyle\int F(x,y,\overrightarrow{S}_{T,sing})\, d\|S_{T,sing}\| \end{aligned}$$

**proof:** Since $\xi$ orients the tangent plane of an $n$-dimensional completely vertical cycle, modulo an orthogonal transformation, we can assume that $N = n$, in the definition of $f$-mass. Consequently it suffices to consider $n$-covectors in $\bigwedge^n(\mathbf{R}^n \times \mathbf{R}^N)$ and linear transformations $G : \mathbf{R}^n \to \mathbf{R}^n$. From Hadamard's determinant theorem

$$(\det G)^2 \ \leq \prod_{j=1}^{n} \left( \sum_{i=1}^{n} a_{ij}^2 \right), \quad G = (a_{ij})$$

we then deduce the optimal isoperimetric inequality

$$(6) \qquad |\det G| \ \leq \ n^{-n/2} |G|^n \ .$$

In particular

$$\|\omega\|_f \geq |\omega|\ , \qquad \|\xi\|_f \leq |\xi|\ ,$$

and, by considering the linear map

$$\eta \ \longrightarrow \ \left( \frac{\xi}{|\xi|}, \eta \right) =: < \omega_\xi, \eta > \ ,$$

since $\|\omega_\xi\| \leq 1$, we deduce that $\|\xi\|_f \geq \|\xi\|$, hence $\|\xi\|_f = |\xi|$. From this the claim follows at once. □

The functional $\mathcal{D}(T)$ is clearly coercive with respect to the $\mathcal{D}$-norm, moreover, by theorem 3 of section 5 of [3], $\mathcal{D}(T)$ is sequentially lower semicontinuous with respect to the $\mathcal{D}$-weak convergence; finally, passing to the homology map is a "continuous" operation with respect to the $\mathcal{D}$-weak convergence. Therefore proving existence theorems for variational problems for $\mathcal{D}(T)$ in $\mathcal{D}$-weakly closed subclasses of $\text{cart}^n(\Omega, \mathcal{Y})$ is just a trivial matter. We only state one such an existence theorem.

**Theorem 1** *Let $\mathcal{X}$ and $\mathcal{Y}$ be two compact, boundaryless, oriented Riemannian manifolds of dimension respectively $n$ and $m \geq n$, and let $T_0$ be an element of $\text{cart}^n(\mathcal{X}, \mathcal{Y})$. Then the infimum of $\mathcal{D}(T)$ in the class*

$$\left\{ T \in \text{cart}^n(\mathcal{X}, \mathcal{Y}) \; : \; T_* = T_{0*} \right\}$$

*is attained. Moreover, if $T$ is a minimizer, we have*

$$T = [\![G_{u_T}]\!] + \sum_{i=1}^{k} [\![x_i]\!] \times \gamma_i \; ,$$

*where $\gamma_i$ is a rectifiable cycle in $\mathcal{Y}$ of the type $S^n$ with least area in its homology class.*

In the case $\mathcal{Y} = S^n$, as a special case of the previous theorem we get

**Theorem 2** *For any integer $m$ there exists a minimizer of $\mathcal{D}(T)$ in the class*

$$E_m := \left\{ T \in \text{cart}^n(\mathcal{X}, S^n) \; : \; \textit{degree of } T = m \right\}$$

*If we set*

$$\lambda_m \; := \; \inf \left\{ \mathcal{D}(T) \; : \; T \in E_m \right\}$$

*we obviously have*

$$\lambda_\ell \; \leq \; \lambda_m + \mathcal{H}^n(S^n)|k - \ell| \; ;$$

moreover, compare [4] [6],

**Theorem 3** *Let $T$ be a minimizer of $\mathcal{D}$ in $E_m$. If for $\ell \neq m$ and $|\ell - m| \leq m$*

$$\lambda_m \ < \ \lambda_\ell + \mathcal{H}^n(S^n)|\ell - m| \ ,$$

*then $T$ has no vertical part, i.e., $T = [\![G_{u_T}]\!]$ for some $u_T \in H^{1,n}(\mathcal{X}, S^n)$*

**proof:** Let $\ell$ be the degree of $[\![G_{u_T}]\!]$, and consequently $m - \ell$ the degree of $S_T$. We have for $x_0 \in S^n$

$$\begin{aligned} n^{-n/2} \textstyle\int_{\mathcal{X}} |du_T|^n \, dvol_{\mathcal{X}} \quad &+ |m - \ell|\mathcal{H}^n(S^n) = \mathcal{D}(T) \leq \\ &\mathcal{D}(m[\![x_0]\!] \times [\![S^n]\!]) = m\mathcal{H}(S^n) \ , \end{aligned}$$

in particular

$$|m - \ell| \ \leq \ m \ ,$$

thus, if $\ell \neq m$, by our assumption and since $[\![G_{u_T}]\!]$ minimizes $\mathcal{D}$ in $E_\ell$, we find

$$\lambda_\ell + |m - \ell|\mathcal{H}^n(S^n) = \lambda_m < \lambda_\ell + |m - \ell|\mathcal{H}^n(S^n) \ ,$$

a contradiction. □

# 3 Final remarks.

By theorem 4 of section 1, every cartesian current in $\text{cart}^n(\Omega, S^n)$ can be approximated $\mathcal{D}$-weakly and in energy by a sequence of smooth mappings $u_k$

$$[\![G_{u_k}]\!] \ \overset{\mathcal{D}}{\rightharpoonup} \ T$$

$$n^{-n/2} \int_\Omega |du_k|^n \, dvol_{\mathcal{X}} \ \to \ \mathcal{D}(T) \ .$$

This shows in particular that $\mathcal{D}(T)$ is the greatest lower semicontinuous extension of $n^{-n/2} \int_\Omega |du|^n$ to $\text{cart}^n(\Omega, S^n) = \text{Cart}^n(\Omega, S^n)$.

We are not able to prove a similar result in the general case. Going through the proof of theorem 4 of section 1, we easily sees that the point is to prove that for every rectifiable cycle of the type $S^n$ there exists an "*instanton*", i.e., a smooth map $u : \mathbf{R}^n \to \mathcal{Y}$ with values in $C$ such that

$$n^{-n/2} \int_{\mathbf{R}^n} |du|^n \, dx \ = \ \mathbf{M}(C) \ ,$$

or even to prove that there is a sequence of smooth maps $u_k$ such that

$$[\![G_{u_k}]\!] \xrightarrow{\mathcal{D}} C, \qquad \mathcal{D}([\![G_{u_k}]\!] \to \mathbf{M}(C) .$$

However, every cartesian current $T$ in $\text{cart}^n(\Omega, \mathcal{Y})$ can be $\mathcal{D}$-weakly and homologically approximated by smooth mappings. This means that for every $T \in \text{cart}^n(\Omega, \mathcal{Y})$ there exists a sequence of smooth mappings $u_k$ such that

$$[\![G_{u_k}]\!](\omega) \to T(\omega) \qquad \forall \omega \in \mathcal{Z}^n(\Omega \times \mathcal{Y}) .$$

Consider in fact $T = [\![G_{u_k}]\!] + \sum_{i=1}^{k} [\![x_i]\!] \times C_i$ in $\text{cart}^n(\Omega, \mathcal{Y})$. Since the $C_i$'s are of the type $S^n$ we can find cycles $\tilde{C}_i$ homologous to $C_i$ and mappings $\psi_i : S^n \to \tilde{C}_i$ such that $\psi_{i\#}[\![S^n]\!] = \tilde{C}_i$, and obviously, the cartesian current

$$\tilde{T} := [\![G_{u_k}]\!] + \sum_{i=1}^{k} [\![x_i]\!] \times \tilde{C}_i$$

is homologically equivalent to $T$, in the sense that

$$\tilde{T} = T \qquad \text{on } \mathcal{Z}^n(\Omega \times \mathcal{Y}) .$$

Now, by the same procedure of theorem 4 section 1, and taking into account the fact that $\text{Cart}^n(\Omega, S^n) = \text{cart}^n(\Omega, S^n)$, it is not difficult to show that there exists a sequence of smooth mappings $\{u_k\}$ such that

$$[\![G_{u_k}]\!] \xrightarrow{\mathcal{D}} \tilde{T}$$

i.e. $[\![G_{u_k}]\!](\omega) \to T(\omega)$ for all $\omega \in \mathcal{Z}^n(\Omega \times \mathcal{Y})$.

# References


[1] BREZIS H., CORON J.M., *Large solutions for harmonic maps in two dimensions.* Commun. Math. Phys. **92** (1983) 203-215.

[2] FEDERER H., *Geometric measure theory.* Springer-Verlag, New York, 1969.

[3] GIAQUINTA M., MODICA G., SOUČEK J., *Cartesian currents, weak diffeomorphisms and existence theorems in nonlinear elasticity.* Archive for Rat. Mech. Anal. **106** (1989) 97-159. *Erratum and addendum.* Archive for Rat. Mech. Anal. **109** (1990) 385-392.

[4] GIAQUINTA M., MODICA G., SOUČEK J., *Cartesian currents and variational problems for mappings into spheres.* Annali S.N.S. Pisa **16** (1989) 393-485.

[5] GIAQUINTA M., MODICA G., SOUČEK J., *The Dirichlet integral for mappings between manifolds: cartesian currents and homology.* Preprint.

[6] LIONS P.L., *The concentration compactness principle in the calculus of variations. The limit case,* part 2. Revista Matematica Iberoamericana **1** (1985) 45-121.

[7] SACKS J., UHLENBECK K., *The existence of minimal immersions of 2-spheres.* Ann. of Math. **113** (1981) 1-24.

[8] SCHOEN R., UHLENBECK K., *Boundary regularity and miscellaneous results on harmonic maps.* J. Diff. Geom. **18** (1983) 253-268.

[9] UHLENBECK K., *Minimal spheres and other conformal variational problems* in *Seminar on minimal submanifolds,* Bombieri Ed., Annals of Math. Studies **103**, Princeton Univ. Press, New Jersey.

M. GIAQUINTA, G. MODICA
Dip. di Matematica Applicata
Università di Firenze
Via S.Marta, 3
I-50139 Firenze
Italy

J. SOUČEK
Československá Akademie Věd
Matematický Ústav
Žitná, 25
11567 Praha
Czechoslovakia

June 1991

R HARDT*

# Spaces of harmonic maps with fixed singular sets

Questions concerning the nature and location of singularities of harmonic maps are quite difficult. For 3 dimensional domains there are a surprisingly large number of harmonic maps with isolated singularities at a variety of locations, as indicated by recents works of F.Bethuel, H.Brezis, J.-M.Coron, R.Hardt, F.H.Lin, L.Mou, and C.Poon [**BBC**], [**BB**], [**HLP**], [**M**], [**P**]. Here we consider various spaces of harmonic maps having a fixed singular set and controlled behavior near the singular set. Recent perturbation studies [**HM**], [**Sm2**] in these spaces provide new classes of harmonic maps. Under suitable hypotheses, energy minimality or strict stability is preserved under such perturbations. For smooth harmonic maps we find some results on uniqueness and finiteness for generic boundary data. There are many interesting examples involving moving singularities. Here we describe a family $\{u_t\}$ of harmonic maps from $\mathbf{B}^3$ to $\mathbf{S}^2$, with the same boundary data, but with $\operatorname{sing} u_t = \{(0,0,\pm t)\}$. As $t \to 0$, $u_t$ converges strongly in $H^1$ to a smooth harmonic map. Thus there are harmonic maps from $\mathbf{B}^3$ to $\mathbf{S}^2$ with exactly two singularities near 0 of arbitrarily small energy.

Suppose $\Omega$ is a smooth domain in $\mathbf{R}^m$ and, $N$ is a compact smooth Riemannian submanifold of $\mathbf{R}^p$. An $H^1$ map $u : \Omega \to N$ is a *harmonic map* if $u$ is a critical point for the energy integrand $E(u) = \int_\Omega |\nabla u|^2 dx$ under variations of the image of $u$ in $N$. So

$$\frac{d}{dt}\Big|_{t=0} E(\Pi_N(u + t\zeta)) = 0$$

for all $\zeta \in C_0^1(\Omega, \mathbf{R}^p)$ where $\Pi_N$ is the nearest point retraction mapping of some neighborhood $U$ of $N$ onto $N$. Note that for $|t|$ sufficiently small,e.g.

$$|t| < \frac{\operatorname{dist}(N, \mathbf{R}^p \setminus N)}{1 + sup|\zeta|},$$

each point $u(x) + t\zeta(x)$ lies in $U$ so that the variation is well-defined. From this we obtain the harmonic map equation

$$\Delta u + A_u(\nabla u, \nabla u) = 0$$

where $A_{u(x)}$ is the trace of the second fundamental form of $N$ evaluated at $u(x)$. In case $N = \mathbf{S}^n$, $\Pi_N(y) = \frac{y}{|y|}$, and this system of partial differential equations becomes

$$\Delta u + |\nabla u|^2 u = 0.$$

The *existence* of a harmonic map with prescribed boundary data $g : \partial\Omega \rightarrow M$ is easy to show whenever there is at least one finite energy map with boundary values $g$. The point is that under weak convergence in $H^1$, energy is lower semi-continuous, the boundary trace is fixed, and the resulting strong convergence in $L^2$ preserves the constraint of mapping into $N$. There are many examples of *nonuniqueness* for solutions of the Dirichlet problem for the harmonic map equation. [**HKL**] even contains an example of a one parameter family of distinct energy-minimizing harmonic maps from $\mathbf{B}^3$ to $\mathbf{S}^2$ which all have the same Dirichlet boundary data.

Next we briefly discuss the *regularity* of harmonic maps. In case $m = 1$, a harmonic map is an absolutely continuous constant speed geodesic and so is smooth, as smooth as $N$. For $m = 2$,the smoothness of weak solutions of the harmonic map equation was proven just last year by F. Hélein [**H**]. This followed earlier 2-dimensional work by C.B.Morrey [**M**] for energy minimizing maps and by M.Grüter [**G1**] ,[**G2**] and R.Schoen [**Sc**] for stationary harmonic maps. A harmonic map is *stationary* if it has energy first variation zero under smooth variations of the domain. For $m \geq 3$ there are also several conditions guaranteeing the regularity of harmonic maps. One, by J.Eells and J.H.Sampson [**ES**], is that the target manifold $N$ have nonpositive sectional curvature. Another, by S.Hildebrandt, H.Kaul,and K.O.Widman [**HKW**], involves the assumption that the image be contained in a set that is convex in a weak sense. But in general, there may exist singularities in harmonic maps. One should keep in mind the following example:

**Example 1.** Suppose $q : \mathbf{C} \rightarrow \mathbf{C}$ is a rational function and $\omega = \omega_q$ is the corresponding conformal map from $\mathbf{S}^2$ to $\mathbf{S}^2$ , i.e. $\omega_q = \Pi^{-1} \circ q \circ \Pi$ where $\Pi$ is stereographic projection. Then $h_q : \mathbf{B}^3 \rightarrow \mathbf{S}^2, h_q = \omega_q(\frac{x}{|x|})$, is a homogeneous harmonic map which is, for nonconstant $q$ , singular at 0.

An important general question is the structure of singularities of harmonic maps. For an energy minimizing harmonic map, R.Schoen and K.Uhlenbeck [**SU**] and (with some restrictions on $N$) M.Giaquinta and E.Giusti [**GG**] proved, in the early eighties, that the singular set is isolated for $m = 3$ and of Hausdorff dimension $\leq m - 3$ for $m \geq 3$. For a stationary harmonic map whose target is a sphere, L.C.Evans [**E**] has recently proved that the singular set has $m - 2$ dimensional Hausdorff measure zero. But there exist many harmonic maps that are not minimizing or not stationary. A particularly simple example is:

**Example 2.** [**HKLu**] Here the smooth horizontal vectorfield

$$u : \mathbf{B}^3 \to \mathbf{S}^2, u(x_1, x_2, x_3) = (\cos \lambda x_3, \sin \lambda x_3, 0)$$

is not energy minimizing for $\lambda$ sufficiently large. This map is stationary as are all smooth harmonic maps.

Another class of non-minimizers comes from Example 1.

**Example 3.** H.Brezis, J-M.Coron, and E.Lieb [**BCL**] proved that $h_q$ is energy minimizing if and only if $\omega_q$ is either a constant or a rotation. Thus, $q$ must have degree $\leq 1$, and the energy density of $\omega_q$ must be "balanced". In particular, $h_{z^2}$ is not energy minimizing while $h_{2z}$ is not even stationary because moving the origin may produce a non zero first variation of energy.

Libin Mou and I have begun studying the structure of the *space* of harmonic maps. Our goal is to obtain some kind of stratified structure with Banach manifold strata similar to the beautiful theory of branched minimal surfaces due to R.Böhme and A.Tromba [**BT**]. Our results so far [**HM**] only include a manifold structure for harmonic maps with a *fixed* isolated singularity near a homogeneous harmonic map. Also for smooth harmonic maps we obtain results similar to those of B.White [**W**] for smooth minimal immersions. The presence of singularities in most parts of [**HM**] required various estimates and lead to several interesting examples of singular Jacobi fields and families of harmonic maps.

Our general setup is as follows: Let $Z$ be a fixed compact subset of $\Omega$ and $d(x) = \mathrm{dist}(x, Z)$. We assume that

$$C = \sup_{r>0} \frac{\mathrm{meas}\{x : d(x) < r\}}{r^3} < \infty.$$

This means that $Z$ has finite $m-3$ dimensional Minkowski content [**F**]. This holds, for example, if $Z$ is an $m-3$ dimensional Lipschitz submanifold. For $k \in \{1,2,...\}$ and $0 \le \alpha < 1$ we will use the weighted norm

$$\|u\| \equiv \|u\|_{k,\alpha} = \sum_{j=0}^{k} \|d^j \nabla^j u\|_{C^0} + \sup_{x \neq y} \inf\{d(x), d(y)\}^{j+\alpha} \frac{\|\nabla^j u(x) - \nabla^j u(y)\|}{|x-y|^\alpha}.$$

Note that

$$\begin{aligned} E(u) &\le \int_{\{d \ge 1\}} d^2 |\nabla u|^2 dx + \sum_{i=1}^{\infty} \int_{\{2^{-i} \le d \le 2^{-i+1}\}} d^2 \frac{|\nabla u|^2}{d^2} dx \\ &\le \|u\|_{1,0}^2 \cdot \left( \text{meas}\,(\Omega) + \sum_{i=1}^{\infty} 2^{2i} \cdot C \cdot 2^{-3i+3} \right) \\ &\le \text{const} \cdot \|u\|_{k,\alpha}^2 . \end{aligned}$$

We now define the space

$$\mathcal{H} = \{\text{harmonic maps } u : \Omega \to N : \|u\|_{k,\alpha} < \infty\},$$

and roughly state two of the results of [**HM**].

**Theorem 1.** *Suppose $\Omega = \mathbf{B}^m$ and $u_0 \in C^{k,\alpha}(\mathbf{B}^m \setminus \{0\}, N)$ is a homogeneous harmonic map. Then, near $u_0$ (in an appropriate sense), $\mathcal{H}$ is a Banach manifold and the map*

$$p : \mathcal{H} \to C^{k,\alpha}(\partial\Omega, N), \quad p(u) = u|_{\partial\Omega},$$

*is locally Fredholm.*

**Theorem 2.** *Except for a set of finite codimension ( = index of p) any $C^2$ small perturbation of a harmonic map $\omega : \mathbf{S}^2 \to \mathbf{S}^2$ is boundary data for some harmonic map $u : \mathbf{B}^3 \to \mathbf{S}^2$ which is singular only at 0.*

Such a weighted norm was used by L.Caffarelli, R.Hardt, and L.Simon [**CHS**] to construct a compact non-cone minimal hypersurface. It was constructed as a normal perturbation of a given compact minimal cone and approached this cone asymptotically on approach to the vertex. Simon [**Si**] carried over this construction for harmonic maps and other variational partial differential equations. N.Smale [**Sm**] was able to use several singularities simultaneously in constructing bridged minimal surfaces with many cone-like singularities. L.Mou [**M1**] treated a similar problem with harmonic maps. In all these papers "quasi-balanced" perturbations of the boundary data were used. That is, restrictions on some of the lower order Fourier coefficients of the boundary data guaranteed the asymptotic decay. Later [**HS**] Hardt and Simon showed how small such "quasi-balanced" perturbations could preserve the area-minimizing property. The importance of these conditions has been studied carefully in the recent work [**Sm2**] whose results include the above Theorem 2. On the other hand, [**HS**] showed that when considering area-minimizers, singularities will always disappear under any small perturbation of the boundary which is entirely on one side of the given minimizing cone. R.MacIntosh [**Mc**] generalized this to "mostly 1-sided" perturbations. A recent preprint [**MSm**] of N. Smale and R. Mazzeo gives such a result even with a higher dimensional singular set. For harmonic maps, Simon and MacIntosh [**MS**] also gave an analogue which included a mostly 1-sided perturbation of the equator map.

Two other results of [**HM**] concern *generic* boundary data for *smooth* harmonic maps

**Theorem 3.** (finiteness) *Let $g \in C^{k,\alpha}(\partial\Omega, N)$ be a regular value of $p$. For each positive number $I$, there exists an integer $J$ and a $C^{k,\alpha}$ neighborhood $G$ of $g$ so that for all $\gamma \in G$*

$$\mathrm{card}\{u \in \mathcal{H} \ : \ \|u\|_{k,\alpha} \leq I, u|_{\partial\Omega} = \gamma\} \ \leq \ J \ .$$

**Theorem 4.** (uniqueness) *The set of all $g \in C^{k,\alpha}(\partial\Omega, N)$ that serve as boundary data for two distinct smooth harmonic maps of the same energy is of first Baire category.*

Concerning the generic uniqueness, L.Mou [M] showed how, even in the presence of singularities, the boundary data of nonuniqueness for *energy-minimizers* is of measure 0. Much of this work involved constructing the appropriate measure on the space of boundary data. Concerning the generic finiteness, there are examples in [**HKL**] and [**BBC**] of maps $g : \mathbf{S}^2 \to \mathbf{S}^2$ which are boundary data for infinitely many distinct harmonic maps. The distinct maps in [**HKL**] have the same energy because they are minimizing. Moreover, all boundary maps $C^1$ close to such $g$ also have these properties. But this does not contradict Theorems 3 or 4 because, in [**HKL**] and [**BBC**],the constructions of infinitely many harmonic maps involve *moving* the singularities whereas they are fixed in the theorems of [**HM**].

**Remarks on proofs.**

*Theorem 1.* For a map $u : \Omega \to N$, a *tangent vectorfield along* $u$ is a map $\kappa : \Omega \to \mathbf{R}^p$ such that $\kappa(x) \in T_{u(x)}N$ for all $x \in \Omega$. Computing the second variation of energy of a harmonic map $u : \Omega \to N$ in the direction $\kappa$ gives the *Jacobi operator*

$$J_u\kappa = \Delta\kappa - DA_u(\kappa, du, du) - 2A_u(d\kappa, du).$$

A solution of $J_u\kappa = 0$ is called a *Jacobi field* of $u$. For $u \in \mathcal{H}$, one uses the vector space $K$ of *bounded* Jacobi fields $\kappa$ along $u$ whose boundary values are restricted to a suitable finite dimensional space. Here various elliptic estimates show that $\dim K < \infty$ and that the boundedness of a Jacobi field $\kappa$ is equivalent to the condition $\|\kappa\|_{1,0} < \infty$. Near $u_0$ , the space $\mathcal{H}$ can be shown, by an implicit function theorem argument, to correspond to a submanifold of $K \times C^{k,\alpha}(\partial\Omega, N)$ of codimension $\dim K$.

*Theorem 2.* For $u = \omega(\frac{x}{|x|})$ and $\zeta$ an $H^1$ tangent vectorfield along $u$ we prove the strict stability inequality

$$\frac{d^2}{dt^2}\Big|_{t=0} \int_{\mathbf{B}} \Big|\nabla\Big(\frac{u + t\zeta}{|u + t\zeta|}\Big)\Big|^2\, dx \geq \frac{1}{2}\int_{\mathbf{B}} \frac{|\zeta|^2}{r^2}\, dx.$$

*Theorem 3.* This uses an elementary covering space argument.

*Theorem 4.* Assume $u_1$ and $u_2$ belong to $\mathcal{H}$ and $g = u_1|_{\partial\Omega} = u_2|_{\partial\Omega}$. If Theorem 4 is false, then, we may, by the Smale Sard Theorem, assume that $g$ is a regular value of the projection $p$. Let $F_1$, $F_2$ be local inverses of $p$ near $u_1$, $u_2$, and consider

$$Q(\psi) = \int_B |\nabla F_1(\psi)|^2 - |\nabla F_2(\psi)|^2\, dx.$$

Then

$$\langle\frac{\partial u_1}{\partial n} - \frac{\partial u_2}{\partial n}, DQ(g)\rangle = \int_{\mathbf{B}} \Big|\frac{\partial u_1}{\partial n} - \frac{\partial u_2}{\partial n}\Big|^2\, dx \neq 0$$

by uniqueness for the Cauchy problem. So the bad set $Q^{-1}\{0\}$ is, by the implicit function theorem, a submanifold of codimension one near $g$.

**Examples without suitable gradient bounds.** Here we will discuss various families of harmonic maps $u$ from $\mathbf{B}^3$ to $\mathbf{S}^2$ for which the above discussion does *not* apply because their gradients fail to satisfy a uniform bound

$$|\nabla u| \leq \frac{c}{d} .$$

(i). *From Example 1* The mappings $u_{\lambda z}$ approach a constant mapping weakly in $H^1$ as $\lambda \to 0$. This convergence is not strong in $H^1$ or any local norm.

(ii). *A degree 0 singularity.* By [**HLP**] there exists a harmonic map $u \in C^\infty(\mathbf{B}^3 \setminus \{0\}, \mathbf{S}^2)$ which is singular at 0 but has

$$\deg(u|\partial \mathbf{B}_r) = 0 \text{ for all } r > 0 .$$

Here $u(r(\cdot))$ approaches a constant as $r \to 0$. Moreover, $u \notin \mathcal{H}$ because $|\nabla u| \not\leq \frac{c}{d}$ . The existence of $u$ is based on an axially symmetric constructiondiscussed below.

(iii). *Singularity cancellation.* Below we will also use other constructions from [**HLP**] to show that:

*There exist a smooth harmonic map $u_0 : \mathbf{B}^3 \to \mathbf{S}^2$ which is the strong $H^1$ limit, as $t \to \infty$ , of harmonic maps $u_t : \mathbf{B}^3 \to \mathbf{S}^2$ where*

$$\operatorname{sing} u_t = \{(0,0,\pm t)\} \text{ and } u_t|_{\partial \mathbf{B}} = u_0|_{\partial \mathbf{B}} .$$

Such merging and cancellation of singularities is not possible for energy-minimizers by [**AL**] or [**HL**] . In light of [**HM**] an interesting question concerns the correct topology to use to understand this example.

**Axially symmetric constructions.** A map $u : \mathbf{B}^3 \to \mathbf{S}^2$ is *axially symmetric* if it can be written, in terms of cylindrical coordinates on the domain, as

$$u(r,\theta,z) = (\cos\phi\, \cos\theta, \cos\phi\, \sin\theta, \sin\phi)$$

for some scalar function $\phi = \phi(r,z)$. It was observed in [**HLP**] that there are maps $g : \mathbf{S}^2 \to \mathbf{S}^2$ which admit extensions to maps from $\mathbf{B}^3$ to $\mathbf{S}^2$ that are either continuous or are axially symmetric but not both. A simple such $g$ is given in spherical coordinates by sending $(\phi,\theta)$ to $(2\phi,\theta)$. The functional

$$L(u) = (4\pi)^{-1}\sup_{\xi:\Omega\to\mathbf{R},\,\|\nabla\xi\|_\infty\le 1}\Big\{\int_\Omega D(u)\cdot\nabla\xi\,dx - \int_{\partial\Omega}(\operatorname{Jac}\phi)\,\xi\,d\sigma\Big\}\ ,$$

introduced by Bethuel, Brezis, and Coron [**BBC**] , roughly measures the distance between the singularities of $u$. Following [**BBC**] and [**HLP**] one may find a function $u:\mathbf{B}^3\to\mathbf{S}^2$ which minimizes $E+8\pi L$ among axially symmetric maps. Then $u$ is harmonic, and $u$ must have singularities, which form, by [**HLP**] , a finite subset of the $Z-axis$. The tangent map at such a singularity is a constant, and the restriction of $u$ to any small sphere about the singularity has degree 0.

To obtain the singularity cancellation phenomenon we first fix any smooth axially symmetric boundary data $g:\mathbf{S}^2\to\mathbf{S}^2$ which has image in the open upper hemisphere. Then the map $u_0:\mathbf{B}^3\to\mathbf{S}^2$ which minimizes energy among axially symmetric maps having boundary values $g$ also has image in this hemisphere and is unique and smooth (see e.g.[**HKW**] ). For each $t>0$, choose any axially symmetric map $v_t$ in

$$C^\infty(\mathbf{B}^3\setminus\{(0,0,t),(0,0,-t)\},\mathbf{S}^2)$$

which has singularities at $(0,0,\pm t)$ of degree $\pm1$. As in Section 9 of [**HLP**] one may find a mapping $u_t$ with boundary data $g$ that minimizes, among axially symmetric maps, the functional $E+8\pi L(\cdot,v_t)$ where

$$L(u,v) = (4\pi)^{-1}\sup_{\xi:\Omega\to\mathbf{R},\,\|\nabla\xi\|_\infty\le 1}\Big\{\int_\Omega (D(u)-D(v))\cdot\nabla\xi\,dx\Big\}\ .$$

As in [**HLP**] $u_t$ is harmonic, belongs to $C^\infty(\mathbf{B}^3\setminus\{(0,0,t),(0,0,-t)\},\mathbf{S}^2)$, and has singularities at $(0,0,\pm t)$ of degree $\pm1$. It is easy to verify the inequalities

$$E(u_0)\le E(u_t)\le E(u_0)+2\cdot 4\pi\cdot t$$

By lower semicontinuity of energy under weak $H^1$ convergence and the uniqueness property of $u$, we find that

$$\lim_{t\to 0} u_t = u_0$$

with the convergence being strong in $H^1$ because $\lim_{t\to 0}E(u_t)=E(u_0)$.

**Failure of small-energy regularity.** A frequent statement in regularity theory is:

*There exists a positive* $\varepsilon_0$ *so that if* $u \in \mathcal{U}$ *and* $\int_{\mathbf{B}_1} |\nabla u|^2\, dx \le \varepsilon_0$, *then* $u|\mathbf{B}_{1/2}$ *is smooth.*

This is true for a family $\mathcal{U}$ of harmonic maps from $\mathbf{B}_1^m$ to $N$ in case each member of $\mathcal{U}$ :

is energy minimizing [**SU**] or

is smooth away from $\{0\}$ [**L**] or

is stationary and $N = \mathbf{S}^n$ [**E**].

However it is not true in general. For any positive $\varepsilon_0$ we may, using (iii), choose first a positive $r$ so that the map $w_0 \equiv u_0(r\cdot)$ has $\int_{\mathbf{B}_1} |\nabla w_0|^2\, dx \le \frac{1}{2}\varepsilon_0$. Then chose $t \le \frac{r}{3}$ sufficiently small so that the map $w_t \equiv u_t(r\cdot)$ has $\int_{\mathbf{B}_1} |\nabla w_t|^2\, dx \le \varepsilon_0$. Here $w_t$ has, despite its small energy, two singularities in $B_{1/2}$.

## REFERENCES


[AL] F.J.Almgren Jr. and E.Lieb, *Singularities of energy minimizing maps from the ball to the sphere: examples, counterexamples, and bounds.* Ann. of Math. 128 (1988), 483–530.

[BB] F.Bethuel and H.Brezis, *Regularity of minimizers of relaxed problems for harmonic maps.* Preprint.

[BBC] F.Bethuel, H.Brezis, and J.-M.Coron, *Relaxed energies for harmonic maps.* Progress in nonlinear differential equations and their applications, Variational Methods, Volume 4, Birkhauser, 1990, 37-52.

[BCL] H.Brezis, J.-M.Coron, and E.Lieb, *Harmonic maps with defects.* Comm. Math. Physics 107(1986), 649-705.

[BT] R.Böhme and A.Tromba, *The index theorem for classical minimal surfaces.* Ann. of Math.113(1981), 447-499.

[CHS] L.Caffarelli, R.Hardt, and L.Simon, *Minimal surfaces with isolated singularities.* Manuscripta Math. 48(1984), 1-18.

[E] L.C.Evans, *Partial regularity for stationary harmonic maps into spheres.* Preprint.

[ES] J.Eells and Sampson, *Harmonic maps of Riemannian manifolds.* Amer.J.Math. 86(1964), 109-160.

[F] H.Federer, *Geometric measure theory.* Springer-Verlag, Berlin, Heidelberg, and New York, 1969.

[G1] M.Grüter, *Regularity of weak H-surfaces.* J.Reine Angew.Math.329(1981), 1-15.

[G2] M.Grüter, *Eine Bemerkung zur Regularität stationärer Punkte von konform invarianten Variationsintegralen.* manuscripta math.55(1986), 451-453.

[GG] M.Giaquinta and E.Giusti, *The singular set of the minima of certain quadratic functionals.* Ann.Sc.Norm.Pisa11(1984), 45-55.

[H] F.Hélein, *Regularité des applications faiblement harmoniques entre une surface et une variété Riemannienne.* To appear in Comptes Rendus Ac. Sc.

[HKL] R.Hardt, D.Kinderlehrer and F.H.Lin, *The variety of configurations of static liquid crystals.* Progress in nonlinear differential equations and their applications, Variational Methods, Volume 4, Birkhauser, 1990, 115-132.

[HKLu] R.Hardt, D.Kinderlehrer and M.Luskin, *Remarks about the mathematical theory of liquid crystals* in *Calculus of Variations.* Hildebrandt, Kinderlehrer, and Miranda, ed., Springer Lecture Notes in Math.134, 123-138.

[HKW] S.Hildebrandt, H.Kaul, and K.Widman, *An existence theory for harmonic maps of Riemannian manifolds.* Acta Math.188(1977), 1-16.

[HL] R.Hardt and F.H.Lin, *Stability of singularities of minimizing harmonic maps.* J. Diff. Geom. 29(1987), 113-123.

[HLP] R.Hardt, F.H.Lin, and C.Poon, *Axially symmetric harmonic maps minimizing a relaxed energy.* To appear in Comm.Pure Appl.Math.

[HM] R.Hardt and L.Mou, *Harmonic maps with fixed singular sets.* To appear in J. Geometric Analysis.

[HS] R.Hardt and L.Simon, *Area minimizing hypersurfaces with isolated singularities,* J.Reine Angew.Math.362(1985), 102-129.

[L] G.Liao, *A regularity theorem for harmonic maps with small energy.* J.Diff.Geom. 22(1985), 233-241.

[MSm] R.Mazzeo and N.Smale, *Perturbing away higher dimensional singularities from area minimizing hypersurfaces*, Preprint.

[M] C.B.Morrey,Jr., *The problem of Plateau in a Riemannian manifold*, Annals of Math. 49(1948),807-851.

[M1] L.Mou, *Harmonic maps with prescribed finite singularities.* Comm.in P.D.E. Vol. 14, 11(1989), 1509-1540.

[M2] L.Mou, *Uniqueness of energy minimizing maps for almost all smooth boundary data.* Indiana Univ. Math. Jour. 40,no.1(1991), 363-392.

[Mc] R.MacIntosh, *Singular area minimizing hypersurfaces.* Australian Math.Soc.Gaz.22(1985), 233-241.

[MS] R.MacIntosh and L.Simon, *Perturbing away singularities of harmonic maps.* Manuscripta Math.67(1990), 113-124.

[P] C.Poon, *Some new harmonic maps from $B^3$ to $S^2$*. To appear in J.Diff.Geom., 1991.

[Sc] R. Schoen, *Analytic aspects fo the harmonic map problem.* M.S.R.I. Public. 2, Springer, Berlin 1984, 321-358.

[Si] L.Simon, *Isolated singularities for extrema of general variational problems.* Lecture Notes in Mathematics 1161, Springer-Verlag, 1985.

[Sm1] N.Smale, *Minimal surfaces with many isolated singularities.* Ann. of Math.130(1989), 603-642.

[Sm2] N.Smale, *Geometric P.D.E.'s with isolated singularities.* Preprint.

[SU] R.Schoen and K.Uhlenbeck, *A regularity theory for harmonic maps.* J. Diff. Geom. 17(1982), 307-335.

[W] B.White, *The space of m-dimensional surfaces that are stationary for a parametric elliptic functional.* Indiana Univ. Math. Jour. Vol. 36, 3(1987),567–602.

*Research partially supported by the National Science Foundation

Mathematics Department, Rice University, Houston, TX 77251 USA

R D JAMES AND D KINDERLEHRER

# Frustration and microstructure: an example in magnetostriction

**Contents**



## 1. Introduction

Microstructural properties of materials, especially crystalline solids, are implicated in many of their properties. Vice versa, there are macroscopic environments which limit microstructural configurations. Certain iron/rare earth alloys, eg, $TbDyFe_2$, display both a huge magnetostriction and frustration, i.e., minimum energy not achieved, in which microstructure plays an important, if puzzling, role. We discuss this example in the framework of continuum thermoelasticity theory, where symmetry demands energy densities which are highly degenerate[1]. This leads to novel analytical and computational issues, many of which we have been unable to resolve.

Crystals are idealized as materials with a high degree of configurational order. As a consequence, the continuum energy densities ascribed to them are invariant under discrete groups and have multiple potential wells. Such densities are not lower semicontinuous. The infimum of energy may be obtained only in some generalized sense, while a minimizing sequence may develop successively finer oscillations. The limit deformation alone need not be sufficient to characterize many of the properties of the limit configuration. Martensitic materials, in particular, exhibit fine structure in the form of fine twinned microstructure, often appearing as layers or layers within layers.

A remarkable feature of ferromagnetic materials is that the single domain state is generally unstable. This constrasts with martensite, where the single variant configuration is stable for arbitrarily large samples. In the blue phase of cholesteric liquid crystals, the failure of stability of the uniform state relative to an array of defects is termed *frustration*, cf. Sethna [62]. Our calculations here could be interpreted as one possible interpretation of this phenomenon at a macroscopic scale. The frustration in our system arises from the competition of an anisotropy energy which demands constant magnetization strength and direction with an induced field energy which prefers to tend to zero. A consequence of this is to promote development of a fine scale structure which seeks to compromise the constraint of constant magnetization strength. A different mechanism is given by Sethna for the blue phase.

Certain iron/rare earth alloys display both frustration and a huge magnetostriction. There are cubic Laves phase $RFe_2$ (R = rare earth) compounds, for example, where magnetically induced strains "overwhelm the conventional thermal expansion of the material", Clark [16]. $TbDyFe_2$ (terfenol) solidifies from the melt with a textured microstructure which plays an important, if puzzling, role in its magnetostrictive properies. Our objective in this note is to describe briefly a theory of magnetoelastic interactions based on the micromagnetics of W. F. Brown, Jr. [10,11,12] and the symmetry considerations introduced by Ericksen [23-31]. It has some similarities with Toupin's theory of the elastic dielectric [70]. We shall then illustrate how the equilibrium microstructure of $TbDyFe_2$ is consistent with this theory. Our information about the properties of $TbDyFe_2$ comes primarily from Lord [53].

For relatively rigid materials one may assume the free energy to depend on magnetization alone, [39,40,51]. The theory in this case gives good qualitative agreement with experiment, explaining why cubic magnets have a few large domains and why uniaxial ones have a fine structure. Domain refinement at the boundary is also predicted when the normal to the boundary has a suitable orientation with relative to the crystal axes, in agreement with observations.

The analysis introduced to study the micromagnetic theory is based on the study of minimizing sequences, or devices used to summarize their oscillatory behavior. This gives a reasonable description of microscopic aspects of domain structure and macroscopic state functions. The particular averaging device used by us is the Young measure, Young [72], and first introduced in partial differential equations by Tartar [68,69]. The Young measure is particularly useful for predicting where in the body fine structure will occur. We refer to Ball [3], Ball and James [4,5], Chipot [14], Chipot and Kinderlehrer [13], Collins and Luskin [17,18,19], Collins, Kinderlehrer, and Luskin [20], Firooze and Kohn [32], Fonseca [33,34,35], James [36,37], James and Kinderlehrer [38], Kinderlehrer [43], Kohn [48,49], Matos [57], Pedregal [58,59], Sverak [64-67], and Zhang [73,74].

In addition to Brown's work, general references to the theory of ferromagnetism and ferromagnetic domain structure include Clark [16], Craik and Tebble [21], Kléman [47], Landau and Lifshitz [50], Landau, Lifshitz and Piatevskii [51], and Lifshitz [52]. Recent mathematical analysis includes Anzellotti, Baldo, and Visintin [1], Brandon and Rogers [9], Rogers [60,61], and Visintin [71]. Computational aspects of micromagnetics have been studied by Luskin and Ma [54] and Ma [55].

## 2. Energy of magnetostriction

Equilibrium configurations of the system are interpreted as stationary points of a variational principle which consists of the sum of a stored energy and the induced magnetic field energy. In this section we describe the energy of a configuration and in §3 we discuss a variational principle. The stored energy density of the material will depend on the deformation gradient $F \in \mathbb{M}$, $3 \times 3$ matrices, magnetization (per unit mass) $m \in \mathbb{R}^3$, and temperature $\theta \in \mathbb{R}$. We suppose it given by a nonnegative function

$$W(F, m, \theta) \qquad F \in D, \ m \in \mathbb{R}^3, \theta \in \mathbb{R}, \tag{2.1}$$

where $D \subset \mathbb{M}$ is a suitable domain of matrices with positive determinant. It is subject to the condition of frame indifference

$$W(QF, mQ^T, \theta) = W(F, m, \theta), \qquad Q \in SO(3), \tag{2.2}$$

and $F, m, \theta$ as in (2.1). We also impose a condition of material symmetry which is derived from a Cauchy-Born rule applied to the symmetry imputed to the underlying crystal lattice. This is explained in [41] and relies on the ideas set forth by Ericksen [24]. This symmetry is that

$$W(FP, m, \theta) = W(F, m, \theta), \qquad P \in \mathbb{P}, \tag{2.3}$$

where $\mathbb{P}$ is a crystallographic point group. We are hesitant to impose full magnetic symmetry including invariance under time reversals for reasons explained in [41].

In the spatial configuration, Maxwell's equations hold. Let y denote the spatial variable and B, H, and M denote the magnetic induction, the magnetic field, and the magnetization (dipole moment per unit volume), respectively. Then, for an appropriate choice of units,

$$B = H + M, \tag{2.4}$$

$$\mathrm{div}_y B = 0 \quad \text{and} \quad \mathrm{curl}_y H = 0 \quad \text{in } \mathbb{R}^3.$$

Introducing $U(y)$ for which $H = -\nabla_y U$, we obtain that (2.4) is equivalent to

$$\mathrm{div}_y(-\nabla_y U + M) = 0 \quad \text{in } \mathbb{R}^3. \tag{2.5}$$

The field energy density is given by

$$\frac{1}{2}|H|^2 = \frac{1}{2}|\nabla_y U|^2.$$

The material is assumed magnetically saturated, leading to the constraint

$$\left|\frac{M}{\rho}\right| = f(\theta) \quad \text{in the body}, \tag{2.6}$$

where $\rho$ is the density, cf. Brown [11], James and Müller [42], Landau and Lifschitz [50].

Assume now that initially the material occupies a reference configuration $\Omega \subset \mathbb{R}^3$ and has constant density $\rho_o$. As discussed below, $\Omega$ is interpreted as an undistorted single crystal above the Curie temperature. By an abuse of notation, let $y(x)$ denote the deformation of $\Omega$ to $y(\Omega)$, assumed for the purposes of discussion to be 1:1. Since $\rho(x) = \rho_o / \det \nabla y(x)$, the magnetization per unit mass previously introduced,

$$m = \frac{1}{\rho_o} \det \nabla y \, M,$$

so the constraint (2.6) assumes the form

$$|m| = f(\theta).$$

For our purposes it suffices to assume that $\rho_o = 1$, $m = m(x)$ and

$$\begin{aligned} m &= 0 && \text{if } \theta > \theta_0 \text{ and} \\ |m| &= 1 && \text{in } \Omega \text{ at } \theta < \theta_0, \end{aligned} \tag{2.7}$$

where $\theta_0$ is the Curie point (associated with the onset of magnetization) and $\theta$ is fixed for our purposes.

In this fashion we may write the virtual energy of the configuration $y = y(x)$, $m = m(x)$ in the mixed reference/spatial form

$$E(y,m) \;=\; \int_{\Omega} W(\nabla y, m, \theta)\, dx \;+\; \frac{1}{2}\int_{\mathbb{R}^3} |\nabla_y U|^2\, dy \tag{2.8}$$

subject to the constraints, cf. (2.4) and (2.7),

$$\mathrm{div}_y\,(-\nabla_y U + \frac{1}{\det \nabla y}\, m) \;=\; 0 \quad \text{in } \mathbb{R}^3. \tag{2.9}$$

$$|m| \;=\; 1 \quad \text{in } y(\Omega).$$

From (2.9), we may also write the energy in the form

$$E(y,m) \;=\; \int_{\Omega} W(\nabla y, m, \theta)\, dx \;+\; \frac{1}{2}\int_{\Omega} \frac{1}{\det \nabla y}\, m\cdot\nabla_y U\, dy \;. \tag{2.10}$$

To express this in terms of reference variables alone, introduce $u(x) = U(y(x))$, so $\nabla u(x) = \nabla_y U(y(x))F(x)$, $F(x) = \nabla y(x)$. With $C = F^T F$, the constraint equation (2.9) becomes

$$\mathrm{div}(\, -\nabla u\, C^{-1}\det F \;+\; mF^{-T}\,) \;=\; 0 \quad \text{in } \mathbb{R}^3, \tag{2.11}$$

and the saturation condition is simply

$$|m| \;=\; 1 \quad \text{in } \Omega. \tag{2.12}$$

The virtual energy of $y = y(x)$, $m = m(x)$ in reference form is

$$E(y,m) \;=\; \int_{\Omega} W(\nabla y, m, \theta)\, dx \;+\; \frac{1}{2}\int_{\mathbb{R}^3} \nabla u\; C^{-1}\cdot\nabla u\, \det F\, dx, \tag{2.13}$$

subject to (2.11) and (2.12). Analogous to (2.10), we may also write (2.13) as

$$E(y,m) \;=\; \int_{\Omega} W(\nabla y, m, \theta)\, dx \;+\; \frac{1}{2}\int_{\mathbb{R}^3} \nabla u\cdot mF^{-T}\, dx. \tag{2.14}$$

We wish to note here in a parenthetical fashion that in (2.11), (2.13) and (2.14) we have conveniently ignored the behavior of $y$ outside of the region $\Omega$ occupied by the material. Without entering into a complete discussion of this issue, let us consider the most naive point of view. Suppose that $y$ is a 1:1 deformation of $\Omega$ defined on all of $\mathbb{R}^3$ and that $y'(x) = y(\eta(x))$ where $\eta(x) = x$ in $\Omega$. The potential $U(y)$ is then independent of the choice of mapping $y$ or $y'$ and so is the expression (2.10). Thus the energy of a configuration does not depend on the particular extension of $y(x)$ if $y|_{\Omega}$ is 1:1.

Moreover, as we shall illustrate shortly, the infimum of $E(y,m)$ depends only on $y|_{\Omega}$ in situations of interest.

The symmetry condition (2.3) induces a potential well structure on W. Our schema for understanding this well structure begins by choosing for $\mathbb{P}$ the symmetry group of a putative high temperature non-magnetic parent phase of the material. For example, in the case we shall consider here, $\mathbb{P}$ is the cubic group of order 24: relative to a cubic basis, these are the proper orthogonal matrices of the form $P = (p_{ij})$, $p_{ij} = \pm 1$ or 0. This is the appropriate assumption for $TbDyFe_2$. For $\theta < \theta_o$, we assume there exists a pair $(U_1, m_1)$ with $|m_1| = 1$ and $U_1 = U_1^T$ positive definite satisfying

$$W(U_1,m_1,\theta) \leq W(F,m,\theta) \quad \text{for } F \in D, |m| = 1. \tag{2.15}$$

Generally, $U_1$ and $m_1$ depend on temperature. The conditions (2.7) and (2.8) imply the existence of other minima by (2.9). We shall assume that *the full set of minima is determined by the orbits of* $(U_1,m_1)$ *under these actions.* Thus

$$\begin{aligned} \inf W = W(RU_1H,m_1R^T) < W(F,m) \quad &\text{for } R \in SO(3), H \in \mathbb{P} \\ &\text{and } F \in \mathbb{M}, |m| = 1, \text{ with } (F,m) \neq (RU_1H,m_1R^T). \end{aligned} \tag{2.16}$$

The potential wells may be described as

$$\begin{aligned} &(RU_1,m_1R^T), \quad R \in SO(3), \\ &(RU_2,m_2R^T), \quad R \in SO(3), \\ &\qquad \vdots \\ &(RU_n,m_nR^T), \quad R \in SO(3), \end{aligned} \tag{2.17}$$

where

$$\{(U_1,m_1), (U_2,m_2), \dots (U_n,m_n)\} = \{(QU_1Q^T,m_1Q^T): Q \in \mathbb{P}\}.$$

An orbit of the form $(RU_i,m_iR^T)$, $R \in SO(3)$, will be called a *variant*.

## 3. A variational principle

We would like to investigate variational principles compatible with minimizing the functional (2.8) or (2.13). A first requirement is that a variational principle be capable of delivering the possible minimum energy configurations determined by the well structure described in the preceding section. We formulate here a requirement for this which is a slight modification of our treatment of the rigid ferromagnet [40]. In this section we suppress the dependence of various quantities on temperature $\theta$.

THEOREM 3.1 *Assume that there exists a pair* $(F_o, m_o)$ *with* $\det F_o > 0$ *and* $|m_o| = 1$ *such that*

$$W(F_o, m_o) = W(F_o, -m_o) = \min W.$$

*Then there is a sequence* $(y^k, m^k)$ *such that*

$$y^k : \mathbb{R}^3 \to \mathbb{R}^3 \text{ is 1:1 and } m^k : \Omega \to \mathbb{S}^2$$

*with* $\det \nabla y^k = \det F_o$ *such that*

$$\lim_{k \to \infty} E(y^k, m^k) = \min W |\Omega|. \tag{3.1}$$

PROOF. In fact, we choose $y^k(x) = y_o(x) \equiv F_o x$ for all k. Let $n \in \mathbb{S}^2$ satisfy $n \cdot m_o F_o^{-T} = 0$. Set

$$\vartheta(t) = \begin{cases} -1 & 0 \le t < \frac{1}{2} \\ +1 & \frac{1}{2} \le t < 1 \end{cases},$$

and extend $\vartheta$ to be periodic of period 1 on $\mathbb{R}$. Define

$$f^k(x) = \vartheta(kn \cdot x)\, m_o F_o^{-T}, \quad k = 1,2,3,\ldots \quad \text{and}$$

$$m^k(x) F_o^{-T} = \chi_\Omega f^k(x) = \vartheta(kn \cdot x)\, \chi_\Omega m_o F_o^{-T}, \quad k = 1,2,3,\ldots$$

Note that by the choice of $\vartheta$ and n,

$$f^k \to 0 \quad \text{in } L^\infty(\mathbb{R}^3;\mathbb{R}^3) \text{ weak* and} \tag{3.2}$$

$$\operatorname{div} f^k = 0 \quad \text{in } H^{-1}_{loc}(\mathbb{R}^3). \tag{3.3}$$

Now let us note the lemma below, cf. Rogers [61] or [41].

LEMMA 3.2 *If* $(f^k)$ *satisfy* (3.2) *and* (3.3), *then*

$$\operatorname{div} \chi_\Omega f^k \to 0 \quad \text{in } H^{-1}(\mathbb{R}^3).$$

For the proof of the lemma, we refer to [41]. To continue the proof of the theorem, note that $C_0^{-1} \det F_0$ is positive definite, hence there is a solution

$$u^k \in V: \ \operatorname{div}(-\nabla u^k C_0^{-1} \det F_0 + m^k F_0^{-T}) = 0 \quad \text{in } H^{-1}, \text{ where}$$

$$V = \{ v \in H^1_{loc}(\mathbb{R}^3) : \nabla v \in L^2(\mathbb{R}^3) \},$$

which satisfies

$$\| \nabla u^k \|_{L^2(\mathbb{R}^3)} \le \text{const} \, \| m^k F_0^{-T} \|_{L^2(\mathbb{R}^3)} \le M.$$

Finally,

$$\min W \, |\Omega| \le E(y^k, m^k) = \min W \, |\Omega| + \frac{1}{2} \int_{\mathbb{R}^3} \nabla u^k \cdot m^k F_0^{-T} \, dx$$

$$\le \min W \, |\Omega| + \frac{1}{2} \| \nabla u^k \|_{L^2(\mathbb{R}^3)} \| \operatorname{div} m^k F_0^{-T} \|_{H^{-1}(\mathbb{R}^3)}$$

$$= \min W \, |\Omega| + \frac{1}{2} \| \nabla u^k \|_{L^2(\mathbb{R}^3)} \| \operatorname{div} f^k \chi_\Omega \|_{H^{-1}(\mathbb{R}^3)} \, .$$

Applying the lemma to the last term,

$$\lim_{k \to \infty} E(y^k, m^k) = \min W \, |\Omega|. \qquad \text{QED}$$

Since the right hand side of (3.1) is the minimum possible value of E(y,m), the theorem serves us as a criterion in several ways. Any variational principle must recover the infimum of the functional. Also, later on, we can use THEOREM 3.1 to check that a given configuration is of minimum energy.

Rather than survey all the possibilities for minimum principles, let us adopt a point of view convenient for analytical purposes by choosing a reference formulation. In finite elasticity we do not generally require that the admissible deformations be 1:1, although there are occasions where this is feasible to prove (Ball [2], Ciarlet and Necas [15], Fonseca [35]), but we do ask that local orientation be preserved. So one generally imposes the condition that either $\det \nabla y > 0$ for an admissible deformation $y$ or that

$$W(A,m) \;=\; \infty \quad \text{when} \quad \det A \le 0.$$

In the present situation, we are also asked to resolve the constraint equation (2.11), which we interpret to mean, cf. LEMMA 3.2,

$$u \in V\colon\ \operatorname{div}(-\nabla u\, C^{-1}\det F + m\,F^{-T}) = 0 \quad \text{in } H^{-1}(\mathbb{R}^3)\,, \text{ where} \tag{3.4}$$

$$V = \{\, v \in H^1_{loc}(\mathbb{R}^3)\colon\ \nabla v \in L^2(\mathbb{R}^3), \quad \int_{\{|x| \le 1\}} v\,dx = 0 \}\,,$$

when $F = \nabla y$, with $y$ an admissible variation. For this it is convenient to assure that the matrix $C^{-1}\det F$ is positive definite and that the term $\operatorname{div}(m^k F^{-T})$ is in $H^{-1}$. Our technique is to adopt a van der Waals condition and to assume in addition that $y$ has bounded derivatives. This will permit us to infer, for example, that

(i) if $u \in V$ satisfies (3.4), then $\| u \|_V \le$ const. and (3.5)

(ii) if $\frac{1}{2} \int_{\mathbb{R}^3} \nabla u^k\, (C^k)^{-1} \cdot \nabla u^k \det F^k\, dx \to 0$, then $u^k \to 0$ in $V$ (3.6)

As we have been suggesting, there are many ways to achieve these conditions, but we should like to consider one which has been under discussion for some time, although it may not have appeared explicitly in the literature, and is common in the study of duality theory. Recently it has been taken up by Ball and James [5] and Kinderlehrer and Pedregal [44,45].

We shall assume that there is a subset $D \subset \mathbb{M}$ such that

$$W(A,m) \begin{cases} < \infty & A \in D \\ = +\infty & A \notin D \end{cases} \tag{3.7}$$

About $D$ we impose these requirements:

$$\Sigma = \{A\colon\ W(A,m) = \inf W\} \subset D\,, \tag{3.8}$$

$$D \subset \{A\colon\ \det A \ge \delta\}\,, \text{ where } \delta > 0 \text{ is given,} \tag{3.9}$$

$D\,\mathbb{P} \subset D$, i.e., $D$ is invariant under the symmetry group $\mathbb{P}$, and (3.10)

$D$ is the closure of a bounded open convex set. (3.11)

Let us assume that the symmetry group $\mathbb{P} \subset SO(3)$. Suppose that any A in the potential wells defined by (2.17) satisfies

$$\left| \operatorname{tr}(A^TA - \mathbb{1}) \right| = \left| |A|^2 - 3 \right| \leq r \tag{3.12}$$

with r so small that (3.12) ensures that $\det F \geq \delta > 0$. We let the domain D where W(F,m) is defined as a function of F be determined by (3.12). It is invariant under the action of $\mathbb{P}$ and is convex. Thus all the properties (3.8) - (3.11) are satisfied. (3.9) and (3.11) imply that the constraint equation is well behaved, (3.5) and (3.6). In [5] it is shown how to obtain a D satisfying (3.8) - (3.10) with a general well structure.

A first advantage of (3.12) is that it permits us to understand the relaxation of the energy functional. In general, let K be the closure of a bounded open convex set. Given $\psi \in C(K)$, set

$$\hat{\psi}(A) = \begin{cases} \psi(A) & A \in K \\ \infty & \text{otherwise} \end{cases} . \tag{3.13}$$

Let

$$\hat{\psi}^{\#}(A) = \inf_{H_0^{1,\infty}(\Omega;\mathbb{R}^3)} \frac{1}{|\Omega|} \int_\Omega \hat{\psi}(A+\nabla\zeta)\, dx , \qquad A \in \mathbb{M} \tag{3.14}$$

Then $\hat{\psi}^{\#}(A) = +\infty$ for $A \notin K$,

$\hat{\psi}^{\#}(A)$ is quasiconvex, and

$$\Psi^{\#}(v) = \int_\Omega \hat{\psi}^{\#}(\nabla v)\, dx, \quad v \in H_0^{1,\infty}(\Omega;\mathbb{R}^3),$$

is sequentially weak* lower-semicontinuous [44]. In addition a relaxation result is valid. Suppose that

$$y_o \in H^{1,\infty}(\Omega;\mathbb{R}^3): \int_\Omega \hat{\psi}(\nabla y_o)\, dx < +\infty .$$

Then

$$\inf_{A} \int_{\Omega} \hat{\psi}(\nabla y)\, dx \;=\; \inf_{A} \int_{\Omega} \hat{\psi}^{\#}(\nabla y)\, dx, \tag{3.15}$$

$$A \;=\; \{ y \in H^{1,\infty}(\Omega;\mathbb{R}^3) :\; y = y_o \text{ on } \partial\Omega \}.$$

We have not at present identified the relaxation of a functional of the form

$$\int_{\Omega} \psi(\nabla y, m)\, dx, \qquad y \in H^{1,\infty}(\Omega;\mathbb{R}^3),\; m \in L^{\infty}(\Omega;\mathbb{S}^2)$$

nor of

$$\int_{\Omega} \hat{\psi}(\nabla y, m)\, dx, \qquad y \in H^{1,\infty}(\Omega;\mathbb{R}^3),\; m \in L^{\infty}(\Omega;\mathbb{S}^2).$$

However, it is possible to give the partial result that, for $m \in L^{\infty}(\Omega;\mathbb{S}^2)$ fixed,

$$\inf_{A} \int_{\Omega} \hat{\psi}(\nabla y, m)\, dx \;=\; \inf_{A} \int_{\Omega} \hat{\psi}^{\#}(\nabla y, m)\, dx, \tag{3.16}$$

$$A \;=\; \{ y \in H^{1,\infty}(\Omega;\mathbb{R}^3) :\; y = y_o \text{ on } \partial\Omega \},$$

where for each fixed unit vector $\mu$,

$$\hat{\psi}^{\#}(A,\mu) \;=\; \inf_{H_o^{1,\infty}(\Omega;\mathbb{R}^3)} \frac{1}{|\Omega|} \int_{\Omega} \hat{\psi}(A + \nabla\zeta, \mu)\, dx\,, \qquad A \in \mathbb{M}. \tag{3.17}$$

This can be proved by modification of a known method, Marcellini [56], Dacorogna [22].

We next wish to investigate the limit configurations available to the energy $E(y,m)$. These are given by the posssible minimizing sequences in terms of the Young measures they define. Suppose that $(y^k, m^k)$, $\nabla y^k = F^k$, is a minimizing sequence with the property

$$(y^k, m^k) \;\to\; (y, \bar{m}) \quad \text{in } H^{1,\infty}(\mathbb{R}^3;\mathbb{R}^3) \times L^{\infty}(\Omega;\mathbb{S}^2) \text{ weak*}. \tag{3.18}$$

Then there is a family $\nu = (\nu_x)_{x \in \mathbb{R}^3}$ of probability measures such that whenever $\psi \in C(\mathbb{M} \times \mathbb{S}^2)$,

$$\psi(F^k, m^k) \;\to\; \bar{\psi} \quad \text{in } L^{\infty}(\mathbb{M} \times \mathbb{S}^2;\mathbb{R}) \text{ weak*, where}$$

$$\bar{\psi}(x) \;=\; \int_{\mathbb{M}\times\mathbb{S}^2} \psi(A,\mu)\, d\nu_x(A,\mu) \quad \text{in } \mathbb{R}^3 \text{ a.e.}$$

Let us isolate several basic features of the variational principle in this context. Since

$$\lim_{k\to\infty} E(y,m) \;=\; |\,\Omega\,| \min W,$$

it is immediate that

$$\bar{W}(x) \;=\; \min W \quad \text{and} \quad \operatorname{supp} \nu\,|_{\Omega} \;\subset\; \{(A,\mu)\colon\; W(A,\mu) \;=\; \min W\,\} \;\equiv\; \Sigma. \tag{3.19}$$

i.e., the support of $\nu$ is in the energy wells, and, since we have already constructed one sequence for which the field energy tends to zero,

$$\frac{1}{2}\int_{\mathbb{R}^3} \nabla u^k\,(C^k)^{-1}\cdot\nabla u^k \det F^k\, dx \;\to\; 0, \tag{3.20}$$

whence $u^k \to 0$ in $V$.

The limit deformation $y(x)$ has gradient

$$F(x) \;=\; \int_{\mathbb{M}\times\mathbb{S}^2} A\, d\nu_x(A,\mu) \quad \text{in } \mathbb{R}^3 \text{ a.e. and}$$

$$F(x) \;=\; \int_{\Sigma\times\mathbb{S}^2} A\, d\nu_x(A,\mu) \quad \text{in } \Omega \text{ a.e.} \tag{3.21}$$

so that

$$F(x) \in \text{convex hull}\,\Sigma \;\subset\; D. \tag{3.22}$$

This suggests several questions. First consider any gradient Young measure $\nu = (\nu_x)_{x\in\Omega}$ with $\operatorname{supp}\nu \subset \Sigma$. Is it true that there is a sequence $(u^k)$ with

$$\operatorname{range} \nabla u^k \;\subset\; D \tag{3.23}$$

such that $(\nabla u^k)$ generates $\nu$ ? What is known is that there is such a sequence with

$$\operatorname{range} \nabla u^k \;\subset\; t\,\Sigma, \tag{3.24}$$

where $t \geq 1$ depends only on the well structure, [44]. It has also been established that if $\Sigma$ consists of two variants, then any $F(x)$ satifying (3.21) may be achieved by a $\nu$ which consists of a convex combination of 3 ([5]) or 4 ([46]) Dirac masses. The associated sequences $( u^k )$ satisfy (3.24) with $t = 1 + \varepsilon$, for $\varepsilon$ chosen arbitrarily small. Also in some interesting cases of self-accomodation, (3.23) may be shown to hold, Bhattacharya [7]. A general open question is whether any function y whose gradient satisfies (3.21) is a limit of finite rank laminates with support in D.

Let us now consider briefly the magnetostatic energy. In the limit, this term vanishes according to (3.20). It follows that

$$m^k F^{k-T} \to \alpha \quad \text{in } L^\infty(\mathbb{R}^3;\mathbb{R}^3) \text{ weak*}, \quad \alpha = 0 \text{ for } x \notin \Omega, \text{ and}$$

$$\operatorname{div}(m^k F^{k-T}) \to 0 \quad \text{in } H^{-1}_{loc}(\mathbb{R}^3). \tag{3.25}$$

Thus

$$\operatorname{div} \alpha = 0 \quad \text{in } H^{-1}(\mathbb{R}^3). \tag{3.26}$$

It need not be true in general that $\alpha = 0$. We briefly inquire about the relationship between $\alpha$ and

$$\bar{m} = \int_{\Sigma\times\mathbb{S}^2} \mu \, d\nu_x(A,\mu) \quad .$$

To a product of the form

$$\beta \, \nabla y^T = (\beta \cdot \nabla y_1, \beta \cdot \nabla y_2, \beta \cdot \nabla y_3)$$

we may seek to apply the div-curl lemma [68] provided $\beta$ is the limit of quantities $\beta^k$ with div $\beta^k$ compact in $H^{-1}$. In our situation, $\beta^k = m^k F^{k-T}$ satisfies this condition, (3.25), so

$$\beta^k \cdot \nabla y_i^k \to \alpha \cdot \nabla y_i \text{ in } \mathcal{D}'.$$

Since $( m^k F^{k-T})$ and $( \nabla y^k )$ are bounded,

$$\bar{m} = \alpha \, F^T \text{ or } \quad \alpha = \bar{m} \, F^{-T}. \tag{3.27}$$

We shall use this relation in the next section to illustrate the necessity of magnetic fine structure in certain configurations.

## 4. Description of the equilibrium microstructure

The magnetostrictive material $Tb_xDy_{1-x}Fe_2$, $x \approx .27$, in equilibrium exhibits a herringbone configuration, with two sets of laminar fine structures separated by a (111) plane[2], cf. Figure 1. We shall focus attention on a single set of lamellae, eg., that below the indicated plane of separation in the region labelled $\Omega^-$. Ignoring dependence on temperature, as usual, we assume that W(F,m) is invariant under the group $\mathbb{P}$, the cubic group of order 24. As we have noted

$$\mathbb{P} = \{ P \in SO(3): P = (p_{ij}), \ p_{ij} = \pm 1 \text{ or } 0 \}. \tag{4.1}$$

We choose the pair $(U_1, m_1)$ with

$$U_1 = \mathbb{1} + \varepsilon\, m_1 \otimes m_1, \quad m_1 = \frac{1}{\sqrt{3}}(1,1,1), \ |\varepsilon| \text{ small.} \tag{4.2}$$

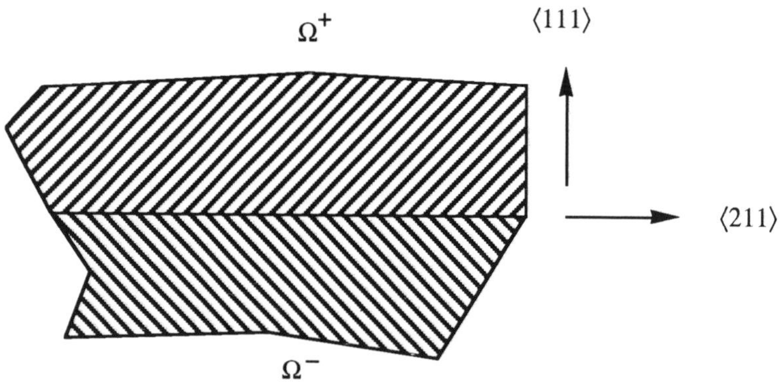


Figure 1 Schematic diagram of microstructure in $TbDyFe_2$, illustrating herringbone structure of two sets of laminar fine structures. Crystallographic directions are indicated.

Here we have made a special choice of reference configuration (see [41] for details.)Thus the low temperature phase derives from the high temperature phase by a stretch or contraction along a principal diagonal. One may easily calculate that there are eight potential wells. With

$$m_2 = \frac{1}{\sqrt{3}}(1,-1,-1), \quad m_3 = \frac{1}{\sqrt{3}}(1,-1,1), \quad m_4 = \frac{1}{\sqrt{3}}(-1,-1,1), \tag{4.3}$$

these are given by the SO(3) orbits of

$$(U_i,m_i) \text{ and } (U_i,-m_i), \quad U_i = \mathbb{1} + \varepsilon m_i \otimes m_i, \quad i = 1,\ldots,4, \tag{4.4}$$

according to (2.17). The conclusion of Theorem 3.1 obviously holds in this situation. We now consider the variant structure, for which we prove a special case of [4], Theorem 7. To understand the statement of this theorem, we recall a few terms. Two orbits $SO(3)M_1$ and $SO(3)M_2$ are *mechanically compatible*, or simply, *compatible*, provided there is at least one matrix $F_1 \in SO(3)M_1$ and one matrix $F_2 \in SO(3)M_2$ such that $F_2 - F_1$ is rank one. If $F_2 - F_1 = a \otimes n$, then there is a continuous piecewise affine deformation $y(x)$ such that

$$\nabla y(x) = \begin{cases} F_1 & n \cdot x < \gamma \\ F_2 & n \cdot x > \gamma \end{cases}, \text{ for any given } \gamma.$$

In fact, if for one $F_1$ there is one $F_2$, there are two such $F_2$'s and this property holds for every $F_1 \in SO(3)M_1$. The pairs $(F_1,m_1)$ and $(F_2,m_2)$ are *mechanically and magnetically compatible* provided that $F_2 - F_1 = a \otimes n$, as before, and

$$(m_2 F_2^{-T} - m_1 F_1^{-T}) \cdot n = 0.$$

This means that the vector field

$$\alpha(x) = \begin{cases} m_1 F_1^{-T} & n \cdot x < \gamma \\ m_2 F_2^{-T} & n \cdot x > \gamma \end{cases},$$

satisfies

$$\operatorname{div} \alpha = 0 \text{ in } H^{-1}(\mathbb{R}^3),$$

and, does not induce any field energy in the functional E, and is a first step toward constructing a minimizing sequence. The compatibility of the minimum energy wells of W is assured by the result below, cf. [41].

THEOREM 4.1 *Suppose that*

$$U_1 = \mathbb{1} + \varepsilon m_1 \otimes m_1 \textit{ and } U_2 = \mathbb{1} + \varepsilon m_2 \otimes m_2, \tag{4.5}$$

$$|m_i| = 1 \textit{ and } m_1, m_2 \textit{ independent.}$$

*Then*

$$SO(3)U_1 \textit{ and } SO(3)U_2 \textit{ are compatible wells.}$$

*There are rotations* $R^{\pm}$ *with axis* $p = m_1 \wedge m_2$ *such that*

$$U_1 = R^{\pm}U_2(\mathbb{1} + a^{\pm}\otimes n^{\pm}), \tag{4.6}$$

*with* $n^+ \parallel p \wedge (m_1 - m_2)$, $n^- \parallel p \wedge (m_1 + m_2)$, *and* $a^{\pm} \cdot n^{\pm} = 0$.

*The pairs*

$$\{(U_1,m_1)\,,\,(R^{\pm}U_2,\pm m_2(R^{\pm})^T\}$$

*are mechanically and magnetically compatible across planes* $n^{\pm} \cdot x = \gamma$.

For example, with $m_1$ and $m_2$ given above, $n^+ = \langle 100\rangle$ and $n^- = \langle 011\rangle$, in agreement with the data of D. Lord. The Theorem applies to other transitions as well; $m_i$ could be $\langle 100\rangle$ or $\langle 110\rangle$ directions and the result specifies the twin planes for more common cubic/tetragonal, etc., transitions.

We now exhibit a minimizing sequence which has Young measure

$$\nu_x = \tfrac{1}{2}(1-\lambda)(\delta_{(U_1,m_1)} + \delta_{(U_1,-m_1)}) + \tfrac{1}{2}\lambda(\delta_{(R^+U_2,m_2(R^+)^T)} + \delta_{(R^+U_2,-m_2(R^+)^T)}),\ x \in \Omega^-. \tag{4.7}$$

where $0 \le \lambda \le 1$. For convenience of notation, denote by $\Omega \subset \mathbb{R}^3$ be the region occupied by the material, instead of $\Omega^-$, and suppose it has a sufficiently regular boundary. Set $n = n^+$ and $R = R^+$ and define the functions

$$\vartheta(t) = \begin{cases} -1 & 0 \le t < \frac{1}{2} \\ +1 & \frac{1}{2} \le t < 1 \end{cases}, \text{ and}$$

$$\eta(t) = \begin{cases} 1 & 0 \le t < \lambda \\ 0 & \lambda \le t < 1 \end{cases},$$

and extend $\vartheta$ and $\eta$ to be periodic of period 1 on $\mathbb{R}$. Define $y^k(x)$ by $y^k(0) = 0$ and

$$\nabla y^k = F^k = (1 - \eta(kx\cdot n))U_1 + \eta(kx\cdot n)RU_2, \ x \in \mathbb{R}^3. \tag{4.9}$$

Now in each layer where $F^k = U_1$, say, $j + \lambda \le kx\cdot n \le j + 1$, define

$$m^k(x) = \vartheta(kp\cdot x)m_1,$$

and in each layer where $F^k = RU_2$, define

$$m^k(x) = \vartheta(kp\cdot x)m_2R^T.$$

Hence,

$$m^k(x) = \vartheta(kp\cdot x)((1 - \eta(kx\cdot n))m_1 + \eta(kx\cdot n)m_2), \quad x \in \mathbb{R}^3. \tag{4.10}$$

According to this construction,

$$f^k(x) = m^k(x)\, F^k(x)^{-T} = \frac{\vartheta(kp\cdot x)}{1 + \varepsilon}((1 - \eta(kx\cdot n))m_1 + \eta(kx\cdot n)m_2), \quad x \in \mathbb{R}^3, \tag{4.11}$$

satisfies

$$\operatorname{div} f^k = 0 \ \text{ in } H^{-1}(\mathbb{R}^3) \ \text{ and } \ f^k \to 0 \ \text{ in } L^\infty(\mathbb{R}^3) \text{ weak*}.$$

Hence by Lemma 3.2,

$$\operatorname{div} \chi_\Omega f^k \to 0 \ \text{ in } H^{-1}(\mathbb{R}^3).$$

Since $W(F^k,m^k) = \min W$, we have that for this sequnce $(y^k,m^k)$,

$$\lim_{k\to\infty} E(y^k,m^k) = |\Omega| \min W.$$

It is not necessary to be so precise in the construction of the minimizing sequence. It is possible to have a "slow" deformation variable and a "fast" magnetization variable, for example, and to exploit Lemma 3.2 in such a way that the magnetic compatibility across planes $x \cdot n$ = const. is not used.

## 5. Magnetic fine structure

Using (3.27), we can investigate the magnetization distribution associated with specific mechanical microstructures. We give two illustrations of this. We shall show that (4.7) is the unique Young measure whose underlying deformation gradient is the constant matrix

$$F = (1-\lambda)U_1 + \lambda R U_2 \quad \text{in } \Omega, \tag{5.1}$$

where $R = R^+$ and whose support is given by (5.3) below. Consequently, any equilibrium configuration of the form described by $\Omega^-$ in Figure 1 necessarily has magnetic fine structure. We then extend this to the composite $\Omega^+ \cup \Omega^-$. Indeed, in both cases our objective is to show that

$$\bar{m} = 0 \quad \text{in } \Omega. \tag{5.2}$$

Let us assume that $\nu = (\nu_x)_{x \in \Omega}$ is a Young measure generated by a minimizing sequence $(y^k, m^k)$ of the functional $E$ with the properties

$$\operatorname{supp} \nu \subset X = \{(A,\mu): A = QU_i, \mu = m_i Q^T, Q \in SO(3), i = 1,2\} \tag{5.3}$$

where

$$U_i = \mathbb{1} + \varepsilon m_i \otimes m_i, \ |m_i| = 1, i = 1,2, \text{ with } m_1, m_2 \text{ independent.} \tag{5.4}$$

We further assume that the underlying deformation gradient is given by (5.1) in a neighborhood $\Omega$. In addition, we assume that $|\varepsilon|$ is small. First of all, it is known ([5],[46]) and easily shown that under the conditions of (4.8), (4.9) the deformation portion of the Young measure whose support is given by (5.3) is unique and given by a convex combination of Dirac masses. Hence in view of the restriction on the support of $\nu$ given by (5.3),

$$\nu_x = (1-\lambda)\{(1-\gamma_1(x))\, \delta_{U_1} \otimes \delta_{m_1} + \gamma_1(x)\, \delta_{U_1} \otimes \delta_{-m_1}\} +$$
$$\lambda\{(1-\gamma_2(x))\, \delta_{RU_2} \otimes \delta_{m_2 R^T} + \gamma_2(x)\, \delta_{RU_2} \otimes \delta_{-m_2 R^T}\}, \tag{5.5}$$

where $0 \le \gamma_i(x) \le 1$. Now

$$\bar{m}(x) = \int_X \mu \, d\nu_x(A,\mu) \quad \text{in } \Omega \text{ a.e. and} \tag{5.6}$$

$$\alpha(x) = \int_X \mu A^{-T} \, d\nu_x(A,\mu) \quad \text{in } \Omega \text{ a.e..} \tag{5.7}$$

Thus

$$\overline{m} = ((1-\lambda)(1-2\gamma_1)m_1 + \lambda(1-2\gamma_2)m_2R^T)\chi_\Omega \tag{5.8}$$

while on the other hand

$$\alpha = (1-\lambda)\{(1-\gamma_1)\, m_1U_1^{-T} - \gamma_1 m_1 U_1^{-T}\}\chi_\Omega +$$

$$\lambda\{(1-\gamma_2)\, m_2R^T(RU_2)^{-T} - \gamma_2\, m_2R^T(RU_2)^{-T}\}\chi_\Omega$$

Since $U_i^{-T} = U_i^{-1}$, the above simplifies to

$$\alpha = \{(1-\lambda)(1-2\gamma_1)\, m_1U_1^{-1} + \lambda(1-2\gamma_2)\, m_2U_2^{-1}\}\chi_\Omega \tag{5.9}$$

We now seek to identify the quantities in the expression $\overline{m} = \alpha F^T$, cf. (3.27). Setting $\beta_i = (1-2\gamma_i)$,

$$\alpha F^T = \{(1-\lambda)\beta_1\, m_1U_1^{-1} + \lambda\beta_1\, m_2U_2^{-1}\}\{(1-\lambda)U_1 + \lambda U_2R^T\} \quad \text{in } \Omega.$$

Since this expression must equal (5.9),

$$\lambda(1-\lambda)\{\beta_1 m_1 (\mathbb{1} - U_1^{-1}U_2R^T) + \beta_2 m_2 (R^T - U_2^{-1}U_1)\} = 0. \tag{5.10}$$

The only case of interest is $0 < \lambda < 1$. If the two (constant) vectors

$$q_1 = m_1(\mathbb{1} - U_1^{-1}U_2R^T) \quad \text{and} \quad q_2 = m_2(R^T - U_2^{-1}U_1) \tag{5.11}$$

are independent, then $\beta_1 = \beta_2 = 0$. If they are dependent, then the functions $\beta_i(x)$ are proportional: there is a scalar $c \in \mathbb{R}$ for which

$$\beta_2(x) = c\,\beta_1(x) \quad \text{or} \quad \beta_1(x) = 0 \quad \text{in } \Omega, \tag{5.12}$$

Hence, since $m_iU_i^{-1} = \frac{1}{1+\varepsilon} m_i$,

$$\alpha = \frac{\beta_1}{1+\varepsilon}((1-\lambda)m_1 + \lambda c m_2)\,\chi_\Omega. \tag{5.13}$$

Suppose at this point that (5.1) is satisfied in the entire region occupied by the material, $\Omega$. Thus $\alpha$ has constant direction and satisfies

$$\operatorname{div} \alpha = 0 \quad \text{in } H^{-1}(\mathbb{R}^3).$$

This implies that $\alpha = 0$. In fact any mapping of the form

$$\zeta \to \int_{\mathbb{R}^3} f \nabla \zeta \, dx$$

where $f \in L^2(\mathbb{R}^3)$ has compact support either has full rank or $f$ vanishes identically, cf. [40] Lemma 4.1. By (5.13),

$$\int_{\mathbb{R}^3} \frac{\beta_1}{1 + \varepsilon} \chi_\Omega \nabla \zeta \, dx \cdot ((1 - \lambda)m_1 + \lambda c m_2) = 0,$$

so

$$f = \frac{\beta_1(x)}{1 + \varepsilon} = 0.$$

Consequently, $\beta_1 = \beta_2 = 0$ which implies that $\gamma_1 = \gamma_2 = \frac{1}{2}$. This verifies (5.2).

In fact, $q_1$ and $q_2$ of (5.11) are always dependent. Manipulation of equation (5.10) reveals that it is equivalent to

$$(\beta_1 m_1 U_1^{-1} - \beta_2 m_2 U_2^{-1})(U_1 - U_2 R^T) = 0,$$

or

$$\frac{1}{1 + \varepsilon} (\beta_1 m_1 - \beta_2 m_2)(U_1 - U_2 R^T) = 0. \tag{5.14}$$

Now

$$U_1 - U_2 R^T = n \otimes R U_2 a$$

is a rank one matrix. Since $m_1$ and $m_2$ are independent, it is always possible to find $\beta_i$ such that (5.14) holds. In fact, some additional algebra shows that $\beta_1 + \beta_2 = 0$.

Let us now consider the composite material described in Figure 1, assuming that the variant proportion is constant in the top and the bottom. An expression for the deformation identical to (5.1) holds in each of $\Omega^+$ and $\Omega^-$. We find by the preceding reasoning that $\alpha$ has constant direction in each of $\Omega^-$ and $\Omega^+$. Arguing in a manner similar to the single laminate case, we conclude again that $\alpha = 0$.

## References


[1] Anzellotti, G., Baldo, S., and Visintin, A. 1991 Asymptotic behavior of the Landau-Lifshitz model of ferromagnetism, Applied Mathematics and Optimization, 23, 171-192

[2] Ball, J. M. 1981 Global invertibility of Sobolev functions and the interpenetration of matter, Proc. R. Soc. Edin. 88A, 315-328

[3] Ball, J. M. 1989 A version of the fundamental theorem for Young measures, *PDE's and continuum models of phase transitions*, Lecture Notes in Physics, 344,(Rascle, M., Serre, D., and Slemrod, M., eds.) Springer, 207-215

[4] Ball, J. M. and James, R. 1987 Fine phase mixtures as minimizers of energy, Arch. Rat. Mech. Anal.,100, 15-52

[5] Ball, J. M. and James, R. 1991 Proposed experimental tests of a theory of fine microstructure and the two well problem, Phil. Trans. Roy. Soc. Lond. (to appear)

[6] Ball, J. M. and Zhang, K. 1990 Lower semicontinuity of multiple integrals and the biting lemma, Proc. Royal Soc. Edinburgh, 114A, 367-379

[7] Battacharya, K. Self accomodation in martensite, Arch. Rat. Mech. Anal. (to appear)

[8] Battacharya, K. Wedge-like microstructure in martensite, (to appear)

[9] Brandon, D. and Rogers, R. The coercivity paradox and nonlocal ferromagnetism, (to appear)

[10] Brown, W.F. 1962 *Magnetostatic Principles in Ferromagnetism*, Vol. 1 of Selected Topics in Solid State Physics (ed. E.P. Wohlfarth), North-Holland.

[11] Brown, W.F. 1963 *Micromagnetics*, John Wiley and Sons, New York.

[12] Brown, W.F. 1966 *Magnetoelastic Interactions*, Vol. 9 of Springer Tracts in Natural Philosophy (ed. C. Truesdell), Springer-Verlag.

[13] Chipot, M. and Kinderlehrer, D. 1988 Equilibrium configurations of crystals, Arch. Rat. Mech. Anal. 103, 237-277

[14] Chipot, M. Numerical analysis of oscillations in nonconvex problems,(to appear)

[15] Ciarlet, P. and Necas, J. 1987 Injectivity and self contact in nonlinear elasticity, Arch. Rat. Mech. Anal., 19, 171-188

[16] Clark, A. E. 1980 Magnetostrictive rare earth - $Fe_2$ compounds, *Ferromagnetic Materials, Vol 1* (Wohlfarth, E. P. ed) North Holland, 532 - 589

[17] Collins, C. and Luskin, M 1989 The computation of the austenitic-martensitic phase transition, Lecture Notes in Physics 344 (ed. M. Rascle, D. Serre and M. Slemrod), Springer-Verlag, 34-50.

[18] Collins, C. and Luskin, M. Numerical modeling of the microstructure of crystals with symmetry-related variants, *Proc. ARO US-Japan Workshop on Smart/Intelligent Materials and Systems*, Technomic

[19] Collins, C. and Luskin, M. Optimal order error estimates for the finite element approximation of the solution of a nonconvex variational problem, to appear

[20] Collins, C., Kinderlehrer, D., and Luskin, M. Numerical approximation of the solution of a variational problem with a double well potential, SIAM J. Numer. Anal.

[21] Craik, D.J. and Tebble, R. S. 1965 *Ferromagnetism and Ferromagnetic Domains*, North-Holland.

[22] Dacorogna, B. 1989 *Direct methods in the Calculus of Variations*, Springer

[23] Ericksen, J. L. 1979 On the symmetry of deformable crystals, Arch. Rat. Mech. Anal. 72, 1-13

[24] Ericksen, J. L. 1980 Some phase transitions in crystals, Arch. Rat. Mech. Anal. 73, 99-124

[25] Ericksen, J. L. 1981 Changes in symmetry in elastic crystals, IUTAM Symp. Finite Elasticity (Carlson, D.E. and Shield R.T., eds.) M. Nijhoff, 167-177

[26] Ericksen, J. L. 1982 Crystal lattices and sublattices, Rend. Sem. Mat. Padova, 68, 1-9

[27] Ericksen, J. L. 1984 The Cauchy and Born hypotheses for crystals, *Phase Transformations and Material Instabilities in Solids*, (Gurtin, M., ed) Academic Press, 61-78

[28] Ericksen, J. L. 1986 Constitutive theory for some constrained elastic crystals, Int. J. Solids Structures, 22, 951 - 964
[29] Ericksen, J. L. 1987 Twinning of crystals I, *Metastability and Incompletely Posed Problems*, IMA Vol. Math. Appl. 3,(Antman, S., Ericksen, J.L., Kinderlehrer, D., Müller, I.,eds) Springer, 77-96
[30] Ericksen, J. L. 1988 Some constrained elastic crystals, *Material Instabilities in Continuum Mechanics*, (Ball, J. ed.) Oxford, 119 - 136
[31] Ericksen, J. L. 1989 Weak martensitic transformations in Bravais lattices, Arch. Rat. Mech. Anal, 107, 23 - 36
[32] Firooze, N. and Kohn, R. 1991 Geometric parameters and the relaxation of multiwell energies, IMA preprint Series 765
[33] Fonseca, I. 1988 The lower quasiconvex envelope of the stored energy function for an elastic crystal, J. Math. pures et appl, 67, 175-195
[34] Fonseca, I. Lower semicontinuity of surface measures (to appear)
[35] Fonseca, I. The Wulff Theorem revisited (to appear)
[36] James, R. D. 1988 Microstructure and weak convergence, *Proc. Symp. Material Instabilities in Continuum Mechanics*, Heriot-Watt, (Ball, J. M., ed.), Oxford, 175-196
[37] James, R. D. 1989 Relation between microscopic and macroscopic properties of crystals undergoing phase transformation, in *Proc. 7th Army Conf. on Applied Mathematics and Computing* (ed. F. Dressel).
[38] James, R. D. and Kinderlehrer, D. 1989 Theory of diffusionless phase transitions, *PDE's and continuum models of phase transitions*, Lecture Notes in Physics, 344,(Rascle, M., Serre, D., and Slemrod, M., eds.) Springer, 51-84
[39] James, R. D. and Kinderlehrer, D. 1990 An example of frustration in a ferromagnetic material, Nematics: Mathematical and Physical Aspects, (Coron, J.-M., Ghidaglia, J.-M., and Hélein, F., eds), Kluwer NATO ASI series, 201-222
[40] James, R. D. and Kinderlehrer, D. 1990 Frustration in ferromagnetic materials, Cont. Mech. Therm. 2, 215-239
[41] James, R. D. and Kinderlehrer, D. A theory of magnetostriction with application to $TbDyFe_2$ (to appear)
[42] James, R.D. and Müller, S. to appear
[43] Kinderlehrer, D. 1988 Remarks about the equilibrium configurations of crystals, *Proc. Symp. Material instabilities in continuum mechanics*, Heriot-Watt (Ball, J. M. ed.) Oxford, 217-242
[44] Kinderlehrer, D. and Pedregal, P. 1991 Characterizations of Young measures generated by gradients, Arch. Rat. Mech. Anal. 115, 329-365
[45] Kinderlehrer, D. and Pedregal, P. Charactérisation des mesures de Young associées à un gradient, C.R.A.S. Paris (to appear)
[46] Kinderlehrer, D. and Pedregal, P. Remarks about Young measures supported on two wells (to appear)
[47] Kléman, M. 1983 *Points, Lines and Walls*, John Wiley and Sons, New York.
[48] Kohn, R. V. 1991 The relaxation of a double-well energy, Cont. Mech. Therm., 3, 193-236
[49] Kohn, R.V. 1989 The relationship between linear and nonlinear variational models of coherent phase transitions, in *Proc. 7th Army Conf. on Applied Mathematics and Computing* (ed. F. Dressel).
[50] Landau, L.D. and Lifshitz, E. M.1935 *Physik. Z. Sowjetunion* **8**, 337–346.
[51] Landau, L.D., Lifshitz, E. M., and Pitaevskii, L. P. 1984 *Electrodynamics of continuous media*, Vol. 8 of Course of Theoretical Physics, Pergamon Press.
[52] Lifshitz, E.M. 1944 On the magnetic structure of iron, *J. Physics* **8**, 337–346.
[53] Lord, D. 1990 Magnetic domain observations in $TbDyFe_2$, IMA lecture
[54] Luskin, M. and Ma, L. 1990 Analysis of the finite element approximation of microstructure in micromagnetics, UMSI report 90/164
[55] Ma, L. to appear
[56] Marcellini, P. 1985 Approximation of quasiconvex functions and lower semicontinuity of certain quasiconvex integrals, Manu. Math., 51, 1-28
[57] Matos, J. The absence of fine microstructure in $\alpha$–$\beta$ quartz, (to appear)
[58] Pedregal, P. 1989 Thesis, University of Minnesota
[59] Pedregal, P. 1989 Weak continuity and weak lower semicontinuity for some compensation operators, Proc. Royal Soc. Edin. 113, 267 - 279

[60] Rogers, R.C. 1988 Nonlocal variational problems in nonlinear electromagneto-elastostatics, SIAM J. Math. Anal. 19, 1329–1347.
[61] Rogers, R.C. 1990 A nonlocal model for the exchange energy uin ferromagnetic materials, J. Int. Eqns. Appl. (to appear)
[62] Sethna, J. 1987 Theory of the blue phases of chiral nematic liquid crystals, in *Theory and Applications of Liquid Crystals* (ed. J.L. Ericksen and D. Kinderlehrer), IMA Vol. Math. Appl. 5, Springer, 305-324
[63] Stoner, E.C. 1945 The demagnetizing factors for ellipsoids, Phil. Mag. 36, 803–821.
[64] Sverak, V. 1991 Quasiconvex functions with subquadratic growth, Proc. R. Soc. Lond., 433, 723-725
[65] Sverak, V. On Tartar's conjecture (to appear)
[66] Sverak, V. On the problem of two wells, (to appear)
[67] Sverak, V. On the regularity of the Monge-Ampère equation without convexity, (to appear)
[68] Tartar, L. 1979 Compensated compactness and applications to partial differential equations, *Nonlinear analysis and mechanics: Heriot Watt Symposium, Vol I V*(Knops, R., ed.) Pitman Res. Notes in Math. 39, 136-212
[69] Tartar, L. 1983 The compensated compactness method applied to systems of conservation laws, *Systems of nonlinear partial differential equations* (Ball, J. M., ed) Riedel
[70] Toupin, R. 1956 The elastic dielectric, *J. Rat. Mech. Anal.*, **5**, 849 - 915
[71] Visintin, A. 1985 On Landau-Lifshitz equations in ferromagnetism, Japan. J. Appl. Math., 2, 69-84
[72] Young, L. C. 1969 *Lectures on calculus of variations and optimal control theory*, W.B. Saunders
[73] Zhang, K. A construction of quasiconvex functions with linear growth at infinity (to appear)
[74] Zhang, K. Rank-one connections and the three "well" problem, (to appear)

R.D. James
Department of Aerospace
Engineering and Mechanics
University of Minnesota
Minneapolis, MN 55455

D. Kinderlehrer
Department of Mathematics and
Center for Nonlinear Analysis
Carnegie Mellon University
Pittsburgh, PA 15213-3890

---

[1] Research group *Transitions and Defects in Ordered Materials*, funded by the NSF and the AFOSR (DMS 87-18881) and by the ARO (DAAL 03 88 K 0010).

2 Crystallographic directions are referred to the putative high temperature cubic configuration.

J R OCKENDON

# Some macroscopic models for superconductivity

## 1. Introduction and Physical Background

This talk will comprise 3 sections. First there will be a review of the salient physical evidence, together with some elementary macroscopic models. Then we will discuss the celebrated "Ginzburg-Landau" model which highlights the shortcomings of the elementary models and finally we will catalogue some conjectures posed by this modelling discussion. Several of the concepts mentioned here are discussed in greater detail in [1].

Mathematically it is most convenient to discuss the transition from normal to superconducting in terms of the response of a specimen to changes in its external magnetic field, rather than the more popular conception of changes is its ambient temperature. We need to recall the fundamental observations of Onnes [2] that, when the imposed magnetic field $H_0$ is decreased through a value $H_c$ which depends on the temperature $T$, the material can change from being normal (in which case its current is related to the electric field by Ohm's Law) to being superconducting; in the latter case Ohm's law does not apply and some new information is needed to close Maxwell's equations. The most important evidence for this new information is the Meissner effect [3] which states that the magnetic field is expelled from a superconducting specimen. All this evidence is summarized in Fig. 1. In particular Fig. 1d plots the magnetization, here defined to be the difference between the mean magnetic field in the specimen and $H_0$ , as a function of $H_0$; however this figure is not true for all superconductors as we shall see later.

Although there is a weak coupling between the thermal and electromagnetic effects in supercondutors, we will ignore heat flow during this talk. We will also ignore displacement currents and assume that the dimensionless Maxwell equations

$$\nabla\cdot H=0,\nabla\cdot E=0,\nabla\times H=j,\nabla\times E=-\frac{\partial H}{\partial t} \tag{1a-d}$$

relate the electric field E, the magnetic field $H$ and the current $j$ everywhere. Thus, following [4], we can construct a very simple model for a cylinder aligned in the $z$-direction undergoing a superconducting phase transition as in Fig. 2. The magnetic field only has a component $H_3(x,y,t)$ and so, if we assume (and we will see later that this assumption is not always justified) that the wire is in an <u>intermediate state</u> with a normal region $N$ surrounding a superconducting region (or vice versa), then, in the normal region, Ohm's law

$$j = E \tag{2}$$

gives

$$\frac{\partial H_3}{\partial t}=\Delta H_3 \tag{3}$$

there. The Meissner effect gives $H_3 = 0$ in the superconducting region and the Onnes critical field-condition is modelled by writing

$$H_3 \downarrow H_c \tag{4}$$

as we approach the phase boundary from $N$.

Also, the conservation of magnetic flux (1d), namely

$$\frac{\partial H_3}{\partial t} + \nabla \cdot (E_2, -E_1, 0) = 0 \quad ,$$

gives the second "free boundary" condition

$$\frac{\partial H_3}{\partial n} = -H_c V_n \tag{5}$$

as we approach the boundary from $N$, where $V_n$ is the normal velocity away from $N$. Now (3)-(5) are nothing more than the classical one-phase "Stefan Model" for melting or solidification and this model is well-known [5] to be well-posed only if $N$ is expanding (i.e. the wire is being "switched off"). Otherwise the model needs to be regularized and this is traditionally achieved (but not yet proved to be achieved) by adding to $H_c$ in (4) terms involving $V_n$ or the curvature of the phase boundary. However we also recall that the phase boundary can be smoothed using the phase-field model [6]

$$\frac{\partial H_3}{\partial t} + \frac{H_c}{2}\frac{\partial F}{\partial t} = \Delta H_3 \qquad (6)$$

$$\alpha \frac{\partial F}{\partial t} = \alpha \xi^2 \Delta F + \frac{1}{2a}(F - F^3) + 2H_3; \qquad (7)$$

here $F \in [-1,1]$ is an order parameter measuring the fraction of material transformed and $\xi$ measures the width of the "smoothed-out" transition region. Formally (3-5) can be retrieved from (6,7) by letting the parameters $\alpha$, $\xi$ and a tend to zero appropriately.

The above ideas can be quickly generalized to three-dimensional configurations. Then, in the normal region, (1,2) give

$$\frac{\partial H}{\partial t} = \Delta H; \qquad (8)$$

(4) generalizes to

$$|H| \downarrow H_c \qquad (9)$$

and, since $\frac{\partial H}{\partial t} + div\begin{pmatrix} 0 & -E_3 & E_2 \\ E_3 & 0 & -E_1 \\ -E_2 & E_1 & 0 \end{pmatrix} = 0$, the conservation condition at the phase boundary is

$$E \times n \ (= (\nabla \times H) \times n) = -H\ V_n \qquad (10)$$

where n is the outward normal to the normal region; (9) and (10) are to be imposed as we approach the phase boundary from the normal region but we will now have an underdetermined problem unless we also impose the free boundary condition

$$\nabla \cdot H = 0 \tag{11}$$

there. However, (11) would be unnecessary if $\nabla \cdot H = 0$ had been appended to (8).

A formal stability analysis [7] reveals that (8-11) seem to have the same well-posedness properties as (3-5), i.e. that we only expect stability where $N$ is expanding, but we have the interesting situation that the phase boundary is a torus and that nontrivial steady states are possible by using models from inviscid cavitation theory,[1].

## 2. Ginzburg-Landau Models

In [8], superconductivity was modelled on a "meso-scale" by using the same philosophy as later adapted for the phase field theory but with the crucial assumption that the "macroscopic" quantum effects can be accounted for by writing equations for a complex order parameter

$$\Psi = f\, e^{i\chi} \qquad 0 < f \le 1. \tag{12}$$

Here $f^2$ is interpreted as the density of superconducting electrons. The freedom of choice in the phase $\chi$ is then associated with the freedom of choice of the magnetic vector potential, say $A$, so the Ginzburg-Landau free energy density is not just a polynomial in $|\Psi|$, $|H|$ and $|\nabla\Psi|$ but rather involves $(\nabla - iA)\Psi$. In fact, the choice of energy density

$$-|\Psi|^2+\frac{1}{2}|\Psi|^4+\gamma^2|H|^2+|(\xi\nabla-i\frac{\gamma}{\lambda}A)\Psi|^2$$

gives Euler-Lagrange equations

$$(\xi\nabla-i\frac{\gamma}{\lambda}A)^2\Psi+\Psi(1-|\Psi|^2)=0 \qquad (13)$$

$$-\lambda^2\nabla\times(\nabla\times A)=\frac{i\xi\lambda}{2\gamma}(\Psi^*\nabla\Psi-\Psi\nabla\Psi^*)+A|\Psi|^2 \qquad (14)$$

where $\nabla \times A = H$ partially defines $A$ and $\Psi^*$ is the complex conjugate of $\Psi$; (13) is anlogous to (7) and (14) models the electromagnetic effects in the phase transition. Also $\xi$, $\lambda$ and $\gamma$ are constants to be discussed later. As long as $f \neq 0$, these equations can be greatly simplified by choosing $A$ so that $\nabla \cdot A = 0$ and writing

$$Q=A-\frac{\lambda\xi}{\gamma}\nabla\chi. \qquad (15)$$

Then

$$\xi^2\Delta f = f^3-f+\frac{\gamma^2}{\lambda^2}f|Q|^2 \qquad (16)$$

and

$$-\lambda^2\nabla \times (\nabla \times Q) = f^2 Q \tag{17}$$

are real equations for $f$ and $Q$, and (17) clearly measures the current flow. We will not discuss boundary conditions for (16, 17) here but merely note that:

(i) There are solutions in which $f$ vanishes at a point. This can be seen by writing

$$\Psi = f(r)\, e^{in\theta},\, Q = Q(r)\, e_\theta \ , \ n = 1,2, \ \ldots \ .$$

in cylindrical polar coordinates $(r,\ \theta,\ z)$, [9], and studying the resulting coupled second-order differential equations for $f$ and $Q$. The current, which flows in what is called a superconducting "vortex" is purely azimuthal and the magnetic field is along the z-axis with a net flux proportional to n; in fact, when $n = 1$ we have a single "fluxon" of strength $2\pi\xi\lambda/\gamma$.

(ii) Evolution models analogous to (16,17) have been written down in [10]; these cannot be derived as easily as (13,14) but instead rely on a more detailed averaging of quantum mechanical models. The end result is that terms proportional to $\frac{\partial f}{\partial t}$ and $\frac{\partial Q}{\partial t} + \nabla\left(\varphi + \frac{\xi\lambda}{\gamma}\frac{\partial \chi}{\partial t}\right)$ must be added to (16,17) respectively, where the electric potential is given by $E + \frac{\partial A}{\partial t} = -\nabla\varphi$. Finally, the result $\nabla \cdot f^2 Q = 0$, which is a trivial consequence (13,14) in the steady state, becomes the evolution equation

$$\alpha f^2\left(\varphi+\frac{\xi\lambda}{\gamma}\frac{\partial\chi}{\partial t}\right)+\nabla\cdot f^2 Q=0,$$

so that there is a space charge in this case and the second equation in (1) does not apply.

(iii) The parameters $\xi$ and $\lambda$ can be interpreted as "penetration dephts" for the order parameter and the magnetic field respectively. Typically they give dimensional values of about $1\mu m$.

From both the physical and the mathematical modelling viewpoint the Ginzburg-Landau equations and their unsteady generalisation have two dramatic consequences.

A. Travelling wave solutions. If a propagating phase boundary exists, we expect the local solution to be described by a travelling wave solution of the evolution forms of (16,17). Taking z to be the normal to the phase boundary and $Q = (0, Q(z), 0)$, we find that the structure of the phase transition in the travelling wave is described by

$$f'' = \kappa^2(f^3-f+fQ^2) \qquad '=\frac{d}{dz} \tag{18}$$

$$Q'' = f^2 Q \tag{19}$$

where $\kappa = \lambda/\xi$ is called the Ginzburg-Landau parameter. The conditions that the material is normal and superconducting on either side of the transition are

$$f \to 0 \text{ as } z \to +\infty$$

$$Q \to 0,\ f \to 1 \text{ as } z \to -\infty$$

respectively. It is then easy to show [11] that $Q' \to \frac{1}{\sqrt{2}}$ as $z \to +\infty$ and hence the theory states that if the phase transition occurs through the mechanism of a propagating phase boundary, the value of $|H|$ in the normal region (called $H_c$ in the previous section) is $\frac{1}{\sqrt{2}}$.

B. Asymptotics as $\lambda,\ \xi \to 0$. A formal asymptotic analysis can be carried out for (16,17) (and their evolution forms) in the same way as for the phase field (6,7), [7]. The result is that we retrieve the vector Stefan model (8-11) but, when we proceed to second order terms in the formal expansion we find that (9) must be corrected by small terms linear in the curvature and normal velocity of the phase boundary. The surprise is that the coefficients of these terms are such that they are only both stabilising when $\kappa < \frac{1}{\sqrt{2}}$. Thus, it is only when $\kappa < \frac{1}{\sqrt{2}}$ that the G-L model offers a hope for regularising the ill-posed ($N$ contracting) configurations for (8-11). Indeed, when $\kappa > \frac{1}{\sqrt{2}}$, the G-L model suggests that any phase boundaries which are present are even more unstable than they would be without the presence of non-zero $\xi$, $\lambda$.

## 3. Type I and Type II Superconductors

The most interesting evidence for what happens when $\kappa > \frac{1}{\sqrt{2}}$ comes from considering steady-state bifurcations from the normal configuration $f = 0$, $Q = (0, -H_0 z, 0)$. When $f$ is everywhere small and the magnetic field is $H_0$ at $z = \pm\infty$, we find that any non-zero solution satisfies

$$\xi^2 f'' + [1-(H_0\, z/\lambda)^2]\, f = 0 \tag{20}$$

with $f'(\pm\infty) = 0$. As $H_0$ is progressively decreased, we find [12] that an acceptable solution first exists when

$$H_0 = H_{c_2}\ , \text{ say}$$

where $H_{c_2} > \frac{1}{\sqrt{2}}$ when $\kappa > \frac{1}{\sqrt{2}}$ and $H_{c_2} < \frac{1}{\sqrt{2}}$ when $\kappa < \frac{1}{\sqrt{2}}$.

A weakly nonlinear analysis then reveals that the bifurcation is subcritical/supercritical depending on the sign of $\kappa - \frac{1}{\sqrt{2}}$ (Fig.3). Accordingly, superconductors with $\kappa < \frac{1}{\sqrt{2}}$ and $\kappa > \frac{1}{\sqrt{2}}$ are called <u>Type I</u> and <u>Type II</u> respectively.

Now the above lowest-order bifurcating solution gives an eigensolution f whose form is as in Fig. 4, with corresponding magnetic field $Q'$ and superconducting current $Q''$.

The superconducting phase is localized near the plane $z = 0$ and the superconducting current flows in the $y$-direction (the direction of Q) and is the same in any plane $x$ = const. A much more interesting configuration is possible when we consider two-dimensional bifurcations. In this case we can allow $\Psi$ to vanish at isolated points by writing

$$\Psi = e^{imy}g(z) + e^{-imy}g(-z)$$

where g also satisfies (20) but now $\Psi = 0$ at $z = 0$, $y=\left(n+\frac{1}{2}\right)\frac{\pi}{m}$. Thus the associated superconducting current which flows in vortices near these zeros, is approximately $\left(0, \frac{|\Psi|^2\xi}{\lambda\gamma}\nabla\chi, 0\right)$ where $\chi$ swings through $2\pi$ around the zero (Fig. 4b). Several studies have been carried out with more complicated arrays of these vortices (see e.g.[13]).

This bifurcation analysis suggests strongly that the transition from normal to superconducting in a Type II superconductor takes place not through the propagation of a phase boundary at applied fields near $H_0 = H_c$, but through the growth of superconducting regions almost everywhere except for discrete zeros of $\Psi$, where there are vortices. Such growth can occur for values of $H_0 > H_c$ and it is easy to see that when the material is nearly perfectly superconducting everywhere, these vortices have spatial extent of $O(\xi)$. If we further conjecture that as $H_0$ is decreased, the vortices move towards the boundary of the superconductor and vanish, we can explain the existence of the critical field $H_{c_1}$, in Fig. 5, which is the analogue of Fig. 1d for Type II superconductors. When $H_{c_1}<H_0<H_{c_2}$, the Type II superconductor is said to be in a <u>mixed state</u> as was first predicted in [14].

## 4. Conclusion.

We can crudely summarize the response of superconductors to transitions induced by varying $H_0$ by Fig. 6. We emphasize that this is only for quasistatic situations and that it ignores important real-world effects such as hysteresis, the effects of boundaries and the effects of thermal coupling. Nonetheless the scenario we have presented offers many opportunities for further mathematical work, and in particular the development of homogenized models which avoid knowledge of too many details of the microstructure. Clearly these models will be very different for Type I and Type II materials, and many open questions remain concerning the behavior of materials with $\kappa \approx 1/\sqrt{2}$.

Acknowledgement. The author would like to thank Mr. S. J. Chapman and Dr. S. D. Howison for many helpful contributions to this discourse.

Figure 1. Observations of Onnes and Meissner-Ochsenfeld

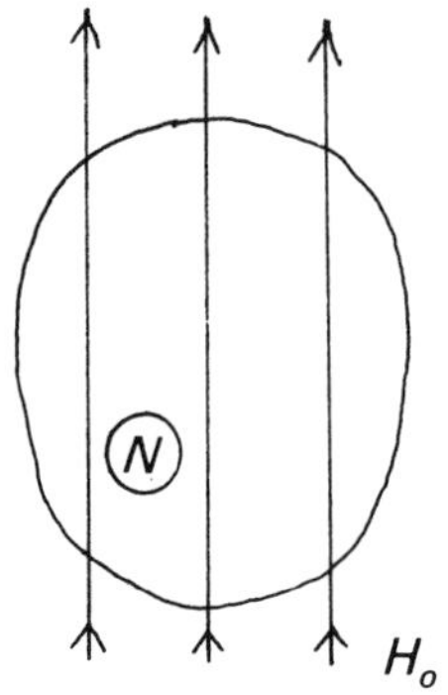


$H_o > H_c(T)$

Fig. 1(a)

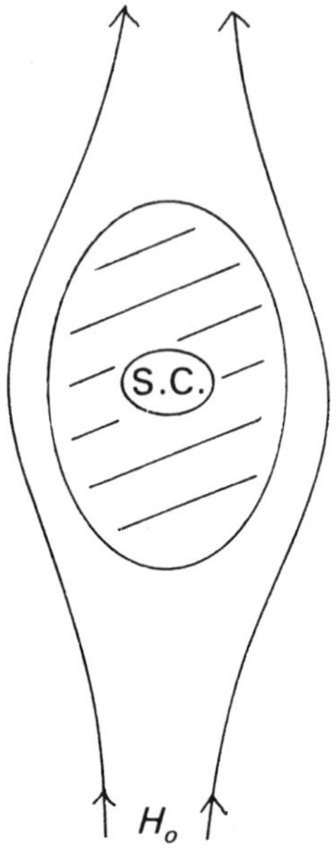


$H_o < H_c(T)$

Fig. 1(b)

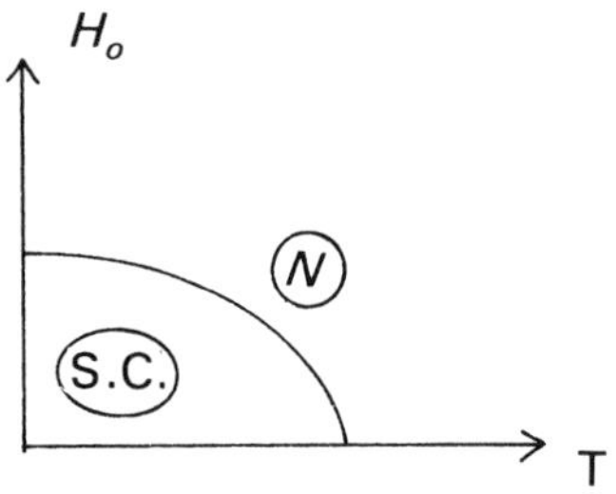


Fig. 1(c)

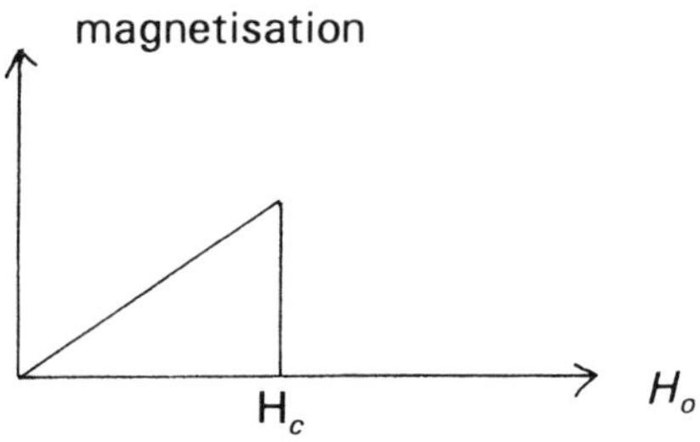


Fig. 1(d)

Figure 2. Intermediate State in a Cylinder

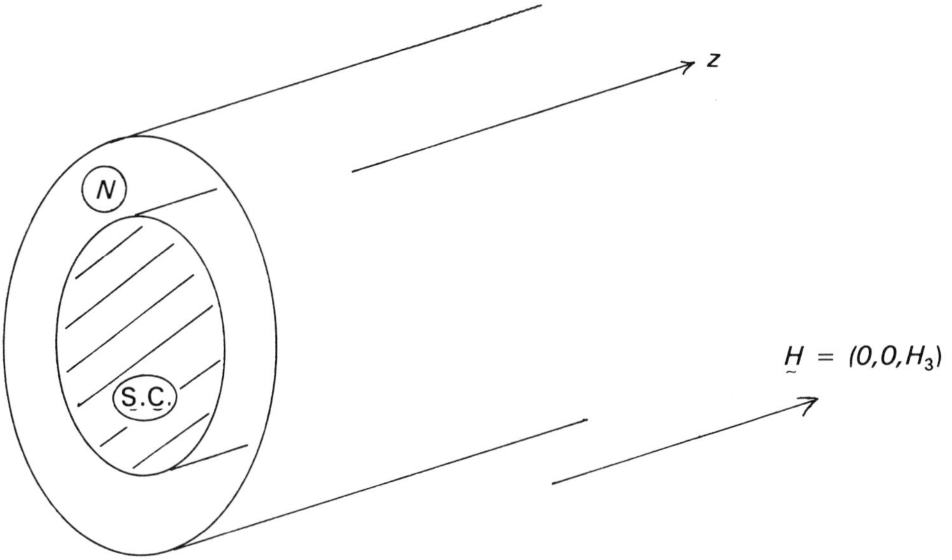


Figure 3. Bifurcation from Normal State

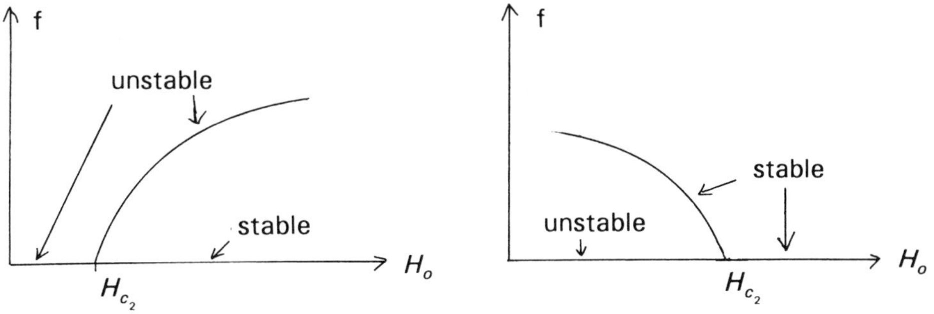


$\kappa < \frac{1}{\sqrt{2}}$ : *TYPE I* $\qquad$ $\kappa > \frac{1}{\sqrt{2}}$ : *TYPE II*

Figure 4

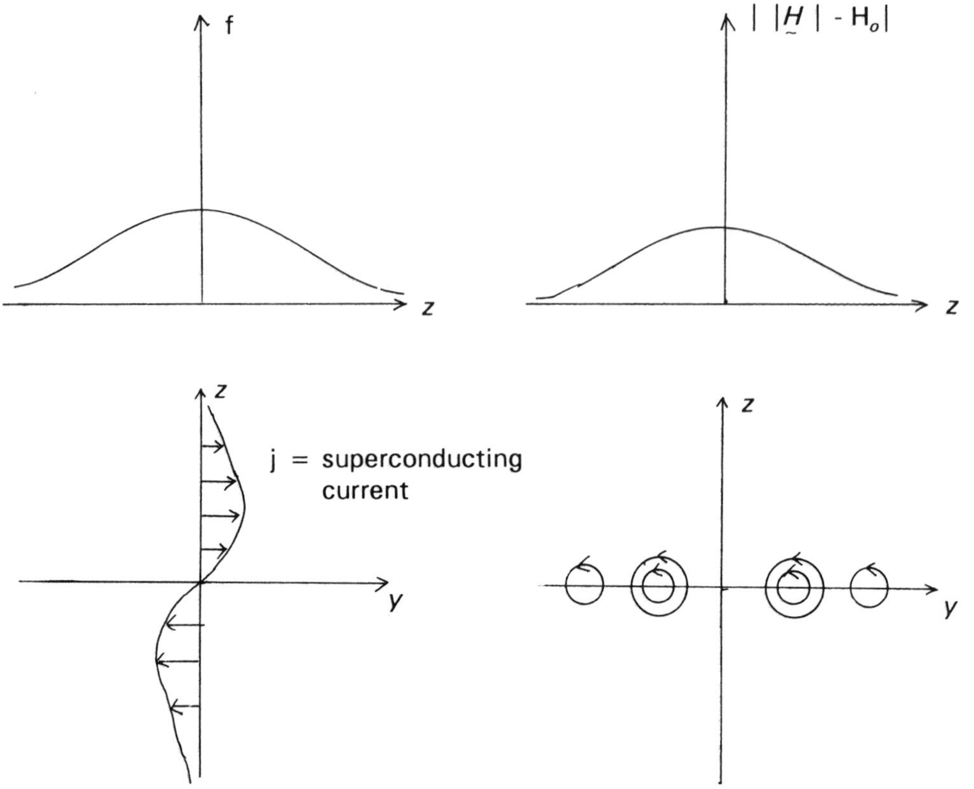


Fig. 4(a). One-dimensional bifurcation

Fig. 4(b). Two-dimensional bifurcation

Figure 5. Response of Type II superconductors

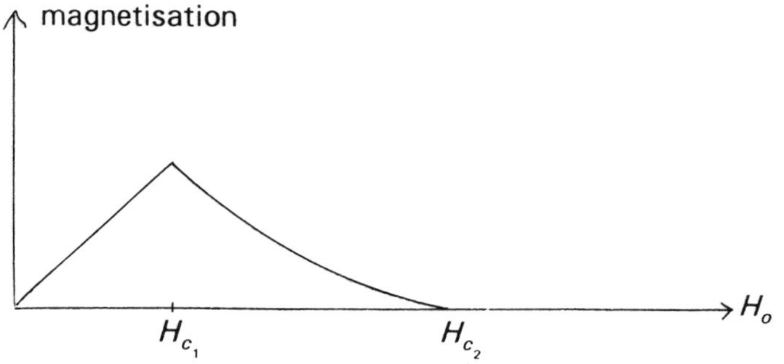

Figure 6. Superconductor Classification

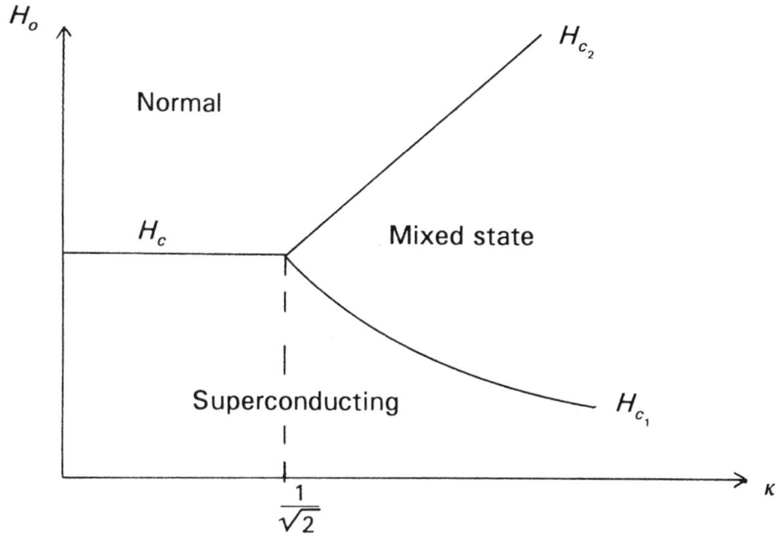


<u>References</u>


1. S. J. Chapman, S. D. Howison, J.R. Ockendon: Macroscopic Models for Superconductivity, submitted to SIAM Rev. (1991)

2. Onnes, H. K.: Leiden Comm. <u>139</u> F (1914)

3. Meissner, W., Ochsenfeld, R.: Naturwissenschaften <u>21</u> 787 (1933)

4. Keller, J. B.: Propagation of a Magnetic Field into a Superconductor. Phys. Rev. <u>III</u>, 1497 (1958)

5. Crank, J. C.: Free and Moving Boundary Problems, Oxford, 1984.

6. Caginalp, G.: The Dynamics of a Conserved Phase Field System, IMA J. Appl. Math. <u>44</u>, 77(1990)

7. Chapman, S. J.: M. Sc. Thesis, Oxford Univ. (1990)

8. Ginzburg, V. L., Landau, L. D.: On the Theory of Superconductivity. JETP 20, 1064 (1950)

9. Berger, M. S., Chen, Y. Y.: Symmetric Vortices for the Ginzburg-Landau Equations. J. Funct. Anal. 82, 259 (1989)

10. Gor'kov, L. P., Eliashberg, G. M.: Generalisation of the Ginzburg-Landau equations for non-stationary problems. Sov. Phys. JETP 27, 328 (1968)

11. Chapman, S. J., Harrison S. D., Mcleod J. B., Ockendon, J. R.: Normal-Superconducting Transitions in Ginzburg-Landau Theory. Proc. Roy. Soc. Edin. (1991) (to appear)

12. Odeh, F.: Existence and bifurcation theorems for the Ginzburg-Landau equations. J. Math. Phys. 8 4351(1967)

13. Kleiner, W. H., Roth, L. M., Autler, S. M.: Bulk solution of Ginzburg-Landau equations for Type II superconductors. Phys. Rev. 133, 5A, 1226 (1964)

14. Abrikosov, A. A.: On the magnetic properties of superconductors of the second kind. Sov. Phys. JETP 5, 1124 (1952)

L SIMON*

# The singular set of minimal submanifolds and harmonic maps

The question of what can be said about the structure of the singular set of minimal surfaces and the extrema of other geometric variational problems has remained largely open. Indeed, for minimal surfaces, apart from various upper bounds on the possible dimension of the singular set (see e.g.: [DeG], [AF1,2], [FH2], [AW1], [G], [SL3], [SS]), little has been known beyond the work of Jean Taylor [TJ1,2] and Brian White [WB1,2] concerning mod $p$ and "$(M, \epsilon, \delta)$" minimizing hypersurfaces, where the tangent cones are of very special (and unvarying) type, and there are topological obstructions to perturbing away the singularities. Similarly for harmonic maps, almost nothing has been known about the structure of the singular set.

Here we describe some recent work which establishes rectifiablity and local finiteness of measure of the singular set for various classes of minimal submanifolds and harmonic maps, including for the first time cases where the tangent cones (or tangent maps) may have varying type and when there is no topological obstruction to perturbing away the singularities. For example, the results described here include the $(n-2)$-rectifiablity for the interior singular set of any mod 2 minimizing current of arbitrary codimension, and local finiteness for the $(n-2)$-dimensional measure of the "top dimensional" part of this singular set. There are also results for harmonic maps, including for example the $(n-3)$-rectifiability and local finiteness of measure of the singular set of an energy minimizing map between compact Riemannian manifolds $M$, $N$, provided the target manifold has dimension 2. (The assumption that the target has dimension 2 is needed in order to check that the "integrability" assumption in the main theorem (Theorem 2 of §2) below is satisfied; it is presently open whether or not this assumption can be removed without significantly changing the conclusions.)

Here we shall merely state the main results and make a few general comments about the method of proof; detailed proofs of the results described here are to be found in [SL1,4].

## 1. Main results for minimal submanifolds.

We let $\mathcal{M}$ be a "multiplicity one" class of minimal submanifolds $M$ embedded in $\mathbf{R}^{n+k}$. Thus $\mathcal{M}$ is a collection of smooth properly embedded $n$-dimensional submanifolds $M \subset \mathbf{R}^{n+k}$, and corresponding to each $M \in \mathcal{M}$ we assume there is an open set $U_M \supset M$ such that:

(i) $$\mathcal{H}^n(M \cap K) < \infty \quad \forall \text{ compact } K \subset U_M ,$$

* Research partly supported by NSF grant DMS-9012718 at Stanford University.

(ii) Every $M \in \mathcal{M}$ is stationary in $U_M$ in the usual sense that $\int_M \operatorname{div}_M \Phi = 0$ for every smooth $\Phi : U_M \to \mathbf{R}^{n+k}$ with support contained in a compact subset of $U_M$, where $\operatorname{div}_M$ denotes tangential divergence relative to $M$. (See [SL1] for further discussion.)

(iii) $\mathcal{M}$ is closed under rigid motions and homotheties in a manner which respects the correspondence $M \to U_M$; thus we require $M \in \mathcal{M} \Rightarrow q\eta_{Y,\rho} M \in \mathcal{M}$ and $q\eta_{Y,\rho} U_M = U_{q\eta_{Y,\rho} M}$ for each $Y \in \mathbf{R}^{n+k}$ and each $\rho > 0$, and for each orthogonal $q \in \mathrm{SO}(\mathbf{R}^{n+k})$. Here $\eta_{Y,\rho}$ denotes the transformation $X \mapsto \rho^{-1}(X - Y)$.

(iv) $\mathcal{M}$ is weakly compact in the sense that if $\{M_j\} \subset \mathcal{M}$, if $U \subset \mathbf{R}^{n+k}$ is open with $U \subset U_{M_j}$ $\forall j$, and if $\sup_j \mathcal{H}^n(M_j \cap K) < \infty$ $\forall$ compact $K \subset U$, then there is a subsequence $M_{j'}$ and an $M \in \mathcal{M}$ such that $U_M \supset U$ and $M_{j'} \to M$ in the measure theoretic (or varifold) sense that $\int_{M_{j'}} f\, d\mathcal{H}^n \to \int_M f\, d\mathcal{H}^n$ for each fixed continuous $f : U \to \mathbf{R}$ with compact support.

For $M \in \mathcal{M}$ and $X \in U_M$, (iv) above, together with the monotonicity formula guarantees that for each sequence $\rho_j \downarrow 0$ there is a subsequence $\rho_{j'}$ such that $\eta_{X,\rho_{j'}} M \to \mathbf{C} \in \mathcal{M}$ with $\mathbf{C}$ a cone with vertex at 0; thus $\eta_{0,\lambda}\mathbf{C} = \mathbf{C}$ for each $\lambda > 0$. (See the discussion in [SL1] for details.) We let $\operatorname{Tan}_X M$ denote the set of all such cones corresponding to all such sequences $\rho_j$, $\rho_{j'}$. Furthermore, again by (iv) and the monotonicity formula, we know that $\Theta_M(X) = \lim_{\rho\downarrow 0}(\omega_n \rho^n)^{-1}\mathcal{H}^n(M \cap B_\rho(X))$ exists for all $X \in \overline{M} \cap U_M$ and equals $\Theta_{\mathbf{C}}(0)$ for any $\mathbf{C} \in \operatorname{Tan}_X M$. The singular set, $\operatorname{sing} M$ of $M \in \mathcal{M}$ is defined by

$$\operatorname{sing} M = \{X \in \overline{M} \cap U_M : \Theta_M(X) > 1\},$$

and (by (iv) and Allard's regularity theorem) corresponds exactly to the set of points $X \in \overline{M} \cap U_M$ such that $\operatorname{Tan}_X M$ contains at least one (hence a unique) $n$-dimensional subspace of $\mathbf{R}^{n+k}$.

Furthermore, using the "stratification of singularities by tangent cone type" [AF1, §1.28] (which is easily modified to the setting adopted here—see [SL1]), we know that there is a "top dimension" $m$ for the singular sets of $M \in \mathcal{M}$ in the sense that there is an integer $m \le n - 1$ such that

**1.1** $$m = \max\{\dim \operatorname{sing} M : M \in \mathcal{M}\},$$

and, for any $M \in \mathcal{M}$, there is a set $S \subset \operatorname{sing} M$ of Hausdorff dimension $m - 1$ (discrete if $m = 1$) such that if $X \in \operatorname{sing} M \backslash S$ then there is a cylindrical cone $q(\mathbf{C}_0 \times \mathbf{R}^m) \in \operatorname{Tan}_X M$, where $q \in \mathrm{SO}(\mathbf{R}^{n+k})$, and where $\mathbf{C}_0$ an $(n-m)$-dimensional cone in $\mathbf{R}^{n-m+k}$ with $\operatorname{sing} \mathbf{C}_0 = \{0\}$ such that $\mathbf{C}_0 \cap S^{n-m+k-1}$ is a smooth compact $(n - m - 1)$-dimensional submanifold of $S^{n-m+k-1}$ (a finite set of points when $m = n - 1$).

For a detailed discussion of all these points we refer to [SL1]. * For the main structure theorem concerning the singular set we use the notation that

$$\operatorname{sing}_\alpha M = \{X \in \operatorname{sing} M \backslash S : \Theta_M(X) = \alpha\},$$

and we have to assume that all cylindrical cones $\mathbf{C}_0 \times \mathbf{R}^m \in \mathcal{M}$ have cross-section $\mathbf{C}_0$ which satisfies an "integrability condition" of a kind first introduced by Allard and Almgren [AA] in their work on asymptotics for minimal submanifolds near isolated singular points. Specifically, we have to assume that for all such $\mathbf{C}_0$ that all homogeneous degree one solutions $v = r\varphi(\omega)$ of the Jacobi-field equation $\mathcal{L}_{\mathbf{C}_0} v = 0$ are accounted for as initial velocities of 1-parameter families of minimal cones $\{\mathbf{C}_t\}_{t\in(-1,1)}$, where each $\mathbf{C}_t$ is a cone with vertex at 0, and where the initial velocity at $x_0 \in \mathbf{C}_0$ is defined by $\frac{\partial u(x,t)}{\partial t}|_{t=0}$, where $u(x,t)$ is the section of the normal bundle of $\mathbf{C}_0$ whose graph (i.e. $\{x + u(x,t) : x \in \mathbf{C}_0\}$) gives $\mathbf{C}_t$; it is assumed that such $u(x,t)$ exist and are smooth in $(x,t)$. Here $\mathcal{L}_{\mathbf{C}_0}$ is the Jacobi-field operator on the cone $\mathbf{C}_0$, obtained by linearizing (at 0) the area functional obtained by taking areas of graphs of smooth sections of the normal bundle $(T\mathbf{C}_0)^\perp$.

Then we have:

**Theorem 1 (Main structure theorem).** *Suppose $m$ is as in 1.1. Suppose also that, for each cylindrical cone $\mathbf{C} = \mathbf{C}_0 \times \mathbf{R}^m \in \mathcal{M}$, the cross-section $\mathbf{C}_0$ satisfies the integrability condition referred to above. Then for each $M \in \mathcal{M}$, $\operatorname{sing} M$ is countably $m$-rectifiable, and for each $\alpha > 1$ there is an open set $V_\alpha \supset \operatorname{sing}_\alpha M$ such that $\{X \in U_M : \Theta_M(X) \geq \alpha\}$ has locally finite $\mathcal{H}^m$-measure in $V_\alpha$; further any compact $K \subset U_M$ intersects $\operatorname{sing}_\alpha M$ for at most finitely many $\alpha$.*

An important point is that the troublesome integrability hypothesis in the above theorem is automatically satisfied if $m = n-1$ or $m = n-2$. For example if $m = n-2$ then any cylindrical cone $\mathbf{C} = \mathbf{C}_0 \times \mathbf{R}^m \in \mathcal{M}$ has 2-dimensional cross-section $\mathbf{C}_0$, so $\mathbf{C}_0$ must consist of a finite union of 2-dimensional planes $\cup_{j=1}^N P_j$, where each $P_j$ passes through the origin and where $P_j \cap P_j = \{0\}$ for $i \neq j$. (Because the only smooth connected compact embedded 1-dimensional minimal submanifolds of $S^{n+k-1}$ are the finite unions of pairwise disjoint great circles.) It is then straightforward to check that the integrability condition is satisfied. Likewise for $m = n-1$ (when $\mathbf{C}_0$ is simply a finite union of rays emanating from the origin), the integrability condition is easily checked.

Thus we have the following corollary of Theorem 1:

**Corollary 1.** *If $m$ is as in 1.1 and either $m = n-2$ or $m = n-1$, then for each $M \in \mathcal{M}$, $\operatorname{sing} M$ is countably $m$-rectifiable, and $\operatorname{sing}_\alpha M$ has locally finite $\mathcal{H}^m$-measure for each $\alpha$; in fact there is an open $V_\alpha \supset \operatorname{sing}_\alpha M$ such that $V_\alpha \cap \{X : \Theta_M(X) \geq \alpha\}$ has locally finite $\mathcal{H}^m$-measure in $V_\alpha$.*

Notice in particular that the class $\mathcal{T}_2$ of the regular sets of mod 2 minimizing currents in $\mathbf{R}^{n+k}$ form a multiplicity one class in the sense discussed above (by [FW], [R], [FH2]), and have $m = n-2$ (by [FH2]) for any $k \geq 2$. Furthermore (by [MF]) any cylindrical cone $\mathbf{C}_0 \times \mathbf{R}^{n-2} \in \mathcal{T}_2$ is such that $\mathbf{C}_0$ consists of a union of a collection of $j$ pairwise mutually orthogonal 2-planes in $\mathbf{R}^{k+2}$ (any pair of which have only the origin in common), where $2 \le j \le k/2+1$. We therefore also conclude from Corollary 1 the following:

**Corollary 2.** *Suppose $M$ is the interior regular set of a current $T$ which is mod 2 minimizing in $\mathbf{R}^{n+k}$. Then $\operatorname{sing} M (\equiv \overline{M} \setminus (M \cup \operatorname{spt} \partial_2 T)$, where $\partial_2 T$ is the mod 2 boundary of $T$) is countably $(n-2)$-rectifiable and, with $S_j$ denoting the set of all points $X \in \operatorname{sing} M$ such that $\operatorname{Tan}_X M$ contains a cylindrical cone $q(\mathbf{C}_0 \times \mathbf{R}^{n-2})$, with $q \in \mathrm{SO}(\mathbf{R}^{n+k})$ and $\mathbf{C}_0$ is a union of $j$ pairwise mutually orthogonal 2-planes in $\mathbf{R}^{k+2}$, $\dim(\operatorname{sing} M \setminus (\cup_{2 \le j \le k/2+1} S_j)) \le n-3$, $\operatorname{sing} M \setminus (\cup_{2 \le j \le k/2+1} S_j)$ is discrete for $n = 3$, and $S_j$ has locally finite $\mathcal{H}^{n-2}$-measure for each $j$.*

**Remark:** Notice that Corollary 1 actually implies the stronger result that for each $j$ there is an open $V_j \supset S_j$ such that $\operatorname{sing} M \cap \{X \in V_j : \Theta_M(X) \ge j\}$ has locally finite $\mathcal{H}^{n-2}$-measure in $V_j$.

All these theorems are a consequence of a technical decay lemma and the decomposition theorem described very briefly in §3 of this report. Some especially interesting results are obtained in the special case when it is possible to a *priori* rule out the first alternative of the technical lemma. One such result is the following:

**Corollary 3.** *If $\mathbf{V}$ is an $n$-dimensional stationary integral varifold in some open set $U \subset \mathbf{R}^{n+k}$ and if $X_0 \in U$ with $1 < \Theta_{\mathbf{V}}(X_0) < 2$, then, for some $\rho > 0$, $\operatorname{sing} \mathbf{V} \cap B_\rho(X_0)$ is the union of an embedded $(n-1)$-dimensional $C^{1,\alpha}$ manifold and a closed set of dimension $\le n-2$. If $n = 2$ we have the more precise conclusion that there is $\rho > 0$ such that either $\operatorname{sing} \mathbf{V} \cap B_\rho(X_0)$ is a properly embedded $C^{1,\alpha}$ Jordan arc with endpoints in $\partial B_\rho(X_0)$ or else is a finite union of properly embedded locally $C^{1,\alpha}$ Jordan arcs of finite length, each with one endpoint at $X_0$ and one endpoint in $\partial B_\rho(X_0)$.*

**Remark:** By a properly embedded locally $C^{1,\alpha}$ Jordan arc $\Gamma$ we mean a homeomorphic image of $[0,1]$ such that for each compact subarc $K \subset \Gamma$ not containing either of the endpoints of $\Gamma$ there is a $C^{1,\alpha}$ diffeomorphism of $[0,1]$ onto $K$.

Of course all of the above results extend to multiplicity one classes in a general $(n+k)$-dimensional Riemannian manifold; in view of the Nash embedding theorem, this can be achieved by simply allowing suitable non-zero term on the right in the first variation identity in (ii) above. For more details we refer to the discussion in §7 of [SL1].

## 2. Harmonic maps

The results for minimizing harmonic maps are completely analogous to the results of §1 above for minimal submanifolds. We let $N$ be a compact Riemannian manifold of dimension $p \geq 2$. Without loss of generality we assume by the Nash embedding theorem that $N$ is embedded in a Euclidean space $\mathbf{R}^P$. We let $U$ be any open subset of $\mathbf{R}^n$, equipped with a metric $g = \sum_{i,j=1}^n g_{ij}(X)dX^i dX^j$, where $(g_{ij}(X))$ is a positive definite matrix for each $X \in U$ and where each $g_{ij}$ of at least class $C^{2,\mu}$ on $U$ for some $\mu \in (0,1)$; henceforth $\mu$ is a fixed constant in $(0,1)$.

As usual (see [SU]) by a minimizing harmonic map $u : (U,g) \to N$ we mean a map $u : U \to N$ such that $u^j \equiv e_j \cdot u$, considered as a real-valued function on $U$, is in the Sobolev space $W^{1,2}_{loc}(U)$ and $\mathcal{E}_K(u) \leq \mathcal{E}_K(v)$ whenever $K$ is a compact subset of $U$ and whenever $v : U \to N$ with $v \equiv u$ outside $K$; here $\mathcal{E}_K(v)$ is the energy functional, defined by $\mathcal{E}_K(v) = \int_K \sum_{k=1}^P \sum_{i,j=1}^n g_{ij}(x)(D_i v^k)(D_j v^k)\sqrt{g}$, where $v^k \equiv e_k \cdot v$, assumed in $W^{1,2}_{loc}(U)$, and $g = \det(g_{ij})$.

We let $\mathcal{H}(N)$ denote any class of energy minimizing maps from open subsets $U \subset \mathbf{R}^n$, equipped with $C^{2,\mu}$ metrics $g$ as described above; $\mathcal{H}(N)$ is assumed to be closed under composition with rigid motions and homotheties of the domain, and also to be weakly compact in the appropriate sense. More precisely, we assume:

(i) $$u : (U,g) \to N \in \mathcal{H}(N) \Rightarrow u \circ \eta_{Y,\rho}^{-1} \circ q^{-1} : (q \circ \eta_{Y,\rho} U, \tilde{g}) \to N \in \mathcal{H}(N)$$

for any $Y \in \mathbf{R}^{n+k}$, $\rho > 0$, and $q \in \mathrm{SO}(\mathbf{R}^n)$; here $\tilde{g}$ denotes the naturally scaled metric $(q^{-1})^*(\sum_{i,j=1}^n g_{ij}(Y+\rho X))dX^i dX^j)$ on $q\eta_{Y,\rho}U$, written as the pull-back relative to $q^{-1}$ of the metric $\sum_{i,j=1}^n g_{ij}(Y+\rho X))dX^i dX^j$ on $\eta_{Y,\rho}U$.

(ii) If $u_j : (U_j, g^{(j)}) \to N \in \mathcal{H}(N)$, $j = 1,2,\ldots$, are such that $U_j \supset U$ ($U \subset R^n$ a fixed open set), if $\sup_j \sup_K \mathcal{E}_K(u_j)$, $\sup_j [g^{(j)}_{k\ell}]_{2,\mu,K}$, $\sup_j \sup_K \lambda_j^{-1} < \infty$ for each compact $K \subset U$, where $\lambda_j(X)$ is the minimum eigenvalue of $(g^{(j)}_{k\ell}(X))$ for each $X \in U_j$ and $[g^{(j)}_{k\ell}]_{2,\mu}$ is the usual $C^{2,\mu}$-norm of $g^{(j)}_{k\ell}$, then there is a subsequence $u_{j'}$ and a map $u : (\tilde{U}, \tilde{g}) \to N \in \mathcal{H}(N)$ with $\tilde{U} \supset U$, $u_{j'} \to u$ in $L^2_{loc}(U)$ and $g^{(j')}_{k\ell} \to \tilde{g}_{k\ell}$ relative to the $C^2$ norm on $U$.

(Notice that by the compactness theory of [SU], this is automatic if we select $\mathcal{H}(N)$ to be *all* the harmonic maps from open subsets of $\mathbf{R}^n$ (equipped with $C^{2,\mu}$ metrics) into $N$.)

Analogous to the minimal surface case we know (ii) and the monotonicity formula guarantee that for each $u : U \to N \in \mathcal{H}(N)$, each $X \in U$, and each sequence $\rho_j \downarrow 0$, there is a subsequence $\rho_{j'}$ such that $u_{\rho_{j'}} \to v$ in $L^2_{loc}(\mathbf{R}^n)$, where $u_\rho(Y) \equiv u(X + \rho Y)$ and where $v$ is a homogeneous degree zero map $\mathbf{R}^n \to N$. Such maps $v$ are called tangent maps of $u$ at $X$, and the set of all such (corresponding to all such sequences $\rho_j$, $\rho_{j'}$) is denoted $\mathrm{Tan}_X u$.

Analogous to the minimal submanifold case there is an integer $m$ with

**2.1** $$m = \max\{\dim \operatorname{sing} u \,:\, u \in \mathcal{H}(N)\},$$

and there are maps (called henceforth $m$-cylindrical maps) $\varphi : \mathbf{R}^{n-m} \times \mathbf{R}^m \to N$ in $\mathcal{H}(N)$ such that $\varphi(x,y) \equiv \varphi_0(|x|^{-1}x)$ for all $(x,y) \in (\mathbf{R}^{n-m}\backslash\{0\}) \times \mathbf{R}^m$, where $\varphi_0 : S^{n-m-1} \to N$ is a smooth harmonic map, henceforth called the cross-sectional map corresponding to the $m$-cylindrical map $\varphi$. In fact (by the analogue of the stratification result for the minimal case) we know that there is a set $S$ of Hausdorff dimension $m-1$ (discrete if $m = 1$) such that for all $X \in \operatorname{sing} u\backslash S$ there is (at least modulo composition with an isometry) such an $m$-cylindrical map $\varphi \in \operatorname{Tan}_X M$. For $\alpha > 0$ we let

$$\operatorname{sing}_\alpha u = \{X \in \operatorname{sing} u\backslash S \,:\, \Theta_u(X) = \alpha\}.$$

Analogous to the integrability condition for minimal cones described in §1, in the following theorem we need to assume that if $\varphi_0$ is the cross-sectional map corresponding to an $m$-cylindrical map $\varphi \in \mathcal{H}(N)$, and if $v$ is a smooth section of the pulled back tangent bundle $\varphi_0^* TN$ which satisfies the equation $\mathcal{L}_{\varphi_0} v = 0$, where $\mathcal{L}_{\varphi_0}$ is the linearization at $\varphi_0$ of the harmonic map operator (i.e. the the linearization at $\varphi_0$ of the Euler Lagrange operator of the energy functional for maps $S^{n-m-1} \to N$), then $v$ is generated as initial velocity of a 1-parameter family $\{\varphi_t\}_{t\in(-1,1)}$ of harmonic maps $S^{n-m-1} \to N$. Thus each $\varphi_t$ a smooth harmonic map of $S^{n-m-1} \to N$, $\varphi_t(x)$ depends smoothly on the joint variables $(x,t)$, and $v = \frac{\partial \varphi_t(x)}{\partial t}\big|_{t=0}$.

Then analogous to Theorem 1 of §1 we have the following:

**Theorem 2.** *Suppose $u : U \to N$ is in $\mathcal{H}(N)$, $m$ is as in 2.1, and all $m$-cylindrical maps $\varphi \in \mathcal{H}(N)$ are such that the above integrability condition holds. Then* $\operatorname{sing} u$ *is countably $m$-rectifiable, and for each $\alpha > 0$ there is an open set $V_\alpha \subset U$ such that $\operatorname{sing}_\alpha u \subset V_\alpha$ and $\{X \in U : \Theta_u(X) \geq \alpha\}(\supset \operatorname{sing}_\alpha u)$ has locally finite $m$-dimensional Hausdorff measure in $V_\alpha$. Furthermore for each compact $K \subset U$ we have $\operatorname{sing}_\alpha u \cap K \neq \emptyset$ for at most finitely many $\alpha$.*

Gulliver and White [GW] have shown that the above integrability hypothesis is always satisfied in case $m = n-3$ and $\dim N = 2$, so as a corollary of the above theorem we have the following:

**Corollary 4.** *If $\mathcal{H}(N)$ is the set of all minimizing harmonic maps from open subsets $U \subset \mathbf{R}^n$, equipped with $C^{2,\mu}$ Riemannian metrics, into $N$, if $\dim N = 2$, and if $u : U \to N \in \mathcal{H}(N)$, then* $\operatorname{sing} u$ *is $(n-3)$-rectifiable and and for each $\alpha > 0$ there is an open set $V_\alpha$ such that $\operatorname{sing}_\alpha u \subset V_\alpha \subset U$ and $\{X \in V_\alpha : \Theta_u(X) \geq \alpha\}(\supset \operatorname{sing}_\alpha u)$ has locally finite $(n-3)$-dimensional Hausdorff measure in $V_\alpha$.*

Harmonic maps also admit analogues of the more precise results exemplified for minimal submanifolds by Corollary 3. For example:

**Corollary 5.** *If $\mathcal{H}(N)$ is as in Corollary 4, and if either $N = S^2$ with its standard metric or with a metric sufficiently close in the $C^2$ sense to the standard metric, then for any $u \in \mathcal{H}(N)$, $\operatorname{sing} u$ is the disjoint union of an embedded $(n-3)$-dimensional submanifold and a closed set of dimension $\leq n-4$. If $n = 4$ then the singular set is the union of finitely many $C^{1,\alpha}$ Jordan arcs of finite length together with a discrete set of points.*

The proof of Corollary 5 is based on Corollary 4 and a result of Brezis, Coron and Lieb, which asserts that a homogeneous degree zero locally minimizing harmonic map from $\mathbf{R}^3$ into $S^2$ is either a constant or else restricts to $S^2$ to give a conformal transformation of $S^2$ which is topologically of degree 1.

We should mention here that in the setting of the above corollary, in the case $n = 4$, Hardt and Lin [HL] have previously established that the singular set consists of a finite union of $C^{0,\alpha}$ curves together with a discrete set.

### 3. Remarks on the proofs.

The key ingredient, on which all the results above depend, is a technical decay lemma. In the case of minimal submanifolds, this lemma says roughly that, if $M \subset \mathcal{M}$ and if $M$ is close to $\mathbf{C}$ in a ball $B_\rho(0)$ in a suitable $L^2$ sense (made precise in [SL1]), where $\mathbf{C} = \mathbf{C}_0 \times \mathbf{R}^m$ is a cylindrical cone having cross-section $\mathbf{C}_0$ satisfying the integrability condition of Theorem 1 above, then either there is a significant "gap" in the part of the singular set consisting of points $X \in B_\rho$ where the density $\Theta_M(X)$ of $M$ at $X \geq$ the density $\Theta_{\mathbf{C}}(0)$ of $\mathbf{C}$ at 0, or else there is a cylindrical cone $\tilde{\mathbf{C}}$ close to $\mathbf{C}$ such that the quantity $\rho^{-n-2}\int_{M\cap B_\rho} \operatorname{dist}^2(X, \tilde{\mathbf{C}})$ decays by a fixed factor as we reduce radius by a fixed factor. (For a precise statement, the reader is referred to [SL1]; the analogous lemma for harmonic maps appears in [SL4].)

We shall not give any details about the proof of the technical lemma, except to say that it is proved by capitalizing on the fact that if the first alternative *fails*, then very good $L^2$ estimates (measuring deviation of $M$ away from cylindrical cones $\mathbf{C}_0 \times \mathbf{R}^m$) can be obtained, thus making it feasible to use a "blowup" argument to prove that the second alternative must hold.

We emphasize that methods involving "improvement of excess" as in the second alternative of the above are by now quite standard in regularity theory (see e.g. [DeG], [AF2], [G], [AW1,2], [SS], [SU], [GG]); however, a result like the above lemma (which says that either we get excess improvement or else there is a significant gap in the singular set) has not, as far as we are aware, been previously utilized.

By making careful use of the alternatives of the above lemma in balls $B_\rho(Y)$, where $\rho \leq \rho_0/2$ and $Y \in \{X \in B_{\rho_0}(X_0) : \Theta_M(X) \geq \alpha\}$, where $X_0 \in \operatorname{sing}_\alpha M$ and $\rho_0$ is chosen suitably small, we can iteratively apply the above technical lemma as long as the alternative (i) fails. Thus (with fixed $\theta \in (0, 1/4)$ chosen suitably) we see that if $Y \in T_\infty$, where $T_\infty \subset \operatorname{sing} M$ is the set where, after a translation taking $Y$ to 0, the first alternative fails at a sequence $\rho = \rho_0\theta^i$, $i = 1, 2, \ldots$, then

$$\theta^{-(i+1)(n+2)} \int_{M_0 \cap B_{\theta^{i+1}\rho_0}(0)} \operatorname{dist}^2(X, \mathbf{C}_{i+1}) \le 2^{-2i}\epsilon^2 \rho_0^{n+2}$$

for a suitable sequence $\{\mathbf{C}_i\}$ of cylindrical cones, where $\epsilon > 0$ is as small as we please (provided $\rho_0$ is taken small enough, depending on $\epsilon$ and $X_0$), and where $M_0$ is the image of $M$ under the translation $X \mapsto X - Y$. It then follows (by more or less standard arguments) that $T_\infty$ is contained in an embedded $C^1$ manifold $L$. On the other hand, the sets $T_j$ where the first alternative fails at a sequence $\rho = \theta^i \rho_0$, $i = 1, 2, \ldots, j-1$, and where the first alternative holds at $\rho = \rho_0\theta^j$ can be (with the aid of a covering lemma—making use of the "gaps" in the singular set guaranteed by the first alternative) covered by balls $\{B_{\rho_k}(Y_k)\}$ such that $\sum_k \rho_k^m \le (1-\delta)\rho_0^m$. Thus in a suitably small neighbourhood of each point $X_0 \in \operatorname{sing}_\alpha M$ we obtain a "decomposition theorem" which says that, for suitable $\delta \in (0,1)$,

$$\{X \in B_{\rho_0}(X_0) : \Theta_M(X) \ge \Theta_{\mathbf{C}}(0)\} = \Gamma_1 \cup \Gamma_2,$$

$\Gamma_1 \subset L$, $L$ an $m$-dimensional embedded $C^{1,\alpha}$ manifold with $\operatorname{vol}(L) \le \omega_m \rho_0^m$, and $\Gamma_2 \subset \cup_j B_{\rho_j}(X_j)$ for some family $B_{\rho_j}(X_j)$ of balls with $\sum_{j=1}^N \rho_j^m \le (1-\delta)\rho_0^m$. The nature of this result suggests the possibility of repeated iteration, starting at the second stage with a suitable scaling and translation of $M \cap B_{\rho_j}(X_j)$ in place of $M \cap B_{\rho_0}(X_0)$. Such an iteration is indeed possible under the appropriate circumstances (the main point is that one must be able to check the starting hypotheses at each new stage), and the main theorem about the structure of the singular set (Theorem 1 of §1) is obtained in exactly this way.

The proof of the results of §2 for harmonic maps are entirely analogous, depending again on a technical decay lemma of exactly the same type, and a consequent decomposition theorem.

For complete details of the arguments, the reader is referred to [SL1,4].

## References

[AA] W. Allard & F. Almgren, *On the radial behavior of minimal surfaces and the uniqueness of their tangent cones*, Ann. of Math. **113** (1981), 215–265.

[AW1] W. Allard, *On the first variation of a varifold*, Annals of Math. **95** (1972), 417–491.

[AF1] F. Almgren, *Q-valued functions minimizing Dirichlet's integral and the regularity of of area minimizing rectifiable currents up to codimension two*, Preprint.

[AF2] F. Almgren, *Existence and regularity almost everywhere of solutions to elliptic variational problems among surfaces of varying topological type and singularity structure,* Annals of Math. **87** (1968), 321–391.

[BCL] H. Brezis, J.-M. Coron, & E. Lieb, *Harmonic maps with defects,* Comm. Math. Physics **107** (1986), 82–100.

[DeG] E. De Giorgi, *Frontiere orientate di misura minima,* Sem. Mat. Scuola Norm. Sup. Pisa (1961), 1–56.

[FH1] H. Federer, Geometric Measure Theory, Springer-Verlag, Berlin–Heidelberg–New York (1969).

[FH2] H. Federer, *The singular sets of area minimizing rectifiable currents with codimension one and of area minimizing flat chains modulo two with arbitrary codimension,* Bull. A.M.S. **76** (1970), 767–771.

[FW] W. Fleming, *Flat chains over a finite coefficient group,* Trans. A.M.S. **121** (1966), 160–186.

[G] E. Giusti, Minimal surfaces and functions of bounded variation, Birkhäuser, Boston, 1984.

[GG] M. Giaquinta & E. Giusti, *The singular set of the minima of certain quadratic functionals,* Ann. Scuola Norm. Sup. Pisa **11** (1984), 45–55

[HL] R. Hardt & F.-H. Lin, *The singular set of an energy minimizing map from $B^4$ to $S^2$*, Preprint (1990).

[MF] F. Morgan, *On the singular structure of two-dimensional area minimizing surfaces in $\mathbf{R}^n$*, Math. Annalen **261** (1982), 101–110.

[R] R. E. Reifenberg, *Solution of the Plateau problem for m-dimensional surfaces of varying topological type,* Acta. Math. **104** (1960), 1–92.

[SS] R. Schoen & L. Simon, *Regularity of stable minimal hypersurfaces,* Comm. Pure Appl. Math. **34** (1981), 741–797.

[SU] R. Schoen & K. Uhlenbeck, *A regularity theory for harmonic maps,* J. Diff. Geom. **17** (1982), 307–336.

[SL1] L. Simon, *Cylindrical Tangent Cones and the Singular Set of Minimal Submanifolds*, Preprint, 1991

[SL2] L. Simon, *Entire solutions of the minimal surface equation*, J. Diff. Geom. **30** (1989), 643–688.

[SL3] L. Simon, Lectures on Geometric Measure Theory, Proceedings of the Centre for Mathematical Analysis, Australian National University, **3** (1983).

[SL4] L. Simon, *On the singularities of harmonic maps* (In preparation).

[TJ1] J. E. Taylor, *Regularity of the singular sets of of two dimensional area minimizing flat chains modulo 3 in* $\mathbf{R}^3$, Inventiones Math. **22** (1973), 119–139.

[TJ2] J. E. Taylor, *The structure of singularities in soap bubbles and soap-film-like minimal surfaces,* Ann. of Math. **103** (1976), 489–539.

[WB1] B. White, *Regularity of the singular sets in immiscible fluid interfaces and solutions to other Plateau-type problems,* Proc. C.M.A. (Canberra), **10** (1985), 244–249.

[WB2] B. White, To appear.

G ALLAIRE

# Homogenization of the unsteady Stokes equations in porous media

**0) Introduction.**

In [7] J.L. Lions studied the homogenization of the evolution Stokes problem in a periodic porous medium $\Omega_\varepsilon$ (of period $\varepsilon$)

$$\begin{cases} \dfrac{\partial u_\varepsilon}{\partial t} + \nabla p_\varepsilon - \varepsilon^2 \Delta u_\varepsilon = f \ , \quad div\ u_\varepsilon = 0 \quad in\ \Omega_\varepsilon \\ u_\varepsilon = 0 \quad on\ \partial\Omega_\varepsilon \ , \quad u_\varepsilon(t{=}0,x) = a_\varepsilon(x) \end{cases} \tag{0.1}$$

where $u_\varepsilon$ and $p_\varepsilon$ denote the velocity and pressure of the fluid, $f$ the density of forces acting on the fluid, and $a_\varepsilon$ an initial condition for the velocity. By means of formal asymptotic expansions (see [5], [12]) he derived the homogenized problem for (0.1) as $\varepsilon$ goes to zero

$$\begin{cases} u(t,x) \ = \ a(t,x) + \displaystyle\int_0^t A(t-s)[f - \nabla p](s,x)\, ds \quad in\ [0,T]\times\Omega \\ div\ u = 0 \quad in\ \Omega, \quad u.n \ = \ 0 \quad on\ \partial\Omega \end{cases} \tag{0.2}$$

where $u$ and $p$ denote the limit velocity and pressure, $a$ is an initial condition which depends on $a_\varepsilon$ and decays exponentially in time, and $A(t)$ is a symmetric permeability tensor. Problem (0.2) is a Darcy's law with memory which generalizes the usual Darcy's law obtained by homogenization of the steady Stokes equations [1], [6], [7], [12], [14].

The purpose of the present paper is to rigorously prove the convergence of the homogenization process, i.e. the convergence of the solutions $(u_\varepsilon, p_\varepsilon)$ of (0.1) to the solution $(u, p)$ of (0.2) (see theorems 3.1 and 3.2). To this end, we use the new "two-scale convergence method" which was first introduced by G. Nguetseng [11], and further developed by the author [3], [4]. Loosely speaking, it is a rigorous justification of two-scale asymptotic expansions (see [5], [6], [12]), and thus, it is an alternative to the so-called "energy method" of L. Tartar [13]. Actually, besides the homogenization result itself, the main interest of the present paper is to demonstrate the power and the simplicity of the two-scale convergence method in the homogenization of a concrete example. The paper is organized as follows : section 1 is devoted to the setting of the problem, basic facts about two-scale convergence are introduced in section 2, while the main results are proved in section 3.

## 1) Setting of the problem.

As in [5], or [12], a periodic porous medium is defined by a domain $\Omega$ and an associated microstructure, or periodic cell $Y = [0;1]^N$, which is made of two complementary parts : the fluid part $Y_f$, and the solid part $Y_s$ ($Y_f \cup Y_s = Y$ and $Y_f \cap Y_s = \emptyset$). More precisely, we assume that $\Omega$ is a smooth, bounded, connected set in $\mathbb{R}^N$, and that $Y_f$ is a subset of $Y$ which is smooth and connected in the unit torus, i.e. $Y$ with periodic boundary condition (equivalently, the $Y$-periodic subset of $\mathbb{R}^N$, of period $Y_f$, is smooth and connected). The microscale of a porous medium is a (small) positive number $\varepsilon$. The domain $\Omega$ is covered by a regular mesh of size $\varepsilon$ : each cell $Y_i^\varepsilon$ is of the type $[0;\varepsilon]^N$, and is divided in a fluid part $Y_{f_i}^\varepsilon$ and a solid part $Y_{s_i}^\varepsilon$, i.e. is similar to the unit cell $Y$ rescaled to size $\varepsilon$. The fluid part $\Omega_\varepsilon$ of a porous medium is defined by

$$\Omega_\varepsilon = \Omega - \bigcup_{i=1}^{N(\varepsilon)} Y_{s_i}^\varepsilon = \Omega \cap \bigcup_{i=1}^{N(\varepsilon)} Y_{f_i}^\varepsilon \tag{1.1}$$

where the number of cells is $N(\varepsilon) = |\Omega| \varepsilon^{-N} [1+o(1)]$. Throughout the present paper, we assume that $\Omega_\varepsilon$ is a smooth, connected set in $\mathbb{R}^N$.

**Remark 1.1.**

This assumption on $\Omega_\varepsilon$ is of no fundamental importance in the sequel, but it appeals some comments from a technical point of view. It is automatically satisfied if the solid part $Y_s$ is strictly included in the cell $Y$, and if we removed the solid parts $Y_{s_i}^\varepsilon$ which meet the boundary $\partial\Omega$ (see [12], and [14]). However, this is not the case when the solid part $Y_s$ meets the boundary of the cell $Y$ (near the boundary $\partial\Omega$, there may be some small connected components of $\Omega_\varepsilon$, and the boundary of $\Omega_\varepsilon$ may be not smooth due to "wild" intersections between $\partial\Omega$ and $\partial Y_{f_i}^\varepsilon$, see [1]). Fortunately, the assumption on $\Omega_\varepsilon$, being smooth and connected, is by no means necessary for the sequel, but, since avoiding it introduces some technicalities, we are going to use it anyway, in order to simplify the exposition.

We consider the unsteady Stokes equations in the fluid domain $\Omega_\varepsilon$ with a Dirichlet boundary condition. We denote by $u_\varepsilon$ and $p_\varepsilon$ the velocity and pressure of the fluid, $f$ the density of forces acting on the fluid, and $a_\varepsilon$ an initial condition for the velocity. We assume that the density of the fluid is equal to 1, while its viscosity is very small, and indeed is exactly $\varepsilon^2$ (where $\varepsilon$ is the microscale). The system of equations is

$$\begin{cases} \dfrac{\partial u_\varepsilon}{\partial t} + \nabla p_\varepsilon - \varepsilon^2 \Delta u_\varepsilon = f \ , \quad div\ u_\varepsilon = 0 \quad in\ \Omega_\varepsilon \\ u_\varepsilon = 0 \quad on\ \partial\Omega_\varepsilon \ , \quad u_\varepsilon(t{=}0,x) = a_\varepsilon(x). \end{cases} \tag{1.2}$$

**Remark 1.2.**

The scaling $\varepsilon^2$ of the viscosity is not surprising : indeed it is well-known (see [6], [7], and [12]), that it is the precise scaling which gives a non-zero limit for the velocity $u_\varepsilon$ as $\varepsilon$ goes to zero. The scaling 1 of the density is the precise one that keeps a dependence on time for the limit problem. With these scalings, system 1.2 was studied by J.L. Lions [7], using formal asymptotic expansions. A. Mikelic [10] studied (1.2) with an $\varepsilon^2$ scaling for the density, leading to a limit problem, different from ours, and with no inertial terms.

In (1.2), the force $f(t,x)$ is given in $[L^2([0,T]\times\Omega)]^N$, and the initial condition $a_\varepsilon(x)$ belongs to $[H_0^1(\Omega_\varepsilon)]^N$. Furthermore, denoting by $\tilde{\cdot}$ the extension operator by zero in $\Omega-\Omega_\varepsilon$, we assume that $\tilde{a}_\varepsilon$ satisfies

$$\|\tilde{a}_\varepsilon\|_{L^2(\Omega)} + \varepsilon\,\|\nabla\tilde{a}_\varepsilon\|_{L^2(\Omega)} \leq C \quad \textit{and} \quad \textit{div}\ a_\varepsilon = 0 \quad \textit{in}\ \Omega_\varepsilon\,. \tag{1.3}$$

**Proposition 1.3.**

The Stokes equations (1.2) admits a unique solution $u_\varepsilon \in L^2(\,[0,T]\,;\,H_0^1(\Omega_\varepsilon)^N\,)$, and $p_\varepsilon \in L^2(\,[0,T]\,;\,L^2(\Omega_\varepsilon)/\mathbb{R}\,)$. Furthermore, the extension by zero of the velocity $\tilde{u}_\varepsilon$ satisfies the a priori estimates

$$\|\tilde{u}_\varepsilon\|_{L^\infty([0,T];L^2(\Omega))} + \varepsilon\,\|\nabla\tilde{u}_\varepsilon\|_{L^\infty([0,T];L^2(\Omega))} \leq C\ , \quad \textit{and} \quad \left\|\frac{\partial\tilde{u}_\varepsilon}{\partial t}\right\|_{L^2([0,T]\times\Omega)} \leq C \tag{1.4}$$

where the constant $C$ does not depend on $\varepsilon$. (The proof is left to the reader.)

**Proposition 1.4.**

There exists an extension $P_\varepsilon$ of the pressure defined in $L^2(\,[0,T]\,;\,L^2(\Omega)/\mathbb{R}\,)$ by

$$P_\varepsilon = p_\varepsilon \quad \textit{in}\ \Omega_\varepsilon\ , \quad \textit{and} \quad P_\varepsilon = \frac{1}{|Y^\varepsilon_{f_i}|}\int_{Y^\varepsilon_{f_i}} p_\varepsilon \quad \textit{in each}\ Y^\varepsilon_{s_i} \tag{1.5}$$

and a constant $C$, which does not depend on $\varepsilon$, such that

$$\|P_\varepsilon\|_{L^2([0,T];L^2(\Omega)/\mathbb{R})} \leq C. \tag{1.6}$$

**Proof.**

Proposition 1.4 is a mere combination of previous results of [14], [1], and [9]. We briefly sketch its proof. Introducing a projection operator $R_\varepsilon$ from $H_0^1(\Omega)^N$ in $H_0^1(\Omega_\varepsilon)^N$, the extension $P_\varepsilon$ is defined, a.e. in time, by

$$< \nabla P_\varepsilon, v >_{H^{-1},H_0^1(\Omega)} \; = \; < \nabla p_\varepsilon, R_\varepsilon v >_{H^{-1},H_0^1(\Omega_\varepsilon)} \quad \text{for any } v \in H_0^1(\Omega)^N. \tag{1.7}$$

Due to properties of the operator $R_\varepsilon$ (see [14] in the case of isolated obstacles, and [1] in the case of connected obstacles), definition (1.7) makes sense. Estimate (1.6) is deduced from (1.7) by integration by parts, and using the estimates (1.4) on the velocity. Finally, the equivalent definition (1.5) is obtained from (1.7) by choosing suitable functions $v$ with compact support in $Y_i^\varepsilon$ and $Y_{s_i}^\varepsilon$ (see [9]). We point out that the assumption on $\Omega_\varepsilon$, being smooth and connected, is used only here (without that assumption, the extension $P_\varepsilon$ would be merely defined and bounded in $L^2_{loc}(\Omega)$).

Since (extensions of) the velocity $u_\varepsilon$ and the pressure $p_\varepsilon$ are bounded sequences as $\varepsilon$ goes to zero, we can extract a subsequence such that they converge to a limit velocity $u$ and pressure $p$. The homogenization process amounts to find a system of equations (the homogenized problem) satisfied by $u$ and $p$. For this purpose, we introduce in the next section a new method of homogenization, called the two-scale convergence method.

**2) Two-scale convergence.**

Let $C_\#^\infty(Y)$ be the space of infinitely differentiable functions in $\mathbb{R}^N$ which are periodic of period $Y$. Denote by $L_\#^2(Y)$ (resp. $H_\#^1(Y)$) its completion for the norm of $L^2(Y)$ (resp. $H^1(Y)$). (Remark that $L_\#^2(Y)$ actually coincides with the space of functions in $L^2(Y)$ extended by $Y$-periodicity to the whole of $\mathbb{R}^N$.)

Following the lead of G. Nguesteng [11], we introduce the following

**Definition 2.1.**

A sequence of functions $u_\varepsilon$ in $L^2(\Omega)$ is said to *two-scale converge* to a limit $u_0(x,y)$ belonging to $L^2(\Omega\times Y)$ if, for any function $\psi(x,y)$ in $D[\Omega;C_\#^\infty(Y)]$, we have

$$\lim_{\varepsilon\to 0} \int_\Omega u_\varepsilon(x)\psi(x,\frac{x}{\varepsilon})\,dx = \iint_{\Omega Y} u_0(x,y)\psi(x,y)\,dxdy\ . \tag{2.1}$$

This new notion of "two-scale convergence" makes sense because of the next compactness theorem.

**Theorem 2.2.**

From each bounded sequence $u_\varepsilon$ in $L^2(\Omega)$ one can extract a subsequence, and there exists a limit $u_0(x,y) \in L^2(\Omega\times Y)$ such that this subsequence two-scale converges to $u_0$.

Theorem 2.2 is proved in [3], [4], [11]. The main idea of two-scale convergence is that, if a sequence $u_\varepsilon(x)$ is given as an expansion of the type

$u_0(x,\frac{x}{\varepsilon}) + \varepsilon u_1(x,\frac{x}{\varepsilon}) + \varepsilon^2 u_2(x,\frac{x}{\varepsilon}) + \cdots$, where the functions $u_i(x,y)$ are $Y$-periodic in $y$, then the first term of the expansion actually coincides with the two-scale limit of $u_\varepsilon$. Loosely speaking, two-scale convergence captures the oscillations of a sequence which are in resonance with that of the test functions $\psi(x,\frac{x}{\varepsilon})$. For a given sequence $u_\varepsilon$, there is more information in its two-scale limit $u_0$ than in its weak-$L^2$ limit $u$, since $u_0$ contains some knowledge on the periodic oscillations of $u_\varepsilon$, while $u$ is just an "average" of $u_\varepsilon$. These claims are made rigorous in the next proposition which establishes a link between two-scale and weak-$L^2$ convergences.

**Proposition 2.3.**

Let $u_\varepsilon$ be a sequence of functions in $L^2(\Omega)$ which two-scale converges to a limit $u_0(x,y) \in L^2(\Omega \times Y)$. Then $u_\varepsilon$ converges also to $u(x) = \int_Y u_0(x,y)\, dy$ in $L^2(\Omega)$ weakly. Furthermore, we have

$$\lim_{\varepsilon \to 0} \|u_\varepsilon\|_{L^2(\Omega)} \geq \|u_0\|_{L^2(\Omega \times Y)} \geq \|u\|_{L^2(\Omega)} . \tag{2.2}$$

**Proof.**

By taking test functions $\psi(x)$, which depends only on $x$, in (2.1), we immediately obtain that $u_\varepsilon$ weakly converges to $u(x) = \int_Y u_0(x,y)\, dy$ in $L^2(\Omega)$. Let $\psi(x,y)$ be a smooth $Y$-periodic function

$$\int_\Omega [u_\varepsilon(x) - \psi(x,\frac{x}{\varepsilon})]^2\, dx = \int_\Omega u_\varepsilon(x)^2\, dx + \int_\Omega \psi(x,\frac{x}{\varepsilon})^2\, dx - 2\int_\Omega u_\varepsilon(x)\psi(x,\frac{x}{\varepsilon})\, dx \geq 0.$$

Passing to the limit as $\varepsilon$ goes to zero yields

$$\lim_{\varepsilon \to 0} \int_\Omega u_\varepsilon(x)^2\, dx \geq 2\int_\Omega\int_Y u_0(x,y)\psi(x,y)\, dxdy - \int_\Omega\int_Y \psi(x,y)^2\, dxdy .$$

Then, using a sequence of smooth functions which converges strongly to $u_0$ in $L^2(\Omega \times Y)$ leads to the desired result.

The next theorem shows that, if a two-scale limit contains all the oscillations of a sequence (condition (2.3)), then one obtains a corrector-type result, i.e. a strong convergence for $u_\varepsilon(x) - u_0(x,\frac{x}{\varepsilon})$.

**Theorem 2.4.**

Let $u_\varepsilon$ be a sequence of functions in $L^2(\Omega)$ which two-scale converges to a limit $u_0(x,y) \in L^2(\Omega \times Y)$. Assume that

$$\lim_{\varepsilon \to 0} \| u_\varepsilon \|_{L^2(\Omega)} = \| u_0 \|_{L^2(\Omega \times Y)} \tag{2.3}$$

and that $u_0(x,y)$ is sufficiently smooth (see remark 2.5), then

$$\lim_{\varepsilon \to 0} \| u_\varepsilon(x) - u_0(x, \frac{x}{\varepsilon}) \|_{L^2(\Omega)} = 0. \tag{2.4}$$

A proof of theorem 2.4 may be found in [3], [4].

**Remark 2.5.**

In the definition 2.1 of two-scale convergence, we consider very smooth test functions $\psi(x,y)$ (which are also $Y$-periodic in $y$). Their regularity can be weakened, but not too much since $\psi(x, \frac{x}{\varepsilon})$ needs to be measurable. We emphasize that this problem of measurability is not purely technical, but is linked to possible counter-examples of the well-known convergence result for periodic functions which says that $\psi(x, \frac{x}{\varepsilon})$ converges to $\int_Y \psi(x,y)\, dy$ in a suitable weak topology. For more details, we refer the interested reader to [4]. Here, it is enough to know that the regularity assumption on the test function $\psi(x,y)$ in definition 2.1, or on the two-scale limit $u_0(x,y)$ in theorem 2.4, can be, e.g., either $L^2[\Omega; C_\#(Y)]$, or $L^2_\#[Y; C(\overline{\Omega})]$ (roughly speaking, continuity is needed in only one variable).

**Remark 2.6.**

Two-scale convergence also applies to sequences $u_\varepsilon(t,x)$ which depends on a dummy variable $t$ (here, $t$ stands for the time variable, and dummy means that the test functions do not oscillate with respect to $t$). Theorem 2.2 is easily generalized as follows: for any sequence $u_\varepsilon(t,x)$ bounded in $L^2([0,T] \times \Omega)$, there exists a function $u_0(t,x,y)$ in $L^2([0,T] \times \Omega \times Y)$ such that, up to a subsequence and for any $\phi(t) \in C^\infty([0,T])$ and $\psi(x,y) \in D[\Omega; C^\infty_\#(Y)]$, one has

$$\lim_{\varepsilon \to 0} \int_0^T \int_\Omega u_\varepsilon(t,x) \phi(t) \psi(x, \frac{x}{\varepsilon})\, dt dx = \int_0^T \int_\Omega \int_Y u_0(t,x,y) \phi(t) \psi(x,y)\, dt dx dy \,. \tag{2.5}$$

In the two-scale limit (2.5), the variable $t$ is merely a parameter, and the two-scale limit $u_0(t,x,y)$ does not capture any possible oscillations in $t$ of the sequence $u_\varepsilon$.

## 3) Main results.

This section is devoted to the homogenization of the unsteady Stokes equations (1.2). The proof of convergence of the homogenization process is based on the two-scale convergence results obtained in section 2. In theorem 3.1, the limit problem is presented as a "two-scale homogenized" problem. In theorem 3.2, the same limit problem is proved to be equivalent to the "usual" homogenized problem combined with the cell problem. Both formulations of the limit problem have their pros and cons as discussed in remark 3.3. All the results of this section are proved under the assumption that the entire sequence $\tilde{a}_\varepsilon$ (the initial conditions of the Stokes problem (1.2)) two-scale converges to a unique limit $a_0(x,y)$. Remark that the only point in this assumption is the uniqueness of the two-scale limit. This is a very natural assumption, which is automatically satisfied if $a_\varepsilon$ is itself the unique solution of a steady Stokes problem in $\Omega_\varepsilon$ (with a given force independent of $\varepsilon$).

**Theorem 3.1.**

The extension $(\tilde{u}_\varepsilon, P_\varepsilon)$ of the solution of (1.2) two-scale converges to the unique solution $(u_0(x,y), p(x))$ of the two-scale homogenized problem

$$\begin{cases} \dfrac{\partial u_0}{\partial t}(x,y) + \nabla_y p_1(x,y) + \nabla_x p(x) - \Delta_{yy} u_0(x,y) = f(x) \quad in\ [0,T]\times\Omega\times Y_f \\ div_y u_0(x,y) = 0 \quad in\ \Omega\times Y_f \quad \text{and} \quad div_x \left[ \int_Y u_0(x,y)\, dy \right] = 0 \quad in\ \Omega \\ u_0(x,y) = 0 \quad in\ \Omega\times Y_s \quad \text{and} \quad \left[ \int_Y u_0(x,y)\, dy \right].n = 0 \quad on\ \partial\Omega \\ y \rightarrow u_0, p_1 \quad Y\text{-periodic} \\ u_0(t=0) = a_0(x,y). \end{cases} \tag{3.1}$$

**Theorem 3.2.**

The extension $(\tilde{u}_\varepsilon, P_\varepsilon)$ of the solution of (1.2) converges, weakly in $[L^2(\Omega)]^N \times [L^2(\Omega)/I\!R]$, to the unique solution $(u,p)$ of the homogenized problem

$$\begin{cases} u(t,x) = a(t,x) + \int_0^t A(t-s)[f - \nabla p](s,x)\, ds \quad in\ [0,T]\times\Omega \\ div\ u(t,x) = 0 \quad in\ [0,T]\times\Omega \\ u(t,x).n = 0 \quad on\ [0,T]\times\partial\Omega \end{cases} \tag{3.2}$$

where $a(t,x)$ is an initial condition which depends only on the sequence $a_\varepsilon$ and on the microstructure $Y_f$, and $A(t)$ is a symmetric, positive definite, (permeability) tensor which depends only on the microstructure $Y_f$ (their precise form is to be found in the proof of the present theorem). Furthermore, the two-scale homogenized problem (3.1) is equivalent to (3.2) complemented with the cell problems (3.13)-(3.14), and $u(t,x) = \int_{Y_f} u_0(t,x,y)\, dy$, while the pressure $p(t,x)$ is the same in (3.1) and (3.2).

**Remark 3.3.**

The two-scale homogenized problem is also called a two pressures Stokes system (see [7]). The homogenized problem (3.2) is a Darcy's law with memory (due to the convolution in time). It is not difficult to check that both $a(t,x)$ and $A(t,x)$ decay exponentially in time. Thus, if the force $f$ is steady (i.e. does not depend on $t$), asymptotically, for large time $t$, we recover the usual steady Darcy's law for $u$ and $p$. In homogenization, the limit problem is usually presented as (3.2) (i.e. only macroscopic variables are used). However, in the present case, the elimination of the microscopic variable $y$ induces a complicate, integro-differential, type for (3.2). Thus, for establishing that the limit problem is well-posed (i.e. existence and uniqueness of solutions), the "two-scale" form (3.1) of the limit problem is preferable. Furthermore, compared to (3.2), (3.1) contains some supplementary informations (namely, the so-called cell problem is included in (3.1)), which yields a corrector result for the velocity (theorem 3.5). The two approaches (3.1) or (3.2) of the limit problem were also discussed earlier by J.L. Lions (see chapter 2.5 in [7]).

**Remark 3.4.**

The homogenization of the evolution Stokes problem (1.2) can also be considered in a domain $\Omega_\varepsilon$ with isolated obstacles $Y_{s_i}^\varepsilon$ of size $a_\varepsilon$ much smaller than the period $\varepsilon$. Using our previous results [2], it is easily seen that, when the obstacles are smaller than $\varepsilon$, but also larger than a given critical size (in 3-D, we require $\varepsilon^3 \ll a_\varepsilon \ll \varepsilon$), the corresponding homogenized system is a time dependent Darcy's law

$$\begin{cases} \dfrac{\partial u}{\partial t} + Mu + \nabla p = f \;, \quad div\; u = 0 \;\; in\;\; [0,T]\times\Omega \\ u.n = 0 \quad on\;\; [0,T]\times\partial\Omega \;, \quad u(t{=}0,x) = \bar{a}(x) \end{cases} \tag{3.3}$$

where $M$ is a constant tensor, and $\bar{a}$ is an initial condition. We emphasize that the two situations (obstacles of size, either $\varepsilon$, or much smaller than $\varepsilon$) are completely different : in particular, the homogenized problem (3.2) can not be written under the form (3.3).

**Theorem 3.5.**

Assume that the initial condition satisfies $\lim_{\varepsilon\to 0}\int_\Omega |\tilde{a}_\varepsilon(x)|^2 dx = \iint_{\Omega Y} |a_0(x,y)|^2 dxdy$. Then, the convergence of the velocity is improved : $\lim_{\varepsilon\to 0} \| u_\varepsilon(t,x) - u_0(t,x,\frac{x}{\varepsilon}) \|_{L^2([0,T]\times\Omega)} = 0.$

The remaining part of this section is devoted to the proofs of the previous results. In view of the estimates (1.4) on the velocity $u_\varepsilon$, we can state the following

**Lemma 3.6.**

There exists a limit $u_0(t,x,y) \in L^2([0,T]\times\Omega\ ;\ H^1_\#(Y)^N)$ such that, up to a subsequence, the sequences $\tilde{u}_\varepsilon$, $\varepsilon\nabla\tilde{u}_\varepsilon$, and $\partial\tilde{u}_\varepsilon/\partial t$ two-scale converge to $u_0$, $\nabla_y u_0$, and $\partial u_0/\partial t$ respectively. Furthermore, $u_0$ satisfies

$$\begin{cases} div_y u_0(t,x,y) = 0 \ \ in \ \Omega\times Y, \ \ and \quad div_x[\int_Y u_0(t,x,y)\, dy] = 0 \ \ in \ \Omega \\ u_0(t,x,y) = 0 \ \ in \ \Omega\times Y_s\ , \ \ and \quad [\int_Y u_0(t,x,y)\, dy].n = 0 \quad on \ \partial\Omega. \end{cases} \tag{3.4}$$

**Proof.**

By application of theorem 2.2 and remark 2.6, there exists three functions $u_0(t,x,y)$, $\xi_0(t,x,y)$, and $\zeta_0(t,x,y)$ in $L^2([0,T]\times\Omega\times Y)$ such that

$$\begin{cases} \lim_{\varepsilon\to 0}\int_0^T\int_\Omega u_\varepsilon(t,x).\phi(t)\psi(x,\frac{x}{\varepsilon})\, dtdx = \int_0^T\int_\Omega\int_Y u_0(t,x,y).\phi(t)\psi(x,y)\, dtdxdy \\ \lim_{\varepsilon\to 0}\int_0^T\int_\Omega \varepsilon\nabla u_\varepsilon(t,x).\phi(t)\Xi(x,\frac{x}{\varepsilon})\, dtdx = \int_0^T\int_\Omega\int_Y \xi_0(t,x,y).\phi(t)\Xi(x,y)\, dtdxdy \\ \lim_{\varepsilon\to 0}\int_0^T\int_\Omega \frac{\partial u_\varepsilon}{\partial t}(t,x).\phi(t)\psi(x,\frac{x}{\varepsilon})\, dtdx = \int_0^T\int_\Omega\int_Y \zeta_0(t,x,y).\phi(t)\psi(x,y)\, dtdxdy \end{cases} \tag{3.5}$$

for any $\psi(x,y) \in D[\Omega;C^\infty_\#(Y)]^N$, $\Xi(x,y) \in D[\Omega;C^\infty_\#(Y)]^{N^2}$, and $\phi(t) \in D([0,T])$. Integrating by parts and passing to the two-scale limit in the two last lines of (3.5) yields

$$\begin{cases} \lim_{\varepsilon\to 0}\int_0^T\int_\Omega u_\varepsilon\phi(t).div_y\Xi(x,\frac{x}{\varepsilon})\, dtdx = -\int_0^T\int_\Omega\int_Y \xi_0.\phi(t)\Xi(x,y)\, dtdxdy = \int_0^T\int_\Omega\int_Y u_0.\phi(t) div_y\Xi(x,y)\, dtdxdy \\ \lim_{\varepsilon\to 0}\int_0^T\int_\Omega u_\varepsilon.\frac{\partial\phi(t)}{\partial t}\psi(x,\frac{x}{\varepsilon})\, dtdx = -\int_0^T\int_\Omega\int_Y \zeta_0.\phi(t)\psi(x,y)\, dtdxdy = \int_0^T\int_\Omega\int_Y u_0.\frac{\partial\phi(t)}{\partial t}\psi(x,y)\, dtdxdy \end{cases}$$

Desintegrating by parts leads to $\xi_0 = \nabla_y u_0$ and $\zeta_0 = \partial u_0/\partial t$. Moreover, the incompressibility condition $div\ u_\varepsilon = 0$ yields $div_y u_0(x,y) = 0$ and $div_x[\int_Y u_0(x,y)dy] = 0$, by integrating by parts the first line of (3.5) with $\psi(x,y)$ successively equal to $\nabla_y \theta(x,y)$ and $\nabla_x \theta(x)$. The other properties (3.4) are also easily obtained by a proper choice of test functions in (3.5).

**Proof of theorem 3.1.**

Let $\phi(t) \in C^\infty([0,T])$ with $\phi(T) = 0$. Let $\psi(x,y) \in D[\Omega;C^\infty_\#(Y)]^N$ with $\psi(x,y) \equiv 0$ in $\Omega \times Y_s$ (thus, $\psi(x,\frac{x}{\varepsilon}) \in [H^1_0(\Omega_\varepsilon)]^N$). Multiplying equation (1.2) by $\varepsilon\phi(t)\psi(x,\frac{x}{\varepsilon})$ and integrating by parts in the space variable $x$ gives a single non-zero term when passing to the limit

$$\lim_{\varepsilon \to 0} \int_0^T\int_\Omega P_\varepsilon \phi(t) div_y \psi(x,\frac{x}{\varepsilon})\, dtdx = 0. \tag{3.6}$$

Since $P_\varepsilon$ is a bounded sequence in $L^2([0,T]\,;\,L^2(\Omega)/\mathbb{R})$ (see proposition 1.4), it admits a two-scale limit $p_0(t,x,y)$. Passing to the limit in (3.6), we deduce

$$\int_0^T\int_\Omega\int_Y p_0(t,x,y)\phi(t) div_y \psi(x,y)\, dtdxdy = 0,$$

which implies that $p_0$ does not depend on $y$ in $Y_f$. Using the particular form (1.5) of the extension $P_\varepsilon$ in $\Omega - \Omega_\varepsilon$, we obtain the same result in $Y_s$, namely $p_0(t,x,y) = p(t,x)$.

Next, we add to the previous assumptions on $\psi(x,y)$ the incompressibility condition $div_y \psi(x,y) = 0$. Multiplying equation (1.2) by $\phi(t)\psi(x,\frac{x}{\varepsilon})$, integrating by parts, and passing to the two-scale limit yields

$$\int_\Omega\int_Y a_0(x,y).\phi(0)\psi(x,y)\, dxdy - \int_0^T\int_\Omega\int_Y u_0(t,x,y).\frac{\partial\phi}{\partial t}(t)\psi(x,y)\, dtdxdy \tag{3.7}$$

$$- \int_0^T\int_\Omega\int_Y p(t,x)\phi(t) div_x \psi(x,y)\, dtdxdy + \int_0^T\int_\Omega\int_Y \nabla_y u_0(t,x,y).\phi(t)\nabla_y \psi(x,y)\, dtdxdy$$

$$= \int_0^T\int_\Omega\int_Y f(t,x)\phi(t).\psi(x,y)\, dtdxdy.$$

Since (3.7) holds for any functions $\phi$, with $\phi(T) = 0$, and $\psi$, with $\psi(x,y) \equiv 0$ in $\Omega \times Y_s$ and $div_y \psi(x,y) = 0$, and recalling that the orthogonal of divergence-free vector-functions is the set of all gradients (see lemma 3.8), there exists a pressure $p_1(t,x,y)$ such that

$$\frac{\partial u_0}{\partial t}(t,x,y) + \nabla_y p_1(t,x,y) + \nabla_x p(t,x) - \Delta_{yy} u_0(t,x,y) = f(t,x) \quad in \ [0,T]\times\Omega\times Y_f \, . \quad (3.8)$$

Together with (3.4) equation (3.8) is just the two-scale homogenized system (3.1). If (3.1) admits a unique solution, then the entire sequence ( $\tilde{u}_\varepsilon, P_\varepsilon$ ) converges to its unique solution ( $u_0(x,y)$ , $p(x)$ ). Thus, the proof of theorem 3.1 is completed by the next lemma 3.7.

**Lemma 3.7.**

There exists a unique solution $(u_0, p, p_1)$ of the two-scale homogenized system (3.1).

**Proof.**

Denote by $H^1_{0\#}(Y_f)$ the subspace of $H^1_\#(Y_f)$ composed of the functions which are zero on $\partial Y_f \cap \partial Y_s$. Let us define the Hilbert spaces

$$V = \left\{ v(x,y) \in L^2(\Omega; H^1_{0\#}(Y_f)^N) \ / \ div_y v = 0,\ div_x [\int_{Y_f} v dy] = 0,\ [\int_{Y_f} v dy].n_x = 0 \ on \ \partial\Omega \right\}, \quad (3.9)$$

$H$, the completion of $V$ in $[L^2(\Omega\times Y_f)]^N$, and, denoting by $V'$ the dual space of $V$,

$$E = \left\{ v(t,x,y) \ / \ v \in L^2([0,T];V),\ \frac{\partial v}{\partial t} \in L^2([0,T];V') \right\}, \text{ and } \ E_0 = \left\{ v \in E \ / \ v(T) = 0 \right\}.$$

Multiplying the equation (3.1) by a function $v \in E_0$, and integrating by parts leads to

$$\int_0^T\int_\Omega\int_{Y_f} \nabla_y u_0 . \nabla_y v \ dtdxdy - \int_0^T\int_\Omega\int_{Y_f} u_0 . \frac{\partial v}{\partial t} \ dtdxdy = \int_0^T\int_\Omega\int_{Y_f} f.v \ dtdxdy + \int_\Omega\int_{Y_f} a_0 . v(0) \ dxdy. \quad (3.10)$$

Since the left hand side of (3.10) is coercive on $E_0$, by application of the Lions lemma (see theorem 1.1, chapter 3, [8]), there exists a unique solution $u_0$ in $E \cap C([0,T];H)$ of the variational formulation (3.10). Furthermore, since $a_0 \in V$ and $f \in [L^2([0,T]\times\Omega)]^N$, the regularity of the solution is improved : $u_0 \in L^2([0,T]\times\Omega; H^2_\#(Y_f)^N)$ and $\partial u_0/\partial t \in L^2([0,T];H)$. It remains to prove that the variational formulation (3.10) is actually equivalent to the two-scale homogenized problem (3.1). The only difficulty is to obtain the two pressures $\nabla_x p(t,x) + \nabla_y p_1(t,x,y)$ when desintegrating by parts (3.10) : this is the purpose of the next lemma 3.8.

**Lemma 3.8.**

The orthogonal $V^\perp$ of the Hilbert space $V$, defined in (3.9), has the following characterization

$$V^\perp = \left\{ v(x,y) = \nabla_x \phi(x) + \nabla_y \phi_1(x,y) \text{ with } \phi \in H^1(\Omega), \text{ and } \phi_1 \in L^2(\Omega; L^2_\#(Y_f)) \right\}. \quad (3.11)$$

**Proof.**

Remark that $V = V_1 \cap V_2$ with

$$V_1 = \left\{ v(x,y) \in L^2(\Omega; H^1_{0\#}(Y_f)^N) \;/\; div_y v = 0 \right\}$$

$$V_2 = \left\{ v(x,y) \in L^2(\Omega; H^1_{0\#}(Y_f)^N) \;/\; div_x [\int_{Y_f} v dy] = 0, \; [\int_{Y_f} v dy].n_x = 0 \text{ on } \partial\Omega \right\}.$$

It is a well-known result (see, e.g., [15], [16]) that

$$V_1^\perp = \left\{ \nabla_y \phi_1(x,y) \;/\; \phi_1 \in L^2(\Omega; L^2_\#(Y_f)) \right\}, \text{ and } V_2^\perp = \left\{ \nabla_x \phi(x) \;/\; \phi \in H^1(\Omega) \right\}.$$

Since $V_1$ and $V_2$ are two closed subspaces, it is equivalent to say $(V_1 \cap V_2)^\perp = V_1^\perp + V_2^\perp$ or $V_1 + V_2 = \overline{V_1 + V_2}$. Indeed, we are going to prove that $V_1 + V_2$ is equal to $L^2(\Omega; H^1_{0\#}(Y_f)^N)$, which establishes that $V_1 + V_2$ is closed, and thus (3.11).

For $1 \le i \le N$, denote by $v_i(y)$ the unique solution in $[H^1_{0\#}(Y_f)]^N$ of the steady Stokes problem

$$\begin{cases} \nabla s_i - \Delta v_i = e_i \;, \; div\; v_i = 0 \text{ in } Y_f \\ v_i = 0 \text{ on } \partial Y_f \cap \partial Y_s \;, \; s_i, v_i \; Y\text{-periodic.} \end{cases}$$

For a given $v(x,y) \in L^2(\Omega; H^1_{0\#}(Y_f)^N)$, there exists a unique solution $p(x)$ in $H^1(\Omega)/\mathbb{R}$ of the Neuman problem

$$\begin{cases} div_x \left[ \sum_{i=1}^{N} \int_{Y_f} v_i(y) dy \; \frac{\partial p}{\partial x_i}(x) - \int_{Y_f} v(x,y) dy \right] = 0 \quad in\ \Omega \\ \left[ \sum_{i=1}^{N} \int_{Y_f} v_i(y) dy \; \frac{\partial p}{\partial x_i}(x) - \int_{Y_f} v(x,y) dy \right].n = 0 \quad on\ \partial\Omega \end{cases}$$

Remark that the constant matrix $( \int_{Y_f} v_i(y)\, dy )_{1 \le i \le N}$ is positive definite since $\int_{Y_f} v_i.e_j = \int_{Y_f} \nabla v_i . \nabla v_j$ . Then, decomposing $v$ as

$$v(x,y) = \sum_{i=1}^{N} v_i(y)\frac{\partial p}{\partial x_i}(x) + \left[ v(x,y) - \sum_{i=1}^{N} v_i(y)\frac{\partial p}{\partial x_i}(x) \right], \tag{3.12}$$

it is easy to see that the first term in the right hand side of (3.12) belongs to $V_1$, while the second one belongs to $V_2$.

Q.E.D.

**Proof of theorem 3.2.**

First, by virtue of proposition 2.3, the sequence $(\tilde{u}_\varepsilon, P_\varepsilon)$ converges to $( \int_Y u_0(x,y)dy \ , p(x) )$ (the average, with respect to $y$, of its two-scale limit) in $[L^2(\Omega)]^N \times [L^2(\Omega)/I\!R]$ weakly. Second, to obtain the homogenized problem (3.2), we separate the variables $x$ and $y$ in the two-scale homogenized problem (3.1). We decompose its solution $u_0$ in two parts $u_1 + u_2$ where $u_1$ is just the evolution (without any forcing term) of the initial condition $a_0$. Thus $u_1$ is the unique solution of

$$\begin{cases} \frac{\partial u_1}{\partial t}(t,x,y) + \nabla_y q(t,x,y) - \Delta_{yy} u_1(t,x,y) \ = \ 0 \quad in \ \Omega \times Y_f \\ div_y u_1(t,x,y) = 0 \quad in \ \Omega \times Y_f \\ u_1 \ = \ 0 \quad on \ \partial Y_f \cap \partial Y_s \ , \ \ y \rightarrow u_1, q \quad Y\text{-periodic} \\ w_i(t{=}0,x,y) = a_0(x,y). \end{cases} \tag{3.13}$$

The average of $u_1$ in $y$ is just $a(t,x)$ (the initial condition in the homogenized system (3.2)). On the other hand, $u_2$ is given by

$$u_2(t,x,y) \ = \ \int_0^t \sum_{i=1}^{N} [f_i \ - \ \frac{\partial p}{\partial x_i}](s,x)\frac{\partial w_i}{\partial t}(t-s,y) \ ds \tag{3.14}$$

where, for $1 \le i \le N$, $w_i$ is the unique solution of the cell problem

$$\begin{cases} \frac{\partial w_i}{\partial t}(t,y) + \nabla_y q_i(t,y) - \Delta_{yy} w_i(t,y) \ = \ e_i \quad in \ Y_f \\ div_y w_i \ = 0 \quad in \ Y_f \\ w_i \ = 0 \ \ on \ \partial Y_f \cap \partial Y_s \ , \ \ y \rightarrow w_i, q_i \quad Y\text{-periodic} \\ w_i(t{=}0,y) = 0. \end{cases} \tag{3.15}$$

Introducing the matrix $A$ defined by

$$A_{ij}(t) \ = \ \int_{Y_f} \frac{\partial w_i}{\partial t}(t,y) e_j \ dy, \tag{3.16}$$

we deduce (3.2) from (3.1), by averaging $u_1$ and $u_2$ with respect to $y$ (actually, (3.1) is equivalent to (3.2) combined with (3.13)-(3.16)). Eventually, using semi-group theory, one can prove that $A$ is symmetric, positive definite, and decays exponentially in time.

**Proof of theorem 3.5.**

Multiplying the Stokes equation (1.2) by $u_\varepsilon$ leads to

$$\frac{1}{2}\int_\Omega |\tilde{u}_\varepsilon(T)|^2 - \frac{1}{2}\int_\Omega |\tilde{a}_\varepsilon|^2 + \varepsilon^2 \int_0^T\int_\Omega |\nabla \tilde{u}_\varepsilon|^2 = \int_0^T\int_\Omega f.\tilde{u}_\varepsilon . \tag{3.17}$$

Multiplying the two-scale homogenized equation (3.1) by $u_0$ yields

$$\frac{1}{2}\int_\Omega\int_Y |u_0(T)|^2 - \frac{1}{2}\int_\Omega\int_Y |a_0|^2 + \int_0^T\int_\Omega\int_Y |\nabla_y u_0|^2 = \int_0^T\int_\Omega\int_Y f.u_0 . \tag{3.18}$$

The right hand side of (3.17) converges to that of (3.18), and by assumption so does $\int_\Omega |\tilde{a}_\varepsilon|^2$ to $\int_\Omega\int_Y |a_0|^2$. Thus, as $\varepsilon$ goes to zero,

$$\frac{1}{2}\int_\Omega |\tilde{u}_\varepsilon(T)|^2 + \varepsilon^2 \int_0^T\int_\Omega |\nabla \tilde{u}_\varepsilon|^2 \to \frac{1}{2}\int_\Omega\int_Y |u_0(T)|^2 + \int_0^T\int_\Omega\int_Y |\nabla_y u_0|^2 . \tag{3.19}$$

By virtue of proposition 2.3, the limit of each term on the left hand side of (3.19) is greater than its corresponding term in the right hand side. Thus

$$\lim_{\varepsilon\to 0} \int_\Omega |\tilde{u}_\varepsilon(T)|^2 = \int_\Omega\int_Y |u_0(T)|^2 .$$

By application of theorem 2.4, we obtain the desired result.

*Note added in proof.* After this work has been completed, I learned that similar results have been recently and independently obtained by M. Avellaneda and A. Mikelic.

**References.**

[1] G. Allaire, *Homogenization of the Stokes flow in a connected porous medium,* Asymptotic Analysis 2, pp.203-222 (1989).

[2] G. Allaire, *Homogenization of the Navier-Stokes equations in open sets perforated with tiny holes I-II,* Arch. Rat. Mech. Anal. 113, pp.209-259, pp.261-298 (1991).

[3] G. Allaire, *Homogénéisation et convergence à deux échelles, application à un problème de convection diffusion,* C. R. Acad. Sci. Paris, t. 312, I, pp.581-586 (1991).

[4] G. Allaire, *Homogenization and two-scale convergence,* in preparation.

[5] A. Bensoussan, J.L. Lions, G. Papanicolaou, *Asymptotic analysis for periodic structures,* North-Holland (1978).

[6] J.B. Keller, *Darcy's law for flow in porous media and the two-space method,* Lecture Notes in Pure and Appl. Math., 54, Dekker, New York (1980).

[7] J.L. Lions, *Some methods in the mathematical analysis of systems and their control,* Science Press, Beijing, Gordon and Breach, New York (1981).

[8] J.L. Lions, E. Magenes, *Problème aux limites non homogènes et applications, vol.1,* Dunod, Paris (1968).

[9] R. Lipton, M. Avellaneda, *A Darcy law for slow viscous flow past a stationary array of bubbles,* Proc. Roy. Soc. Edinburgh, 114A, pp.71-79 (1990).

[10] A. Mikelic, *Homogenization of Nonstationary Navier-Stokes equations in a Domain with a Grained Boundary,* to appear in Annali Mat. Pura ed Applicata.

[11] G. Nguetseng, *A general convergence result for a functional related to the theory of homogenization,* SIAM J. Math. Anal., vol.20 (3), pp.608-623 (1989).

[12] E. Sanchez-Palencia, *Non homogeneous media and vibration theory,* Lecture notes in physics 127, Springer Verlag (1980).

[13] L. Tartar, *Cours Peccot au Collège de France,* unpublished (1977).

[14] L. Tartar, *Convergence of the homogenization process,* Appendix of [12].

[15] L. Tartar, *Topics in Nonlinear Analysis,* Publications mathématiques d'Orsay 78.13, Université de Paris-Sud (1978).

[16] R. Temam, *Navier-Stokes equations,* North-Holland (1979).

Commissariat à l'Energie Atomique

LETR/SERMA/DMT

C.E.N. Saclay, F-91191 GIF sur YVETTE

G BELLETTINI, M PAOLINI AND C VERDI

# Numerical minimization of functionals with curvature by convex approximations

**1. Introduction.** We address the numerical minimization of the functional

$$(1.1)\qquad \mathcal{F}(v) := \int_\Omega |Dv| + \int_{\partial\Omega} \mu v \, d\mathcal{H}^{n-1} - \int_\Omega \kappa v \, dx, \qquad \forall\, v \in BV(\Omega; \{-1,1\}),$$

where $\Omega \subset \mathbf{R}^n$ $(n \geq 2)$ is a $C^{0,1}$ open bounded set, $\kappa \in L^\infty(\Omega)$, and $\mu \in L^\infty(\partial\Omega; [-1,1])$. It is well known [13] that any minimum of $\mathcal{F}$ is the characteristic function of a set $A \subseteq \Omega$ whose boundary has prescribed mean curvature $\kappa$ and contact angle $\arccos(\mu)$ at $\partial\Omega$.

The minimization of the functional $\mathcal{F}$ is just viewed as a model of geometrical type problems in the calculus of variations, that involve unknown interfaces and the related surface energy. Such problems may arise in important applicative fields, such as phase transition theories [7] and computer vision theory [22] (see also [9]), and their numerical solution seems quite difficult, because of the lack of convexity and regularity of the functionals at hand (see, e.g., [1,2,3,4,6,21]).

The relaxation of the functional $\mathcal{F}$ via a double well potential has been proposed in [20]. This leads to the numerical minimization of the regular, nonconvex, functionals

$$(1.2)\qquad \mathcal{G}_\sigma(v) := \int_\Omega \left[\sigma|\nabla v|^2 + \frac{1}{\sigma}(1-v^2) - \frac{\pi}{2}\kappa v\right] dx, \qquad \forall\, v \in H^1(\Omega; [-1,1]),$$

under suitable prescribed boundary conditions. In [2,3], we have discretized $\mathcal{G}_\sigma$ by linear finite elements and proved, under the relation $h = o(\sigma)$ between the meshsize $h$ and the relaxation parameter $\sigma$, the $\Gamma$-convergence of the discrete functionals $\mathcal{G}_{\sigma,h}$ to $\mathcal{F}$ in $L^1(\Omega)$, as $\sigma \to 0$.

A different approximation has been investigated in [5]. Noting that the minima of $\mathcal{F}$ in $BV(\Omega; \{-1,1\})$ can be found in terms of the minima of $\mathcal{F}$ on the larger, closed, convex, space $BV(\Omega; [-1,1])$, the (nonstrict) convexity of $\mathcal{F}$ can be exploited for its numerical minimization via finite element discretizations. Since the numerical algorithms perform better for strictly convex regular functionals, $\mathcal{F}$ is preliminarily regularized by

$$(1.3)\qquad \mathcal{F}_\varepsilon(v) = \int_\Omega \sqrt{\varepsilon^2 + |Dv|^2} + \int_{\partial\Omega} \mu v \, d\mathcal{H}^{n-1} - \int_\Omega \kappa v \, dx, \qquad \forall\, v \in BV(\Omega; [-1,1]),$$

which, in turn, are discretized by continuous linear finite elements. Letting $\varepsilon$ and $h$ go to 0 independently, in [5] we proved that $\Gamma\text{-}\lim \mathcal{F}_{\varepsilon,h} = \mathcal{F}$ in $L^1(\Omega)$, so that any family of discrete minima $\{u_{\varepsilon,h}\}_{\varepsilon,h}$ admits a subsequence converging to a minimum point $u$ of $\mathcal{F}$.

We stress that no relation between $\varepsilon$ and $h$ is required for the limit procedure and the stability of the convex minimization algorithm, whereas the nonconvex approximation converges if $h = o(\sigma)$ and is even unstable if $h > C^\star\sigma$, where $C^\star \leq 1$ is a precise stability constant depending on the finite element mesh [3]. Moreover, the relaxed solutions exhibit a $\mathcal{O}(\sigma)$-wide transition layer across the interfaces, which may make the numerical approximation quite inaccurate; this effect is absent in the convex approximations (see §5).

In §4 we describe the constrained Newton-like algorithm used for the minimization of the convex functionals $\mathcal{F}_{\varepsilon,h}$ and, in §5, we present several numerical experiments.

**2. The setting.** We state precisely the continuous and discrete functionals and recall some basic properties. Let $\mathcal{H}^{n-1}$ denote the $(n-1)$-dimensional Hausdorff measure in $\mathbf{R}^n$ [12] and $|\cdot|$ be the Lebesgue measure in $\mathbf{R}^n$. Let $BV(\Omega)$ be the space of the bounded variation functions in $\Omega$ and denote by $v \in L^1(\partial\Omega)$ the trace of $v \in BV(\Omega)$ on $\partial\Omega$. Let $\int_\Omega |Dv|$ denote the *total variation* in $\Omega$ and $\int_\Omega \sqrt{1+|Dv|^2}$ the *area* of any function $v \in BV(\Omega)$ [16, Defs. 1.1, 14.1]. For any set $E \subseteq \Omega$, let $\chi_E$ be its characteristic function, namely, $\chi_E(x) := 1$ if $x \in E$, $\chi_E(x) := -1$ if $x \in \Omega \setminus E$. Let $\widetilde{\mathcal{K}} := BV(\Omega;\{-1,1\})$ be the space of the characteristic functions of sets of finite perimeter in $\Omega$ and $\mathcal{K} := BV(\Omega;[-1,1])$. Finally, for any $v \in BV(\Omega)$, set $\{v > t\} := \{x \in \Omega : v(x) > t\}$ and note that $\chi_{\{v>t\}} \in \widetilde{\mathcal{K}}$, for a.e. $t \in \mathbf{R}$ [16].

The original functional $\mathcal{F}$, defined in (1.1) for $v \in BV(\Omega)$, admits at least a minimum point $u \in \mathcal{K}$, because $\mathcal{F}$ is bounded from below and lower semicontinuous in $\mathcal{K}$ with respect to the topology of $L^1(\Omega)$ [5,19]. We stress that $\min_{v\in\widetilde{\mathcal{K}}} \mathcal{F}(v) = \min_{v\in\mathcal{K}} \mathcal{F}(v)$ and that the minimum points of $\mathcal{F}$ in $\mathcal{K}$ give the minimum points of $\mathcal{F}$ in $\widetilde{\mathcal{K}}$, because [5]:

*if $u \in \mathcal{K}$ is a minimum point of $\mathcal{F}$ in $\mathcal{K}$, then, for a.e. $t \in [-1,1]$, the characteristic function $\chi_{\{u>t\}} \in \widetilde{\mathcal{K}}$ is a minimum point of $\mathcal{F}$ in $\widetilde{\mathcal{K}}$ and $\mathcal{F}(u) = \mathcal{F}(\chi_{\{u>t\}})$.*

In fact, using the coarea formula [16, Thm. 1.23] and the Cavalieri formula, we get

$$\mathcal{F}(v) = \frac{1}{2}\int_{-1}^{1} \mathcal{F}(\chi_{\{v>t\}})dt, \quad \text{that is} \quad \int_{-1}^{1} (\mathcal{F}(\chi_{\{v>t\}}) - \mathcal{F}(v))dt = 0, \qquad \forall\, v \in \mathcal{K}.$$

Then, the minimality of $u$ in $\mathcal{K}$ entails $\mathcal{F}(\chi_{\{u>t\}}) - \mathcal{F}(u) \geq 0$, whence $\mathcal{F}(u) = \mathcal{F}(\chi_{\{u>t\}})$, for a.e. $t \in [-1,1]$. In particular, $\mathcal{F}$ has a unique minimum point in $\widetilde{\mathcal{K}}$ if and only if $\mathcal{F}$ has a unique minimum in $\mathcal{K}$, and they coincide. Note that $\mathcal{F}$ may have relative minima in $\widetilde{\mathcal{K}}$: in view of the convexity of $\mathcal{F}$ in $\mathcal{K}$, they are no longer relative minima of $\mathcal{F}$ in $\mathcal{K}$.

Let us present some examples.

*Example 1.* In the trivial case $\mu, \kappa := 0$, $\chi_\emptyset$ and $\chi_\Omega$ are the absolute minima of $\mathcal{F}$ in $\widetilde{\mathcal{K}}$ so that, for any $0 \leq \lambda \leq 1$, $u^\lambda := 2\lambda - 1$ is an absolute minimum of $\mathcal{F}$ in $\mathcal{K}$. Any "minimum diameter" of $\Omega$ corresponds to a relative minimum of $\mathcal{F}$ in $\widetilde{\mathcal{K}}$.

*Example 2.* Let $\Omega := (-2,2)^2$, $\mu := 0$ on $|x_2| = 2$, $\mu = 1$ on $x_1 = -2$, $\mu := -1$ on $x_1 = 2$, and $\kappa := 0$. Then, for any $-2 \leq a \leq 2$, $u^a := \chi_{\{x_1 \geq a\}}$ is an absolute minimum of $\mathcal{F}$ in $\widetilde{\mathcal{K}}$, whereas any $x_1$-nondecreasing $x_2$-independent function is a minimum of $\mathcal{F}$ in $\mathcal{K}$.

*Example 3.* Let $\Omega := (-2,2)^2$, $\mu := 1$ (tangential contact at $\partial\Omega$), and $\kappa := r \in \mathbf{R}^+$. The functional $\mathcal{F}$ has one absolute minimum, $\chi_{A^r}$, where $A^r := \{([|x_1| - (2-\frac{1}{r})]_+)^2 + ([|x_2| - (2-\frac{1}{r})]_+)^2 \le \frac{1}{r^2}\}$, for any $r > \frac{2+\sqrt{\pi}}{4} =: r^\star$, and $\chi_\emptyset$, for any $0 < r < r^\star$; for $r = r^\star$, both $\chi_{A^{r^\star}}$ and $\chi_\emptyset$ are absolute minima in $\widetilde{\mathcal{K}}$, so that, for any $0 \le \lambda \le 1$, $u^\lambda := \lambda(\chi_{A^{r^\star}} + 1) - 1$ is a minimum of $\mathcal{F}$ in $\mathcal{K}$. Note that $\chi_\emptyset$ is a relative minimum of $\mathcal{F}$ in $\widetilde{\mathcal{K}}$, for any $r > r^\star$.

*Example 4.* Let $\Omega := (-2,2)^2$, $\mu := -1$ on $\Gamma_1 := \partial\Omega \cap \{x_1 x_2 \le 0\}$, $\mu := 1$ on $\Gamma_2 := \partial\Omega \setminus \Gamma_1$, and $\kappa := 0$. The functional $\mathcal{F}$ has two absolute minima in $\widetilde{\mathcal{K}}$, $\chi_A$ and $\chi_B$, where $A := \Omega \cap \{|x_1 + x_2| \le 2\}$ and $B := \Omega \cap \{|x_2 - x_1| \ge 2\}$; then, for any $0 \le \lambda \le 1$, $u^\lambda := \chi_A + \lambda(\chi_B - \chi_A)$ is a minimum of $\mathcal{F}$ in $\mathcal{K}$.

Since the regularized functional $\mathcal{F}_\varepsilon$, defined in (1.3) for $v \in BV(\Omega)$, is bounded from below and $L^1(\Omega)$-lower semicontinuous in $\mathcal{K}$, $\mathcal{F}_\varepsilon$ has a minimum point $u_\varepsilon \in \mathcal{K} \cap W^{1,1}_{loc}(\Omega)$ [16,18]. Moreover, since $\mathcal{F}_\varepsilon$ is strictly convex in $(BV(\Omega) \cap W^{1,1}_{loc}(\Omega))/\mathbf{R}$, the minimum is unique up to a possible additive constant. More precisely, $u_\varepsilon$ is unique if and only if either $\int_\Omega \kappa \ne \int_{\partial\Omega} \mu$ or $\sup_\Omega u_\varepsilon = 1$ and $\inf_\Omega u_\varepsilon = -1$. For instance, $\{u_\varepsilon^\lambda := u^\lambda = 2\lambda - 1\}_{0 \le \lambda \le 1}$ are the minima of $\mathcal{F}_\varepsilon$ in Ex. 1, whereas the minimum of $\mathcal{F}_\varepsilon$ is unique in Exs. 2,3,4, even if the identity $\int_\Omega \kappa = \int_{\partial\Omega} \mu$ holds in Exs. 2,4, and, for $r = 1$, in Ex. 3, because $\sup_\Omega u_\varepsilon = 1$ and $\inf_\Omega u_\varepsilon = -1$ (e.g., $u_\varepsilon := \frac{x_1}{2}$ is the unique absolute minimum of $\mathcal{F}_\varepsilon$ in Ex. 2).

Let $\{\mathcal{S}_h\}_{h>0}$ denote a *regular* family of partitions of $\Omega$ into simplices [8, p. 132] and $h_S \le h$ be the diameter of any $S \in \mathcal{S}_h$. For simplicity, we assume that $\bar\Omega = \cup_{S \in \mathcal{S}_h} S$. Let $\mathbf{V}_h \subset H^1(\Omega)$ be the piecewise linear finite element space over $\mathcal{S}_h$ and $\Pi_h$ be the usual Lagrange interpolation operator. In addition, define $\mathcal{K}_h := \mathbf{V}_h \cap \mathcal{K} = \{v \in \mathbf{V}_h : |v| \le 1 \text{ in } \Omega\}$.

We approximate $\mu$ and $\kappa$ by continuous, piecewise linear over $\mathcal{S}_h$, functions $\mu_h$ and $\kappa_h$, respectively, so that [8]

$$(2.1) \qquad \|\mu_h\|_{L^\infty(\partial\Omega)} \le 1, \quad \|\nabla\mu_h\|_{L^1(\partial\Omega)} = o(h^{-1}), \quad \mu_h \underset{h\to 0}{\to} \mu \text{ in } L^1(\partial\Omega),$$

$$(2.2) \qquad \|\kappa_h\|_{L^\infty(\Omega)} \le \|\kappa\|_{L^\infty(\Omega)}, \quad \|\nabla\kappa_h\|_{L^1(\Omega)} = o(h^{-1}), \quad \kappa_h \underset{h\to 0}{\to} \kappa \text{ in } L^1(\Omega).$$

For instance, letting $\{\delta_h\}_h$ be a family of mollifiers defined by $\delta_h(x) := \eta_h^n \delta(\eta_h x)$, where $\eta_h = o(h^{-1})$, we can define $\mu_h := \Pi_h(\mu \star \delta_h)$ and $\kappa_h := \Pi_h(\kappa \star \delta_h)$. If $\mu$ and $\kappa$ are more regular, e.g., bounded variation piecewise continuous functions, then we can define $\mu_h := \Pi_h \mu$ and $\kappa_h := \Pi_h \kappa$ (and we have $\|\nabla\mu_h\|_{L^1(\partial\Omega)}, \|\nabla\kappa_h\|_{L^1(\Omega)} = \mathcal{O}(1)$).

We define the discrete functionals as follows:

$$(2.3) \quad \mathcal{F}_h(v) := \int_\Omega |\nabla v| dx + \int_{\partial\Omega} \Pi_h(\mu_h v)\, d\mathcal{H}^{n-1} - \int_\Omega \Pi_h(\kappa_h v)\, dx, \qquad \forall\, v \in \mathbf{V}_h,$$

$$(2.4) \quad \mathcal{F}_{\varepsilon,h}(v) := \int_\Omega \sqrt{\varepsilon^2 + |\nabla v|^2} dx + \int_{\partial\Omega} \Pi_h(\mu_h v) d\mathcal{H}^{n-1} - \int_\Omega \Pi_h(\kappa_h v) dx, \quad \forall\, v \in \mathbf{V}_h.$$

Since $\mathcal{F}_h$ and $\mathcal{F}_{\varepsilon,h}$ are continuous over $\mathbf{V}_h$, they admit minimum points $u_h$ and $u_{\varepsilon,h} \in \mathcal{K}_h$, respectively, because $\mathcal{K}_h$ is a compact subset of a finite dimensional space. The minimum of $\mathcal{F}_h$ may be not unique. For instance, in Ex. 1 and, for a suitable mesh $\mathcal{S}_h$ and datum $\mu_h$, in Exs. 2,4, $\mathcal{F}_h$ has a continuum of minima. On the other hand, since $\mathcal{F}_{\varepsilon,h}$ is strictly convex in $\mathbf{V}_h/\mathbf{R}$, the minimum $u_{\varepsilon,h}$ is unique up to a possible additive constant. More precisely, $u_{\varepsilon,h}$ is unique if and only if either $\int_\Omega \kappa_h \neq \int_{\partial\Omega} \mu_h$ or $\sup_\Omega u_{\varepsilon,h}=1$ and $\inf_\Omega u_{\varepsilon,h}=-1$. For instance, in Exs. 2,3,4, the minimum $u_{\varepsilon,h}$ is unique; see §5.

**3. Convergence.** We recall the convergence results proved in [5], namely,

$$(3.1) \quad |\mathcal{F}_\varepsilon(v) - \mathcal{F}(v)| \leq \varepsilon|\Omega|, \ \forall\, v \in \mathcal{K}, \qquad |\mathcal{F}_{\varepsilon,h}(v) - \mathcal{F}_h(v)| \leq \varepsilon|\Omega|, \ \forall\, v \in \mathcal{K}_h, \ h>0,$$

$$(3.2) \quad |\mathcal{F}_h(v_h) - \mathcal{F}(v_h)| = o_h(1), \quad |\mathcal{F}_{\varepsilon,h}(v_h) - \mathcal{F}_\varepsilon(v_h)| = o_h(1), \quad \forall\, \{v_h \in \mathcal{K}_h\}_h, \ \varepsilon>0,$$

$$(3.3) \qquad \Gamma\text{-}\lim_{h\to 0} \mathcal{F}_h = \mathcal{F}, \qquad \Gamma\text{-}\lim_{h\to 0} \mathcal{F}_{\varepsilon,h} = \mathcal{F}_\varepsilon, \qquad in\ L^1(\Omega),$$

and, in particular, letting $\varepsilon$ and $h$ go to 0 independently,

$$(3.4) \qquad \Gamma\text{-}\lim_{(\varepsilon,h)\to(0,0)} \mathcal{F}_{\varepsilon,h} = \mathcal{F}, \qquad in\ L^1(\Omega).$$

The estimate (3.1) follows from the inequality [16]:

$$0 \leq \int_\Omega \sqrt{\varepsilon^2 + |Dv|^2} - \int_\Omega |Dv| = \varepsilon \left( \int_\Omega \sqrt{1 + \left|D\left(\frac{v}{\varepsilon}\right)\right|^2} - \int_\Omega \left|D\left(\frac{v}{\varepsilon}\right)\right| \right) \leq \varepsilon|\Omega|, \ \forall\, v \in BV(\Omega).$$

Now, considering $\mathcal{F}_h = \mathcal{F}_{\varepsilon,h}$ and $\mathcal{F} = \mathcal{F}_\varepsilon$ with $\varepsilon=0$, for all $\varepsilon \geq 0$ and $v_h \in \mathcal{K}_h$, we have:

$$\begin{aligned} \mathcal{F}_{\varepsilon,h}(v_h) - \mathcal{F}_\varepsilon(v_h) &= \int_{\partial\Omega} [\Pi_h(\mu_h v_h) - \mu v_h]\, d\mathcal{H}^{n-1} - \int_\Omega [\Pi_h(\kappa_h v_h) - \kappa v_h]\, dx \\ &= \int_{\partial\Omega} [\Pi_h(\mu_h v_h) - \mu_h v_h]\, d\mathcal{H}^{n-1} + \int_{\partial\Omega} (\mu_h - \mu) v_h d\mathcal{H}^{n-1} \\ &+ \int_\Omega [\Pi_h(\kappa_h v_h) - \kappa_h v_h]\, dx + \int_\Omega (\kappa_h - \kappa) v_h dx =: I_1 + I_2 + II_1 + II_2. \end{aligned}$$

Since $|v_h| \leq 1$ in $\bar{\Omega}$, we have $|I_2| \leq \|\mu_h - \mu\|_{L^1(\partial\Omega)}$ and $|II_2| \leq \|\kappa_h - \kappa\|_{L^1(\Omega)}$. Using a well known interpolation estimate and the local inverse inequality $\|\nabla v_h\|_{L^\infty(T)} \leq C h_S^{-1} \|v_h\|_{L^\infty(T)}$, where either $T = \partial S$ or $T = S \in \mathcal{S}_h$ [8, p.140], we get

$$\begin{aligned} |I_1| &\leq C \sum_{S\in\mathcal{S}_h} h_S^2 \|D^2(\mu_h v_h)\|_{L^1(\partial S\cap\partial\Omega)} \\ &\leq C \sum_{S\in\mathcal{S}_h} h_S^2 \|\nabla\mu_h \cdot \nabla v_h\|_{L^1(\partial S\cap\partial\Omega)} \leq Ch\|\nabla\mu_h\|_{L^1(\partial\Omega)} \end{aligned}$$

and, similarly, $|II_1| \leq Ch\|\nabla\kappa_h\|_{L^1(\Omega)}$. Hence, (3.2) follows from (2.1) and (2.2).

Next, we observe that $\mathcal{F}(v)$ and $\mathcal{F}_\varepsilon(v)$, for $v \in \mathcal{K}$, can be approximated by $\{\mathcal{F}(v_h)\}_h$ and $\{\mathcal{F}_\varepsilon(v_h)\}_h$, respectively, for a suitable sequence $\{v_h \in \mathcal{K}_h\}_h$, as $h \to 0$. In fact, given a ball $B$ containing $\bar{\Omega}$, let $\widetilde{v} \in W^{1,1}(B \backslash \bar{\Omega}; [-1,1])$ be a function with trace $v$ on $\partial\Omega$ [14], and denote again by $v \in BV(\mathbf{R}^n; [-1,1])$ the function $v(x) := v(x)$ if $x \in \Omega$, $v(x) := \widetilde{v}(x)$ if $x \in B \backslash \Omega$, $v(x) := 0$ if $x \in \mathbf{R}^n \backslash B$. Set $\widehat{v}_h(x) := (v \star \delta_h)(x)$, for all $x \in B$, and $v_h := \Pi_h \widehat{v}_h \in \mathcal{K}_h$. Noting that $\|D^2\widehat{v}_h\|_{L^1(\Omega)} \leq \eta_h$, using a well known interpolation estimate, we have $\|v_h - \widehat{v}_h\|_{W^{1,1}(\Omega)} \leq C[h^2 + h]\|D^2\widehat{v}_h\|_{L^1(\Omega)} = o_h(1)$. Hence, since [16, Prop. 1.15]

$$\lim_{h\to 0} \|\widehat{v}_h - v\|_{L^1(\Omega)} = 0 \qquad \text{and} \qquad \lim_{h\to 0} \int_\Omega |\nabla\widehat{v}_h| dx = \int_\Omega |Dv|,$$

using also the inequality $|\int_\Omega |\nabla v_h| dx - \int_\Omega |\nabla\widehat{v}_h| dx| \leq \int_\Omega |\nabla(v_h - \widehat{v}_h)| dx$, we get

$$\lim_{h\to 0} \|v_h - v\|_{L^1(\Omega)} = 0 \qquad \text{and} \qquad \lim_{h\to 0} \int_\Omega |\nabla v_h| dx = \int_\Omega |Dv|.$$

This entails [16, Thm. 2.11]

$$\lim_{h\to 0} \|v_h - v\|_{L^1(\partial\Omega)} = 0$$

and, using the inequality $|\int_\Omega \sqrt{\varepsilon^2 + |Dv|^2} - \int_\Omega \sqrt{\varepsilon^2 + |\nabla v_h|^2} dx| \leq |\int_\Omega |Dv| - \int_\Omega |\nabla v_h| dx|$,

$$\mathcal{F}(v) = \lim_{h\to 0} \mathcal{F}(v_h) \qquad \text{and} \qquad \mathcal{F}_\varepsilon(v) = \lim_{h\to 0} \mathcal{F}_\varepsilon(v_h), \qquad \forall\, v \in \mathcal{K}. \tag{3.5}$$

Now, using the semicontinuity of $\mathcal{F}$ and $\mathcal{F}_\varepsilon$, (3.2), and (3.5), we get (3.3) and, using also (3.1), we get (3.4). Let us show the latter property. The functionals $\mathcal{F}$ and $\mathcal{F}_\varepsilon$ ($\mathcal{F}_h$ and $\mathcal{F}_{\varepsilon,h}$, respectively) are set to $+\infty$ in $L^1(\Omega) \backslash \mathcal{K}$ ($L^1(\Omega) \backslash \mathcal{K}_h$, respectively). We have:

*(i).* Let $v \in L^1(\Omega)$ and $\{v_{\varepsilon,h} \in \mathcal{K}_h\}_{\varepsilon,h}$ be any sequence converging to $v$ in $L^1(\Omega)$, as $(\varepsilon, h) \to (0,0)$. Using the semicontinuity of $\mathcal{F}$, (3.2), and (3.1), we have

$$\mathcal{F}(v) \leq \liminf_{(\varepsilon,h)\to(0,0)} \mathcal{F}(v_{\varepsilon,h}) = \liminf_{(\varepsilon,h)\to(0,0)} \mathcal{F}_h(v_{\varepsilon,h}) = \liminf_{(\varepsilon,h)\to(0,0)} \mathcal{F}_{\varepsilon,h}(v_{\varepsilon,h}).$$

*(ii).* Let $v \in \mathcal{K}$ and $\{v_h \in \mathcal{K}_h\}_h$ be the sequence defined in (3.5). Using (3.5), (3.2), and (3.1), we have

$$\mathcal{F}(v) = \lim_{h\to 0} \mathcal{F}(v_h) = \lim_{h\to 0} \mathcal{F}_h(v_h) = \lim_{(\varepsilon,h)\to(0,0)} \mathcal{F}_{\varepsilon,h}(v_h).$$

REMARK 3.1. Let $u_{\varepsilon,h}$ be a minimum of $\mathcal{F}_{\varepsilon,h}$. We have $\mathcal{F}_{\varepsilon,h}(u_{\varepsilon,h}) \le \mathcal{F}_{\varepsilon,h}(0) = \varepsilon|\Omega|$, whence, using (2.1) and (2.2), $\int_\Omega |Du_{\varepsilon,h}| \le \int_\Omega \sqrt{\varepsilon^2 + |Du_{\varepsilon,h}|^2} \le \mathcal{H}^{n-1}(\partial\Omega) + |\Omega|(1 + \|\kappa\|_{L^\infty(\Omega)})$, for all $0 < \varepsilon \le 1$ and $h > 0$. Then, by the compactness theorem in $BV(\Omega)$ [16, Thm. 1.19], the family $\{u_{\varepsilon,h}\}_{\varepsilon,h}$ admits a subsequence converging to some $u \in \mathcal{K}$ in $L^1(\Omega)$ and, in view of (3.4) [10], $u$ is a minimum point of $\mathcal{F}$.

**4. Discrete algorithm.** We describe the constrained Newton-like algorithm [11,15] for the minimization of $\mathcal{F}_{\varepsilon,h}$ in $\mathcal{K}_h$. The condition $|v| \le 1$, for all $v \in \mathcal{K}_h$, naturally gives rise to a constrained optimization problem. On the other hand, since $\mathcal{F}_{\varepsilon,h}$ is nonstrictly convex (linear) along the directions defined by the constant functions, and so the Hessian matrix is singular at any $v \in \mathbf{V}_h$, then the Newton steps can be performed only in nonconstant directions. It turns out that the definition of the subspaces of admissible, strictly convex, directions for $\mathcal{F}_{\varepsilon,h}$, where seeking for suitable descent directions, is the most delicate part of the algorithm. We point out that the quadrature formulae in (2.4) allow the direct implementation on a computer of the minimization algorithm. For the numerical solution of the nonparametric minimal surfaces, see also [17,23] and the papers cited therein.

*4.1. Notation.* Let $\mathcal{N}_h := \{x_j\}_{j=1}^J$ be the nodes of $\mathcal{S}_h$ and $\{\varphi_j\}_{j=1}^J$ be the hat functions, defined by $\varphi_j(x_i) = \delta_{ij}$ (Kronecker's symbol). For all $1 \le j \le J$, set $q_j := \nabla\varphi_j$ and $q_j^S := q_{j|S}$, for all $S \in \mathcal{S}_h$. Let $\mathbf{M}$ and $\mathbf{B}$ denote the (diagonalized) mass matrices, with elements $m_{jj} := \int_\Omega \varphi_j dx$ and $b_{jj} := \int_{\partial\Omega} \varphi_j d\mathcal{H}^{n-1}$, respectively, and define

$$c_j := b_{jj}\mu_h(x_j) - m_{jj}\kappa_h(x_j), \qquad \forall\, 1 \le j \le J.$$

Any function $v \in \mathbf{V}_h$ is identified to the vector $\mathbf{v} := \{v_j := v(x_j)\}_{j=1}^J$ of its nodal values. Let $\mathbf{l} := 1$, i.e., $l_j := 1$ for all $1 \le j \le J$, and $D := \{\alpha\mathbf{l}\}_{\alpha\in\mathbf{R}}$ be the subspace of the constant directions. For any $v \in \mathbf{V}_h$, let us define $q_v^S := \nabla v_{|S} = \sum_{j\in S} v_j q_j^S$ ("$j \in S$" is a shorthand for "the node $x_j \in S$"), and $\gamma_v^S := \sqrt{\varepsilon^2 + |q_v^S|^2}$. Hence, we have

$$\mathcal{F}_{\varepsilon,h}(v) = \sum_{S\in\mathcal{S}_h} |S|\gamma_v^S + \sum_{j=1}^J c_j v_j, \qquad \forall\, v \in \mathbf{V}_h, \tag{4.1}$$

and, after easy calculations, we get the gradient $\nabla\mathcal{F}_{\varepsilon,h}$:

$$\frac{\partial\mathcal{F}_{\varepsilon,h}(v)}{\partial v_j} = \sum_{S\ni j} |S| \frac{q_j^S \cdot q_v^S}{\gamma_v^S} + c_j, \qquad \forall\, 1 \le j \le J, \tag{4.2}$$

and the Hessian matrix $H\mathcal{F}_{\varepsilon,h}$:

$$\frac{\partial^2\mathcal{F}_{\varepsilon,h}(v)}{\partial v_i \partial v_j} = \sum_{S\ni i,j} |S| \frac{q_j^S \cdot q_i^S - (q_j^S \cdot q_v^S)(q_i^S \cdot q_v^S)/(\gamma_v^S)^2}{\gamma_v^S}, \qquad \forall\, 1 \le i,j \le J. \tag{4.3}$$

Obviously, $\nabla\mathcal{F}_{\varepsilon,h}$ and $H\mathcal{F}_{\varepsilon,h}$ do not change along the constant directions, that is,

$$\nabla\mathcal{F}_{\varepsilon,h}(v+\alpha)=\nabla\mathcal{F}_{\varepsilon,h}(v) \quad\text{and}\quad H\mathcal{F}_{\varepsilon,h}(v+\alpha)=H\mathcal{F}_{\varepsilon,h}(v), \qquad \forall\, v\in\mathbf{V}_h,\ \alpha\in\mathbf{R}.$$

In addition, note that, for all $v\in\mathbf{V}_h$,

$$\nabla\mathcal{F}_{\varepsilon,h}(v)\cdot\mathbf{1}=\sum_{j=1}^{J}\frac{\partial\mathcal{F}_{\varepsilon,h}(v)}{\partial v_j}=\sum_{j=1}^{J}c_j=\mathbf{c}\cdot\mathbf{1}=\int_{\partial\Omega}\mu_h-\int_{\Omega}\kappa_h,\quad H\mathcal{F}_{\varepsilon,h}(v)\,\mathbf{1}=\sum_{j=1}^{J}\frac{\partial^2\mathcal{F}_{\varepsilon,h}(v)}{\partial v_i\partial v_j}=0,$$

and that $H\mathcal{F}_{\varepsilon,h}$ is a sparse matrix, because $\frac{\partial^2\mathcal{F}_{\varepsilon,h}(v)}{\partial v_i\partial v_j}=0$ for all nonadjacent nodes $x_i,x_j$.

*4.2. Minimization algorithm.* The constrained Newton-like algorithm reads as follows:

S0. Let $v^0\in\mathcal{K}_h$ be the initial guess. Set $k:=0$ (iterations count).

S1. Compute $F^k:=\mathcal{F}_{\varepsilon,h}(v^k)$, $\mathbf{g}^k:=\nabla\mathcal{F}_{\varepsilon,h}(v^k)$, and $\mathbf{E}^k:=H\mathcal{F}_{\varepsilon,h}(v^k)$.

S2. Define $\mathcal{C}^k:=\{x_j\in\mathcal{N}_h:|v_j^k|=1 \text{ and } v_j^k g_j^k\le 0\}$ and $\mathcal{W}^k:=\mathcal{N}_h\setminus\mathcal{C}^k$
(the sets of the constrained and movable nodes with respect to the $-\mathbf{g}^k$ direction),
and $W^k:=\{\mathbf{p}\in\mathbf{R}^J:\ p_j=0 \text{ for all } x_j\in\mathcal{C}^k\}$
(the subspace where a suitable admissible descent direction is sought).

S3. IF $\mathcal{W}^k=\emptyset$, THEN $u_{\varepsilon,h}:=v^k$ is an absolute minimum of $\mathcal{F}_{\varepsilon,h}$, STOP
(since $W^k=\{0\}$, there is no admissible strict descent direction for $\mathcal{F}_{\varepsilon,h}$).

S4. Define a suitable descent direction $\mathbf{p}^k\in W^k$ and a scalar displacement $\alpha_0^k$ as follows:

S41. IF $\mathcal{W}^k=\mathcal{N}_h$ (a Newton step cannot be performed, because $\det(\mathbf{E}^k)=0$), THEN

S411. IF $\mathbf{g}^k\cdot\mathbf{1}<0$ (or $\mathbf{g}^k\cdot\mathbf{1}>0$), THEN set $\mathbf{p}^k:=\mathbf{1}$ (or $\mathbf{p}^k:=-\mathbf{1}$), $\alpha_0^k:=+\infty$, CONTINUE TO S45
($\mathbf{p}^k=\pm\mathbf{1}$ corresponds to a "degenerate" Newton direction, because $\mathcal{F}_{\varepsilon,h}$ is linear along $\pm\mathbf{1}$, and so $v^k$ will be pushed against a barrier $\pm\mathbf{1}$).

S412. IF $\mathbf{g}^k\cdot\mathbf{1}=0$ (note that $\mathcal{F}_{\varepsilon,h}(v^k+\alpha)=F^k$, $\forall\ \alpha\in\mathbf{R}$, because $\mathbf{c}\cdot\mathbf{1}=0$), THEN
IF $g_{j_M}^k<0$, where $v_{j_M}^k=\max_{1\le j\le J}v_j^k$ (or $g_{j_m}^k>0$, where $v_{j_m}^k=\min_{1\le j\le J}v_j^k$),
THEN set $\mathbf{v}^k:=\mathbf{v}^k+(1-v_{j_M}^k)\mathbf{1}$ (or $\mathbf{v}^k:=\mathbf{v}^k-(1+v_{j_m}^k)\mathbf{1}$), GO TO S2
(the new set of the constrained nodes $\mathcal{C}^k$ will be nonempty);
ELSE set $\mathbf{p}^k:=-\mathbf{g}^k$, $\alpha_0^k:=+\infty$, CONTINUE TO S5 (see Remark *i)* below).

S42. IF $\mathcal{W}^k\ne\mathcal{N}_h$, THEN project $\mathbf{g}^k$ and $\mathbf{E}^k$ on $W^k$, namely,
for any $x_j\in\mathcal{C}^k$, set $g_j^k:=0$ and $e_{ij}^k=e_{ji}^k:=\delta_{ij}$, for any $1\le i\le J$
(since $\mathbf{1}\notin W^k$, $\mathcal{F}_{\varepsilon,h}$ is strictly convex along the directions in $W^k$,
so that the projected $H\mathcal{F}_{\varepsilon,h|W^k}=\mathbf{E}^k$ is positive definite and
$\mathbf{p}^k$ can be defined by $\mathbf{E}^k\mathbf{p}^k=-\mathbf{g}^k$ [note that $p_j^k=0$, if $x_j\in\mathcal{N}_h\setminus\mathcal{W}^k$]).

S43. Compute the incomplete Choleski factorization $\mathbf{LDL}^T$ of $\mathbf{E}^k$, where
$\mathbf{L}$ is lower triangular with unit diagonal entries and $\mathbf{D}$ is positive diagonal
(if $\mathbf{E}^k$ is almost singular, the factorization may be inaccurate or even fail);
IF the factorization fails, THEN set $\mathbf{p}^k:=-\mathbf{g}^k$, $\alpha_0^k:=+\infty$, CONTINUE TO S5.

S44. Solve the linear system $\mathbf{E}^k\mathbf{p}^k = -\mathbf{g}^k$ by the preconditioned conjugate gradient method, performing at most $\mathcal{O}(\sqrt{J})$ iterations ($\mathbf{p}^k$ is well approximated except the factorization mildly failed); set $\alpha_0^k := 1$.

S45. Define $\mathcal{C}^k := \{x_j \in \mathcal{W}^k : |v_j^k| = 1 \text{ and } v_j^k p_j^k > 0\}$ (note that $\mathcal{C}^k \neq \mathcal{W}^k$, because $\mathbf{p}^k \cdot \mathbf{g}^k < 0$ and, for all $x_j \in \mathcal{W}^k$, $v_j^k g_j^k > 0$ if $|v_j^k| = 1$), update $\mathcal{W}^k := \mathcal{W}^k \setminus \mathcal{C}^k$ and set $W^k := \{\mathbf{p} \in W^k : p_j = 0 \text{ for all } x_j \in \mathcal{C}^k\}$; IF $\mathcal{C}^k \neq \emptyset$, THEN GO TO S42.

S5. Set $v^{k+1} := v^k$.

S6. Let $\alpha_M^k$ be the largest scalar for which $|\mathbf{v}^{k+1} + \alpha_M^k \mathbf{p}^k|_\infty \leq 1$ and define $\alpha^k : \min_{\alpha \in [0, \alpha_M^k]} \mathcal{F}_{\varepsilon,h}(\mathbf{v}^{k+1} + \alpha \mathbf{p}^k) = \mathcal{F}_{\varepsilon,h}(\mathbf{v}^{k+1} + \alpha^k \mathbf{p}^k)$; the optimal $\alpha^k \in [0, \alpha_M^k]$ is computed by a "linear search" [11] with cubic Hermite interpolant polynomials starting from 0 and $\alpha_M^k \wedge \alpha_0^k$.

S7. Set $\mathbf{v}^{k+1} := \mathbf{v}^{k+1} + \alpha^k \mathbf{p}^k$ (note that $\alpha^k = \alpha_0^k = 1$ corresponds to a Newton step).

S8. IF $\alpha^k = \alpha_M^k$, THEN define $\mathcal{C}^k := \{x_j \in \mathcal{W}^k : |v_j^{k+1}| = 1\}$ (note that $\mathcal{C}^k \neq \emptyset$), update $\mathcal{W}^k := \mathcal{W}^k \setminus \mathcal{C}^k$, set $p_j^k := 0$ if $x_j \in \mathcal{C}^k$, and compute $\mathbf{g}^{k+1} := \nabla \mathcal{F}_{\varepsilon,h}(v^{k+1})$; IF $\mathbf{g}^{k+1} \cdot \mathbf{p}^k < 0$, THEN set $\alpha_0^k := +\infty$, GO TO S6.

S9. IF $|\mathbf{v}^{k+1} - \mathbf{v}^k|_\infty \leq \eta$ $(\simeq 10^{-6})$, THEN $u_{\varepsilon,h} := v^{k+1}$, STOP; ELSE $k := k+1$, GO TO S1.

REMARKS. *i)* If $\mathbf{1} \notin W^k$ (i.e., $\mathcal{W}^k \neq \mathcal{N}_h$), we have

$$\mathcal{F}_{\varepsilon,h}(\mathbf{v}^k + \mathbf{p}) = F^k + \mathbf{g}^k \cdot \mathbf{p} + \frac{1}{2}\mathbf{p}^T \mathbf{E}^k \mathbf{p} + \mathcal{O}(|\mathbf{p}|^3) =: Q^k(\mathbf{p}) + \mathcal{O}(|\mathbf{p}|^3), \quad \forall\, \mathbf{p} \in W^k.$$

In that case, the projected Hessian matrix $\mathbf{E}^k$ is positive definite, and the Newton step S44 corresponds to the exact unconstrained minimization of the quadratic part $Q^k(\mathbf{p})$ of $\mathcal{F}_{\varepsilon,h}(\mathbf{v}^k + \mathbf{p})$ on $W^k$. The case $W^k = \mathbf{R}^J$, item S41 (i.e., all the nodes are movable along the steepest descent $-\mathbf{g}^k$ direction), basically may take place because of either the initial guess or the nonuniqueness of the minimum of $\mathcal{F}_{\varepsilon,h}$. In that case, a Newton step cannot be performed, because $\mathbf{E}^k \mathbf{p} = 0$, for all $\mathbf{p} \in D$, and so the quadratic form $Q^k(\mathbf{p})$ can be unbounded from below. Then the algorithm may select either the constant direction $\mathbf{p}^k = \mathbf{1}$ (or $\mathbf{p}^k = -\mathbf{1}$), step S411, or the steepest descent direction $\mathbf{p}^k = -\mathbf{g}^k$, step S412, according to the following arguments. Since $\mathbf{c} \cdot \mathbf{1} = \mathbf{g}^k \cdot \mathbf{1}$, from (4.1) we get $\mathcal{F}_{\varepsilon,h}(\mathbf{v}^k + \mathbf{p}) = F^k + \mathbf{g}^k \cdot \mathbf{p}$, for all $\mathbf{p} \in D$; hence, the constant direction $\mathbf{p}^k = \mathbf{1}$ ($\mathbf{p}^k = -\mathbf{1}$, respectively) is a global descent direction if $\mathbf{g}^k \cdot \mathbf{1} < 0$ ($\mathbf{g}^k \cdot \mathbf{1} > 0$, respectively), and may be considered as a "degenerate" Newton direction. On the other hand, since $\mathbf{p}^T \mathbf{E}^k \mathbf{p} > 0$ for all $\mathbf{p} \notin D$, then $\mathcal{F}_{\varepsilon,h}(\mathbf{v}^k + \mathbf{p}) > F^k$, as $|\mathbf{p}|$ becomes large, where $\mathbf{p}$ is any nonconstant direction: thus the steepest descent step $\mathbf{p}^k = -\mathbf{g}^k$, selected if $\mathbf{g}^k \cdot \mathbf{1} = 0$, can perform only a small displacement.

In the later case, the steepest descent direction should be effectively improved,e.g.,by constraining the functional on $\mathbf{V}_h/\mathbf{R}$, i.e., projecting the direction $\mathbf{p}^k = -\mathbf{g}^k$ and the Hessian matrix $\mathbf{E}^k$ on $\{\mathbf{p} \in \mathbf{R}^J : \mathbf{p} \cdot \mathbf{1} = 0\}$. More precisely, we set $g_j^k := g_j^k - g_J^k$ and $e_{ij}^k := e_{ij}^k - e_{Jj}^k - e_{iJ}^k + e_{JJ}^k$, for all $1 \leq i, j \leq J-1$. The projected $(J-1) \times (J-1)$ Hessian matrix is positive definite, so that a Newton step can be performed on that subspace.

Note that, since $\nabla \mathcal{F}_{\varepsilon,h}(v^k + \alpha) = \mathbf{g}^k$, for all $\alpha \in \mathbf{R}$, the selection of either one of the constant directions, step S411, as well as the straight movement of $v^k$ against a barrier $+1$ or $-1$, step S412, give rise to constrain some nodes in view of the immediately successive execution of a Newton step on $W^k$.

*ii)* For $\varepsilon = 0$, $\nabla \mathcal{F}_h$ and $H\mathcal{F}_h$ are undefined at any function $v \in \mathbf{V}_h$ which is constant on at least one triangle $S \in \mathcal{S}_h$: in that case, $\gamma_v^S = |q_v^S| = 0$, and the definitions (4.2) and (4.3) are void for $j \in S$. Moreover, the functional $\mathcal{F}_h$ may be nonstrictly convex even along nonconstant admissible descent directions (e.g., if $\mathcal{F}_h$ has not a unique minimum), so that the projected Hessian matrix $\mathbf{E}^k$ is singular. On the other hand, for $\varepsilon > 0$, the functional $\mathcal{F}_{\varepsilon,h}$ may exhibit almost flat directions in $W^k$, even if its minimum is unique; for instance, if $\mathcal{F}$ has a relative minimum in $\widetilde{\mathcal{K}}$ with value approximatively equal to the absolute minimum value or if $\mathcal{F}$ has not a unique minimum, then the projected Hessian matrix $\mathbf{E}^k$ is tremendously ill-conditionned for small values of $\varepsilon$. Hence, the Newton step S44 may be very unstable for small values of $\varepsilon$. To make more robust the algorithm, a dynamic reduction of $\varepsilon$ has been implemented, namely: letting $h$ be fixed, we start with $\varepsilon = \varepsilon_0 \approx h$ and, once the stop test in step S9 is satisfied, we reduce $\varepsilon$, iterating until a given threshold $\bar{\varepsilon}$ has been lowered. Thus, the algorithm above deals with very small $\varepsilon$'s only when the iterates $v^k$ are close to a minimum of $\mathcal{F}_h$. Moreover, if a Newton step is expected to be unstable because the incomplete Choleski factorization fails, then a steepest descent step S43 is executed just to go through the topic situation.

*iii)* The algorithm is convergent also in the case that $\mathcal{F}_{\varepsilon,h}$ has not a unique minimum, i.e., $\mathcal{F}_{\varepsilon,h}$ has a continuum $\{u_{\varepsilon,h}^\lambda\}_{0 \leq \lambda \leq 1}$ of minima defined up to additive constants. In that case, $\nabla \mathcal{F}_{\varepsilon,h}(u_{\varepsilon,h}^\lambda) = 0$, for any $0 \leq \lambda \leq 1$, and $\mathbf{c} \cdot \mathbf{1} = 0$, so that the algorithm should always select the steepest descent step S412 and oscillations among different minima should not take place. Nevertheless, in our tests we have experienced nonuniqueness of the minimum of $\mathcal{F}_{\varepsilon,h}$ only in the trivial case $\mu, \kappa = 0$ of Ex. 1 (see §§2,5).

*iv)* In conclusion, the numerical experiments show that the algorithm is robust and reaches the numerical minimum in a few Newton-like iterations. Likely, the inefficient steepest descent steps as well as the expensive updatings of the Newton direction, necessary if $\mathcal{C}^k \neq \emptyset$ in step S45, are performed very rarely. We also would stress that the iterations through the "linear search", performed in step S8, are extremely important, because they allow a very fast construction of the final shape of the discrete minimum, pushing $v^k$ against the barriers $+1$ and $-1$, with inexpensive updatings of the descent direction $\mathbf{p}^k$. Finally, we observe that if the algorithm stops at step S3, then the found discrete minimum verifies $|u_{\varepsilon,h}| = 1$ at the nodes, namely either $u_{\varepsilon,h} = \chi_\emptyset$ or $u_{\varepsilon,h} = \chi_\Omega$ or, very rarely, $u_{\varepsilon,h}$ has a one-triangle-wide transition layer across the interface.

**5. Numerical experiments.** In this section we comment on various examples. Here $\varepsilon_0 := h$; $\bar{\varepsilon}$ is simply denoted by $\varepsilon$. Since the discrete minimum $u_{\varepsilon,h}$ of $\mathcal{F}_{\varepsilon,h}$ is unique in Exs. 2 to 6 below, the function $v^0 := \chi_\emptyset = -1$ is set as the initial guess in those examples. The discrete solutions $u_{\sigma,h}$ obtained via the relaxation approach (1.2), so-called "relaxed" minima, are taken from [3]. We denote by **t** the computing CPU time in seconds.

5.1. *Example 1.* See Ex. 1 in §2. Let $\Omega := (-2,2)^2 \setminus \{4x_1^2 + (2|x_2| - 7)^2 \le 25\}$. The functional $\mathcal{F}_{\varepsilon,h}$ has a continuum $\{u_{\varepsilon,h} := 2\lambda - 1\}_{0 \le \lambda \le 1}$ of minima. If the initial guess $v^0$ is a constant, the algorithm obviously stops directly. Starting, e.g., from $v^0 := \Pi_h \chi_{\{x_1 > 0\}}$, which interpolates on $\mathcal{S}_h$ a relative minimum of $\mathcal{F}$ in $\widetilde{\mathcal{K}}$, we get convergence, with no oscillations, to a minimum of $\mathcal{F}_{\varepsilon,h}$. Here, $\varepsilon = 0.1$ and $h = 0.1$. As expected, the algorithm always selects the steepest descent direction, step S412, thus leading to a quite slow convergence, because in all iterations all the nodal values are unconstrained, $|v_j^k| < 1$.

5.2. *Example 2.* See Ex. 2 in §2. Let $\mu_h := \Pi_h \mu$. Fig. 5.1 shows the level lines $\{u_{\varepsilon,h} = i0.1\}$, $-10 \le i \le 10$, of the discrete minimum, for $\varepsilon = 0.1$ and $h = 0.1$; they are straight lines, even if the mesh $\mathcal{S}_h$ is unstructured, because the discrete minimum $u_{\varepsilon,h}$ is a linear function and coincides with the minimum $u_\varepsilon = \frac{x_1}{2}$ of $\mathcal{F}_\varepsilon$. The absolute minima $\{u^a = \chi_{\{x_1 \ge a\}}\}_{-2 \le a \le 2}$ of $\mathcal{F}$ in $\widetilde{\mathcal{K}}$ can thus be precisely recovered as $\{\chi_{\{u_{\varepsilon,h} > t\}}\}_{-1 \le t \le 1}$.

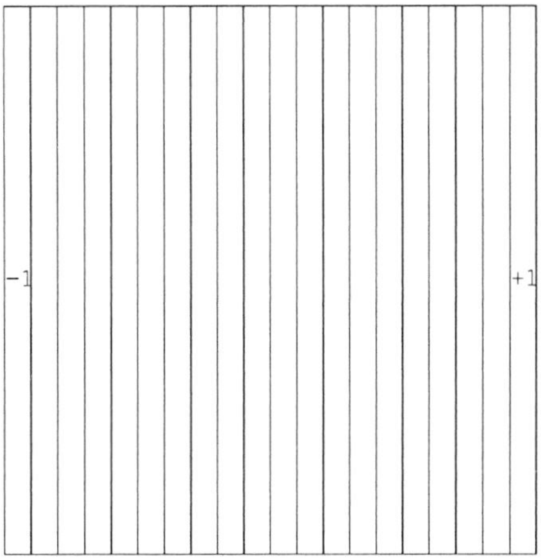


FIGURE 5.1. Ex. 2: level lines $\{u_{\varepsilon,h} = i0.1\}$, $-10 \le i \le 10$, of the discrete minimum [$\varepsilon = 0.1$, $h = 0.1$].

5.3. *Example 3.* See Ex. 3 in §2. Fig. 5.2 shows, for $r = 1$, the exact minimum $A^1$ (dashed lines), the relaxed minimum $A^1_{\sigma,h} := \{u_{\sigma,h} = 0\}$ (dotted line), for $h = 0.08$ and $\sigma = 0.16$ [**t** = 288], and the discrete minimum $A^1_{\varepsilon,h} := \{u_{\varepsilon,h} > 0\}$ (solid lines) for $h = 0.1$ and $\varepsilon = 0.05$ [**t** = 261]. The inaccuracy of the relaxed minimum $A^1_{\sigma,h}$ is basically due to the $\mathcal{O}(\sigma)$-wide transition layer of $u_{\sigma,h}$ across the interface, which prevents the set $A^1_{\sigma,h}$ from matching sharply the Dirichlet boundary condition $u_{\sigma,h} = -1$. This effect of the relaxation approach

FIGURE 5.2. Ex. 3 ($r = 1$): exact minimum $A^1$ (dashed lines), relaxed minimum $A^1_{\sigma,h}$ [$\sigma = 0.16$, $h = 0.08$] (dotted line), and discrete minimum $A^1_{\varepsilon,h}$ [$\varepsilon = 0.05$, $h = 0.1$] (solid lines).

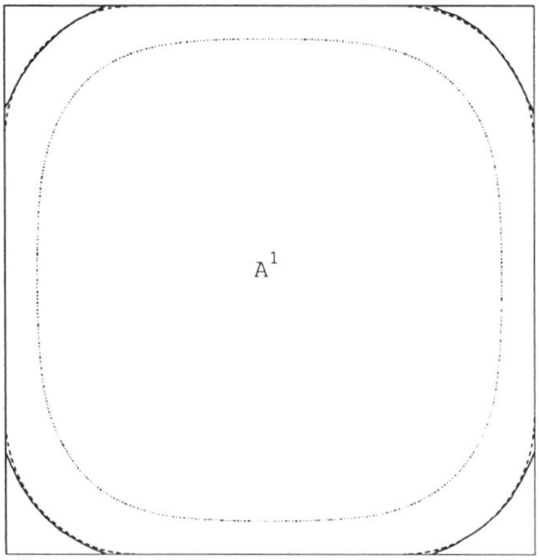


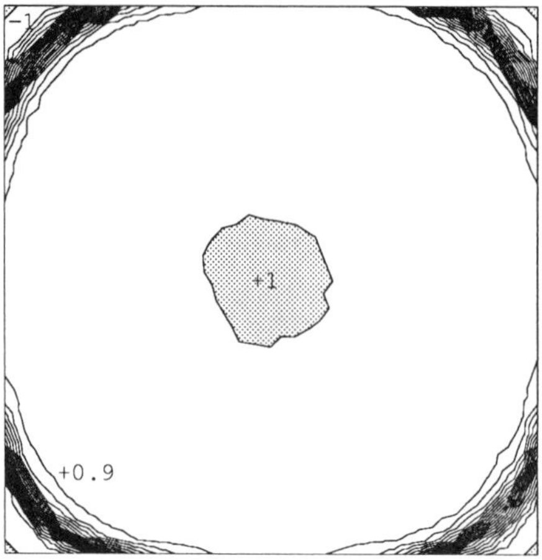


FIGURE 5.3. Ex. 3 ($r = 1$): level lines $\{u_{\varepsilon,h} = i0.1\}$, $-10 \le i \le 10$, of the discrete minimum [$\varepsilon = 0.05$, $h = 0.1$].

is absent in the convex approximation. In fact, the variational inequality corresponding to the minimization of $\mathcal{F}_{\varepsilon,h}$ has a Neumann condition at the boundary, namely, formally, $\nabla(\frac{v}{\varepsilon}) \cdot \nu + \mu\sqrt{1 + |\nabla(\frac{v}{\varepsilon})|^2} = 0$. Moreover, for $\varepsilon$ sufficiently small (say $\varepsilon \le h$), the solution $u_{\varepsilon,h}$ basically does not change (see (3.1)), so that the transition layer of $u_{\varepsilon,h}$ across the interface is just a space discretization effect. Fig. 5.3 shows the level lines $\{u_{\varepsilon,h} = i0.1\}$, $-10 \le i \le 10$, of the discrete solution; we stress that most of them are bunched near $\partial A^1_{\varepsilon,h}$.

For any $r > r^\star$, the functional $\mathcal{F}$ has two minima $\chi_{A^r}, \chi_\emptyset \in \widetilde{\mathcal{K}}$, with $\mathcal{F}(\chi_{A^r}) < \mathcal{F}(\chi_\emptyset)$, whereas $\mathcal{F}(\chi_{A^{r^\star}}) = \mathcal{F}(\chi_\emptyset)$ (i.e., $\mathcal{F}$ has a flat line from $\chi_{A^{r^\star}}$ to $\chi_\emptyset$, for $r = r^\star$). The relaxed minima may approximate either the absolute minimum $\chi_{A^r}$ or the relative minimum $\chi_\emptyset$, depending on the initial guess, whereas the $\mathcal{F}_{\varepsilon,h}$'s have a unique minimum, which always converges to the absolute minimum $\chi_{A^r}$ of $\mathcal{F}$. The convex approach thus allows an accurate numerical evaluation of the critical value $r^\star$. In fact, taking for instance $h = 0.1$ and $\varepsilon = 0.05$, we see that $u_{\varepsilon,h} \simeq \chi_\emptyset$, for $r \le 0.95$ (e.g., for $r = 0.95$, $\{u_{\varepsilon,h} > -0.65\} = \emptyset$ and $\{-0.9 \le u_{\varepsilon,h} \le -0.8\}$ is a thin layer across $\partial A^r$), and $u_{\varepsilon,h} \simeq \chi_{A^r}$, for $r \ge 0.955$. Hence, the numerical critical value $r^\star_{\varepsilon,h} \in [0.95, 0.955]$ ($r^\star := \frac{2+\sqrt{\pi}}{4} \simeq 0.943$).

Finally, we give some data on the performance of the minimization algorithm. For $r = 1$, $h = 0.1$, and $\varepsilon = 0.05$, we get convergence in 18 Newton-like iterations (in number of 13 with $\alpha^k = 1$), with 3 updatings of the Newton direction and no steepest descent steps. Note that $u_{\varepsilon,h} = 1$ in numerous nodes (see Fig. 5.3): the iterations through the "linear search" in step S8 (in number of 114) precisely serve to push, cheapily, the iterates against the barrier $+1$, from the initial guess $v^0 = -1$.

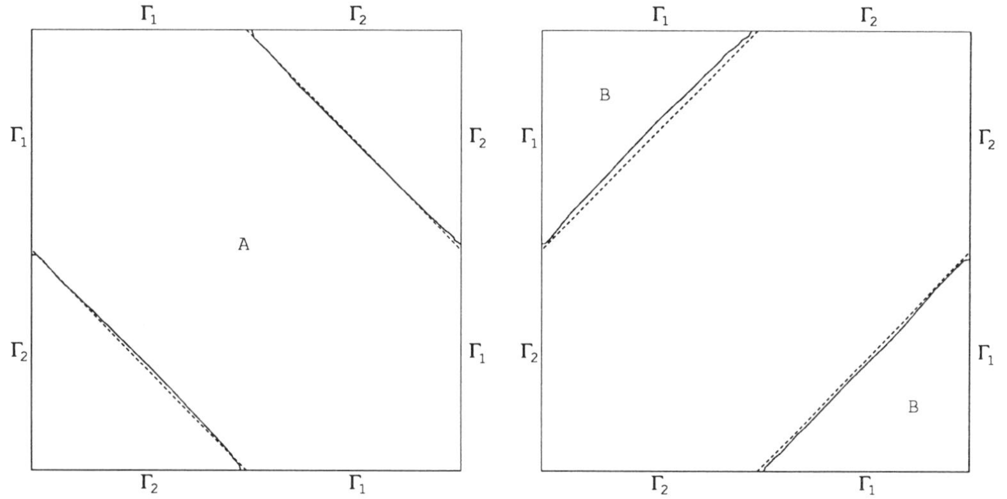


FIG. 5.4. Ex. 4: Exact $A, B$ (dashed lines) and discrete $A_{\varepsilon,h}$, $B_{\varepsilon,h}$ [$\varepsilon=0.1$, $h=0.1$] (solid lines) minima.

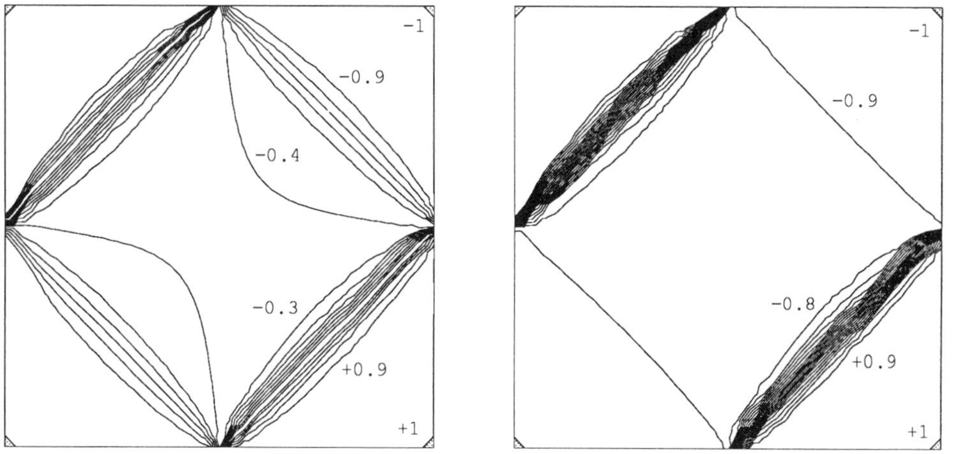


FIGURE 5.5. Ex. 4: level lines $\{u_{\varepsilon,h} = i0.1\}$, $-10 \leq i \leq 10$, of the discrete minimum [$h = 0.1$ and $\varepsilon = 0.05$, $\varepsilon = 0.01$, respectively].

5.4. *Example 4.* See Ex. 4 §2. The discrete boundary datum is defined by $\mu_h := \Pi_h \mu$. Figs. 5.4a,b show both the exact minima $A$, $B$ (dashed lines) and the discrete ones $A_{\varepsilon,h} := \{u_{\varepsilon,h} > -0.5\}$, $B_{\varepsilon,h} := \{u_{\varepsilon,h} > 0.5\}$ (solid lines), where $u_{\varepsilon,h}$ is the unique discrete minimum of $\mathcal{F}_{\varepsilon,h}$, for $\varepsilon=0.1$ and $h=0.1$. We stress that, in general, $\mathcal{F}_h(A) \neq \mathcal{F}_h(B)$, because of the nonsymmetry of the mesh $\mathcal{S}_h$; hence, for $\varepsilon$ very small, the unique discrete minimum $u_{\varepsilon,h}$ may select, independently of the initial guess, either $A$ or $B$ (see Figs. 5.5a,b, where $h=0.1$ and $\varepsilon=0.05$, $\varepsilon=0.01$, respectively). On the contrary, in [3], the relaxed minima $A_{\sigma,h}$ and $B_{\sigma,h}$ were obtained iterating from different initial guesses.

FIGURE 5.6. Ex. 5 ($r = 1$): exact minimum $A$ (dashed line), relaxed minimum $A_{\sigma,h}$ [$\sigma = 0.17$, $h = 0.1$] (dotted line), and discrete minimum $A_{\varepsilon,h}$ [$\varepsilon = 0.02$, $h = 0.1$] (solid line).

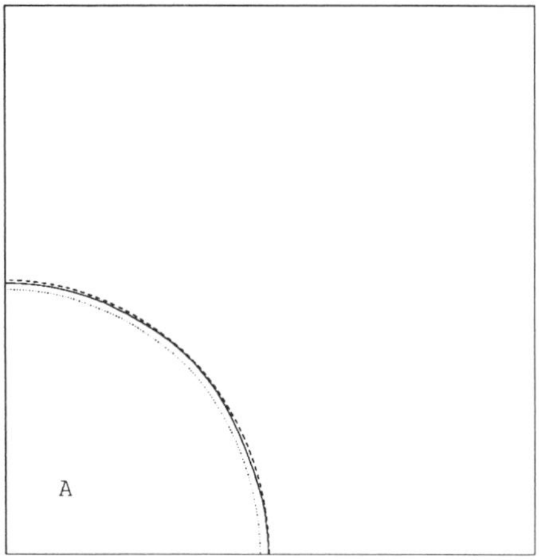


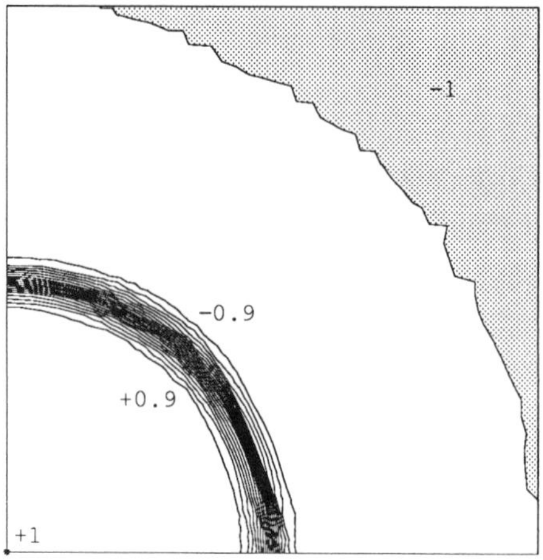


FIGURE 5.7. Ex. 5 ($r = 0.76$): level lines $\{u_{\varepsilon,h} = i0.1\}$, $-10 \le i \le 10$, of the discrete minimum [$\varepsilon = 0.005$, $h = 0.1$].

5.5. *Example 5.* Let $\Omega := (0,4)^2$, $\mu := 0$ (normal contact or reflection condition) on $x_1, x_2 = 0$, $\mu := 1$ on $x_1, x_2 = 4$, and $\kappa(x) := -r|x| + 2r + 0.5$, $r \in \mathbf{R}^+$. Define $\mu_h := \Pi_h \mu$ and $\kappa_h := \Pi_h \kappa$. The functional $\mathcal{F}$ has one absolute minimum, $\chi_A$, where $A := \{|x| \le 2\}$, for any $r > 0.75 =: r^\star$, and $\chi_\emptyset$, for any $0 < r < r^\star$; for $r = r^\star$, both $\chi_A$ and $\chi_\emptyset$ are absolute minima in $\widetilde{\mathcal{K}}$. Note that $\chi_\emptyset$ is a relative minimum of $\mathcal{F}$ in $\widetilde{\mathcal{K}}$, for any $r > r^\star$, and $\chi_A$ is a relative minimum, for any $0.25 < r < r^\star$. Let $r = 1$. Fig. 5.6 shows $A$ (dashed line), the relaxed minimum $A_{\sigma,h} := \{u_{\sigma,h} = 0\}$ (dotted line), for $h = 0.1$ and $\sigma = 0.17$ [$\mathbf{t} = 439$], and the discrete minimum $A_{\varepsilon,h} := \{u_{\varepsilon,h} > 0\}$ (solid line), for $h = 0.1$ and $\varepsilon = 0.02$ [$\mathbf{t} = 169$]. Note the accuracy of $A_{\varepsilon,h}$ with respect to $A_{\sigma,h}$, and compare $\mathbf{t}$!

As in Ex. 3, also in this case the convex approach gives an accurate approximation of the critical value $r^\star$. Taking $h = 0.1$ and $\varepsilon = 0.005$, we get $u_{\varepsilon,h} \simeq \chi_\emptyset$, if $r \le 0.755$ (e.g., for $r = 0.755$, $\{u_{\varepsilon,h} > -0.8\} = \emptyset$ and $\{-0.9 \le u_{\varepsilon,h} \le -0.8\}$ is a thin layer across $\partial A$), and $u_{\varepsilon,h} \simeq \chi_A$, if $r \ge 0.76$ (e.g., for $r = 0.76$, Fig. 5.7 shows the level lines $\{u_{\varepsilon,h} = i0.01\}$, $-10 \le i \le 10$). Hence, the numerical critical value $r^\star_{\varepsilon,h} \in [0.755, 0.76]$.

*Example 6.* Let $\Omega := (-1,1) \times (-1.5, 1.5)$, $\mu := 1$, and $\kappa := -40(x_1^2 + x_2^2(x_2^2 - 1)) + r$, $r \in \mathbf{R}$. Define $\kappa_h := \Pi_h \kappa$. No exact absolute minimum is known. The empty set is a relative minimum for any $r$. The numerical experiments show that there exists a critical value $r^\star \in (0.4, 0.5)$ for which $\mathcal{F}$ has two absolute minima. For $r < r^\star$, $\mathcal{F}$ has one absolute minimum $\chi_{A^r}$, where $A^r$ is the nonconnected set depicted by dashed lines in Fig. 5.8, for $r = r_1 := 0.4$ (actually, $A^{r_1}$ has been obtained by the front-tracking method introduced in [4]); the dotted line contours a relative minimum, $B^{r_1}$, of $\mathcal{F}$ in $\widetilde{\mathcal{K}}$ (note that dropping one component of $A^{r_1}$ gives a new relative minimum); the solid lines show the discrete

FIGURE 5.8. Ex. 6 ($r = 0.4$): front-tracked absolute minimum $A^1$ (dashed lines), relative minimum $B^1$ (dotted line) and discrete minimum $A^1_{\varepsilon,h}$ [$\varepsilon = 0.02$, $h = 0.1$] (solid lines).

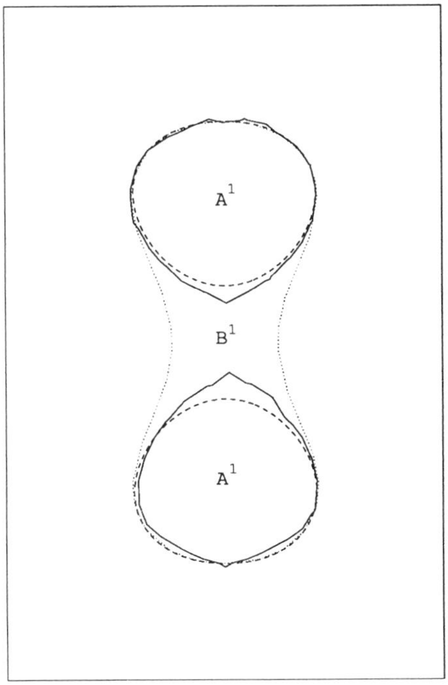


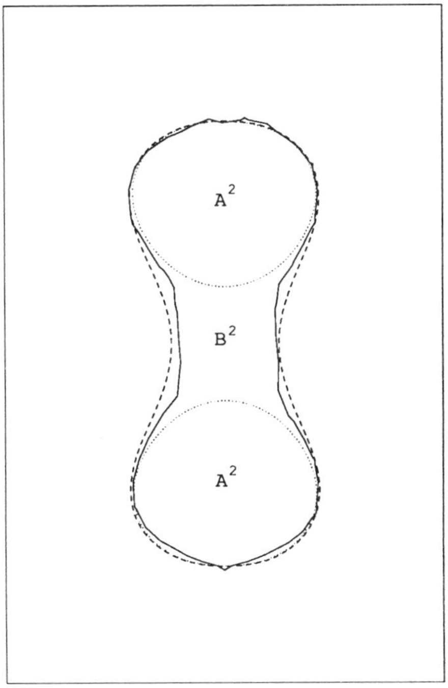


FIGURE 5.9. Ex. 6 ($r = 0.5$): front-tracked absolute minimum $B^2$ (dashed line), relative minimum $A^2$ (dotted lines) and discrete minimum $B^2_{\varepsilon,h}$ [$\varepsilon = 0.02$, $h = 0.1$] (solid line).

absolute minimum $A^{r_1}_{\varepsilon,h}$, for $h=0.1$ and $\varepsilon=0.02$. On the other hand, for $r>r^\star$, $\mathcal{F}$ has one absolute minimum $\chi_{B^r}$, where, for $r=r_2:=0.5$, the front-tracked $B^{r_2}$ is depicted by a dashed line in Fig. 5.9; the dotted lines contour the relative minimum $A^{r_2}$; the solid line shows the discrete absolute minimum $B^{r_2}_{\varepsilon,h}$, for $h=0.1$ and $\varepsilon=0.02$. For $r=r^\star$, $\chi_{A^{r^\star}}$ and $\chi_{B^{r^\star}}$ are the two absolute minima of $\mathcal{F}$ in $\widetilde{\mathcal{K}}$.

ACKNOWLEDGEMENTS. This work was partially supported by MURST (Progetto Nazionale "Equazioni di Evoluzione e Applicazioni Fisico-Matematiche" and "Analisi Numerica e Matematica Computazionale"), by CNR (IAN, Contract 89.01785.01, and Progetto Finalizzato "Sistemi Informatici e Calcolo Parallelo", Sottoprogetto "Calcolo Scientifico per Grandi Sistemi"), and by SISSA/ISAS, Italy.

## REFERENCES


[1] R. ALMGREN, *Computation of evolving phase interfaces with Gibbs-Thomson effect*, preprint (1991).

[2] G. BELLETTINI, M. PAOLINI, AND C. VERDI, *Γ-convergence of discrete approximations to interfaces with prescribed mean curvature*, Atti Accad. Naz. Lincei Rend. Cl. Sci. Fis. Mat. Natur. (9), 1 (1990), pp. 317–328.

[3] G. BELLETTINI, M. PAOLINI, AND C. VERDI, *Numerical minimization of geometrical type problems related to calculus of variations*, Calcolo (to appear).

[4] G. BELLETTINI, M. PAOLINI, AND C. VERDI, *Front-tracking and variational method to approximate interfaces with prescribed mean curvature*, in Proc. Numerical Methods for Free Boundary Problems (Jyväskylä, 1990, P. Neittaanmäki ed.), Birkhäuser, Basel, 1991, pp. 94–103.

[5] G. BELLETTINI, M. PAOLINI, AND C. VERDI, *Convex approximations of functionals with curvature*, Atti Accad. Naz. Lincei Rend. Cl. Sci. Fis. Mat. Natur. (9) (1991) (to appear).

[6] J.F. BLOWEY AND C.M. ELLIOTT, *The Cahn-Hilliard gradient theory for phase separation with non-smooth free energy Part II: numerical analysis*, Euro. J. Appl. Math. (1991) (to appear).

[7] G. CAGINALP, *The dynamics of a conserved phase field system: Stefan-like, Hele-Shaw, and Cahn-Hilliard models as asymptotic limits*, IMA J. Appl. Math., 44 (1990), pp. 77–94.

[8] P.G. CIARLET, *The Finite Element Method for Elliptic Problems*, North-Holland, Amsterdam, 1978.

[9] E. DE GIORGI, *Free discontinuity problems in calculus of variations*, in Proc. Meeting in honour of J.L. Lions, North-Holland, Amsterdam, 1988, to appear.

[10] E. DE GIORGI AND T. FRANZONI, *Su un tipo di convergenza variazionale*, Atti Accad. Naz. Lincei Rend. Cl. Sci. Fis. Mat. Natur. (8), 58 (1975), pp. 842–850.

[11] J.E. DENNIS AND R.B. SCHNABEL, *Numerical Methods for Unconstrained Optimization and Nonlinear Equations*, Prentice-Hall, New Jersey, 1983.

[12] H. FEDERER, *Geometric Measure Theory*, Springer-Verlag, Berlin, 1968.

[13] R. FINN, *Equilibrium Capillary Surfaces*, Springer-Verlag, Berlin, 1986.

[14] E. GAGLIARDO, *Caratterizzazioni delle tracce sulla frontiera relative ad alcune classi di funzioni in n variabili*, Rend. Sem. Mat. Univ. Padova, 27 (1957), pp. 284–305.

[15] P.E. GILL AND W. MURRAY, *Numerical Methods for Constrained Optimization*, Academic Press, London, 1974.

[16] E. GIUSTI, *Minimal Surface and Functions of Bounded Variation*, Birkhäuser, Boston, 1984.

[17] C. JOURON, *Resolution numérique du problème des surfaces minima*, Arch. Rational Mech. Anal., 59 (1975), pp. 311–341.

[18] U. MASSARI AND M. MIRANDA, *Minimal Surfaces of Codimension One*, North-Holland, Amsterdam, 1984.

[19] L. MODICA, *Gradient theory of phase transitions with boundary contact energy*, Ann. Inst. H. Poincaré Anal. Non Linéaire, 4 (1987), pp. 487–512.

[20] L. MODICA AND S. MORTOLA, *Un esempio di Γ-convergenza*, Boll. Un. Mat. Ital. B (5), 14 (1977), pp. 285–299.

[21] J. MOREL AND S. SOLIMINI, *Segmentation of images by variational methods: a constructive approach*, Revista Matematica Univ. Complutense Madrid, 1 (1988), pp. 169–182.

[22] D. MUMFORD AND J. SHAH, *Optimal approximations by piecewise smooth functions and associated variational problems*, Comm. Pure Appl. Math., 42 (1989), pp. 577–685.

[23] R.H. NOCHETTO, *Pointwise accuracy of a finite element method for nonlinear variational inequalities*, Numer. Math., 54 (1989), pp. 601–618.



G. Bellettini: International School for Advanced Studies SISSA/ISAS, 34014 TRIESTE.

M. Paolini: Istituto di Analisi Numerica del CNR, 27100 PAVIA.

C. Verdi: Dipartimento di Meccanica Strutturale, Università di Pavia, 27100 PAVIA.

C M BRAUNER, P FIFE, G NAMAH AND C SCHMIDT-LAINE

# Homogenization of propagative combustion processes

## 1 - Introduction

Despite the vast number of investigations into principles and techniques of homogenization in various contexts, nothing has been done, to our knowledge, concerning homogenization of propagative combustion processes. Nevertheless, propagating flame fronts in striated media do exist. Our basic example will be the combustion of propellant in certain rocket motors where striations may arise during the propellant casting. One may refer to [1], [3] and [7] where such propagation and a resulting phenomenon known as the "hump effect" are discussed. This latter anomaly appears as an overpressure in the combustion chamber and in fact has been hypothesized in [3] to be related to the presence of thin striations in the propellant.

With the goal of setting up a framework in this context, this paper will deal with the propagation of a flame front in a vertically striated medium. In the next section we shall write the equations governing such a propagation, and present some numerical results for a given wavelength. We recover a result proved in [7], namely the existence of a periodic solution in time, in a front-fixed frame. Finally, by using homogenization techniques, we show in the last section that the periodic solution converges to a travelling wave solution with constant velocity, as the period tends to zero.

## 2 - The Equations and Numerical Results

Let $x = \xi^\varepsilon(t)$ be the position of the flame front at time $t$ . Then the propagation of the front in a vertically striated medium is governed by the following equations

$$c\,\frac{\partial u^\varepsilon}{\partial t} - \frac{\partial}{\partial x}\,(d^\varepsilon\,\frac{\partial u^\varepsilon}{\partial x}\,) = 0 \quad , \quad x < \xi^\varepsilon(t) \tag{2.1}$$

$$\frac{d\xi^\varepsilon}{dt} = -\frac{1}{\rho}\; R_o^\varepsilon\, K(u^\varepsilon) \quad , \qquad x = \xi^\varepsilon(t) \tag{2.2}$$

and the boundary conditions

$$d^{\varepsilon}\frac{\partial u^{\varepsilon}}{\partial t} = \theta\,\beta\,R_o^{\varepsilon}\,K(u^{\varepsilon})\ , \qquad x = \xi^{\varepsilon}(t) \tag{2.3}$$

$$u^{\varepsilon}(x,t) \longrightarrow 0 \ \ as \qquad x \to -\infty\ . \tag{2.4}$$

Here $u^{\varepsilon}$ represents the temperature, and the inhomogeneity of the medium is characterised by the physical parameter $d^{\varepsilon}$ (thermal diffusivity), together with the chemical parameter $R_o^{\varepsilon}$. $K$ is an Arrhenius type function, and the other parameters $c$, $\rho$, $\beta$, and $\theta$ represent respectively, heat capacity, molar density, heat release, and the fraction of energy production which serves to heat the solid.

For the rest of the paper, the striations will be assumed to consist of two types of layers alternately placed in a periodic fashion. The parameters $d^{\varepsilon}$ and $R_o^{\varepsilon}$ will then have a periodic dependence on the spatial coordinate.

To solve equations (2.1)-(2.4) numerically for a given $\varepsilon$, it is convenient to consider them in a front-fixed frame, using the transformation $z = x - \xi^{\varepsilon}(t)$. The equations then become

$$c\,\frac{\partial u^{\varepsilon}}{\partial t} - c\,\frac{d\xi^{\varepsilon}}{dt}\,\frac{\partial u^{\varepsilon}}{\partial z} - \frac{\partial}{\partial z}\,(d^{\varepsilon}\,(z+\xi^{\varepsilon}(t))\,\frac{\partial u^{\varepsilon}}{\partial z}\,) = 0\ ,\ z < 0 \tag{2.5}$$

$$\frac{d\xi^{\varepsilon}}{dt} = -\frac{1}{\rho}\,R_o^{\varepsilon}(\xi^{\varepsilon}(t))\,K(u^{\varepsilon}(0,t)) \tag{2.6}$$

together with the boundary conditions

$$d^{\varepsilon}(\xi^{\varepsilon}(t))\,\frac{\partial u^{\varepsilon}}{\partial z} = \theta\,\beta\,R_o^{\varepsilon}(\xi^{\varepsilon}(t))\,K(u^{\varepsilon})\ ,\ z = 0 \tag{2.7}$$

$$u^{\varepsilon}(z,t) \longrightarrow 0\ ,\ \ as\ \ z \to -\infty\ . \tag{2.8}$$

Figure (2.1) shows a result obtained by using a finite difference scheme of Tikhonov and Samarkii's type [6]. For initial conditions, we have taken $\xi^{\varepsilon}(0) = 0$ and $u^{\varepsilon}(z,0) = u_o(z)$ with $u_o$, the steady state solution of the homogeneous problem. The function $K$ is chosen to be of exponential type.

The right hand side curves show temperature against time plots at the front (the uppermost curve) and at two other values of $z$ ($z=-0.5$, $z=-1.0$). The curves on the left represent temperature against distance plots for different values of time, including the initial condition. As proved in [7], the established temperature profiles are seen to be periodic in time.

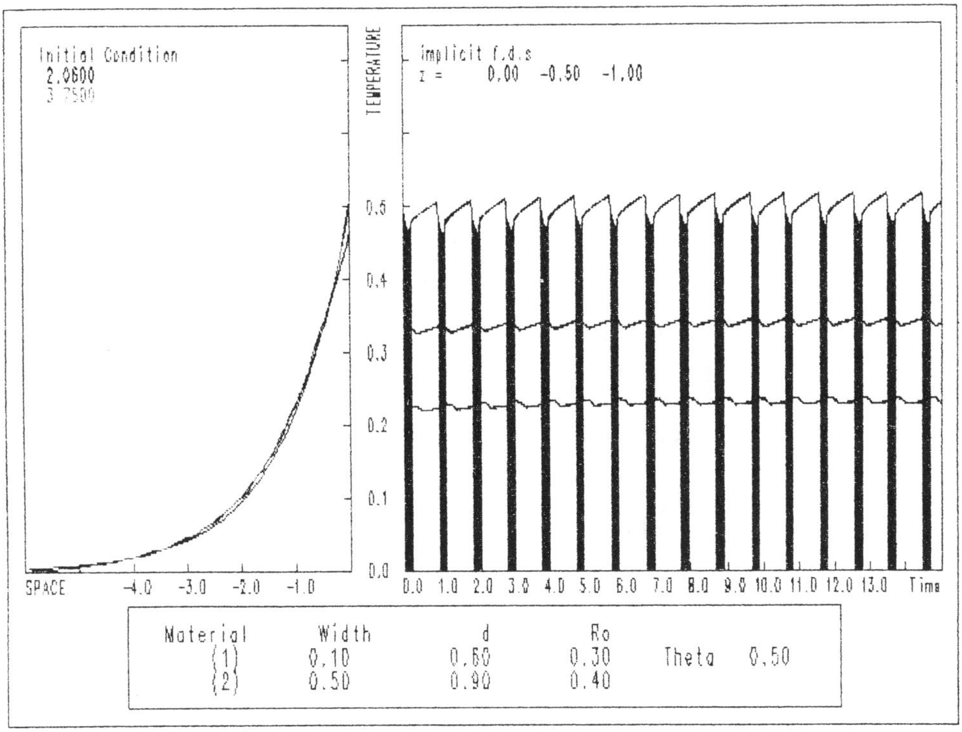


Fig: 2.1

## 3 - Homogenization process

3.a) Setting up of the problem

From now on, we assume $d^\varepsilon$ , $R_o^\varepsilon$ and $K$ to be positive, continuous and bounded real functions. Let $\Omega = (-\infty, 0)$ and $T > 0$, a fixed number. We then define

$$H = L^2(\Omega)\,, \quad V = H^1(\Omega)\,, \quad Q = \Omega \times (0, T) \; and$$

$$\theta^\varepsilon = \{(x, t) \in Q \, ; x < \xi^\varepsilon(t)\} \, .$$

We now define the microscopic variable $y$ as

$$y = \frac{x}{\varepsilon} \tag{3.1}$$

and consider the two functions $R_o$ and $d$ both bounded and periodic in $y$ . We next set

$$R_o^\varepsilon(x) = R_o\left(\frac{x}{\varepsilon}\right) \; and \; d^\varepsilon(x) = d\left(\frac{x}{\varepsilon}\right). \tag{3.2}$$

3.b) Ansatz expansions

We can try to obtain formal homogenized equations of the system (2.5)-(2.8) by using Ansatz expansions. For this purpose, we consider the following asymptotic expansions

$$u^{\varepsilon}(x, y, t) = u_o(x, t) + \varepsilon\, u_1(x, y, t) + \varepsilon^2\, u_2(x, y, t) + \dots \tag{3.3a}$$

$$\xi^{\varepsilon}(t) = \xi_o(t) + \varepsilon\, \xi_1(t) + \dots \tag{3.3b}$$

and proceed as in [2] to obtain equations satisfied by $u_o$ and $\xi_o$. As one can expect, $u_o$ is found to satisfy

$$c\,\frac{\partial u_o}{\partial t} - \frac{1}{m_y(\frac{1}{d})}\,\frac{\partial^2 u_o}{\partial x^2} = 0\ ,\ x < \xi_o(t) \tag{3.4}$$

but the homogenized speed is not obtained in an explicit way. In fact, we get

$$\frac{d\xi_o}{dt} = -\frac{1}{\rho}\, R_{oo}\, K\,(u_o(\xi_o(t), t)) \tag{3.5}$$

where $R_{oo}$ is the zeroth order term in a formal expansion of $R_o^{\varepsilon}\,(\xi_o)$. At first sight, it is tempting to believe that

$$R_{oo} = m_y(R_o) \tag{3.6}$$

but as we show in the next paragraph, $R_{oo}$ is in fact the harmonic mean of $R_o$, i.e.

$$R_{oo} = \frac{1}{m_y(\frac{1}{R_o})}\ . \tag{3.7}$$

($m_y$ ( ) represents the mean over one period).

3.c) Convergence results

THEOREM - *Under the assumptions of* (3.a), *we have the following convergence results as* $\varepsilon$ *tends to zero* :

$$u^{\varepsilon} \to u \quad \textit{weakly in}\ \ L^2(0, T\,; V)$$

$$\xi^{\varepsilon} \to \xi \ \ \textit{uniformly on}\ \ [0, T]$$

*with* $(u, \xi)$ *satisfying the following equations*

$$c\,\frac{d\xi}{dt}\,\frac{du}{dz} + \frac{1}{m_y(\frac{1}{d})}\,\frac{d^2u}{dz^2} = 0\ ,\ z < 0 \tag{3.8}$$

$$\frac{d\xi}{dt} = - \frac{\rho^{-1}}{m_y(\frac{1}{R_o})} K(u(0)) \tag{3.9}$$

*subject to the boundary conditions*

$$\frac{1}{m_y(\frac{1}{d})} \frac{du}{dz} = \theta \beta \frac{1}{m_y(\frac{1}{R_o})} K(u(0)), \ z = 0 \tag{3.10}$$

$$u(z) \longrightarrow 0 \ \ as \ \ z \to -\infty \ . \tag{3.11}$$

Note that $z$ represents the spatial coordinate in the front-fixed frame.

*Proof*: First we recall an existence theorem proved in [7]. Consider the problem (2.5)-(2.8) subject to the conditions

$$\xi^{\varepsilon}(0) = 0,$$
$$u^{\varepsilon}(z,0) = u^{\varepsilon}(z,T^{\varepsilon}),$$

with $T^{\varepsilon}$ = the time taken by the front to cover one spatial period ($\varepsilon Y$).

PROPOSITION 3.1 - *Under the assumptions of* 3(*a*), *the above problem admits a solution* $(u^{\varepsilon}, \xi^{\varepsilon}, T^{\varepsilon})$ *with*

$$u^{\varepsilon} \in L^2(0, T^{\varepsilon}; V) \cap L^{\infty}(0, T^{\varepsilon}; H),$$

$$\xi^{\varepsilon} \in W^{1,\infty}(0, T^{\varepsilon}), \quad T^{\varepsilon} > 0,$$

*and such that* $u^{\varepsilon}$ *is* $T^{\varepsilon}$*–periodic in time.*

In this paragraph, we are going to use the above result and the estimates obtained in [7]. Subsequently, we have the following convergences (up to an extraction)

$$u^{\varepsilon} \longrightarrow u \ \ weakly\ in\ \ L^2(0, T; V) \tag{3.12}$$

$$\xi^{\varepsilon} \longrightarrow \xi \ \ uniformly\ on \ \ [0, T] \tag{3.13}$$

$$\frac{\partial u^{\varepsilon}}{\partial t} \longrightarrow \frac{\partial u}{\partial t} \ \ weakly\ in\ \ L^2(0, T; V') \tag{3.14}$$

$$\frac{d\xi^{\varepsilon}}{dt} \longrightarrow \frac{d\xi}{dt} \ \ weakly\ in\ \ L^{\infty}(0, T)\ w.s \tag{3.15}$$

$$K(u^{\varepsilon}(0, .)) \longrightarrow K(u(0, .))\ strongly\ in\ \ L^p(0, T), 1 \leq p < +\infty . \tag{3.16}$$

We start by proving that the limit of $u^\varepsilon$ is independent of time. This amounts to proving that for $\varphi \in L^2(0, T; V)$

$$< \frac{\partial u^\varepsilon}{\partial t}, \varphi >_{L^2(0,T;V'),L^2(0,T;V)} \longrightarrow 0 \quad as \;\; \varepsilon \to 0 \ . \tag{3.17}$$

This is obtained from the fact that $u^\varepsilon$ is $T^\varepsilon$-periodic in time.

We now proceed by constructing a suitable test function. Given $P(y)$ as a first degree polynomial in $y$, we define $w(y)$ as a solution of

$$\frac{\partial}{\partial y}(d(y) \frac{\partial \omega}{\partial y}) = 0 \tag{3.18}$$

and where $\omega - P$ is a Y-periodic function in $y$.

We then define

$$\omega^\varepsilon(x) = \varepsilon\, \omega(\frac{x}{\varepsilon}) \tag{3.19}$$

and observe that

$$\frac{\partial}{\partial x}(d^\varepsilon(x) \frac{\partial \omega^\varepsilon}{\partial x}) = 0$$

i.e.

$$\frac{\partial}{\partial z}(d^\varepsilon(z+\xi^\varepsilon(t)) \frac{\partial w^\varepsilon}{\partial z}(z+\xi^\varepsilon(t)) = 0 \ , \ z < 0 \ . \tag{3.20}$$

We now set

$$\hat{w}^\varepsilon(z, t) = w^\varepsilon(z+\xi^\varepsilon(t)) \ .$$

For any $\varphi \in C_o^\infty(Q)$, we multiply (2.5) by $\varphi \hat{w}^\varepsilon$ and (3.20) by $\varphi u^\varepsilon$. We then integrate over $Q$ and the difference of the two results gives

$$\int_Q c\,( \frac{\partial u^\varepsilon}{\partial t} - \frac{d\xi^\varepsilon}{dt}\frac{\partial u^\varepsilon}{\partial z})\, \varphi\, \hat{w}^\varepsilon\, dz\, dt =$$

$$\int_Q d^\varepsilon(z+\xi^\varepsilon(t)) \frac{\partial \hat{w}^\varepsilon}{\partial z} u^\varepsilon \frac{\partial \varphi}{\partial z} dz\, dt - \int_Q d^\varepsilon(z+\xi^\varepsilon(t))\, \hat{w}^\varepsilon \frac{\partial u^\varepsilon}{\partial z}\frac{\partial \varphi}{\partial z} dz\, dt \ . \tag{3.21}$$

It is in this equation that we are going to pass to the limit. In addition to a classical procedure (cf. [2]), here we will be brought to handle the difficulties due to the presence of $\xi^\varepsilon$ in the above terms. To overcome this inconveniency, we will proceed via the initial frame, the overall idea being to put the term $\xi^\varepsilon$ in the test function.

Let us consider the first term. In the initial frame, it becomes (we revert to the $x$ variable by $x = z + \xi^\varepsilon(t)$)

$$X_1^\varepsilon = \int_Q c\,[\frac{\partial u^\varepsilon}{\partial t} - \frac{d\xi^\varepsilon}{dt}\frac{\partial u^\varepsilon}{\partial z}]\,\varphi\,\hat{w}^\varepsilon dz\,dt = \int_{\theta^\varepsilon} c\,\frac{\partial u^\varepsilon}{\partial t}\,w^\varepsilon(x)\,\varphi(x-\xi^\varepsilon(t),t)\,dx\,dt$$

$$= -\int_{\theta^\varepsilon} c\,u^\varepsilon\,w^\varepsilon\,(\frac{\partial\varphi}{\partial t}(x-\xi^\varepsilon, t) - \frac{d\xi^\varepsilon}{dt}\frac{\partial\varphi}{\partial x}(x-\xi^\varepsilon(t), t))\,dx\,dt\,.$$

The latter integral can be rewritten as

$$X_1^\varepsilon = -\int_Q c\,\tilde{u}^\varepsilon\,w^\varepsilon\,\chi_{\theta^\varepsilon}\,[\frac{\partial\tilde{\varphi}}{\partial t}(x-\xi^\varepsilon, t) - \frac{d\xi^\varepsilon}{dt}\frac{\partial\tilde{\varphi}}{\partial x}(x-\xi^\varepsilon(t), t)]\,dx\,dt \qquad (3.22)$$

with

$$\chi_{\theta^\varepsilon} = 1 \quad if \quad (x, t)\in\theta^\varepsilon \quad and \ 0 \ otherwise$$

$$\tilde{u}^\varepsilon(x, t) = u^\varepsilon(x, t)\,,\ x < \xi^\varepsilon(t)\,,$$

$$= u^\varepsilon(\xi^\varepsilon(t), t)\,,\ \xi^\varepsilon(t) \le x < 0\,.$$

It is in this reformulated form of (3.22) that we will pass to the limit. From (3.13), we have

$$\chi_{\theta^\varepsilon} \to \chi_\theta \quad strongly\ in\ L^P(Q)\,,\ 1\le p < +\infty \qquad (3.23)$$

where $\chi_\theta$ is the characteristic function of the set $\theta = \{x < \xi(t)\}$ . From (3.12), we have

$$\tilde{u}^\varepsilon \to \tilde{u} \quad weakly\ in\ L^2(0, T; V) \qquad (3.24)$$

when $\tilde{u}$ is the corresponding extension of $u$ . Note that $Q$ can be replaced by the compact support of $\tilde{\varphi}$ in (3.22), leading to a strong convergence of $\tilde{u}^\varepsilon$ .

From the definition of $w^\varepsilon$ , one can see that

$$w^\varepsilon \longrightarrow P \quad strongly\ in\ L^2(\Omega)\,. \qquad (3.25)$$

Therefore in the limit, (3.22) becomes

$$X_1 = -\int_Q c\,\tilde{u}\,P\,\chi_\theta\,[\frac{\partial\tilde{\varphi}}{\partial t}(x-\xi, t) - \frac{d\xi}{dt}\cdot\frac{\partial\tilde{\varphi}}{\partial x}(x-\xi(t), t)]\,dx\,dt$$

which can be rewritten as

$$X_1 = -\int_\theta c\,u\,P\,\frac{\partial}{\partial t}\varphi(x-\xi(t), t)\,dx\,dt\,. \qquad (3.26)$$

We then integrate w.r.t. time at least in a weak sense and retransform the resulting term in a front-fixed frame. Note that $u$ being independent of time, the limit of the first term reads finally

$$X_1 = -\int_Q c\,\frac{du}{dz}\frac{d\xi}{dt}\,P(z+\xi(t))\,\varphi\,dz\,dt\,. \qquad (3.27)$$

The two other terms of (3.21) are treated through classical arguments (cf. [2]) together with the techniques used above. This leads to the final homogenized equation

$$c\,\frac{d\xi}{dt}\,\frac{du}{dz}+\frac{1}{m_y(\frac{1}{d})}\,\frac{d^2u}{dz^2}=0\,,\quad z<0\,. \tag{3.28}$$

Now, it still remains to find the homogenized velocity $\frac{d\xi}{dt}$. We state the following result.

PROPOSITION 3.2 - $\displaystyle \frac{d\xi}{dt}=\frac{-\rho^{-1}}{m_y(\frac{1}{R_o})}\,K(u(0))\,.$

Proof. By dividing on both sides by $R_o^\varepsilon(\xi^\varepsilon(t))$, the velocity equation (2.6) becomes

$$\frac{1}{R_o^\varepsilon(\xi^\varepsilon(t))}\,\frac{d\xi^\varepsilon}{dt}=-\,\rho^{-1}\,K(u^\varepsilon(0,t))\,.$$

Recall that from (3.16) we have

$$K(u^\varepsilon(0,.))\longrightarrow K(u(0))\ \textit{strongly in}\ L^p(0,T)\,,\ 1\leq p<+\infty\,.$$

Next, let

$$X_\varepsilon=\int_0^T\frac{1}{R_o^\varepsilon(\xi^\varepsilon(t))}\,\frac{d\xi^\varepsilon}{dt}\,\psi(t)\,dt \tag{3.29}$$

with $\psi$, a test function on $[0,T]$.

Through a change of variable $u=\xi^\varepsilon(t)$, equation (3.29) becomes

$$X_\varepsilon=\int_0^{\xi^\varepsilon(T)}\frac{1}{R_o^\varepsilon(u)}\,\psi((\xi^\varepsilon)^{-1}(u))\,du\,. \tag{3.30}$$

Using (3.13) and the fact that

$$\frac{1}{R_o^\varepsilon}\longrightarrow m_y\,(\frac{1}{R_o})\ \ in\ L^\infty(\Omega)\ w.s\,, \tag{3.31}$$

one can easily show that

$$X_\varepsilon\longrightarrow X_o=\int_0^{\xi(T)}m_y\,(\frac{1}{R_o})\,\psi\,(\xi^{-1}(u))\,du\,. \tag{3.32}$$

By a reverse change of variable $t = \xi^{-1}(u)$, we have

$$X_o = \int_0^T m_y \left(\frac{1}{R_o}\right) \frac{d\xi}{dt} \psi(t)\, dt . \qquad (3.33)$$

This finally leads to

$$m_y \left(\frac{1}{R_o}\right) \frac{d\xi}{dt} = -\rho^{-1} K(u(0)) \qquad (3.34)$$

and this completes the proof of proposition 3.2.

The proof of the theorem is now completed by deriving the homogenized boundary condition.

The homogenized boundary condition. Let us consider the initial problem (2.5)-(2.8) and let $\varphi \in L^2(0, T; V)$. We multiply (2.5) by $\varphi$ and integrate by parts w.r.t. $z$ over $Q$. We obtain

$$\int_Q c \frac{\partial u^\varepsilon}{\partial t} \varphi\, dz\, dt + \int_Q \Gamma^\varepsilon \frac{\partial \varphi}{\partial z} dz\, dt - \int_0^T \Gamma^\varepsilon(0, t)\, \varphi(0, t)\, dt = 0 \qquad (3.35)$$

with

$$\Gamma^\varepsilon = d^\varepsilon(\xi^\varepsilon(t)) \frac{\partial u^\varepsilon}{\partial z} + c \frac{d\xi^\varepsilon}{dt} u^\varepsilon$$

and where $\Gamma^\varepsilon(0, t)$ will be given by (cf. (2.7))

$$\Gamma^\varepsilon(0, t) = \theta\, \beta\, R_o^\varepsilon(\xi^\varepsilon(t))\, K(u^\varepsilon(0, t)) + c \frac{d\xi^\varepsilon}{dt} u^\varepsilon(0, t) . \qquad (3.36)$$

By using proposition (3.2) and the fact that $\frac{\partial u}{\partial t} = 0$, in the limit (3.35) gives

$$\int_Q \Gamma \frac{\partial \varphi}{\partial z} dz\, dt - \int_0^T [\theta\, \beta \frac{1}{m_y(\frac{1}{R_o})} K(u(0)) + c \frac{d\xi}{dt} u(0)]\, \varphi(0, t)\, dt = 0 , \qquad (3.37)$$

with

$$\Gamma = \frac{1}{m_y(\frac{1}{d})} \frac{du}{dz} + c \frac{d\xi}{dt} u \quad (cf.\ 3.28)) .$$

After integrating the first term by parts w.r.t. $z$, equation (3.37) reduces to

$$\int_0^T \frac{1}{m_y(\frac{1}{d})} \frac{du}{dz}(0)\, \varphi(0, t)\, dt = \int_0^T \theta\, \beta \frac{1}{m_y(\frac{1}{R_o})} K(u(0))\, \varphi(0, t)\, dt . \qquad (3.38)$$

Equation (3.38) holding for all $\varphi \in L^2(0, T; V)$, we thus have

$$\frac{1}{m_y(\frac{1}{d})} \frac{du}{dz}(0) = \theta \beta \frac{1}{m_y(\frac{1}{R_o})} K(u(0)) \tag{3.39}$$

which is the homogenized boundary condition.

This ends the proof of the theorem.

Acknowledgements.

This work was supported in part through a contract with the SNPE, France. The authors are thankful to Dr B. Gossant and G. Uhrig for helpful discussions.

REFERENCES

[1] C.W. Beckman, R.L. Geisler, *Ballistic Anomaly trends in subscale solid motors*, 18th Joint Propulsion Conference, June 1982, Ohio.

[2] A. Bensoussan, J.L. Lions, G. Papanicolaou, *Asymptotic analysis for periodic structures* (North-Holland).

[3] C.M. Brauner et al., *Modelisation of the "Hump effect"*. To appear.

[4] C.M. Brauner, P. Fife, G. Namah, Cl. Schmidt-Lainé, *Propagation of a flame front in a striated solid medium*. To appear.

[5] J.L. Lions, E. Magenes, *Problèmes aux limites non homogènes et applications*, vol. 1 et 2, Paris, Dunod, 1968.

[6] A.R. Mitchell, *Computational Methods in partial differential equations*, p.23, John Wiley & Sons.

[7] G. Namah, *Etude de deux modèles de combustion en phase gazeuse et en milieu solide strié*, Thèse de l'Université Bordeaux I, 1990.

Addresses

C.M. BRAUNER, G. NAMAH
Centre de Recherche en Mathématiques de Bordeaux, Université Bordeaux I
351, Cours de la Libération, 33405 Talence Cedex - France.

P. FIFE
Department of Mathematics, University of Utah, Salt Lake City
UT 84 112 - U.S.A.

Cl. SCHMIDT-LAINE
CNRS, UMR 128, Ecole Normale Supérieure de Lyon
Laboratoire de Mathématiques
46, Allée d'Italie , 69364 Lyon Cedex 07 - France

B BRIGHI AND M CHIPOT

# Approximation in nonconvex problems

## 1. Introduction and notation

Let $\varphi : \mathbf{R}^n \to \mathbf{R}$ be a continuous function. Let us denote by $\varphi^{**}$ the convex envelope of $\varphi$ -i.e. the function defined by

$$\varphi^{**}(\alpha) = \sup \{ \, g(\alpha) \ : \ g \text{ convex} \ , \ g \leq \varphi \, \}. \tag{1.1}$$

We will assume all along that there exists a convex function $g$ bounding $\varphi$ from below in such a way that $\varphi^{**}$ is finite.

Let $\Omega$ be some bounded, polygonal domain of $\mathbf{R}^n, n \geq 1$, with a boundary $\Gamma$. If $W_0^{1,\infty}(\Omega)$ denotes the space of Lipschitz continuous functions vanishing on $\Gamma$, see [17], it is well known (see for instance [14]) that

$$\varphi^{**}(\alpha) = \inf_{v \in W_0^{1,\infty}(\Omega)} \{ \frac{1}{|\Omega|} \int_\Omega \varphi(\alpha + \nabla v(x)) \, dx \}. \tag{1.2}$$

Of course, this result implies in particular that the right hand side of (1.2) is independent of $\Omega$.

Let us denote by $\tau$ a triangulation of $\Omega$ into simplices $K$ of mesh size

$$h = \operatorname*{Max}_{K \in \tau} diam \ K$$

where *diam* $K$ denotes the diameter of the simplex $K$. Denote by $P_1(K)$ the set of polynomials of degree 1 on $K$ and set

$$V_h^0 = \{ v : \Omega \to \mathbf{R} \ : \ v \text{ is continuous, } v|_K \in P_1(K) \ \ \forall K \in \tau, \ v = 0 \ \text{ on } \Gamma \}$$

($v|_K$ denotes the restriction of $v$ to $K$).

Then let us define the approximated convex envelope of $\varphi$ by

$$\varphi_h^{**}(\alpha) = \inf_{v \in V_h^0} \{ \frac{1}{|\Omega|} \int_\Omega \varphi(\alpha + \nabla v(x)) \, dx \}. \tag{1.3}$$

One has clearly

$$\varphi_h^{**}(\alpha) \geq \varphi^{**}(\alpha) \tag{1.4}$$

and the infimum in (1.3) makes sense. Now, of course this infimum depends on $\Omega$ and the triangulation at hand. For simplicity we have dropped this dependence in the notation $\varphi_h^{**}(\alpha)$.

In this note, we would like to derive estimates for the difference

$$\varphi_h^{**} - \varphi^{**}$$

in terms of the mesh size $h$. This kind of results were introduced in [9], [6], [5], [10], [11] ,[12], [13] in a slightly different context.

## 2. One dimensional results

For simplicity we would like to restrict ourselves to the one dimensional case. We refer the reader to [2] for results in higher dimensions.

So, assume that

$$\Omega = (\omega_-, \omega_+)$$

and denote by $x_0, x_1, ..., x_{n+1}$ a subdivision of $(\omega_-, \omega_+)$ such that

$$\omega_- = x_0 < x_1 < ... < x_n < x_{n+1} = \omega_+ \tag{2.1}$$

$$h = \max_{i=0,\dots,n} x_{i+1} - x_i. \tag{2.2}$$

Then we have :

**THEOREM 1**: Assume that

$$\lim_{|\xi|\to\infty} \frac{\varphi(\xi)}{|\xi|} = +\infty \tag{2.3}$$

then under the above assumption there exists a constant $C = C(\alpha, \varphi)$ such that

$$0 \leq \varphi_h^{**}(\alpha) - \varphi^{**}(\alpha) \leq \frac{C}{|\Omega|} \cdot h \tag{2.4}$$

where $|\Omega| = \omega_+ - \omega_-$.

We will need some lemmas :

**Lemma 2.1** : Let $\varphi : \mathbf{R} \to \mathbf{R}$ be a continuous function. Let $a \in \mathbf{R}$ such that $\varphi^{**}(a) = \varphi(a)$. If there exists $b \in [-\infty, +\infty]$ such that

$$\varphi^{**}(x) < \varphi(x) \quad \forall\, x \in (a,b) \quad (\text{or} \quad (b,a)) \tag{2.5}$$

then $\varphi^{**}$ is affine on $(a, b)$.

**Proof :** There is no loss of generality in assuming that $b \in (a, +\infty]$.
Assume first that $b < +\infty$. Let us denote by $g$ the function that is affine on $(a, b)$ and agrees with $\varphi^{**}$ outside of $(a, b)$. Of course, $g$ is convex and

$$g \geq \varphi^{**}. \tag{2.6}$$

Next, remark that

$$g = \varphi^{**} \leq \varphi \qquad \text{outside of} \quad (a, b).$$

We claim that

$$g \leq \varphi. \tag{2.7}$$

If not, it would exist $z_0 \in (a, b)$ such that

$$\eta = \inf_{[a,b]} \varphi - g = \varphi(z_0) - g(z_0) < 0.$$

Then, $g + \eta$ is a convex function such that

$$g + \eta \leq \varphi$$

and thus

$$g + \eta \leq \varphi^{**}.$$

But, then at the point $z_0$ one would have

$$\varphi^{**}(z_0) \geq g(z_0) + \eta = \varphi(z_0) \geq \varphi^{**}(z_0)$$

which contradicts (2.5). From (2.7) we derive

$$g \leq \varphi^{**}$$

and by (2.6)

$$g = \varphi^{**}.$$

This completes the proof since if (2.5) holds on $(a, +\infty)$ then, $\varphi^{**}$ is affine on any finite interval included in $(a, +\infty)$ and thus on $(a, +\infty)$.

**Lemma 2.2 :** Let $\hat{\varphi}$ be a continuous, nonnegative function such that :

$$\hat{\varphi}(\omega_1) = \hat{\varphi}(\omega_2) = 0.$$

Let $\alpha \in [\omega_1, \omega_2]$, then there exists $u_h \in V_h^0$, and a constant $C = C(\alpha, \hat{\varphi})$ such that :

$$\frac{1}{|\Omega|} \int_\Omega \hat{\varphi}(\alpha + u_h'(x))\, dx \;\leq\; \frac{C}{|\Omega|} h \tag{2.8}$$

$$\alpha + u'_h(x) \in [\omega_1, \omega_2] \quad \text{a.e. in } \Omega. \tag{2.9}$$

Recall that $|\Omega| = \omega_+ - \omega_-$.

**Proof** : First, replacing $\hat{\varphi}$ by

$$\beta \to \hat{\varphi}(\alpha + \beta)$$

there is no loss of generality to assume that $\alpha = 0$. Next, if $\omega_1$ or $\omega_2 = 0$, $u_h = 0$ does it. So we can assume

$$\omega_1 < 0 < \omega_2.$$

Then we can define

$$u = \omega_2(x - \omega_-) \wedge \omega_1(x - \omega_+)$$

where $\wedge$ denotes the minimum of two functions, and

$$u_h = \text{the interpolate of } u.$$

Clearly,

$$u'_h = \omega_i$$

except maybe on some interval $(x_k, x_{k+1})$ where

$$u'_h \in (\omega_1, \omega_2),$$

since on this interval

$$u'_h(x) = \beta = \frac{1}{x_{k+1} - x_k} \int_{x_k}^{x_{k+1}} u'_h(x)dx = \frac{1}{x_{k+1} - x_k} \int_{x_k}^{x_{k+1}} u'(x)dx ,$$

and thus $u'_h(x) \in (\omega_1, \omega_2)$. It then follows that

$$\int_\Omega \hat{\varphi}(u'_h(x))\, dx = \int_{x_k}^{x_{k+1}} \hat{\varphi}(u'_h(x))\, dx \le \hat{\varphi}(\beta)h.$$

This concludes the proof of the lemma.

We are now able to give a proof of the Theorem 1.

**Proof of Theorem 1** : Set

$$\mathcal{A} = \{a \in \mathbf{R} : \varphi(a) = \varphi^{**}(a)\}.$$

If $co\mathcal{A}$ denotes the convex hull of $\mathcal{A}$ we have

$$co\mathcal{A} = \mathbf{R}. \tag{2.10}$$

Indeed, if not we can assume that

$$a_1 = sup\ \mathcal{A} < +\infty.$$

(We would argue the same way if we had $inf \mathcal{A} > -\infty$).

Since $\mathcal{A}$ is closed one has clearly

$$\varphi^{**}(a_1) = \varphi(a_1) \quad , \quad \varphi^{**}(\beta) < \varphi(\beta) \quad \forall\ \beta > a_1.$$

By Lemma 2.1 it follows that $\varphi^{**}$ is affine on $[a_1, +\infty)$ which means that for some $\lambda$

$$\varphi^{**}(\beta) = \lambda(\beta - a_1) + \varphi(a_1), \quad \forall\ \beta \geq a_1.$$

By (2.3), for any positive constant $C$, there exists a constant $\beta'$ such that

$$\varphi(\beta) \geq C(\beta - a_1) \quad \forall\ \beta \geq \beta' \geq a_1$$

and thus a constant $C'$ such that

$$\varphi(\beta) \geq C(\beta - a_1) + C' \quad \forall\ \beta \tag{2.11}$$

(it is enough to choose $C' = \inf_{(-\infty, a_1]} \varphi$). But then, since the right hand side of (2.11) is a convex function,

$$\varphi^{**}(\beta) = \lambda(\beta - a_1) + \varphi(a_1) \geq C(\beta - a_1) + C' \quad \forall\ \beta$$

which is clearly impossible if one chooses $C > \lambda$. This proves (2.10).

Let $\alpha \in \mathbf{R}$. If $\alpha \in \mathcal{A}$, then one has

$$\varphi(\alpha) = \varphi^{**}(\alpha) = \varphi_h^{**}(\alpha)$$

and (2.4) follows. If $\alpha \notin \mathcal{A}$, then by (2.10) there exists $\omega_1, \omega_2 \in \mathcal{A}$ such that

$$\alpha \in (\omega_1, \omega_2) \text{ and } \varphi^{**} < \varphi \text{ on } (\omega_1, \omega_2).$$

By Lemma (2.1), $\varphi^{**}$ is affine on $(\omega_1, \omega_2)$, and by lemma 2.2 applied with

$$\hat{\varphi} = \varphi - \varphi^{**}$$

one has for some $u_h$

$$\frac{1}{|\Omega|} \int_\Omega \varphi(\alpha + u_h'(x))\, dx \ - \ \frac{1}{|\Omega|} \int_\Omega \varphi^{**}(\alpha + u_h'(x))\, dx \ \leq \frac{C}{|\Omega|} h$$

hence

$$\varphi_h^{**}(\alpha) - \varphi^{**}\Big(\frac{1}{|\Omega|} \int_\Omega (\alpha + u_h'(x))\, dx\ \Big) \leq \frac{C}{|\Omega|} h$$

which is

$$\varphi_h^{**}(\alpha) - \varphi^{**}(\alpha) \leq \frac{C}{|\Omega|} h.$$

This completes the proof.

**Remark 1** : If $\mathbf{R} \setminus \mathcal{A}$ is a bounded set of $\mathbf{R}$, then the constant $C$ does not depend on $\alpha$. It is the case when $\varphi$ is convex at infinity.

**Remark 2** : The estimate (2.4) is sharp. Indeed, if (2.3) fails one can even construct examples for which (2.4) fails for any power of $h$. For a more precise analysis of this phenomenon and complementary results see [2], [1].

**Remark 3** : In higher dimension one can obtain estimates of $\varphi_h^{**} - \varphi^{**}$ in $h^{\frac{1}{2}}$ provided that (2.3) holds. More precisely there exists a constant $C = C(\alpha, \varphi, \Omega)$ such that

$$0 \leq \varphi_h^{**}(\alpha) - \varphi^{**}(\alpha) \leq C h^{\frac{1}{2}}$$

The method is based on the results of [5] and a careful analysis, see[1].

Note for instance that it requires an extension of Lemma 2.1.

**Remark 4** : Minimizing sequences of (1.3) develop oscillations that occur in numerous physical setting- see for instance [3], [4], [7], [16].

Their study provides nice applications of the theory of Young measures (see [15], [19]). We refer the reader to [9], [10], [11], [12], [13], [6], [5] for complements on this subject.

## REFERENCES


[1] B. Brighi : Thesis University of Metz, in preparation.

[2] B. Brighi and M. Chipot : Approximated convex envelope of a function. In preparation.

[3] J. M. Ball and R. D. James : Fine phase mixtures as minimizers of energy. Arch. Rational Mech. Anal., 100, (1987), p. 13-52.

[4] J. M. Ball and R. D. James : Proposed Experimental Tests of a Theory of Fine Microstructures and the Two-Well Problem. (1991), preprint.

[5] M. Chipot : Numerical analysis of oscillations in nonconvex problems. Numerische Mathematik, 59, (1991), p. 747-767.

[6] M. Chipot and C. Collins : Numerical approximation in variational problems with potential wells. (1990), preprint. (To appear in SIAM J. Numer. Anal.).

[7] M. Chipot and D. Kinderlehrer : Equilibrium configurations of crystals. Arch. Rational Mech. Anal., 103, (1988), p. 237-277.

[8] C. Collins : Thesis, University of Minnesota, 1990.

[9] C. Collins, D. Kinderlehrer and M. Luskin : Numerical approximation of the solution of a variational problem with a double well potential. IMA preprint # 605, (1990). (To appear in SIAM J. Numer. Anal.).

[10] C. Collins and M. Luskin : The computation of the austenitic-martensitic phase transition. In *Partial Differential Equations and Continuum Models of Phase Transitions*, Lecture Notes in Physics # 344, M. Rascle, D.Serre and M. Slemrod, eds., Springer-Verlag, Berlin, New York, (1989), p. 34–50.

[11] C. Collins and M. Luskin : Computational results for phase transitions in shape memory materials. In *Smart Materials, Structures, and Mathematical Issues*, C. Rogers, ed. Technomic Publishing Co., Lancaster, Pennsylvania, (1989), p. 198–215.

[12] C. Collins and M. Luskin : Numerical modeling of the microstructure of crystals with symmetry-related variants. In *Proceedings of the ARO US-Japan Workshop on Smart/ Intelligent Materials*, Technomic Publishing Co., Lancaster, Pennsylvania, (to appear).

[13] C. Collins and M. Luskin : Optimal order error estimates for the finite element approximation of the solution of a nonconvex variational problem. Preprint, (1990).

[14] B. Dacorogna : *Direct Methods in the Calculus of Variations.* Applied math. Sciences # 78, Springer Verlag (1989).

[15] L. C. Evans : *Weak Convergence Methods for Nonlinear Partial Differential Equations.* A.M.S. Regional Conference Series in Mathematics # 74, (1989).

[16] I. Fonseca : The lower quasiconvex envelope of the stored energy function for an elastic crystal. J. Math. Pures et Appl., 67, (1988), p. 175–195.

[17] D. Gilbarg and N. S. Trudinger : *Elliptic Partial Differential Equations of Second Order.* Springer Verlag, (1985).

[18] R. Kohn : The relationship between linear and nonlinear variational models of coherent phase transitions. In *Proceedings of the Seventh Army Conference on Applied Mathematics and Computing*, West Point, June 1989.

[19] L. Tartar : Compensated compactness and application to partial differential equations In *Nonlinear analysis and mechanics: Heriot–Watt Symp IV*, R.J. Knops ed., Pitman, (1979), 136–212.

B. Brighi & M. Chipot
Université de Metz
Département de Mathématiques
Ile de Saulcy, 57045 METZ-CEDEX 01
(FRANCE)

A BRILLARD

# Asymptotic flow of a viscous and incompressible fluid through a plane sieve

## I - INTRODUCTION

A bounded, smooth and open subset $\Omega$ of $\mathbb{R}^3$ is separated in two open subsets $\Omega^+$ and $\Omega^-$, by the plane $\{x_3 = 0\}$. On $\Sigma = \Omega\cap\{x_3 = 0\}$, are $\varepsilon$-periodically disposed identical $r_\varepsilon$-homothetics of an open subset T of the unit ball $B_2(1)$ of $\mathbb{R}^2$, with : $0 < r_\varepsilon < \varepsilon/2$ (see fig. 1, below).

A viscous and incompressible fluid slowly flows in a stationary motion, either in $\Omega_{\varepsilon D} = \Omega\backslash\bigcup_i T_{\varepsilon i}$, with homogeneous Dirichlet boundary conditions, or in $\Omega_{\varepsilon N} = \Omega^+\cup\Omega^-\cup(\bigcup_i T_{\varepsilon i})$, with homogeneous Neumann boundary conditions, under the action of exterior forces $\vec{f}$ ($\vec{f} \in (L^2(\Omega))^3$).

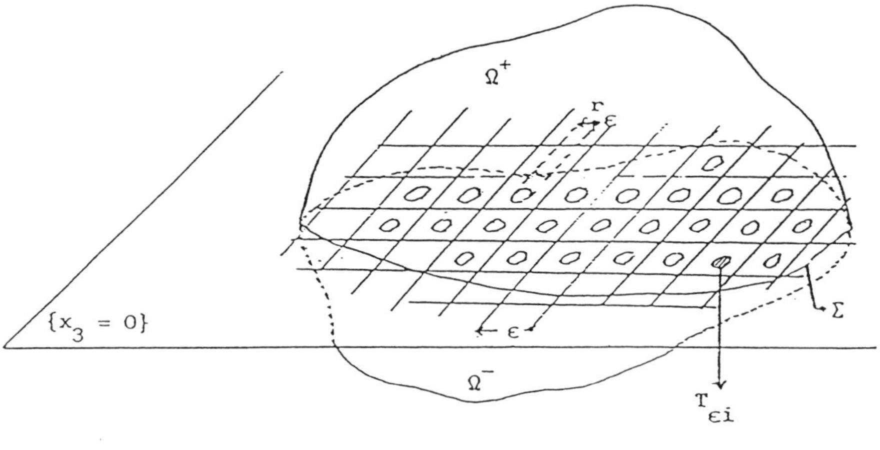


fig. 1 : the porous media

In the first case, the velocity $\vec{u}_{\varepsilon D}$ of the fluid is the solution of :

$$\left|\begin{array}{lll} -\Delta\vec{u}_{\varepsilon D} = -\nabla p_{\varepsilon D} + \vec{f} & \text{in } \Omega_{\varepsilon D}, & \\ \operatorname{div}(\vec{u}_{\varepsilon D}) = 0 & \text{in } \Omega_{\varepsilon D}, & \quad (1) \\ \vec{u}_{\varepsilon D|\partial\Omega} = \vec{0}\ ;\ \vec{u}_{\varepsilon D|\Sigma} = \vec{0} & \text{on } \bigcup_i T_{\varepsilon i}, & \end{array}\right.$$

where $p_{\varepsilon D}$ represents the internal pressure of the fluid. For simplicity, the viscosity coefficient of the fluid has been normalized to 1. The fluid is stuck on $\partial\Omega$ and, along $\Sigma$, on the union of identical solid pieces of size $r_\varepsilon$.

In the second case, the velocity $\vec{u}_{\varepsilon N}$ of the fluid is the solution of :

$$
\left|\begin{array}{ll}
-\Delta\vec{u}_{\varepsilon N} + \vec{u}_{\varepsilon N} = -\nabla p_{\varepsilon N} + \vec{f} & \text{in } \Omega_{\varepsilon N}, \\
\mathrm{div}(\vec{u}_{\varepsilon N}) = 0 \quad \text{in } \Omega_{\varepsilon N}, & \\
\dfrac{\partial\vec{u}_{\varepsilon N}}{\partial\nu} - p_{\varepsilon N}.\vec{\nu} = \vec{0} \quad \text{on } \partial\Omega \ ; & \dfrac{\partial\vec{u}_{\varepsilon N}}{\partial n} - p_{\varepsilon N}.\vec{n} = \vec{0} \quad \text{on } \Sigma\setminus\bigcup_i T_{\varepsilon i},
\end{array}\right. \tag{2}
$$

where $\vec{\nu}$ denotes the outer normal to $\Omega$ and $\vec{n}$ is equal to $(0,0,-1)$. The fluid slowly flows through the Neumann strainer, whose apertures are of size $r_\varepsilon$.

The purpose of this work is to study the behaviour of these two flows, when the parameter $\varepsilon$ goes to 0. The total number $I(\varepsilon)$ of $r_\varepsilon$-homothetics of $T$ included in $\Sigma$, grows as $\mathrm{meas}(\Sigma)/\varepsilon^2$, while their common size $r_\varepsilon$ decreases to 0. Hence, the boundary conditions on $\Sigma$ become more and more oscillating.

In [3], [7], [8], see also the references therein, the asymptotic behaviour of the solutions $u_{\varepsilon D}$ and $u_{\varepsilon N}$ of :

$$
\left|\begin{array}{lll}
-\Delta u_{\varepsilon D} = f, & \text{in } \Omega_{\varepsilon D} & (f \in L^2(\Omega)) \\
u_{\varepsilon D|\partial\Omega} = 0 \ ; \ u_{\varepsilon D|\Sigma} = 0 & \text{on } \bigcup_i T_{\varepsilon i}, &
\end{array}\right. \tag{3}
$$

$$
\left|\begin{array}{ll}
-\Delta u_{\varepsilon N} + u_{\varepsilon N} = f, & \text{in } \Omega_{\varepsilon N} \\
\dfrac{\partial u_{\varepsilon N}}{\partial\nu} = 0 \quad \text{on } \partial\Omega \ ; & \dfrac{\partial u_{\varepsilon N}}{\partial n} = 0 \quad \text{on } \Sigma\setminus\bigcup_i T_{\varepsilon i},
\end{array}\right. \tag{4}
$$

was studied, when $\varepsilon$ goes to 0. A critical size $r_\varepsilon^c = \varepsilon^2$ of the zones was exhibited and it was proved that the asymptotic behaviour of the two sequences $(u_{\varepsilon D})_\varepsilon$ and $(u_{\varepsilon N})_\varepsilon$ is quite analogous, since one has :

**THEOREM 1.** ([8], Theorem 2.1)
*$(u_{\varepsilon D})_\varepsilon$ converges, in the weak topology of $H^1_0(\Omega)$, to $u_{0D}$ solution of :*

$$
\operatorname*{Min}_{u\in H^1_0(\Omega)} \left( \int_\Omega |\nabla u|^2\,dx + a.C.\int_\Sigma |u_{|\Sigma}|^2\,d\sigma - 2.\int_\Omega f.u\,dx \right),
$$

$$\text{where : } a = \lim_{\varepsilon\to 0} (r_\varepsilon . \varepsilon^{-2}), \tag{5}$$

$$C = \operatorname*{Min}_{\substack{w\in H^1(\mathbb{R}^3)\\ w_{|\Sigma} = 1 \text{ on } T}} \int_{\mathbb{R}^3} |\nabla w|^2 \, dx.$$

**THEOREM 2.** ([8], Theorem 2.2)

$(u_{\varepsilon N})_\varepsilon$ *converges, in the weak topology of* $H^1(\Omega^+\cup\Omega^-)$, *to* $u_{ON}$ solution of :

$$\operatorname*{Min}_{u\in H^1(\Omega^+\cup\Omega^-)} \left( \int_{\Omega^+\cup\Omega^-} (|\nabla u|^2 + |u|^2)\, dx + \frac{a}{4}.C.\int_\Sigma [u]^2 \, d\sigma - 2.\int_\Omega f.u \, dx \right),$$

*where* $[u]$ *represents the jump of* $u$ *accross* $\Sigma$, *that is the difference between the traces* $u^+$ *(on* $\Sigma^+$*) and* $u^-$ *(on* $\Sigma^-$*) of the function* $u$ *in* $H^1(\Omega^+\cup\Omega^-)$.

In the next paragraph, we study the case of a low density of zones, that is when $\lim_{\varepsilon\to 0} (r_\varepsilon . \varepsilon^{-1})$ is equal to 0 and we establish an analogy on the asymptotic behaviour of the sequences $(\vec{u}_{\varepsilon D})_\varepsilon$ and $(\vec{u}_{\varepsilon N})_\varepsilon$, similar to the above-described one (see Theorems 3, 8). Then, we consider the case of a high density of zones, taking $r_\varepsilon$ equal to $\alpha.\varepsilon$ $(0 < \alpha < 1/2)$ and we precise these behaviours (Theorems 14, 16). Finally, we briefly indicate some possible extensions of these results.

## II - ASYMPTOTIC BEHAVIOUR OF THE FLOWS WHEN $\lim_{\varepsilon\to 0} r_\varepsilon.\varepsilon^{-1} = 0$

In order to decribe the asymptotic behaviour of $(\vec{u}_{\varepsilon D})_\varepsilon$ and $(\vec{u}_{\varepsilon N})_\varepsilon$, we introduce the solution $(\vec{W}^k, q^k)$, $k = 1, 2$ or $3$, of the Stokes problem :

$$\left|\begin{array}{ll} -\Delta\vec{W}^k = -\nabla q^k & \text{in } \mathbb{R}^3\backslash T, \\ \operatorname{div}(\vec{W}^k) = 0 & \text{in } \mathbb{R}^3\backslash T, \\ \vec{W}^k_{|T} = \vec{e}^k, & (\vec{e}^k \text{ is the } k\text{-th canonical vector of } \mathbb{R}^3) \\ \vec{W}^k(y) \xrightarrow[|y|\to+\infty]{} 0 \; ; \; D_i\vec{W}^k(y) \xrightarrow[|y|\to+\infty]{} 0 \; ; \; q^k(y) \xrightarrow[|y|\to+\infty]{} 0, & \end{array}\right. \tag{6}$$

and the positive definite and symmetric matrix $\mathcal{C}$ associated to these solutions by :

$$\mathcal{C}_{k\ell} = \int_{\mathbb{R}^3\backslash T} \nabla\vec{W}^k . \nabla\vec{W}^\ell \, dy \qquad (k, \ell = 1, 2 \text{ or } 3). \tag{7}$$

The existence of $\vec{W}^k$, $q^k$ may be proved by means of the classical methods, based on the variational formulation of (6).

**A) CASE OF HOMOGENEOUS DIRICHLET BOUNDARY CONDITIONS**

The asymptotic flow crucially depends on the value of the constant $a$ defined in (5) and is described in the following theorem :

**THEOREM 3.**

*1) Let $a$, defined in (5), be equal to 0. Then, the sequence $(\vec{u}_{\varepsilon D})_\varepsilon$ converges in the weak topology of $(H^1_o(\Omega))^3$, to $\vec{u}^\circ_{oD}$, solution of :*

$$\begin{cases} -\Delta\vec{u}^\circ_{oD} = -\nabla p^\circ_{oD} + \vec{f} & \text{in } \Omega, \\ \operatorname{div}(\vec{u}^\circ_{oD}) = 0 & \text{in } \Omega, \\ \vec{u}^\circ_{oD}|_{\partial\Omega} = \vec{0}. \end{cases}$$

*2) Suppose that $a$ is equal to $+\infty$. Then, the sequence $(\vec{u}_{\varepsilon D})_\varepsilon$ converges, in the weak topology of $(H^1_o(\Omega^+\cup\Omega^-))^3$ to $\vec{u}^*_{oD}$, solution of :*

$$\begin{cases} -\Delta\vec{u}^*_{oD} = -\nabla p^*_{oD} + \vec{f} & \text{in } \Omega^+\cup\Omega^-, \\ \operatorname{div}(\vec{u}^*_{oD}) = 0 & \text{in } \Omega^+\cup\Omega^-, \\ \vec{u}^*_{oD}|_{\partial\Omega} = \vec{0}\ ;\ \vec{u}^*_{oD}|_{\Sigma} = \vec{0}. \end{cases}$$

*3) Suppose that $a$ is strictly positive and finite. Then, the sequence $(\vec{u}_{\varepsilon D})_\varepsilon$ converges in the weak topology of $(H^1_o(\Omega))^3$, to the solution $\vec{u}_{oD}$ of :*

$$\begin{cases} -\Delta\vec{u}_{oD} = -\nabla p_{oD} + \vec{f} & \text{in } \Omega^+\cup\Omega^-, \\ \operatorname{div}(\vec{u}_{oD}) = 0 & \text{in } \Omega^+\cup\Omega^-, \\ \left[\dfrac{\partial\vec{u}_{oD}}{\partial n} - p_{oD}.\vec{n}\right] + a.\mathscr{C}.\vec{u}_{oD}|_{\Sigma} = \vec{0}, \end{cases}$$

*where $\mathscr{C}$ is the matrix defined by (7).*

In order to prove these result, let us first establish the variational formulation of (1). The solution $\vec{u}_{\varepsilon D}$ of (1) is the solution of the minimization problem :

$$\min_{\vec{u}\in(H^1_o(\Omega))^3} \{F_{\varepsilon D}(\vec{u}) - 2.\int_{\Omega_{\varepsilon D}} \vec{f}.\vec{u}\, dx\}, \tag{8}$$

where $F_{\varepsilon D}$ is the functional defined on $(H^1_o(\Omega))^3$ by :

$$F_{\varepsilon D}(\vec{u}) = \int_{\Omega_{\varepsilon D}} |\nabla\vec{u}|^2\, dx + \delta_{V_{\varepsilon D}}(\vec{u}), \tag{9}$$

$\delta_{V_{\varepsilon D}}$ denoting the indicator function of the closed subspace $V_{\varepsilon D}$ of $(H^1_o(\Omega))^3$ :

$$V_{\varepsilon D} = \{\vec{u} \in (H^1_o(\Omega))^3 \ / \ \mathrm{div}(\vec{u}) = \vec{0} \text{ in } \Omega \ ; \ \vec{u}_{|\Sigma} = \vec{0} \text{ on } \bigcup_i T_{\varepsilon i}\}. \tag{10}$$

Taking into account this variational formulation (8) of (1), the asymptotic behaviour of $(\vec{u}_{\varepsilon D})_\varepsilon$ may be deduced from the asymptotic behaviour of the sequence $(F_{\varepsilon D})_\varepsilon$, thanks to the use of epi-convergence methods :

**DEFINITION AND THEOREM 4.** (see [2], Theorem 1.10) *Let* $(F_\varepsilon)_\varepsilon$ *and* F *be functionals from a metric vector space* $(X,\tau)$ *into* $\bar{\mathbb{R}}$. $(F_\varepsilon)_\varepsilon$ *epi-converges to* F, *in the topology* $\tau$, *if and only if the two following assertions are fulfilled :*

$$\forall\, x \in X,\ \exists\ (x^o_\varepsilon)_\varepsilon\ \tau\text{-converging to } x : \limsup_{\varepsilon \to 0} F_\varepsilon(x^o_\varepsilon) \le F(x), \tag{11}$$

$$\forall\, x \in X,\ \forall\ (x_\varepsilon)_\varepsilon\ \tau\text{-converging to } x : \liminf_{\varepsilon \to 0} F_\varepsilon(x_\varepsilon) \ge F(x). \tag{12}$$

*Suppose that* $x_\varepsilon$ *is a minimizer of* $F_\varepsilon$ : $F_\varepsilon(x_\varepsilon) = \mathrm{Min}_{x\in X} F_\varepsilon(x)$, $(x_\varepsilon)_\varepsilon$ *is* $\tau$*-relatively compact and* $(F_\varepsilon)_\varepsilon$ *epi-converges to* F *in the topology* $\tau$. *Then, every limit point* $\bar{x}$ *of* $(x_\varepsilon)_\varepsilon$ *is a minimizer of* F *and, moreover,* $\lim_{\varepsilon\to 0} F_\varepsilon(x_\varepsilon) = F(\bar{x})$.

**REMARK 5.** This variational convergence is well-fitted to the asymptotic analysis of minimization problems and is a special case of the Γ-convergence introduced in [5]. For the properties of the epi-convergence, we refer to [2].

Theorem 3 is a consequence, through the Definition 4, of the following theorem, which has to be compared to Theorem 1.

**THEOREM 6.** *Let* $F_{\varepsilon D}$ *be the functional defined by* (9). *Then,* $(F_{\varepsilon D})_\varepsilon$ *epi-converges, in the weak topology of* $(H^1_o(\Omega))^3$, *to* $F_{oD}$ *defined by :*

$$F_{oD}(\vec{u}) = \int_{\Omega_{\varepsilon D}} |\nabla\vec{u}|^2\, dx + a.\sum_{k\ell} \mathscr{C}_{k\ell}.\int_\Sigma u_{k|\Sigma}.u_{\ell|\Sigma}\, d\sigma + \delta_{V_{oD}}(\vec{u}),$$

*where :*

$$V_{oD} = \{\vec{u} \in (H^1_o(\Omega))^3 \ / \ \mathrm{div}(\vec{u}) = 0 \text{ in } \Omega\}.$$

<u>Sketch of the proof of Theorem 6</u> (see [4] for the details)

This proof is based on the construction of appropriate test-functions satisfying (11) :

$$\vec{u}^{o}_{\varepsilon D}(x) = \begin{cases} \vec{u}(x) - \sum_{k} \mathrm{curl}(\hat{\vec{W}}^{k}_{\varepsilon i}.\psi_{\varepsilon i})(x).u_{k}(x_{\varepsilon i}) - \mathrm{curl}(\hat{\vec{u}}_{\varepsilon i}.\phi_{\varepsilon i})(x), & \\ & \text{in } B_{\varepsilon i} = B_3(x_{\varepsilon i},\frac{\varepsilon}{2}), \\ \vec{u}(x) & \text{in } Y_{\varepsilon i}\backslash B_{\varepsilon i}, \end{cases}$$

for every smooth function $\vec{u}$ in $V_{OD}\cap(C^1(\bar{\Omega}))^3$, where :

$x_{\varepsilon i}$ is the center of the i-th $\varepsilon$-cell $Y_{\varepsilon i}$ : $Y_{\varepsilon i} = x_{\varepsilon i} + \varepsilon Y$, Y denoting the unit square of $\mathbb{R}^2$ : $Y = ]-\frac{1}{2},\frac{1}{2}[\times]-\frac{1}{2},\frac{1}{2}[$,

$\hat{\vec{W}}^{k}_{\varepsilon i}$ is such that : $\mathrm{curl}(\hat{\vec{W}}^{k}_{\varepsilon i})(x) = \vec{W}^{k}_{\varepsilon i}(x) = \vec{W}^{k}(\frac{x-x_{\varepsilon i}}{r_\varepsilon})$, in $B_3(x_{\varepsilon i},\frac{\varepsilon}{4}+r_\varepsilon)$ and satisfies the estimates :

$$\|\hat{\vec{W}}^{k}_{\varepsilon i}\|_{(L^2(B_3(x_{\varepsilon i},\frac{\varepsilon}{4}+r_\varepsilon)))^3} \le K.\varepsilon.\|\vec{W}^{k}_{\varepsilon i}\|_{(L^2(B_3(x_{\varepsilon i},\frac{\varepsilon}{4}+r_\varepsilon)))^3}$$

$$\|\nabla\hat{\vec{W}}^{k}_{\varepsilon i}\|_{(L^2(B_3(x_{\varepsilon i},\frac{\varepsilon}{4}+r_\varepsilon)))^9} \le K.\|\vec{W}^{k}_{\varepsilon i}\|_{(L^2(B_3(x_{\varepsilon i},\frac{\varepsilon}{4}+r_\varepsilon)))^3}$$

(see Theorem 4.9 of [6]),

$\hat{\vec{u}}_{\varepsilon i}$ is such that $\mathrm{curl}(\hat{\vec{u}}_{\varepsilon i})(x) = \vec{u}(x) - \vec{u}(x_{\varepsilon i})$, in $B_3(x_{\varepsilon i},r_\varepsilon^{2/3})$, and satisfies the estimates :

$$\|\hat{\vec{u}}_{\varepsilon i}\|_{(L^2(B_3(x_{\varepsilon i},r_\varepsilon^{2/3})))^3} \le K.r_\varepsilon^{2/3}.\|\vec{u}_{\varepsilon i}\|_{(L^2(B_3(x_{\varepsilon i},r_\varepsilon^{2/3})))^3}$$

$$\|\nabla\hat{\vec{u}}_{\varepsilon i}\|_{(L^2(B_3(x_{\varepsilon i},r_\varepsilon^{2/3})))^9} \le K.\|\vec{u}_{\varepsilon i}\|_{(L^2(B_3(x_{\varepsilon i},r_\varepsilon^{2/3})))^3}$$

$\psi_{\varepsilon i}$ is a cut-off function with support in $B_3(x_{\varepsilon i},\frac{\varepsilon}{4}+r_\varepsilon)$ and identically equal to 1 in $B_3(x_{\varepsilon i},\frac{\varepsilon}{8}+r_\varepsilon)$,

$\phi_{\varepsilon i}$ is a cut-off function with support in $B_3(x_{\varepsilon i},r_\varepsilon^{2/3})$ and identically equal to 1 in $B_3(x_{\varepsilon i},r_\varepsilon)$.

The verification of (11) also requires the following pointwise estimates on the solution $\vec{W}^{k}$, $q^{k}$ of (6) :

**LEMMA 7.** (see [4] and also Annexe C of [1]). *There exists a constant* K *such that for every* y *satisfying* : $d(y,T) > c$ $(c > 0)$ :

$$|\vec{W}^k(y)| \le K.\left(\frac{1}{d(y,T)} + \frac{1}{d(y,T)^2}\right),$$

$$|D_i\vec{W}^k(y)| \le K.\left(\frac{1}{d(y,T)^2} + \frac{1}{d(y,T)^3}\right), \qquad (i = 1,\ 2 \text{ or } 3),$$

$$|q^k(y)| \le K.\left(\frac{1}{d(y,T)^2} + \frac{1}{d(y,T)^3}\right).$$

Verification of (11)

Suppose first that $\alpha$ is finite and $\vec{u}$ belongs to $V_{OD}\cap(C^1(\bar{\Omega}))^3$. In this case, we notice that $\vec{u}^o_{\varepsilon D}$ belongs to $V_{\varepsilon D}$, defined in (10), thanks to the cut-off functions $\psi_{\varepsilon i}$ and $\phi_{\varepsilon i}$. From the above-indicated estimates on $\hat{\vec{u}}_{\varepsilon i}$ or $\hat{\vec{W}}^k_{\varepsilon i}$, one infers the following properties :

$$\sum_i \text{curl}(\hat{\vec{u}}_{\varepsilon i}.\phi_{\varepsilon i}) \xrightarrow[\varepsilon\to 0]{} 0, \text{ in the strong topology of } (H^1(\Omega))^3,$$

$$\left(\sum_i \sum_k \text{curl}(\hat{\vec{W}}_{\varepsilon i}.\psi_{\varepsilon i}).u_k(x_{\varepsilon i})\right)_\varepsilon \text{ is bounded in } (H^1(\Omega))^3.$$

Hence, the sequence $(\vec{u}^o_{\varepsilon D})_\varepsilon$ is bounded in $(H^1_o(\Omega))^3$. Since :

$$\chi_{\Omega\setminus\cup_i B_{\varepsilon i}}(x).(\vec{u} - \vec{u}^o_{\varepsilon D})(x) \equiv 0,$$

one proves that $(\vec{u}^o_{\varepsilon D})_\varepsilon$ converges to $\vec{u}$ in the weak topology of $(H^1_o(\Omega))^3$. Then

$$F_{\varepsilon D}(\vec{u}^o_{\varepsilon D}) = \int_{\Omega_{\varepsilon D}} |\nabla\vec{u}|^2\,dx + \sum_{k\ell}\sum_i u_k(x_{\varepsilon i}).u_\ell(x_{\varepsilon i})\times$$
$$\times\int_{B_{\varepsilon i}} \nabla\text{curl}(\hat{\vec{W}}^k_{\varepsilon i}.\psi_{\varepsilon i}).\nabla\text{curl}(\hat{\vec{W}}^\ell_{\varepsilon i}.\psi_{\varepsilon i})\,dx + o_\varepsilon,$$

with $\lim_{\varepsilon\to 0} o_\varepsilon = 0$. Taking into account the smoothness of $\vec{u}$, one writes :

$$F_{\varepsilon D}(\vec{u}^o_{\varepsilon D}) = \int_{\Omega_{\varepsilon D}} |\nabla\vec{u}|^2\,dx + \sum_{k\ell}\sum_i \left(\int_{Y_{\varepsilon i}} u_k(x).u_\ell(x)\,dx\right)\times$$
$$\times\frac{1}{\varepsilon^2}.\int_{B_{\varepsilon i}} \nabla\text{curl}(\hat{\vec{W}}^k_{\varepsilon i}.\psi_{\varepsilon i}).\nabla\text{curl}(\hat{\vec{W}}^\ell_{\varepsilon i}.\psi_{\varepsilon i})\,dx + o_\varepsilon.$$

Let $A_{\varepsilon i}$ be equal to $\int_{B_{\varepsilon i}} \nabla(\text{curl}(\hat{\vec{W}}^k_{\varepsilon i}.\psi_{\varepsilon i})).\nabla(\text{curl}(\hat{\vec{W}}^\ell_{\varepsilon i}.\psi_{\varepsilon i}))\,dx.$

$$A_{\varepsilon i} = \int_{B_{\varepsilon i}} \nabla\vec{W}^k_{\varepsilon i}.\nabla\vec{W}^\ell_{\varepsilon i}.(\psi_{\varepsilon i})^2\,dx + \int_{B_{\varepsilon i}} \vec{W}^k_{\varepsilon i}.\vec{W}^\ell_{\varepsilon i}.\nabla\psi_{\varepsilon i}.\nabla\psi_{\varepsilon i}\,dx +$$

$$+ \int_{B_{\varepsilon i}} \nabla\hat{\vec{W}}^{k}_{\varepsilon i}.\nabla\hat{\vec{W}}^{\ell}_{\varepsilon i}.\nabla\psi_{\varepsilon i}.\nabla\psi_{\varepsilon i}\ dx + \int_{B_{\varepsilon i}} \hat{\vec{W}}^{k}_{\varepsilon i}.\hat{\vec{W}}^{\ell}_{\varepsilon i}.\nabla(\nabla\psi_{\varepsilon i}).\nabla(\nabla\psi_{\varepsilon i})\ dx.$$

Thanks to the pointwise estimates of Lemma 7, one derives :

$$\left|\int_{B_{\varepsilon i}} \nabla\vec{W}^{k}_{\varepsilon i}.\nabla\vec{W}^{\ell}_{\varepsilon i}.((\psi_{\varepsilon i})^2 - 1)\ dx\right| \le K.\varepsilon^3 \ ; \ \left|\int_{B_{\varepsilon i}} \vec{W}^{k}_{\varepsilon i}.\vec{W}^{\ell}_{\varepsilon i}.\nabla\psi_{\varepsilon i}.\nabla\psi_{\varepsilon i}\ dx\right| \le K.\varepsilon^3.$$

Moreover the above-indicated estimates on $\hat{\vec{W}}^{k}_{\varepsilon i}$ imply similar estimates for the two last terms of $A_{\varepsilon i}$. Finally, one obtains :

$$F_{\varepsilon D}(\vec{u}^{o}_{\varepsilon D}) = \int_{\Omega_{\varepsilon D}} |\nabla\vec{u}|^2\ dx + \sum_{k\ell}\sum_{i}\left(\int_{Y_{\varepsilon i}} u_k(x).u_\ell(x)\ d\sigma\right)\times$$

$$\times\frac{1}{\varepsilon^2}.\int_{B_{\varepsilon i}} \nabla\vec{W}^{k}_{\varepsilon i}.\nabla\vec{W}^{\ell}_{\varepsilon i}\ dx + o_\varepsilon.$$

Hence :

$$\lim_{\varepsilon\to 0} F_{\varepsilon D}(\vec{u}^{o}_{\varepsilon D}) = \int_{\Omega_{\varepsilon D}} |\nabla\vec{u}|^2\ dx + a.\sum_{k\ell} \mathscr{C}_{k\ell}.\int_{\Sigma} u_k(x).u_\ell(x)\ d\sigma,$$

using the definition of $\vec{W}^{k}_{\varepsilon i}$ and the definition (7) of $\mathscr{C}_{k\ell}$.

The verification of (11) in the case of a function $\vec{u}$ in $V_{OD}$, is proved by means of a standard diagonalization argument ([2], Corollary 1.16). The case $a$ equal to $+\infty$ is deduced from the preceding proof, by means of a comparison principle on the functional $F_{\varepsilon D}$.

<u>Verification of (12)</u>

Suppose that $a$ is finite and $\vec{u}$ belongs to $V_{OD}$. The verification of (12) is based on a sub-differential inequality. Let $(\vec{u}_n)_n$ (resp. $(\vec{u}_\varepsilon)_\varepsilon$) be a sequence of functions in $V_{OD}\cap(C^1(\bar{\Omega}))^3$ (resp. in $V_{\varepsilon D}$), converging to $\vec{u}$, in the strong topology of $(H^1_o(\Omega))^3$ (resp. in the weak topology of $(H^1_o(\Omega))^3$). We write :

$$F_{\varepsilon D}(\vec{u}_\varepsilon) \ge F_{\varepsilon D}((\vec{u}_n)^{o}_{\varepsilon D}) + 2.\int_{\Omega_{\varepsilon D}} \nabla((\vec{u}_n)^{o}_{\varepsilon D}).\nabla(\vec{u}_\varepsilon - (\vec{u}_n)^{o}_{\varepsilon D})\ dx.$$

Notice that $\vec{o}_{\varepsilon n} = \vec{u}_\varepsilon - (\vec{u}_n)^{o}_{\varepsilon D}$ is such that $(\vec{o}_{\varepsilon n})_\varepsilon$ converges to $\vec{u} - \vec{u}_n$, in the weak topology of $(H^1_o(\Omega))^3$.

$$\int_{\Omega_{\varepsilon D}} \nabla((\vec{u}_n)^o_{\varepsilon D}).\nabla(\vec{o}_{\varepsilon n})\, dx = \int_{\Omega} \nabla\vec{u}_n.\nabla(\vec{u} - \vec{u}_n)\, dx -$$

$$- \sum_{k} \sum_{i} (\vec{u}_n)_k(x_{\varepsilon i}).\int_{B_{\varepsilon i}} \nabla \mathrm{curl}(\hat{\vec{W}}^k_{\varepsilon i}.\psi_{\varepsilon i}).\nabla\vec{o}_{\varepsilon n}\, dx + o_\varepsilon.$$

Thanks to the preceding estimates, one proves, in the same way as for the verification of (11), that :

$$\int_{\Omega_{\varepsilon D}} \nabla((\vec{u}_n)^o_{\varepsilon D}).\nabla(\vec{o}_{\varepsilon n})\, dx = \int_{\Omega} \nabla\vec{u}_n.\nabla(\vec{u} - \vec{u}_n)\, dx -$$

$$- \sum_{k} \sum_{i} (\vec{u}_n)_k(x_{\varepsilon i}).\int_{B_{\varepsilon i}} \nabla\vec{W}^k_{\varepsilon i}.\nabla\vec{o}_{\varepsilon n}.\psi_{\varepsilon i}\, dx + o_\varepsilon.$$

Let us integrate by parts this last integral :

$$\int_{B_{\varepsilon i}} \nabla\vec{W}^k_{\varepsilon i}.\nabla\vec{o}_{\varepsilon n}.\psi_{\varepsilon i}\, dx = - \int_{B_{\varepsilon i}} \Delta\vec{W}^k_{\varepsilon i}.\vec{o}_{\varepsilon n}.\psi_{\varepsilon i}\, dx - \int_{B_{\varepsilon i}} \nabla\vec{W}^k_{\varepsilon i}.\vec{o}_{\varepsilon n}.\nabla\psi_{\varepsilon i}\, dx$$

$$= \int_{B_{\varepsilon i}} q^k_{\varepsilon i}.\vec{o}_{\varepsilon n}.\nabla\psi_{\varepsilon i}\, dx - \int_{B_{\varepsilon i}} \nabla\vec{W}^k_{\varepsilon i}.\vec{o}_{\varepsilon n}.\nabla\psi_{\varepsilon i}\, dx.$$

Taking into account Lemma 7 and Lemma 2.4 of [6], one obtains :

$$\limsup_{\varepsilon \to 0} \Big|\sum_{k} \sum_{i} (\vec{u}_n)_k(x_{\varepsilon i}).\int_{B_{\varepsilon i}} \nabla\vec{W}^k_{\varepsilon i}.\nabla\vec{o}_{\varepsilon n}.\psi_{\varepsilon i}\, dx\Big| \le$$

$$\le K.\|\vec{u}_n\|_{(L^2(\Sigma))^3}.\|\vec{u}-\vec{u}_n\|_{(L^2(\Sigma))^3}.$$

Hence :

$$\liminf_{\varepsilon \to 0} F_{\varepsilon D}(\vec{u}_\varepsilon) \ge F_{OD}(\vec{u}_n) - K.\|\vec{u}_n\|_{(L^2(\Sigma))^3}.\|\vec{u}-\vec{u}_n\|_{(L^2(\Sigma))^3}.$$

Finally, let n increase to +∞ and use the property of $(\vec{u}_n)_n$ : (12) is proved, when $a$ is finite. The case $a$ equal to +∞ is again proved by means of a comparison principle. ∎

**B) CASE OF HOMOGENEOUS NEUMANN BOUNDARY CONDITIONS**

**THEOREM 8.**

*1) Let $a$, defined in (5), be equal to 0. Then, the sequence $(\vec{u}_{\varepsilon N})_\varepsilon$ converges in the weak topology of $(H^1(\Omega^+ \cup \Omega^-))^3$, to $\vec{u}^o_{ON}$, solution of :*

$$\begin{cases} - \Delta\vec{u}^o_{ON} + \vec{u}^o_{ON} = - \nabla p^o_{ON} + \vec{f} & \text{in } \Omega^+ \cup \Omega^-, \\ \mathrm{div}(\vec{u}^o_{ON}) = 0 & \text{in } \Omega^+ \cup \Omega^-, \end{cases}$$

$$\left| \frac{\partial \vec{u}^{\circ}_{ON}}{\partial \nu} - p^{\circ}_{ON}.\vec{\nu} = \vec{0}, \quad on\ \partial\Omega \ ; \quad \frac{\partial \vec{u}^{\circ}_{ON}}{\partial n} - p^{\circ}_{ON}.\vec{n} = \vec{0}, \quad on\ \Sigma^{+}\ and\ on\ \Sigma^{-}. \right.$$

*2) Suppose that $a$ is equal to $+\infty$. Then, the sequence $(\vec{u}_{\varepsilon N})_{\varepsilon}$ converges, in the weak topology of $(H^1(\Omega^{+}\cup\Omega^{-}))^3$ to $\vec{u}^{*}_{ON}$, solution of :*

$$\left| \begin{array}{ll} -\Delta\vec{u}^{*}_{ON} + \vec{u}^{*}_{ON} = -\nabla p^{*}_{ON} + \vec{f} & in\ \Omega, \\ div(\vec{u}^{*}_{ON}) = 0 & in\ \Omega, \\ \dfrac{\partial \vec{u}^{*}_{ON}}{\partial \nu} - p^{*}_{ON}.\vec{\nu} = \vec{0}, & on\ \partial\Omega, \end{array} \right.$$

*3) Suppose that $a$ is strictly positive and finite. Then, the sequence $(\vec{u}_{\varepsilon N})_{\varepsilon}$ converges in the weak topology of $(H^1(\Omega^{+}\cup\Omega^{-}))^3$, to the solution $\vec{u}_{ON}$ of :*

$$\left| \begin{array}{ll} -\Delta\vec{u}_{ON} + \vec{u}_{ON} = -\nabla p_{ON} + \vec{f} & in\ \Omega^{+}\cup\Omega^{-}, \\ div(\vec{u}_{ON}) = 0 & in\ \Omega^{+}\cup\Omega^{-}, \\ \dfrac{\partial \vec{u}^{*}_{ON}}{\partial \nu} - p^{*}_{ON}.\vec{\nu} = \vec{0}, \quad on\ \partial\Omega \ ; & \pm\dfrac{\partial \vec{u}_{ON}}{\partial n} \mp p_{ON}.\vec{n} + \dfrac{1}{4}\, a.\mathscr{C}.[\vec{u}_{ON}] = \vec{0}, \quad on\ \Sigma^{\pm}, \end{array} \right.$$

*where $\mathscr{C}$ is the matrix defined by (7).*

**REMARK 9.** Let us point out that $\varepsilon^2$ is the critical size of the solid pieces or holes:

- when $a$ is equal to 0, the influence of the solid pieces or holes asymptotically vanishes : $\vec{u}^{\circ}_{OD}$ is the solution of the Stokes problem in $\Omega$, with homogeneous Dirichlet boundary conditions on $\partial\Omega$, while $\vec{u}^{\circ}_{ON}$ is the solution of the Stokes problem in the two completely separated domains $\Omega^{+}$ and $\Omega^{-}$, with homogeneous Neumann boundary conditions on $\partial\Omega^{+}$ and $\partial\Omega^{-}$,
- when $a$ is equal to $+\infty$, the influence of the solid pieces or holes is asymptotically extended to the whole $\Sigma$ : $\vec{u}^{*}_{OD}$ is the solution of the Stokes problem in $\Omega^{+}$ and in $\Omega^{-}$, with homogeneous Dirichlet boundary conditions on $\partial\Omega^{+}$ and $\partial\Omega^{-}$, while $\vec{u}^{*}_{ON}$ is the solution of the Stokes problem in $\Omega$, with homogeneous Neumann conditions on $\partial\Omega$.

In order to obtain the variational formulation of (2), we denote by $V_{\varepsilon N}$ the closed subspace of $(H^1(\Omega))^3$, corresponding to the homogeneous Neumann boundary conditions :

$$V_{\varepsilon N} = \{\vec{u} \in (H^1(\Omega^+ \cup \Omega^-))^3 \ / \ \mathrm{div}(\vec{u}) = 0 \text{ in } \Omega_{\varepsilon N} \ ; \ [\vec{u}] = 0 \text{ on } \bigcup_i T_{\varepsilon i}\}.$$

Then, $\vec{u}_{\varepsilon N}$ is the solution of :

$$\underset{\vec{u} \in (H^1(\Omega^+ \cup \Omega^-))^3}{\mathrm{Min}} \{F_{\varepsilon N}(\vec{u}) - 2.\int_{\Omega_{\varepsilon N}} \vec{f}.\vec{u}\, dx\},$$

where $F_{\varepsilon N}$ is defined by : $F_{\varepsilon N}(\vec{u}) = \int_{\Omega^+ \cup \Omega^-} (|\nabla\vec{u}|^2 + |\vec{u}|^2)\, dx + \delta_{V_{\varepsilon N}}(\vec{u})$.

Theorem 8 is therefore a consequence of the following theorem :

**THEOREM 10.** *The sequence* $(F_{\varepsilon N})_\varepsilon$ *epi-converges, in the weak topology of* $(H^1(\Omega^+ \cup \Omega^-))^3$*, to* $F_{ON}$ *:*

$$F_{ON}(\vec{u}) = \int_{\Omega^+ \cup \Omega^-} (|\nabla\vec{u}|^2 + |\vec{u}|^2)\, dx + \frac{a}{4}.\sum_{k\ell} \mathscr{C}_{k\ell}.\int_\Sigma [u_k].[u_\ell]\, d\sigma + \delta_{V(\Omega^+ \cup \Omega^-)}(\vec{u}),$$

*where :*

$$V(\Omega^+ \cup \Omega^-) = \{\vec{u} \in (H^1(\Omega^+ \cup \Omega^-))^3 \ / \ \mathrm{div}(\vec{u}) = 0 \quad \text{in } \Omega^+ \cup \Omega^-\}.$$

<u>Sketch of the proof of Theorem 10</u>

The construction of the appropriate test-function, satisfying (11), in the present case is similar to the case of homogeneous Dirichlet boundary conditions :

$$\vec{u}^{\,o}_{\varepsilon N}(x) = \begin{cases} \vec{u}(x) - \sum_k \mathrm{curl}(\hat{\vec{W}}^k_{\varepsilon i}.\psi_{\varepsilon i})(x).U^{\pm}_k(x_{\varepsilon i}) - \mathrm{curl}(\hat{\vec{u}}_{\varepsilon i}.\phi_{\varepsilon i})(x), & \text{in } B_3(x_{\varepsilon i}, \frac{\varepsilon}{2}), \\ \vec{u}(x), & \text{in } Y_{\varepsilon i} \backslash B_3(x_{\varepsilon i}, \frac{\varepsilon}{2}), \end{cases}$$

for every function $\vec{u}$ in $V(\Omega^+ \cup \Omega^-) \cap (C^1(\bar{\Omega}^+ \cup \bar{\Omega}^-))^3$, where $\vec{U}^{\pm}$ is such that :

$$\mathrm{div}(\vec{U}^{\pm}) = 0 \text{ in } \Omega^+ \cup \Omega^- \ ; \ \vec{U}^{\pm}|_{\Sigma^+} = \frac{1}{2}.[\vec{u}] \ ; \ \vec{U}^{\pm}|_{\Sigma^-} = -\frac{1}{2}.[\vec{u}].$$

The computations for the verification of (11) and (12) will be omitted. ∎

**REMARK 11.**

1) Notice that the coefficient $a$, appearing in the "strange term" of $F_{OD}$, has been changed into $\frac{a}{4}$ in $F_{ON}$ (see Theorems 1 and 2), while the trace of $\vec{u}$ on $\Sigma$ is replaced by the jump of $\vec{u}$ accross $\Sigma$, in this additional term.
2) From Theorems 6, 10, and 3.71, 3.74 of [2], one deduces :
- the convergence of the solutions of the evolution problems associated to

(1) and (2), to the solutions of the evolution problems associated to the limit problems, respectively described in Theorems 3, 8, 3) in the strong topology of $L^2(0,T_o,(L^2(\Omega))^3)$ or $L^2(0,T_o,(L^2(\Omega^+\cup\Omega^-))^3)$ $(T_o > 0)$,
- the convergence of the spectrum of the linked operators (see [4]).

The asymptotic behaviour of the pressures is the following :

**THEOREM 12.** [4]

*1) Suppose that a is equal to 0. Then,* $(\overset{\circ}{p}_{\varepsilon D|\Omega^\pm})_\varepsilon$ *and* $(\overset{\circ}{p}_{\varepsilon N|\Omega^\pm})_\varepsilon$ *converge, in the weak topology of* $L^2(\Omega^\pm)/\mathbb{R}$*, respectively to* $\overset{\circ}{p}_{OD|\Omega^\pm}$ and $\overset{\circ}{p}_{ON|\Omega^\pm}$*, the limit pressures appearing in Theorems 3 and 8, 1).*

*2) Suppose that a is equal to +∞. Then,* $(p^*_{\varepsilon D|\Omega^\pm})_\varepsilon$ *and* $(p^*_{\varepsilon N|\Omega^\pm})_\varepsilon$ *converge, in the weak topology of* $L^2(\Omega^\pm)/\mathbb{R}$*, respectively to* $p^*_{OD|\Omega^\pm}$ and $p^*_{ON|\Omega^\pm}$*, the limit pressures appearing in Theorems 3 and 8, 2).*

*3) Suppose that a is strictly positive and finite. Then,* $(p_{\varepsilon D|\Omega^\pm})_\varepsilon$ *and* $(p_{\varepsilon N|\Omega^\pm})_\varepsilon$ *converge, in the weak topology of* $L^2(\Omega^\pm)/\mathbb{R}$*, respectively to* $p_{OD|\Omega^\pm}$ and $p_{ON|\Omega^\pm}$*, the limit pressures appearing in Theorems 3 and 8, 3).*

**III - ASYMPTOTIC BEHAVIOUR WHEN** $r_\varepsilon = \alpha.\varepsilon$ $(0 < \alpha < \varepsilon/2)$

In this special case, Theorems 3 and 8, 2) imply that the two sequences $(\vec{u}_{\varepsilon D|\Sigma})_\varepsilon$ and $([\vec{u}_{\varepsilon N}])_\varepsilon$ converge to $\vec{0}$, in the strong topology of $(L^2(\Sigma))^3$. The purpose of this paragraph, is to precise the rate of convergence of these sequences. From Lemma 3.4 of [8], one derives, after some easy computations :

**PROPOSITION 13.**

*1)* $(\frac{1}{\varepsilon}.\vec{u}_{\varepsilon D|\Sigma})_\varepsilon$ *is bounded in* $(L^2(\Sigma))^3$.

*2)* $(\frac{1}{\sqrt{\varepsilon}}.(\vec{u}_{\varepsilon D} - \vec{u}^*_{OD}))_\varepsilon$ *converges to* $\vec{0}$*, in the weak topology of* $(H^1_o(\Omega))^3$.

In order to describe the limit of $(\frac{1}{\varepsilon}.\vec{u}_{\varepsilon D|\Sigma})_\varepsilon$, we introduce the problem :

$$\left|\begin{array}{ll} -\Delta\vec{Z}^k = -\nabla Q^k & \text{in } G = Y\times]0,+\infty[, \\ \operatorname{div}(\vec{Z}^k) = 0 & \text{in } G, \\ \vec{Z}^k_{|Y} = \vec{0} & \text{on } \alpha.T, \end{array}\right.$$

$$\left|\begin{array}{l} \dfrac{\partial \vec{Z}^{k}}{\partial n} - Q^{k}.\vec{n} = \vec{e}^{k} \qquad \text{on } Y\backslash\alpha.T, \\[2ex] \vec{Z}^{k} \text{ is Y-periodic, } (\vec{Z}^{k} \text{ has the sames traces on the opposite faces of G).} \end{array}\right.$$

Then, we have :

**THEOREM 14.**

*1)* $(\frac{1}{\varepsilon}.(\vec{u}_{\varepsilon D})_{k|\Sigma})_{\varepsilon}$ *converges, in the weak topology of* $L^2(\Sigma)$, *to :*

$$-\frac{1}{2}.[\frac{\partial\vec{u}^{*}_{OD}}{\partial n} - p^{*}_{OD}.\vec{n}].\int_{Y}\vec{Z}^{k}(y)\ dy \qquad (k = 1,\ 2 \text{ or } 3),$$

*2)* $(\frac{1}{\varepsilon}.\int_{\Omega_{\varepsilon D}}|\nabla(\vec{u}_{\varepsilon D} - \vec{u}^{*}_{OD})|^2\ dx)_{\varepsilon}$ *converges to :*

$$\frac{1}{2}.\int_{\Sigma}[\frac{\partial\vec{u}^{*}_{OD}}{\partial n} - p^{*}_{OD}.\vec{n}].\left(\sum_{k}[\frac{\partial\vec{u}^{*}_{OD}}{\partial n} - p^{*}_{OD}.\vec{n}]_{k}.\int_{Y}\vec{Z}^{k}(y)\ dy\right)\ d\sigma.$$

In the case of homogeneous Neumann boundary conditions, the corresponding estimates are :

**PROPOSITION 15.**

*1)* $(\frac{1}{\varepsilon}.[\vec{u}_{\varepsilon N}])_{\varepsilon}$ *is bounded in* $(L^2(\Sigma))^3$.

*2)* $(\frac{1}{\sqrt{\varepsilon}}.(\vec{u}_{\varepsilon N} - \vec{u}^{*}_{ON}))_{\varepsilon}$ *converges to* $\vec{0}$, *in the weak topology of* $(H^1(\Omega^{+}\cup\Omega^{-}))^3$,

and the asymptotic behaviour is the following :

**THEOREM 16.**

*1)* $(\frac{1}{\varepsilon}.[\vec{u}_{\varepsilon N}]_{k})_{\varepsilon}$ *converges, in the weak topology of* $L^2(\Sigma)$, *to :*

$$-\frac{1}{2}.(\frac{\partial\vec{u}^{*}_{ON}}{\partial n} - p^{*}_{ON}.\vec{n}).\int_{Y}\vec{Z}^{k}(y)\ dy \qquad (k = 1,\ 2 \text{ or } 3),$$

*2)* $(\frac{1}{\varepsilon}.\int_{\Omega^{+}\cup\Omega^{-}}\left(|\nabla(\vec{u}_{\varepsilon N} - \vec{u}^{*}_{ON})|^2 + |\vec{u}_{\varepsilon N} - \vec{u}^{*}_{ON}|^2\right)\ dx)_{\varepsilon}$ *converges to :*

$$2.\int_{\Sigma}(\frac{\partial\vec{u}^{*}_{ON}}{\partial n} - p^{*}_{ON}.\vec{n}).\left(\sum_{k}(\frac{\partial\vec{u}^{*}_{ON}}{\partial n} - p^{*}_{ON}.\vec{n})_{k}.\int_{Y}\vec{Z}^{k}(y)\ dy\right)\ d\sigma.$$

**REMARK 17.**

1) The results exposed in the Theorems 14 and 16 are similar to the corresponding ones, obtained in [8] (Theorems 3.2 and 3.3) and describing the asymptotic behaviour of the solutions of (3) and (4) when $r_\varepsilon = \alpha.\varepsilon$.
2) In [9], the asymptotic behaviour of $\vec{u}_{\varepsilon D}$ is studied in this situation.

Sketch of the proofs of Theorems 14 and 16

From the solution $\vec{Z}^k$, $Q^k$ of (13), we build $\vec{Z}^k_\varepsilon$, $Q^k_\varepsilon$ in the following way :

a) if $k = 1$ or $2$ :

$$\vec{Z}^k_\varepsilon(x) = \vec{Z}^k(\tfrac{x}{\varepsilon}) \quad \text{in } Y_\varepsilon\times]0,+\infty[ \quad ; \quad Q^k_\varepsilon(x) = Q^k(\tfrac{x}{\varepsilon}) \quad \text{in } Y_\varepsilon\times]0,+\infty[,$$

$$Q^k_\varepsilon(x_1,x_2,x_3) = Q^k_\varepsilon(x_1,x_2,-x_3) \qquad \text{in } Y_\varepsilon\times]-\infty,0[.$$

$$(\vec{Z}^k_\varepsilon)_j(x_1,x_2,x_3) = (\vec{Z}^k_\varepsilon)_j(x_1,x_2,-x_3) \qquad \text{in } Y_\varepsilon\times]-\infty,0[, \quad j = 1,\ 2,$$

$$(\vec{Z}^k_\varepsilon)_3(x_1,x_2,x_3) = -(\vec{Z}^k_\varepsilon)_3(x_1,x_2,-x_3) \qquad \text{in } Y_\varepsilon\times]-\infty,0[,$$

b) if $k = 3$, the second members of the two last equalities are multiplied by $-1$.

From Lemma 3.9 of [9], one derives the following properties of the restrictions of $\vec{Z}^k_\varepsilon$ and $Q^k_\varepsilon$ to $\Omega$ :

**LEMMA 18.**

*1)* $(\vec{Z}^k_\varepsilon)_\varepsilon$ *is bounded in* $(L^2(\Omega))^3$,

*2)* $(\sqrt{\varepsilon}.\|\nabla \vec{Z}^k_\varepsilon\|_{(L^2(\Omega))^9})_\varepsilon$ *is bounded,*

*3)* $(\sqrt{\varepsilon}.Q^k_\varepsilon)_\varepsilon$ *is bounded in* $L^2(\Omega)$*, for an appropriate choice of* $Q^k$*, defined up to an additive constant.*

Then, we choose any function $\vec{\phi}$ in $(C^\infty_o(\Omega))^3$ and consider :

$$\int_{\Omega^+\cup\Omega^-} \nabla(\vec{u}_{\varepsilon D} - \vec{u}^*_{OD}).\nabla(\sum_k \vec{Z}^k_\varepsilon.\phi_k)\ dx,$$

or :

$$\int_{\Omega^+\cup\Omega^-} \Big(\nabla(\vec{u}_{\varepsilon N} - \vec{u}^*_{ON}) + (\vec{u}_{\varepsilon N} - \vec{u}^*_{ON})\Big).\nabla(\sum_k \vec{Z}^k_\varepsilon.\phi_k)\ dx,$$

where we let $\varepsilon$ go to 0, taking into account the properties of $(\vec{Z}^k_\varepsilon)_\varepsilon$, exposed in Lemma 18 and the estimates on $(\vec{u}_{\varepsilon D})_\varepsilon$ (resp. $(\vec{u}_{\varepsilon N})_\varepsilon$), given in Proposition 13 (resp. Proposition 15). ∎

## IV - FURTHER RESULTS

In [4], the analogy between the two asymptotic flows, exposed in part II, is also established in the case of a more general repartition of the solid pieces or holes.

The case of an incompressible and viscoplastic Bingham fluid is also studied.

## REFERENCES


[1] ALLAIRE G., Homogénéisation des équations de Stokes et de Navier-Stokes. Thèse Université Paris VI (1989)

[2] ATTOUCH H., Variational convergence for functions and operators. Pitman, London (1984)

[3] ATTOUCH H., PICARD C., Comportement limite de problèmes de transmission à travers des grilles de formes quelconques. Rend. Sem. Mat. Torino Vol 45 1 (1987)

[4] BRILLARD A., Homogénéisation de quelques équations de la mécanique des milieux continus. Thèse d'Etat. Montpellier (1990)

[5] DE GIORGI E., Convergence problems for functions and operators. Proceedings "Recent methods in nonlinear analysis". Rome 1978. Pitagora Editrice, Bologna (1979)

[6] MARCHENKO V.A., HROUSLOV E. Ja., Problèmes aux limites dans des domaines avec frontières finement granulées. Naukova Dumka Kiev (1974)

[7] MURAT F., The Neumann Sieve. Proceedings "Nonlinear variational problems". Isola d'Elba 1983. Research Notes in Math Vol 127. Pitman, London (1985)

[8] PICARD C., Comportement limite de solutions d'inéquations variationnelles associées à une suite de contraintes de type obstacle. Thèse d'Etat. Paris XI (1984)

[9] SANCHEZ-PALENCIA E., Un problème d'écoulement lent d'un fluide incompressible au travers d'une paroi finement perforée. In " Les méthodes de l'homogénéisation : Théorie et applications en physique". Eyrolles, Paris (1985).



Alain BRILLARD
Faculté des Sciences et Techniques
4 Rue des Frères Lumière
F-68093 MULHOUSE Cedex

P COLLI AND M GRASSELLI

# Phase transitions in materials with memory

**1. Introduction.** In a recent paper (cf. [5]) we deal with two phase transition problems accounting for memory effects in the heat conduction phenomenon. The formulation of the related models involves some constitutive assumptions on the thermodynamic fields. Thus, according to a well known and widely investigated approach (see, e.g., [4]), the classical Fourier law is modified by adding a memory term in the heat flux equation. Moreover, as two different phases may appear, we allow the internal energy to depend on the phase variable $\chi$ besides the temperature $\vartheta$ and the past histories of $\vartheta$ and $\chi$. Once the energy balance has been applied, the two models differ in the further relationship between $\vartheta$ and $\chi$ which accounts for the phase transition. First, taking the standard equilibrium condition at the interface between two phases (cf., e.g., [6]), we consider a Stefan problem with memory effects. Next, substituting this equilibrium condition with a relaxation dynamics, we represent superheating and supercooling phenomena. Let us now briefly describe the basic equations of both problems.

Let $\Omega \subset \mathbf{R}^N$ $(N \geq 1)$ be a bounded domain filled up by a sample of material with memory, which is supposed for simplicity to be homogeneous and isotropic. As already stated, the functions $\vartheta : \Omega \times \mathbf{R} \to \mathbf{R}$ and $\chi : \Omega \times \mathbf{R} \to [0,1]$ represent the *absolute temperature* of such a material and the *concentration* of the more energetic phase (i.e., water if a water–ice system is concerned), respectively. By the (linear) constitutive assumptions on the *heat flux* and the *internal energy*, the universal conservation law for energy (*energy balance*) leads to the following integrodifferential equation (cf. [2,4,5])

$$\partial_t \left(\varphi_0\vartheta + \psi_0\chi + \varphi * \vartheta + \psi * \chi\right) = k_0\Delta\vartheta + k * \Delta\vartheta + f \quad \text{in } \Omega\times]0,+\infty[, \tag{1.1}$$

where $\partial_t := \partial/\partial t$, the symbol "$*$" denotes the usual convolution product with respect to time over $]0,t[$, and $\Delta$ stands for the *Laplacian* acting on the space variables. Moreover, $\varphi_0$, $\psi_0$, $k_0$ are given positive constants, $\varphi$, $\psi$, $k : ]0,+\infty[ \to \mathbf{R}$ are the so-called *memory functions*, and $f : \Omega\times]0,+\infty[ \to \mathbf{R}$ is a known function depending on the *heat source* and on the past histories of $\vartheta$ and $\chi$ up to $t = 0$.

Next, we supply the equation (1.1) with a further law relating $\vartheta$ and $\chi$. Assuming that $\vartheta = 0$ be the equilibrium temperature, the well known *equilibrium condition of Stefan type* reads as follows (cf., e.g., [2,6])

$$\chi \in H(\vartheta) \quad \text{in } \Omega\times]0,+\infty[, \tag{1.2}$$

where $H$ denotes the Heaviside graph, that is $H(\xi) = 0$ if $\xi < 0$, $H(0) = [0,1]$, $H(\xi) = 1$ if $\xi > 0$. On the other hand, in order to account for dynamical *supercooling* and *superheating* effects, we alternatively consider a *non equilibrium* condition, given by the following *relaxation dynamics* for the phase variable $\chi$ (see, e.g., [9,10])

$$\alpha\chi_t + H^{-1}(\chi) \ni \beta(\vartheta) \quad \text{in } \Omega\times]0,+\infty[. \tag{1.3}$$

Here the positive constant $\alpha$ represents a *small* kinetic parameter and $\beta : \mathbf{R} \to \mathbf{R}$ is a given continuous function such that $\beta(\cdot)$ is increasing in a neighbourhood of 0 and $\beta(0) = 0$.

Then, the paper [5] is concerned with the problem of finding $\vartheta$ and $\chi$ solving either the equations (1.1–2) or (1.1), (1.3) and satisfying suitable initial and boundary conditions. Letting the function $\beta$ be Lipschitz continuous, the existence and uniqueness of the solution are proved for the related variational formulations.

In this note we extend this analysis along two directions, namely existence and continuous dependence on data. First, assuming $\beta$ just continuous (as it may occur in some applications [9,10]), with the help of an *approximation – a priori estimates – passage to the limit* procedure we show an existence result for the latter *relaxed* problem (corresponding to (1.1) and (1.3)). Then, in the more regular framework (i.e., $\beta$ Lipschitz continuous), by proving *contracting estimates* we deduce the Lipschitz continuous dependence of the solution upon the data for both the former *Stefan* problem (corresponding to (1.1–2)) and the relaxed problem.

**2. Variational formulations and known results.** Here we recall the variational formulations of both problems along with the related existence and uniqueness results proved in [5]. In order to simplify the presentation, we restrict ourselves to the case of homogeneous boundary conditions (however, the results can be extended to more general boundary conditions [5]).

Assume that the boundary $\partial\Omega$ of $\Omega$ be of class $C^{0,1}$. Let $T > 0$ and let $Q := \Omega\times]0,T[$. We set $\mathrm{H} := L^2(\Omega)$, $\mathrm{V} := H_0^1(\Omega)$ and identify H with its dual space, so that $\mathrm{V} \subset \mathrm{H} \subset \mathrm{V}' \equiv H^{-1}(\Omega)$ with dense and compact injections. Also, we introduce the following closed and convex subset of H

$$\mathrm{K} := \{\gamma \in \mathrm{H} \ : \ 0 \leq \gamma \leq 1 \quad \text{a.e. in } \Omega\}. \tag{2.1}$$

In the sequel we will denote by $\langle \cdot, \cdot \rangle$ either the duality pairing between V and V′ or the scalar product in H. Besides, $(\cdot, \cdot)$ and $\|\cdot\|$ will represent the scalar product in $\mathrm{H}^N$ and the norm in H (or in $\mathrm{H}^N$), respectively.

Letting $\vartheta_0$, $\chi_0$ be the initial values of $\vartheta$ and $\chi$ and denoting by $e_0$ the initial energy, for the data we assume that

$$(H1) \qquad \varphi,\ \psi,\ k \in W^{1,1}(0,T),$$
$$(H2) \qquad f \in L^2(0,T;\mathrm{V}'),$$
$$(H3) \qquad \exists\, \Lambda > 0 : \quad |\beta(\vartheta_1) - \beta(\vartheta_2)| \leq \Lambda |\vartheta_1 - \vartheta_2| \quad \forall\, \vartheta_1, \vartheta_2 \in \mathbf{R},$$
$$(H4) \qquad \vartheta_0 \in \mathrm{H},$$
$$(H5) \qquad \chi_0 \in \mathrm{K},$$
$$(H6) \qquad e_0 \in \mathrm{H}.$$

A variational formulation of the Cauchy–Dirichlet problem for the equations (1.1), (1.3) is given by the following

**Problem (P1).** *Find* $\vartheta \in H^1(0,T;\mathrm{V}') \cap L^2(0,T;\mathrm{V})$ *and* $\chi \in H^1(0,T;\mathrm{H})$ *satisfying*

$$\langle \partial_t(\varphi_0\vartheta + \psi_0\chi), v\rangle + \langle \partial_t(\varphi * \vartheta + \psi * \chi), v\rangle$$
$$+(k_0\nabla\vartheta + k * \nabla\vartheta, \nabla v) = \langle f, v\rangle \quad \forall\, v \in \mathrm{V}, \text{ a.e. } in\ ]0,T[, \tag{2.2}$$
$$\chi(\cdot, t) \in \mathrm{K} \quad \forall\, t \in [0,T], \tag{2.3}$$
$$\alpha\langle \chi_t, \chi - \gamma\rangle \leq \langle \beta(\vartheta), \chi - \gamma\rangle \quad \forall\, \gamma \in \mathrm{K}, \text{ a.e. } in\ ]0,T[, \tag{2.4}$$
$$\vartheta(\cdot, 0) = \vartheta_0 \quad \text{a.e. } in\ \Omega, \tag{2.5}$$
$$\chi(\cdot, 0) = \chi_0 \quad \text{a.e. } in\ \Omega. \tag{2.6}$$

**Remark 2.1.** As $\vartheta \in H^1(0,T;\mathrm{V}') \cap L^2(0,T;\mathrm{V})$, then we easily deduce, for instance by interpolation, that $\vartheta \in C^0([0,T];\mathrm{H})$. Therefore, owing also to $\chi \in H^1(0,T;\mathrm{H})$, the initial conditions (2.5–6) make sense.

The existence and uniqueness result (see [5, Thm. 2.1]) for Problem (P1) is stated by the following

**Theorem 2.1.** *Under the assumptions (H1–5) the Problem (P1) has a unique solution.*

Concerning the Stefan problem, i.e. the initial–boundary value problem for (1.1–2), we point out that it suffices to prescribe just the initial value for the internal energy $e_0$. In this case, the variational formulation reads as follows

**Problem (P2).** *Find* $\vartheta \in L^\infty(0,T;\mathrm{H}) \cap L^2(0,T;\mathrm{V})$ *and* $\chi \in L^\infty(Q)$ *satisfying (2.2) and*

$$\partial_t(\varphi_0\vartheta + \psi_0\chi) \in L^2(0,T;\mathrm{V}'), \tag{2.7}$$
$$\chi \in H(\vartheta) \quad \text{a.e. } in\ Q, \tag{2.8}$$
$$(\varphi_0\vartheta + \psi_0\chi)|_{t=0} = e_0 \quad in\ \mathrm{V}'. \tag{2.9}$$

From [5, Thms. 2.2–3] it follows that

**Theorem 2.2.** *Assume that (H1–3) and (H6) hold. Then there exists one and only one solution of Problem (P2).*

**Remark 2.2.** Let us note that existence and uniqueness results analogous to Theorems 2.1–2 hold for more general assumptions on $\psi$, $f$ and for functions $\beta$ also depending on the variable $\chi$ in a Lipschitz way.

**3. Main results.** In this section we state the existence and continuous dependence theorems outlined in the Introduction. Our first result is concerned with the existence of a solution of Problem (P1) when the function $\beta$ is only continuous and linearly bounded. Then we replace the assumption (H3) by the weaker one

$$(H7) \qquad \beta \in C^0(\mathbf{R}), \quad \exists\, \Lambda_0, \Lambda_1 > 0 \ : \quad |\beta(\vartheta)| \le \Lambda_0 |\vartheta| + \Lambda_1 \quad \forall\, \vartheta \in \mathbf{R}.$$

**Remark 3.1.** It is straightforward to verify that any function $\beta$ fulfilling (H3) satisfies (H7). Indeed, it suffices to take, for instance, $\Lambda_0 = \Lambda$ and $\Lambda_1 = |\beta(0)|$.

**Theorem 3.1.** *Under the assumptions (H1–2), (H4–5), (H7) there exists at least one solution of Problem (P1).*

**Remark 3.2.** If the function $\beta$ depends on the variable $\chi$ too, it should be interesting to find sufficient conditions on $\beta(\vartheta, \chi)$ (weaker than the Lipschitz continuity) in order to guarantee the existence of a solution of Problem (P1).

The next two theorems show that the solutions of the Problems (P1) and (P2) continuously depend on the initial data, on the memory functions, and on $f$. The first result is only concerned with Problem (P1). Recalling Theorem 2.1, we have the following

**Theorem 3.2.** *Assuming (H3) hold, let* $\{\varphi_j, \psi_j, k_j, f_j, \vartheta_{0j}, \chi_{0j}\}$, $j = 1,2$, *be two sets of data satisfying the hypotheses (H1–2) and (H4–5). Denoting by* $(\vartheta_j, \chi_j)$, $j = 1,2$, *the corresponding solutions in Problem (P1) and letting* $L$ *be a constant such that*

$$\max\left\{\|f_j\|_{L^2(0,T;V')}, \|\vartheta_{0j}\|, \|\varphi_j\|_{W^{1,1}(0,T)}, \|\psi_j\|_{L^1(0,T)}, \|k_j\|_{W^{1,1}(0,T)}\right\} \le L \tag{3.1}$$

*for* $j = 1,2$, *there exists a positive function* $C_0 \in C^0(]0,+\infty[^2)$ *such that*

$$\begin{aligned} &\|\vartheta_2 - \vartheta_1\|_{L^2(Q)} + \|1 * (\vartheta_2 - \vartheta_1)\|_{C^0([0,T];V)} + \|\chi_2 - \chi_1\|_{C^0([0,T];H)} \\ &\le C_0(L, \alpha^{-1})\big\{\|1 * (f_2 - f_1)\|_{L^2(0,T;V')} + \|\vartheta_{02} - \vartheta_{01}\| + \|\chi_{02} - \chi_{01}\| \\ &\quad + \|\varphi_2 - \varphi_1\|_{L^1(0,T)} + \|\psi_2 - \psi_1\|_{L^1(0,T)} + \|k_2 - k_1\|_{L^1(0,T)}\big\}, \end{aligned} \tag{3.2}$$

where obviously $(1 * u)(\cdot, t) = \int_0^t u(\cdot, \tau)d\tau$ for any $t \in [0,T]$ and for $u \in L^1(0,T;V')$. *Moreover the function* $C_0$ *(also depending on* $\varphi_0$, $\psi_0$, $k_0$, $\Lambda$, $|\beta(0)|$, $T$, $|\Omega|$*) is non decreasing with respect to each of its arguments and such that* $C_0(L, \alpha^{-1}) \nearrow +\infty$ *as* $\alpha \searrow 0$.

**Remark 3.3.** The estimate (3.2) still holds when $\beta$ is a Lipschitz continuous function of $\vartheta$ and $\chi$ (see the later Remark 6.1).

If the function $\beta$ is linear and increasing (cf. Introduction), the estimate (3.2) can be improved with respect to the dependence on $\alpha$ of the Lipschitz constant. This result is stated in the first part of the following theorem, which is also related to Problem (P2) (see Theorem 2.2).

**Theorem 3.3.** *Let* $\{\varphi_j, \psi_j, k_j, f_j, \vartheta_{0j}, \chi_{0j}, e_{0j}\}$, $j = 1,2$, *satisfy (H1–2) and (H4–6). Denote by* $(\vartheta_j, \chi_j)$ $j = 1,2$, *the corresponding solutions to either Problem (P1) with*

$$\beta(\xi) := \Lambda\xi \quad \forall\, \xi \in \mathbf{R} \quad (\Lambda > 0) \tag{3.3}$$

*or Problem (P2). Then, letting* $M$ *be a constant such that*

$$\max\left\{\|f_j\|_{L^2(0,T;V')}, \|e_{0j}\|, \|\varphi_j\|_{W^{1,1}(0,T)}, \|\psi_j\|_{W^{1,1}(0,T)}, \|k_j\|_{W^{1,1}(0,T)}\right\} \le M \tag{3.4}$$

*for* $j = 1,2$, *there exists a positive and non decreasing function* $C_2 \in C^0(]0,+\infty[)$ *such that the solutions of the former problem satisfy*

$$\begin{aligned}
&\|\vartheta_2 - \vartheta_1\|_{L^2(Q)} + \|1 * (\vartheta_2 - \vartheta_1)\|_{C^0([0,T];V)} + C_1(\alpha)\|\chi_2 - \chi_1\|_{C^0([0,T];H)} \\
&\quad + \|\chi_2 - \chi_1\|_{L^2(0,T;V')} \le C_2(M)\big\{\|1 * (f_2 - f_1)\|_{L^2(0,T;V')} + C_1(\alpha)\|\chi_{02} - \chi_{01}\| \\
&\qquad + \|e_{02} - e_{01}\| + \|\varphi_2 - \varphi_1\|_{L^1(0,T)} + \|\psi_2 - \psi_1\|_{L^1(0,T)} + \|k_2 - k_1\|_{L^1(0,T)}\big\},
\end{aligned} \tag{3.5}$$

*where* $C_1(\alpha) := \sqrt{\alpha\psi_0/\Lambda}$ *and* $e_{0j} = \varphi_0\vartheta_{0j} + \psi_0\chi_{0j}$ *for* $j = 1,2$. *Concerning the Problem (P2), the estimate (3.5) holds true with* $\alpha = 0$, *that is*

$$\begin{aligned}
&\|\vartheta_2 - \vartheta_1\|_{L^2(Q)} + \|1 * (\vartheta_2 - \vartheta_1)\|_{C^0([0,T];V)} + \|\chi_2 - \chi_1\|_{L^2(0,T;V')} \\
&\le C_2(M)\big\{\|1 * (f_2 - f_1)\|_{L^2(0,T;V')} + \|e_{02} - e_{01}\| + \|\varphi_2 - \varphi_1\|_{L^1(0,T)} \\
&\qquad + \|\psi_2 - \psi_1\|_{L^1(0,T)} + \|k_2 - k_1\|_{L^1(0,T)}\big\}.
\end{aligned} \tag{3.6}$$

*Moreover* $C_2(M)$ *also depends upon* $\varphi_0$, $\psi_0$, $k_0$, $T$, $|\Omega|$.

**Remark 3.4.** Note that the results expressed by the Theorems 3.1–3 apply *a fortiori* to the *phase relaxation* and *Stefan* problems *without memory* (cf., e.g., [10, 6]), i.e. when $\varphi = \psi = k \equiv 0$.

**4. A priori estimates.** Here we shall establish two a *priori* estimates useful to prove the Theorems 3.1–3. Throughout this section, we suppose that (H1–2) and (H4–6) hold.

**Lemma 4.1.** *Let $\beta$ fulfil the assumption (H7). Then there exists a positive function $C_3 \in C^0(]0,+\infty[)$ such that any solution $(\vartheta,\chi)$ of Problem (P1) satisfies*

$$\|\vartheta\|_{L^\infty(0,T;\mathrm{H})\cap L^2(0,T;\mathrm{V})} + \|\chi\|_{H^1(0,T;\mathrm{H})\cap L^\infty(Q)} \leq C_3(\alpha^{-1}). \tag{4.1}$$

*Moreover $C_3$ depends only on $\varphi_0$, $\psi_0$, $k_0$, $\|\varphi\|_{W^{1,1}(0,T)}$, $\|\psi\|_{L^1(0,T)}$, $\|k\|_{L^2(0,T)}$, $\|\vartheta_0\|$, $\|f\|_{L^2(0,T;\mathrm{V}')}$, $\alpha$, $\Lambda_0$, $\Lambda_1$, $T$, $|\Omega|$, and $C_3(\alpha^{-1}) \nearrow +\infty$ as $\alpha \searrow 0$.*

**Proof.** We choose $v = \vartheta$ in (2.2) and integrate it from 0 to $t \in ]0,T]$. Accounting for the initial condition (2.5), we obtain

$$\frac{\varphi_0}{2}\|\vartheta(\cdot,t)\|^2 + k_0\|\nabla\vartheta\|^2_{L^2(0,t;\mathrm{H}^N)} = \frac{\varphi_0}{2}\|\vartheta_0\|^2 - \sum_{i=1}^{5} I_i(t), \tag{4.2}$$

where

$$I_1(t) := \psi_0\int_0^t \langle\chi_t(\cdot,\tau),\vartheta(\cdot,\tau)\rangle d\tau, \qquad I_2(t) := \int_0^t \langle\partial_t(\psi*\chi)(\cdot,\tau),\vartheta(\cdot,\tau)\rangle d\tau,$$

$$I_3(t) := \int_0^t \langle\partial_t(\varphi*\vartheta)(\cdot,\tau),\vartheta(\cdot,\tau)\rangle d\tau, \quad I_4(t) := \int_0^t ((k*\nabla\vartheta)(\cdot,\tau),\nabla\vartheta(\cdot,\tau))d\tau,$$

$$I_5(t) := -\int_0^t \langle f(\cdot,\tau),\vartheta(\cdot,\tau)\rangle d\tau,$$

for any $t \in [0,T]$. We now estimate each one of these integrals. By applying the Hölder inequality in space and time and the elementary inequality

$$ab \leq (\varepsilon/2)a^2 + (2\varepsilon)^{-1}b^2 \quad \forall\, a,b \in \mathbf{R},\ \forall\,\varepsilon > 0, \tag{4.3}$$

we easily deduce that

$$|I_1(t)| \leq \frac{1}{4}\|\chi_t\|^2_{L^2(0,t;\mathrm{H})} + \psi_0^2\|\vartheta\|^2_{L^2(0,t;\mathrm{H})} \qquad \forall\, t \in [0,T]. \tag{4.4}$$

It is easy to check that $\partial_t(\psi*\chi) = \psi\chi_0 + (\psi*\chi_t)$ a.e. in $Q$. Also, owing to a well known inequality (see, e.g., [7, Thm. 2.2, p. 39]), the following estimate $\|\psi*\chi_t\|_{L^2(0,t;\mathrm{H})} \leq \|\psi\|_{L^1(0,t)}\|\chi_t\|_{L^2(0,t;\mathrm{H})}$ holds. Then, by (H5), (2.1), and (4.3) we have

$$|I_2(t)| \leq \sqrt{|\Omega|}\int_0^t |\psi(\tau)|\,\|\vartheta(\cdot,\tau)\|\,d\tau + \frac{1}{4}\|\chi_t\|^2_{L^2(0,t;\mathrm{H})} + \|\psi\|^2_{L^1(0,t)}\|\vartheta\|^2_{L^2(0,t;\mathrm{H})} \tag{4.5}$$

for any $t \in [0,T]$. Noting that $\partial_t(\varphi * \vartheta) = \varphi(0)\vartheta + (\varphi' * \vartheta)$ a.e. in $Q$ and arguing as before, we infer

$$|I_3(t)| \leq \left\{|\varphi(0)| + \|\varphi'\|_{L^1(0,t)}\right\} \|\vartheta\|^2_{L^2(0,t;\mathrm{H})} \qquad \forall\, t \in [0,T]. \tag{4.6}$$

Next, (3.3) and a further application of the Hölder inequality in time yield

$$|I_4(t)| \leq k_0^{-1} \|k\|^2_{L^2(0,t)} \int_0^t \|\nabla\vartheta\|^2_{L^2(0,\tau;\mathrm{H}^N)}\, d\tau + \frac{k_0}{4} \|\nabla\vartheta\|^2_{L^2(0,t;\mathrm{H}^N)} \tag{4.7}$$

for any $t \in [0,T]$. Recalling (H2) we easily have

$$|I_5(t)| \leq k_0^{-1} \|f\|^2_{L^2(0,t;\mathrm{V}')} + \frac{k_0}{4} \left\{\|\vartheta\|^2_{L^2(0,t;\mathrm{H})} + \|\nabla\vartheta\|^2_{L^2(0,t;\mathrm{H}^N)}\right\} \qquad \forall\, t \in [0,T]. \tag{4.8}$$

On the other hand, from (2.3–4), (H5), and (H7) it follows that (cf., e.g., [3, p. 73])

$$\|\chi_t\|^2_{L^2(0,t;\mathrm{H})} \leq \frac{2\Lambda_0^2}{\alpha^2} \|\vartheta\|^2_{L^2(0,t;\mathrm{H})} + \frac{2\Lambda_1^2|\Omega|t}{\alpha^2} \qquad \forall\, t \in [0,T]. \tag{4.9}$$

By summing (4.2) and (4.9), with the help of (4.4–8) we infer that the following inequality

$$\begin{aligned}
&\frac{\varphi_0}{2} \|\vartheta(\,\cdot\,,t)\|^2 + \frac{k_0}{2} \|\nabla\vartheta\|^2_{L^2(0,t;\mathrm{H})} + \frac{1}{2} \|\chi_t\|^2_{L^2(0,t;\mathrm{H})} \leq \frac{\varphi_0}{2} \|\vartheta_0\|^2 + k_0^{-1} \|f\|^2_{L^2(0,T;\mathrm{V}')} \\
&+ \frac{2\Lambda_1^2|\Omega|T}{\alpha^2} + \left\{\psi_0^2 + \|\psi\|^2_{L^1(0,T)} + |\varphi(0)| + \|\varphi'\|_{L^1(0,T)} + \frac{k_0}{4} + \frac{2\Lambda_0^2}{\alpha^2}\right\} \int_0^t \|\vartheta(\,\cdot\,,\tau)\|^2\, d\tau \\
&+ k_0^{-1} \|k\|^2_{L^2(0,T)} \int_0^t \|\nabla\vartheta\|^2_{L^2(0,\tau;\mathrm{H}^N)}\, d\tau + \sqrt{|\Omega|} \int_0^t |\psi(\tau)|\, \|\vartheta(\,\cdot\,,\tau)\|\, d\tau
\end{aligned} \tag{4.10}$$

holds for any $t \in [0,T]$. Setting now

$$R_{\vartheta,\chi}(t) := \left(\|\vartheta(\,\cdot\,,t)\|^2 + \|\nabla\vartheta\|^2_{L^2(0,t;\mathrm{H})} + \|\chi_t\|^2_{L^2(0,t;\mathrm{H})}\right)^{1/2} \qquad \forall\, t \in [0,T], \tag{4.11}$$

by (4.10) it is easy to see that there are two positive constants $C_4$, $C_5$ and a positive function $C_6 \in L^1(0,T)$ such that

$$R^2_{\vartheta,\chi}(t) \leq C_4 + C_5 \int_0^t R^2_{\vartheta,\chi}(\tau)d\tau + \int_0^t C_6(\tau) R_{\vartheta,\chi}(\tau) d\tau \qquad \forall\, t \in [0,T], \tag{4.12}$$

where $C_4$, $C_5$, $C_6$ have (at most) the same dependences as $C_3$ and $C_4$, $C_5$ blow up as $\alpha$ goes to 0. By applying to (4.12) an extended version of the Gronwall lemma (see, e.g., [1, Teo. 2.1]) we find a constant $C_7$, say $C_7 = 2\left(\sqrt{C_4} + \int_0^T C_6(t)dt\right) \exp\left(\sqrt{2}\, C_5 T\right)$, such that

$$R_{\vartheta,\chi}(t) \leq C_7 \qquad \forall\, t \in [0,T]. \tag{4.13}$$

Finally, (4.11), (4.13), (2.3) and (2.1) imply (4.1) and the lemma is completely proved.

**Lemma 4.2.** *Assume that $\beta$ satisfies (3.3). Then there exists a positive constant $C_8$, independent of $\alpha$, such that any solution $(\vartheta, \chi)$ either to Problem (P1) or to Problem (P2) satisfies*

$$\|\vartheta\|_{L^\infty(0,T;\mathrm{H})\cap L^2(0,T;\mathrm{V})} \leq C_8. \tag{4.14}$$

*Moreover $C_8$ depends only on $\varphi_0$, $\psi_0$, $k_0$, $\|\varphi\|_{W^{1,1}(0,T)}$, $\|\psi\|_{W^{1,1}(0,T)}$, $\|k\|_{L^2(0,T)}$, $\|e_0\|$, $\|f\|_{L^2(0,T;\mathrm{V}')}$, $T$, and $|\Omega|$, where $e_0 := \varphi_0\vartheta_0 + \psi_0\chi_0$ in the case of Problem (P1).*

**Proof.** As it is quite similar to the previous one, let us point out the few differences. We just consider Problem (P1): indeed any (weak) limit point of subsequences of solutions of Problem (P1) as $\alpha \searrow 0$ yields one solution of Problem (P2) (see [5, Section 4]), so that the estimate (4.14) will hold also for the $\vartheta$ limit. From (2.3–4) it follows that (see, e.g., [3, Lemme 3.3, p. 73])

$$\alpha \|\chi_t\|^2_{L^2(0,t;\mathrm{H})} = \Lambda \int_0^t \int_\Omega \vartheta\chi_t \quad \forall\, t \in [0, T]. \tag{4.15}$$

We also have (cf. (4.2))

$$\frac{\varphi_0}{2} \|\vartheta(\cdot, t)\|^2 + k_0 \|\nabla\vartheta\|^2_{L^2(0,t;\mathrm{H})} = \frac{\varphi_0}{2} \|\vartheta_0\|^2 - \psi_0 \int_0^t \int_\Omega \chi_t\vartheta - \sum_{i=2}^{5} I_i(t) \tag{4.16}$$

for any $t \in [0, T]$. It is not difficult to see (cf. (4.3), (2.3), and (2.1)) that

$$|I_2(t)| \leq \frac{t|\Omega|}{2} \left\{ |\psi(0)|^2 + \|\psi'\|^2_{L^1(0,t)} \right\} + \|\vartheta\|^2_{L^2(0,t;\mathrm{H})} \quad \forall\, t \in [0, T]. \tag{4.17}$$

Then, multiplying (4.15) by $\psi_0/\Lambda$ and adding it to (4.16), with the help of (4.6–8) and (4.17) we get a Gronwall type inequality similar to (4.10), where $(1/2)\|\chi_t\|^2_{L^2(0,t;\mathrm{H})}$ replaces $(\alpha\psi_0/\Lambda)\|\chi_t\|^2_{L^2(0,t;\mathrm{H})}$. Now, as $\|\vartheta_0\| \leq \left(\|e_0\| + \psi_0\sqrt{|\Omega|}\right)/\varphi_0$ because of (H5) and (2.1), the estimate (4.14) is an easy consequence of the Gronwall lemma.

**5. Proof of Theorem 3.1.** First, we introduce a sequence $\{\beta_n\}$ of Lipschitz continuous and linearly bounded functions approximating $\beta$. Setting

$$\overline{\beta}_n(\xi) := \begin{cases} \beta(-n) & \text{if } \xi < -n \\ \beta(\xi) & \text{if } -n \leq \xi \leq n \\ \beta(n) & \text{if } \xi > n \end{cases}$$

for any $n \in \mathbf{N}$ and letting $\eta \in C_0^\infty(\mathbf{R})$ be such that $\eta \geq 0$, $\operatorname{supp}(\eta) \subseteq [-1, 1]$, and $\int_{\mathbf{R}} \eta = 1$, we choose, for instance,

$$\beta_n(\xi) := \int_{\mathbf{R}} \overline{\beta}_n(\xi + y/n)\eta(y)dy \quad \forall\, \xi \in \mathbf{R}, \ \forall\, n \in \mathbf{N} \setminus \{0\}.$$

Then, by (H7) it is not difficult to check that $\beta_n \in C^{0,1}(\mathbf{R})$,

$$|\beta_n(\xi)| \le \Lambda_0|\xi| + 2\Lambda_1 \quad \forall\, \xi \in \mathbf{R}, \text{ for } n \text{ large enough,} \tag{5.1}$$

$$\beta_n \to \beta \quad \text{uniformly on compact sets as } n \nearrow \infty. \tag{5.2}$$

Then we can formulate the following approximating problem.

**Problem ($\mathrm{P}_n$).** *Find* $\vartheta_n \in H^1(0,T;\mathrm{V}') \cap L^2(0,T;\mathrm{V})$ *and* $\chi_n \in H^1(0,T;\mathrm{H})$ *satisfying (2.2–3), (2.5–6), and*

$$\alpha\langle \partial_t\chi_n, \chi_n - \gamma\rangle \le \langle \beta_n(\vartheta_n), \chi_n - \gamma\rangle \quad \forall\, \gamma \in \mathrm{K}, \text{ a.e. } in\ ]0,T[. \tag{5.3}$$

Thanks to Theorem 2.1, for any $n \in \mathbf{N}\setminus\{0\}$ there exists a unique solution $(\vartheta_n, \chi_n)$ of Problem ($\mathrm{P}_n$). Also, from (5.1) and Lemma 4.1 it follows that

$$\|\vartheta_n\|_{L^\infty(0,T;\mathrm{H})\cap L^2(0,T;\mathrm{V})} + \|\chi_n\|_{H^1(0,T;\mathrm{H})\cap L^\infty(Q)} \le C_9 \tag{5.4}$$

for some constant $C_9$ independent of $n$. Hence, by comparison in (2.2), it is easy to see (cf. the proof of Lemma 4.1) that

$$\begin{aligned}\|\partial_t\vartheta_n\|_{L^2(0,T;\mathrm{V}')} &\le \varphi_0^{-1}\left\{\sqrt{|\Omega|}\,\|\psi\|_{L^2(0,T)} + \|f\|_{L^2(0,T;\mathrm{V}')}\right\}\\ &+ \varphi_0^{-1}C_9\left\{\psi_0 + |\varphi(0)| + \|\varphi'\|_{L^1(0,T)} + \|\psi\|_{L^1(0,T)} + k_0 + \|k\|_{L^1(0,T)}\right\}.\end{aligned} \tag{5.5}$$

Owing to (5.4–5), there exists a pair $(\vartheta, \chi)$ such that, possibly taking subsequences,

$$\vartheta_n \to \vartheta \quad \text{weakly in } H^1(0,T;\mathrm{V}') \cap L^2(0,T;\mathrm{V}), \tag{5.6}$$

$$\chi_n \to \chi \quad \text{weakly star in } H^1(0,T;\mathrm{H}) \cap L^\infty(Q) \tag{5.7}$$

as $n \nearrow \infty$. Then it is a standard matter to check that $\vartheta$ and $\chi$ satisfy the initial conditions (2.5–6) (cf. Remark 2.1), the variational equality (2.2) and the restriction (2.3) (K, being convex, is closed also with respect to the weak topology of H). In order to deduce that $(\vartheta, \chi)$ yields one solution of Problem (P1), it remains to prove (2.4) or equivalently that

$$\frac{\alpha}{2}\left(\|\chi(\cdot,T)\|^2 - \|\chi_0\|^2\right) = \int_Q \alpha\chi_t\chi \le \int_Q \{\alpha\chi_t\gamma + \beta(\vartheta)(\chi - \gamma)\} \tag{5.8}$$

for any $\gamma \in L^2(Q)$ such that $\gamma(\cdot,t) \in \mathrm{K}$ for a.e. $t \in ]0,T[$.

Now, from (5.6) and the Aubin compactness lemma (see, e.g., [8, p. 58]) it follows that, at least for a subsequence,

$$\vartheta_n \to \vartheta \quad \text{strongly in } L^2(0,T;\mathrm{H}) \text{ and a.e. in } Q \text{ as } n \nearrow \infty. \tag{5.9}$$

Hence, on account of (5.1–2) and the Lebesgue dominated convergence theorem, it is straightforward to verify that

$$\beta_n(\vartheta_n) \to \beta(\vartheta) \quad \text{a.e. in } Q \text{ and strongly in } L^2(Q) \text{ as } n \nearrow \infty. \tag{5.10}$$

On the other hand, taking an arbitrary (cf. (2.1)) $\gamma \in L^\infty(Q)$, $0 \le \gamma \le 1$ a.e. in $Q$, as test function in (5.3), the integration with respect to time gives the inequality (cf. also (5.8))

$$\frac{\alpha}{2}\left(\|\chi_n(\cdot,T)\|^2 - \|\chi_0\|^2\right) \le \int_Q \{\alpha(\partial_t\chi_n)\gamma + \beta_n(\vartheta_n)(\chi_n - \gamma)\}. \tag{5.11}$$

Thanks to (5.7), (5.10), and to the weak lower semicontinuity of the norm in H, it is straightforward to deduce (5.8) from (5.11) and thus conclude the proof.

**Remark 5.1.** On account of Lemma 4.1 and (5.5), it is not difficult to see that the existence result stated by Theorem 3.1 holds under the weaker assumptions $\psi$, $k \in L^2(0,T)$. In fact, it will suffice to take regularizing sequences $\{\psi_n\}$, $\{k_n\}$ in Problem $(\mathrm{P}_n)$ and, due to (5.4), pass to the limit without any difficulty.

**6. Proof of Theorem 3.2.** Taking the difference of the equations (2.2) and of the initial conditions (2.5–6) written for $\vartheta_2, \chi_2$ and $\vartheta_1, \chi_1$, it is easy to check that $\Theta := \vartheta_2 - \vartheta_1$ and $\mathcal{X} := \chi_2 - \chi_1$ satisfy

$$\langle \varphi_0\Theta_t + \psi_0\mathcal{X}_t, v\rangle + \langle \partial_t(\varphi_2 * \Theta + \psi_2 * \mathcal{X}), v\rangle + (k_0\nabla\Theta + k_2 * \nabla\Theta, \nabla v) = \langle \mathcal{F}, v\rangle$$
$$- \langle \partial_t(\Phi * \vartheta_1 + \Psi * \chi_1), v\rangle - (\mathcal{K} * \nabla\vartheta_1, \nabla v) \quad \forall\, v \in \mathrm{V}, \text{ a.e. in } ]0,T[, \tag{6.1}$$
$$\Theta(\cdot,0) = \Theta_0 \quad \text{a.e. in } \Omega, \tag{6.2}$$
$$\mathcal{X}(\cdot,0) = \mathcal{X}_0 \quad \text{a.e. in } \Omega, \tag{6.3}$$

where $\mathcal{F} := f_2 - f_1$, $\Phi := \varphi_2 - \varphi_1$, $\Psi := \psi_2 - \psi_1$, $\mathcal{K} := k_2 - k_1$, $\Theta_0 := \vartheta_{02} - \vartheta_{01}$, and $\mathcal{X}_0 := \chi_{02} - \chi_{01}$. We integrate (6.1) from 0 to $\tau \in ]0,T]$ taking (6.2–3) into account. Then, choosing $v = \Theta(\cdot,\tau)$ and integrating once more in time, we obtain

$$\varphi_0\|\Theta\|^2_{L^2(0,t;\mathrm{H})} + \frac{k_0}{2}\|\nabla(1 * \Theta)(\cdot,t)\|^2 = \sum_{i=6}^{8} I_i(t), \tag{6.4}$$

where

$$I_6(t) := \int_0^t \langle \varphi_0\Theta_0 + \psi_0\mathcal{X}_0 + (1 * \mathcal{F} - \psi_0\mathcal{X} - \varphi_2 * \Theta - \psi_2 * \mathcal{X})(\cdot,\tau), \Theta(\cdot,\tau)\rangle d\tau,$$

$$I_7(t) := -\int_0^t \langle (\Phi * \vartheta_1 + \Psi * \chi_1)(\cdot,\tau), \Theta(\cdot,\tau)\rangle d\tau,$$

$$I_8(t) := -\int_0^t (\nabla(1 * k_2 * \Theta + 1 * \mathcal{K} * \vartheta_1)(\cdot,\tau), \nabla\Theta(\cdot,\tau)) d\tau,$$

for any $t \in [0,T]$. With the help of the Hölder inequality and (4.3) (cf., e.g., (4.4–6) for analogous estimates) it is not difficult to find a positive constant $C_{10}$, depending only on $\varphi_0$, $\psi_0$, and $\|\psi_2\|_{L^1(0,T)}$, such that

$$|I_6(t)| \leq C_{10}\left\{\|\Theta_0\|^2 + \|\mathcal{X}_0\|^2 + \|1 * \mathcal{F}\|^2_{L^2(0,T;V')} + \int_0^t \|\mathcal{X}(\cdot,\tau)\|^2\,d\tau\right\}$$

$$+ \frac{2}{\varphi_0}\|\varphi_2\|^2_{L^2(0,T)}\int_0^t \|\Theta\|^2_{L^2(0,\tau;H)}\,d\tau + \frac{\varphi_0}{4}\|\Theta\|^2_{L^2(0,t;H)} \qquad \forall\, t \in [0,T]. \tag{6.5}$$

As $|\chi_1| \leq 1$ a.e. in $Q$ (cf. (2.3) and (2.1)), similarly we have

$$|I_7(t)| \leq \frac{2}{\varphi_0}\left\{\|\vartheta_1\|^2_{L^2(0,T;H)}\|\Phi\|^2_{L^1(0,T)} + T|\Omega|\,\|\Psi\|^2_{L^1(0,T)}\right\} + \frac{\varphi_0}{4}\|\Theta\|^2_{L^2(0,t;H)} \tag{6.6}$$

for any $t \in [0,T]$. In order to estimate $I_8$, observe that $k_2 * \Theta = k_2(0)(1*\Theta) + k_2' * (1*\Theta)$. Then an integration by parts in time yields

$$I_8(t) = -(\nabla(k_2 * 1 * \Theta + 1 * \mathcal{K} * \vartheta_1)(\cdot,t), \nabla(1*\Theta)(\cdot,t))$$

$$+ \int_0^t (\nabla(k_2(0)(1*\Theta) + k_2' * (1*\Theta) + \mathcal{K} * \vartheta_1)(\cdot,\tau), \nabla(1*\Theta)(\cdot,\tau))\,d\tau,$$

whence it is straightforward to deduce that

$$|I_8(t)| \leq \frac{k_0}{4}\|\nabla(1*\Theta)(\cdot,t)\|^2 + \left\{\frac{2T}{k_0} + \frac{1}{4}\right\}\|\nabla\vartheta_1\|^2_{L^2(0,T;H^N)}\|\mathcal{K}\|^2_{L^1(0,T)}$$

$$+ \left\{\frac{2\,\|k_2\|^2_{L^2(0,t)}}{k_0} + |k_2(0)| + \|k_2'\|_{L^1(0,t)} + 1\right\}\int_0^t \|\nabla(1*\Theta)(\cdot,\tau)\|^2\,d\tau \tag{6.7}$$

for any $t \in [0,T]$. Next, we substitute $\vartheta$, $\chi$ with $\vartheta_j$, $\chi_j$, $j = 2,1$, in (2.4), taking respectively $\gamma = \chi_1$ and $\gamma = \chi_2$. Summing them and integrating in time, owing to (6.3), (H3), and (4.3) we obtain

$$\alpha\,\|\mathcal{X}(\cdot,t)\|^2 - \alpha\|\mathcal{X}_0\|^2 \leq \int_0^t \langle\beta(\vartheta_2(\cdot,\tau)) - \beta(\vartheta_1(\cdot,\tau)), \mathcal{X}(\cdot,\tau)\rangle d\tau$$

$$\leq \frac{\varphi_0}{4}\|\Theta\|^2_{L^2(0,t;H)} + \frac{\Lambda^2}{\varphi_0}\int_0^t \|\mathcal{X}(\cdot,\tau)\|^2\,d\tau \qquad \forall\, t \in [0,T]. \tag{6.8}$$

Now we add (6.8) to (6.4) and estimate the right hand side with the help of (6.5–7): note that the priori bound (4.1) allows us to control the $L^2(0,T;V)$–norm of $\vartheta_1$. Then we infer that (cf. (3.1), Lemma 4.1 and Remark 3.1) there is a constant $C_{11}$ with the same dependences (and properties) of $C_0$ satisfying

$$\|\Theta\|^2_{L^2(0,t;H)} + \|\nabla(1*\Theta)(\cdot,t)\|^2 + \|\mathcal{X}(\cdot,t)\|^2$$

$$\leq C_{11}\left\{\|\Theta_0\|^2 + \|\mathcal{X}_0\|^2 + \|1*\mathcal{F}\|^2_{L^2(0,T;V')} + \|\Phi\|^2_{L^1(0,T)} + \|\Psi\|^2_{L^1(0,T)} + \|\mathcal{K}\|^2_{L^1(0,T)}\right.$$

$$\left. + \int_0^t \left(\|\Theta\|^2_{L^2(0,\tau;H)} + \|\nabla(1*\Theta)(\cdot,\tau)\|^2 + \|\mathcal{X}(\cdot,\tau)\|^2\right) d\tau\right\} \qquad \forall\, t \in [0,T]. \tag{6.9}$$

Finally, by applying the Gronwall lemma in (6.9), we easily deduce (3.2).

**Remark 6.1.** The previous Remark 3.3 becomes clear thanks to the above proof and, in particular, to the estimate (6.8), which is the only step to suitably adjust.

**7. Proof of Theorem 3.3.** Keeping the notations of the previous section, we observe that $\Theta$ and $\mathcal{X}$ still satisfy the equality (6.1). By integrating it in time, accounting for the initial conditions (6.2–3) or (2.9) written for $\vartheta_2, \chi_2$ and $\vartheta_1, \chi_1$, (if Problem (P2) is concerned), and setting $E_0 := e_{02} - e_{01}$, we get the following equality

$$\psi_0 \mathcal{X} + \psi_2 * \mathcal{X} = G \quad \text{in V}', \tag{7.1}$$

where

$$\begin{aligned}\langle G, v\rangle := -\langle \varphi_0 \Theta, v\rangle - (k_0 \nabla(1 * \Theta), \nabla v) + \langle E_0 + 1 * \mathcal{F} - \varphi_2 * \Theta - \Phi * \vartheta_1 - \Psi * \chi_1, v\rangle \\ - (\nabla(1 * k_2 * \Theta + 1 * \mathcal{K} * \vartheta_1), \nabla v) \quad \forall\, v \in \text{V},\end{aligned} \tag{7.2}$$

a.e. in $]0,T[$. As $\psi_2 \in W^{1,1}(0,T)$, then (cf., e.g., [7, Ch. 2, Thm. 3.1]) there is a unique function $\widetilde{\psi}_2 \in W^{1,1}(0,T)$, called *resolvent* of $\psi/\psi_0$, solving the equation

$$\psi_0 \widetilde{\psi}_2 + \psi_2 * \widetilde{\psi}_2 = \psi_2 \quad \text{in } [0,T]. \tag{7.3}$$

Since $\widetilde{\psi}_2(0) = \psi_0^{-1}\psi_2(0)$ and $\psi_0 \widetilde{\psi}_2' = \psi_2' + \widetilde{\psi}_2(0)\psi_2 + \widetilde{\psi}_2' * \psi_2$ a.e. in $]0,T[$ because of (7.3), it is easy to verify that

$$\|\widetilde{\psi}_2\|_{W^{1,1}(0,T)} \leq C_{12} \tag{7.4}$$

for some constant $C_{12}$ depending on $\psi_0$, $\|\psi_2\|_{W^{1,1}(0,T)}$, and $T$. Also, from (7.3) it follows that (see, e.g., [7, Ch. 2, Thm. 3.5]) the equation (7.1) can be rewritten as

$$\langle \psi_0 \mathcal{X}, v\rangle = \langle G - \widetilde{\psi}_2 * G, v\rangle \quad \forall\, v \in \text{V}', \text{ a.e. in } ]0,T[. \tag{7.5}$$

By taking $v = \Theta$ and integrating (7.5) with respect to time, we obtain (cf. (7.2))

$$\begin{aligned}
&\varphi_0 \|\Theta\|^2_{L^2(0,t;\text{H})} + \psi_0 \int_0^t \int_\Omega \mathcal{X}\Theta + \frac{k_0}{2} \|\nabla(1 * \Theta)(\cdot, t)\|^2 \\
&= \int_0^t \langle E_0 + (1 * \mathcal{F} - \widetilde{\psi}_2 * E_0 - \widetilde{\psi}_2 * 1 * \mathcal{F})(\cdot,\tau), \Theta(\cdot,\tau)\rangle d\tau \\
&- \int_0^t \langle (\varphi_2 * \Theta - \varphi_0 \widetilde{\psi}_2 * \Theta - \widetilde{\psi}_2 * \varphi_2 * \Theta)(\cdot,\tau), \Theta(\cdot,\tau)\rangle d\tau \\
&- \int_0^t \langle (\Phi * \vartheta_1 + \Psi * \chi_1 - \widetilde{\psi}_2 * \Phi * \vartheta_1 - \widetilde{\psi}_2 * \Psi * \chi_1)(\cdot,\tau), \Theta(\cdot,\tau)\rangle d\tau \\
&- \int_0^t (\nabla(1 * k_2 * \Theta - k_0 \widetilde{\psi}_2 * 1 * \Theta - \widetilde{\psi}_2 * 1 * k_2 * \Theta)(\cdot,\tau), \nabla\Theta(\cdot,\tau)) d\tau \\
&- \int_0^t (\nabla(1 * \mathcal{K} * \vartheta_1 - \widetilde{\psi}_2 * 1 * \mathcal{K} * \vartheta_1)(\cdot,\tau), \nabla\Theta(\cdot,\tau)) d\tau \quad \forall\, t \in [0,T].
\end{aligned} \tag{7.6}$$

Arguing as in (6.5–7) and then taking (3.4), (7.4), and Lemma 4.2 into account, it is not difficult to find a constant $C_{13}$, having the same dependences as $C_2$, such that

$$\frac{\varphi_0}{4}\|\Theta\|^2_{L^2(0,t;H)} + \psi_0 \int_0^t\int_\Omega \mathcal{X}\Theta + \frac{k_0}{4}\|\nabla(1*\Theta)(\cdot,t)\|^2$$
$$\leq C_{13}\Big\{\|E_0\|^2 + \|1*\mathcal{F}\|^2_{L^2(0,T;V')} + \|\Phi\|^2_{L^1(0,T)} + \|\Psi\|^2_{L^1(0,T)} + \|\mathcal{K}\|^2_{L^1(0,T)}$$
$$+ \int_0^t \Big(\|\Theta\|^2_{L^2(0,\tau;H)} + \|\nabla(1*\Theta)(\cdot,\tau)\|^2\Big)\,d\tau\Big\} \quad \forall t\in[0,T]. \tag{7.7}$$

We first consider Problem (P1). Following the procedure used to deduce (6.8), we easily have

$$\alpha\,\|\mathcal{X}(\cdot,t)\|^2 - \alpha\|\mathcal{X}_0\|^2 \leq \Lambda \int_0^t\int_\Omega \mathcal{X}\Theta \quad \forall t\in[0,T]. \tag{7.8}$$

Multiplying (7.8) by $\psi_0/\Lambda$ and adding it to (7.7), an application of the Gronwall lemma implies the existence of a constant $C_{14}$ such that

$$\|\Theta\|_{L^2(0,T;H)} + \|\nabla(1*\Theta)\|_{C^0([0,T];H^N)} + C_1(\alpha)\|\mathcal{X}\|_{C^0([0,T];H)} \leq C_{14}\{\|E_0\| + C_1(\alpha)\|\mathcal{X}_0\|$$
$$+\|1*\mathcal{F}\|_{L^2(0,T;V')} + \|\Phi\|_{L^1(0,T)} + \|\Psi\|_{L^1(0,T)} + \|\mathcal{K}\|_{L^1(0,T)}\}, \tag{7.9}$$

where $C_1$ is defined in Theorem 3.3 and $C_{14}$ only depends on $C_{13}$, $\varphi_0$, $k_0$, and $T$. Then, by comparison in (7.5) (cf. also (7.2)), it is easy to find a constant $C_{15}$ such that

$$\|\mathcal{X}\|_{L^2(0,T;V')} \leq C_{15}\{C_1(\alpha)\|\mathcal{X}_0\| + \|1*F\|_{L^2(0,T;V')} + \|E_0\|$$
$$+ \|\Phi\|_{L^1(0,T)} + \|\Psi\|_{L^1(0,T)} + \|\mathcal{K}\|_{L^1(0,T)}\}. \tag{7.10}$$

Therefore, the estimate (3.5) follows directly from (7.9–10).

Concerning Problem (P2), by the previous analysis it is not difficult to check that (3.6) holds. Indeed, owing to (2.8) and the monotonicity of the graph $H$, we have

$$\int_0^t\int_\Omega \Theta\mathcal{X} \geq 0 \quad \forall t\in[0,T],$$

so that (7.9) (with $\alpha = 0$) is an easy consequence of (7.7) and the Gronwall lemma.

**Remark 7.1.** The estimates (3.5–6) can be slightly improved with respect to the variation of the variable $\chi$. In fact, thanks to (7.9), we can deduce an analogous bound for $\|G\|_{L^2(0,T;H)+L^\infty(0,T;V')}$, where $G$ is defined by (7.2). Hence, due to (7.5) and (7.4), we can replace $\|\mathcal{X}\|_{L^2(0,T;V')}$ by $\|\mathcal{X}\|_{L^2(0,T;H)+L^\infty(0,T;V')}$ in (7.10) and consequently in (3.5–6).

## REFERENCES


[1] C. BAIOCCHI, *Sulle equazioni differenziali astratte lineari del primo e del secondo ordine negli spazi di Hilbert,* Ann. Mat. Pura Appl. (4) **76** (1967), 233–304.

[2] V. BARBU, *A variational inequality modeling the non Fourier melting of a solid,* An. Ştiinţ. Univ. "Al. I. Cuza" Iaşi Secţ. I a Mat. (N.S.) **28** (1982), 35–42.

[3] H. BRÉZIS, *Opérateurs maximaux monotones et semi-groupes de contractions dans les espaces de Hilbert,* North–Holland, Amsterdam 1973.

[4] B. D. COLEMAN, *Thermodynamics of materials with memory,* CISM Course and Lectures **73**, Springer, Vienna 1971.

[5] P. COLLI AND M. GRASSELLI, *Phase transition problems in materials with memory,* Pubbl. IAN-CNR **781,** Pavia 1991, 1–16.

[6] A. DAMLAMIAN, *Some results on the multi-phase Stefan problem,* Comm. Partial Differential Equations **2** (1977), 1017–1044.

[7] G. GRIPENBERG, S–O. LONDEN, AND O. STAFFANS, *Volterra integral and functional equations,* Encyclopedia Math. Appl. **34**, Cambridge Univ. Press, Cambridge 1990.

[8] J. L. LIONS, *Quelques méthodes de résolution des problèmes aux limites non linéaires,* Dunod, Paris 1969.

[9] A. VISINTIN, *Supercooling and superheating effects in phase transitions,* IMA J. Appl. Math. **35** (1985), 233–256.

[10] A. VISINTIN, *On supercooling and superheating effects in phase transitions,* Boll. Un. Mat. Ital. C (6) **5** (1986), 293–311.



Pierlugi Colli
Dipartimento di Matematica
Università di Pavia
Strada Nuova 65, 27100 Pavia, Italy

Maurizio Grasselli
Istituto di Analisi Numerica del C.N.R.
Corso Carlo Alberto 5, 27100 Pavia, Italy

B GUSTAFSSON, J MOSSINO AND C PICARD

# Limit behaviour of some stratified structures with high conductivity

## 1. INTRODUCTION

Let us consider the homogenization of the elliptic problem

$$\begin{cases} -\operatorname{div} A^{\varepsilon} \nabla u^{\varepsilon} = f \quad \text{in } \Omega, \\ + \text{boundary conditions}, \end{cases} \tag{$1^{\varepsilon}$}$$

where $A^{\varepsilon}$ (and also their inverses) are uniformly elliptic matrices.

Let $\Omega = ]0,1[ \times \Omega'$, where $\Omega'$ is a bounded domain in $\mathbf{R}^{N-1}$ and let us assume that the conductivity matrix $A^{\varepsilon} = (a^{\varepsilon}_{i,j})$ only depends on the first coordinate, say $a^{\varepsilon}_{i,j}(x) = a^{\varepsilon}_{i,j}(x_1)$;

in other words, $\Omega$ represents a stratified structure.

It is well known (cf. [7]) that the problem ($1^{\varepsilon}$) converges to the homogenized problem

$$\begin{cases} -\operatorname{div} A \nabla u = f \quad \text{in } \Omega, \\ + \text{boundary conditions}, \end{cases} \tag{1}$$

if $$\frac{1}{a^{\varepsilon}_{1,1}} \to \frac{1}{a_{1,1}},$$

$$\frac{a^{\varepsilon}_{i,1}}{a^{\varepsilon}_{1,1}} \to \frac{a_{i,1}}{a_{1,1}}, \qquad \frac{a^{\varepsilon}_{1,j}}{a^{\varepsilon}_{1,1}} \to \frac{a_{1,j}}{a_{1,1}}, \quad i,j \geq 2,$$

$$a^{\varepsilon}_{i,j} - \frac{a^{\varepsilon}_{i,1}\, a^{\varepsilon}_{1,j}}{a^{\varepsilon}_{1,1}} \to a_{i,j} - \frac{a_{i,1}\, a_{1,j}}{a_{1,1}}, \quad i,j \geq 2,$$

all of those convergences are in $w^*\text{-}L^{\infty}(\Omega)$.

We are interested in stratified structures with high conductivity, in which case the previous sequences (in the conditions mentioned just above) are not necessarily bounded in $L^\infty(\Omega)$.

In this paper, we consider diagonal matrices $A^\varepsilon$ and we deal with "isotropic" ($A^\varepsilon = a^\varepsilon I$) and "nonisotropic" ($A^\varepsilon = \mathrm{diag}\,(a_i^\varepsilon)$) structures. The main hypothesis allowing very high or high conductivity of the structure are respectively

$$\int_I a_i^\varepsilon(x_1)\, dx_1 \to +\infty \qquad \text{("singular" condition)}$$

or

$$\int_I a_i^\varepsilon(x_1)\, dx_1 \to \int_I a_i(x_1)\, dx_1 \qquad \text{("nonsingular" condition)}$$

for every nondegenerate interval $I$ contained in $[0,1]$. We establish the limit behavior of quasi-linear problems of the form

$$\begin{cases} -\dfrac{\partial}{\partial x_1} g_1\!\left(x, a_1^\varepsilon \dfrac{\partial u^\varepsilon}{\partial x_1}\right) - \displaystyle\sum_{i=2}^{N} a_i^\varepsilon \dfrac{\partial}{\partial x_i} g_i\!\left(\dfrac{\partial u^\varepsilon}{\partial x_i}\right) = f \quad \text{in } \Omega, \\ u^\varepsilon \in W^{1,p}(\Omega) + \text{boundary conditions.} \end{cases}$$

In [6], we prove the convergence of $(1^\varepsilon)$ to $(1)$ for $A^\varepsilon$ symmetric, under the following hypothesis which are weaker than those of [7] recalled above :

$$\frac{1}{a_{1,1}^\varepsilon} \to \frac{1}{a_{1,1}} \quad \text{in } w^*\text{-}L^\infty(\Omega),$$

$$\frac{a_{i,1}^\varepsilon}{a_{1,1}^\varepsilon} \to \frac{a_{i,1}}{a_{1,1}} \quad \text{in } w\text{-}L^2(\Omega),\ i \geq 2,$$

$$\int_I \left( a_{i,j}^\varepsilon - \frac{a_{i,1}^\varepsilon\, a_{j,1}^\varepsilon}{a_{1,1}^\varepsilon} \right) \to \int_I \left( a_{i,j} - \frac{a_{i,1}\, a_{j,1}}{a_{1,1}} \right), \ i, j \geq 2,$$

for every interval $I$ contained in $[0,1]$.

## 2. ISOTROPIC SINGULAR CASE.

Let us consider the following sequence of minimization problems

$$(P^{\varepsilon})\quad \mathrm{Inf}\,\{\ \int_{\Omega} \frac{1}{a^{\varepsilon}(x_1)}\, G(x, a^{\varepsilon}(x_1)\,\nabla v(x))\,dx\ -\ \int_{\Omega} f(x)\,v(x)\,dx\ ;\ v \in W_L^{1,p}(\Omega)\}$$

where

- $\Omega = ]\,0,1[\ x\ \Omega'$, $\Omega'$ is a bounded domain in $\mathbf{R}^{N-1}$, $\Gamma_o = \{0\}\ x\ \Omega'$, $\Gamma_1 = \{1\}\ x\ \Omega'$,

- $a^{\varepsilon} \in L^{\infty}(0,1)$ and there exists $\alpha > 0$ such that $a^{\varepsilon}(x_1) \geq \alpha > 0$ for almost every $x_1 \in ]\,0,1[$ and for every $\varepsilon > 0$,

- $W_L^{1,p}(\Omega) = \{v \in W^{1,p}(\Omega)\ ;\ v = 0 \text{ on } \Gamma_o,\ v = 1 \text{ on } \Gamma_1\}$ $(1 < p < \infty)$,
- $f \in L^{p'}(\Omega)$, $\frac{1}{p} + \frac{1}{p'} = 1$,
- G is a standard function in the calculus of variations, that is :

  - $G : (x, Z) \in \Omega\ x\ \mathbf{R}^N \to G(x, Z) \in \mathbf{R}$ is a Caratheodory function (that is measurable with respect to x , continuous with respect to Z)

  - for almost every $x \in \Omega$, $G(x, .)$ is a strictly convex function which admits a gradient denoted by $g(x, .)$.

  - there exist constants $c$ , $C$ , $C^* > 0$ and $h \in L^1(\Omega)$ such that, for almost every $x \in \Omega$ and for every $Z \in \mathbf{R}^N$,

$$c\,|Z|^p \leq G(x, Z) \leq C\,|Z|^p + h(x),$$

$$|g(x, Z)| \leq C^*\,(1 + |Z|^{p-1}),$$

for example $G(x,Z) = |Z|^p$, where $|.|$ denotes the euclidian norm or the $l^p$-norm.

These assumptions imply that problem $(P^{\varepsilon})$ admits a unique solution $u^{\varepsilon}$ which is also the unique weak solution of the quasilinear problem (or linear problem in the case $G(x,Z) = |Z|^2$ )

$$\begin{cases} -\,\mathrm{div}\ g(x, a^{\varepsilon}(x_1)\,\nabla u^{\varepsilon}) = f \quad \text{in } \Omega, \\ u^{\varepsilon} \in W_L^{1,p}(\Omega) \text{ and satisfying a homogeneous Neuman boundary condition on } \partial\Omega \setminus (\Gamma_0 \cup \Gamma_1). \end{cases}$$

**THEOREM 2.1.** *Assume that* $(a^\varepsilon)$ *satisfies the following hypothesis* :

$(A_1)$ *there exists* $a \in L^\infty(0,1)$ *such that* $\frac{1}{a^\varepsilon} \to \frac{1}{a}$ *in* $w$*-$L^\infty(0,1)$ *as* $\varepsilon \to 0$,

$(A_2)$ *for every nondegenerate interval* $I$ *contained in* $[0,1]$,

$$\int_I (a^\varepsilon)^{p-1}(x_1)\, dx_1 \to +\infty \quad as \quad \varepsilon \to 0 .$$

*Then, as* $\varepsilon \to 0$, *the solution* $u^\varepsilon$ *of* $(P^\varepsilon)$ *converges weakly in* $W^{1,p}(\Omega)$ *to the solution* $u$ *of*

$$(P) \quad \operatorname{Inf}\{ \int_\Omega \frac{1}{a(x_1)} G(x, a(x_1)\nabla v(x))\, dx - \int_\Omega f(x)\, v(x)\, dx \;;$$

$$v \in W^{1,p}_L(\Omega),\ \frac{\partial v}{\partial x_i} = 0 \text{ for } i = 2,\dots,N\} .$$

*Moreover*

$$\int_\Omega \frac{1}{a^\varepsilon(x_1)} G(x, a^\varepsilon(x_1)\nabla u^\varepsilon(x))\, dx \to \int_\Omega \frac{1}{a(x_1)} G(x, a(x_1)\nabla u(x))\, dx .$$

**Remark 2.2.** Actually, the limit problem $(P)$ is equivalent to a one dimensional problem. We refer to [5] for the proof in a similar (slightly more general) setting. This problem $(P)$ can be also obtained as the limit problem for some foliated materials with many slides which are equipotential hypersurfaces (cf. [4]).

## 3. NONISOTROPIC CASE.

In this section we are dealing with both singular and nonsingular conditions. This is the main result of this paper.

Let us consider the following sequence of minimization problems

$$(P^\varepsilon) \quad \operatorname{Inf}\{ J^\varepsilon(v) - \int_\Omega f(x)\, v(x)\, dx \;;\ v \in W^{1,p}_L(\Omega)\}$$

where

$$J^\varepsilon(v) = \int_\Omega \frac{1}{a_1^\varepsilon(x_1)} G_1(x, a_1^\varepsilon(x_1)\frac{\partial v}{\partial x_1}(x))\, dx + \sum_{i=2}^N \int_\Omega a_i^\varepsilon(x_1)\, G_i(\frac{\partial v}{\partial x_i}(x))\, dx.$$

Let us assume that

- $\Omega$ , $W_L^{1,p}(\Omega)$ and f are as in section 2,

- $a_i^\varepsilon \in L^\infty(0,1)$ and there exists $\alpha > 0$ such that $a_i^\varepsilon(x_1) \geq \alpha > 0$ for almost every

$x_1 \in ]0,1[$ , for $\varepsilon > 0$ and for all $i = 1,\ldots,N$,

- $G_1 : (x, z) \in \Omega \times \mathbf{R} \to G_1(x, z) \in \mathbf{R}$ is a Caratheodory function which is strictly convex with respect to the second variable, which admits a gradient denoted by $g_1(x, .)$ and satisfies the following growth properties: there exist constants $\lambda_1, \Lambda_1, \Lambda^*_1 > 0$ and $\gamma_1 \in L^1(\Omega)$ such that

$$\lambda_1 |z|^p \leq G_1(x, z) \leq \Lambda_1 |z|^p + \gamma_1(x) ,$$
$$|g_1(x, z)| \leq \Lambda^*_1 (1 + |z|^{p-1}) ,$$

for almost every $x \in \Omega$ and for every $z \in \mathbf{R}$ ,

- for every $i = 2,\ldots,N$ , $G_i$ is a strictly convex function defined on $\mathbf{R}$ which admits a gradient $g_i$ and there exist positive constants $\lambda_i, \Lambda_i , \Lambda^*_i , \gamma_i$ such that ,

$$\lambda_i |z|^p \leq G_i( z) \leq \Lambda_i |z|^p + \gamma_i ,$$
$$|g_i(x, z)| \leq \Lambda^*_i (1 + |z|^{p-1}) ,$$

for every $z \in \mathbf{R}$ .

Clearly problem $(P^\varepsilon)$ admits a unique solution $u^\varepsilon$ characterized by

$$\begin{cases} -\dfrac{\partial}{\partial x_1} g_1(x, a_1^\varepsilon \dfrac{\partial u^\varepsilon}{\partial x_1}) - \displaystyle\sum_{i=2}^{N} a_i^\varepsilon \dfrac{\partial}{\partial x_i} g_i(\dfrac{\partial u^\varepsilon}{\partial x_i}) = f \text{ in } \Omega \\ u^\varepsilon \in W_L^{1,p}(\Omega) \text{ and satisfying a homogeneous Neuman boundary condition on } \partial\Omega \setminus (\Gamma_0 \cup \Gamma_1). \end{cases}$$

**THEOREM 3.1.** *Let* E , F *be a partition of the set of indices* $\{2, \ldots , N\}$ *(possibly* E *or* F *is empty ). Assume :*

$(H_1)$ *there exists* $a_1 \in L^\infty (0, 1)$ *such that* $\dfrac{1}{a_1^\varepsilon} \to \dfrac{1}{a_1}$ *in* $w^*$- $L^\infty(0, 1)$ *as* $\varepsilon \to 0$ ,

$(H_2)$ *for every* $i \in E$ , *there exists* $a_i \in L^\infty (0, 1)$ *such that for every interval* I *contained in* [0,1] ,

$$\int_I a_i^\varepsilon (x_1)\, dx_1 \to \int_I a_i (x_1)\, dx_1 , \text{ as } \varepsilon \to 0 ,$$

$(H_3)$ *for every* $j \in F$ *and for every non degenerate interval* I *contained in* [0,1] ,

$$\int_I a_j^{\varepsilon}(x_1)\,dx_1 \to +\infty, \quad as \quad \varepsilon \to 0,$$

(H$_4$) *for every* $j \in F$, $G_j(0) = 0$.

*Then, as* $\varepsilon \to 0$, *the solution* $u^{\varepsilon}$ *of* $(P^{\varepsilon})$ *converges weakly in* $W^{1,p}(\Omega)$ *to the solution* *u of*

$$(P) \quad \mathrm{Inf}\{ J(v) - \int_{\Omega} f(x)\,v(x)\,dx \; ; \; v \in W \}$$

*where*

$$W = \{ v \in W_L^{1,p}(\Omega) \; ; \forall j \in F, \frac{\partial v}{\partial x_j} = 0 \}$$

$$J(v) = \int_{\Omega} \frac{1}{a_1(x_1)} G_1(x, a_1(x_1)\frac{\partial v}{\partial x_1}(x))\,dx + \sum_{i \in E} \int_{\Omega} a_i(x_1)\, G_i(\frac{\partial v}{\partial x_i}(x))\,dx.$$

*Moreover* $J^{\varepsilon}(u^{\varepsilon}) \to J(u)$.

**Remark 3.2.** The hypothesis (H$_2$) is weaker than " $a_i^{\varepsilon} \to a_i$ in w-$L^1(0,1)$ ", but it is stronger than " $a_i^{\varepsilon} \to a_i$ weakly in the space $M_b(0,1)$ of bounded measures on $]0,1[$ ".

For instance, suppose that $\Omega$ is a stratified domain with layers $\Sigma_{k,\varepsilon}$ of size $r_\varepsilon$ and of the form $\{(x_1,x') \in \Omega \; ; \; t_k - \frac{r_\varepsilon}{2} \le x_1 \le t_k + \frac{r_\varepsilon}{2}\}$, $t_k$ periodically distributed with period $\varepsilon$ ($\varepsilon >> r_\varepsilon$) along the $x_1$-axis. Let $a_i^{\varepsilon} = a^{\varepsilon}$ for all $i = 1,\dots,N$, with $a^{\varepsilon}(x_1) = \lambda_\varepsilon$ in all the layers $\Sigma_{k,\varepsilon}$ and $a^{\varepsilon}(x_1) = 1$ in $\Omega \setminus \Sigma_{k,\varepsilon}$ and assume $\lambda^{\varepsilon} \to +\infty$. Clearly (H$_1$) is satisfied with $a_1 = 1$. If $\dfrac{r^{\varepsilon}\lambda^{\varepsilon}}{\varepsilon} \to +\infty$ as $\varepsilon \to 0$, then $a^{\varepsilon}$ satisfies (H$_3$). If $\dfrac{r^{\varepsilon}\lambda^{\varepsilon}}{\varepsilon} \to k \in [0,+\infty[$, then $a^{\varepsilon}$ satisfies (H$_2$) with $a_i = 1 + k$, $i \ge 2$, but the sequence $(a^{\varepsilon})$ is not equiintegrable and hence $(a^{\varepsilon})$ does not converge to $1 + k$ in w-$L^1(0,1)$. In this very simple context, the limit behaviour has been studied by Chabi in [2].

**PROOF.** Following De Giorgi (cf.[3] and also [1]), the method is to deduce the convergence of the minimization problems $(P^{\varepsilon})$ from the $\Gamma$- convergence of the functionals $J^{\varepsilon}$. It relies on the three lemmas :

**Lemma 3.3.** *Assume* $(H_1)$ , $(H_2)$ *and* $(H_4)$ . *For every* $v \in C^2(\bar{\Omega}) \cap W$ , *there exists* $v^\varepsilon \in W_L^{1,p}(\Omega)$ *such that* $v^\varepsilon$ *converges to* $v$ *in* $w - W^{1,p}(\Omega)$ *and*

$$\limsup J^\varepsilon(v^\varepsilon) \le J(v) .$$

**Lemma 3.4.** *Assume* $(H_1)$ *and* $(H_2)$ . *If* $v^\varepsilon$ *converges to* $v$ *in* $w - W^{1,p}(\Omega)$ , *with* $v \in W$ , *then*

$$\liminf J^\varepsilon(v^\varepsilon) \ge J(v) .$$

**Lemma 3.5.** *Assume* $(H_3)$ . *If* $v^\varepsilon \in W_L^{1,p}(\Omega)$ *and converges to* $v$ *in* $w - W^{1,p}(\Omega)$ *and if* $\int_\Omega a_j^\varepsilon \left|\frac{\partial v^\varepsilon}{\partial x_j}\right|^p dx$ *is bounded for some* $j \in F$ , *then* $\frac{\partial v}{\partial x_j} = 0$ *on* $\Omega$.

Proof of theorem 3.1. Let $u^\varepsilon$ be the unique solution of $(P^\varepsilon)$. Let $v \in C^2(\bar{\Omega}) \cap W$. By lemma 3.3, there exist $v^\varepsilon \in W_L^{1,p}(\Omega)$ such that $v^\varepsilon$ converge to $v$ in w-$W^{1,p}(\Omega)$ (therefore in $L^p(\Omega)$) and

$$\begin{aligned} J(v) - \int_\Omega f v \, dx &\ge \limsup \left( J^\varepsilon(v^\varepsilon) - \int_\Omega f v^\varepsilon dx \right) \\ &\ge \limsup \left( J^\varepsilon(u^\varepsilon) - \int_\Omega f u^\varepsilon dx\right) \\ &\ge \limsup \int_\Omega \left(\lambda_1 \alpha^{p-1} \left|\frac{\partial u^\varepsilon}{\partial x_1}\right|^p + \sum_{i=2}^N \lambda_i \alpha \left|\frac{\partial u^\varepsilon}{\partial x_i}\right|^p - f u^\varepsilon \right)dx. \end{aligned}$$

Using Poincaré's inequality, we deduce that $(u^\varepsilon)$ is bounded in $W^{1,p}(\Omega)$ and that $\int_\Omega a_j^\varepsilon \left|\frac{\partial u^\varepsilon}{\partial x_j}\right|^p dx$ is bounded for all $j \in F$ . Hence a subsequence of $u^\varepsilon$ , say $u^\varepsilon$ again, converges to some $\underline{u}$ in $w - W_L^{1,p}(\Omega)$ . By lemma 3.5, $\underline{u} \in W$ . By lemma 3.4,

$$\begin{aligned} J(\underline{u}) - \int_\Omega f \underline{u} \, dx &\le \liminf \left(J^\varepsilon(u^\varepsilon) - \int_\Omega f u^\varepsilon dx\right) \\ &\le \limsup \left(J^\varepsilon(u^\varepsilon) - \int_\Omega f u^\varepsilon dx\right) \le J(v) - \int_\Omega f v \, dx , \end{aligned}$$

for every $v \in C^2(\overline{\Omega}) \cap W$, and by density for every $v$ in $W$. It follows that $\underline{u} = u$, the unique solution of $(P\ )$, the whole sequence $(u^\varepsilon)$ converges to $u$ in $w - W^{1,p}_L(\Omega)$ and in $L^p(\Omega)$ and $J^\varepsilon(u^\varepsilon) \to J(u)$.

Proof of lemma 3.3. Let $v \in C^2(\overline{\Omega}) \cap W$. Let $v^\varepsilon$ be defined by

$$v^\varepsilon(x_1,x') = \int_0^{x_1} \frac{a_1}{a_1^\varepsilon}(y_1) \frac{\partial v}{\partial x_1}(y_1,x')\, dy_1 + c^\varepsilon(x') \int_0^{x_1} \frac{1}{a_1^\varepsilon}\, dy_1$$

with $c^\varepsilon(x') = \left(1 - \int_0^1 \frac{a_1}{a_1^\varepsilon}(y_1) \frac{\partial v}{\partial x_1}(y_1,x')\, dy_1\right)\left(\int_0^1 \frac{1}{a_1^\varepsilon}\, dy_1\right)^{-1}$.

We have $v^\varepsilon \in C^o(\overline{\Omega})$, $\frac{\partial v^\varepsilon}{\partial x_1} \in L^\infty(\Omega)$, $\frac{\partial v^\varepsilon}{\partial x_i} \in C^o(\overline{\Omega})$ for $i \geq 2$, $\frac{\partial v^\varepsilon}{\partial x_j} = 0$ for $j \in F$ and $v^\varepsilon \in W$. Using $(H_1)$ and Ascoli's theorem, one can prove that $c^\varepsilon \to 0$ in $C^o(\overline{\Omega})$, $\frac{\partial c^\varepsilon}{\partial x_i} \to 0$ in $C^o(\overline{\Omega})$ for $i \geq 2$. In the same way $v^\varepsilon \to v$ in $C^o(\overline{\Omega})$, $\frac{\partial v^\varepsilon}{\partial x_i} \to \frac{\partial v}{\partial x_i}$ in $C^o(\overline{\Omega})$ for $i \geq 2$. Moreover $\frac{\partial v^\varepsilon}{\partial x_1} = \frac{a_1}{a_1^\varepsilon}\frac{\partial v}{\partial x_1} + \frac{c^\varepsilon}{a_1^\varepsilon}$. Hence

$$\int_\Omega \frac{1}{a_1^\varepsilon} G_1\left(x, a_1^\varepsilon \frac{\partial v^\varepsilon}{\partial x_1}\right) dx = \int_\Omega \frac{1}{a_1^\varepsilon} G_1\left(x, a_1 \frac{\partial v}{\partial x_1} + c^\varepsilon\right) dx .$$

Since $a_1 \frac{\partial v}{\partial x_1} + c^\varepsilon \to a_1 \frac{\partial v}{\partial x_1}$ in $L^\infty(\Omega)$ (hence in $L^p(\Omega)$) and $G_1$ is a Caratheodory function with suitable growth conditions, $G_1(x, a_1 \frac{\partial v}{\partial x_1} + c^\varepsilon) \to G_1(x, a_1 \frac{\partial v}{\partial x_1})$ in $L^1(\Omega)$. By $(H_1)$, it follows that

$$\int_\Omega \frac{1}{a_1^\varepsilon} G_1\left(x, a_1^\varepsilon \frac{\partial v^\varepsilon}{\partial x_1}\right) dx \to \int_\Omega \frac{1}{a_1} G_1\left(x, a_1 \frac{\partial v}{\partial x_1}\right) dx .$$

For $j \in F$, $\frac{\partial v^\varepsilon}{\partial x_j} = 0$, $G_j(\frac{\partial v^\varepsilon}{\partial x_j}) = G_j(0) = 0$ (by $(H_4)$) and

$$\int_\Omega a_j^\varepsilon(x_1)\ G_j(\frac{\partial v^\varepsilon}{\partial x_j})\,dx = G_j(0) \int_\Omega a_j^\varepsilon(x_1)\,dx = 0.$$

For $i \in E$, let us write

$$\int_\Omega a_i^\varepsilon(x_1)\ G_i(\frac{\partial v^\varepsilon}{\partial x_i})\,dx = \int_0^1 a_i^\varepsilon(x_1)\ \phi_i^\varepsilon(x_1)\,dx_1$$

where $\phi_i^\varepsilon(x_1) = \int_\Omega G_i(\frac{\partial v^\varepsilon}{\partial x_i}(x_1,x'))\,dx' \to \phi_i(x_1) = \int_\Omega G_i(\frac{\partial v}{\partial x_i}(x_1,x'))\,dx'$

in $C^o([0,1])$ ( $\frac{\partial v^\varepsilon}{\partial x_i}$ remains in a compact set of $\mathbf{R}$, where the continuous function $G_i$ is effectively uniformly continuous). By $(H_2)$ it follows that

$$\int_0^1 a_i^\varepsilon(x_1)\ \phi_i^\varepsilon(x_1)\,dx_1 \to \int_0^1 a_i(x_1)\ \phi_i(x_1)\,dx_1 = \int_\Omega a_i(x_1)\ G_i(\frac{\partial v}{\partial x_i})\,dx.$$

Hence $\lim J^\varepsilon(v^\varepsilon) = J(v)$.

<u>Proof of lemma 3.4</u>. Suppose that $v^\varepsilon \to v$ in $w - W^{1,p}(\Omega)$ with $v \in W$.

First, by convexity of $G_1$, we have

$$\liminf \int_\Omega \frac{1}{a_1^\varepsilon} G_1(x, a_1^\varepsilon \frac{\partial v^\varepsilon}{\partial x_1})\,dx \geq \liminf \int_\Omega \frac{1}{a_1^\varepsilon} G_1(x, a_1 \frac{\partial v}{\partial x_1})\,dx$$

$$+ \liminf \int_\Omega g_1(x, a_1 \frac{\partial v}{\partial x_1})\,(\frac{\partial v^\varepsilon}{\partial x_1} - \frac{a_1}{a_1^\varepsilon}\frac{\partial v}{\partial x_1})\,dx\,.$$

Using $(H_1)$, we get

$$\liminf \int_\Omega \frac{1}{a_1^\varepsilon} G_1(x, a_1^\varepsilon \frac{\partial v^\varepsilon}{\partial x_1})\,dx \geq \int_\Omega \frac{1}{a_1} G_1(x, a_1 \frac{\partial v}{\partial x_1})\,dx\,.$$

Secondly, for $j \in F$, $\int_\Omega a_j^\varepsilon \, G_j(\frac{\partial v^\varepsilon}{\partial x_j}) \, dx \geq 0$.

Now, let us prove that

$$\liminf \int_\Omega a_i^\varepsilon \, G_i(\frac{\partial v^\varepsilon}{\partial x_i}) \, dx \;\geq\; \int_\Omega a_i \, G_i(\frac{\partial v}{\partial x_i}) \, dx \text{ , for every } i \in E .$$

This is the difficult part. This proof relies on the method developed in [5]. For each $i \in E$, we will approach $v^\varepsilon$ by suitable step functions with respect to $x_1$.
Let $i \in E$ be fixed. Given $n \in \mathbf{N}$, let $I_k = [\frac{k-1}{n}, \frac{k}{n}]$, for $k = 1, ..., n$. Let $w^{\varepsilon,n}$ be defined as follows :

$$w^{\varepsilon,n}(x_1,x') = \sum_{k=1}^{n} X_{I_k}(x_1) \int_{I_k} v^\varepsilon(y_1,x') \, d\mu^{\varepsilon,k}(y_1)$$

where $d\mu^{\varepsilon,k}(y_1) = \dfrac{a_i^\varepsilon(y_1)}{\int_{I_k} a_i^\varepsilon(y_1)\, dy_1} \, dy_1$ on $I_k$ ($\mu^{\varepsilon,k}$ is a probability measure on $I_k$),

and $X_{I_k} = 1$ on $I_k$ and $X_{I_k} = 0$ elsewhere.

As in [5] ,we have

$$\int_0^1 | v^\varepsilon - w^{\varepsilon,n} |^p dx_1 \leq \frac{1}{n^p} \int_0^1 | \frac{\partial v^\varepsilon}{\partial x_1} |^p dx_1$$

and hence, since $v^\varepsilon$ is bounded in $W^{1,p}(\Omega)$,i

$$|| v^\varepsilon - w^{\varepsilon,n} ||_{L^p(\Omega)} \leq \frac{K}{n} \text{ , for some constant } K.$$

As in [5], we also have

$$\int_0^1 | \frac{\partial w^{\varepsilon,n}}{\partial x_i} |^p dx_1 \leq \left( \int_0^1 a_i^\varepsilon \, | \frac{\partial v^\varepsilon}{\partial x_i} |^p dx_1 \right) \max \left\{ \frac{|I_k|}{\int_{I_k} a_i^\varepsilon \, dx_1} \; ; \; k = 1,...,n \right\}.$$

But $\dfrac{|I_k|}{\displaystyle\int_{I_k} a_i^\varepsilon \, dx_1} \leq \alpha^{-1}$ . Hence we get

$$\int_\Omega |\frac{\partial w^{\varepsilon,n}}{\partial x_i}|^p dx \leq \alpha^{-1} \int_\Omega a_i^\varepsilon |\frac{\partial v^\varepsilon}{\partial x_i}|^p dx \leq (\alpha \lambda_i)^{-1} \int_\Omega a_i^\varepsilon G_i(\frac{\partial v^\varepsilon}{\partial x_i}) dx$$

which can be supposed bounded (otherwise the lemma is obvious) . Thus $\frac{\partial w^{\varepsilon,n}}{\partial x_i}$ is bounded in $L^p(\Omega)$.

Let us decompose $\int_\Omega a_i^\varepsilon G_i(\frac{\partial v^\varepsilon}{\partial x_i}) dx - \int_\Omega a_i G_i(\frac{\partial v}{\partial x_i}) dx$ into the sum of three terms :

$$\int_\Omega a_i^\varepsilon \left(G_i(\frac{\partial v^\varepsilon}{\partial x_i}) - G_i(\frac{\partial w^{\varepsilon,n}}{\partial x_i})\right) dx$$

$$+ \int_\Omega G_i(\frac{\partial w^{\varepsilon,n}}{\partial x_i}) (a_i^\varepsilon - a_i) dx$$

$$+ \int_\Omega a_i \left( G_i(\frac{\partial w^{\varepsilon,n}}{\partial x_i}) - G_i(\frac{\partial v}{\partial x_i})\right) dx .$$

The first term is nonnegative since

$$\int_0^1 a_i^\varepsilon \left(G_i(\frac{\partial v^\varepsilon}{\partial x_i}) - G_i(\frac{\partial w^{\varepsilon,n}}{\partial x_i})\right) dx_1 \geq \int_0^1 a_i^\varepsilon g_i(\frac{\partial w^{\varepsilon,n}}{\partial x_i})(\frac{\partial v^\varepsilon}{\partial x_i} - \frac{\partial w^{\varepsilon,n}}{\partial x_i}) dx_1 = 0$$

by convexity of $G_i$ and by definition of $w^{\varepsilon,n}$.

The second term becomes

$$\left| \int_\Omega G_i(\frac{\partial w^{\varepsilon,n}}{\partial x_i}) (a_i^\varepsilon - a_i) dx \right| \leq \sum_{k=1}^n \int_{\Omega'} G_i(\frac{\partial w^{\varepsilon,n}}{\partial x_i}) \left| \int_{I_k} (a_i^\varepsilon - a_i) dx_1 \right| dx'.$$

But, by $(H_2)$, there exists $\varepsilon'(n)$ such that, for $\varepsilon \leq \varepsilon'(n)$,

$$\max \left\{ \left| \int_{I_k} (a_i^\varepsilon - a_i) dx \right| ; k = 1,\dots,n \right\} \leq \frac{1}{n^2} .$$

Hence,

$$\left| \int_\Omega G_i(\frac{\partial w^{\varepsilon,n}}{\partial x_i}) (a_i^\varepsilon - a_i) dx \right| \leq \frac{1}{n} \int_\Omega G_i(\frac{\partial w^{\varepsilon,n}}{\partial x_i}) dx$$

$$\leq \frac{1}{n} \int_\Omega (\Lambda_i |\frac{\partial w^{\varepsilon,n}}{\partial x_i}|^p + \gamma_i) dx \leq \frac{K}{n} ,$$

since $\frac{\partial w^{\varepsilon,n}}{\partial x_i}$ is bounded in $L^p(\Omega)$.

In order to obtain the lim inf of the third term, let us choose $\varepsilon(n) \le \text{Min}\,(\frac{1}{n}, \varepsilon'(n))$ $(\varepsilon(n) \to 0$ as $n \to \infty)$. We have seen that

$$|| v^{\varepsilon(n)} - w^{\varepsilon(n),n} ||_{L^p(\Omega)} \le \frac{K}{n}$$

and (up to extraction of a new subsequence) $v^{\varepsilon(n)} \to v$ in s-$L^p(\Omega)$. Thus, when $n \to \infty$, $w^{\varepsilon(n),n} \to v$ in s-$L^p(\Omega)$.

As $\frac{\partial w^{\varepsilon,n}}{\partial x_i}$ is bounded in $L^p(\Omega)$, we may also suppose that $\frac{\partial w^{\varepsilon(n),n}}{\partial x_i} \to \frac{\partial v}{\partial x_i}$ in w-$L^p(\Omega)$.

By convexity,

$$\liminf \int_\Omega a_i \left( G_i(\frac{\partial w^{\varepsilon(n),n}}{\partial x_i}) - G_i(\frac{\partial v}{\partial x_i})\right) dx \ge 0 .$$

Finally, we get

$$\liminf \int_\Omega a_i^{\varepsilon(n)} G_i(\frac{\partial v^{\varepsilon(n)}}{\partial x_i})\, dx \ge \int_\Omega a_i \; G_i(\frac{\partial v}{\partial x_i})\, dx ,$$

and lemma 3.4 easily follows by contradiction.

<u>Proof of lemma 3.5.</u> As in the proof of lemma 3.4, for each $j \in F$ we consider the function $w^{\varepsilon,n}$ and we get

$$\int_\Omega |\frac{\partial w^{\varepsilon,n}}{\partial x_j}|^p dx \le \left(\int_\Omega a_j^\varepsilon \, |\frac{\partial v^\varepsilon}{\partial x_j}|^p dx\right) \max \left\{\frac{|I_k|}{\int_{I_k} a_j^\varepsilon \, dx_1} ; k = 1,...,n\right\}.$$

By $(H_3)$, there exists $\varepsilon(n)$ ( and we may suppose $\varepsilon(n) \to 0$) such that $\varepsilon \le \varepsilon(n)$ implies

$$\min \left\{ \int_{I_k} a_j^\varepsilon \, dx_1 \; ; k = 1,...,n \right\} \ge 1$$

and then (since the last integral on $\Omega$ is bounded by hypothesis)

$$\int_\Omega |\frac{\partial w^{\varepsilon(n),n}}{\partial x_j}|^p dx \le \frac{K}{n} \to 0 .$$

As previously, $w^{\varepsilon(n),n} \to v$ in s-$L^p(\Omega)$ and we get $\frac{\partial v}{\partial x_j} = O$ .

## REFERENCES.

[1] H. ATTOUCH, Variational Convergence for Functions and Operators, Appl. Math. Series, Pitman, London, 1984.

[2] E. CHABI, Homogénéisation de matériaux composites de forte conductivité, Publication AVAMAC de Perpignan-France (1985), N° 13.

[3] E. DE GIORGI, Convergence problems for functionals and operators, Proceeding "Recent Methods in nonlinear Analysis", Rome 1978, edited by E. De Giorgi, E. Magenes, U. Mosco, Pitagora, Bologna, (1979), p. 131-188.

[4] B. GUSTAFSSON, J. MOSSINO, C. PICARD, Homogenization of foliated annuli, Annali Mat. Pura Applic., to appear (see also C. R. Acad. Sci. Paris, 309 (1989) p. 239-244).

[5] B. GUSTAFSSON, J. MOSSINO, C. PICARD, Stratified materials allowing asymptotically prescribed equipotentials, to appear.

[6] B. GUSTAFSSON, J. MOSSINO, C. PICARD, Homogenization of stratified structures with high conductivity, to appear.

[7] F. MURAT, H-convergence, Séminaire d'Analyse Fonctionnelle et Numérique de l'Université d'Alger, 1977-78, multigraphié.

[8] L. TARTAR, Remarks on homogenization in Homogenization and Effective Moduli of Materials and Media (ed. by J. L. Ericksen, D. Kinderlehrer, R. Kohn, J. L. Lions), Springer-Verlag 1986, p. 228-246.

## AUTHORS' ADDRESSES :

B.G. : Tekniska Högskolan, Matematik, 10044 Stockholm - Suède.

J.M. : CNRS, Laboratoire d'Analyse Numérique, Université de Paris-Sud, Bât. 425, 91405 Orsay - France.

C.P. : U. F. R. de Mathématiques et d'Informatique, Université d'Amiens, 33 rue Saint Leu, 80039 Amiens- France et Laboratoire d'Analyse Numérique, Université de Paris-Sud, Bât. 425, 91405 Orsay - France.

J GWINNER*

# Boundary element convergence for unilateral harmonic problems

## 1 Introduction

In this note we extend the recent convergence analysis given by Han [14] for the harmonic Dirichlet-Signorini boundary value problem in two respects. Firstly we treat the fully mixed Dirichlet-Neumann-Signorini problem and admit the case of only Neumann and Signorini boundary conditions where the associated variational problem is no longer coercive, but the resulting boundary bilinear form satisfies a Gårding inequality with a compact perturbation term. Secondly we do not only consider piecewise linear-affine approximations to the trace of the unknown function, but also investigate piecewise quadratic and piecewise cubic approximations which lead to nonconform boundary element approximation schemes. Here we apply the recent abstract discretization theorem of [10] that extends the discretization theory of Glowinski [7] from elliptic bilinear forms to the more general semicoercive case and also extends the well-known discretization theorem of Hildebrandt and Wienholtz [15] to variational inequalities. Based on this result we establish norm convergence of piecewise polynomial boundary element approximations to those unilateral harmonic boundary value problems without imposing any regularity assumption.

Currently the boundary element method is under study towards the solution of the unilateral boundary value problems that arise from the Signorini boundary condition and where hence the free boundary is part of the boundary. Spann [24] derived error estimates for the harmonic Dirichlet-Signorini

*Fachbereich Mathematik, TH Darmstadt, D-6100 Darmstadt; currently Institut für Angewandte Mathematik, Universität Hannover, D-3000 Hannover, Germany

problem. Schmitz and Schneider [22] and together with Wendland [23] analysed a penalty approach to this latter problem.

## 2 The Unilateral Boundary Value Problem

In this section we describe the unilateral boundary value problem, in particular its equivalent boundary variational inequality, and collect some preliminary results that are useful for the convergence analysis to follow. So let $\Omega \subset \mathbb{R}^2$ be a bounded plane domain with the Lipschitz boundary $\Gamma$ [20, 8]. Then $n$, the outward normal to $\Gamma$, exists almost everywhere and $n \in [L^\infty(\Gamma)]^2$ (see [20, Lemma 2.4.2]).

In this note we consider the simplest elliptic equation

$$-\Delta u = 0 \quad \text{in } \Omega\,. \tag{1}$$

Thus the traction operator $\mathcal{T}$ on $\Gamma$ for elliptic systems is here simply given by

$$\varphi := \mathcal{T}(u) := \frac{\partial u}{\partial n}.$$

To formulate the boundary conditions, let $\Gamma = \overline{\Gamma}_D \cup \overline{\Gamma}_N \cup \overline{\Gamma}_S$, where the open parts $\Gamma_D, \Gamma_N$, and $\Gamma_S$ are mutually disjoint. We prescribe

$$u = 0 \quad \text{on } \Gamma_D\,, \tag{2}$$

$$\mathcal{T}(u) = g \quad \text{on } \Gamma_N\,. \tag{3}$$

On the remaining part $\Gamma_S$, the Signorini's conditions are imposed, i.e.

$$u \le 0\,, \quad \varphi \le h\,, \quad u(\varphi - h) = 0\,, \tag{4}$$

where $h \in H^{-1/2}(\Gamma_S)$ is given. To make the unilateral problem meaningful we assume meas $(\Gamma_S) > 0$, but we do not require meas $(\Gamma_D) > 0$. Note there is no loss of generality to assume homogeneous conditions above. Indeed, more general conditions can be reduced to the form given above by a superposition argument that uses the solution of the linear boundary value problem

$$\Delta u = f \quad \text{in } \Omega$$

$$u = u_D^0 \quad \text{on } \Gamma_D\,, \quad \mathcal{T}(u) = 0 \quad \text{on } \Gamma_N\,, \quad u = u_S^0 \quad \text{on } \Gamma_S$$

and an appropriately redefined right hand side $h$ in (4). To give the variational formulation of the boundary value problem (1) – (4) we introduce the bilinear form

$$\beta(v,w) := \int_\Omega \operatorname{grad} v \cdot \operatorname{grad} w \, dx = \sum_{k=1}^{2} \int_\Omega \frac{\partial v}{\partial x_k} \frac{\partial w}{\partial x_k} \, dx$$

and the linear form

$$\ell(v) := \int_{\Gamma_N} g\, v \, ds + \int_{\Gamma_S} h\, v \, ds$$

on the function space

$$\overset{*}{H}{}^1(\Omega) := \{v \in H^1(\Omega) : v = 0 \quad \text{on } \Gamma_D\} \tag{5}$$

and the convex closed cone

$$\mathcal{K} := \{v \in \overset{*}{H}{}^1(\Omega) : v \le 0 \quad \text{on } \Gamma_S\}\,. \tag{6}$$

Then the variational formulation of (1) – (4) reads (see e.g. [17]): Find $u \in \mathcal{K}$ such that for all $v \in \mathcal{K}$

$$\beta(u, v-u) \ge \ell(v-u)\,. \tag{7}$$

Due to Stampacchia [25] existence and also uniqueness (see also [3, Theorem 7.5, Part I]) of the variational solution to (1) – (4) or to (7) are guaranteed, if

$$\ell(\underline{1}) = \int_{\Gamma_N} g \, ds + \int_{\Gamma_S} h \, ds > 0 \tag{8}$$

holds.

A fundamental solution of (1) is given by

$$\mathcal{F}(x,y) := \frac{1}{2\pi} \log|x-y|\,.$$

Using Green's formula and the jump relations for elastic potentials [18, 19] Han [14] derives

$$\begin{aligned}\beta(u,v) &= \int_\Gamma \mathcal{F}(x,y)\,\frac{du(y)}{ds_y}\,\frac{dv(x)}{ds_x}\,ds_y ds_x \\ &\quad + \int_\Gamma\int_\Gamma (\mathcal{T}_x\mathcal{F}(x,y))\,\varphi(y)\,v(x)\,ds_y ds_x + \frac{1}{2}\int_\Gamma \varphi\,v\,ds \\ &=: a\left(\frac{du}{ds},\frac{dv}{ds}\right) + b(\varphi,v)\,.\end{aligned}$$

Then with the convex cone

$$K := \{v \in H^{1/2}(\Gamma) : v = 0 \text{ on } \Gamma_D\,,\ v \le 0 \text{ on } \Gamma_S\}\,,$$

(7) is shown to be equivalent with the following variational problem: Find $[u,\varphi] \in K \times H^{-1/2}(\Gamma)$ such that

$$(\pi)\quad \begin{cases} a\left(\dfrac{du}{ds},\dfrac{dv}{ds}-\dfrac{du}{ds}\right) + b(\varphi, v-u) \ge \ell(v-u)\,, & \forall v \in K\,; \\ a(\psi,\varphi) - b(\psi,u) = 0\,, & \forall \psi \in H^{-1/2}(\Gamma)\,; \end{cases}$$

Note that $(\pi)$ is equivalent to

$$B([u,\varphi]\,,[v,\psi]-[u,\varphi]) \ge \ell(v-u)\,,\quad \forall [v,\psi] \in K \times H^{-1/2}(\Gamma) \tag{9}$$

with the bilinear form

$$B([u,\varphi],[v,\psi]) := a\left(\frac{du}{ds},\frac{dv}{ds}\right) + a(\psi,\varphi) + b(\varphi,v) - b(\psi,u)\,.$$

Indeed, since the variational equality in $(\pi)$ is equivalent to the variational inequality

$$a(\psi-\varphi,\varphi) - b(\psi-\varphi,u) \ge 0$$

on the space $H^{-1/2}(\Gamma)$, the implication $(\pi) \Rightarrow (9)$ is immediate. On the other hand, $(\pi)$ follows from (9) by the choices $\psi = 0\,,\ v = u\,.$

Now our aim is to establish a Gårding inequality for the bilinear form $B(\cdot,\cdot)$ in the space

$$V := H^{1/2}(\Gamma) \times H^{-1/2}(\Gamma)\,,$$

i.e. positive definiteness up to a compact perturbation term. The boundary integral operators that give rise to the bilinear form $B(\cdot,\cdot)$ can be understood as pseudodifferential operators [6]. Since coordinate transformations do not affect their principal symbol [6], thus contribute only to compact perturbation terms (see e.g. [16] for more detailed arguments of this kind) we need only consider the case of a smooth domain in the subsequent reasoning.

**Lemma 2.1** *There exist a constant $c_0 > 0$ and a compact operator $C_0 : H^{1/2}(\Gamma) \to H^{-1/2}(\Gamma)$ such that*

$$\|\frac{dv}{ds}\|^2_{-1/2,\Gamma} \geq c_0 \|v\|^2_{1/2,\Gamma} - \langle C_0 v, v\rangle_{H^{-1/2}\times H^{1/2}}, \quad \forall v \in H^{1/2}(\Gamma). \qquad (10)$$

*Proof.* Let $\theta = 2\pi s/L$, where $L$ is the boundary length, and we can assume without loss of generality that $\Gamma$ is the unit circle. Then we can argue similar to [14] with the only difference that due to the nontrivial kernel of $\beta$ an extra term enters. More detailed using the Fourier expansion for a smooth function $v$ – what by density suffices to consider –

$$v = \frac{a_0}{2} + \sum_{n=1}^{\infty}(a_n \cos n\theta + b_n \sin n\theta),$$

$$\frac{dv}{d\theta} = \sum_{n=1}^{\infty}(nb_n \cos n\theta - na_n \sin n\theta),$$

one finds

$$\|v\|^2_{1/2,\Gamma} = \frac{a_0^2}{2} + \sum_{n=1}^{\infty}(1+n^2)^{1/2}(a_n^2 + b_n^2),$$

$$\|\frac{dv}{d\theta}\|^2_{-1/2,\Gamma} = \sum_{n=1}^{\infty}(1+n^2)^{-1/2} n^2 (a_n^2 + b_n^2)$$

$$\geq \frac{1}{2}\sum_{n=1}^{\infty}(1+n^2)^{1/2}(a_n^2 + b_n^2),$$

$$a_0^2 = \left[\frac{1}{2\pi}\int_0^{2\pi} v(\theta)d\theta\right]^2 \leq c\,\|v\|^2_{0,\Gamma} \quad (c > 0).$$

Hence

$$\|\frac{dv}{d\theta}\|^2_{-1/2,\Gamma} \geq \frac{1}{2}\|v\|^2_{1/2,\Gamma} - \frac{c}{4}\|v\|^2_{0,\Gamma}\,. \tag{11}$$

Since

$$H^{1/2}(\Gamma) \subset H^0(\Gamma) \equiv L^2(\Gamma) \subset H^{-1/2}(\Gamma)$$

forms a Gelfand triple with *compact* and dense embeddings, the last term in (11) can be replaced by $\langle C_0 v, v\rangle$ with $C_0 : H^{1/2}(\Gamma) \to H^{-1/2}(\Gamma)$ compact concluding the proof. q.e.d.

**Lemma 2.2** *The bilinear form $B(\cdot,\cdot)$ is bounded in $V \times V$; moreover satisfies a Gårding inequality, i.e. there exist a positive constant $c_0$ and a compact operator $C : V \to V^*$ such that*

$$\begin{aligned} &B([v,\psi],[v,\psi]) + \langle C[v,\psi],[v,\psi]\rangle_{V^*\times V} \\ &\geq c_0\|[v,\psi]\|_V^2 := c_0\{\|v\|^2_{H^{1/2}(\Gamma)} + \|\psi\|^2_{H^{-1/2}(\Gamma)}\}\,, \\ &\forall [v,\psi] \in V := H^{1/2}(\Gamma) \times H^{-1/2}(\Gamma)\,. \end{aligned} \tag{12}$$

*Proof.* We have

$$B([v,\psi],[v,\psi]) = a\Big(\frac{dv}{ds},\frac{dv}{ds}\Big) + a(\psi,\psi)\,.$$

By [2, Theorem 1]

$$|a(\psi,\psi)| \leq \text{const}\,\|\psi\|^2_{H^{-1/2}(\Gamma)}\,.$$

Since for any $v \in H^{1/2}(\Gamma)$, $\frac{dv}{ds} = \sum_i \frac{\partial v}{\partial x_i}\dot{x}_i \in H^{-1/2}(\Gamma)$, it follows

$$|a\Big(\frac{dv}{ds},\frac{dv}{ds}\Big)| \leq \text{const}\,\|v\|^2_{H^{1/2}(\Gamma)}\,.$$

Therefore it remains to prove (12). By [2, Theorem 2] the bilinear form $a(\cdot,\cdot)$ satisfies a Gårding inequality on $[H^{-1/2}(\Gamma)]^2$ in the general case of a Lipschitz domain, i.e.

$$a(\psi,\psi) \geq c_a\|\psi\|^2_{H^{-1/2}(\Gamma)} - \langle C_A\psi,\psi\rangle_{H^{1/2}(\Gamma)\times H^{-1/2}(\Gamma)}\,, \quad \forall \psi \in H^{-1/2}(\Gamma)\,, \tag{13}$$

where $c_a > 0$, $C_A : H^{-1/2}(\Gamma) \to H^{1/2}(\Gamma)$ is compact. Hence

$$a\Big(\frac{dv}{ds},\frac{dv}{ds}\Big) \geq c_a\|\frac{dv}{ds}\|^2_{H^{-1/2}(\Gamma)} - \langle C_A\frac{dv}{ds},\frac{dv}{ds}\rangle, \quad \forall v \in H^{1/2}(\Gamma)\,. \tag{14}$$

Combining (13) and (14) with Lemma 2.1 yields (12). q.e.d.

Finally we are concerned with the density relation

$$\overline{K \cap C^\infty(\Gamma)} = K\,, \tag{15}$$

which is essential for our convergence analysis to come. Since the embedding $H^{1/2}(\Gamma) \subset L^1(\Gamma)$ is continuous and $L^1$-convergence implies pointwise convergence almost everywhere for a subsequence, $K$ is closed. Therefore it remains to show

$$K \subset \overline{K \cap C^\infty(\Gamma)}\,.$$

To this end one uses the continuity and surjectivity of the trace operator $\gamma : H^1(\Omega) \to H^{1/2}(\Gamma)$ and applies the analogous inclusion

$$\mathcal{K} \subset \overline{\mathcal{K} \cap C^\infty(\Gamma)}\,,$$

which can be proved [9, Chapter 3] using Friedrich's regularization and the fact that with $\Omega$ a Lipschitz domain, $H = H^1(\Omega)$ is a Dirichlet space and in particular the map $w \in H \to w^+ = \max(0, w)$ is a continuous map into $H$.

# 3 Discretization of the Boundary Variational Inequality and the Convergence Result

In the following we suppose that for simplicity $\Omega$ is polygonal, but not necessarily convex. Let $\Gamma$ be represented by

$$x_i = X_i(s)\,, \quad 0 \le s \le L \quad (i = 1, 2)$$

with $X_i(0) = X_i(L)$ $(i = 1, 2)$. We partition $\Gamma$ into finitely many segments by the points $P_j = \big(X_1(s_j), X_2(s_j)\big)$, $j = 1, \ldots, J$, where the endpoints of $\overline{\Gamma}_D$ and $\overline{\Gamma}_S$ are included and where $s_1 = 0$, $s_{J+1} = L$. The partitioning of $\Gamma$ is characterized by the mesh size

$$h := \max_{j=1,\ldots,J} |s_{j+1} - s_j|\,.$$

Note that the boundary variational inequality (9) splits into a variational equality in $H^{-1/2}(\Gamma)$, which can be discretized in a standard way [21, 26], and a novel variational inequality in the convex cone $K \subset H^{1/2}(\Gamma)$. As an important issue of this paper we want to treat not only piecewise linear, but also piecewise quadratic and piecewise cubic approximations of $K$. To this end we introduce the space $\mathcal{P}^\kappa$ of polynomials of degree less than or equal to $\kappa$ ($\kappa = 1, 2, 3$) and the subsequent finite point sets:

$$\Sigma_1^h := \{s_j : j = 1, \ldots, J\}$$

$$\Sigma_2^h := \{s \in (0, L) : s \text{ is a midpoint of an interval } (s_j, s_{j+1}) \text{ for some } j = 1, \ldots, J\}$$

$$\Sigma_3^h := \{s \in (0, L) : s \text{ divides an interval } (s_j, s_{j+1}) \text{ by the ratio 1:2}\}$$

Moreover

$$\Pi_1^h := \{P_j : j = 1, \ldots, J\} \cap \overline{\Gamma}_S ,$$

where with appropriate $1 \le j_0 \le j_1 < L$

$$\Pi_1^h = \{P_j : j = j_0, \ldots, j_1 + 1\} ,$$

and for $\kappa = 2, 3$

$$\Pi_\kappa^h := \left\{P = \big(X_1(s), X_2(s)\big) : s \in \Sigma_1^h \cup \Sigma_\kappa^h\right\} \cap \overline{\Gamma}_S .$$

Then the trace space of $\overset{*}{H}{}^1(\Omega)$, denoted by $\overset{*}{H}{}^{1/2}(\Gamma)$ can be approximated by the finite dimensional subspace

$$U_{\kappa,\mu}^h := \left\{v^h \in C^\mu(\Gamma) : v^h \circ X \mid (s_j, s_{j+1}) \in \mathcal{P}^\kappa \; (j = 1, \ldots, J) ; \; v^h | \Gamma_D = 0\right\} ,$$

$K$ by the convex cone

$$K_{\kappa,\mu}^h := \{v^h \in U_{\kappa,\mu}^h : v^h(P) \le 0 \, (\forall P \in \Pi_\kappa^h)\} ,$$

and $H^{-1/2}(\Gamma)$ by the finite dimensional subspace

$$\Phi_{\kappa-1,\mu-1}^h := \left\{\psi^h \in C^{\mu-1}(\Gamma) : \psi^h \circ X \mid (s_j, s_{j+1}) \in \mathcal{P}^{\kappa-1} \; (j = 1, \ldots, J)\right\} .$$

Here $\mu \in \mathbb{N}_0$ with $\mu \leq \kappa - 1$ and $C^{-1}(\Gamma)$ denotes the space of piecewise constant functions. Note that $K^h_{1,0} \subset K$ holds for all $h > 0$.

Thus we are led to the following discretized variational problem: Find $[u^h, \varphi^h] \in K^h_{\kappa,\mu} \times \Phi^h_{\kappa-1,\mu-1}$ such that

$$(\pi^h_\kappa) \quad \begin{cases} a\left(\dfrac{du^h}{ds}, \dfrac{dv^h}{ds} - \dfrac{du^h}{ds}\right) + b(\varphi^h, v^h - u^h) \geq \ell(v^h - u^h), & \forall v^h \in K^h_{\kappa,\mu} \\ a(\psi^h, \varphi^h) = b(\psi^h, u^h), \quad \forall \psi^h \in \Phi^h_{\kappa-1,\mu-1}; \end{cases}$$

or equivalently

$$B([u^h, \varphi^h], [v^h, \psi^h] - [u^h, \varphi^h]) \geq \ell(v^h - u^h),$$
$$\forall [v^h, \psi^h] \in K^h_{\kappa,\mu} \times \Phi^h_{\kappa-1,\mu-1}. \tag{16}$$

Let us remark that the condition (8) guarantees also the existence of the solution $[u^h, \varphi^h]$ of the approximate problem $(\pi^h_\kappa)$ because our discretization does not affect the linear form $\ell$. Now we can present our main result.

**Theorem 3.1** *Suppose, there exists a unique solution* $[u, \varphi]$ *to* $(\pi)$ *and also exist solutions* $[u^h_\kappa, \varphi^h_\kappa]$ *to* $(\pi^h_\kappa)$ $(h > 0)$ . *Then for* $\kappa = 1, 2, 3$

$$\lim_{h \to 0} \| [u^h_\kappa, \varphi^h_\kappa] - [u, \varphi] \|_{H^{1/2}(\Gamma) \times H^{-1/2}(\Gamma)} = 0$$

*Proof.* In virtue of Lemma 2.2, the bilinear form $B(\cdot, \cdot)$ satisfies the Gårding inequality (12). Therefore Theorem 4.1 of [10] applies and requires the following hypotheses, due to Glowinski (see [7, Chapter 1]):

**H1** If $\{v^h\}_{h>0}$ weakly converges to $v$, where $v^h \in K^h := K^h_{\kappa,\mu}$, then $v \in K$.

**H2** There exist a subset $M \subset H^{1/2}(\Gamma)$ such that $\overline{M} = K$ and mappings $\rho^h$ : $M \to U^h = U^h_{\kappa,\mu}$ with the property that, for each $w \in M$, $\rho^h w$ strongly converges to $w$ (as $h \to 0+$) and $\rho^h w \in K^h$ for all $0 < h < h_0(w)$.

We note that the analogous hypotheses for the approximation of $\psi \in H^{-1/2}(\Gamma)$ by $\psi^h \in \Phi^h$ are trivally satisfied in view of $\Phi^h \subset H^{-1/2}(\Gamma)$ and well-known density and approximation properties.

*Verification of* (H1). Since $K^h_{1,\mu}$ is contained in the weakly closed set $K$ for all $h > 0$, we have only to consider the cases $\kappa = 2$ and $\kappa = 3$ with $\mu \in \mathbb{N}_0$ such that $\mu \leq \kappa - 1$.

Let the polygonal boundary part $\overline{\Gamma}_S$ be partitioned by

$$\overline{\Gamma}_S = \bigcup_{j=j_0}^{j_1} [P_j, P_{j+1}] ,$$

where the closed line segment $[P_j, P_{j+1}]$ has the intermediate point $P_{j+\frac{1}{2}} \in \Pi_2^h$, respectively the two intermediate points $P_{j+\frac{1}{3}}, P_{j+\frac{2}{3}} \in \Pi_3^h$. For any $\psi \in C^0(\overline{\Gamma}_S)$ with $\psi \geq 0$ we define

$$\psi^h = \sum_{j=j_0}^{j_1} \psi(P_{j+\frac{1}{2}}) \chi_{j+\frac{1}{2}} ,$$

where $\chi_{j+\frac{1}{2}}$ denotes the characteristic function of the open segment $]P_j, P_{j+1}[$. Then $\psi^h \geq 0$ on $\Gamma_S$ ($\kappa = 2, 3$) and by the uniform continuity of $\psi$ on $\overline{\Gamma}_S$

$$\lim_{h \to 0} \|\psi^h - \psi\|_{L^\infty(\Gamma_S)} = 0 . \tag{17}$$

Now let $\{v^h\}_{j>0}$ be a family weakly convergent to $v \in \overset{*}{H}{}^1(\Gamma)$, where $v^h \in K_{\kappa,\mu}^h$ ($\forall h > 0$; $\kappa = 2$ or $\kappa = 3$). Since the embedding $H^{1/2}(\Gamma) \subset L^1(\Gamma_S)$ is weakly continuous, the functions $v^h$ converge weakly to $v$ in $L^1(\Gamma_S)$ and are norm bounded. Therefore by the estimate

$$\left| \int_{\Gamma_S} (v^h \psi^h - v\psi) ds \right| \leq \|v^h\|_{L^1(\Gamma_S)} \|\psi^h - \psi\|_{L^\infty(\Gamma_S)} + \left| \int_{\Gamma_S} (v^h - v)\psi \, ds \right| ,$$

using (17) and $\psi \in L^\infty(\Gamma_S) = \left(L^1(\Gamma_S)\right)^*$, we obtain that

$$\lim_{h \to 0} \int_{\Gamma_S} v^h \psi^h \, ds = \int_{\Gamma_S} v\psi \, ds . \tag{18}$$

From Simpson's rule it follows for $v^h \in K_{2,\mu}^h$ and all $\psi \in C^0(\Gamma)$ with $\psi \geq 0$ that

$$\begin{aligned} \int_{\Gamma_S} v^h \psi^h \, ds &= \sum_{j=j_0}^{j_1} \int_{s_j}^{s_{j+1}} \psi(P_{j+\frac{1}{2}})(v^h \circ X)(s) \, ds \\ &= \frac{1}{6} \sum_{j=j_0}^{j_1} \psi(P_{j+\frac{1}{2}})(s_{j+1} - s_j) \left[ v^h(P_j) + 4v^h(P_{j+\frac{1}{2}}) + v^h(P_{j+1}) \right] \\ &\leq 0 , \end{aligned} \tag{19}$$

whereas from Newton's pulcherrima quadrature rule (see e.g. [13, §7.1.5]) for $v^h \in K^h_{3,\mu}$

$$\int_{\Gamma_S} v^h \psi^h \, ds = \frac{1}{8} \sum_{j=j_0}^{j_1} \psi(P_{j+\frac{1}{2}})\,(s_{j+1} - s_j) \Big[ v^h(P_j) + 3v^h(P_{j+\frac{1}{3}}) + 3v^h(P_{j+\frac{2}{3}}) + v^h(P_{j+1}) \Big]$$

$$\leq 0 \,. \tag{20}$$

Combining (18) and (19), respectively (20) we obtain that for all $\psi \in C^0(\overline{\Gamma}_S)$ with $\psi \geq 0$

$$\int_{\Gamma_S} v\psi \, ds \leq 0 \,,$$

hence $v \leq 0$ almost everywhere on $\Gamma_S$ or $v \in K$. This proves (H1).

*Verification of* (H2). In virtue of (15), we can take $M = K \cap C^\infty(\Gamma)$. Now we define $\rho^h_\kappa : H^{1/2}(\Gamma) \cap C^\infty(\Gamma) \to U^h_{\kappa,\kappa-1} \subseteq U^h_{\kappa,\mu}$ by $L$–periodic spline interpolation subordinated to the partitioning of $\Gamma$. Thus in particular

$$\rho^h_\kappa w(P) = w(P) \,, \quad \forall P \in \Pi^h_\kappa \quad (\kappa = 1, 2, 3) \,.$$

Hence $\rho^h_\kappa w$ belongs to $K^h_{\kappa,\kappa-1} \subseteq K^h_{\kappa,\mu}$ for any $w \in M$, since $\mu \leq \kappa - 1$. Moreover by spline interpolation theory (see e.g. [4, Lemma 4.1]), $U_{\kappa,\kappa-1}$ is a regular family of finite elements in the sense of Babuška and Aziz [1] and therefore we have

$$\|w - \rho^h_\kappa w\|_{H^{1/2}(\Gamma)} \leq c h^{\kappa - 1/2} \, \|w\|_{H^\kappa(\Gamma)} \quad (\kappa = 1, 2, 3)$$

with $c > 0$ independent of $h$ and $w$. Hence we conclude that

$$\lim_{h \to 0} \|w - \rho^h_\kappa w\|_{H^{1/2}(\Gamma)} = 0 \,, \quad \forall w \in M \,;\ \kappa = 1, 2, 3 \,.$$

q.e.d.

**Concluding Remarks** By the proof above (see in particular the estimates (19) and (20)) we have shown that boundary element convergence holds true for arbitrary piecewise polynomial approximations as long as the corresponding Newton-Cotes quadrature formula has positive weights. This is a reasonable restriction for practical computations and is satisfied for the Newton-Cotes formulae up to the order $\kappa = 8$ [5, §6.2.1].

In this note we considered the simplest elliptic equation. The method presented can be extended to more general problems, e.g. the Navier - Lame -system of linear elasticity, where, however, additional considerations are necessary. Here referring to [12] boundary element convergence can be established for the planar contact problem which parallels recently obtained results for the finite element method ([11]).

## References


[1] I. Babuška, A.K. Aziz, *Survey lectures on the mathematical formulation of the finite element method,* in *The Mathematical Foundation of the Finite Element Method* (A.K. Aziz, ed.), Academic Press, New York, 1972, 3–359.

[2] M. Costabel, *Boundary integral operators on Lipschitz domains: Elementary results,* SIAM J. Math. Anal. **19** (1988), 613–626.

[3] G. Duvaut, J.L. Lions, *Inequalities in Mechanics and Physics,* Springer, New York, 1976.

[4] J. Elschner, *On spline approximation for a class of integral equations, I: Galerkin and collocation methods with piecewise polynomials,* Math. Methods in the Applied Sciences **10** (1988), 543–559.

[5] H. Engels, *Numerical quadrature and cubature,* Academic Press, New York, 1980.

[6] G.I. Èskin, *Boundary Value Problems for Elliptic Pseudodifferential Equations,* Translations of Mathematical Monographs, Vol. 52, American Mathematical Society, Providence, 1981.

[7] R. Glowinski, *Numerical methods for nonlinear variational problems,* Springer, New York, 1984.

[8] P. Grisvard, *Elliptic Problems in Nonsmooth Domains,* Pitman, Boston, 1985.

[9] J. Gwinner, *Convergence and error analysis for variational inequalities and unilateral boundary value problems,* Habilitationsschrift, THD-Preprint 1257, Technische Hochschule Darmstadt, 1989.

[10] J. Gwinner, *Discretization of semicoercive variational inequalities,* Aequationes Math. **42** (1991), 72–79.

[11] J. Gwinner, *Finite-element convergence for contact problems in plane linear elastostatics,* to appear in Q. Appl. Math.

[12] J. Gwinner, E.P. Stephan, *A boundary element procedure for contact problems in plane linear elastostatics* (submitted).

[13] G. Hämmerlin, K.H. Hoffmann, *Numerische Mathematik,* Springer, 1989.

[14] H. Han, *A direct boundary element method for Signorini problems,* Math. Computation **55** (1990), 115–128.

[15] S. Hildebrandt, E. Wienholtz, *Constructive proofs of representation theorems in separable Hilbert space,* Comm. Pure Appl. Math. **17** (1964), 369–373.

[16] G.C. Hsiao, E.P. Stephan, W.L. Wendland, *On the Dirichlet problem in elasticity for a domain exterior to an arc,* J. Computational Appl. Mathematics **34** (1991), 1–19.

[17] D. Kinderlehrer, G. Stampacchia, *An Introduction to Variational Inequalities and Their Applications,* Academic Press, New York, 1984.

[18] V.D. Kupradze, *Potential Methods in the Theory of Elasticity,* Israel Program for Scientific Translations, Jerusalem, 1965.

[19] N.I. Muskhelishvili, *Some Basic Problems of the Mathematical Theory of Elasticity,* Noordhoff, Groningen, 1963.

[20] J.Nečas, *Les méthodes directes en théorie des équations élliptiques,* Academia/Masson, Prague/Paris, 1967.

[21] J.C. Nedelec, *Approximation des Equations Intégrales en Mécanique et en Physique,* Lecture Notes, Centre Math. Appl., Ecole polytechnique, Palaiseau, France 1977.

[22] H. Schmitz, G. Schneider, *Boundary element solution of the Dirichlet-Signorini problem by a penalty method,* to appear in Appl. Analysis.

[23] H. Schmitz, G. Schneider, W. Wendland, *Boundary element methods for problems involving unilateral boundary conditions,* in *Nonlinear Computational Mechanics - State of the Art* (W. Wagner, P. Wriggers, eds.), Springer, 1991.

[24] W. Spann, *Fehlerabschätzungen zur Randelementmethode beim Signorini–Problem für die Laplace–Gleichung,* PhD Thesis, Universität München, 1989.

[25] G. Stampacchia, *Variational inequalities,* in *Theory and Applications of Monotone Operators* (A. Ghizetti; ed.), Edizione Odersi, Gubbio, 1969, 101–192.

[26] W.L. Wendland, *On some mathematical aspects of boundary element methods for elliptic problems,* in MAFELAP V (J.R. Whiteman, ed.), Academic Press, New York, 1985, 193–227.

M KUBO AND M LANGLAIS

# Periodic solutions for nonlinear population dynamics models with periodic supply

This note is a continuation of [5] where the corresponding linear problem is analyzed. We are interested in time periodic solutions to the evolution equation

**PROBLEM (1):**

$$\partial_t u + \partial_a u - k\Delta u + \mu(x,t,a,P(x,t))u(x,t,a) = f(x,t,a),\ x\in\ \Omega,\ t>0, a>0;$$

$$u(x,t,0) = \int_0^\infty \beta(x,t,a,P(x,t))\ u(x,t,a)\ da,\ x\in\Omega,\ t>0;$$

$$u(x,t,a) = 0,\ x\in\partial\Omega,\ t>0,\ a>0;$$

$$P(x,t) = \int_0^\infty u(x,t,a)\ da,\ x\in\partial\Omega,\ t>0.$$

This problem arises in age dependent population dynamics problems with spatial structure (see [4,6] for example). In this setting, u(x,t,a) is the density of individuals having age a>0 at time t>0 and location x in $\Omega$, an open domain of $\mathbb{R}^n$, n=1,2,3; P(x,t) is the total population. $\beta(x,t,a,p)$ is the fertility function and $\mu(x,t,a,p)$ is the death rate at age a>0, time t>0 and position x in $\Omega$ when the total population is at level p. The function f(x,t,a) stands for the external supply of individuals.

Next we apply our results to the S-I-R-S epidemic models:

**PROBLEM (2)**

$$\partial_t i + \partial_a i - k\Delta i + \mu(x,t,a,P(x,t))\ i = +\gamma(a,i)\ s - \delta(a)\ i - \sigma(a)\ i \qquad + f_i\ (x,t,a);$$

$$\partial_t s + \partial_a s - k\Delta s + \mu(x,t,a,P(x,t))\ s = -\gamma(a,i)\ s + \delta(a)\ i \qquad + \rho(a)\ r + f_s(x,t,a);$$

$$\partial_t r + \partial_a r - k\Delta r + \mu(x,t,a,P(x,t)\ )r = \qquad + \sigma(a)\ i - \rho(a)\ r + f_r(x,t,a);$$

$$i(x,t,a) = s(x,t,a) = r(x,t,a) = 0,\ x \in \partial\Omega,\ t>0,\ a>0;$$

$$i(x,t,0) = \varepsilon_i \int_0^\infty \beta(x,t,\ a,P(x,t))\ i(x,t,a)\ da$$

$$r(x,t,0) = \varepsilon_r \int_0^\infty \beta(x,t,a,P(x,t))\ r(x,t,a)\ da; \quad s(x,t,0) = u(x,t,0) - i(x,t,0) - r(x,t,0).$$

Here, $\gamma(a,i)$ is the infection force function that may take either of the following forms:

$$\gamma(a,i) = \gamma(a)\ i : \text{intracohort model};$$

$$\gamma(a,i) = \gamma(a) \int_0^\infty i(x,t,a)\ da : \text{intercohort model};$$

$\delta$, $\sigma$, $\rho$ are nonnegative functions modeling the interactions of the three classes (Susceptible, Infective and Removed); $\varepsilon_i$ (resp. $\varepsilon_r$) gives the fraction of offsprings produced by the infective class (removed class) that are actually infective (removed). Lastly, $f_i$, $f_s$ and $f_r$ are the supply of the corresponding classes and verify: $f_i + f_s + f_r = f$ so that upon adding up the equations for i, s, and r we find $i + s + r = u$. See [1,3,5,7,8] for more details on these models.

Main assumptions. Throughout the paper we have: T and k are positive real numbers; $f(x,t+T,a) = f(x,t,a)$; $0 \le f(x,t,a) \le m < +\infty$ and furthermore:

$$0 \le F(x,t) = \int_0^\infty f(x,t,a)\ da \le M < +\infty$$

Next, $\lambda_1$ is the first eigenvalue of the Dirichlet problem for $-\Delta$ in $\Omega$.

In the first three sections we give our results concerning Problem (1) under special assumptions concerning $\beta$ and $\mu$; next we give applications to the intra and inter cohort models i.e. to Problem (2).

1. PROBLEM (1) IN THE LINEAR CASE.

Assumption (H0): $\mu(x,t,a,p) = \mu_n(a) \ge 0$; $0 \le \beta(x,t,a,p) = \beta_n(a) \le \beta < +\infty$; either $\mathrm{supp}\beta_n \subset [0,A]$, $A < +\infty$, or $\beta_n$ and $\mu_n$ are constant.

Let $r^*$ be the unique real root of the so-called characteristic equation:

$$1 = \int_0^\infty \beta_n(a) \ \exp(-\int_0^a \mu_n(\alpha)\, d\alpha)\, e^{-ra}\, da$$

The basic result in [5] is:

Theorem 0. *Assume (H0) holds; then:*

*1). If $r^* < k\lambda_1$, then there is a unique non negative and asymptotically stable T-periodic solution to Problem (1);*

*2). If $r^* \geq k\lambda_1$ then Problem (1) has no non negative T-periodic solution and furthermore any solution to Problem (1) having a nonnegative initial condition at $t=0$ goes to $+\infty$ as $t$ tends to $+\infty$ provided $f(x,t,a)$ be nontrivial.*

2. PROBLEM (1).

In this section we set:

Assumption (H1): $\mu(x,t,a,p) = \mu_e(x,t,p) \geq 0$; $0 \leq \beta(x,t,a,p) = \beta_e(x,t,p) \leq \beta < +\infty$; $\mu_e$ and $\beta_e$ are locally lipschitz continuous functions over $\mathbb{R}^3$ and T-periodic in time.

We introduce the following semilinear parabolic problem which is derived from Problem (1) upon integrating over all ages its first three relations :

$$\partial_t P - k\Delta P + \left[\mu_e(x,t,P(x,t)) - \beta_e(x,t,P(x,t))\right] P = F(x,t),\ x\in\Omega,\ t>0;$$

$$P(x,t) = 0,\ x\in\partial\Omega. \qquad (3)$$

Theorem 1. *Assume (H1) holds and set $\rho^* = Sup_{x,t,p}(\beta_e(x,t,p) - \mu_e(x,t,p))$.*

*When $\rho^* < k\lambda_1$ there is at least one non negative T-periodic solution to Problem (1). Furthermore, if the mapping $p \rightarrow (k\lambda_1 + \mu_e(x,t,p) - \beta_e(x,t,p))p$ is increasing this T-periodic solution is unique and asymptotically stable.*

Remark. When $\mu$ and $\beta$ are independent of x, t, a and p, Theorems 0 and 1 are consistent because $r^* = \rho^*$.

Sketch of the proof. Uniqueness follows from usual computations: take the difference between two T-periodic solutions, multiply the resulting equation by the difference of the two solutions and integrate over $\Omega$x(0,T).

The existence part is a little bit more elaborated: first we prove that (3) has at least one T-periodic solution P(x,t); next, we substitute this P(x,t) back into the first three equations in Problem (1) that becomes a linear problem: a straightforward generalisation of Theorem 0, using the assumption $\rho^* < k\lambda_1$, shows that there is a unique T-periodic solution . Lastly we have to check that

$$P(x,t) = \int_0^\infty u(x,t,a)\, da$$

To this end it is enough to show that both sides are solutions of the linear parabolic problem

$$\partial_\tau z - k\Delta z + \left[\beta_e(x,t,P(x,t)) - \mu_e(x,t,P(x,t))\right] z = F(x,t),\ x\in\Omega,\ t>0;$$
$$z(x,0) = 0,\ x\in\partial\Omega$$
$$z(x,0) = z(x,T),\ x\in\Omega. \qquad (4)$$

because this problem has a unique solution when $\rho^* < k\lambda_1$ .

We prove the first part i.e. the existence of a T-periodic solution to (3). We begin with an a priori estimate.

Lemma. *Assume $\rho^* < k\lambda_1$. There is a constant C>0, depending only on F and $k\lambda_1 - \rho*$ such that for any any T-periodic and nonnegative P(x,t) the solution to (4) satisfies: $0 \leq z(x,t) \leq C$.*

Proof of the lemma: Take a domain $\Omega'$ such that the closure of $\Omega$ lies in $\Omega'$ and such that $\delta = k\lambda_1(\Omega') - \rho^* > 0$, $\lambda_1(\Omega')$ being the first eigenvalue of the Dirichlet problem for $-\Delta$ in $\Omega'$; let w be a corresponding eigenfunction satisfying $1 \leq w(x)$ in $\Omega$. Lastly let y(t) be the unique solution of

$$y'(t) + \delta y(t) = M,\ t>0;\ y(0) = \text{Sup}_x z(x,0),$$

z being the nonnegative and T-periodic solution to (4); we may verify by the comparison principle that $0 \leq z(x,t) \leq w(x)\, y(t)$ for x in $\Omega$ and t>0; hence we obtain from the explicit form of y(t) that for any positive integer n

$$0 \leq \text{Sup}_x z(x,0) = \text{Sup}_x z(x,nT) \leq (e^{-n\delta T}\, \text{Sup}_x z(x,0) + C(\delta,M))\, \text{Sup}_x w(x).$$

The desired estimate follows by choosing n large enough.

End of the proof of Theorem 1. Assume $\rho^* < k\lambda_1$ Given any T-periodic and non negative function P with $0 \leq P(x,t) \leq C$, C as in the above lemma, there is a unique T-periodic solution z of the linear parabolic equation (4) which actually also satisfies the inequalities $0 \leq z(x,t) \leq C$: this follows from a standard contraction argument.

We now define $\mathbb{E}$ as the set of measurable and time periodic with period T functions from $\Omega x(0,T)$ to $\mathbb{R}$ which are square integrable over $\Omega x(0,t)$ for each positive t. Next set $\mathbb{K}$ as the closed convex subset of $\mathbb{E}$ consisting of the fonctions P in $\mathbb{E}$ such that: $0 \leq P(x,t) \leq C$. Lastly let $G : \mathbb{K} \to \mathbb{K}$ be the mapping defined as G(P)=z, the T-periodic solution to (4). Clearly a fixed point of G is a solution to (3) and the existence of such a fixed point will follow from the Schauder's fixed point theorem once we have proved the complete continuity of G. Continuity and compactness are well-known properties of the solution set of the parabolic equation (4) once the a-priori estimate $0 \leq P(x,t) \leq C$ is granted.

When the condition $\rho^* < k\lambda_1$ in Theorem 1 does not hold , neither the existence nor the uniqueness of a T-periodic solution to (1) is granted. We first give a non existence result generalizing that in [4].

Proposition. *Assume $0 \leq \mu(x,t,a,p) \leq \mu$ while $0 < \beta \leq \beta(x,t,a,p)$. When $k\lambda_1 + \mu - \beta < 0$ any solution to Problem (1) having a nonnegative initial condition at $t = 0$ goes to $+\infty$ as t tends to $+\infty$ .*

Proof. It is enough to show that the solution to the linear problem (1) with constant $\mu(x,t,a,p) = \mu$ and $\beta(x,t,a,p) = \beta$, taking the same initial condition at $t = 0$, is a subsolution for the non linear problem; next we may apply Theorem 0.

On the other hand, we may have existence but no uniqueness of T-periodic solutions; this may be seen from (3) when the corresponding stationary problem has two non negative solutions.

Example. Set f(x,t a) =0, $\beta(x,t,a,p) = \beta$ , $\mu(x,t,a,p) = p$; then the semilinear elliptic problem $- k\Delta v = v\,[\beta - v]$ in $\Omega$ and v=0 on the boundary of $\Omega$ has two solutions provided $\beta > k\lambda_1$

3. PROBLEM (2).

We still assume that assumption (H1) holds; the set of conditions at a=0 becomes

$$i(x,t,0) = \varepsilon_i \beta(x,t,P(x,t))\, I(x,t) \;; \quad r(x,t,0) = \varepsilon_r \beta(x,t,P(x,t))\, R(x,t) \;;$$

$$s(x,t,0) = \beta(x,t,P(x,t))\, [\, P(x,t) - \varepsilon_i I(x,t) - \varepsilon_r R(x,t)\, ] \qquad (5)$$

where

$$I(x,t) = \int_0^\infty i(x,t,a)\, da \; ; \; R(x,t) = \int_0^\infty r(x,t,a)\, da.$$

We suppose

Assumption (H2): $\gamma(a)$, $\delta(a)$, $\sigma(a)$ and $\rho(a)$ are non negative and bounded functions; $f_i$, $f_s$ and $f_r$ are also non negative, T-periodic and satisfy: $f_i + f_s + f_r = f$; lastly $\varepsilon_i$ and $\varepsilon_r$ are constants lying in [0,1].

Theorem 2. *Assume (H1), (H2) and* $\rho^* < k\lambda_1$ *hold.*

*Let u be the solution to Problem (1). Then, for both intra and inter cohort models Problem (2) has at least one non negative and T-periodic solution such that* $i + s + r = u$.

Proof: We give a proof in the intercohort case. The intracohort model can be handled by performing slight modifications (see also [5]).

Let u be a solution to Problem (1). Substitute the total population P(x,t) into Problem (2), with the above simplifications (5) in the condition at a=0 implied by (H1). Define E as the set of elements $(I_0, R_0)$ verifying:

$$0 \le I_0 \,,\, 0 \le R_0 \,,\, I_0 + R_0 \le P(x,t), \; I_0 \text{ and } R_0 \text{ are T-periodic (in time).}$$

For each $(I_0, R_0)$ in E consider Problem (2) with $I = I_0$ and $R = R_0$ in the infection force function $\gamma$ and in the condition at a=0. The Cauchy problem on the half space a>0 has a unique non negative solution because it reduces to a linear system of parabolic equations along the charasteristic lines t - a = constant; the solution is T-periodic because the coefficients and the data on a=0 are T-periodic (global existence and nonnegativity follow more or less from the results of [2]). Lastly one may check, using a uniqueness argument, that $s + i + r = u$.

It follows that (I, R) defined as

$$I(x,t) = \int_0^\infty i(x,t,a)\, da \; ; \; R(x,t) = \int_0^\infty r(x,t,a)\, da.$$

lies in E. The existence of a T-periodic solution to Problem (2) follows again from Schauder's theorem.

Remark. A uniqueness result concerning the intracohort model with two classes (i.e. $\sigma = 0$ and $f_r = 0$ ) is given in the linear case in [5]. This may be extended to the above situation for both intra and intercohort models.

4. REFERENCES.


[1] S.Busenberg, K.Cooke and M.Iannelli. *Endemic thresholds and stability in a class of age -structured epidemics.* SIAM J.Appl.Math. 48 (1988) pp.1379-1395.

[2] K.N.Chueh, C.C.Conley and J.A.Smoller. *Positively invariant regions for systems of nonlinear diffusion equations.* Indiana Univ.Journal 26 (1977) pp.373-392.

[3] W.E.Fitzgibbon, J.J.Morgan and S.J.Waggoner. *A quasilinear system modelling the spread of infections.* Preprint.

[4] M.E.Gurtin. *A system of equations for age-dependent population diffusion.* J.Theo.Biol. 40 (1973) pp.389-392.

[5] M.Kubo and M.Langlais. *Periodic solutions for a population dynamics problem with age dependence and spatial structure.* J.Math.Biol. 29 (1991) pp.363-346.

[6] M.Langlais. *Large time behaviour in a nonlinear age dependent population dynamics problem with spatial structure.* J.Math.Biol. 26 (1988) pp. 319-346.

[7] P.Waltman.*Deterministic Threshold models in the theory of epidemics.* Lecture Notes in Biomathematics 1. Springer-Verlag Berlin (1974).

[8] G.F.Webb. *A reaction-diffusion model for a deterministic diffusive epidemic.* J.Math.Anal.Appl.84 (1981) pp.150-161.



Masahiro KUBO* and Michel LANGLAIS

URA CNRS 226 CeReMaB. UFR des Sciences Humaines Appliquées.
Université de Bordeaux II. 146, rue Léo Saignat .
33076 BORDEAUX Cedex. France

*Permanent address: Department of Mathematics, Faculty of Science and Engineering, Saga University, 1 Honjo-machi, SAGA 840, Japan.



M.Kubo is visiting the University of Bordeaux II during the academic year 1990-91 under a grant from the CIES.

This work is partially supported by the MENJS (DRED, Volet International des Contrats Pluriannuels de Recherche).

F LEONETTI

# On the regularity of vector-valued minimizers of some nonconvex functionals with nonstandard growth

**Introduction.** Let $\Omega$ be a bounded open subset of $\mathbb{R}^n$, $n \geq 2$. Let us consider integral functionals

$$I(u;\Omega) = \int_\Omega F(|Du(x)|)\,dx \tag{1}$$

where $u\colon \Omega \to \mathbb{R}^N$, $N \geq 1$ , is vector-valued and $F\colon [0,\infty) \to [0,\infty)$ is continuous. The regularity of minimizers of (1) has been deeply studied [**3**] in the case

$$at^m - b \leq F(t) \leq ct^m + d \qquad \forall t \geq 0 \tag{2}$$

where $a, b, c, d, m$ are nonnegative constants with $m > 1$. In the last few years a special interest has been rising in the case in which different powers appear in (2), namely

$$at^p - b \leq F(t) \leq ct^q + d \qquad \forall t \geq 0 \tag{3}$$

where $p < q$ : inequality (3) is called *nonstandard growth condition* [**4**] , [**7**]. In this paper we present a contribution to the regularity theory in this framework. Our main result is the following monotonicity formula for minimizers $u$ of (1):

$$r^{-\alpha} \int_{B(x^0,r)} F(|Du(x)|)\,dx \leq R^{-\alpha} \int_{B(x^0,R)} F(|Du(x)|)\,dx$$

where $0 < r \leq R$ and $\alpha$ is a positive constant depending on the function $F$, *which is not assumed to be convex* . The previous monotonicity formula gives us the regularity result in Morrey spaces:

$$F(|Du|) \in L^{1,\alpha}_{\text{loc}}(\Omega)$$

**Assumptions and Results.** We study integrals (1) for functions $F$ satisfying

$$F\colon [0,\infty) \to [0,\infty) \text{ is continuous and increasing} \tag{4}$$

$\Omega$ is a bounded open subset of $\mathbb{R}^n$, $n \geq 2$ ; a vector-valued function $u\colon \Omega \to \mathbb{R}^N$, $N \geq 1$ , is said to be a minimizer of the integral (1) if $u \in W^{1,1}(\Omega)$ and

$$F(|Du|) \in L^1(\Omega) \tag{5}$$

$$I(u;B(x^0,t)) \leq I(v;B(x^0,t)) \tag{6}$$

for every $v$ such that $v - u \in W_0^{1,1}(B(x^0,t))$, for every ball $B(x^0,t) = \{x \in \mathbb{R}^n : |x - x^0| < t\} \subset \Omega$. Moreover we assume that there exists a constant $q$ such that

$$1 \leq q < n \tag{7}$$

$$t \mapsto F(t)/t^q \text{ is decreasing in } (0,\infty) \tag{8}$$

Now we can state our main result:

**Theorem 1.** *Let $F$ verify (4) (7) (8); if $u$ minimizes the integral (1), in the sense of (5) (6), then*

$$F(|Du|) \in L^{1,n-q}_{\text{loc}}(\Omega) \tag{9}$$

*and the following estimate holds*

$$r^{q-n} \int\limits_{B(x^0,r)} F(|Du(x)|)\,dx \leq R^{q-n} \int\limits_{B(x^0,R)} F(|Du(x)|)\,dx \tag{10}$$

*for every $r, R : 0 < r \leq R < \frac{1}{2}dist(x^0, \partial\Omega)$, for every $x^0 \in \Omega$.*

**Remark 1.** Under the assumptions (4) (7) (8) of our theorem, we have

$$0 \leq F(t) \leq (t^q + 1)F(1) \qquad \forall t \geq 0 \tag{11}$$

so theorem 1 provides us the regularity result (9) in the case of nonstandard growth (3) with no restriction on the smallest exponent $p$. In this framework we want to quote [**2**] [**8**] where higher integrability results are proved under the restriction $p \leq q < np/(n-p)$ on the orders of nonstandard growth $p$ and $q$.

**Remark 2.** Theorem 1 does not require convexity about $F$ and can be applied in this case :

$$F(t) = \begin{cases} e^{s-1}t & \text{if } t \in [0,e) \\ t^{s+h\sin\log\log t} & \text{if } t \in [e,\infty) \end{cases}$$

where $1 < s < \min\{n/2; \sqrt{2}/(\sqrt{2}-1)\}$ , $h = s/\sqrt{2}$ . We remark that such a function $F$ is neither convex nor concave in $(M,\infty)$ , for every $M > 0$ . This example can be found in [**2**] [**9**].

**Remark 3.** Our theorem 1 can also be applied in the following cases:

$$F(t) = t^q \tag{12}$$

where $1 \leq q < n$ ; for $q \geq 2$ the monotonicity result is already known [**5**] [**3**,p.262] [**6**] [**1**] ;

$$F(t) = \begin{cases} t^{m+1} & \text{if } t \in [0,1) \\ t^m(1+\log t) & \text{if } t \in [1,\infty) \end{cases} \tag{13}$$

where $1 \leq m < n-1$ ; in this case we get (7) (8) with $q = m+1$ ;

$$F(t) = \begin{cases} e^{s-1}t & \text{if } t \in [0,e) \\ t^{s+h\sin\log\log t} & \text{if } t \in [e,\infty) \end{cases} \tag{14}$$

where $1 < s < n$ , $0 < h \leq s/\sqrt{2}$ , $h < (n-s)/\sqrt{2}$ ; here (7) (8) are satisfied with $q = s + h\sqrt{2}$ ; this last example can be found in [**2**] [**9**]. Let us set

$$\phi(t) = t^{q-n} \int_{B(x^0,t)} F(|Du(x)|)\, dx \tag{15}$$

then formula (10) tells us that $\phi$ is monotone increasing, that is

$$\phi(r) \leq \phi(R) \qquad \text{if } r \leq R \tag{16}$$

**Proof of Theorem 1:** we apply the technique used in [**5**] [**3**,p.262]. First of all, let us remark that (4) (7) (8) imply

$$F(\lambda t) \leq \lambda^q F(t) \qquad \forall \lambda \geq 1, \forall t \geq 0 \tag{17}$$

Now we fix $x^0 \in \Omega$ and we set

$$u_t(x) = u(x^0 + t\frac{x-x^0}{|x-x^0|})$$

For almost every $t \in (0, \frac{1}{2}dist(x^0, \partial\Omega))$ we have

$$u_t \in W^{1,1}(B(x^0,t)) \qquad ; \qquad u - u_t \in W_0^{1,1}(B(x^0,t)) \tag{18}$$

$$|Du_t(x)| = t^2|x-x^0|^{-4}\{|(Du)_t(x)|^2|x-x^0|^2 - |< x-x^0, (Du)_t(x) >|^2\} \tag{19}$$

$$\text{where} \qquad (Du)_t(x) = Du(x^0 + t\frac{x-x^0}{|x-x^0|}) \qquad \text{and}$$

$$| < x - x^0, (Du)_t(x) > |^2 = \sum_{\alpha=1}^{N} \{ \sum_{i=1}^{n} (x_i - x_i^0)(D_i u^\alpha)_t(x) \}^2 .$$

$$\int_{S^{n-1}} F(|Du(x^0 + t\omega)|)\, dH_{n-1}(\omega) < \infty \tag{20}$$

$$F(|(Du)_t|) \in L^1(B(x^0, t)) \tag{21}$$

Now we consider the function $\phi$ defined in (15): we have

$$\phi'(t) = (q-n)t^{q-n-1} \int_{B(x^0,t)} F(|Du(x)|)\, dx +$$

$$+ t^{q-1} \int_{S^{n-1}} F(|Du(x^0 + t\omega)|)\, dH_{n-1}(\omega) \tag{22}$$

We will prove that $\phi'(t) \geq 0$ for almost every $t$ ; in order to do that, we use the minimizing property (6) with $v = u_t$ :

$$\int_{B(x^0,t)} F(|Du(x)|)\, dx \leq \int_{B(x^0,t)} F(|Du_t(x)|)\, dx = (I)$$

Since $F$ is increasing and $|Du_t(x)| \leq t|x - x^0|^{-1}|(Du)_t(x)|$, we have

$$(I) \leq \int_{B(x^0,t)} F(t|x - x^0|^{-1}|(Du)_t(x)|)\, dx = (II)$$

Now we use polar coordinates

$$(II) = \int_0^t \int_{S^{n-1}} F(tr^{-1}|Du(x^0 + t\omega)|)\, dH_{n-1}(\omega) r^{n-1}\, dr = (III)$$

Since $tr^{-1} \geq 1$ , we can apply (17)

$$(III) \leq \int_0^t t^q r^{-q} r^{n-1}\, dr \int_{S^{n-1}} F(|Du(x^0 + t\omega)|)\, dH_{n-1}(\omega) =$$

$$= \frac{t^n}{n-q} \int_{S^{n-1}} F(|Du(x^0 + t\omega)|)\, dH_{n-1}(\omega)$$

All the previous calculations tell us that

$$\int_{B(x^0,t)} F(|Du(x)|)\, dx \leq \frac{t^n}{n-q} \int_{S^{n-1}} F(|Du(x^0 + t\omega)|)\, dH_{n-1}(\omega) \tag{23}$$

We insert (23) into (22) and we keep in mind that $q - n < 0$ :

$$\phi'(t) \geq (q-n)t^{q-n-1}\frac{t^n}{n-q}\int\limits_{S^{n-1}} F(|Du(x^0 + t\omega)|)\,dH_{n-1}(\omega) +$$

$$+t^{q-1}\int\limits_{S^{n-1}} F(|Du(x^0 + t\omega)|)\,dH_{n-1}(\omega) = 0$$

So, if $0 < r \leq R < \frac{1}{2}dist(x^0, \partial\Omega)$, we have

$$\phi(R) - \phi(r) = \int_r^R \phi'(t)\,dt \geq 0$$

and inequality (10) is proved; such an inequality tells us that the regularity result (9) is achieved.

## APPENDIX

When we deal with convex $F$ we can estimate, from below, the difference $\phi(R) - \phi(r)$ in this way:

**Theorem 2.** *Let us assume (4) (7) (8); in addition we require*

$$F(0) = 0 \tag{24}$$

$$t \mapsto F(\sqrt{t}) \text{ is convex in } [0, \infty) \tag{25}$$

*If $u$ minimizes the integral (1), in the sense of (5) (6), then*

$$\phi(R) - \phi(r) \geq \frac{n-q}{n-1}\int\limits_{B(x^0,R)\setminus B(x^0,r)} |x - x^0|^{q-n} F(|\frac{du}{d\nu}(x)|)\,dx \tag{26}$$

*for every $r, R : 0 < r \leq R < \frac{1}{2}dist(x^0, \partial\Omega)$, for every $x^0 \in \Omega$; by $\frac{du}{d\nu}$ we mean the derivative with respect to the direction $\nu = \frac{x-x^0}{|x-x^0|}$.*

**Remark 4.** Some monotonicity formulas, similar to (26), are proved in [**5**] [**3**,p.262] [**6**] [**1**].

**Proof of Theorem 2:** we apply the technique used in [**5**] [**3**,p.262]. First of all, let us remark that, under our assumptions on $F$, the following inequalities are true

$$F(\lambda t) \geq \lambda F(t) \qquad \forall \lambda \geq 1, \forall t \geq 0 \tag{27}$$

$$F(\sqrt{a^2-b^2}) \leq F(a) - F(b) \qquad \forall a, b : 0 \leq b \leq a \tag{28}$$

In order to estimate $\phi'(t)$ , we use the minimizing property (6) with $v = u_t$ as before; now we apply (19) and (28) with

$$a = t|x - x^0|^{-1}|(Du)_t(x)|$$

$$b = t|x - x^0|^{-2}| < x - x^0, (Du)_t(x) > |$$

and we have:

$$\int_{B(x^0,t)} F(|Du(x)|)\, dx \leq \int_{B(x^0,t)} F(|Du_t(x)|)\, dx \leq$$

$$\leq \int_{B(x^0,t)} F(t|x - x^0|^{-1}|(Du)_t(x)|)\, dx -$$

$$- \int_{B(x^0,t)} F(t|x - x^0|^{-2}| < x - x^0, (Du)_t(x) > |)\, dx$$

As in theorem 1 we get

$$\int_{B(x^0,t)} F(t|x - x^0|^{-1}|(Du)_t(x)|)\, dx \leq \frac{t^n}{n-q} \int_{S^{n-1}} F(|Du(x^0 + t\omega)|)\, dH_{n-1}(\omega)$$

We use polar coordinates and (27):

$$- \int_{B(x^0,t)} F(t|x - x^0|^{-2}| < x - x^0, (Du)_t(x) > |)\, dx =$$

$$= - \int_0^t \int_{S^{n-1}} F(tr^{-1}| < \omega, Du(x^0 + t\omega) > |)\, dH_{n-1}(\omega) r^{n-1}\, dr \leq$$

$$\leq - \int_0^t tr^{-1} r^{n-1}\, dr \int_{S^{n-1}} F(| < \omega, Du(x^0 + t\omega) > |)\, dH_{n-1}(\omega) =$$

$$= - \frac{t^n}{n-1} \int_{S^{n-1}} F(| < \omega, Du(x^0 + t\omega) > |)\, dH_{n-1}(\omega)$$

Putting together the previous inequalities we get

$$\int_{B(x^0,t)} F(|Du(x)|)\, dx \leq \frac{t^n}{n-q} \int_{S^{n-1}} F(|Du(x^0 + t\omega)|)\, dH_{n-1}(\omega) -$$

$$- \frac{t^n}{n-1} \int_{S^{n-1}} F(| < \omega, Du(x^0 + t\omega) > |)\, dH_{n-1}(\omega) \tag{29}$$

We insert estimate (29) into (22) and we have

$$\phi'(t) \geq \frac{n-q}{n-1} t^{q-1} \int_{S^{n-1}} F(|<\omega, Du(x^0+t\omega)>|)\, dH_{n-1}(\omega)$$

If $0 < r \leq R < \frac{1}{2} dist(x^0, \partial\Omega)$, we get

$$\phi(R) - \phi(r) = \int_r^R \phi'(t)\, dt \geq$$

$$\geq \frac{n-q}{n-1} \int_r^R t^{q-n} \int_{S^{n-1}} F(|<\omega, Du(x^0+t\omega)>|)\, dH_{n-1}(\omega) t^{n-1}\, dt =$$

$$= \frac{n-q}{n-1} \int_{B(x^0,R)\setminus B(x^0,r)} |x-x^0|^{q-n} F(|<\frac{x-x^0}{|x-x^0|}, Du(x)>|)\, dx$$

Since $<\frac{x-x^0}{|x-x^0|}, Du(x)> = \frac{du}{d\nu}(x)$ when $\nu = \frac{x-x^0}{|x-x^0|}$ , the proof of theorem 2 is finished.

**Acknowledgment.** This research was performed when I was visiting the Centre for Mathematical Analysis, Australian National University,on a C.N.R. grant. I gladly take the opportunity to thank L. Simon and J. Hutchinson for introducing me to this subject.

## References

1. N. Fusco - J. Hutchinson, *Partial regularity for minimizers of certain functionals having non quadratic growth*, Ann. Mat. Pura Appl. **155** (1989), 1–24.
2. N. Fusco - C. Sbordone, *Higher integrability of the gradient of minimizers of functionals with nonstandard growth conditions*, Comm. Pure Appl. Math. **43** (1990), 673–683.
3. M. Giaquinta, "Multiple integrals in the calculus of variations and nonlinear elliptic systems," Princeton University Press, Princeton, 1983.
4. M. Giaquinta, *Growth conditions and regularity, a counterexample*, Manuscripta Math. **59** (1987), 245–248.
5. M. Giaquinta - E. Giusti, *The singular set of the minima of certain quadratic functionals*, Ann. Scuola Norm. Sup. Pisa **9** (1984), 45–55.
6. J. Jost - M. Meier, *Boundary regularity for minima of certain quadratic functionals*, Math. Ann. **262** (1983), 549–561.
7. P. Marcellini, *Regularity of minimizers of integrals of the calculus of variations with nonstandard growth conditions*, Arch. Rat. Mech. Anal. **105** (1989), 267–284.
8. C. Sbordone, *On some inequalities and their applications to the calculus of variations*, Boll. Un. Mat. Ital. An. Funz. e Appl. **5** (1986), 73–94.
9. G. Talenti, *Boundedness of minimizers*, Hokkaido Math. J. **19** (1990), 259–279.

Dipartimento di Matematica , Università di L'Aquila, via Vetoio , 67010 Coppito , L'Aquila, Italy.

G ŁUKASZEWICZ

# On diffusion in viscous fluids mixed boundary conditions

## 1. Introduction and Results

In this paper we consider a boundary-value problem for the equations describing stationary motion of a mixture of two viscous fluids, with the absence of heat transfer. The mixture has constant density and occupies a bounded domain $\Omega$ in $R^3$ , with boundary $\partial\Omega$. We assume that $\partial\Omega = \overline{\partial_1\Omega \cup \partial_2\Omega}$, where $\partial_1\Omega$ and $\partial_2\Omega$ are some open and disjoint subsets of $\partial\Omega$, with $\partial_1\Omega \neq \emptyset$. The boundary-value problem reads

$$-\nu\Delta u + (u \cdot \nabla)u + (1/\rho)\nabla p = f + cg \qquad \text{in } \Omega, \qquad (1.1)$$

$$\text{div} u = 0 \qquad \text{in } \Omega, \qquad (1.2)$$

$$-\text{div}(D(c)\nabla c) + u \cdot \nabla c = (1/\rho)\text{div}(K(c)\nabla p) \qquad \text{in } \Omega, \qquad (1.3)$$

$$u = a \qquad \text{on } \partial\Omega, \qquad (1.4)$$

$$c = h_1 \qquad \text{on } \partial_1\Omega, \qquad (1.5;1)$$

$$-J \cdot n = h_2 \circ c \qquad \text{on } \partial_2\Omega. \qquad (1.5;2)$$

The unknown functions $u = (u_1, u_2, u_3)$ , $p$ and $c$ denote mean mass velocity vector, pressure, and concentration of one of the components (say, first component) of the mixture, respectively;$f = (f_1, f_2, f_3)$ is the external force per unit mass acting on the first component, and $g = (g_1, g_2, g_3)$ is the difference between the forces per unit mass acting on the second and the first compoment. If the only external force to act is that of gravitation then $g = 0$. $D$ and $K$ denote diffusion and barodiffusion coefficients, $J$ is the diffusion flux, $n$ the outward unit normal vector to $\partial_2\Omega$, $\nu = const > 0$ is the viscosity coefficient.

By $\nabla, \Delta$ and div we denote the usual gradient, Laplacian and divergence operators, so that $\Delta u, (u \cdot \nabla)u$ and $\nabla p$ are vectors with components $\Delta u_i$, $u_j(\partial/\partial x_j)u_i$ and $(\partial/\partial x_i)p$, respectively ($i = 1, 2, 3$; repeated indices are summed); $\text{div} u = (\partial/\partial x_j)u_j$, $u \cdot \nabla c = u_j(\partial/\partial x_j)c$, etc.

We assume that functions $D$ and $K$ are defined on the real line and satisfy

$$0 < m \leq D(t) \leq M \quad \text{for each} \quad t \in R, \qquad (1.6)$$

$$K(t) = 0 \quad \text{if} \quad t \leq 0 \quad \text{or} \quad t \geq 1, \qquad (1.7)$$

where $m, M$ are some positive constants, $m \leq M$. The first assumption is in agreement with the thermodynamical constraint $D > 0$, and the second reflects the fact that in pure fluid the diffusion flux equals zero [10].

From the definition of $c$ as the concentration of the first component of the mixture we conclude that

$$0 \leq c \leq 1. \qquad (1.8)$$

In fact, a maximum principle for equation (1.3), together with (1.7) and appriopriate assumptions about the functions $h_1$ and $h_2$ in (1.5) give (1.8) for each solution $c$ of (1.3), (1.5).

We notice that if $c \equiv 0$ or 1 in $\Omega$ then, in view of (1.7), equations (1.1)-(1.3) reduce to the Navier-Stokes equations for one of the components of constant density $\rho$.

For the thorough discussion of the diffusion phenomenon and derivation of equations (1.1)-(1.3) we refer to [8], [10], [13], [19].

Below, for convenience of the reader, we sketch the derivation of equations (1.1)-(1.3). Let $\rho_i$ and $u_i$ denote the density and the velocity of the i-th component of the mixture, respectively ($i = 1, 2$). For stationary motion the law of conservation of mass of the i-th component reads

$$\mathrm{div}(\rho_i u_i) = 0\,, \quad (i = 1, 2) \tag{1.9}$$

Denote by $\rho$ and $u$ the total density and the mean mass velocity of the mixture: $\rho = \rho_1 + \rho_2$, $u = (\rho_1 u_1 + \rho_2 u_2)/\rho$. Summing the equations in (1.9) we obtain $\mathrm{div}(\rho u) = 0$. If $\rho = const$, the last equation reduces to (1.2). Now, denote by J the diffusion flux of the first component: $J = \rho_1(u_1 - u)$. Proceeding formally we obtain from (1.9)

$$\rho u \cdot \nabla c = -\mathrm{div} J\,, \tag{1.10}$$

where $c = \rho_1/\rho$. By thermodynamical considerations [10]

$$-J = \alpha \nabla z\,, \tag{1.11}$$

$$\alpha \nabla z = \rho D(c) \nabla c + K(c) \nabla p\,, \tag{1.12}$$

where $\alpha$ is a positive constant and $z$ denotes the chemical potential of the mixture. Combining (1.10)-(1.12) we get (1.3). We obtain equation (1.1), roughly speaking, by adding equations of momentum for the two components. The procedure, however, is rather complicated and we shall not reproduce it, refering the reader to the literature quoted above.

A motivation to study the above model of diffusion comes from the fact that it is the basis of many other, and much more involved, models of mixtures which are of considerable importance in the applied sciences (see [13] and the literature quoted there). Fluid suspensions (for example blood) [14], [15] belong to this type of mixtures. Their densities and temperatures are constant and the diffusion effect is due to changes of pressure and concentrations of the components.

Before stating the results we introduce some notations:

-$\Omega$: a bounded open and simply–connected subset of $R^3$, locally situated on one side of its boundary $\partial\Omega$, a manifold of class $C^2$; $\partial\Omega = \overline{\partial_1\Omega \cup \partial_2\Omega}$, where $\partial_1\Omega$ and $\partial_2\Omega$ are nonempty, mutually disjoined open subsets of $\partial\Omega$;

-$L^r$ = usual $L^r(\Omega)$ space ($1 \le r \le \infty$), with norm

$$|\varphi|_r = (\int_\Omega |\varphi|^r)^{1/r} \quad \text{for} \quad r < \infty\,,$$

and the obvious modification for $r = \infty$;

-$H_0^1$ = closure of smooth functions of compact supports in $\Omega$, in the norm

$$\|\varphi\|_1 = |\nabla\varphi|_2 = \left(\sum_{i=1}^{3}\int_{\Omega}\left|\frac{\partial\varphi}{\partial x_i}\right|^2\right)^{1/2};$$

-$\tilde{W}$ = the set of smooth functions on $\bar{\Omega}$ which are equal to zero on $\partial_1\Omega$;

-$W$ = completion of $\tilde{W}$ in the norm $\|\cdot\|_1$;

-$\tilde{V}$ = the set of smooth and divergence free vector functions in $R^3$, compactly supported in $\Omega$;

-$V$ = closure of $\tilde{V}$ in the norm

$$\|u\|_1 = |\nabla u|_2 = \left(\sum_{i,j=1}^{3}\int_{\Omega}\left|\frac{\partial u_i}{\partial x_j}\right|^2\right)^{1/2};$$

-$W^{m,r}$ = Sobolev space $W^{m,r}(\Omega)(m = 1, 2, 3, \ldots; 1 \le r \le \infty)$ of functions from $L^r$, whose generalized derivatives up to the order $m$ are in $L^r$, with usual norm denoted by $\|\cdot\|_{m,r}$;

-$W_{\sigma,0}^{1,2} = \{u = (u_1, u_2, u_3) \in W^{1,2} : \operatorname{div} u = 0 \ \text{ in } \Omega, \quad u = 0 \ \text{ on } \partial_2\Omega\}$;

-$B^{m-1/r,r} = B^{m-1/r,r}(\partial\Omega)$ - space of traces on $\partial\Omega$ of functions from $W^{m,r}$, with usual norm denoted by $[\cdot]_{m-1/r,r}$;

-$C^0 = C^0(\bar{\Omega})$ - space of continuous functions on $\bar{\Omega}$, with norm $|\cdot|_\infty$.

For a subset $\omega$ of $\Omega$ we define:

-$C_\omega^{0,\alpha} = C^{0,\alpha}(\bar{\omega})$ - space of Hölder continuous functions on $\bar{\omega}$, with usual norm, denoted by $|\cdot|_{0,\alpha,\omega}$, $(0 < \alpha \le 1)$;

-$C^{0,\alpha} = C^{0,\alpha}(\bar{\Omega})$.

For basic properties of the above function spaces see [1], [7], [9], [18].

We notice that since the surface measure of $\partial_1\Omega$ is positive, there exists a constant $C > 0$ such that for all $\varphi \in W$, $|\varphi|_2 \le C\|\varphi\|_1$. In the body of the paper we refer to this inequality as to Poincaré's inequality.

In what follows we assume that $q$ *is an arbitrary but fixed real* $> 3$,

$$f, g \in L^q, \tag{A1}$$

$$D, K : R \to R \quad \text{are continuous functions satisfying} \quad (1.6), (1.7), \tag{A2}$$

$$h_1 \in W^{1/2,2}, \quad 0 \le h_1 \le 1 \quad \text{on} \quad \partial_1\Omega, \tag{A3}$$

$$h_2 \quad \text{is a decreasing and bounded function of} \quad c \in R;\ h_2(0) \ge 0,\ h_2(1) \le 0, \tag{A4}$$

$$a \in B^{2-1/q,q}, \quad a = 0 \quad \text{on} \quad \partial_2\Omega, \quad \int_{\partial\Omega} a \cdot n = 0. \tag{A5}$$

For convenience, we assume also that the density of the mixture equals one.

In this paper we prove the following theorems:

THEOREM 1.1. *(existence). Let the assumptions (A1)-(A5) hold, and let the $L^q$-norms of $f$ and $g$ and the $B^{2-1/q,q}$ -norm of $a$ be small enough. Then there exists a triple of functions*

$$(u,p,c) \in W^{2,q} \times W^{1,q} \times W^{1,2} \tag{1.13}$$

*such that*

$$0 \le c \le 1 \qquad \text{in } \Omega\,, \tag{1.14}$$

$$-\nu\Delta u + (u\cdot\nabla)u + \nabla p = f + cg \qquad \text{a.e. in } \Omega\,, \tag{1.15}$$

$$\mathrm{div} u = 0 \qquad \text{in } \Omega\,, \tag{1.16}$$

*and*

$$\int_\Omega D(c)\nabla c\cdot\nabla\varphi + \int_\Omega u\cdot\nabla c\varphi = -\int_\Omega K(c)\nabla p\cdot\nabla\varphi + \int_{\partial_2\Omega} h_2(c)\varphi \quad \text{for each} \quad \varphi \in W\,, \tag{1.17}$$

*with*

$$u = a \qquad \text{on } \partial\Omega\,, \tag{1.18}$$

$$c = h_1 \qquad \text{on } \partial_1\Omega\,. \tag{1.19}$$

THEOREM 1.2. *(existence). Let the assumptions (A1)-(A5) hold, and let $K$ be Lipschitz continuous, that is*

$$|K(t) - K(s)| \le L_K|t-s| \quad \text{for all} \quad t,s \in R\,, \tag{1.20}$$

*and some positive constant $L_K$. Then there exists a triple of functions $(u,p,c)$ satisfying conditions (1.13)-(1.19).*

THEOREM 1.3. *(uniqueness). Let the assumptions (A1)-(A5) hold, the diffusion coefficient $D$ be a positive constant, $K$ satisfy (1.20), and*

$$|h_2(c_1) - h_2(c_2)| \le \gamma|c_1 - c_2|\,, \quad 0 < \gamma < 1\,. \tag{1.21}$$

*Let $X = |f|_q + |g|_q + [a]_{2-1/q,q}$. Then there exists a continuous, increasing and positive function $F$ of $X > 0$, with $F(X) \to 0$ as $X \to 0$, such that the solution $(u,p,c)$ of problem (1.13)-(1.19) (guaranteed by Theorem 1.2) is unique, provided*

$$F(X)/D + \gamma < 1\,.$$

Observe that by (1.11), (1.12) each classical and smooth up to the boundary solution of problem (1.1)–(1.5) is also a weak solution of the problem in the sense of definition (1.13)–(1.19); inversely, each sufficiently smooth weak solution satisfying (1.13)–(1.19) is a classical solution of problem (1.1)–(1.5).

REMARK. Condition (1.5;2) may be easily extended to more general form, eg. $-J\cdot n = h_2(x, s_1(x), s_2(x), c(x))$ on $\partial_2\Omega$, where $s_1$, $s_2$ are some control functions, $0 \le s_1(x) \le s_2(x) \le 1$, and $h_2(x, s_1, s_2, c) \ge 0$ if $c \le s_1$, and $\le 0$ if $c \ge s_2$. We leave the details to the reader. See also [5], [16].

The plan of the remaining sections of the paper is as follows. In Section 2 we study linearized problem (1.15), (1.16), (1.18) in $(u,p)$. In Section 3 we consider problem (1.17), (1.19) in $c$, with given $u$ and $p$. In Section 4 we prove existence Theorems 1.1 and 1.2, by using Schauder's fixed point theorem and estimates obtained in Sections 2, 3. Section 5 presents the proof of Theorem 1.3.

For convenience, we denote several universal numeric constants by the letter $C$ without bothering to distinguish them with subscripts. Otherwise we write $C(Y)$ to point out that $C$ depends on $Y$.

## 2. Linearized Navier-Stokes system

In this section we consider the boundary-value problem in $(u,p)$:

$$-\nu\Delta u + (v\cdot\nabla)u + \nabla p = f + bg \qquad \text{in } \Omega, \quad (2.1)$$

$$\operatorname{div} u = 0 \qquad \text{in } \Omega, \quad (2.2)$$

$$u = a \qquad \text{on } \partial\Omega, \quad (2.3)$$

where $f, g, b, v$ and $a$ are given functions.

We define, for $f, g \in L^q$ , $b \in C^0$ and $a \in B^{2-1/q,q}$:

$$R = |f|_q + |b|_\infty |g|_q + [a]_{2-1/q,q}, \quad R_0 = R + R^2, \quad R_1 = R + R_0^2. \qquad (2.4)$$

Lemma 2.1. *Let $f, g$ be as in (A1), $a$ be as in (A5) and $b \in C^0$. There exist positive reals $r, r_0$ and $r_1$ such that if $v \in A$,*

$$A = \{v \in W^{1,2}_{\sigma,0} \cap C^0 : \|v\|_1 \le rR, \quad |v|_q \le r_0 R_0, \quad |v|_\infty \le r_1 R_1\}$$

*then problem (2.1)-(2.3) has a unique solution $(u,p) \in (W^{2,q} \cap A) \times W^{1,q}$, with $\int_\Omega p(x)dx = 0$. Moreover,*

$$\|u\|_{2,q} + \|p\|_{1,q} \le C(R + R_1^2). \qquad (2.5)$$

Proof: Fix $f, g \in L^q$, $b \in C^0$, $v \in W^{1,2}_{\sigma,0} \cap C^0$ and $a$ satisfying (A5). We shall show at first the existence of a unique pair $(u,p) \in W^{1,2}_{\sigma,0} \times L^2$, $\int_\Omega p(x)dx = 0$, satisfying (2.1) in the distribution sense. To this end we reduce problem (2.1)–(2.3) to a homogeneous one by introducing the new variable $w = u - \tilde{a}$, where $\tilde{a}$ is an extension to $\Omega$ of the boundary data $a$ such that $\tilde{a} \in W^{1,2}_{\sigma,0}$ [4], [18]. If a pair $(u,p)$ satisfies (2.1)–(2.3) then $w \in V$ and $(w,p)$ satisfies

$$-\nu\Delta w + (v\cdot\nabla)w + \nabla p = f + bg + \nu\Delta\tilde{a} - (v\cdot\nabla)\tilde{a} \qquad \text{in } \Omega, \quad (2.6)$$

$$\operatorname{div} w = 0 \qquad \text{in } \Omega, \quad (2.7)$$

$$w = 0 \qquad \text{on } \partial\Omega. \quad (2.8)$$

It suffices to show that there exists a unique pair $(w,p) \in V \times L^2$, $\int_\Omega p(x)dx = 0$, satisfying (2.6)–(2.8). We multiply both sides of (2.6) by some function $z$ in $\tilde{V}$ and integrate over $\Omega$. After integration by parts we obtain

$$\nu\int_\Omega \nabla w\cdot\nabla z + \int_\Omega (v\cdot\nabla)wz = \int_\Omega (f+bg)z - \nu\int_\Omega \nabla\tilde{a}\nabla z - \int_\Omega (v\cdot\nabla)\tilde{a}z. \qquad (2.9)$$

We notice that [9], [18]

$$\int_\Omega (v\cdot\nabla)wz = -\int_\Omega (v\cdot\nabla)zw\,, \quad \text{for all} \quad v,w\in V. \tag{2.10}$$

Then it is easy to see that the left-hand side of (2.9) defines a continuous and coercive bilinear form in $(w,z)$ on $V\times V$, and the right-hand side defines a continuous linear functional in $z$ on $V$. Thus, by the Lax-Milgram lemma [7], there exists a unique $w\in V$ such that (2.9) holds for each $z\in V$. Now, $\tilde f = -\nu\Delta w - \nu\Delta\tilde a + (v\cdot\nabla)w + \nabla p - f - bg$ belongs to $H^{-1}$, the dual space to $H_0^1$, and $<\tilde f, z> = 0$ for each $z$ in $\tilde V$, which implies [18] that $\tilde f = \nabla p$ in the distribution sense in $\Omega$, for some $p\in L^2$. We normalize $p$ so that $\int_\Omega p(x)dx = 0$. Thus $(w,p)$ is the unique pair in $V\times L^2$ satisfying (2.1) in the distribution sense.

Now we shall show that the obtained solution $(u,p)$ of (2.1)–(2.3) belongs to $W^{2,q}\times W^{1,q}$, and determine constants $r, r_0$ and $r_1$ in the definition of the set $A$ in such a way that $u\in A$ if only $v\in A$, cf. [2], [11]. Our main tool is the well known estimate

$$\|u\|_{k+2,s} + \|p\|_{k+1,s} \le C\left(\|f\|_{k,s} + [a]_{k+2-1/s,s}\right), \tag{2.11}$$

($s>1$, $k$ is an integer $\ge -1$, $\|\cdot\|_{-1,s}$ is the norm in the dual space to $W_0^{1,s'}(\Omega)$, $1/s+1/s'=1$) belonging to Cattabriga [4] (see also [18]) of the solution $(u,p)$, $\int_\Omega p(x)\,dx = 0$ of the Stokes problem

$$\begin{aligned} -\nu\Delta u + \nabla p &= f && \text{in } \Omega,\\ \operatorname{div} u &= 0 && \text{in } \Omega,\\ u &= a && \text{on } \partial\Omega. \end{aligned}$$

At first we shall estimate $u$ in the $\|\cdot\|_1$ norm. We assume that the extension $\tilde a$ of $a$ has the following property:

$$\left|\int_\Omega (v\cdot\nabla)\tilde a w\right| \le (\nu/2)\cdot\|v\|_1\cdot\|w\|_1 \tag{2.12}$$

for all $v\in W^{1,2}$ such that $\operatorname{div} v = 0$, and $w\in V$ (see [6], [18]). Let $1/t = 1/q + 1/3$ and $C_1>0$ be such that

$$\max\{[a]_{1/2,2}, [a]_{4/3,3/2}, [a]_{2-1/t,t}\} \le C_1[a]_{2-1/q,q}. \tag{2.13}$$

Setting $z=w$ in (2.9) and using (2.10), (2.12), (2.13) we obtain

$$\begin{aligned} \nu\|w\|_1^2 &= \int_\Omega (f+bg)w - \nu\int_\Omega \nabla\tilde a\cdot\nabla w - \int_\Omega (v\cdot\nabla)\tilde a w\\ &\le C(|f|_q + |b|_\infty|g|_q)\|w\|_1 + \nu\|\tilde a\|_1\|w\|_1 + \nu/2\|v\|_1\|w\|_1\\ &\le C(C_1)\cdot R\cdot\|w\|_1 + \nu/2\|v\|_1\|w\|_1 \end{aligned} \tag{2.14}$$

with $R$ as in (2.4). As $u = w + \tilde{a}$, and by (2.13) we have $\|u\|_1 \le \|w\|_1 + C(C_1)[a]_{2-1/q,q}$, and by (2.14)

$$\|u\|_1 \le C(C_1) \cdot R/\nu + (1/2)\|v\|_1 + C(C_1)[a]_{2-1/q,q} \le C(\nu, C_1) \cdot R + (1/2)\|v\|_1 .$$

Let $\|v\|_1 \le 2C(\nu, C_1) \cdot R = rR$. Then

$$\|u\|_1 \le rR . \tag{2.15}$$

We shall assume that $\|v\|_1 \le rR$ (cf. the definition of the set $A$).

Now, by Hölder's inequality, the inequality $|u|_6 \le C\|u\|_1$ for $u \in W^{1,2}_{\sigma,0}$, and by (2.15) we have

$$|(v \cdot \nabla)u|_{3/2} \le |v|_6 \|u\|_1 \le C\|v\|_1 \|u\|_1 \le CR^2 .$$

Cattabriga's estimate (2.11) applied to problem (2.1)-(2.3) with $\tilde{f} = f + bg - (v \cdot \nabla)u$, $k = 0$ and $s = 3/2$ gives

$$\|u\|_{2,3/2} + \|p\|_{1,3/2} \le C(R^2 + R) = CR_0 .$$

Since $W^{2,3/2} \hookrightarrow W^{1,3} \hookrightarrow L^q$ for each $q > 3$, there exists a positive constant $r_0$ such that $|u|_q \le r_0 R_0$. We shall assume that $|v|_q \le r_0 R_0$. Now, with $1/t = 1/q + 1/3$, and by Hölder's inequality and the above imbeddings we have

$$|(v \cdot \nabla)u|_t \le C|v|_q |\nabla u|_3 \le CR_0^2 .$$

We apply (2.11) again to obtain

$$\|u\|_{2,t} + \|p\|_{1,t} \le C(R_0^2 + R) = CR_1 .$$

Since $W^{2,t} \hookrightarrow W^{1,q} \hookrightarrow C^0$, there exists a constant $r_1$ such that $|u|_\infty \le r_1 R_1$. We shall assume that $|v|_\infty \le r_1 R_1$. In the end

$$|(v \cdot \nabla)u|_q \le C|v|_\infty |\nabla u|_q \le CR_1^2 ,$$

and using Cattabriga's estimate again we obtain inequality (2.5). Moreover, if $v \in A$ then $u \in A$. ▮

Now we shall show that the map $(v, b) \to (u, p)$, where $(u, p)$ is the unique solution of the boundary-value problem (2.1)-(2.3) from Lemma 2.1, is continuous in certain topologies. More precisely, let $M_1$ be a positive real and

$$B = \{\, b \in C^0 \; : \quad |b|_\infty \le M_1 \,\}.$$

In view of further applications, we consider the map $(v, b) \to (u, p)$ on the product $A \times B$, where $A$ is the set from Lemma 2.1.

LEMMA 2.2. *The map*

$$\Phi : C^0 \times C^0 \supset A \times B \ni (v,b) \to (u,p) \in C^0 \times W^{1,2}$$

*is continuous.*

PROOF: Let $(v,b)$, $(v_n,b_n)$, $n = 1,2,3,\dots$ be in $A \times B$, and let $\Phi(v_n,b_n) = (u_n,p_n)$, $\Phi(v,b) = (u,p)$. Then $(u-u_n, p-p_n)$ is the solution of the problem

$$-\nu\Delta(u-u_n) + \nabla(p-p_n) = \tilde{f}_n \qquad \text{in } \Omega, \tag{2.16}$$

$$\operatorname{div}(u-u_n) = 0 \qquad \text{in } \Omega, \tag{2.17}$$

$$u - u_n = 0 \qquad \text{on } \partial\Omega, \tag{2.18}$$

where $\tilde{f} = (b-b_n)g + ((v_n - v)\cdot\nabla)u_n + (v\cdot\nabla)(u_n - u)$. Multiplying both sides of (2.16) by $u - u_n$ and integrating over $\Omega$ we obtain

$$\nu\|u-u_n\|_1^2 = \int_\Omega (b-b_n)g(u-u_n) + \int_\Omega ((v_n - v)\cdot\nabla)u_n(u-u_n).$$

Using Hölder's and Poincaré's inequalities we estimate the right-hand side by

$$C\{|b-b_n|_\infty |g|_2 \|u-u_n\|_1 + |v-v_n|_\infty \|u_n\|_1 \|u-u_n\|_1\}.$$

Hence

$$\|u-u_n\|_1 \le (C/\nu)\{|b-b_n|_\infty |g|_2 + |v-v_n|_\infty \|u_n\|_1\}.$$

Let $(v_n,b_n) \to (v,b)$ in $C^0 \times C^0$, as $n \to \infty$. Since $\|u_n\|_1 \le rR$ by (2.15), we conclude that $u_n \to u$ in $H_0^1$, as $n \to \infty$, and, in concequence, $\tilde{f}_n \to 0$ in $L^2$. We apply Cattabriga's estimate (2.11) to problem (2.16)-(2.18), obtaining $u_n \to u$ in $W^{2,2}$ (hence uniformly), and $p_n \to p$ in $W^{1,2}$. This proves the continuity of $\Phi$. ∎

We shall use Lemmas 2.1 and 2.2 in Section 4.

## 3. EQUATION OF DIFFUSION

In this section we consider the following problem in $c$:

$$c \in W^{1,2}, \tag{3.1}$$

$$\int_\Omega D(\tilde{b})\nabla c\cdot\nabla\varphi + \int_\Omega u\cdot\nabla c\varphi = -\int_\Omega K(c)\nabla p\cdot\nabla\varphi + \int_{\partial_2\Omega} h_2(c)\varphi \text{ for each } \varphi \in W, \tag{3.2}$$

$$c - \xi \in W, \tag{3.3}$$

where

$$\xi \in W^{1,2}, \quad \text{with} \quad \xi = h_1 \quad \text{on} \quad \partial_1\Omega, \tag{3.4}$$

$$\tilde{b} \in C^0, \quad u \in W^{1,2}_{\sigma,0} \cap C^0, \quad p \in W^{1,q}, \tag{3.5}$$

$D$ and $K$ are as in (A2), and $h_1$, $h_2$ are as in (A3) and (A4), respectively.

Our aim is to prove existence of solutions of problem (3.1)-(3.3), estimate them in $C^0$ and $C^{0,\alpha}$ norms (under suitable assumptions about $h_1$), and prove the unique solvability of the problem, provided $K$ is Lipschitz continuous.

We begin with the linearized problem

$$c \in W^{1,2}, \tag{3.6}$$

$$\int_\Omega D(\tilde{b})\nabla c \cdot \nabla\varphi + \int_\Omega u \cdot \nabla c\varphi = -\int_\Omega K(b)\nabla p \cdot \nabla\varphi + \int_{\partial_2\Omega} h_2(b)\varphi \text{ for each } \varphi \in W, \tag{3.7}$$

$$c - \xi \in W. \tag{3.8}$$

LEMMA 3.1. *Let (3.4),(3.5) and (A2)-(A4) hold, and $b, \tilde{b} \in C^0$. Then there exists a unique solution of problem (3.6)-(3.8). Moreover*

$$\|c\|_1 \leq C(|K|_\infty + [h_1]_{1/2,2,\partial_1\Omega})(|u|_\infty + |\nabla p|_2) + C\{(M+1)[h_1]_{1/2,2,\partial_1\Omega} + |h_2|_{\infty,\partial_2\Omega}\} \equiv \tilde{C}_1 . \tag{3.9}$$

PROOF: Since $u \in W^{1,2}_{\sigma,0}$, we have

$$\int_\Omega u \cdot \nabla c\varphi = -\int_\Omega u \cdot \nabla\varphi c \quad \text{for all} \quad c \in W^{1,2} \quad \text{and} \quad \varphi \in W. \tag{3.10}$$

Thus, in particular, the left-hand side of (3.7) defines a continuous and coercive bilinear form on $W \times W$. We introduce the new variable $\tilde{c} = c - \xi$ reducing the problem to the following one: find $\tilde{c} \in W$ such that

$$\int_\Omega D(\tilde{b})\nabla\tilde{c} \cdot \nabla\varphi + \int_\Omega u \cdot \nabla\tilde{c}\varphi = -\int_\Omega K(b)\nabla p\nabla\varphi - \int_\Omega D(\tilde{b})\nabla\xi\nabla\varphi - \int_\Omega u \cdot \nabla\xi\varphi + \int_{\partial_2\Omega} h_2(b)\varphi ,$$

for each $\varphi \in W$. The existence of a unique solution $\tilde{c} \in W$ follows from the Lax-Milgram lemma. Let $\|\xi\|_1 \leq C[h_1]_{1/2,2,\partial_1\Omega}$. Setting $\varphi = \tilde{c}$ in the above integral identity and using (1.6), (3.10) and Poincaré's inequality we easily obtain

$$\begin{aligned} m\int_\Omega |\nabla\tilde{c}|^2 &\leq \int_\Omega |K(b)\nabla p \cdot \nabla\tilde{c}| + \int_\Omega |D(\tilde{b})\nabla\xi \cdot \nabla\tilde{c}| + \int_\Omega |u \cdot \nabla\xi\tilde{c}| + \int_{\partial_2\Omega} |h_2(b)\tilde{c}| \\ &\leq C\{|K|_\infty|\nabla p|_2\|\tilde{c}\|_1 + M[h_1]_{1/2,2,\partial_1\Omega}\|\tilde{c}\|_1 + |u|_\infty[h_1]_{1/2,2,\partial_1\Omega}\|\tilde{c}\|_1 \\ &\quad + |h_2(b)|_{2,\partial_2\Omega}\|\tilde{c}\|_1\} , \end{aligned}$$

from which we conclude (3.9). ∎

LEMMA 3.2. *Let $c$ be the solution of problem (3.6)-(3.8). Then $c \in C^{0,\beta}_\omega$ for each subdomain $\omega$ of $\Omega$, separated from $\partial\Omega$, and*

$$|c|_{0,\beta,\omega} \leq C_0\{|c|_2 + (1/m)|K(b)\nabla p|_q\}. \tag{3.11}$$

*The constant $C_0$ depends on $dist(\omega, \partial\Omega)$, $|u|_\infty$, and $\beta$ depends on $dist(\omega, \partial\Omega)$.*

*Moreover, if $h_1 \in C^{0,1}(\partial_1\Omega)$ then $c \in C^{0,\alpha}$ for some $\alpha$, $0 < \alpha < 1$, and*

$$|c|_\infty \le C(|K|_\infty + \tilde{C}_1)(|u|_\infty + |\nabla p|_{q_0}) + C\{|h_1|_{\infty,\partial_1\Omega} + |h_2|_{\infty,\partial_2\Omega}\} \equiv \tilde{C}_2\,, \tag{3.12}$$

$$|c|_{0,\alpha,\Omega} \le C(|K|_\infty + \tilde{C}_1)(|u|_\infty + |\nabla p|_{q_0}) + C\{|h_1|_{0,1,\partial_1\Omega} + |h_2|_{\infty,\partial_2\Omega}\} \equiv \tilde{C}_3\,, \tag{3.13}$$

*where $q_0 = min\{6, q\}$, and $\tilde{C}_1$ is as in (3.9).*

PROOF: Inequality (3.11) follows directly from general results concerning local estimates of weak solutions of elliptic problems ( see Theorem 8.24, in [7], for example).

To prove (3.12), (3.13) we use (3.10) and rewrite (3.7) in the form

$$\int_\Omega D(\tilde{b})\nabla c \cdot \nabla\varphi = \int_\Omega \{uc - K(b)\nabla p\}\nabla\varphi + \int_{\partial_2\Omega} h_2(b)\varphi \quad \text{for each} \quad \varphi \in W.$$

Let $q_0 = \min\{6, q\} > 3$, and $s > 2$. Using Stampacchia's estimates in $C^0$ and $C^{0,\alpha}$ for weak solutions of the mixed problem for elliptic equations [17], [12] (see also Lemma 2 in [5] for the explicit dependence of the relevant estimates on the right–hand side of the equation and boundary conditions) we obtain

$$|c|_\infty \le C\{|uc - K(b)\nabla p|_{q_0} + |h_1|_{\infty,\partial_1\Omega} + |h_2(b)|_{s,\partial_2\Omega}\}$$

and

$$|c|_{0,\alpha,\Omega} \le C\{|uc - K(b)\nabla p|_{q_0} + |h_1|_{0,1,\partial_1\Omega} + |h_2(b)|_{s,\partial_2\Omega}\}.$$

As $q_0 \le 6$, $|uc|_{q_0} \le C|u|_\infty\|c\|_1$, and from the above estimates we easily obtain (3.12), (3.13). ∎

LEMMA 3.3. *Let (3.4),(3.5) and (A2)–(A4) hold, and let $h_1 \in C^{0,1}(\partial_1\Omega)$. Then there exists a solution of problem (3.1)-(3.3). Moreover, $c \in C^{0,\alpha}$ for some $\alpha$, $0 < \alpha < 1$, and*

$$|c|_{0,\alpha,\Omega} \le \tilde{C}_3\,, \tag{3.14}$$

*where $\tilde{C}_3$ is as in (3.13).*

PROOF: To prove existence of the solution we apply Schauder's fixed point theorem [7] to the map $\Phi_1 : C^0 \supset B_1 \ni b \to c \in C^0$, where

$$B_1 = \{b \in C^0 \;:\; |b|_\infty \le \tilde{C}_2\},$$

$\tilde{C}_2$ is as in (3.12), and $c$ is the unique solution of problem (3.6)-(3.8) from Lemma 3.1. From (3.12) it follows that $\Phi_1(B_1) \subset B_1$, and inequality (3.13) implies compactness of $\Phi_1(B_1)$ in $C^0$. We shall prove that the map $\Phi_1$ is continuous. Let $b_n \to b$ in $C^0$, $b, b_n \in B_1$ for $n = 1.2.3, \ldots$, and $c_n = \Phi_1(b_n)$, $c = \Phi_1(b)$. From (3.9) and (3.13) it follows the existence of a subsequence $(c_\mu)$ such that

$$c_\mu \to \tilde{c} \quad \text{uniformly on} \quad \bar{\Omega}\,, \quad \text{and weakly in} \quad W^{1,2}.$$

Passing to the limit in

$$\int_\Omega D(\tilde{b})\nabla c_\mu \cdot \nabla\varphi + \int_\Omega u \cdot \nabla c_\mu \varphi = -\int_\Omega K(b_\mu)\nabla p \cdot \nabla\varphi + \int_{\partial_2\Omega} h_2(b_\mu)\varphi \quad \text{for each} \quad \varphi \in W\,,$$

we conclude that $\tilde{c} = c$, and that the whole sequence $(c_n)$ converges uniformly to $c$. Thus, $\Phi_1$ is continuous in the uniform topology. Other conclusions of the lemma are obvious. ∎

LEMMA 3.4. *Let (3.4),(3.5) and (A2)–(A4) hold. Let us assume that $K$ is Lipschitz continuous (as in (1.20)), and that $h_1 \in C^{0,1}(\partial_1\Omega)$, with $0 \le h_1 \le 1$. Than the solution of the problem (3.1)-(3.3), given by Lemma 3.3, is unique. Moreover*

$$0 \le c \le 1 \quad in \quad \Omega\,. \tag{3.15}$$

PROOF: To prove that the solution is unique we assume, on the contrary, that there exist two different solutions $c_1$ and $c_2$. Let $\tau = c_1 - c_2$. Using (3.10) we obtain

$$\int_\Omega D(\tilde{b})\nabla\tau\cdot\nabla\varphi = \int_\Omega F\cdot\nabla\varphi + \int_{\partial_2\Omega}(h_2(c_1)-h_2(c_2))\varphi \quad \text{for each} \quad \varphi\in W\,, \tag{3.16}$$

where $F = \tau u + (K(c_2) - K(c_1))\nabla p$. By our assumptions

$$|F| \le \{|u| + L_K|\nabla p|\}|\tau| \equiv |F_1|\cdot|\tau|\,, \tag{3.17}$$

with $F_1 \in L^2$. Let $\varphi^+ = \max\{\varphi, 0\}$. For $\delta > 0$ we set (cf. [3]; see also [5], [16]) $\varphi = (\tau-\delta)^+/\tau$ in (3.16) ($\varphi \in W$, and $\nabla\varphi = \delta\cdot\nabla\tau/\tau^2$ on the set $\Omega_\delta = \{\, x\in\Omega : \tau(x) > \delta\,\}$). By the monotonicity of $h_2$ and by (3.17) we have

$$\int_\Omega D(\tilde{b})\nabla\tau\cdot\nabla\varphi \le \int_\Omega |F_1|\cdot|\tau|\cdot|\nabla\varphi| \quad \text{for each} \quad \varphi\in W\,.$$

Thus

$$\int_{\Omega_\delta}\frac{D(\tilde{b})|\nabla\tau|^2}{\tau^2} \le \int_{\Omega_\delta}\frac{|F_1|\cdot|\nabla\tau|}{|\tau|}$$

Since $D(\tilde{b}) \ge m > 0$, by Schwartz' inequality we obtain

$$\int_{\Omega_\delta}\frac{|\nabla\tau|^2}{\tau^2} \le L\,, \qquad L = \frac{2}{m^2}\int_\Omega |F_1|^2\,,$$

hence

$$\int_\Omega \left|\nabla \ln\left(1+\frac{(\tau-\delta)^+}{\delta}\right)\right|^2 \le L\,.$$

Now, by Poincaré's inequality

$$\int_\Omega \left|\ln\left(1+\frac{(\tau-\delta)^+}{\delta}\right)\right|^2 \le CL\,,$$

independently of $\delta > 0$. Let $\delta \to 0$ and we conclude that $\tau \le 0$ *a.e.* in $\Omega$. Thus $c_1 \le c_2$ *a.e.* in $\Omega$. Similarly we show that $c_2 \le c_1$ *a.e.* in $\Omega$, so that $c_1 = c_2$ *a.e.* in $\Omega$. We have come to the contradiction with our assumption $c_1 \ne c_2$. This proves the uniqueness.

To prove (3.15), set $\varphi = c^- = \min\{c, 0\}$ in (3.2) ($\varphi \in W$, as $c \geq 0$ on $\partial_1\Omega$). We obtain

$$\int_\Omega D(\tilde{b})|\nabla c^-|^2 = 0\,, \tag{3.18}$$

as $\int_\Omega u \cdot \nabla c^- c^- = 0$ by (3.10), $K(c)\nabla c^- = 0$ by (1.7), and $\int_{\partial_2\Omega} h_2(c)c^- \leq 0$ by (A4). As $c^- = 0$ on $\partial_1\Omega$, and $D(\tilde{b})$ is positive, (3.18) implies that $c^- = 0$ in $\Omega$. Hence $c \geq 0$ in $\Omega$. Similarly, taking $\varphi = (c-1)^+$ we obtain $c \leq 1$ in $\Omega$. This proves (3.15). ∎

Now we are in a position to prove the existence of a solution of the main problem in the paper.

## 4. Existence Theorems

In this section we prove Theorems 1.1 and 1.2.

Proof of Theorem 1.1: Let the assumptions of Theorem 1.1 hold. For convenience, we shall keep the temporary assumption

$$h_1 \in C^{0,1}(\partial_1\Omega)\,, \tag{4.1}$$

and release from it at the end of the section. We use Schauder's fixed point theorem. Let $A \subset C^0$ be the set defined in Section 2 ( see Lemma 2.1 ). Let $B = \{\, b \in C^0 \,:\, |b|_\infty \leq M_1 \,\}$ for an arbitrary number $M_1$ such that

$$C\{|h_1|_{\infty,\partial_1\Omega} + |h_2|_{\infty,\partial_2\Omega}\} < M_1$$

(with $C$ as in (3.12)). We consider the map

$$\Psi : C^0 \times C^0 \supset A \times B \ni (v, b) \to (u, c) \in C^0 \times C^0\,,$$

constructed as follows. For $(v, b) \in A \times B$, $\Psi(v, b) = (u, c)$, where $(u, p, c)$ is the unique solution of the problem

$$\begin{aligned} -\nu\Delta u + (v\cdot\nabla)u + \nabla p &= f + bg && \text{in } \Omega\,,\\ \operatorname{div} u &= 0 && \text{in } \Omega\,,\\ u &= a && \text{on } \partial\Omega\,, \end{aligned}$$

$$\int_\Omega D(b)\nabla c\cdot\nabla\varphi + \int_\Omega v\cdot\nabla c\varphi = -\int_\Omega K(b)\nabla p\cdot\nabla\varphi + \int_{\partial_2\Omega} h_2(b)\varphi \quad \text{for each} \quad \varphi \in W\,,$$

$$c - \xi \in W\,, \quad \xi = h_1 \quad \text{on} \quad \partial_1\Omega\,.$$

Lemmas 2.1, 3.1 and 3.2 guarantee that the map $\Psi$ is well defined. From Lemma 2.1 it follows that $u \in A$. By Lemma 3.2 $c \in B$, provided the norms $|f|_q$, $|g|_q$, and $[a]_{2-1/q,q}$ are small enough (see inequalities (2.4), (2.5), and (3.12)). Hence, with $|f|_q$, $|g|_q$ and $[a]_{2-1/q,q}$ small enough, $\Psi(A\times B) \subset A \times B$. In view of (2.5) and (3.13), $\Psi(A\times B)$ is a compact subset of $C^0 \times C^0$. We shall show that the map $\Psi$ is continuous in the uniform topologies. Let $(v,b)$, $(v_n,b_n)$, $n=1,2,3,\dots$ be in $A\times B$, $(v_n,b_n)\to(v,b)$ in $C^0\times C^0$, as $n\to\infty$, $\Psi(v_n,b_n)=(u_n,c_n)$, $\Psi(v,b)=(u,c)$. We have to prove that $(u_n,c_n)\to(u,c)$ in $C^0\times C^0$, as $n\to\infty$. By Lemma 2.2 we have

$$u_n\to u \quad \text{in} \quad C^0, \qquad \nabla p_n\to\nabla p \quad \text{in} \quad W^{1,2}. \tag{4.2}$$

To show that $c_n\to c$ in $C^0$, consider the identities

$$\int_\Omega D(b_n)\nabla c_n\cdot\nabla\varphi+\int_\Omega v_n\cdot\nabla c_n\varphi=-\int_\Omega K(b_n)\nabla p_n\cdot\nabla\varphi+\int_{\partial_2\Omega} h_2(b_n)\varphi \qquad \varphi\in W, \quad (4.3)_n$$

$n=1,2,3,\dots$. As $(c_n)$ is a bounded sequence in $W^{1,2}$ and in $C^{0,\alpha}$, for some $\alpha$, $0<\alpha<1$, there exists a subsequence $(c_\mu)$ such that

$$c_\mu\to\tilde c \quad \text{in} \quad C^0, \quad \text{and weakly in} \quad W^{1,2}. \tag{4.4}$$

By our assumptions, (4.2) and (4.4), we can pass to the limit in $(4.3)_\mu$, obtaining

$$\int_\Omega D(b)\nabla\tilde c\cdot\nabla\varphi+\int_\Omega v\cdot\nabla\tilde c\varphi=-\int_\Omega K(b)\nabla p\cdot\nabla\varphi+\int_{\partial_2\Omega} h_2(b)\varphi \quad \text{for each} \quad \varphi\in W. \tag{4.5}$$

Now, as (4.5) is uniquely solvable in $\tilde c$, we conclude that $\tilde c=c$, and $c_n\to c$ in $C^0$. This completes the proof of Theorem 1.2, under the additional assumption (4.1). ∎

PROOF OF THEOREM 1.2: The proof is very similar to that of Theorem 1.1. Let the assumptions of Theorem 1.2 hold, together with (4.1). Let $B=\{b\in C^0 : \ |b|_\infty\le 1\}$, and

$$\Psi_1 : C^0\times C^0\supset A\times B\ni(v,b)\to(u,c)\in C^0\times C^0$$

be defined as follows. For $(v,b)\in A\times B$ let $\Psi_1(v,b)=(u,c)$, where $(u,p,c)$ is the unique solution of the problem

$$\begin{aligned} -\nu\Delta u+(v\cdot\nabla)u+\nabla p&=f+bg && \text{in} \quad \Omega,\\ \operatorname{div} u&=0 && \text{in} \quad \Omega,\\ u&=a && \text{on} \quad \partial\Omega, \end{aligned}$$

$$\int_\Omega D(b)\nabla c\cdot\nabla\varphi+\int_\Omega u\cdot\nabla c\varphi=-\int_\Omega K(c)\nabla p\cdot\nabla\varphi+\int_{\partial_2\Omega} h_2(c)\varphi \quad \text{for each} \quad \varphi\in W, \tag{4.6}$$

$$c-\xi\in W, \qquad \xi=h_1 \quad \text{on} \quad \partial_1\Omega. \tag{4.7}$$

In view of Lemmas 2.1 and 3.4, the map $\Psi_1$ is well defined, and $\Psi_1(A\times B)\subset A\times B$. By (2.5) and (3.14) $\Psi_1(A\times B)$ is compact in $C^0\times C^0$. The continuity of $\Psi_1$ in the uniform topologies is obvious due to the unique solvability of problem (4.6), (4.7) (Lemma 3.4). We omit the details. ∎

To complete the proofs of Theorems 1.1 and 1.2 we have to release from the additional assumption (4.1). Let $h \in W^{1/2,2}(\partial\Omega)$. We take a sequence $(\xi_n) \subset W^{1,2}$ such that $\xi_n \in C^{0,1}$ and $\xi_n \to \xi$ in $W^{1,2}$. Then $\xi_n \in C^{0,1}(\partial_1\Omega)$ and $\xi_n|_{\partial_1\Omega} \to h$ in $W^{1/2,2}(\partial_1\Omega)$, as $n \to \infty$. Let $(u_n, p_n, c_n)$, $n = 1, 2, 3, \ldots$ be solutions as in Theorems 1.1 and 1.2, corresponding to boundary data $c_n = \xi_n$ on $\partial_1\Omega$. In view of estimates (2.5), (3.11) we can select a subsequence $(u_\mu, p_\mu, c_\mu)$ such that for some $(u, p, c) \in (W^{2,q} \cap V) \times W^{1,q} \times W^{1,2}$

$$
\begin{aligned}
u_\mu &\to u \quad \text{uniformly on } \bar{\Omega}, \text{ and in } W^{1,2}, \\
p_\mu &\to p \quad \text{weakly in } W^{1,2}, \\
c_\mu &\to c \quad \text{uniformly on compacts in } \Omega, \text{ pointwise in } \Omega, \text{ and weakly in } W^{1,2}.
\end{aligned}
$$

Now, by standard argument we show that $(u, p, c)$ is a solution of problem (1.14)-(1.19). This completes the proofs of Theorems 1.1 and 1.2.

## 5. Uniqueness

In this section we prove Theorem 1.3. Assume that $(u_1, p_1, c_1)$ and $(u_2, p_2, c_2)$ are two different solutions of problem (1.15)-(1.19). Then the difference $(u_1 - u_2, p_1 - p_2, c_1 - c_2)$ satisfies the following integral identities

$$
\nu \int_\Omega \nabla(u_1 - u_2) \cdot \nabla v + \int_\Omega (u_1 \cdot \nabla)(u_1 - u_2) v = \int_\Omega (c_1 - c_2) g v + \int_\Omega ((u_2 - u_1) \cdot \nabla) u_2 v\,, \quad (5.1)
$$

for each $v \in V$, and

$$
D \int_\Omega \nabla(c_1 - c_2) \cdot \nabla\varphi = \int_\Omega G \cdot \nabla\varphi + \int_{\partial_2\Omega} (h_2(c_1) - h_2(c_2))\varphi \quad (5.2)
$$

for each $\varphi \in W$, where

$$
G = c_2(u_1 - u_2) + (c_1 - c_2)u_2 + (K(c_2) - K(c_1))\nabla p_2 + K(c_1)(\nabla p_2 - \nabla p_1)\,. \quad (5.3)
$$

Since $c_1 - c_2 \in W$, from (5.2) and (3.12) we have

$$
|c_1 - c_2|_\infty \le (C/D)|G|_r + |h_2(c_1) - h_2(c_2)|_{\infty,\partial_2\Omega} \quad (r > 3 \quad \text{arbitrary}),
$$

and by (1.21)

$$
|c_1 - c_2|_\infty \le (C/D)|G|_r + \gamma|c_1 - c_2|_\infty\,. \quad (5.4)
$$

Our aim now is to estimate $|G|_r$ by $F_1(X) \cdot |c_1 - c_2|_\infty$, where $X = |f|_q + |g|_q + [a]_{2-1/q,q}$, and $F_1$ has the same properties as the function $F$ in Theorem 1.3. This, together with (5.4) would lead to a contradiction, provided $(C/D)F_1(X) + \gamma < 1$. Let $3 < r \le \min\{6, q\}$. From (5.3) and our assumptions

$$
|G|_r \le |u_1 - u_2|_r + |u_2|_r|c_1 - c_2|_\infty + |\nabla p_2|_r L_K |c_1 - c_2|_\infty + |K|_\infty |\nabla p_2 - \nabla p_1|_r. \quad (5.5)
$$

Now we shall estimate the first term on the right-hand side of (5.5). We have: $|u_1-u_2|_r \le C|\nabla(u_1-u_2)|_2$. From (5.1) with $v = u_1 - u_2$ we obtain

$$\nu\int_\Omega |\nabla(u_1-u_2)|^2 = \int_\Omega (c_2-c_1)g(u_1-u_2) + \int_\Omega ((u_1-u_2)\cdot\nabla)u_2(u_1-u_2)\,. \tag{5.6}$$

From (2.15) and (2.4) with $b = c$

$$\|u_2\|_1 \le CX\,, \quad X = |f|_q + |g|_q + [a]_{2-1/q,q}\,. \tag{5.7}$$

From (5.6) and (5.7), by Hölder's and Poincaré's inequalities, we obtain

$$\nu|\nabla(u_1-u_2)|_2^2 \le CX|c_2-c_1|_\infty|\nabla(u_1-u_2)|_2 + CX|\nabla(u_1-u_2)|_2^2\,.$$

Assuming that $CX \le \nu/2$ we have

$$|\nabla(u_1-u_2)|_2 \le \frac{2}{\nu}CX|c_2-c_1|_\infty\,,$$

hence

$$|u_1-u_2|_r \le CX|c_2-c_1|_\infty\,, \quad 3 < r \le \min\{6,q\}. \tag{5.8}$$

Now, we shall estimate the last term on the right-hand side of (5.5). We have

$$\begin{aligned} -\nu\Delta(u_1-u_2) + \nabla(p_1-p_2) &= S && \text{in } \Omega\,,\\ \operatorname{div}(u_1-u_2) &= 0 && \text{in } \Omega\,,\\ u_1-u_2 &= 0 && \text{on } \partial\Omega\,,\end{aligned}$$

where $S = (c_1-c_2)g + (u_1\cdot\nabla)(u_2-u_1) + ((u_2-u_1)\cdot\nabla)u_2$. From Cattabriga's estimate (2.11) we obtain

$$|\nabla(p_1-p_2)|_r \le X|c_1-c_2|_\infty + |u_1|_\infty|\nabla(u_1-u_2)|_r + |((u_2-u_1)\cdot\nabla)u_2|_r.$$

We have $|u_1|_\infty$, $|\nabla u_2|_\infty \le F_1(X)$, by (2.5) and (2.4), so that by (5.8)

$$|\nabla(p_1-p_2)|_r \le X|c_1-c_2|_\infty + F_1(X)|\nabla(u_1-u_2)|_r + F_1(X)|c_1-c_2|_\infty.$$

To estimate $|\nabla(u_1-u_2)|_r$, we use Cattabriga's estimate (2.11) with $k=-1$. We obtain

$$|\nabla(u_1-u_2)|_r \le C\|S\|_{-1,r}.$$

Since $S \in L^q$, $q \ge r > 3$, we have, with $s = r/(r-1)$

$$\begin{aligned}\|S\|_{-1,r} &= \sup\{\left|\int_\Omega S\varphi\right| : \|\varphi\|_{1,s} \le 1\}\\ &\le \sup\{|g|_r|c_1-c_2|_\infty|\varphi|_s + |u_1|_\infty|u_1-u_2|_r\|\varphi\|_{1,s}\\ &\qquad + |u_1-u_2|_r|\nabla u_2|_\infty|\varphi|_s : \|\varphi\|_{1,s} \le 1\}\\ &\le F_1(X)|c_1-c_2|_\infty\,.\end{aligned}$$

Combining the above inequalities we conclude that

$$|\nabla(p_1 - p_2)|_r \leq F_1(X)|c_1 - c_2|_\infty,$$

which gives, together with (5.5) and (5.8)

$$|G|_r \leq F_1(X)|c_1 - c_2|_\infty,$$

and by (5.4)

$$|c_1 - c_2|_\infty \leq \{\frac{C}{D}F_1(X) + \gamma\}|c_1 - c_2|_\infty.$$

In conclusion, if $(C/D)F_1(X)+\gamma \equiv F(X)/D+\gamma < 1$, the considered problem is uniquely solvable. The proof of Theorem 1.3 is complete.

## References


1. R.A. Adams, "Sobolev Spaces," Academic Press, New York, 1975.
2. H. Beirão da Veiga, *On the stationary motion of granulated media*, Rend. Sem. Mat. Univ. Padova **77** (1987), 243–253.
3. H. Brezis, G. Kinderlehrer and G. Stampacchia, *Sur une nouvelle formulation du problème de l'ecoulememt à travers une digue*, C. Ren. Acad. Paris **287, Série A** (1978), 711–714.
4. L. Cattabriga, *Su un problema al contorno relativo al sistema di equazioni di Stokes*, Ren. Mat. Sem. Univ. Padova **31** (1961), 308–340.
5. M. Chipot and J.-F. Rodrigues, *On the steady-state continuous casting Stefan problem with non-linear cooling*, Quarterly of Applied Mathematics **40** (1983), 476–491.
6. C. Foias and R. Temam, *Some analytic and geometric properties of the solutions of the evolution Navier-Stokes equations*, J. Math. Pures et Appl. **58** (1979), 339–368.
7. D. Gilbarg and N. S. Trudinger, "Elliptic partial differential equations of second order ," Springer-Verlag, Berlin-Heidelberg-New York-Tokio, 1983.
8. S. R. de Groot and P. Mazur, "Non-equilibrium thermodynamics," North-Holland Publishing Company, Amsterdam, 1962.
9. O. A. Ladyzhenskaya, "The mathematical theory of viscous incompressible flow," Gordon and Breach, New York, 1969.
10. L. D. Landau and E. M. Lifshitz, "Mechanics of continuous media," Gos. Izd. Tech.-Teor. Lit., Moscow, 1954 (in Russian).
11. G. Lukaszewicz, *On an inequality associated with stationary flow of viscous incompressible fluids*, Rend. Accad. Naz. Sci. XL, Mem. Mat. **XI** (1987), 65–76.
12. M. K. V. Murthy and G. Stampacchia, *A variational inequality with mixed boundary conditions*, Israel J. of Math. **13** (1972), 188–224.
13. L. G. Petrosyan, "Some problems of mechanics of fluids with antisymmetric stress tensor," Izd. Erev. Univ., Erevań, 1984 (in Russian).
14. A. S. Popel, *On the hydrodynamics of suspensions*, Izv. AN.SSSR **4** (1969), 24–30 (in Russian).
15. A. S. Popel, S. A. Regirer and P. I. Usick, *A continuum model of blood flow*, Biorheology **XI** (1974), 427–437.
16. J.-F. Rodrigues, *A steady-state Boussinesq-Stefan problem with continuous extraction*, Annali di Mat. Pura Appl. **144** (1986), 203–218.
17. G. Stampacchia, *Problemi al contorno ellittici con dati discontinui dotati di soluzioni holderiane*, Annali di Mat. Pura Appl. **51** (1960), 1–32.
18. R. Temam, "Navier-Stokes equations. Theory and numerical analysis," North-Holland, Amsterdam-New York-Oxford, 1979.
19. C. Truesdall and R. A. Toupin, *The classical field theories*, in "Encyclopedia of Physics, vol III, No. 1, S. Flugge (ed.) Springer-Verlag, Berlin-Göttingen-Heidelberg, 1960," pp. 226–793.


Warsaw University, Department of Mathematics, ul. Banacha 2, 00–913 Warsaw 59, Poland

A MIKELIČ AND M PRIMICERIO

# Homogenization of heat conduction in materials with periodic inclusions of a perfect conductor

## 1. Introduction

In this paper we study a class of problems of linear heat transfer in composite materials with spatially periodic structure and we investigate the limit behaviour of the material as the period tends to zero.

Let Y be the unit cell in $\mathbb{R}^n$ and let $K \subset Y$ be a fixed closed set with Lipschitz boundary (we assume that K is connected for simplicity). Reduce the dimensions of Y and of K by scale factors $\epsilon$ and $r_\epsilon$ respectively ($r_\epsilon \leq \epsilon$) and make the periodic repetition of this cell: we denote by $Y^i_\epsilon$ and by $K^i_{r_\epsilon}$, $i \in \mathbb{Z}^n$ the generic transformed cell and the generic transformed "hole".

Given a (small) domain $\Omega \subset \mathbb{R}^n$ we can cover it by this mesh and denote by

$$T_\epsilon = \bigcup_i \{K^i_{r_\epsilon} : Y^i_\epsilon \subset \bar{\Omega}\} .$$

We study heat conduction in $\Omega$ assuming that $T_\epsilon$ and $\tilde{\Omega} = \Omega \backslash T_\epsilon$ are occupied by two different materials the first of which (filling $T_\epsilon$) has a much larger conductivity.

Under these conditions the conduction problem is well approximated by assuming that the medium filling the "holes" is a perfect conductor and then that its temperature does not depend on the position $\underline{x}$ in each of the $K^i_{r_\epsilon} \subset T_\epsilon$ . Boundary conditions describing the case of contact with perfect conductors (or well-stirred fluids) are presented e.g. in [1] p.22.

Therefore, we are led to study the following problem: to find a function $u^\epsilon(\underline{x},t)$, $\underline{x} \in \tilde{\Omega}$, $t \in (0,T)$ and functions $V^\epsilon_i(t)$, $t \in (0,T)$ (for i=1, 2, ... $N_\epsilon$, where $N_\epsilon$ is the number of holes in $\Omega$ and is of the order of $\epsilon^{-n}$meas $\Omega$) such that:

$$\frac{\partial u^\epsilon}{\partial t} = k\Delta u^\epsilon , \qquad \underline{x} \in \tilde{\Omega} , \ t \in (0,T) ; \tag{1.1}$$

$$u^\epsilon(x,t)=0 , \qquad \underline{x} \in \partial\Omega , \ t \in (0,T) ; \tag{1.2}$$

$$u^\epsilon(\underline{x},0)=u_{0\epsilon}(\underline{x}) , \qquad \underline{x} \in \partial\tilde{\Omega} ; \tag{1.3}$$

$$u^\epsilon(\underline{x},t)=V_i^\epsilon(t)\ , \qquad \underline{x}\in\partial K^i_{r_\epsilon}\ ,\ t\in(0,T)\ ; \tag{1.4}$$

$$\frac{dV_i^\epsilon(t)}{dt}=-C^\epsilon\int_{\partial K^i_{r_\epsilon}} k\,\frac{\partial u^\epsilon}{\partial n}\,d\sigma + f_\epsilon(t)\ , \qquad x\in\partial K^i_{r_\epsilon}\ ,\ t\in(0,T)\ ; \tag{1.5}$$

$$V_i^\epsilon(0)=V_{i0}^\epsilon \tag{1.6}$$

$i=1,\ 2,\ \ldots..\ N_\epsilon$ .

Here $V_{i0}^\epsilon$ are the (prescribed) initial temperatures in the holes and (1.5) expresses a energy balance for the material filling them, $f_\epsilon$ playing the role of a prescribed heat source.

We define the following function spaces:

$$E^\epsilon=\{v\in H^1(\Omega),\ v=0 \text{ on } \partial\Omega\ ,\ v \text{ constant on each connected part of } T_\epsilon\}.$$

$$H^\epsilon=\{v\in L^2(\Omega),\ v \text{ constant on each connected part of } T_\epsilon\}$$

and we assume

$$f_\epsilon\in L^2(0,T)\ , \tag{1.7}$$

$$u_{0\epsilon}\in H^\epsilon\ , \tag{1.8}$$

$$k,\ C^\epsilon>0\ . \tag{1.9}$$

We define the scalar products in $E^\epsilon$ and $H^\epsilon$ by

$$(F,\phi)_{E^\epsilon} = (\nabla F,\nabla\phi)_{L^2(\Omega)} + \frac{1}{C^\epsilon}\sum_{i=1}^{N_\epsilon}\frac{1}{|\partial T^i_{r_\epsilon}|}\int_{\partial T^i_{r_\epsilon}} F\,\phi\,d\sigma\ ;$$

and

$$(G,\phi)_{H^\epsilon} = (G,\phi)_{L^2(\Omega)} + \frac{1}{C^\epsilon}\sum_{i=1}^{N_\epsilon}\frac{1}{|\partial T^i_{r_\epsilon}|}\int_{\partial T^i_{r_\epsilon}} F\,\phi\,d\sigma\ .$$

The variational form of problem (1.1)-(1.6) to which we will always refer is standard:

to find $u^\epsilon\in L^2(0,T;E^\epsilon)$ such that $u^\epsilon\in C([0,T];H^\epsilon)$ , $u_t^\epsilon\in L^2((0,T);(E^\epsilon)')$ and the following equation hold

$$<u_t^\epsilon\ ,\ \phi>_{(E^\epsilon)',E^\epsilon} + k\int_\Omega \nabla u^\epsilon\,\nabla\phi\,dx = \frac{f_\epsilon}{C^\epsilon}\sum_{i=1}^{N_\epsilon}\frac{1}{|\partial T^i_{r_\epsilon}|}\int_{\partial T^i_{r_\epsilon}}\phi\,d\sigma\ ,$$

for any $\phi \in E^{\epsilon}$, a.e. in (0,T); $u^{\epsilon}(x,0) = u_{0\epsilon}$ in $H^{\epsilon}$.

It can be shown that this problem possesses a unique solution under the assumptions above. Throughout the paper, by solution to problem (1.1)-(1.6) we will always mean a solution in the sense specified above.

For the well-posedness in a classical sense of the same problem (with stronger assumptions on the data) see [4].

In this paper we will consider homogenization of problem (1.1)-(1.6) when $r_{\epsilon} \ll \epsilon$ ; our results extend to our nonstandard parabolic case the results obtained by [3] in the elliptic case and thus some of our arguments era strictly analogous to the corresponding ones in [3]. We also recall papers [2], [7] in which a model similar to problem (1.1)-(1.6) is studied in the context of different physical situations.

For a more complete bibliography, the reader can refer to the literature mentioned in the papers [2], [3], [6], [7] quoted above.

## 2. Formulation of the auxiliary problems and statement of the results

We will consider the situation when $r_{\epsilon}/\epsilon \to 0$ , as $\epsilon \to 0$ . We introduce several parameters as follows. Let b be a constant such that $0<b \le n$ and let $\theta_{b,\epsilon} = r_{\epsilon}^{b}/\epsilon^{n}$ . Now we define $\theta_{b}$ , the "b-dimensional volume density of holes", by

$$\theta_{b} = \lim_{\epsilon \to 0} \theta_{b,\epsilon} \ , \quad 0 \le \theta_{b} \le +\infty \ . \tag{2.1}$$

Note that the notion of $\theta_{b}$ is analogous to the notion of the b-dimensional Hausdorff measure.

Now let us define auxiliary problems. First we denote by $B_1$ a ball of radius $\frac{1}{2}$ with a center at the center of the cube $]0,1[^{n}$. Obviously, $\bar{K}_0 \subset B_{\epsilon/r_{\epsilon}}$ (ball with the same center but with radius $\epsilon/r_{\epsilon}$). We define the $H^1$-capacity of the $A \subset B$ in $\mathbb{R}^n$ by

$$\mathrm{cap}(A,B) = \inf_{v} \left\{ \int_{\mathbb{R}^n} |\nabla v|^2 \, dy \ , \ \forall v \in H_0^1(B) \ , \ v \equiv 1 \text{ on } A \text{ in the } H^1\text{-sense} \right\}$$

and set

$$\mathrm{cap}_{\epsilon} = \mathrm{cap}(K_0, B_{\epsilon/r_{\epsilon}}) \ . \tag{2.2}$$

Note that for $n \ge 3$ , $0<C_1 \le \mathrm{cap}_{\epsilon} \le C_2<+\infty$ and for $n = 2$ , $\mathrm{cap}_{\epsilon}$ is equivalent to $2\pi/\log \frac{\epsilon}{r_{\epsilon}}$ . We denote by $\psi_{\epsilon}$ the capacity potential of $K_0$ in $B_{\epsilon/r_{\epsilon}}$.

Then $\psi_\epsilon$ satisfies

$$\begin{aligned} & -\Delta\psi_\epsilon = 0 && \text{in } B_{\epsilon/r_\epsilon}\backslash\overline{K}_0 , \\ & \psi_\epsilon = 0 && \text{on } \partial B_{\epsilon/r_\epsilon} , \\ & \psi_\epsilon = 1 && \text{on } \partial K_0 , \\ & \psi_\epsilon \in H^1 (B_{\epsilon/r_\epsilon}) . \end{aligned} \tag{2.3}$$

Our auxiliary parabolic problems are to be the analogue of the elliptic ones from [3], pages 642-645.

For $x \in B_\epsilon$ we set

$$w_\epsilon(x,t) = \psi_\epsilon\left(\frac{x}{r_\epsilon}\right) e^{-\Lambda_\epsilon t} , \tag{2.4}$$

$$\Lambda_\epsilon = kC^\epsilon r_\epsilon^{n-2} \mathrm{cap}_\epsilon , \tag{2.5}$$

and extend $w_\epsilon$ by periodicity of period $\epsilon\mathbb{Z}^n$ to obtain an element of $H^1_{loc}(\mathbb{R}^n)$ , still denoted by $w_\epsilon$ , which satisfies

$$\begin{aligned} & -k\Delta w_\epsilon = 0 && \text{in } \bigcup_{i \in \mathbb{Z}^n} \{B^i_\epsilon\backslash\overline{T}^i_{r_\epsilon}\} , \\ & w_\epsilon = 0 && \text{in } \mathbb{R}^n\backslash \bigcup_{i \in \mathbb{Z}^n} B^i_\epsilon , \\ & \int_{\partial T^i_{r_\epsilon}} \left(\frac{1}{C^\epsilon r_\epsilon^{n-1} \, |\partial T^i_{r_\epsilon}|} \frac{\partial w_\epsilon}{\partial t} + k\frac{\partial w_\epsilon}{\partial \nu}\right) d\sigma = 0 \quad \forall i \in \mathbb{Z}^n , \\ & w_\epsilon \text{ depends just on t on each } \partial T^i_{r_\epsilon}, i \in \mathbb{Z}^n , \\ & w_\epsilon(x,0) = 1 \quad \text{on } \partial T^i_{r_\epsilon} . \end{aligned} \tag{2.6}$$

Now let us formulate our conditions on the size of the holes. The most interesting case is

$$C^\epsilon = C_0\epsilon^{-n} ; \quad \Lambda_\epsilon = \frac{r_\epsilon^{n-2}}{\epsilon^n} \mathrm{cap}_\epsilon \, C_0 \to \alpha \quad \text{as } \epsilon \to 0 , \quad \text{where } 0 \leq \alpha < +\infty . \tag{2.7}$$

In order to simplify the proof, we also suppose

$$u_{0\epsilon} = 0 \quad \text{on } T^i_{r_\epsilon}, \quad i \in \{1,\dots,N_\epsilon\} \tag{2.8}$$

$$\tilde{u}_{0\epsilon} \rightarrow u_0 \quad \text{weakly in } L^2(\Omega).$$

Concerning $f_\epsilon$ , we suppose

$$f_\epsilon \rightarrow f \quad \text{weakly in } L^2(0,T). \tag{2.9}$$

We will prove the following result.

**THEOREM** 2.1. Let $u^\epsilon$ be a solution to problem (1.1)-(1.6) and let (2.7), (2.8) and (2.9) hold true.

Furthermore, let $u^*$ be a unique solution to the problem

$$\frac{\partial u^*}{\partial t} - k\Delta u^* + \alpha u^* - c_0\, \alpha^2 e^{-c_0 \alpha t} * u^* = \alpha \int_0^t f\, d\tau - c_0\, \alpha^2 e^{-c_0 \alpha t} * \int_0^t f\, d\tau \qquad \text{in } \Omega x(0,T)$$

$$u^*(x,) = u_0 \qquad \text{in } \Omega , \tag{2.10}$$

$$u^* = 0 \qquad \text{on } \partial\Omega x(0,T) .$$

Then

$$\tilde{u}^\epsilon \rightarrow u^* \quad \text{weakly} \quad \text{in } L^2(0,T;\, H^1_0(\Omega)) , \tag{2.11}$$

$$\tilde{u}^\epsilon \overset{*}{\rightarrow} u^* \quad \text{weak}^* \quad \text{in } L^\infty(0,T;\, L^2(\Omega)) , \tag{2.12}$$

$$\int_0^t \tilde{u}^\epsilon\, d\tau \rightarrow \int_0^t u^*\, d\tau \qquad \text{in } C([0,T];\, L^2(\Omega)). \tag{2.13}$$

Note that '$*$' denotes the time convolution,

$$z*w(t) = \int_0^t z(t-\tau)\, w(\tau) d\tau ,$$

and $\tilde{u}^\epsilon = P^\epsilon u^\epsilon$ where $P^\epsilon$ is the extension operator from $\Omega \backslash T_\epsilon$ to $\Omega$ , see [2].

## 3. Auxiliary results

In this section we consider the behavior of solution to (2.6) when $\epsilon \to 0$ .

We start by proving two propositions (which correspond to Proposition 3.2 of [3]). The first result does not make use of the assumption (2.7).

**PROPOSITION 3.1** : Let $C^\epsilon = C_0 \epsilon^{-q}$ with $q \geq n$ and let $w_\epsilon$ be given by (2.4). Then $w_\epsilon \to 0$ weakly in $L^2(0,T;H^1_{loc}(\mathbb{R}^n))$ . Furthermore, if we suppose

$$C^\epsilon = C_0 \epsilon^{-q}, \quad q \geq n \text{ and } \Lambda_\epsilon = C^\epsilon r_\epsilon^{n-2} \operatorname{cap}_\epsilon \to 0 , \tag{3.1}$$

as $\epsilon \to 0$ , then $w_\epsilon \to 0$ in $L^2(0,T;H^1_{loc}(\mathbb{R}^n))$ . Similarily, the same statement holds if we suppose $q > n$ instead of (3.1).

PROOF: We have

$$k \int_0^t \int_{B^i_\epsilon \setminus \bar{T}^i_{r_\epsilon}} |\nabla w_\epsilon|^2 \, dx \, d\tau = \frac{1}{2C^\epsilon} \left(1 - e^{-2\Lambda_\epsilon t}\right).$$

Let us choose any bounded domain $O$ . Then

$$k \int_0^t \int_O |\nabla w_\epsilon|^2 \, dx \, d\tau = \frac{|O| \epsilon^{-n}}{2C^\epsilon} \left(1 - e^{-2\Lambda_\epsilon t}\right) + R_\epsilon, \tag{3.2}$$

where $R_\epsilon$ is higher order in $\epsilon$ . At this point, the inequality

$$0 \leq w_\epsilon(x,t) \leq e^{-\Lambda_\epsilon t} \leq 1$$

allows us to use the arguments of [3] (page 8, proof of Proposition3.4) to conclude the proof.

Q.E.D.

The second result uses the assumption (2.7):

**PROPOSITION 3.2:** Let us assume that

$$\frac{r_\epsilon^{n-2}}{\epsilon^n} \operatorname{cap}_\epsilon \leq C \quad . \tag{3.3}$$

Then $w_\epsilon \to 0$ weakly in $L^2(0,T;H^1_{loc}(\mathbb{R}^n))$. Furthermore, let us assume

$$\frac{r_\epsilon^{n-2}}{\epsilon^n} \, cap_\epsilon \to 0 \,, \quad \text{as } \epsilon \to 0 \,. \tag{3.4}$$

Then $w_\epsilon \to 0$ in $L^2(0,T;H^1_{loc}(\mathbb{R}^n))$ .

PROOF: We just use the equality

$$\frac{\epsilon^{-n}}{C^\epsilon}\left(1 - e^{-2\Lambda_\epsilon t}\right) = \frac{r_\epsilon^{n-2} \, cap_\epsilon}{\epsilon^n} \, \frac{1 - e^{-2\Lambda_\epsilon t}}{2\Lambda_\epsilon}$$

and the inequality $\frac{1-e^{-x}}{x} \le 1$ for $x>0$ . The rest is the same as in the proof of PROPOSITION 3.1

Q.E.D.

Now we consider the convergence of measures supported on $\bigcup_{i \in \mathbb{Z}^n} B^i_\epsilon$ . Set $\beta_\epsilon = \bigcup_{i \in \mathbb{Z}^n} B^i_\epsilon$ and

$$\mu^*_\epsilon = -k \frac{\partial w_\epsilon}{\partial \nu} \Big|_{\partial \beta_\epsilon} \delta_{\partial \beta_\epsilon} \,, \tag{3.5}$$

where $\delta$ denotes the $n-1$-dimensional surface measure. As in the time-independent case ([3], pages 645-646), we investigate the strong compactness of $\mu^*_\epsilon$ in $H^{-1}(\Omega)$ for fixed $t \in [0,T]$ . Note that

$$\mu^*_\epsilon(t) = -e^{-\Lambda_\epsilon t} \, k \, \frac{\partial \psi_\epsilon\left(\frac{x}{r_\epsilon}\right)}{\partial \nu} \Big|_{\partial \beta_\epsilon} \delta_{\partial \beta_\epsilon} \,.$$

**PROPOSITION 3.3:** Let us assume that

$$e^{-\Lambda_\epsilon t} \, \frac{\epsilon^{-n} \Lambda_\epsilon}{C^\epsilon} \le C \quad \left(\text{i.e. } \frac{r_\epsilon^{n-2}}{\epsilon^n} \, cap_\epsilon \, e^{-\Lambda_\epsilon t} \le C\right) \quad \forall t \,. \tag{3.6}$$

Then $\{\mu^*_\epsilon(t)\}$ is a compact set of $H^{-1}(\Omega)$, $\forall t \in [0,T]$.

Furthermore, if there exists $\alpha > 0$ such that

$$\frac{r_\epsilon^{n-2}}{\epsilon^n} \, cap_\epsilon = \frac{\epsilon^{-n} \Lambda_\epsilon}{C^\epsilon} \to \alpha \tag{3.7}$$

and

$$\Lambda_\epsilon = C^\epsilon r_\epsilon^{n-2} \, cap_\epsilon \to c_0 \, \alpha \quad , \quad \text{as} \ \ \epsilon \to 0, \tag{3.8}$$

then

$$\mu_\epsilon^*(t) \to \alpha \, e^{-\alpha c_0 t} \, dx \quad \text{strongly in} \ \ H^{-1}(\Omega), \ \ \forall t \in [0,T]. \tag{3.9}$$

PROOF: We follow the proof from [3], pages 645-646. The only difference in proving the first part of PROPOSITION 3.3 is that we have $e^{-\Lambda_\epsilon t}$ instead of their $\lambda_\epsilon$.

The second assertion of PROPOSITION 3.3 is somewhat more complicated. We need make an explicit calculation:

$$\int_\Omega d\mu_\epsilon^* = \frac{1}{|\Omega|} \int_{\partial\beta_\epsilon} -k \frac{\partial w_\epsilon}{\partial \nu} \, d\sigma = \frac{\epsilon^{-n}(1+O(1))}{|\Omega|} \int_{r_\epsilon \partial K_0} k \frac{\partial w_\epsilon}{\partial \nu} \, d\sigma =$$

$$\frac{\epsilon^{-n}(1+O(1))}{|\Omega|} \ (-1) \int_{r_\epsilon \partial K_0} \frac{1}{C^\epsilon r_\epsilon^{n-1} |\Sigma|} \ \frac{\partial w_\epsilon}{\partial t} \ d\sigma =$$

$$= \frac{\epsilon^{-n}(1+O(1))}{|\Omega|} \ (-1) \ \frac{1}{C^\epsilon r_\epsilon^{n-1} |\Sigma|} \ \Lambda_\epsilon \, e^{-\Lambda_\epsilon t} \, r_\epsilon^{n-1} |\Sigma| = \frac{\epsilon^{-n}(1+O(1))}{|\Omega|} \, e^{-\Lambda_\epsilon t} \frac{\Lambda_\epsilon}{C^\epsilon} \ ,$$

which implies $\mu^* = \alpha \, e^{-c_0 \alpha t} dx|_\Omega$ .

Q.E.D.

## 4. Proof of THEOREM 2.1

We start recalling, without proof, the so-called first a-priori estimate for problem (1.1)-(1.6).

**LEMMA 4.1:** Let $u^\epsilon$ be a weak solution for (1.1)-(1.6).

Then we have

$$k \, \| \nabla u^\epsilon \|^2_{L^2(0,T;L^2(\Omega^\epsilon)^n)} + \tfrac{1}{2} \, \| u^\epsilon \|^2_{L^\infty(0,T;L^2(\Omega^\epsilon))} +$$

$$+ \frac{1}{4C^\epsilon r_\epsilon^{n-1} |\Sigma|} \sup_{0 \le t \le T} \sum_{i=1}^{N_\epsilon} \int_{\partial T^i_{r_\epsilon}} |u^\epsilon(t)|^2 \, d\sigma \le \frac{C'T}{C^\epsilon \epsilon^n} \int_0^T |f_\epsilon(t)|^2 \, dt + \tag{4.1}$$

$$+ \tfrac{1}{2} \| u_{0\epsilon} \|^2_{L^2(\Omega^\epsilon)} + \frac{1}{2C^\epsilon r_\epsilon^{n-1} |\Sigma|} \sum_{i=1}^{N_\epsilon} \int_{\partial T^i_{r_\epsilon}} |u_{0\epsilon}|^2 \, d\sigma$$

Next, we have

**LEMMA 4.2.:** Let all assumptions from THEOREM 2.1 hold and let $u^\epsilon$ be a weak solution for (1.1)-(1.6). Then there exists a subsequence of $\{\bar{u}^\epsilon\}$, again denoted by $\{\bar{u}^\epsilon\}$, and a function $u^* \in L^2(0,T;H^1{}_0(\Omega)) \bigcap L^\infty(0,T;L^2(\Omega))$ such that

$$\tilde{u}^\epsilon \to u^* \text{ weakly} \quad \text{in } L^2(0,T;\, H^1_0(\Omega)) , \tag{4.2}$$

$$\tilde{u}^\epsilon \overset{*}{\to} u^* \text{ weak*} \quad \text{in } L^\infty(0,T;\, L^2(\Omega)) , \tag{4.3}$$

$$\int_0^t \tilde{u}^\epsilon \, d\tau \to \int_0^t u^* \, d\tau \quad \text{in } C([0,T];\, L^2(\Omega)), \text{ as } \epsilon\to 0. \tag{4.4}$$

PROOF: This is an immediate consequence of LEMMA 4.1.

Q.E.D.

Now, we prove

**LEMMA 4.3.:** Let all assumptions from THEOREM 2.1. hold true. Let $w_\epsilon$ be defined by (2.6) and let $\phi$ be an approximation for $\phi_\epsilon \in H^1_0(\Omega)$ in $E^\epsilon$. Then

$$k \int_\Omega \nabla \int_0^t \tilde{w}_\epsilon * \nabla \int_0^t \tilde{u}^\epsilon \phi_\epsilon + \frac{1}{C^\epsilon r_\epsilon^{n-1} |\Sigma|} \sum_{i=1}^{N_\epsilon} \int_{\partial T^i_{r_\epsilon}} \phi_\epsilon (w_\epsilon(t) - 1) *$$
$$* \int_0^t \left( u^\epsilon - \int_0^\tau f_\epsilon \right) \to \int_\Omega \phi \frac{\phi}{c_0} (1 - e^{-\alpha c_0 t}) * \int_0^t \left( u^* - \int_0^\tau f_\epsilon \right). \tag{4.5}$$

Here '$*$' denotes the time convolution.

PROOF: We start by using $\phi_\epsilon \int_0^t \left( u^\epsilon - \int_0^\tau f_\epsilon \right)$ as a test function for problem (2.6). Then we get

$$k \int_\Omega \int_0^t \nabla \tilde{w}_\epsilon * \int_0^t \left( \tilde{u}^\epsilon - \int_0^\tau f_\epsilon \right) \nabla \phi_\epsilon + k \int_\Omega \nabla \int_0^t \tilde{w}_\epsilon * \nabla \int_0^t \tilde{u}^\epsilon \phi_\epsilon +$$

$$+\frac{1}{C^\epsilon r_\epsilon^{n-1}|\Sigma|}\sum_{i=1}^{N_\epsilon}\int_{\partial T^i_{r_\epsilon}}\phi_\epsilon[w_\epsilon(t)-1]*\int_0^t\left(\tilde{u}^\epsilon-\int_0^\tau f_\epsilon\right)=$$

$$=k\int_{\beta_\epsilon}\int_0^t\frac{\partial w_\epsilon}{\partial\nu}*\int_0^t\left(\tilde{u}^\epsilon-\int_0^\tau f_\epsilon\right)\phi_\epsilon=<-\int_0^t\mu_\epsilon^**\int_0^t\left(\tilde{u}^\epsilon-\int_0^\tau f_\epsilon\right),\phi_\epsilon>$$

Now let us recall that $\phi_\epsilon\to\phi$ in $H_0^1(\Omega)$ (see [3] or [5]). Using that result, (2.4) and PROPOSITION 3.1, we get

$$k\int_\Omega\nabla\int_0^t\tilde{w}_\epsilon*\int_0^t\left(\tilde{u}^\epsilon-\int_0^\tau f_\epsilon\right)\nabla\phi_\epsilon\to 0\quad,\quad\text{as }\epsilon\to 0. \tag{4.6}$$

$$<\int_0^t\mu_\epsilon^*(\tau)*\int_0^t\left(\tilde{u}^\epsilon-\int_0^\tau f_\epsilon\right),\phi_\epsilon>\to\int_\Omega\left(\int_0^t\alpha e^{-\alpha c_0\tau}*\int_0^t\left(u^*-\int_0^\tau f\right)\right)\phi=$$
$$=\int_\Omega\frac{\phi}{c_0}[1-e^{-\alpha c_0 t}]*\int_0^t\left(u^*-\int_0^\tau f\right)\qquad\text{for }\alpha>0. \tag{4.7}$$

Now (4.6) and (4.7) imply (4.5).

Q.E.D.

We also have

**LEMMA 4.4.:** Let all assumptions from THEOREM 2.1 hold true. Then

$$\frac{1}{C^\epsilon r_\epsilon^{n-1}|\Sigma|}\sum_{i=1}^{N_\epsilon}\int_{\partial T^i_{r_\epsilon}}\phi_\epsilon*\int_0^t\left(u^\epsilon-\int_0^\tau f_\epsilon\right)\to-\int_\Omega\frac{\phi}{c_0}[1-e^{-\alpha c_0 t}]*\int_0^t\left(u^*-\int_0^\tau f\right) \tag{4.8}$$

as $\epsilon\to 0$ .

PROOF: We start by using $\phi_\epsilon\int_0^t w_\epsilon$ as a test function for problem (1.1)-(1.6). Then we get

$$k\int_\Omega\nabla\int_0^t\tilde{u}^\epsilon*\nabla\int_0^t\tilde{w}^\epsilon\phi_\epsilon+k\int_\Omega\nabla\int_0^t\tilde{u}^\epsilon*\int_0^t\tilde{w}_\epsilon\nabla\phi_\epsilon+$$

$$\int_\Omega \chi_{\Omega^\epsilon}\ u^\epsilon * \int_0^t w_\epsilon\ \phi_\epsilon\ -\ \int_\Omega \chi_{\Omega^\epsilon}\, u_{0\epsilon} * \int_0^t w_\epsilon\ \phi_\epsilon\ + \tag{4.9}$$

$$+\ \frac{1}{C^\epsilon r_\epsilon^{n-1}\,|\Sigma|}\ \sum_{i=1}^{N_\epsilon} \int_{\partial T^i_{r_\epsilon}} (u^\epsilon - u_{0\epsilon}) * \int_0^t w_\epsilon\ \phi_\epsilon\ =$$

$$=\ \frac{1}{C^\epsilon r_\epsilon^{n-1}\,|\Sigma|} \int_0^t f_\epsilon * \sum_{i=1}^{N_\epsilon} \int_{\partial T^i_{r_\epsilon}} \phi_\epsilon \int_0^t w_\epsilon\ -\ \int_\Omega \chi_{\Omega^\epsilon} \int_0^t f_\epsilon * \int_0^t w_\epsilon \phi_\epsilon\ .$$

Because of PROPOSITION 3.2, we have

$$k \int_\Omega \nabla \int_0^t \tilde{u}^\epsilon * \int_0^t \tilde{w}^\epsilon\ \nabla\phi_\epsilon \to 0\ . \tag{4.10}$$

A simple corollary of estimates in the proof of PROPOSITION 3.1 is the estimate

$$\frac{1}{C^\epsilon r_\epsilon^{n-1}\,|\Sigma|}\ \sum_{i=1}^{N_\epsilon} \int_{\partial T^i_{r_\epsilon}} w_\epsilon^2(t)\ \le\ \frac{C'}{C^\epsilon \epsilon^n}\ .$$

PROPOSITION 3.1 also implies

$$\int_\Omega \chi_{\Omega^\epsilon}\ u^\epsilon * \int_0^t w_\epsilon\ \psi_\epsilon \to 0 \tag{4.11}$$

and

$$\int_\Omega \chi_{\Omega^\epsilon}\ u_{0\epsilon} * \int_0^t w_\epsilon\ \psi_\epsilon \to 0 \tag{4.12}$$

as $\epsilon \to 0$ .

Now (4.10), (4.11), (4.12) and PROPOSITION 3.3 imply (4.8), i.e.

$$\frac{1}{C^\epsilon r_\epsilon^{n-1}\,|\Sigma|}\ \sum_{i=1}^{N_\epsilon} \int_{\partial T^i_{r_\epsilon}} \psi_\epsilon * \int_0^t \left(u^\epsilon - \int_0^\tau f_\epsilon\right) \to \int_\Omega \frac{\psi}{c_0}\ [1\ e^{-\alpha c_0 t}] * \int_0^t \left(u^* - \int_0^\tau f\right)$$

Q.E.D.

Now we can prove THEOREM 2.1. We consider the integrated problem (1.1)-(1.6) with $t\phi_\epsilon$ as a test function, i.e.

$$\int_{\Omega^\epsilon} (u^\epsilon - u_{0\epsilon}) * t\phi_\epsilon + \frac{1}{C^\epsilon r_\epsilon^{n-1} |\Sigma|} \sum_{i=1}^{N_\epsilon} \int_{\partial T^i_{r_\epsilon}} \left(u^\epsilon - \int_0^t f_\epsilon\right) * t\phi_\epsilon +$$

$$+ k \int_{\Omega^\epsilon} \nabla \int_0^t u^\epsilon * t\nabla\phi_\epsilon = 0 .$$

Note that LEMMA 4.4 allows us to limit the boundary term. Other terms are simple. We get

$$\int_\Omega \phi * \int_0^t (u^* - u_0) + \frac{1}{c_0} \int_\Omega \phi\, (1 - e^{-\alpha c_0 t}) * \int_0^t \left(u^* - \int_0^\tau f\right) +$$

$$+ k \int_\Omega \nabla \int_0^t u^* * t\nabla\phi = 0 \quad \text{, i.e.}$$

$$\int_\Omega \phi * \left\{\int_0^t u^* - tu_0\right\} + \frac{\phi}{c_0} (1 - e^{-\alpha c_0 t}) * \int_0^t \left(u^* - \int_0^\tau f\right) - \phi * k\, \Delta \int_0^t \int_0^\tau u^* = 0.$$

This implies

$$- k\Delta \int_0^t u^* + u^* - u_0 + \alpha e^{-\alpha c_0 t} * \left(u^* - \int_0^t f\right) = 0 \qquad \text{in } H^{-1}(\Omega)$$

and finally

$$\frac{\partial u^*}{\partial t} - k\Delta u^* + \alpha u^* - \alpha^2 c_0 e^{-\alpha c_0 t} * u^* = \alpha \int_0^t f - \alpha^2 c_0 e^{-\alpha c_0 t} * \int_0^t f$$

This concludes the proof of Theorem 2.1.

Q.E.D.

## REFERENCES


[1] H. S. Carslaw, J. C. Jaeger: Conduction of Heat in Solids, Clarendon Press, Oxford, 1959.

[2] D. Cioranescu, J. Saint Jean Paulin: Homogenization in Open Sets with Holes, J. Math. Anal. Appl. 71 (1979), 590-607.

[3] A. Damlamian, P. Donato: Homogenization with small perforations of increasingly complicated shapes, SIAM J. Math. Anal. 22 (1991), 639-652.

[4] R. Gianni: Well-posedness of initial-boundary value problems for parabolic equations under a class of non-local boundary conditions, to appear.

[5] S. Kaizu: Behavior of solutions of the Poisson equation under fragmentation of the boundary of the domain, Japan J. Appl. Math. 7 (1990), 77-102.

[6] A. Mikelič, M. Primicerio: Homogenization of the heat equation for a domain with a network of pipes with a well-mixed fluid, to appear.

[7] J. Saint Jean Paulin: Etude de quelques problèmes de mécanique et d'electrotechnique liés aux methodes d'homogenisation, Thèse d' Etat, Université P. et M. Curie, Paris 1981.



Andro Mikelič - Rudjer Boscovic Intitute,
P.O. Box 1016 - 41001 Zagreb, Croatia,
Yugoslavia.

Mario Primicerio - Dipartimento di Matematica "U. Dini"
Viale Morgagni 67/A - 50134 Firenze,
Italia.

F NATAF

# Paraxial approximations of the steady advection-diffusion equation. Padé approximants for operators

## 1. Introduction

The purpose of this paper is to propose a paraxial (or parabolic) approximation of the steady advection-diffusion equation (i.e. an equation which is an evolution equation in the direction x),

$$\mathcal{L}(u) = a(y)\frac{\partial u}{\partial x} - \nu\left(\frac{\partial^2 u}{\partial x^2} + \frac{\partial^2 u}{\partial y^2}\right) = 0 \qquad x \geq 0\,,\ y \in \mathbf{R} \quad a(y) \geq \alpha > 0 \tag{1}$$

$$u(0,y) = u_o(y) \ \text{ at } x=0 \quad \text{and} \quad u \text{ is bounded at infinity.} \tag{2}$$

when the positive advection coefficient a depends only on the direction perpendicular to the advection term. It is a generalization of the case where a is a constant which has been considered in [8]. This kind of approximations is motivated by numerical and physical reasons. Equation (1) is interesting in itself since it models for instance the concentration in pollutant or in colorant in natural environmental flows (see [1] and [3]). The advantage of paraxial approximations of (1) is to be solved faster than (1) and to demand less computer memory. It is also mathematically worth of interest since the related mathematical problem is the approximation of a pseudo-differential operator by a series of "fractions" of differential operators. This approximation is made for $\nu$ tending to zero and so also for small Fourier numbers k and is based on Padé approximants of the symbol (see §1).

More precisely, when a is a positive constant, it can be shown that u is also the solution to a parabolic equation in x,

$$\frac{\partial u}{\partial x} - \Lambda(u) = 0 \qquad x \geq 0\,,\ y \in \mathbf{R}$$

$$u(0,y) = u_o(y)$$

where $\Lambda$ is an operator in the y direction only and whose symbol is

$$\frac{a}{2\nu}\left(1 - \sqrt{1 + \frac{4\,k^2\,\nu^2}{a^2}}\right)$$

For small ν, this pseudo-differential operator is approximated by a series of "rational" operators $(\Lambda_n)_{n\geq 1}$ such that the problems

$$\frac{\partial u_n}{\partial x} - \Lambda_n(u_n) = 0 \qquad x \geq 0\,,\ y \in \mathbf{R} \tag{3}$$

$$u_n(0,y) = u_o(y)$$

are well-posed. $u_n$ is an approximation to u in the sense that we have error estimates of the kind

$$\left\|\frac{\partial(u_n - u)}{\partial x}\right\|_{L^2(\mathbf{R}^2_+)} \leq C_n \left(\frac{\nu}{a}\right)^{2n+1/2} \left\|\frac{\partial^{2n+1} u_o}{\partial y^{2n+1}}\right\|_{L^2(\mathbf{R})}$$

where $C_n$ is a constant which depends only on n.

In §1, we recall the results of [8] in the case where a is a constant. Then a series of paraxial approximations is proposed in the case where a depends on y which is a generalization of the constant case. The difficulty comes from the arbitrariness of the generalization. In §2, we show that the proposed paraxial approximations are well-posed. For this, we use the Hille-Yosida theorem. In §3, we establish an error estimate which has the same order in ν than in the case where a is constant. In the latter case, the exact solution was directly compared to the approximate solution in the Fourier Variable. Here we do not know the exact solution, but instead we write a non homogeneous equation satisfied by the error, for which we obtain a priori estimates.

## 1. The approximants.

For a good understanding of the method, it is necessary to start with the case a constant. Let us write a series of parabolic approximations of the advection-diffusion equation (whose solution is unique) in the half-space $x \geq 0$,

$$a\frac{\partial u}{\partial x} - \nu\left(\frac{\partial^2 u}{\partial x^2} + \frac{\partial^2 u}{\partial y^2}\right) = 0 \qquad x \geq 0\,,\ y \in \mathbf{R} \tag{1.1}$$

$$u(0,y)=u_o(y) \text{ and u is bounded at infinity.} \tag{1.2}$$

Here, a is a positive constant. For this, we shall solve explicitly (1.1) on the Fourier line.

Notation: the partial Fourier transform in the y direction is used in an extensive manner. Let u(x,y) be a function or distribution depending on x and y, its partial Fourier transform with respect to y is denoted by û(x,k) where k is the dual variable of y. û will also be denoted by $\mathcal{F}(u)$ and $\mathcal{F}^{-1}(\hat{u}) = u$.

By Fourier transform in y, (1.1) is reduced to a linear differential equation in x:

$$a\,\hat{u}_x = \nu\left(\hat{u}_{xx} - k^2\hat{u}\right) \tag{1.3}$$

For a fixed k the solution to this differential equation can be written as $\alpha_+(k)\, e^{\lambda^+(k)\,x} + \alpha_-(k)\, e^{\lambda^-(k)\,x}$. $\lambda^{\pm}(k)$ are the roots of the characteristic polynomial,

$$\mathcal{P}(\lambda) = -\,a\,\lambda + \nu\lambda^2 - \nu\, k^2. \tag{1.4}$$

$$\lambda^+(k) = \frac{a}{2\nu}\left(1 + \sqrt{1 + \frac{4k^2\nu^2}{a^2}}\right) \geq 0 \quad \text{and} \quad \lambda^-(k) = \frac{a}{2\nu}\left(1 - \sqrt{1 + \frac{4k^2\nu^2}{a^2}}\right) \leq 0 \tag{1.5}$$

Since the solution is bounded at infinity, for any k, $\alpha_+(k) = 0$. Taking into account the boundary condition at x = 0, the solution û has the following form:

$$\hat{u}(x,k) = \hat{u}_o(k)\, e^{\lambda^-(k)\,x} \tag{1.6}$$

so that û is a solution to the following parabolic equation in x,

$$\frac{\partial \hat{u}}{\partial x} = \lambda^-(k)\,\hat{u}$$

This equation can not be interpreted in the physical space as a partial differential equation because of the square root in the expression of $\lambda^-(k)$. Nevertheless, for small ν it can be approximated by a partial differential equation as we shall see now. To design a series of approximations of increasing order, $\lambda^-(k)$ is approximated at an increasing order in ν by a series of rational fractions defined as follows (see [5] et [6]):

$$\lambda_1^-(k) = -\,\nu\, k^2$$

$$\lambda_{n+1}^-(k) = \frac{\nu\, k^2}{\nu\,\lambda_n^-(k) - a} \tag{1.7}$$

$\lambda_n^-$ is a Padé approximant of $\lambda^-$ in $\nu$ of order [n,n-1] when n is odd and of order [n-1,n-1] when n is even. We now consider the series of approximate problems, $\frac{\partial \hat{u}}{\partial x} = \lambda_n^-(k)\, \hat{u}$ . To ease their interpretation in terms of partial differential equations, we introduce two series of polynomials $P_n$ and $Q_n$ such that $\lambda_n^- = Q_n^{-1} P_n$. The polynomials $P_n$ and $Q_n$ are defined by

$$P_1(k) = -\nu k^2 \qquad\qquad P_{n+1} = -\nu k^2 Q_n$$

$$Q_1(k) = a \qquad\qquad Q_{n+1} = a Q_n - \nu k^2 P_n$$

The equation can be written as

$$Q_n(k) \frac{\partial \hat{u}}{\partial x} = P_n(k)\, \hat{u} \tag{1.8}$$

$P_n$ and $Q_n$ are polynomials in $k^2$. They can be considered as symbols of differential operators in the y direction. The orders of derivation are always even since the polynomial depends only on $k^2$. $P_n(-i\,\partial_y)$ and $Q_n(-i\,\partial_y)$ denote the related differential operators. The inverse Fourier transform of (1.8) gives:

$$Q_n(-i\,\partial_y) \frac{\partial u}{\partial x} - P_n(-i\,\partial_y)\, u = 0 \tag{1.9}$$

This is the paraxial approximation of (1). The polynomials have the following properties:

$$\forall\ n \geq 1\ \forall\ k,\ P_n(k) \leq 0 \text{ and } (P_n(k) = 0 \iff k = 0)$$

and $\quad \forall\ n \geq 1\ \forall\ k,\ \ Q_n(k) > 0$

thus, $\quad \forall\ n \geq 1\ \forall\ k,\ \ \lambda_n^-(k) \leq 0.$

$P_{2n-1}$ is of degree 2n in k and $Q_{2n-1}$ is of degree 2(n-1) in k. $P_{2n}$ is of degree 2n in k et $Q_{2n}$ is of degree 2n in k. The proof of these properties is easy and can be made by induction. $\lambda_n^-(k)$ is non positive as is $\lambda^-(k)$, which is fundamental for the solutions to be bounded at infinity (see [5] and [6]). Had we had taken, for instance, a Taylor expansion of order 2, it would not be the case and it would lead to ill-posed problems. We have the following error estimate

***Theorem 1.***

*Let* n *be a positive integer, there exists a constant* $C_n$ *(depending only on n) such that for any positive* $\nu$ *and for any* $u_o$ *in* $H^{2n+1}$,

$$\left\| \frac{\partial (u - u_n)}{\partial x} \right\|_{L^2(\mathbf{R}_+^2)} \leq C_n \left(\frac{\nu}{a}\right)^{2n+1/2} \left\| \frac{\partial^{2n+1} u_o}{\partial y^{2n+1}} \right\|_{L^2(\mathbf{R})} \tag{1.10}$$

*where* $u_n$ *is the solution to* (3) *and* u *is the solution to* (1).

The proof is not given here and can be found in [8]. It is based on a direct estimate of

$$\frac{\partial \hat{e}_n}{\partial x}(x,k) = \hat{u}_o(k)\,(\lambda^- e^{\lambda^- x} - \lambda_n^- e^{\lambda_n^- x})$$

We shall now extend the strategy when a depends on y.

Notations Let B denote the operator $-\dfrac{\partial^2}{\partial y^2}$ and A the operator of multiplication by a(y).

We can not use any more the Fourier transform to solve (1.1). We shall extend formula (1.7) by the following sequence of operators,

$$\Lambda_1 = -\nu A^{-1}B \qquad (1.11.a)$$

$$\Lambda_{n+1} = -\nu A^{-1}(I - \nu \Lambda_n A^{-1})^{-1} B \qquad (1.11.b)$$

It is obvious that (1.11) reduces to (1.7) when a is a constant.

Remark Definition (1.11) is of course arbitrary and we could have taken

$$\Lambda_1 = -\nu A^{-1}B$$

$$\Lambda_{n+1} = -\nu (I - \nu \Lambda_n A^{-1})^{-1} A^{-1} B$$

When a is a constant, we still have $\lambda_n^-(\partial_y) = \Lambda_n$. The choice made for $\Lambda_n$ will be justified in the next section, we shall show that the approximation of order n

$$\frac{\partial w_n}{\partial x} - \Lambda_n(w_n) = 0 \qquad (1.13)$$

$$w_n(0,y) = u_o(y)$$

is well-posed and in §3, we establish error estimates which are of the same order as when a is a constant.

## 2. Well-posedness of the associated problems.

Notations: Let (u,v) denote the $L^2$ scalar product integral on **R**.

**Hypothesis 1:** In the following, we make the following assumptions for a:

i) $a \in W^{\infty,\infty} = \{u \in L^\infty(\mathbf{R}) \,/\, \forall\, n \geq 1, \dfrac{\partial u^n}{\partial x^n} \in L^\infty(\mathbf{R})\}$

ii) There exists $\alpha$ in **R** such that for any y in **R**, $a(y) \geq \alpha > 0$.

## 2.1. Study of the operator $\Lambda_n$.

Let us give first a definition of $\Lambda_n$ which will be more suitable for the study of the n-th order approximation of order n. Instead of a direct study of $\Lambda_n$, which is not a differential operator, we study a sequence of differential operators $Q_n$ defined by:

$$\begin{aligned} Q_o &= I \\ Q_1 &= A \\ Q_{n+1} &= Q_n A + \nu^2 Q_{n-1} B \quad n \geq 1 \end{aligned} \tag{2.1}$$

$\Lambda_n$ has then the following expression,

$$\Lambda_n = - \nu Q_n^{-1} Q_{n-1} B \tag{2.2}$$

An accurate knowledge of $Q_n$ is necessary for (2.2) to define $\Lambda_n$ and to study the approximation (1.13).

***Lemma 1.***

$Q_n$ *is an operator from* $H^{m+\beta(n)}(\mathbf{R})$ *in* $H^m(\mathbf{R})$ *for any integer* m, *where*

$$\beta(n) = n \textit{ for even } n$$

$$\beta(n) = n-1 \textit{ for odd } n.$$

Proof From (2.1), it can be shown that $Q_n$ has the following expression

$$Q_n = \sum_{n \leq 2k \leq 2n} \quad \sum_{\substack{(i_1,\ldots,i_k) \\ \text{s.t} \\ \sum_{j=1}^{k} i_j = n-k,\ i_j=0 \text{ or } 1}} \quad \prod_{j=1}^{k} C^{i_j} \qquad \text{where } C^o = A \text{ and } C^1 = \nu^2 B \tag{2.3}$$

so that $Q_n$ is formally self-adjoint for the scalar product in $L^2$. For even n, the dominant term in $Q_n$ is $\nu^n B^{n/2} = \nu^n (-1)^{n/2} \frac{\partial^n}{\partial y^n}$ while for odd n, it is $\frac{n+1}{2} A \nu^{n-1} \frac{\partial^{n-1}}{\partial y^{n-1}}$. Hence, $Q_n$ is an operator from $H^{m+\beta(n)}$ in $H^m$ for any integer m. The Fourier symbol of $Q_n$, $SQ_n(y,k)$, depends in fact only on y and on $\nu^2 k^2$ and has the following strong property of global ellipticity

$\forall$ n $\exists C_{n1}, C_{n2} / \forall y \in \mathbf{R}$ $\quad C_{n1}(1+\nu|k|)^{\beta(n)} \leq SQ_n(y,k) \leq C_{n2}(1+\nu|k|)^{\beta(n)}$

We can apply results on pseudo-differential operators with small parameter (see e.g [10], [7]) and we have the

***Theorem 1.***

*Let* a *satisfying hypothesis* 1, *let* $n \geq 1$, *for sufficiently small* $\nu$, $Q_n$ *is a continuous invertible operator from* $H^{s+\beta(n)}$ *into* $H^s$ *for any real* s.

The dependance of $\beta(n)$ on the parity gives the

***Theorem 2.***

*For* n *even and sufficiently small* $\nu$, $\Lambda_n$ *is a continuous linear operator from* $H^s$ *to* $H^s$ *for any real* s. *For* n *odd and sufficiently small* $\nu$, $\Lambda_n$ *is a continuous linear operator from* $H^{s+2}$ *to* $H^s$ *for any real* s.

## 2.2. Well-posedness of the approximation of order n

The purpose of this section is to show that the problem

$$\frac{\partial w_n}{\partial x} - \Lambda_n(w_n) = 0 \tag{2.4}$$

$$w_n(0,y) = u_o(y)$$

is well posed. We want to use the Hille-Yosida thery on evolution problems. By using once more the results on pseudo-differential operators with small parameter we have that

$\forall n\ \forall \mu\ \exists \nu_o > 0$ / for any $0 < \nu < \nu_o$ $\ \mu - \Lambda_n$ is a maximal monotone operator from $H^s$ in $H^s$ for n even and from $H^{s+2} \subset H^s$ in $H^s$ for n odd.

Thus, problem (2.4) is well posed for $\nu$ small enough and $u_o$ regular enough. As for the decay at infinity it has to be proven directly on the equation and we have the

*Lemma 3.*

*For any* n *and for* $w_o$ *in* $H^{\frac{n+5}{2}}$ *for* n *odd and in* $H^{\frac{n}{2}}$ *for* $n \geq 4$ *even (for* $n = 2$ $w_o$ *is in* $H^2$*), the quantity*

$$\int_{\mathbf{R}} \left(\frac{\partial w_n}{\partial x}\right)^2 (x,y)\, dy \qquad x \geq 0$$

*tends to zero as* x *tends to infinity.*

Proof Apply to (2.4) the operator $Q_{n-1}^{-1} Q_n$ to get

$$Q_{n-1}^{-1} Q_n \frac{\partial w_n}{\partial x} + \nu\, B w_n = 0 \tag{2.6}$$

Multiply by $\frac{\partial w_n}{\partial x}$ and integrate by parts over x and y on $[0,X] \times \mathbf{R}$,

$$\int_{\mathbf{R}} \int_0^X Q_{n-1}^{-1} Q_n \frac{\partial w_n}{\partial x} \frac{\partial w_n}{\partial x} \leq \frac{\nu}{2} \int_{\mathbf{R}} \left(\frac{\partial w_o}{\partial y}\right)^2$$

Hence, by the symmetry of $Q_n$ for the $L^2$ norm,

$$\int_{\mathbf{R}} \int_0^X Q_{n-1} Q_{n-1}^{-1} \frac{\partial w_n}{\partial x}\; Q_n Q_{n-1}^{-1} \frac{\partial w_n}{\partial x} \leq \frac{\nu}{2} \int_{\mathbf{R}} \left(\frac{\partial w_o}{\partial y}\right)^2 \tag{2.7}$$

By arguing as for $q_n$, it is easy to show that what ever the parity of n is, there exists a constant $\delta$ such that for sufficiently small $\nu$,

$$\int_{\mathbf{R}} Q_n v\, Q_{n-1} v \geq \delta\, \|v\|_{H^{n-1}}$$

Then (2.7) yields,

$$\delta \int_0^X \left\|Q_{n-1} \frac{\partial w_n}{\partial x}\right\|_{H^{n-1}} dx \leq \frac{\nu}{2} \int_{\mathbf{R}} \left(\frac{\partial w_o}{\partial y}\right)^2 \tag{2.8}$$

When n is even, $Q_{n-1}$ is an invertible operator from $H^{n-1}$ to $H^1$. Thus there exists $\beta > 0$ such that

$$\delta\,\beta \int_0^X \| \frac{\partial w_n}{\partial x} \|_{H^1} dx \ \leq \frac{\nu}{2} \int_{\mathbf{R}} \left(\frac{\partial w_o}{\partial y}\right)^2$$

When n is odd, $Q_{n-1}$ is an invertible operator from $H^{n-1}$ to $L^2$. Thus there exists $\gamma > 0$ such that

$$\delta\,\gamma \int_0^X \| \frac{\partial w_n}{\partial x} \|_{L^2} dx \ \leq \frac{\nu}{2} \int_{\mathbf{R}} \left(\frac{\partial w_o}{\partial y}\right)^2$$

Finally, what ever the parity of n, $\frac{\partial w_n}{\partial x}$ belongs to $L^2(\mathbf{R}_+^2)$. In the same way, it can be proved that $\frac{\partial^2 w_n}{\partial x^2}$ belongs to $L^2(\mathbf{R}_+^2)$. Let f be the function defined by:

$$f: \mathbf{R}_+ \longrightarrow \mathbf{R}_+$$
$$x \longrightarrow \int_{\mathbf{R}} \left(\frac{\partial w_n}{\partial x}\right)^2 (x,y)\, dy$$

f and $\frac{\partial f}{\partial x}$ belong to $L^2(\mathbf{R}_+)$, thus f tends to zero as x tends to infinity.

Remark 3. The existence of a unique solution to (1) has been proved in [9] and we have

***Theorem 3.***

*Let* a *be satisfying hypothesis* 1, *for any* $u_o$ *belonging to* $H^{3/2}(\mathbf{R})$, *there exists a unqiue* u *such that* $\frac{\partial u}{\partial x}, \frac{\partial^2 u}{\partial x^2}, \frac{\partial^2 u}{\partial x \partial y}$ *and* $\frac{\partial^2 u}{\partial y^2}$ *belong to* $L^2(\mathbf{R})$ *and* u *is a solution to* (1).

The proof is not given here and is based on the results in [4].

## 3. Error estimates.

Let us recall the definition of the parabolic approximations,

$$\Lambda_o = 0 \tag{3.1.a}$$

$$\Lambda_{n+1} = -\nu\, A^{-1}(I - \nu\, \Lambda_n\, A^{-1})^{-1}\, B \tag{3.1.b}$$

$w_n$ is a solution to the approximate problem (2.4) with Dirichlet boundary condition $w_o$ and u is a solution to equation (1.1) with the same Dirichlet boundary condition $w_o$ . $e_n$ is the error u - $w_n$. Let us denote the operator $G_{n,\nu}$

$$G_{n,\nu} = \partial_y\Big(\prod_{j=1}^{n} Q_j^{-1} Q_{j-1} B\Big) = \partial_y Q_1^{-1} Q_o B Q_2^{-1} Q_1 B \ldots Q_n^{-1} Q_{n-1} B$$

***Theorem 1.***

*Let* a *be satisfying hypothesis* 1 *and let* $n \geq 1$; *there exists* $\nu_o > 0$ *such that for every* $w_o$ *in* $H^{2n+1}$, *we have for any* $\nu$ *in* $]0,\nu_o[$,

$$\iint \left( a \left(\frac{\partial e_n}{\partial x}\right)^2 + \nu^2 \frac{(\Delta e_n)^2}{a} \right) dx\, dy + \nu \int_R \left(\frac{\partial e_n}{\partial x}\right)^2 (0,y)\, dy \leq \frac{\nu^{4n+1}}{(\inf a)^{2n}} C(n,a) \, \|w_o\|^2_{H^{2n+1}} \qquad (3.2)$$

*where* C(n,a) *depends on* n *and on* a *and its derivatives.*

Remark: The error estimate is thus in $\nu^{4n+1}$, which identical to the case where a is constant.

Proof: In the case where a is a constant, we solve explicitly with Fourier transform both Eq. (1) and (3). Here the principle of the proof is to show that the error $e_n = u - w_n$ satisfies

$$A \frac{\partial e_n}{\partial x} - \nu \, \Delta \, e_n = \nu \, (\Lambda_{n-1} - \Lambda_n) \Lambda_n \, (w_n) \qquad (3.3)$$

and to use this equation to get error estimates.

***Lemma 1.***

*The error* $e_n$ *satisfies equation* (3.3) *for any* $n \geq 1$.

Proof:

We apply $\nu(\partial_x - \frac{A}{\nu} + \Lambda_n)$ to the operator $(\partial_x - \Lambda_n)$ and we evaluate the difference with $- A\partial_x + \nu \, \Delta$,

$$\nu(\partial_x - \frac{A}{\nu} + \Lambda_n) \circ (\partial_x - \Lambda_n) - (-A\partial_x + \nu \, \Delta) = \nu \, [\partial_{xx} - \frac{A}{\nu}\partial_x + \frac{A}{\nu}\Lambda_n - (\Lambda_n)^2] - [-A\partial_x + \nu \, \Delta]$$

By using expression (3.1.b) for $\Lambda_n$, we have

$$= \nu \, [B - (I - \nu \, \Lambda_{n-1} A^{-1})^{-1} B - \nu^2 (A^{-1}(I - \nu \, \Lambda_n A^{-1})^{-1} B)^2]$$
$$= \nu \, [(I - \nu \, \Lambda_{n-1} A^{-1})^{-1} (- \nu \, \Lambda_{n-1} A^{-1} B) - \nu^2 (A^{-1}(I - \nu \, \Lambda_n A^{-1})^{-1} B)^2]$$
$$= \nu \, [ - \nu \, \Lambda_{n-1} A^{-1}(I - \nu \, \Lambda_{n-1} A^{-1})^{-1} B - \nu^2 (A^{-1}(I - \nu \, \Lambda_n A^{-1})^{-1} B)^2]$$
$$= \nu \, [ \Lambda_{n-1} \Lambda_n - (\Lambda_n)^2] = \nu \, (\Lambda_{n-1} - \Lambda_n) \, \Lambda_n$$

Thus, $w_n$ is a solution to

$$(A \, \partial_x - \nu \, \Delta) \, (w_n) = - \nu \, ((\Lambda_{n-1} - \Lambda_n) \, \Lambda_n(w_n)$$

By subtracting

$$(A \, \partial_x - \nu \, \Delta) \, (u) = 0,$$

we have (3.3). We can now obtain our first error estimate.

***Lemma 2:***

*For any* n ≥ 1, *we have*

$$\iint a\left(\frac{\partial e_n}{\partial x}\right)^2 + \nu^2\frac{(\Delta e_n)^2}{a} + \nu\int_{\mathbf{R}}\left(\frac{\partial e_n}{\partial x}\right)^2(0,y) \leq \nu^2\iint \frac{1}{a}\left[(\Lambda_{n-1} - \Lambda_n)\Lambda_n(w_n)\right]^2 \tag{3.4}$$

Proof:

By taking the square of (3.3) and applying $A^{-1}$, we obtain

$$A\left(\frac{\partial e_n}{\partial x}\right)^2 - 2\nu\frac{\partial e_n}{\partial x}\Delta e_n + \nu^2 A^{-1}(\Delta e_n)^2 = \nu^2 A^{-1}\left[(\Lambda_{n-1} - \Lambda_n)\Lambda_n(w_n)\right]^2 \tag{3.5}$$

Thus by integrating by parts, we get (3.4).

To end the proof of theorem 1, the main difficulty is the evaluation of the right hand-side of (3.4) as a function of $w_o$. For this, an operator $D_n$ in the direction y (to be determined) is applied to (2.4)

$$\frac{\partial D_n(w_n)}{\partial x} - D_n\Lambda_n(w_n) = 0 \tag{3.6}$$

(3.6) is multiplied by $D_n(w_n)$ and is integrated by parts on the half-space

$$\frac{1}{2}\int_{\mathbf{R}}[D_n(w_o)]^2 \geq -\iint D_n\Lambda_n(w_n)\, D_n(w_n) \tag{3.7}$$

"Ideally", we wish to have $-{}^tD_n\, D_n\, \Lambda_n = {}^t\Lambda_n\, ({}^t\Lambda_{n-1} - {}^t\Lambda_n)\, A^{-1}\, (\Lambda_{n-1} - \Lambda_n)\, \Lambda_n$. In fact, even for n=1, we cannot get such an equality and we merely have

$$-{}^tD_1\, D_1\, \Lambda_1 = {}^t\Lambda_1\, {}^t\Lambda_1\, A\;\; \Lambda_1\, \Lambda_1 \text{ where } D_1 = \nu^{3/2}\frac{\partial}{\partial y}(A^{-1}B)$$

Nevertheless, we have the following result,

***Lemma 3:***

*There exist two operators* $D_n$ *and* $K_n$ *such that*

$$- {}^t D_n D_n = {}^t\Lambda_n ({}^t\Lambda_{n-1} - {}^t\Lambda_n) K_n (\Lambda_{n-1} - \Lambda_n)$$

(3.8)

*and then,*

$$\frac{1}{2}\int_R [D_n(w_o)]^2 \geq \int\int K_n(\Lambda_{n-1} - \Lambda_n)\Lambda_n(w_n) \cdot (\Lambda_{n-1} - \Lambda_n)\Lambda_n(w_n) \qquad (3.9)$$

Proof:

To show that $D_n$ exists, it is sufficient to prove that there exists $K_n$ such that the right hand-side of (3.8) is self-adjoint. The following relations will be needed:

$$\Lambda_{n-1} - \Lambda_n = - \nu A^{-1}(I - \nu \Lambda_{n-2} A^{-1})^{-1} (\Lambda_{n-1} - \Lambda_{n-2}) \Lambda_n \qquad (3.10)$$

$${}^t\Lambda_{n-1} - {}^t\Lambda_n = - \nu\, {}^t\Lambda_{n-1} ({}^t\Lambda_{n-1} - {}^t\Lambda_{n-2}) (I - \nu A^{-1}\, {}^t\Lambda_{n-1})^{-1} A^{-1} \qquad (3.11)$$

Their proof is straightforward by using definition (3.1).

Let us introduce $\mathcal{A}_n = {}^t\Lambda_n ({}^t\Lambda_{n-1} - {}^t\Lambda_n) K_n (\Lambda_{n-1} - \Lambda_n)$. With the help of (3.10) and (3.11), it is easy to see that

$\mathcal{A}_n = - \nu^{2n-2}\, {}^t\Lambda_n\, {}^t\Lambda_{n-1} \cdots {}^t\Lambda_1\; {}^t\Lambda_1(I - \nu A^{-1}\, {}^t\Lambda_1)^{-1} A^{-1} (I - \nu A^{-1}\, {}^t\Lambda_2)^{-1} A^{-1} \ldots (I - \nu A^{-1}\, {}^t\Lambda_{n-1})^{-1} A^{-1} K_n A^{-1} (I - \nu \Lambda_{n-2} A^{-1})^{-1} A^{-1} (I - \nu \Lambda_{n-3} A^{-1})^{-1} \ldots\ldots A^{-1} (I - \nu \Lambda_1 A^{-1})^{-1} A^{-1} \Lambda_1\Lambda_2 \ldots\ldots \Lambda_{n-1}\Lambda_n$.

For $\mathcal{A}_n$ to be self-adjoint, it is sufficient according to the previous expression that,

$${}^t\Lambda_1(I - \nu A^{-1}\, {}^t\Lambda_1)^{-1} A^{-1} \ldots (I - \nu A^{-1}\, {}^t\Lambda_{n-1})^{-1} A^{-1} K_n A^{-1} (I - \nu \Lambda_{n-2} A^{-1})^{-1} \ldots A^{-1} (I - \nu \Lambda_1 A^{-1})^{-1} A^{-1}$$

is self-adjoint (let us recall that ${}^t\Lambda_1 = - \nu B A^{-1}$). By setting

$$K_n = A (I - \nu A^{-1}\, {}^t\Lambda_{n-1})^{-1} A \ldots (I - \nu A^{-1}\, {}^t\Lambda_1)^{-1} A\; A(I - \nu \Lambda_1 A^{-1})^{-1} \ldots A(I - \nu \Lambda_{n-2} A^{-1})^{-1} A \qquad (3.12)$$

$\mathcal{A}_n$ is self-adjoint and has the following simple expression:

$$\mathscr{A}_n = \nu^{2n-1}\, {}^t\Lambda_n\, {}^t\Lambda_{n-1} \cdots {}^t\Lambda_1\, B\, \Lambda_1\Lambda_2 \cdots\cdots \Lambda_{n-1}\Lambda_n$$

and, we can set

$$D_n = \nu^{n-1/2}\, \partial_y\, \Lambda_1\Lambda_2 \cdots\cdots \Lambda_{n-1}\Lambda_n = \nu^{2n-1}\, G_{n,\nu} \tag{3.13}$$

where $G_{n,\nu}$ has been defined at the beginning of section 3. Estimate (3.9) comes from (3.7) and (3.13). To go on with the proof of theorem 1 we need

***Lemma 4.***

*For any* $n \geq 1$, *we have, for* $\nu$ *small enough*

$$\iint K_n(\Lambda_{n-1} - \Lambda_n)\Lambda_n(w_n) \times (\Lambda_{n-1} - \Lambda_n)\Lambda_n(w_n) \geq \frac{(\inf a)^{2n-1}}{2} \iint \left[(\Lambda_{n-1} - \Lambda_n)\Lambda_n(w_n)\right]^2 \tag{3.14}$$

Proof

Let us prove first that $K_n$ is a partial differential operator. Indeed, let study

$$n\geq 1 \quad R_n = (I - \nu\, \Lambda_o\, A^{-1})A(I - \nu\, \Lambda_1\, A^{-1})A(I - \nu\, \Lambda_2\, A^{-1}) \cdots\cdots A(I - \nu\, \Lambda_{n-1}\, A^{-1})A \tag{3.15}$$

$$(R_o = I)$$

We have

$$K_n = {}^tR_n\, R_{n-1}\,. \tag{3.16}$$

$R_n$ verifies an induction

$$\begin{aligned} R_{n+1} &= R_{n-1}\,(I - \nu\, \Lambda_{n-1}\, A^{-1})\, A\, (I - \nu\, \Lambda_n\, A^{-1})\, A \\ &= R_{n-1}\,(I - \nu\, \Lambda_{n-1}\, A^{-1})\, A\, (I + \nu^2\, A^{-1}(I - \nu\, \Lambda_n\, A^{-1})^{-1} B A^{-1})\, A \\ &= R_n\, A + \nu^2\, R_{n-1} B \end{aligned}$$

Since $R_1 = A$ and $R_2 = A^2 + \nu^2 B$, it is clear from the induction that $R_n$ equals $Q_n$ (see (2.1)) for any n. By global ellipticity, we have, for $\nu$ small enough, that

$$(K_n u,u) \geq \frac{1}{2} \int_{\mathbf{R}} A^{2n-1} u^2 \geq \frac{(\inf a)^{2n-1}}{2} \int_{\mathbf{R}} u^2$$

so that lemma 4 is proved. Then, (3.4) and (3.9) yield

$$\int\int a\left(\frac{\partial e_n}{\partial x}\right)^2 + \nu^2\frac{(\Delta e_n)^2}{a} + \nu\int_{\mathbf{R}}\left(\frac{\partial e_n}{\partial x}\right)^2(0,y) \leq \frac{\nu^{4n+1}}{(\inf a)^{2n}}\int\left(\partial_y Q_1^{-1}Q_o B Q_2^{-1}Q_1 B \ldots Q_n^{-1}Q_{n-1}B(w_o)\right)^2$$

To end the proof of theorem 1, we need the

***Lemma 5.***

*There exists a constant* C(n,a) (*independent of* $\nu$) *which depends on* n *and on* a *and its derivatives such that for* $\nu$ *small enough,*

$$\int\left(\partial_y Q_1^{-1}Q_o B Q_2^{-1}Q_1 B \ldots Q_n^{-1}Q_{n-1}B(w_o)\right)^2 \leq C(n,a)\,\|w_o\|^2_{H^{2n+1}}$$

Proof: It is based on results on commutators of pseudo-differential operators with small parameter. Let F be a pseudo-differential operator with small parameter of non positive order, then

$$[\partial_y,F] = \frac{1}{\nu}\,[\nu\partial_y,F] = M$$

where M is also a pseudo-differential operator with small parameter whose norm as a continuous operator from $L^2$ in $L^2$ is bounded independtly of $\nu$ for $\nu$ small enough.

Since $Q_i^{-1}Q_{i-1}$ is an operator of order 0 or -2 according to the parity of i, we can use this property to transfer the derivatives in y to the right and finally get lemma 5. For instance, we can write

$$BQ_n^{-1}Q_{n-1} = -\,\partial_y\,Q_n^{-1}Q_{n-1}\,\partial_y + \partial_y\,M_o = Q_n^{-1}Q_{n-1}\,B + M_1\,\partial_y + M_o\,\partial_y + M_2$$

where $M_i$ denotes a pseudo-differential operator with small parameter of order 0.

Acknowledgments: I wish to acknowledge the advices and encouragements of L.Halpern and the help of B.Helffer.

## References

[1] G.K.Batchelor, *An Introduction to fluid dynamic* (Cambridge University Press, 1967).

[2] H.Brezis, *Analyse fonctionnelle. Théorie et applications* (Masson, 1983).

[3] P.C.Chatwin et C.M.Allen, Mathematical models of dispersion in rivers and estuaries, *Ann. Rev. Mech. 17* (1985) 119-149.

[4] D.Gilbarg et N.S.Trudinger, *Elliptic Partial Differential Equations of Second Order* (Springer-Verlag, 1983).

[5] L.Halpern, Artificial Boundary Conditions for the Advection-Diffusion Equation, *Math of Comp. 46*, Number 174, (1986) 425-438.

[6] L.Halpern et M.Schatzman, Artificial Boundary Conditions for Incompressible Viscous Flows, *SIAM J. Math. Analysis 20*, n° 2, (1989) 308-354.

[7] B.Helffer, *Théorie spectrale pour des opérateurs globalement elliptiques,* Astérisque 112, (SMF, 1984)

[8] F.Nataf, Paraxialisation des équations de Navier-Stokes, Rapport interne CMAP, (Janvier 1988).

[9] F.Nataf, Approximation paraxiale pour les fluides incompressibles, Etude mathématique et numérique, Thèse de Doctorat de l'Ecole Polytechnique, France(1989).

[10] M.A.Shubin, *Pseudodifferential Operators and Spectral Theory*, (Springer-Verlag, 1980)

Frédéric NATAF

Ecole Polytechnique, Centre de mathématiques Appliquées, 91128, Palaiseau Cedex, FRANCE

S NICAISE

# Regularity of the weak solution of the Lamé system in nonsmooth domains

## 1. INTRODUCTION.

This paper is devoted to the regularity of the solution of the Lamé system in a polygonal domain of the plane or a polyhedral domain of the space. The interior datum is assumed to be in $L^2$, and the boundary conditions are mixed and non-homogeneous. This means that on a part of the boundary we impose Dirichlet boundary conditions (i.e. the displacement vector field is fixed) and on the remainder of the boundary, we impose Neumann boundary conditions, in the sense that the normal traction is fixed. We give the singular behaviour of the weak solution of this system near the corners and, in dimension 3, also along the edges. In dimension 2, this is proved by P. Grisvard in [6]. In dimension 3, partial results were given in [6] and [16] ; here adapting Dauge's techniques of [2], we show that the weak solution is the sum of a singular and regular part, the latter being in $H^{3/2+\varepsilon}$, for some $\varepsilon > 0$ (and not necessarily in $H^2$).

With these results, it is possible to find geometrical conditions on the domain which ensure the regularity $H^{3/2+\varepsilon}$ for some $\varepsilon > 0$, for the weak solution. As classicaly (see [18], [5], [12], [8]), to get this regularity result, it suffices to establish the existence of a strip free of pole. When the boundary conditions are purely of Dirichlet type, the study of such strips is wellknown (see [18], [3], [17] in dimension 2 and [12], [8], [9] in dimension 3). When the boundary conditions are mixed, it seems to be new. In dimension 2, our conditions are necessary and sufficient, while in dimension 3, in view of Grisvard's results about the Laplace operator in [5], we think that it is perhaps possible to improve them.

As an application of these results, we shall study in [14] the regularity of the solution of a coupled problem between the linear elasticity system in the unit cube of $\mathbf{R}^3$ with a plane crack and the plate equation on a plane domain. This problem differs only from the problem obtained in [1] by the boundary conditions. Nevertheless, we may say that we answer to the question of regularity raised in paragraph 6 of [2]. Our coupled problem is similar to the model problem studied in [13] but the obtained regularity results and the methods of proof are different since the Laplace operator is more convenient than the Lamé system.

In [15], we shall consider the exact controllability of the associated dynamical problems. As in [5] and [13], the regularity results obtained here will be useful in order to adapt the Hilbert Uniqueness Method of J.-L. Lions [10].

Let us now introduce some notations. Let $\Omega$ be a bounded open connected subset of $\mathbf{R}^n$, $n \in \{2,3\}$. We suppose that the boundary $\partial\Omega$ of $\Omega$ is the union of a finite number of faces $\overline{\Gamma}_k$, $k \in \mathcal{F}$ ; where in dimension 2, each $\Gamma_k$ is actually a linear segment, while in dimension 3, $\Gamma_k$ is a plane face (it is more convenient to assume that $\Gamma_k$ is open !). If $\Omega$ has slits, we assume that each slit is split up into two faces.

In order to consider mixed boundary conditions, we fix a partition of $\mathcal{F}$ into $\mathcal{D} \cup \mathcal{N}$, where $\mathcal{D}$ will correspond to Dirichlet boundary conditions, while $\mathcal{N}$ to Neumann boundary conditions.

Given a function $w$ or a vector field $\boldsymbol{\mu}$ defined on $\partial\Omega$, it will be convenient to denote by $w^{(k)}$, respectively $\boldsymbol{\mu}^{(k)}$, its restriction to $\Gamma_k$, for all $k \in \mathcal{F}$. Moreover, for a vector $\mathbf{u}$ of $\mathbf{R}^n$ we denote by $u_i$ its $i^{\text{th}}$ component, for all $i \in \{1, \ldots, n\}$, i.e. $\mathbf{u} = (u_i)_{i=1}^n$.

We associate with the displacement vector field $\mathbf{u}$ the linearized strain tensor $\varepsilon(\mathbf{u})$ defined by

$$\varepsilon_{ij}(\mathbf{u}) = (D_j u_i + D_i u_j)/2, \ \forall i, j = 1, \ldots, n,$$

and the linearized stress tensor $\sigma(\mathbf{u})$ given by Hooke's law, using the Lamé coefficients $\lambda$ and $\mu$ ($\lambda$ and $\mu$ are always assumed to be positive) :

$$\sigma_{ij}(\mathbf{u}) = 2\mu\varepsilon_{ij}(\mathbf{u}) + \lambda tr\varepsilon(\mathbf{u})\delta_{ij}, \ \forall i, j = 1, \ldots, n \, .$$

We introduce the Lamé operator

$$L\mathbf{u} = (\sum_{j=1}^{n} D_j \sigma_{ij}(\mathbf{u}))_{i=1}^n \, .$$

For all $k \in \mathcal{F}$, we also denote by $\gamma_k$ the trace operator on the face $\Gamma_k$, $\boldsymbol{\nu}^{(k)}$ the outward normal unit vector on $\Gamma_k$ and

$$T^{(k)}\mathbf{u} = (\sum_{j=1}^{n} \gamma_k \sigma_{ij}(\mathbf{u}) \nu_j^{(k)})_{i=1}^n \, .$$

Given a vector field $\mathbf{f} \in (L^2(\Omega))^n$ (which represents the force density applied to the body $\Omega$) and $\mathbf{g}^{(k)} \in (H^{1/2}(\Gamma_k))^n$, for all $k \in \mathcal{N}$, we consider the weak solution $\mathbf{u} \in (H^1(\Omega))^n$ of the Lamé system

$$L\mathbf{u} = -\mathbf{f} \quad \text{in} \quad \Omega, \tag{1.1}$$

with mixed boundary conditions

$$\gamma_k \mathbf{u} = \mathbf{0} \quad \text{on} \quad \Gamma_k, \ \forall k \in \mathcal{D} \, , \tag{1.2}$$

$$T^{(k)}\mathbf{u} = \mathbf{g}^{(k)} \quad \text{on} \quad \Gamma_k, \ \forall k \in \mathcal{N} \, . \tag{1.3}$$

This problem admits the following variational formulation : we introduce the Hilbert space

$$V = \{u \in (H^1(\Omega))^n \text{ fulfilling } (1.2)\},$$

and the continuous sesquilinear form

$$a_\Omega(\mathbf{u}, \mathbf{v}) = \int_\Omega \sum_{i,j=1}^{n} \sigma_{ij}(\mathbf{u}) \varepsilon_{ij}(\overline{\mathbf{v}}) dx, \ \forall \mathbf{u}, \mathbf{v} \in V \, .$$

Therefore, we shall say that $\mathbf{u}$ is a weak solution of problem (1.1)-(1.3), if $\mathbf{u} \in V$ is a solution of

$$a_\Omega(\mathbf{u}, \mathbf{v}) = \int_\Omega (\mathbf{f}, \mathbf{v}) dx + \sum_{k \in \mathcal{N}} \int_{\Gamma_k} (\mathbf{g}^{(k)}, \gamma_k \mathbf{v}) d\sigma, \forall \mathbf{v} \in V, \tag{1.4}$$

where, from now on, $(\cdot, \cdot)$ denotes the inner product in $\mathbf{C}^n$.

In all this paper, we shall use the Sobolev spaces $W^{s,p}(\Omega)$ defined, for instance, in paragraph 1.3.2 of [4], when $s \in \mathbf{R}$ and $p > 1$. When $p = 2$, they are usually denoted by $H^s(\Omega)$. Moreover, we also use the weighted Sobolev spaces $H^s_\gamma(\Gamma)$ defined in (AA.2) of [2], when $s \geq 0$, $\gamma \in \mathbf{R}$ and $\Gamma$ is a cone of $\mathbf{R}^n$.

## 2. REGULARITY OF THE SOLUTION IN DIMENSION 2.

The behaviour of a solution $\mathbf{u}$ of (1.4) near the vertices of $\Omega$ are wellknown, using Theorem I of [6], we obtain immediately the following :

**Theorem 2.1.** *Let $\mathbf{u} \in V$ be a solution of (1.4) with data $\mathbf{f} \in (L^2(\Omega))^2$, $\mathbf{g}^{(k)} \in (H^{1/2}(\Gamma_k))^2$, $\forall k \in \mathcal{N}$. Let us fix $j, k \in \mathcal{N}$ such that $\overline{\Gamma}_j \cap \overline{\Gamma}_k \neq \emptyset$ and let us denote by $S$ their common vertex and by $\omega$ the interior angle between $\Gamma_j$ and $\Gamma_k$. Then there exist coefficients $c_{\alpha,\nu}$ such that*

$$\mathbf{u} - \sum_{\alpha} \sum_{\nu=1}^{N(\alpha)} c_{\alpha,\nu} \boldsymbol{\sigma}^{\alpha,\nu} \in (W^{2,p}(W))^2, \tag{2.1}$$

*where $W$ is a neighbourhood of $S$, the sum extends to all roots $\alpha \in \mathbf{C}$ of*

$$\sin^2 \alpha\omega = \alpha^2 \sin^2 \omega, \tag{2.2}$$

*in the strip $\Re(\alpha) \in ]0, 2 - 2/p[$. $N(\alpha)$ is the multiplicity of $\alpha$ in (2.2) ($N(\alpha) = 1$ or 2, see [18]). Finally, $\boldsymbol{\sigma}^{\alpha,\nu}$ are the so-called singular functions defined by (1.4) of [6]. This result holds for all $p < 2$ such that the equation (2.2) has no root on the line $\Re(\alpha) = 2 - 2/p$.*

*If $j, k \in \mathcal{D}$, this result remains true if we replace (2.2) by*

$$\sin^2 \alpha\omega = \frac{(\lambda + \mu)^2}{(\lambda + 3\mu)^2} \alpha^2 \sin^2 \omega \ , \tag{2.3}$$

*in that case, the $\boldsymbol{\sigma}^{\alpha,\nu}$'s are defined in paragraph 6.1 of [6].*

*If $j \in \mathcal{N}$, $k \in \mathcal{D}$ or $j \in \mathcal{D}$, $k \in \mathcal{N}$, then again this result still holds when (2.2) is replaced by*

$$\sin^2 \alpha\omega = \{(\lambda + 2\mu)^2 - (\lambda + \mu)^2 \alpha^2 \sin^2 \omega\} / \{(\lambda + \mu)(\lambda + 3\mu)\}, \tag{2.4}$$

*the $\boldsymbol{\sigma}^{\alpha,\nu}$'s being defined in paragraph 6.2 of [6].*

In view of this theorem, if we want to get a maximal regularity for $\mathbf{u}$, it is necessary to show that a strip $\Re(\alpha) \in ]0, 2-2/p[$ has no root of (2.2), (2.3) or (2.4). For the equation (2.2), we can use § 5 of [3] ; for the other equations, analogous arguments show the

**Theorem 2.2.** *If $\omega \in ]0, 2\pi[$, then the equations (2.2) and (2.3) have no root in the strip $\Re(\alpha) \in ]0, \frac{1}{2}]$. On the other hand, the equation (2.4) has no root in the same strip if $\omega \in ]0, \pi[$.*

As a consequence, we deduce the

**Theorem 2.3.** *If $\Omega$ satisfies the assumption*
*($H_2$) $\forall j, k \in \mathcal{F}$ such that $\overline{\Gamma}_j \cap \overline{\Gamma}_k \neq \emptyset$, the interior angle $\omega$ between $\Gamma_j$ and $\Gamma_k$ fulfils $\omega < 2\pi$ and moreover, if $j \in \mathcal{D}$ and $k \in \mathcal{N}$, $\omega < \pi$.*

*Then a solution $\mathbf{u} \in V$ of (1.4) with data $\mathbf{f} \in (L^2(\Omega))^2$ and $\mathbf{g}^{(k)} \in (H^{1/2}(\Gamma_k))^2$, $\forall k \in \mathcal{N}$ satisfies*

$$\mathbf{u} \in (H^{3/2+\varepsilon}(\Omega))^2, \text{ for some } \varepsilon > 0 \, . \tag{2.5}$$

**Proof :** By Theorem 2.2 and the hypothesis $(H_2)$, the strip $\Re(\alpha) \in ]0, \frac{1}{2}]$ is free of root at each vertex of $\Omega$. Moreover, it is wellknown (see paragraph 7 of [2], for instance) that in a fixed strip $\Re(\alpha) \in [a, b]$, with $a, b \in \mathbf{R}$, the equations (2.2) to (2.4) have only a finite number of isolated roots ; therefore there exists $p \in ]4/3, 2[$ (sufficiently closed to 4/3 if necessary) such that the strip $\Re(\alpha) \in ]0, 2 - 2/p]$ is free of root at each vertex of $\Omega$. Owing to Theorem 2.1, we deduce that $\mathbf{u} \in (W^{2,p}(\Omega))^2$, for such a $p$. Using the Sobolev imbedding theorem (see Theorem 1.4.4.1 of [4]), we obtain (2.5) since the assumption $(H_2)$ implies that $\Omega$ has a Lipschitz boundary. ■

**Remark 2.4 :** The geometrical assumptions made in Theorem 2.3 to get the regularity result (2.5) are exactly the same as for the Laplace operator with mixed boundary conditions made by P. Grisvard in [5]. Moreover, thery are in accordance with some figures given in [17] for some particular examples. They are our motivations to establish Theorems 2.2 and 2.3. Moreover, they are necessary in the sense that if $(H_2)$ fails then there exist singularities which do not belong to $(H^{3/2+\varepsilon}(\Omega))^2$ . ■

## 3. VERTEX AND EDGE SINGULARITIES IN DIMENSION 3.

In dimension 3, the behaviour of a solution $\mathbf{u}$ of problem (1.4) along the edges was given by P. Grisvard in [6]. Moreover, it is possible to prove a general regularity result at the vertices and along the edges as Theorem 17.13 of [2] when the boundary conditions (1.2)-(1.3) are homogeneous (adapting paragraphs 17, 22, 23 and 24 of [2] to this problem). A sketch of the proof was given in paragraph 1 of [16]. Since we are interested in non-homogeneous boundary conditions and since we allow cracked domains, it is impossible to use a trace theorem to go back to homogeneous boundary conditions. Therefore, we shall show that Theorem 17.13 of [2] still holds for our system (1.1)-(1.3) but only with a regular part in $H^{3/2+\varepsilon}(\Omega)$ for some $\varepsilon > 0$ (instead of $H^2$). Fortunately, it is sufficient for the applications to the exact controllability (see [5]).

Let us start with the singularities at the vertices. To do that, we fix a vertex $S$ of $\Omega$. In a sufficiently small neighbourhood of $S$, $\Omega$ coincides with a polyhedral cone $\Gamma_S$ of $\mathbf{R}^3$. We denote by $\Omega_S$ the intersection between $\Gamma_S$ and the unit sphere centered at $S$. We shall also use spherical coordinates $(r, \omega)$ with origin at $S$ ; in that way, we have

$$\Omega_S = \{\omega \in S_2 : (r, \omega) \in \Gamma_S\} .$$

Let us denote by $\mathcal{F}_S$, the set of faces of $\Gamma_S$ i.e. $\mathcal{F}_S = \{k \in \mathcal{F} : S \in \overline{\Gamma}_k\}$. For each $k \in \mathcal{F}_S$, we shall denote by $\Gamma'_k$ the face of $\Gamma_S$ containing the face $\Gamma_k$ of $\Omega$ ; $\Gamma''_k$ will be the corresponding arc of the boundary $\partial\Omega_S$ of $\Omega_S$. Finally, we misuse the notation $\gamma_k$ for the trace operator on $\Gamma'_k$ or $\Gamma''_k$, for all $k \in \mathcal{F}_S$.

Obviously, the partition $\mathcal{D} \cup \mathcal{N}$ of $\mathcal{F}$ induces a partition $D_S \cup \mathcal{N}_S$ of $\mathcal{F}_S$. We are now able to set

$$V(\Gamma_S) = \{\mathbf{u} \in (H^1(\Gamma_S))^3 \quad \text{fulfilling} \quad \gamma_k \mathbf{u} = \mathbf{0} \quad \text{on} \quad \Gamma'_k, \forall k \in \mathcal{D}_S\},$$

$$V(\Omega_S) = \{\mathbf{u} \in (H^1(\Omega_S))^3 \quad \text{fulfilling} \quad \gamma_k \mathbf{u} = \mathbf{0} \quad \text{on} \quad \Gamma''_k, \forall k \in \mathcal{D}_S\} .$$

Using a cut-off function, to study the behaviour of a solution $\mathbf{u}$ of (1.4) near the vertex $S$, we may suppose that $\mathbf{u}$ has a compact support, let us say

$$\operatorname{supp} \mathbf{u} \subset B(S, 1),$$

and that it fulfils

$$\int_{\Gamma_S} \sum_{i,j=1}^{3} \sigma_{ij}(\mathbf{u})\varepsilon_{ij}(\bar{\mathbf{v}})dx = \int_{\Gamma_S} (\mathbf{f},\mathbf{v})dx + \sum_{k\in\mathcal{N}_S} \int_{\Gamma'_k} (\mathbf{g}^{(k)}, \gamma_k \mathbf{v})d\sigma, \tag{3.1}$$

for all $\mathbf{v} \in V(\Gamma_S)$ ; where $\mathbf{f} \in (L^2(\Gamma_S))^3$, $\mathbf{g}^{(k)} \in (H^{1/2}(\Gamma'_k))^3$, for all $k \in \mathcal{N}_S$, have a compact support.

As usual [7], [11], the asymptotic behaviour of $\mathbf{u}$ near $S$ depends on a family of operators $\mathcal{A}_S(\alpha)$, with complex parameter $\alpha$, that we now introduce (in a variational way) : we write the operator $D_j$ in spherical coordinates and we set

$$\mathcal{D}_j(\omega, r\partial_r, D_\omega) = rD_j, \ \forall j \in \{1,2,3\} .$$

For $\alpha \in \mathbf{C}$ and a vector field $\mathbf{v}$, we set

$$\mathcal{E}_{ij}(\omega,\alpha,D_\omega)\mathbf{v} = (\mathcal{D}_i(\omega,\alpha,D_\omega)v_j + \mathcal{D}_j(\omega,\alpha,D_\omega)v_i)/2,$$
$$\mathcal{S}_{ij}(\omega,\alpha,D_\omega)\mathbf{v} = 2\mu\mathcal{E}_{ij}(\omega,\alpha,D_\omega)\mathbf{v} + \lambda \operatorname{tr}\mathcal{E}(\omega,\alpha,D_\omega)\mathbf{v}\delta_{ij}, \ \forall i,j \in \{1,2,3\} .$$

For all $\alpha \in \mathbf{C}$, we introduce the continuous sesquilinear form $a_S(\alpha)$ on $V(\Omega_S)$ defined by

$$a_S(\alpha)\{\mathbf{u},\mathbf{v}\} = \int_{\Omega_S} \sum_{i,j=1}^{3} \mathcal{S}_{ij}(\omega,\alpha,D_\omega)\mathbf{u}\mathcal{E}_{ij}(\omega,-(\alpha+1),D_\omega)\bar{\mathbf{v}}d\omega, \ \forall \mathbf{u},\mathbf{v} \in V(\Omega_S) .$$

Finally, the operator $\mathcal{A}_S(\alpha) : V(\Omega_S) \to V(\Omega_S)'$ is defined by

$$\mathcal{A}_S(\alpha)\mathbf{u}(\mathbf{v}) = a_S(\alpha)\{\mathbf{u},\mathbf{v}\} .$$

Arguing as in Proposition 8.4 of [2] and using the fact that Korn's inequality holds on $\Gamma_S$, we can show that $\mathcal{A}_S(\alpha)^{-1}$ is meromorphic on $\mathbf{C}$ and that in a fixed strip $\Re(\alpha) \in [\beta,\gamma]$, $\mathcal{A}_S(\alpha)$ is invertible except for a finite number of exceptional values of $\alpha$.

This allows us to give a result analogous to Lemma 17.4 of [2], its proof is similar but using the variational formulation of our problem as in Proposition 24.1 of [2].

**Theorem 3.1.** *Let $\mathbf{f} \in (L^2(\Gamma_S))^3$, $\mathbf{g}^{(k)} \in (H^{1/2}(\Gamma'_k))^3$, $\forall k \in \mathcal{N}_S$ and let $\mathbf{u} \in V(\Gamma_S)$ be a solution of (3.1) with a compact support. Then there exists $\varepsilon > 0$ and a function $\mathbf{u}_0 \in (H^1_{-\frac{1}{2}-\varepsilon}(\Gamma_S))^3$ such that*

$$\mathbf{u} = \mathbf{u}_0 + \sum_{\alpha} \boldsymbol{\sigma}^\alpha, \tag{3.2}$$

*where the sum extends to all $\alpha$ in the strip $\Re(\alpha) \in ]-\frac{1}{2},\varepsilon[$ such that $\mathcal{A}_S(\alpha)^{-1}$ does not exist; the function $\boldsymbol{\sigma}^\alpha$ belongs to $(H^1(\Gamma_S))^3 \setminus (H^1_{-\frac{1}{2}-\varepsilon}(\Gamma_S))^3$, admits the following expansion*

$$\boldsymbol{\sigma}^\alpha(r,\omega) = r^\alpha \sum_{q=0}^{Q(\alpha)} (\log r)^{Q(\alpha)-q} \varphi^{\alpha,q}(\omega) . \tag{3.3}$$

*for some* $Q(\alpha) \in \mathbf{N}$ *and functions* $\varphi^{\alpha,q}$ *defined on* $\Omega_S$, *and belonging to* $(H^1(\Omega_S))^3$, $q \in \{1, ..., Q(\alpha)\}$ . *Finally,* $\boldsymbol{\sigma}^\alpha$ *satisfies*

$$\begin{cases} L\boldsymbol{\sigma}^\alpha = 0 & in \quad \Gamma_S, \\ \gamma_k \boldsymbol{\sigma}^\alpha = 0 & on \quad \Gamma'_k, \forall k \in \mathcal{D}_S, \\ T^{(k)}\boldsymbol{\sigma}^\alpha = 0 & on \quad \Gamma'_k, \forall k \in \mathcal{N}_S . \end{cases} \tag{3.4}$$

Now, in order to get edge singularities up to the vertex $S$, let us introduce some notations (see § 17.B of [2]) :

• $A(\Omega_S)$ denotes the set of vertices of $\Omega_S$ (it is the set of edges of $\Gamma_S$).

• If $x \in A(\Omega_S)$, there exists a local chart $\chi_x$ sending a neighbourhood of $x$ in $\Omega_S$ onto a neighbourhood of 0 in a cone $C_x$ of $\mathbf{R}^2$ with opening $\omega_x$. Since $x$ corresponds to the common edge between $\Gamma_k$ and $\Gamma_j$, for some $j, k \in \mathcal{F}_S$, $\omega_x$ is the interior dihedral angle between $\Gamma_j$ and $\Gamma_k$. We shall denote by $z_x$ the cartesian coordinates in $C_x$. $\boldsymbol{\sigma}_x^{\alpha,\nu}$ will be the singularities introduced in paragraph 2 associated with the Lamé system in the cone $C_x$ with boundary conditions induced by the boundary conditions imposed on $\Gamma_j$ and $\Gamma_k$, when $\alpha$ is a solution of (2.2), (2.3) or (2.4) with $\omega = \omega_x$. In the same way, for the radial component (see [6] where an analogous phenomenon occurs for the tangential component in a dihedral cone), we need to introduce the singularities $\sigma_x^{\alpha'}$ of the Laplace operator in the cone $C_x$ with boundary conditions induced by the boundary conditions imposed on $\Gamma_j$ and $\Gamma_k$. More precisely, using polar coordinates $(r_x, \theta_x)$ in the cone $C_x$ such that $\theta_x = 0$ on $\Gamma_k$ and $\theta_x = \omega_x$ on $\Gamma_j$, we set

i) If $j, k \in \mathcal{D}$, then $\alpha' = m\pi/\omega_x$, for all $m \in \mathbf{N}^*$ and

$$\sigma_x^{\alpha'}(r_x, \theta_x) = r_x^{\alpha'} sin(\alpha'\theta_x) . \tag{3.5}$$

ii) If $j \in \mathcal{D}$, $k \in \mathcal{N}$, then $\alpha' = (m - \frac{1}{2})\pi/\omega_x$ for all $m \in \mathbf{N}^*$ and

$$\sigma_x^{\alpha'}(r_x, \theta_x) = r_x^{\alpha'} \cos(\alpha'\theta_x) . \tag{3.6}$$

iii) If $j \in \mathcal{N}$, $k \in \mathcal{D}$, then $\alpha' = (m - \frac{1}{2})\pi/\omega_x$, for all $m \in \mathbf{N}^*$ and $\sigma_x^{\alpha'}$ is defined by (3.5).

iv) If $j$, $k \in \mathcal{N}$, then $\alpha' = m\pi/\omega_x$, for all $m \in \mathbf{N}^*$ and $\sigma_x^{\alpha'}$ is defined by (3.6).

For $\varepsilon > 0$, we set

$\Lambda_x(\varepsilon) = \{(\alpha, \nu) : \alpha$ is a solution of (2.2), (2.3) or (2.4) such that $\Re(\alpha) \in ]0, \frac{1}{2} + \varepsilon[$ and $\nu \in \{1, \ldots, N(\alpha)\}\}$,

$\Lambda'_x(\varepsilon) = \{\alpha'$ equal to $m\pi/\omega_x$ or $(m - \frac{1}{2})\pi/\omega_x$ such that $\alpha' \in ]0, \frac{1}{2} + \varepsilon[\}$.

Finally, we introduce the smoothing operator $\mathcal{R}_x$ defined by

$$\mathcal{R}_x(c)(r, \omega) = \varphi_x(\omega) r^\varepsilon [c \star_t \phi](\ln r, z_x) ,$$

where $\varphi_x$ is a cut-off function defined on $\Omega_S$ such that $\varphi_x = 1$ in a neighbourhood of $x$ and $\varphi_x = 0$ in a neighbourhood of the other vertices. $\phi$ is the function introduced by M. Dauge in (16.6) of [2] i.e.

$$\phi(t, z_x) = (-2\pi)^{-1} \int_{\mathbf{R}} e^{it\xi} r(\xi, z_x) d\xi \ ,$$

when $r(\xi, z_x) = \varphi(|z_x|\chi(\xi))$, $\chi$ is a continuous function on $\mathbf{R}$ such that $\chi \geq 1$ on $\mathbf{R}$ and $\chi(t) = |t|$ if $t \geq t_0 > 0$ and $\varphi$ is a rapidly decreasing function on $\mathbf{R}^+$ such that $\varphi = 1$ in a neighbourhood of 0. By $c \star_t \phi$, we mean

$$(c \star_t \phi)(t, z_x) = \int_{\mathbf{R}} c(s) \phi(t - s, z_x) ds \ .$$

- We also introduce the matrix

$$A = \begin{pmatrix} \sin\theta\cos\varphi & \cos\theta\cos\varphi & -\sin\varphi \\ \sin\theta\sin\varphi & \cos\theta\sin\varphi & \cos\varphi \\ \cos\theta & -\sin\theta & 0 \end{pmatrix} .$$

This matrix allows to pass from $\mathbf{u}$ to $(u_r, u_\theta, u_\varphi)$, the projections of the vector $\mathbf{u}$ in cartesian coordinates onto the spherical basis i.e.

$$\mathbf{u} = \begin{pmatrix} u_1 \\ u_2 \\ u_3 \end{pmatrix} = A \begin{pmatrix} u_r \\ u_\theta \\ u_\varphi \end{pmatrix} .$$

Now, we are ready to give the analogue of Theorem 17.13 of [2] to our system.

**Theorem 3.2.** *Let* $\mathbf{f} \in (L^2(\Gamma_S))^3$, $\mathbf{g}^{(k)} \in (H^{1/2}(\Gamma'_k))^3$, $\forall k \in \mathcal{N}_S$ *and let* $\mathbf{u} \in V(\Gamma_S)$ *be a solution of (3.1) with a compact support. Then there exists* $\varepsilon > 0$ *such that*

$$\mathbf{u} = \mathbf{u}_r + \sum_\alpha \boldsymbol{\sigma}^\alpha + \sum_{x \in A(\Omega_S)} \{ \sum_{(\alpha,\nu) \in \Lambda_x(\varepsilon)} \mathcal{R}_x(c_x^{\alpha,\nu}) A \begin{pmatrix} 0 \\ \boldsymbol{\sigma}_x^{\alpha,\nu}(z_x) \end{pmatrix} \qquad (3.7)$$

$$+ \sum_{\alpha' \in \Lambda'_x(\varepsilon)} \mathcal{R}_x(c_x^{\alpha'}) A \begin{pmatrix} \sigma_x^{\alpha'}(z_x) \\ 0 \\ 0 \end{pmatrix} \},$$

*where* $\mathbf{u}_r \in (H^{3/2+\varepsilon}(\Omega))^3$, $c_x^{\alpha,\nu} \in H^{1/2+\varepsilon-\Re(\alpha)}(\mathbf{R})$, $c_x^{\alpha'} \in H^{1/2+\varepsilon-\alpha'}(\mathbf{R})$.

## 4. MAXIMAL REGULARITY FOR THE LAMÉ SYSTEM IN DIMENSION 3.

Theorem 3.2 shows that if we want to give a maximal regularity for a solution $\mathbf{u}$ of problem (1.4), we need to control the edge and vertex singularities. The edge singularities do not pose any problem since they correspond to vertex singularities in dimension 2. It remains the vertex singularities. When the boundary conditions on all the faces are of Dirichlet type, an estimate of a strip free of pole for $\mathcal{A}_S(\alpha)^{-1}$ can be deduced from [12] :

**Lemma 4.1.** *Let $S$ be a fixed vertex of $\Omega$. If $\bar{\Omega}_S$ is different of the unit sphere $S_2$ and $\mathcal{N}_S = \emptyset$, then $\mathcal{A}_S(\alpha)^{-1}$ exists for all $\alpha$ in the strip $\Re(\alpha) \in [-1, 0]$.*

**Proof :** Let us suppose that there exists $\alpha$ in the strip $\Re(\alpha) \in [-1, 0]$ such that $\mathcal{A}_S(\alpha)^{-1}$ does not exist. In that case, Theorem 3.1 shows that there exists a function $\varphi^{\alpha,0}$ on $\Omega_S$ such that $r^\alpha \varphi^{\alpha,0}$ fulfils (3.4). But Theorem 1 of [12] excludes the existence of such a solution in the strip

$$|\Re(\alpha) + \frac{1}{2}| \le \alpha_0 + \frac{1}{2} ,$$

for some $\alpha_0 > 0$. This is the contradiction since this strip is larger than ours. ∎

Unfortunately, Theorem 1 of [12] uses in a basic way the Dirichlet boundary conditions and it seems to be impossible to extend it to mixed boundary conditions. For purely Neumann boundary conditions, using a different method, Mazya and Kozlov prove in Theorem 3 of [8] that, if $\Omega_S$ has no crack, then the conclusion of Lemma 4.1 still holds. Under a geometrical assumption, we can prove that their method can be adapted to mixed boundary conditions. For a fixed vertex $S$ of $\Omega$, let us set

$$C_{S,D} = \{ \sum_{k \in \mathcal{D}_S} \lambda_k \boldsymbol{\nu}^{(k)} : \lambda_k \ge 0, \quad \text{not all zero}\},$$

$$C_{S,N} = \{ \sum_{k \in \mathcal{N}_S} \lambda_k \boldsymbol{\nu}^{(k)} : \lambda_k \ge 0, \quad \text{not all zero}\},$$

with the agreement that $C_{S,D}$ (resp. $C_{S,N}$) is empty if $\mathcal{D}_S$ (resp. $\mathcal{N}_S$) is empty.

**Theorem 4.2.** *Let $S$ be a fixed vertex of $\Omega$. If $\Omega_S$ has no crack and $C_{S,D} \cap C_{S,N} = \emptyset$, then*

*i) If $\mathcal{D}_S \neq \emptyset$, $\mathcal{A}_S(\alpha)^{-1}$ exists for all $\alpha$ in the strip $\Re(\alpha) \in [-1, 0]$.*

*ii) If $\mathcal{D}_S = \emptyset$, $\mathcal{A}_S(\alpha)^{-1}$ exists for all $\alpha$ in the strip $\Re(\alpha) \in [-1, 0]$ except for $\alpha = 0$ and $-1$, where $\ker \mathcal{A}_S(\alpha) = \mathbf{C}^3$.*

**Proof :** The case $\mathcal{D}_S = \emptyset$ is precisely Theorem 3 of [8] (see Remark 2 of [8]). So from now on, we can suppose that $\mathcal{D}_S \neq \emptyset$. We firstly establish that $\mathcal{A}_S(\alpha)^{-1}$ exists for all $\alpha$ on the line $\Re(\alpha) = 0$. To do that, as in Lemma 4.1, we show that a function $\mathbf{u} \neq \mathbf{0}$ in the form

$$\mathbf{u}(r, \omega) = r^\alpha \varphi(\omega) , \tag{4.1}$$

with some function $\varphi$ defined on $\Omega_S$ and $\Re(\alpha) = 0$ can not be a solution of (3.4).

Let us suppose the contrary. Then the assumption that $\Omega_S$ has no crack insure that the following Green formula has a meaning for $\mathbf{u}$ :

$$\int_{\Gamma_{S\varepsilon}} (L\mathbf{u}, \frac{\partial \mathbf{u}}{\partial x_m}) dx = - \int_{\Gamma_{S\varepsilon}} \sum_{i,j=1}^{3} \sigma_{ij}(\mathbf{u}) \varepsilon_{ij}(\frac{\partial \bar{\mathbf{u}}}{\partial x_m}) dx \tag{4.2}$$

$$+ \sum_{k \in \mathcal{F}_S} \int_{\Gamma_{k\varepsilon}} (T^{(k)}\mathbf{u}, \frac{\partial \mathbf{u}}{\partial x_m}) d\sigma,$$

for all $m \in \{1,2,3\}$, all $\varepsilon \in ]0,1[$, when we set

$$\Gamma_{S\varepsilon} = \{(r,\omega) \in \Gamma_S : \varepsilon < r < 1\},\ \Gamma_{k\varepsilon} = \{(r,\omega') \in \Gamma'_k : \varepsilon < r < 1\}.$$

Let us remark that the boundary terms corresponding to $r = \varepsilon$ and $r = 1$ cancel since $\Re(\alpha) = 0$.

Let us fix $m \in \{1,2,3\}$ and $\varepsilon \in ]0,1[$. Taking the real part of (4.2) and since we assume that $\mathbf{u}$ fulfils (3.4), we get

$$0 = -\int_{\Gamma_{S\varepsilon}} \Re(\sum_{i,j=1}^{3} \sigma_{ij}(\mathbf{u})\varepsilon_{ij}(\frac{\partial \overline{\mathbf{u}}}{\partial x_m}))dx + \sum_{k\in\mathcal{D}_S} \int_{\Gamma_{k\varepsilon}} \Re((T^{(k)}\mathbf{u}, \frac{\partial \mathbf{u}}{\partial x_m}))d\sigma\ . \quad (4.3)$$

Now, using the easily checked identity

$$\Re(\sum_{i,j=1}^{3} \sigma_{ij}(\mathbf{u})\varepsilon_{ij}(\frac{\partial \overline{\mathbf{u}}}{\partial x_m})) = \frac{1}{2}\frac{\partial}{\partial x_m}\{\sum_{i,j=1}^{3} \sigma_{ij}(\mathbf{u})\varepsilon_{ij}(\overline{\mathbf{u}})\}$$

and integrating by parts, (4.3) becomes

$$0 = -\frac{1}{2}\sum_{k\in\mathcal{F}_S} \int_{\Gamma_{k\varepsilon}} \sum_{i,j=1}^{3} \sigma_{ij}(\mathbf{u})\varepsilon_{ij}(\overline{\mathbf{u}})\nu_m^{(k)} d\sigma + \sum_{k\in\mathcal{D}_S} \int_{\Gamma_{k\varepsilon}} \Re((T^{(k)}\mathbf{u}, \frac{\partial \mathbf{u}}{\partial x_m}))d\sigma\ . \quad (4.4)$$

It is obvious that

$$\sum_{i,j=1}^{3} \sigma_{ij}(\mathbf{u})\varepsilon_{ij}(\overline{\mathbf{u}}) = 2\mu \sum_{i,j=1}^{3} |\varepsilon_{ij}(\mathbf{u})|^2 + \lambda|\mathrm{tr}\varepsilon(\mathbf{u})|^2\ . \quad (4.5)$$

Moreover using the fact that

$$\frac{\partial u_i}{\partial x_m} = \nu_m^{(k)}\frac{\partial u_i}{\partial \nu^{(k)}} \quad \text{on } \Gamma'_k, \forall k \in \mathcal{D}_S\ ,$$

we can prove the following identity

$$(T^{(k)}\mathbf{u}, \frac{\partial \mathbf{u}}{\partial x_m}) = \nu_m^{(k)}\{2\mu \sum_{i,j=1}^{3} |\varepsilon_{ij}(\mathbf{u})|^2 + \lambda|\mathrm{tr}\varepsilon(\mathbf{u})|^2\} \text{ on } \Gamma'_k, \forall k \in \mathcal{D}_S\ . \quad (4.6)$$

For all $k \in \mathcal{F}_S$, let us set

$$\lambda_{k\varepsilon} = \int_{\Gamma_{k\varepsilon}} \{2\mu \sum_{i,j=1}^{3} |\varepsilon_{ij}(\mathbf{u})|^2 + \lambda|\mathrm{tr}\,\varepsilon(\mathbf{u})|^2\}d\sigma\ . \quad (4.7)$$

Then using (4.5) to (4.7) into (4.4), we arrive to

$$\sum_{k \in \mathcal{N}_S} \lambda_{k\varepsilon} \boldsymbol{\nu}^{(k)} = \sum_{k \in \mathcal{D}_S} \lambda_{k\varepsilon} \boldsymbol{\nu}^{(k)} . \tag{4.8}$$

Therefore the assumption $C_{S,D} \cap C_{S,N} = \emptyset$ imply that

$$\lambda_{k\varepsilon} = 0, \quad \forall k \in \mathcal{F}_S .$$

Since $\varepsilon$ is arbitrary in $]0,1[$, we finally obtain

$$2\mu \sum_{i,j=1}^{3} |\varepsilon_{ij}(\mathbf{u})|^2 + \lambda |\operatorname{tr} \varepsilon(\mathbf{u})|^2 = 0 \text{ on } \Gamma'_k, \forall k \in \mathcal{F}_S . \tag{4.9}$$

At this step, we follow Theorem 3 of [8]. The function

$$v = \operatorname{tr} \varepsilon(\mathbf{u})$$

fulfils (owing to (4.9) and (3.4))

$$\begin{cases} \Delta v = 0 \text{ in } \Gamma_S, \\ \gamma_k v = 0 \text{ on } \Gamma'_k, \forall k \in \mathcal{F}_S . \end{cases} \tag{4.10}$$

Since $v$ has the form

$$v(r,\omega) = r^{\alpha-1} \psi(\omega), \tag{4.11}$$

with some function $\psi$ defined on $\Omega_S$ ; using Theorem 4.3 hereafter, we deduce that

$$v = 0 .$$

Therefore, for all $i,j \in \{1,2,3\}$ the function $\varepsilon_{ij}(\mathbf{u})$ fulfils (4.10) (owing to (4.9) and (3.4)) and admits the expansion (4.11). So again Theorem 4.3 implies that

$$\varepsilon_{ij}(\mathbf{u}) = 0 .$$

This shows that the displacement field $\mathbf{u}$ is a rigid body motion. But this is incompatible with (4.1) except if $\alpha = 0$. In that last case, we deduce that there exists a vector $\mathbf{a} \in \mathbf{C}^3$ such that

$$\mathbf{u}(r,\omega) = \mathbf{a} .$$

Since $\mathcal{D}_S \neq \emptyset$, we arrive to

$$\mathbf{u} = \mathbf{0} .$$

This proves that $\mathcal{A}_S(\alpha)^{-1}$ exists for all $\alpha$ on the line $\Re(\alpha) = 0$. But using the definition of $\mathcal{A}_S(\alpha)$, we see that

$$\mathcal{A}_S(\alpha)^* = \mathcal{A}_S(-(\bar{\alpha}+1)) .$$

Therefore, $\mathcal{A}_S(\alpha)^{-1}$ exists also for all $\alpha$ on the line $\Re(\alpha) = -1$.

For all $t \in [0,1]$, let us set $\mathcal{A}_S^t(\alpha)$ the family of operators (defined on $\Omega_S$ analogously to $\mathcal{A}_S(\alpha)$) associated with the following boundary value problem :

$$\begin{cases} (1-t)L\mathbf{u} + t\Delta\mathbf{u} = \mathbf{f} \quad \text{in} \quad \Gamma_S, \\ \gamma_k \mathbf{u} = \mathbf{0} \quad \text{on} \quad \Gamma_k', \forall k \in \mathcal{D}_S, \\ (1-t)T^{(k)}\mathbf{u} + t\gamma_k \dfrac{\partial \mathbf{u}}{\partial \nu^{(k)}} = \mathbf{g}^{(k)} \quad \text{on} \quad \Gamma_k', \forall k \in \mathcal{N}_S . \end{cases}$$

Using the previous argument, we can show that $\mathcal{A}_S^t(\alpha)^{-1}$ exists for all $\alpha$ on the lines $\Re(\alpha) = 0$ and $\Re(\alpha) = -1$, for any $t \in [0,1]$. Moreover, Theorem 4.3 hereafter shows that $\mathcal{A}_S^1(\alpha)^{-1}$ exists for all $\alpha$ in the strip $\Re(\alpha) \in [-1,0]$. Arguing as at the end of the proof of Theorem 1 of [8], we conclude that $\mathcal{A}_S^t(\alpha)^{-1}$ exists for all $\alpha$ in the same strip. ∎

We need to study the family of operators $\mathcal{B}_S(\alpha)$ with complex parameter $\alpha$ associated with the following boundary value problem, when $S$ is a fixed vertex of $\Omega$ :

$$\begin{cases} \Delta u = f \quad \text{in} \quad \Gamma_S, \\ \gamma_k u = 0 \quad \text{on} \quad \Gamma_k', \forall k \in \mathcal{D}_S, \\ \gamma_k \dfrac{\partial u}{\partial \nu^{(k)}} = 0 \quad \text{on} \quad \Gamma_k', \forall k \in \mathcal{N}_S . \end{cases} \tag{4.12}$$

It is defined variationally as follows : we set

$$W(\Omega_S) = \{u \in H^1(\Omega_S) : \gamma_k u = 0 \quad \text{on} \quad \Gamma_k'', \forall k \in \mathcal{D}_S\},$$

$$b_S(\alpha)\{u,v\} = \int_{\Omega_S} \{\nabla_\omega u \cdot \nabla_\omega \bar{v} - \alpha(\alpha+1)u\bar{v}\} d\omega, \forall u,v \in W(\Omega_S),$$

when $\nabla_\omega u = \left(\frac{\partial u}{\partial \theta}, \frac{1}{\sin\theta}\frac{\partial u}{\partial \varphi}\right)$. Then $\mathcal{B}_S(\alpha)$ is the operator from $W(\Omega_S)$ into its dual $W(\Omega_S)'$ defined by

$$(\mathcal{B}_S(\alpha)u)(v) = b_S(\alpha)\{u,v\}, \forall u,v \in W(\Omega_S) .$$

**Theorem 4.3.** *Let $S$ be a fixed vertex of $\Omega$. If $\mathcal{D}_S \neq \emptyset$, then $\mathcal{B}_S(\alpha)^{-1}$ exists for all $\alpha$ in the strip $\Re(\alpha) \in [-1,0]$ ; while if $\mathcal{D}_S = \emptyset$, the same holds except for $\alpha = 0$ and $\alpha = -1$, where* $\ker \mathcal{B}_S(\alpha) = \mathbf{C}$.

**Proof :** Let us denote by $\{\lambda_k\}_{k\in\mathbf{N}}$ the sequence of eigenvalues (in increasing order) of the Laplace-Beltrami operator $\mathcal{B}_S(0)$ (let us recall that it is a nonnegative selfadjoint operator with a compact resolvant). Since $\mathcal{B}_S(\alpha) = \mathcal{B}_S(0) - \alpha(\alpha+1)I$, we see that $\mathcal{B}_S(\alpha)$ is one-to-one if and only if

$$\alpha(\alpha+1) \neq \lambda_k, \quad \forall k \in \mathbf{N} .$$

This proves the result since $\lambda_0 > 0$ if $\mathcal{D}_S \neq \emptyset$ and $\lambda_0 = 0$ is of multiplicity 1 when $\mathcal{D}_S = \emptyset$. ∎

**Remarks 4.4 :** Theorem 4.3 is implicitly proved in paragraph 5.1 of [5] and it precisely proves the fact that no vertex singularity for the Laplace operator appear in the strip $\Re(\alpha) \in [-1, 0]$ without any geometrical assumption on $\Omega_S$. So we conjecture that the conclusions of Theorem 4.2 still holds without the geometrical assumptions made in Theorem 4.2.

Let us mention two particular situations where the assumption $C_{S,D} \cap C_{S,N} = \emptyset$ is fulfilled :

i) if $\Gamma_S$ is a nondegenerate trihedral cone, then for every choice of $\mathcal{D}_S$ and $\mathcal{N}_S$, this assumption is true.

ii) If card $\mathcal{D}_S \leq 1$ or card $\mathcal{N}_S \leq 1$, and if $\Gamma_S$ is convex, then it holds; while if card $\mathcal{D}_S \geq 2$ and card $\mathcal{N}_S \geq 2$, it may fail. ∎

Collecting the previous results, we arrive to the

**Theorem 4.5.** *Let* $\mathbf{u} \in V$ *be a solution of problem (1.4) with data* $\mathbf{f} \in (L^2(\Omega))^3$, $\mathbf{g}^{(k)} \in (H^{1/2}(\Gamma_k))^3$, $\forall k \in \mathcal{N}$. *If the assumptions* $(H_3E)$ *and* $(H_3V)$ *hereafter are fulfilled, then*

$$\mathbf{u} \in (H^{3/2+\varepsilon}(\Omega))^3, \quad \textit{for some} \quad \varepsilon > 0\,. \tag{4.15}$$

$(H_3E)$ $\forall j, k \in \mathcal{F}$ *such that* $\bar{\Gamma}_j \cap \bar{\Gamma}_k \neq \emptyset$, *the interior dihedral angle* $\omega_{jk}$ *between* $\Gamma_j$ *and* $\Gamma_k$ *belongs to* $]0, 2\pi[$ *and if moreover* $j \in \mathcal{D}$ *and* $k \in \mathcal{N}$, *then* $\omega_{jk} < \pi$.

$(H_3V)$ *For all vertex* $S$ *of* $\Omega$, *either* $\mathcal{N}_S = \emptyset$ *and* $\bar{\Omega}_S \neq S_2$ *or* $\Omega_S$ *has no crack and* $C_{S,N} \cap C_{S,D} \neq \emptyset$.

## REFERENCES


[1] **P.G. Ciarlet, H. Le Dret and R. Nzengwa,** Junctions between three-dimension and two-dimensional linearly elastic structures, J. Math. Pures et Appl., 68, 1989, p. 261-295.

[2] **M. Dauge,** Elliptic boundary value problems on corner domains, Lecture Notes in Math., 1341, Springer-Verlag, 1988.

[3] **M. Dauge,** Stationary Stokes and Navier-Stokes systems on two-or three-dimensional domains with corners I : Linearized equations, SIAM J. Math. Anal., Vol. 20, 1989, p. 74-97.

[4] **P. Grisvard,** Elliptic problems in nonsmooth domains, Monographs and studies in Math., 24, Pitman, 1985.

[5] **P. Grisvard,** Contrôlabilité exacte des solutions de l'équation des ondes en présence de singularités, J. Math. Pures et Appl., 68, 1989, p. 215-259.

[6] **P. Grisvard,** Singularités en élasticité, Archive for rational mechanics and analysis, Vol. 107, 1989, p. 157-180.

[7] **V.A. Kondratiev,** Boundary value problems for elliptic equations in domains with conical or angular points, Trans. Moscow Math. Soc., 16, 1967, p. 227-313.

[8] **V.A. Kozlov and V.G. Maz'ya,** Spectral properties of the operator bundles generated by elliptic boundary value problems in a cone, Functional Analysis and its applications, Vol. 22, 1988, p. 114-121.

[9] **V.A. Kozlov, V.G. Maz'ya and C. Schwab,** On the first boundary value problem of $3-D$ elasticity on conical domains, Preprint University of Maryland, 1989.

[10] **J.-L. Lions,** Contrôlabilité exacte, perturbations et stabilisation de systèmes distribués, tome 1, RMA 8, Masson, 1988.

[11] **V.G. Maz'ya and B.A. Plamenevskii,** Estimates in $L_p$ and in Hölder classes and the Miranda-Agmon maximum principle for solutions of elliptic boundary value problems in domains with singular points on the boundary, Amer. Math. Soc. Transl. (2), 123, 1984, p. 1-56.

[12] **V.G. Maz'ya and B.A. Plamenevskii,** On properties of solutions of three-dimensional problems of elasticity theory and hydrodynamics in domains with isolated singular points, Amer. Math. Soc. Transl. (2), 123, 1984, p. 109-124.

[13] **S. Nicaise,** Exact controllability of a pluridimensional coupled problem, Revista Matematica de la Universidad Complutense de Madrid, to appear.

[14] **S. Nicaise,** About the Lamé system in a polygonal or a polyhedral domain and a coupled problem between the Lamé system and the plate equation I : Regularity of the solutions, Pub. IRMA, Lille, Vol. 22, N°V, 1990.

[15] **S. Nicaise,** About the Lamé system in a polygonal or a polyhedral domain and a coupled problem between the Lamé system and the plate equation II : Exact contollability, Pub. IRMA, Lille, Vol. 24, N°III, 1991.

[16] **T. von Petersdorff,** Randwertprobleme der Elastizitätstheorie für polyeder-Singularitäten und approximation mit randelementmethoden, Thesis, Darmstadt (FRG), 1989.

[17] **A.M. Sändig, U. Richter and R. Sändig,** The regularity of boundary value problems for the Lamé equations in a polygonal domain, Rostocker Math. Kolloq., 36, 1989, p. 21-50.

[18] **J.B. Seif,** On the Green's function for the biharmonic equation in an infinite wedge, Trans. Amer. Math. Soc., 182, 1973, p. 241-260.

Université des Sciences et Techniques de Lille Flandres Artois
U.F.R. de Mathématiques Pures et Appliquées
U.R.A C.N.R.S. 751
F-59655 - VILLENEUVE D'ASCQ CEDEX (France)

G PORRU AND F RAGNEDDA

# A convexity property for functionals defined on the level sets of solutions to some non linear equations

## 1. Introduction

Let $M_t$, $a<t<b$, be a family of smooth closed n-hypersurfaces in the Euclidean space $R^{n+1}$, let $S_r$, $r = 1,\dots,n$, be the r-th elementary symmetric function of the principal curvatures $k_1,\dots,k_n$ of $M_t$, and let $\lambda=\nu^i\partial x^i/\partial t$, where $x=(x^1,\dots,x^{n+1})$ is a point in $M_t$ and $\nu = (\nu^1,\dots,\nu^{n+1})$ is the outer unit normal to $M_t$ at that point. Here and in the sequel the summation convention (from 1 to n+1) over repeated indices is in effect. We set $S_0=1$ and $S_{n+1}=0$.

For a function f of n variables the following formula was proved by R. C. Reilly in [9]:

$$\frac{d}{dt}\int_{M_t} f(S_1,\dots,S_n)dV = \int_{M_t}\lambda\Big(S_1 f(S_1,\dots,S_n) - \tag{1.1}$$

$$- \sum_r^{1,n}[S_r S_1-(r+1)S_{r+1}]D_r f(S_1,\dots,S_n) - \sum_r^{1,n}\sum_{i,j}^{1,n}\nabla_{ij}[D_r f(S_1,\dots,S_n)]T^{ij}_{r-1}\Big)dV,$$

where $D_r f(S_1,\dots,S_n)$ is the derivative of f with respect to $S_r$, $\nabla_{ij}$ indicate covariant differentiation on $M_t$ and $[T^{ij}_r]$ is the r-th Newton tensor associated with the matrix of the shape operator of $M_t$.

The proof of formula (1.1) given by Reilly in [9] is quite long. In section **2** of this paper we give an alternative proof in case $M_t$ are the level sets of a smooth function u(x). In our result, the last sum in the right hand side of (1.1) has a slight different representation. Moreover, we allow f to depend also on $\lambda$. In section **3** we apply the previous formula to obtain a result that may be considered as a natural generalization of a work by Philippin-Payne [7]. Namely, let $M_a$ and $M_b$ be two smooth hypersurfaces in $R^{n+1}$ enclosing convex domains and let $\Omega$ be the domain bounded internally by $M_a$ and externally by $M_b$. Let u(x) be the solution of the Dirichlet problem

$$\left(g(q^2)u_i\right)_i = 0 \tag{1.2}$$

$$u|_{M_a}=a, \quad u|_{M_b}=b.$$

Here (and in the sequel) $u_i$ denotes the derivative of u with respect to $x^i$, $i=1,\dots,n+1$, $q^2=u_iu_i$, and $g(q^2)$ is a smooth positive function satisfying

$$G(q^2) = g(q^2)+2\dot{g}(q^2)q^2 > 0, \tag{1.3}$$

where $\dot{g}(q^2)$ is the derivative of g with respect to $q^2$.

Let

$$M_t = \{x\in R^{n+1}: u(x)=t\}. \tag{1.4}$$

If F(t) is the n-dimensional measure of $M_t$, in [7] it is proved that

$$F(t)F''(t)-\varepsilon[F'(t)]^2 \geq 0, \tag{1.5}$$

where $F'(t)$ is the derivative of F(t) with respect to t, $F''(t)$ is the second derivative and $\varepsilon$ is defined by

$$\varepsilon = \min g(q^2)[G(q^2]^{-1}. \tag{1.6}$$

We generalize equation (1.2) by considering, for $r=0,\dots,n-1$, the equation

$$\left(g(q^2)T^i_{r,j}(D^2u)u_i\right)_j = 0, \tag{1.7}$$

where $[T^i_{0,j}(D^2u)]=I$ (the identity matrix), $[T^i_{r,j}(D^2u)] = T_r(D^2u)$, $r\geq 1$, is the r-th Newton matrix associated with the Hessian matrix $D^2u$, and $g(q^2)$ satisfies

$$G_r(q^2) = (r+1)g(q^2)+2\dot{g}(q^2)q^2 > 0. \tag{1.8}$$

If $S_0=1$ and $S_r$, $r\geq 1$, is the r-th elementary symmetric function of the principal curvatures of $M_t$ relative to a solution u of equation (1.7) we define

$$F_r(t) = \int_{M_t} S_r\,dV$$

and we prove that, for $r=0,\dots,n-1$ it results

$$F_r(t)F''_r(t) - \varepsilon[F'_r(t)]^2 \geq 0,$$

where $\varepsilon=\min g(q^2)[G_r(q^2)]^{-1}$.

Since $G_0(q^2)=G(q^2)$ and $F_0(t)=F(t)$ for $r=0$ our problem coincides with that one investigated by M. Longinetti [4] in dimension two and by Philippin-Payne [7] in n dimensions.

Equation (1.7) has been investigated by several authors. For $u\in R^2$ $(r=1)$ we refer to [11]. For $u\in R^{n+1}$ see [12] and [8]. In case $g(q^2)=1$, (1.7) may be written as $S_{r+1}(D^2u)=0$, $S_r(D^2u)$ being the r-th elementary symmetric function of the eigenvalues of $D^2u$. For this kind of equations we refer to [1,5,6].

## 2 Reilly's formula

Let $u(x)$ be a smooth function of n+1 variables such that, for $a<t<b$, its level hypersurfaces $M_t$ are smooth and closed. Suppose $M_t$ encloses $M_\tau$ when $t>\tau$. If $\Omega=\{x\in R^{n+1}: a<u(x)<b\}$ and $Du$ is the gradient of $u$ we assume $q=|Du|>0$ in $\Omega$. The outer unit normal $\nu$ at a point of $M_t$ is $\nu=q^{-1}Du$. We denote by $\nu^i$ the i-th component of $\nu$ ($\nu^i = q^{-1}u_i$), and by $\nu^i_j$ the derivative of $\nu^i$ with respect to $x^j$ $(i,j=1,\dots,n+1)$. The $(n+1)\times(n+1)$ matrix $B = [\nu^i_j-\nu^i_s\nu^s\nu^j]$ is the well known curvature matrix. One eigenvector of B is $\nu$, and the corresponding eigenvalue is zero. The n other eigenvalues of B are the principal curvatures $k_1,\dots,k_n$ of $M_t$. For our purposes the matrix B is not convenient, we prefer to operate with the matrix $A = [\nu^i_j]$. Let us prove the following

**Lemma 2.1** *Let* $A = [\nu^i_j]$, $B = [\nu^i_j-\nu^i_s\nu^s\nu^j]$. *The matrices* A *and* B *have the same eigenvalues.*

**Proof.** We consider $\nu$ as a $(n+1)\times 1$ matrix and denote by $\nu^T$ the transposed of of $\nu$. We have $\nu\nu^T=[\nu^i\nu^j]$ and $B = A-A\nu\nu^T$. Let us show that

$$B^r = A^r-A^r\nu\nu^T, \quad r=1,2,\dots. \tag{2.1}$$

For r=1 (2.1) is true by definition. Suppose it is true for r-1. Then we have

$$B^r = (A^{r-1}-A^{r-1}\nu\nu^T)(A-A\nu\nu^T) = A^r-A^r\nu\nu^T-A^{r-1}\nu\nu^T A+A^{r-1}\nu\nu^T A\nu\nu^T. \qquad (2.2)$$

Since $\nu$ is a unit vector, $\nu^i\nu^i=1$. As a consequence, $\nu^i\nu^i_j=0$ for $j=1,\ldots,n+1$. In matrix notations we have $\nu^T A=0$. Hence, the last two terms in (2.2) vanish, and (2.1) follows by induction. Now, let us note that $\mathrm{trace}(A^r\nu\nu^T) = \nu^{i_1}_{j_1}\nu^{j_1}_{j_2}\cdots\nu^{j_{r-1}}_{j_r}\nu^{j_r}\nu^{i_1}=0$. (The last equality holds because $\nu^{i_1}_{j_1}\nu^{i_1}=0$ for $j_1=1,\ldots,n+1$). Hence, by (2.1) it follows that $\mathrm{trace}(B^r)=\mathrm{trace}(A^r)$, $r=1,2,\ldots$. It is well known that these equalities for $r=1,\ldots,n+1$ imply that A and B have the same eigenvalues. The lemma is proved.

To the matrix $A=[\nu^i_j]$ we associate the r-th Newton matrix $T_r(A)$ by setting $T_0(A)=I$ (the identity matrix) and, for $r=1,\ldots,n$,

$$T_r(A) = S_r I-T_{r-1}(A)A, \qquad (2.3)$$

where $S_r$ is the r-th elementary symmetric function of the eigenvalues of A. By Lemma 2.1 the eigenvalues of A are $0,k_1,\ldots,k_n$, hence $S_r$, $r=1,\ldots,n$, is the r-th elementary symmetric function of the principal curvatures of $M_t$ and $S_{n+1}=0$. We also set $S_0=1$. Since the matrix $T_r(A)$ is a polynomial in A, it results $T_r(A)A = AT_r(A)$. As a consequence, since $\nu^T A=0$ we have

$$\nu^T T_r(A) = S_r\nu^T. \qquad (2.4)$$

If $[T^i_{r,j}(A)]=T_r(A)$ then it results

$$\left(T^i_{r,j}(A)\right)_i = 0, \quad j=1,\ldots,n+1. \qquad (2.5)$$

The proof of (2.5) makes use of the Schwarz theorem $(\nu^i_j)_s=(\nu^i_s)_j$. For details we refer to [10]. In [10] it is also proved that

$$\mathrm{trace}\left(T_r(A)A\right) = (r+1)S_{r+1}, \quad r=0,\ldots,n. \qquad (2.6)$$

**Theorem 2.1** (Reilly's formula) *If f is a smooth function of n+1 variables then it results*

$$\frac{d}{dt}\int_{M_t} f(S_1,\dots,S_n,q)dV = \int_{M_t} q^{-1}\Big(S_1 f(S_1,\dots,S_n,q)- \tag{2.7}$$

$$-\sum_r^{1,n}\left[S_r S_1-(r+1)S_{r+1}\right]D_r f(S_1,\dots,S_n,q)-\sum_r^{1,n}\left(D_r f(S_1,\dots,S_n,q)\right)_i T^i_{r-1,j}(A)\nu^j_s\nu^s+$$

$$+D_{n+1}f(S_1,\dots,S_n,q)q_s\nu^s\Big)dV,$$

*where* $D_{n+1}f(S_1,\dots,S_n,q)$ *is the derivative of* f *with respect to* q, *and the subscripts* i *and* s *denote partial differentiation with respect to* $x^i$ *and* $x^s$ *respectively.*

**Proof.** Let

$$G(t) = \int_{M_t} f(S_1,\dots,S_n,q)dV. \tag{2.8}$$

If we define

$$\Omega(\tau,t) = \{x\in R^{n+1}:\tau<u(x)<t\}\ ,a<\tau<t<b,$$

then we have

$$G(t)-G(\tau) = \int_{\partial\Omega(\tau,t)} f(S_1,\dots,S_n,q)dV, \tag{2.9}$$

where $\partial\Omega(\tau,t) = M_\tau \cup M_t$ with the normal $\nu$ oriented externally with respect to the domain $\Omega(\tau,t)$. (This follows by the assumption that, being $t>\tau$ , $M_t$ encloses $M_\tau$). In virtue of the divergence theorem, (2.9) implies

$$G(t)-G(\tau) = \int_{\Omega(\tau,t)} \left(f(S_1,\dots,S_n,q)\nu^s\right)_s dx = \tag{2.10}$$

$$= \int_{\Omega(\tau,t)}\left(\sum_r^{1,n} D_r f\ S_{r,s}\ \nu^s + D_{n+1} f\ q_s\nu^s + f\nu^s_s\right)dx,$$

where $S_{r,s}$ is the derivative of $S_r$ with respect to $x^s$, and the arguments of f are understood in the last integral. By (2.6), $S_r = r^{-1}T^i_{r-1,j}(A)\nu^j_i$. As a consequence (see [9] Lemma A)

$$S_{r,s} = T^i_{r-1,j}(A)(\nu^j_i)_s\ . \tag{2.11}$$

The last equality, integration by parts and use of (2.5) lead to

$$\int_{\Omega(\tau,t)} \sum_r^{1,n} D_r f \; S_{r,s} \nu^s dx = \int_{\Omega(\tau,t)} \sum_r^{1,n} D_r f \; T^i_{r-1,j}(A)(\nu^j_s)_i \nu^s dx = \tag{2.12}$$

$$= \int_{\partial\Omega(\tau,t)} \sum_r^{1,n} D_r f \; T^i_{r-1,j}(A)\nu^j_s \nu^s \nu^i dV - \int_{\Omega(\tau,t)} \sum_r^{1,n} (D_r f)_i T^i_{r-1,j}(A)\nu^j_s \nu^s dx-$$

$$- \int_{\Omega(\tau,t)} \sum_r^{1,n} D_r f \; T^i_{r-1,j}(A)\nu^j_s \nu^s_i dx.$$

Equality (2.4) (with r-1 instead of r) together with the equality $\nu^T A=0$ imply $\nu^T T_{r-1}(A)A=0$. The s-th component of this vector is $\nu^i T^i_{r-1,j}(A)\nu^j_s$, hence the integral over $\partial\Omega(\tau,t)$ in (2.12) vanishes. In order to evaluate the last integral in (2.12) let us note that $T^i_{r-1,j}(A)\nu^j_s\nu^s_i$ is the trace of $T_{r-1}(A)A^2$. By (2.3), $T_{r-1}(A)A^2=S_r A-T_r(A)A$. Hence, by also using equality (2.6), we find

$$T^i_{r-1,j}(A)\nu^j_s\nu^s_i = S_r S_1 -(r+1)S_{r+1}.$$

Therefore, by (2.12) we obtain

$$\int_{\Omega(\tau,t)} \sum_r^{1,n} D_r f \; S_{r,s} \nu^s dx = -\int_{\Omega(\tau,t)} \sum_r^{1,n} (D_r f)_i T^i_{r-1,j}(A)\nu^j_s \nu^s dx - \tag{2.13}$$

$$-\int_{\Omega(\tau,t)} \sum_r^{1,n} D_r f \; \left[S_r S_1 -(r+1)S_{r+1}\right] dx.$$

Insertion of (2.13) into (2.10) leads to

$G(t)-G(\tau) =$

$$=\int_{\Omega(\tau,t)} \left( - \sum_r^{1,n} (D_r f)_i T^i_{r-1,j}(A)\nu^j_s\nu^s - \sum_r^{1,n} D_r f \; \left[S_r S_1 -(r+1)S_{r+1}\right] + D_{n+1} f \; q_s \nu^s + f S_1 \right) dx=$$

$$=\int_\tau^t d\theta \int_{M_\theta} q^{-1} \left( - \sum_r^{1,n} (D_r f)_i T^i_{r-1,j}(A)\nu^j_s\nu^s - \sum_r^{1,n} D_r f \left[S_r S_1 -(r+1)S_{r+1}\right] + D_{n+1} f q_s \nu^s + f S_1 \right) dV,$$

where the Federer coarea formula has been used in the last step. By deriving with respect to t in this equation we obtain (2.7) and the theorem is proved.

**Corollary 2.1.** *If* $\alpha$ *is a real number and* $r=0,\ldots,n$, *we have*

$$\frac{d}{dt}\int_{M_t} q^{-\alpha} S_r\, dV = \int_{M_t} q^{-\alpha-1}\Big((r+1)S_{r+1} + \alpha\big[T^i_{r-1,j}(A) q_i \nu^j \nu^s q^{-1} - S_r q_s \nu^s q^{-1}\big]\Big) dV.$$

**Proof.** It follows by Theorem 2.1 when $f(S_1,\dots,S_n,q)=q^{-\alpha}S_r$.

**Remarks.** The assumption that $M_t$ encloses $M_\tau$ when $t>\tau$ is not essential. In the opposite case we can prove Theorem 2.1 and its Corollary by setting $\nu=-q^{-1}Du$. The function $\lambda$ that appears in formula (1.1) is $q^{-1}$ in our situation.

## 3 Convexity results

In the sequel we need the following

**Lemma 3.1.** *Let* B *be a symmetric* n×n *positive definite matrix with eigenvalues* $k_1,\dots,k_n$. *If* $T_r(B)$ *is the* r-th *Newton matrix relative to* B, *then it results*

$$S_r T_r(B) \geq S_{r+1} T_{r-1}(B), \qquad r=1,\dots,n-1, \tag{3.1}$$

*where* $S_r$ *is the* r-th *elementary symmetric function of* $k_1,\dots,k_n$.

**Proof.** For r=1 the proof of (3.1) is easy, so we take $r\geq 2$. Since $T_r(B)$ and $T_{r-1}(B)$ have the same eigenvectors, we may assume that both matrices in (3.1) are in diagonal form. Let $p_{r,n}$ be the eigenvalue of $T_r(B)$ which corresponds to the eigenvalue $k_n$ of B. In order to prove (3.1) it is enough to show that

$$S_r p_{r,n} \geq S_{r+1} p_{r-1,n}\,. \tag{3.2}$$

Let us verify that

$$p_{r,n} = \sum k_{i_1},\dots,k_{i_r}, \tag{3.3}$$

where the sum is extended over all indices satisfying $1\leq i_1<\dots<i_r\leq n-1$. Indeed, for r = 1 the assertion follows by the equality $T_1(B) = S_1 I - B$. Suppose (3.3) holds for r-1. Then, by $T_r(B) = S_r I - T_{r-1}(B)B$ we obtain

$$p_{r,n} = S_r - p_{r-1,n}k_n = S_r - \sum k_{i_1},\dots,k_{i_{r-1}} k_n = \sum k_{i_1},\dots,k_{i_r},$$

and (3.2) follows by induction. We have,

$$S_r = p_{r,n}+k_n p_{r-1,n}\ , \quad S_{r+1}= p_{r+1,n}+k_n p_{r,n}. \tag{3.4}$$

Insertion of (3.4) into (3.2) leads to

$$[p_{r,n}]^2 \geq p_{r+1,n}p_{r-1,n}. \tag{3.5}$$

Inequality (3.5) (that involves only positive terms) can be proved by verifying that each term of its right hand side is also present in the left hand side. (Note that the inequality is not sharp). The lemma is proved.

From now on $\Omega$ is assumed to be a ring-shaped domain in $R^{n+1}$ bounded internally by $M_a$ and externally by $M_b$, where $M_a$ and $M_b$ are smooth hypersurfaces enclosing convex domains. Let $u=u(x)$ be a smooth function defined in $\Omega$ and let $D^2u$ be its Hessian matrix. For $r=1,\dots,n$ we associate to $D^2u$ the r-th Newton matrix

$$T_r(D^2u) = S_r(D^2u)I-T_{r-1}(D^2u)D^2u, \tag{3.6}$$

where $S_r(D^2u)$ is the r-th elementary symmetric function of the eigenvalues of $D^2u$ and, as usual, $T_0(D^2u)=I$.

For a fixed r, $0\leq r\leq n-1$, let us consider in $\Omega$, the following Dirichlet problem

$$\left(g(q^2)T^i_{r,j}(D^2u)u_i\right)_j = 0, \tag{3.7}$$

$$u|_{M_a} = a, \quad u|_{M_b} = b, \qquad a<b, \tag{3.8}$$

where, as in the previous section, $u_i$ is the derivative of u with respect to $x^i$, $q^2=u_iu_i$, $\left[T^i_{r,j}(D^2u)\right]=T_r(D^2u)$ and $g(q^2)>0$ is a smooth function satisfying

$$G_r(q^2) = (r+1)g(q^2)+2\dot{g}(q^2)q^2 > 0, \tag{3.9}$$

$\dot{g}(q^2)$ being the derivative of $g(q^2)$ with respect to $q^2$. We continue to assume the summation convention from 1 to n+1 over repeated indices.

Let us show that equation (3.7) is invariant for rotations and translations.

**Lemma 3.2.** *Equation* (3.7) *is invariant under the linear transformation* $y=Cx+z$, *where* $C$ *is a* $(n+1)\times(n+1)$ *constant orthonormal matrix and* $z$ *is a fixed vector in* $R^{n+1}$.

**Proof.** Since $\left(T^{i}_{r,j}(D^2u)\right)_j=0$ for $i=1,\dots,n+1$ ([10]), equation (3.7) may be rewritten as

$$g(q^2)T^{i}_{r,j}(D^2u)u_{ij}+2\dot{g}(q^2)T^{i}_{r,j}(D^2u)u_{sj}u_s u_i = 0, \tag{3.10}$$

where the identities $qq_j=u_{sj}u_s$ have been used. Since $u_{ij}=u_{ji}$, by using matrix notations, (3.10) reads as

$$g(q^2)\operatorname{trace}\left[T_r(D^2u)D^2u\right]+ 2\dot{g}(q^2)DuT_r(D^2u)D^2u(Du)^T = 0, \tag{3.11}$$

where $Du$ is interpreted as a $1\times(n+1)$ matrix and $(Du)^T$ is its transposed. Let $\nabla u$ denote the gradient of $u$ with respect to $y$ and, similarly, let $\nabla^2u$ denote the Hessian matrix of $u$ with respect to $y$. Then we have $Du = \nabla uC$ and $D^2u = C^T\nabla^2uC$. Consequently, $q^2=Du(Du)^T=\nabla u(\nabla u)^T$ and

$$\operatorname{trace}\left[T_r(D^2u)D^2u\right]=(r+1)S_{r+1}(D^2u) = (r+1)S_{r+1}(\nabla^2u) = \operatorname{trace}\left[T_r(\nabla^2u)\nabla^2u\right]. \tag{3.12}$$

In proving (3.12) we made use of equality (2.6) for the matrices $D^2u$ and $\nabla^2u$. (That equality is proved in [10]). Since $T_r(D^2u)$ is a polynomial in $D^2u$, we also have

$$DuT_r(D^2u)D^2u(Du)^T= \nabla uCT_r(C^T\nabla^2uC)C^T\nabla^2uCC^T(\nabla u)^T= \nabla uT_r(\nabla^2u)\nabla^2u(\nabla u)^T. \tag{3.13}$$

By (3.11), (3.12) and (3.13) the lemma follows.

Now we are in a position to obtain equation (3.10) in normal coordinates. At a point $P\in\Omega$, let $M_t$ be the level set of $u$ at $P$. We may suppose $P$ is the origin of the axes. Let us perform a rotation so that the outer normal $\nu=q^{-1}Du$ to $M_t$ at $P$ coincides with the $x^{n+1}$ axis. Then, at this point we have

$$u_i=0,\ i=1,\dots,n;\ u_{n+1}=q;\ u_{i,n+1}=q_i,\ i=1,\dots,n+1,$$

where $u_{i,n+1}$ denotes the derivative of $u_i$ with respect to $x^{n+1}$ and $q_i$ is the derivative of q with respect to $x^i$. If $x^{n+1} = -\phi(x^1,\dots,x^n)$ is a local representation of $M_t$, then $u(x^1,\dots,x^n,-\phi(x^1,\dots,x^n))=t$. Consequently,

$$u_{ij} = \begin{cases} q\phi_{ij} & 1\le i,j\le n \\ q_i & i=1,\dots,n+1;\ j=n+1. \end{cases} \tag{3.14}$$

It is well known that the eigenvalues of the n×n matrix $D^2\phi=[\phi_{ij}]$ are the principal curvatures $k_1,\dots,k_n$ of $M_t$ at P. Since the eigenvalues of the matrix $A=[\nu^i_j]$ are $0,k_1,\dots,k_n$, the elementary symmetric functions of the eigenvalues of $D^2\phi$ are $S_r$, the same introduced in section **2**. If $S_r(D^2u)$ denotes the r-th elementary symmetric function of the matrix $D^2u$ we have, for $r=0,\dots,n-1$:

$$S_{r+1}(D^2u) = \left[q^{r+1}S_{r+1}+q_{n+1}q^rS_r - q^{r-1}\sum_{i,j}^{1,n} T^i_{r-1,j}(D^2\phi)q_iq_j\right], \tag{3.15}$$

where $T_r(D^2\phi)$, $r=0,\dots,n-2$, is the r-th Newton matrix associated with the n×n matrix $D^2\phi$, $T_{-1}(D^2\Phi)$ vanishes and $S_0=1$. Equality (3.15) is clear for r=0 and easy to prove for r=1. In order to prove it for r≥2 let us represent $S_{r+1}(D^2u)$ by using the generalized Kronecker symbol $\begin{pmatrix} i_1,\dots,i_r \\ j_1,\dots,j_r\end{pmatrix}$, where $i_1,\dots,i_r$ are distinct integers between 1 and n+1. The value of this symbol is 1 if $j_1,\dots,j_r$ is an even permutation of $i_1,\dots,i_r$, is -1 if such a permutation is odd, and is 0 otherwise. With this notation in mind we have ([10]):

$$S_{r+1}(D^2u) = [(r+1)!]^{-1}\begin{pmatrix} i_1,\dots,i_{r+1} \\ j_1,\dots,j_{r+1}\end{pmatrix}u_{i_1j_1}\dots u_{i_{r+1}j_{r+1}}.$$

Let us split this sum into three parts. First we take $i_h\le n$, $h=1,\dots,r+1$, and obtain the first sum in (3.15). After we take $i_h=n+1$ for some value of h and $j_h=n+1$ for the same value of h. Since $u_{n+1,n+1}=q_{n+1}$, we find the second sum in (3.15). Finally, we take the terms where $i_h=n+1$ for some value of h and $j_{h'}=n+1$ for h' different from h. Since $u_{n+1,i}=q_i$, $u_{j,n+1}=q_j$ and ([9,10])

$$T^{i}_{r-1,j}(D^2\phi) = [(r-1)!]^{-1}\begin{pmatrix} i_1,\dots,i_{r-1},i \\ j_1,\dots,j_{r-1},j\end{pmatrix}\phi_{i_1j_1}\cdots\phi_{i_{r-1}j_{r-1}},$$

we find the third sum in (3.15). We note that, (due to the fact that $D^2\phi$ is a nxn matrix) all indices $i, j, i_h$ and $j_h$ in the expression of $T^{i}_{r-1,j}(D^2\phi)$ run over $1,\dots,n$.

In order to evaluate the second sum of (3.10) let us recall that at our point P, $u_i=0$ for $i=1,\dots,n$ and $u_{n+1}=q$. Hence,

$$T^{i}_{r,j}(D^2u)u_{sj}u_su_i = T^{n+1}_{r,j}(D^2u)q_jq^2. \tag{3.16}$$

By [10] and (3.14) we have

$$T^{n+1}_{r,n+1}(D^2u) = (r!)^{-1}\begin{pmatrix} i_1,\dots,i_r,n+1 \\ j_1,\dots,j_r,n+1\end{pmatrix}u_{i_1j_1}\cdots u_{i_rj_r} = \tag{3.17}$$

$$= (r!)^{-1}\begin{pmatrix} i_1,\dots,i_r \\ j_1,\dots,j_r\end{pmatrix}\phi_{i_1j_1}\cdots\phi_{i_rj_r}q^r = S_rq^r,$$

where, in the last sum, the indices $i_h$, $j_h$ run over $1,\dots,n$. Finally, for $j=1,\dots,n$, it results

$$T^{n+1}_{r,j}(D^2u) = (r!)^{-1}\begin{pmatrix} i_1,\dots,i_r,n+1 \\ j_1,\dots,j_r,\ j\end{pmatrix}u_{i_1j_1}\cdots u_{i_rj_r} = \tag{3.18}$$

$$= [(r-1)!]^{-1}\begin{pmatrix} i_1,\dots,i_{r-1},i,n+1 \\ j_1,\dots,j_{r-1},n+1,j\end{pmatrix}\phi_{i_1j_1}\cdots\phi_{i_{r-1}j_{r-1}}q_iq^{r-1} =$$

$$= - T^{i}_{r-1,j}(D^2\phi)q_iq^{r-1},$$

where, as in the previous case, the indices i and j run over $1,\dots,n$. Since $T^{i}_{r,j}(D^2u)u_{ij} = (r+1)S_{r+1}(D^2u)$, by (3.10), (3.15)-(3.18) we find the desired form of equation (3.10) in normal coordinates:

$$\sum_{i,j}^{1,n} T^{i}_{r-1,j}(D^2\phi)q_iq_jq^{-1} - S_rq_{n+1} = g(q^2)[G_r(q^2)]^{-1}(r+1)S_{r+1}q, \tag{3.19}$$

with $G_r(q^2)$ defined by (3.9).

Now we prove the main result of this section.

**Theorem 3.1.** *For a fixed* r, $0\le r\le n-1$, *let* $u(x)$ *be a smooth solution of problem* (3.7)-(3.8) *such that the level sets* $M_t=\{x\in\Omega:\ u(x)=t\}$, *for* $a<t<b$, *enclose convex domains. If* $0<\varepsilon\le g(q^2)[G_r(q^2)]^{-1}$ *then it results*

$$F_r(t)F''_r(t) - \varepsilon[F'_r(t)]^2 \ge 0, \tag{3.20}$$

*where*

$$F_r(t) = \int_{M_t} S_r dV. \tag{3.21}$$

**Proof.** By Corollary 2.1 with $\alpha=0$ we have

$$F'_r(t) = (r+1)\int_{M_t} q^{-1}S_{r+1}dV. \tag{3.22}$$

Again by Corollary 2.1 with $\alpha=1$ and r replaced by r+1 we find

$$F''_r(t) \ge (r+1)\int_{M_t} q^{-3}\left[T^i_{r,j}(A)q_i\nu^j_s\nu^s - S_{r+1}q_s\nu^s\right]dV, \tag{3.23}$$

where the inequality $S_{r+2}\ge0$ (due to the convexity assumptions) has been used. Let $r\ge1$. If we are in the situation considered for obtaining equation (3.19) then (3.14) hold. Furthermore, at the point P we have $\nu=(0,\dots,0,1)$ and

$$\nu^{n+1}_j=0,\ j=1,\dots,n+1;\ \ \nu^i_{n+1}=q_iq^{-1},\ i=1,\dots,n;\ \ \nu^i_j=u_{ij}q^{-1}=\phi_{ij},\ i,j=1,\dots,n.$$

Hence,

$$T^i_{r,n+1}(A)\nu^{n+1}_s\nu^s = 0, \quad i=1,\dots,n+1,$$

$$T^{n+1}_{r,j}(A) = (r!)^{-1}\begin{pmatrix} i_1,\dots,i_r,n+1 \\ j_1,\dots,j_r,\ j\end{pmatrix}\nu^{j_1}_{i_1}\dots\nu^{j_r}_{i_r} = 0,\ j=1,\dots,n.$$

The last equalities are true because one $j_h$ is equal to n+1 and $\nu^{n+1}_{i_h}=0$. For $i,j=1,\dots,n$ we have

$$T^i_{r,j}(A) = (r!)^{-1}\begin{pmatrix} i_1,\dots,i_r,i \\ j_1,\dots,j_r,j\end{pmatrix}\nu^{j_1}_{i_1}\dots\nu^{j_r}_{i_r}.$$

When $j_h=n+1$ in the previous sum, the corresponding term vanishes (because

$\nu_h^{n+1}=0$), hence we may suppose $j_h$ and $i_h$ less then or equal to n. In this case $\nu^i_j=\phi_{ij}$ and, consequently, $T^i_{r,j}(A)=T^i_{r,j}(D^2\phi)$ for $i,j=1,..,n$. Therefore we have

$$T^i_{r,j}(A)q_i\nu^j_s\nu^s = \sum_{i,j}^{1,n} T^i_{r,j}(D^2\phi)q_iq_jq^{-1} \geq S_{r+1}[S_r]^{-1}\sum_{i,j}^{1,n} T^i_{r-1,j}(D^2\phi)q_iq_jq^{-1}, \quad (3.24)$$

where Lemma 3.1 (with $B=D^2\phi$) has been used in the last step. Insertion of (3.24) and (3.19) into (3.23) leads to

$$F''_r(t) \geq (r+1)\int_{M_t} q^{-3}\Big(S_{r+1}[S_r]^{-1}\big[T^i_{r-1,j}(D^2\phi)q_iq_iq^{-1} - S_rq_{n+1}\big]\Big)dV = \quad (3.25)$$

$$= (r+1)^2\int_{M_t} q^{-2}S^2_{r+1}[S_r]^{-1}g(q^2)[G_r(q^2)]^{-1}dV \geq \varepsilon(r+1)^2\int_{M_t} q^{-2}S^2_{r+1}[S_r]^{-1}dV,$$

where the hypothesis $g(q^2)[G_r(q^2)]^{-1} \geq \varepsilon$ has been used. Finally, by using (3.22), Holder inequality, (3.21) and (3.25) we find

$$[F'_r(t)]^2=(r+1)^2\left(\int_{M_t} q^{-1}S_{r+1}dV\right)^2\leq\int_{M_t} S_r dV(r+1)^2\int_{M_t} q^{-2}S^2_{r+1}(S_r)^{-1}dV\leq F_r(t)\varepsilon^{-1}F''_r(t),$$

from which the theorem follows when $r\geq1$. For $r=0$ the computation is much more easy and is left to the reader.

**Remark.** Condition $a<b$ in (3.8) is not essential. If $a>b$ we can prove Theorem 3.1 by setting $\nu=-q^{-1}Du$.

## References


[1] L. Caffarelli, L.Nirenberg, J.Spruck. *The Dirichlet problem for nonlinear second order elliptic equations, III: Functions of the eigenvalues of the Hessian,* Acta Math. **155** (1985), 261-301.

[2] G. Chiti, M. Longinetti. *Differential inequalities for the Minkowski functionals of level sets.* To appear in Proceedings Oberwolfach "General Inequalities" (1990) Birkhauser-Verlag.

[3] B. Kawol. *Rearrangements and convexity of level sets in P.D.E.*, Lectures Notes in Math., **1150**, Springer-Verlag (1985).

[4] M. Longinetti. *Some isoperimetric inequalities for the level curves of capacity and Green's functions on convex plane domains,* SIAM J.Math Anal. **19** (1988), 377-389.

[5] V. I. Oliker. *On the linearized Monge-Ampère equations related to the boundary value Minkowski problem and its generalizations,* Indam, Seminar on Monge-Ampère equations and related topics, Roma (1982), 79-112.

[6] V. I.Oliker. *Hypersurfaces in* $R^{n+1}$ *with prescribed Gaussian curvature and related equations of Monge-Ampère type,* Comm.Part.Diff.Eq.(1984),807-838.

[7] G.A. Philippin, L.E. Payne. *On the conformal capacity problem,* Indam, Symposia Math. Geometry of Sol. to PDE, Ac. Press, London (1989).

[8] G. Porru, S. Vernier. *On symmetrization and nonlinear variational equations*, to appear in Rev. Roumaine de Math. Pures and Appl.

[9] R.C. Reilly. *Variational properties of functions of the mean curvatures for hypersurfaces in space forms,* J. Differ. Geom. **8** (1973), 465-477.

[10] R.C.Reilly.*On the Hessian of a function and the curvatures of its graph,* Michigan Math. J., **20** (1973-74), 373-383.

[11] G. Talenti.*Some estimates of solutions to Monge-Ampère type equations in dimension two,* Ann. Mat. Scuola Norm. Sup. Pisa **8**, ser.4 (1981),183-230.

[12] K. Tso. *On symmetrization and Hessian equations,* J. d'Analyse Mathèmatique **52** (1989), 94-106.

Giovanni Porru, Francesco Ragnedda

Dipartimento di Matematica,

Via Ospedale 72

09124 Cagliari, Italy.

B D REDDY

# Existence of solutions to a quasistatic problem in elastoplasticity

## 1 Introduction

The purpose of this contribution is to examine the question of existence and uniqueness of solutions to a problem arising in the description of quasistatic behaviour of elastoplastic bodies. The quasistatic (as opposed to simply static or steady) nature of the problem is due to the fact that plastic behaviour can only be correctly described in terms of rates of change of certain variables (such as plastic strain); thus these contribute to the presence of rate quantities, and the problem is not therefore merely a boundary-value problem. On the other hand processes are assumed to occur sufficiently slowly so that inertial effects may be ignored. Thus acceleration does not appear in the problem. The quasistatic problem, while an approximation, is an important special case both mathematically as well as from a practical point of view, as the many papers on both of these aspects will confirm.

The first systematic study of the problem at hand is that of Duvaut and Lions [2], who considered the problem for a perfectly plastic material. Johnson [4] subsequently extended the analysis in [2] by approaching the problem in two stages; in the first stage the velocity is eliminated and the problem becomes a variational inequality posed on a time-dependent convex set. The second stage involves the solution for the velocity. A drawback of the two works [2] and [4] is the fact that, while the formulations adopted are convenient mathematically, they bear little relation to those used in practice, in computational approaches, for example. The contributions of Duvaut-Lions and Johnson also predated, and were therefore not in a position to draw on, the important works of Matthies, Strang, Temam and others [8,9,14] on existence for the displacement problem in perfect plasticity; this work gave rise to the definition and study of the space $BD(\Omega)$ of functions of bounded deformation, which are central to a proper study of the existence problem for perfectly plastic materials.

We make use of a formulation which has been extensively treated both theoretically and computationally over the last decade by Martin, Reddy and their coworkers [6,11,12,13]. The chief characteristic of this formulation is that, unlike conventional formulations in elastoplasticity (such as that presented, for example, in [2]) it is a logical extension of the standard displacement problem of linear elasticity in the sense that it reduces to this problem in the event that the body behaves elastically. We confine this study to one involving materials which undergo kinematic hardening; thus solutions are sought in Sobolev spaces. The corresponding problem for perfectly plastic materials will be approached separately.

The problem to be studied here has close parallels with quasistatic problems of frictional contact of elastic bodies ([1], [5], [7]). Certainly a superficial comparison confirms that the two problems have a similar structure, in that they are both variational inequalities of a parabolic nature, and the inequality arises from the nondifferentiability of a functional representing the internal dissipation. In this sense this problem (and the friction problem) differs from that studied in [2] and [4] in that these latter problems are both parabolic variational inequalities, the inequalities arising because the problems are posed on convex sets.

A further feature of the present approach is that existence is studied by first discretising in time, then by showing that the sequence of time- discretised solutions converges to the solution of the original problem. This approach will be of interest to those involved in computational studies of this problem since this is precisely the approach taken in such studies (see, for example, [12]). It is of interest to note that Andersson [1] has recently discussed a version of the friction problem using this approach.

The plan of the rest of this work is as follows. In Section 2 we give full details of the initial-boundary value problem, arriving at a suitable variational formulation. Then in Section 3 we approach the problem of establishing the existence and uniqueness of solutions to this problem. Finally, in Section 4 we conclude with some remarks concerning extensions of the theory presented here.

# 2 Formulation of the problem

We consider the initial-boundary value problem for quasistatic behaviour of an elastoplastic body which occupies a bounded domain $\Omega$ with Lipschitz boundary $\Gamma$. The plastic behaviour of the material is assumed to be describable within the classical framework of a convex yield surface coupled with the normality law. We adopt the form of the flow law in which the dissipation function, rather than the yield function, is employed. The advantages of this formulation have received comprehensive treatment in the works [6,11,12].

The material is assumed to undergo linear kinematic hardening. The assumption of a hardening material, apart from the fact that it represents realistic material behaviour, serves also to allow for a complete analysis within a Sobolev space framework, the case of perfect plasticity requiring special treatment (see, for example, [13,14]). The model incorporates also the classical assumption of no volume change accompanying plastic deformation.

Suppose that the system is initially at rest, and that it is initially undeformed as well as unstressed. A time-dependent field of body force $f(t) = f(x,t)$ is given, with $f(0) = 0$. We are required to find the displacement field $u(t) = u(x,t)$ and plastic strain field $p(t) = p(x,t)$ which satisfy, for $0 \le t \le T$, the equilibrium equation

$$\text{div } \sigma(u(t), p(t)) + f(t) = 0 \ , \tag{2.1}$$

the constitutive equations

$$\sigma(u,p) \ = \ C(\epsilon(u) - p) \ , \tag{2.2}$$

$$\sigma^D - hp \ \in \ \partial D(\dot{p}) \ , \tag{2.3}$$

the strain-displacement relation

$$\epsilon(u) = \tfrac{1}{2}(\nabla u + (\nabla u)^T) \tag{2.4}$$

and the condition of plastic incompressibility

$$\text{tr}p := I.p = 0 \tag{2.5}$$

or $p_{kk} = 0$ . Here and henceforth summation is implied on repeated indices, unless otherwise stated.

Equations (2.1) - (2.5) are required to hold on $\Omega$; here $\sigma$ is the stress tensor, $\sigma^D := \sigma - \frac{1}{3}(\text{tr } \sigma)I$ the stress deviator, $\epsilon$ is the strain tensor, $u$ the displacement vector and $p$ is the plastic strain tensor. A superposed dot denotes differentiation with respect to time. The quantity $C$ is a fourth order tensor of elastic coefficients and $D$ is a positively homogeneous convex function, the dissipation function. Thus $D$ has the properties

$$D(\theta p + (1-\theta)q) \ \leq \ \theta D(p) + (1-\theta)D(q) \ , \quad 0 < \theta < 1 \ \text{ and } p, q \in M^3, \tag{2.6}$$

$$D(\alpha p) \ = \ \alpha D(p) \ , \quad 0 < \alpha \in R, \tag{2.7}$$

where $M^3$ is the set of all symmetric $3 \times 3$ matrices, and we further assume that

$$D(q) \geq 0 \ , \quad D(0) = 0, \tag{2.8}$$

this last assumption being dictated by physical considerations. A simple example of a dissipation function is that corresponding to the von Mises yield condition, for which

$$D(q) = k|q| = k\sqrt{q_{ij}q_{ij}} \ , \tag{2.9}$$

$k$ being a positive scalar.

The material undergoes linear kinematic hardening, as mentioned earlier, and this is represented by the term $hp$ appearing in (2.3). This term is the back-stress, and $h$ is a scalar-valued hardening function (see, for example, [3]). We assume that $h \in L^\infty(\Omega)$, and that there is a constant $h_0 > 0$ such that

$$h(x) \geq h_0 > 0, \quad \text{a.e in } \Omega. \tag{2.10}$$

The elasticity tensor $C$ has the symmetry properties

$$C_{ijkl} = C_{jikl} = C_{klij}, \tag{2.11}$$

and we assume that

$$C_{ijkl} \in L^\infty(\Omega) \tag{2.12}$$

and that $C$ is strongly elliptic: there exists a constant $c_0 > 0$ such that

$$C_{ijkl}(x)\, \zeta_{ij}\, \zeta_{kl} \geq c_0|\zeta|^2 \quad \forall\, \zeta \in M^3\,, \quad a.e. \text{ in } \Omega\,. \tag{2.13}$$

Finally, we take the boundary condition to be

$$u = 0 \quad \text{on } \Gamma\,, \tag{2.14}$$

while the initial conditions are assumed to be

$$u(0) = 0 \quad \text{and} \quad p(0) = 0. \tag{2.15}$$

We will later seek the plastic strain in a class of traceless functions, that is, in a space $Q_0 = \{q : \text{tr } q = 0\}$ ($Q_0$ has of course to be specified more carefully in order to be able to achieve a existence result, but we leave this for later). Then (2.3) reads

$$D(q) - D(p) - (\sigma^D - hp).(q - p) \geq 0 \quad \forall q \in Q_0, \tag{2.16}$$

where the inner product on $M^3$ is defined by $p.q = p_{ij}q_{ij}$. From the definition of $\sigma^D$ and $Q$, though, we see that $\sigma^D.q = \sigma.q$ for any $q \in Q_0$, so that (2.16) (and (2.3)) may be replaced by

$$D(q) - D(p) - (\sigma - hp).(q - p) \geq 0 \quad \forall\, q \in Q_0. \tag{2.17}$$

We are now ready to present a preliminary form of the variational problem of interest. First we define the spaces

$$V = H_0^1(\Omega)^3, \qquad Q = \{q = (q_{ij}) : \ q_{ij} \in L^2(\Omega),\ q_{ji} = q_{ij}\},$$

and

$$Q_0 = \{q \in Q : \ \text{tr } q = 0\},$$

where $H_0^1(\Omega)$ is the space of distributions which together with their first derivatives are in $L^2(\Omega)$, and whose traces on $\Gamma$ vanish. Both $V$ and $Q$ are Hilbert spaces with inner products

$$(u, v)_V = \int_\Omega \frac{\partial u_i}{\partial x_j}\frac{\partial v_i}{\partial x_j}\, dx \quad \text{and} \quad (p, q)_Q = \int_\Omega p.q\; dx = \int_\Omega p_{ij}q_{ij} dx\,,$$

and norms $||v||_V = (v, v)^{\frac{1}{2}}$, $||q||_Q = (q, q)^{\frac{1}{2}}$. Furthermore, $Q_0$ is a closed subspace of $Q$.

We define also the product space $W = V \times Q$ which is a Hilbert space with the inner product

$$(z, w)_W \ := (u, v)_V + (p, q)_Q$$

and norm $||z||_W = (z, z)_W^{\frac{1}{2}}$, where $z = (u, p)$ and $w = (v, q)$, and the subspace $Z = V \times Q_0$, which is closed in the norm $||.||_W$. The topological dual of a Hilbert space $H$ is denoted by $H'$.

For any Hilbert space $H$ we denote by $C(0,T;H)$ the space of continuous functions $u:[0,T]\to H$ with the norm

$$||u||_{C(0,T;H)} = \max_{0\leq t\leq T} ||u(t)||_H, \tag{2.18}$$

and by $L^2(0,T;H)$ the space of all measurable functions $u:(0,T)\to H$ with the norm

$$||u||_{L^2(0,T;H)} = \left(\int_0^T ||u(t)||_H^2\, dt\right)^{\frac{1}{2}}. \tag{2.19}$$

The space of measurable functions $u:(0,T)\to H$ which are essentially bounded is denoted by $L^\infty(0,T;H)$, and is endowed with the norm

$$||u||_{L^\infty(0,T;H)} = \text{ess sup}_{0\leq t\leq T}||u(t)||_H. \tag{2.20}$$

The spaces $C(0,T;H)$ and $L^\infty(0,T;H)$ are Banach spaces, while $L^2(0,T;H)$ is a Hilbert space ([15], Chapter 23).

Given a Hilbert space H, we denote by $W^1(0,T;H)$ the space of functions $f\in L^2(0,T;H)$ with the property that $\dot{f}\in L^2(0,T;H)$. This space is a Hilbert space with norm given by

$$||f||^2_{W^1(0,T;H)} = ||f||^2_{L^2(0,T;H)} + ||\dot{f}||^2_{L^2(0,T;H)}.$$

We record here the fundamental inequality

$$||f(t)-f(s)||_H \leq \int_s^t ||\dot{f}(\tau)||_H\, d\tau \tag{2.21}$$

which holds for $s<t$ and $f\in W^1(0,T;H)$ ([15], page 446), and note also that $W^1(0,T;H)\subset C(0,T;H)$, the imbedding being continuous.

We introduce the bilinear form $a: W\times W\to R$ defined by

$$\begin{aligned} a(w,z) &= \int_\Omega C(\epsilon(u)-p^D).(\epsilon(v)-q^D)+hp^D.q^D\ dx \\ &= \int_\Omega C_{ijkl}\,(\epsilon_{ij}(u)-p^D_{ij})(\epsilon_{kl}(v)-q^D_{kl})+hp^D_{ij}q^D_{ij}\ dx\ , \end{aligned} \tag{2.22}$$

the linear functional

$$l(t)\ :\ W\to R\ ,\quad \langle l,z\rangle = \int_\Omega f(t).v\ dx$$

and the functional

$$j\ :\ W\to R\ ,\quad j(z) = \int_\Omega D(q)(x)\ dx\ , \tag{2.23}$$

where as before $w=(u,p)$ and $z=(v,q)$ .
The functionals $l(t)$ and $j(.)$ are easily shown to be bounded and, from the properties of $D$, $j(.)$ is a convex, positively homogeneous, nonnegative continuous functional. Note,

however, that $j$ *is not differentiable.*

We have the following result.

LEMMA 1. The bilinear form $a(.,.)$ is continuous on $W$ and $Z-$elliptic: there exist constants $\beta > 0$ and $\alpha > 0$ such that

$$|a(w,z)| \leq \beta ||w||_W ||z||_W \quad \text{for all } w, z \in W,$$

and

$$a(z,z) \geq \alpha ||z||_W^2 \quad \text{for all } z \in Z,$$

where the constant $\alpha$ is given by

$$\alpha = \tfrac{1}{2} h_0 \min\left\{1, \frac{K c_0}{c_0 + \frac{1}{2} h_0}\right\},$$

$K$ being the constant in Korn's inequality.

PROOF. Continuity is straightforward, and has been proved in [11]. Ellipticity is also verified there, but for the case in which $p^D$ and $q^D$ in the definition (2.22) of $a(.,.)$ are replaced by $p$ and $q$. In the problem considered in [11] the requirement tr $p = 0$ is not imposed, so that it is possible there to verify that the form is $W-$elliptic. For the present case we observe that, for any $z = (v,q) \in Z$,

$$\begin{aligned}
a(z,z) &\geq c_0 \int_\Omega |\epsilon(v) - q^D|^2 \, dx + h_0 \int_\Omega |q^D|^2 \, dx \\
&= c_0 \int_\Omega |\epsilon(v) - q|^2 \, dx + h_0 \int_\Omega |q|^2 \, dx \\
&= c_0 \int_\Omega \theta |\epsilon(v)|^2 + \left|\sqrt{1-\theta}\,\epsilon(v) - \frac{1}{\sqrt{1-\theta}} q\right|^2 + (h_0 - \frac{\theta}{1-\theta})|q|^2 \, dx \\
&\geq c_0 \int_\Omega \theta |\epsilon(v)|^2 + (h_0 - \frac{\theta}{1-\theta})|q|^2 \, dx
\end{aligned}$$

for any $\theta \in (0,1)$; here we have also used (2.10), (2.13) and the fact that $q^D = q$ for $q \in Z$. The result follows by using Korn's inequality [2] and by choosing $\theta = h_0/(2c_0 + h_0)$. □

REMARK. It is worth noting here that the bilinear form defined by (2.22) is *not* $W-$*elliptic*; indeed, $a(z,z) = 0$ for any $z$ of the form $z = (0, \alpha I)$, where $\alpha \in R$.

We are now ready to define the first variational problem.

PROBLEM P. Given $l \in W^1(0,T;Z')$ with $l(0) = 0$, find $w = (u,p) : [0,T] \to Z$ such that

$$a(w(t), z - \dot{w}(t)) + j(z) - j(\dot{w}(t)) - \langle l, z - \dot{w}(t)\rangle \geq 0 \tag{2.24}$$

for all $z \in Z$.

The formal equivalence of Problem P to the classical problem defined by (2.1) - (2.5) is readily established (see, for example, [12]). We take as fundamental the variational problem P, though, and investigate the question of existence and uniqueness of solutions to this problem.

## 3 Existence and uniqueness

The general problem is addressed in two stages: first, we discretise in time and establish the existence of a family of solutions $\{w_n\}_{n=1}^N$ to the discrete problems. The second stage entails the construction of a linear interpolate in time of the discrete solutions, and finally the demonstration that the limit, as the step size goes to zero, of the sequence of interpolates corresponds to the solution to problem P.

We begin by examining a time-discrete version of Problem P. The time interval $[0, T]$ is partitioned by $0 = t_0 < t_1 < ... < t_N = T$, where $t_n - t_{n-1} = \epsilon$. Given $l \in W^1(0, T; Z')$ we set $l_n = l(t_n)$ with $l_0 = 0$, and denote by $\Delta w_n$ the backward difference $w_n - w_{n-1}$ corresponding to a sequence $\{w_n\}_{n=0}^N$. Then we have

LEMMA 2. There exists a sequence $\{w_n\}_{n=0}^N$ in $Z$, with $w_0 = 0$, such that

$$a(w_n, z - \Delta w_n) + j(z) - j(\Delta w_n) - \langle l_n, z - \Delta w_n\rangle \geq 0 \tag{3.1}$$

for all $z \in Z$, for given $\{l_n\}_{n=0}^N \in Z'$ with $l_0 = 0$. Furthermore, corresponding to each $l_n$ the solution $u_n$ is unique, and there is a constant $c$, independent of $\epsilon$, such that

$$||\Delta w_n||_Z \leq c||\Delta l_n||_{Z'}. \tag{3.2}$$

PROOF. The inequality (3.1) may be rewritten as

$$a(\Delta w_n, z - \Delta w_n) + j(z) - j(\Delta w_n) \geq \langle l_n, z - \Delta w_n\rangle - a(w_{n-1}, z - \Delta w_n). \tag{3.3}$$

We now proceed inductively. For $n = 1$ the problem (3.3) has a unique solution $\Delta w_n = w_1$ since the bilinear form $a(.,.)$ is continuous and $Z-$ elliptic (by Lemma 1), the functional $j(.)$ is convex and continuous, and the functional on the righthand side of (3.3) is bounded and linear; existence and uniqueness follow from the standard theory of variational inequalities. Assuming now that the solution $w_{n-1}$ is known, we proceed in the same manner to show that a unique solution $w_n = \Delta w_n + w_{n-1}$ exists.

To derive the estimate (3.2) we set $z = 0$ in (3.1) to obtain

$$a(\Delta w_n, \Delta w_n) \leq \langle \Delta l_n, \Delta w_n\rangle + a(w_{n-1}, \Delta w_n) - j(\Delta w_n) + \langle l_{n-1}, \Delta w_n\rangle.$$

We show that $a(w_{n-1}, \Delta w_n) - j(\Delta w_n) + \langle l_{n-1}, \Delta w_n\rangle \leq 0$. Indeed, by replacing $n$ by $(n-1)$ and setting $z = \Delta w_{n-1} - \Delta w_n$ in (3.1) we obtain

$$\begin{aligned} 0 &\geq a(w_{n-1}, \Delta w_n) + \langle l_{n-1}, \Delta w_n\rangle + j(\Delta w_{n-1} - \Delta w_n) - j(\Delta w_n) \\ &\geq a(w_{n-1}, \Delta w_n) + \langle l_{n-1}, \Delta w_n\rangle - j(\Delta w_n); \end{aligned}$$

we use here the convexity and positive homogeneity of $j$, which give $j(\Delta w_{n-1}) \leq j(\Delta w_{n-1} - \Delta w_n) + j(\Delta w_n)$. Thus we arrive at the inequality

$$a(\Delta w_n, \Delta w_n) \leq \langle \Delta l_n, \Delta w_n \rangle;$$

the estimate (3.2) now follows from the $Z$−ellipticity of $a(.,.)$ and the boundedness of $\Delta w_n$. □

LEMMA 3. There exist constants $C_1,\ C_2 > 0$ such that

$$\max_{1\leq n\leq N} ||w_n||_Z \leq C_1, \tag{3.4}$$

$$\sum_{n=1}^{N} ||\Delta w_n||_Z^2 \leq C_2\epsilon. \tag{3.5}$$

PROOF. From (3.2) and (2.21) we have

$$\begin{aligned} ||w_n||_Z &= ||\sum_{k=1}^{n} \Delta w_k||_Z \\ &\leq \sum_{k=1}^{n} ||\Delta w_k||_Z \\ &\leq c\sum_{k=1}^{n} ||\Delta l_k||_Z \\ &\leq c\int_0^T ||\dot{l}(\tau)||_{Z'}\, d\tau. \end{aligned}$$

The inequality (3.3) now follows by taking the maximum over $n$.
To derive (3.5) we again begin by using (2.21) to get

$$||\Delta w_n||_Z \leq \int_{t_{n-1}}^{t_n} ||\dot{l}(\tau)||_{Z'}\, d\tau;$$

thus

$$\left|\left|\frac{\Delta w_n}{\epsilon}\right|\right|_Z^2 \leq \epsilon^{-1} \int_{t_{n-1}}^{t_n} ||\dot{l}(\tau)||_{Z'}^2\, d\tau,$$

using the Schwarz inequality. We now sum to obtain

$$\sum_{n=1}^{N} \left|\left|\frac{\Delta w_n}{\epsilon}\right|\right|_Z^2 \epsilon \leq \int_0^T ||\dot{l}(\tau)||_{Z'}^2\, d\tau = C_2,$$

as desired. □

We construct the linear interpolate $w_\epsilon$ of $\{w_n\}$ by setting

$$w_\epsilon(t) = (u_\epsilon(t), p_\epsilon(t)) = w_{n-1} + \frac{\Delta w_n}{\epsilon}(t - t_{n-1})$$

for $t_{n-1} \leq t \leq t_n$. Clearly $w_\epsilon$ belongs to $L^\infty(0,T;Z))$ while $\dot{w}_\epsilon \in L^2(0,T;Z)$. The next step is to establish that $w_\epsilon$ satisfies the variational inequality

$$
\begin{aligned}
0 \leq J_\epsilon \;\equiv\; & \int_0^T [a(w_\epsilon(t), z - \dot{w}_\epsilon(t)) + j(z) - j(\dot{w}_\epsilon(t)) - \langle l_\epsilon(t), z - \dot{w}_\epsilon(t)\rangle]\, dt \\
& + \tfrac{1}{2}a(w_N, z)\epsilon + \tfrac{1}{2}\langle l_N, z\rangle\epsilon + \tfrac{1}{2}c\epsilon \int_0^T ||\dot{l}(\tau)||^2_{Z'}\, d\tau \qquad (3.6)
\end{aligned}
$$

for all $z \in Z$, a.e. in $(0,T)$, where $l_\epsilon(t)$ represents the linear interpolate of $\{l_n\}_{n=1}^N$ and $c$ is the constant appearing in (3.2).

For this purpose we return to (3.1); we divide throughout by $\epsilon$, make use of the positive homogeneity of $j(.)$, and replace the arbitrary $z/\epsilon$ by $z$. Finally we multiply throughout by $\epsilon$ and sum to obtain

$$
\sum_{n=1}^N \epsilon\,[a(w_n, z - \delta w_n) + j(z) - j(\delta w_n) - \langle l_n, z - \delta w_n\rangle] \geq 0 \qquad (3.7)
$$

where $\delta w_n = \Delta w_n/\epsilon$. Now

$$
\begin{aligned}
\sum_{n=1}^N a(w_n, z)\epsilon &= \sum_{n=1}^N \tfrac{1}{2}a(w_n + w_{n-1}, z)\epsilon + \tfrac{1}{2}a(w_N, z)\epsilon \\
&= \sum_{n=1}^N \tfrac{1}{2}a(w_n - w_{n-1}, z)\epsilon + \sum_{n=1}^N a(w_{n-1}, z)\epsilon + \tfrac{1}{2}a(w_N, z)\epsilon \\
&= \sum_{n=1}^N \int_{t_{n-1}}^{t_n} a(w_{n-1} + (t - t_{n-1})\delta w_n, z)\, dt + \tfrac{1}{2}a(w_N, z)\epsilon \\
&= \int_0^T a(w_\epsilon, z)\, dt + \tfrac{1}{2}a(w_N, z)\epsilon.
\end{aligned}
$$

In the same way we find, after routine but tedious manipulations, that

$$
\begin{aligned}
\int_0^T a(w_\epsilon(t), \dot{w}_\epsilon(t))\, dt &= \sum_{n=1}^N a(w_n, \delta w_n)\epsilon - \tfrac{1}{2}\sum_{n=1}^N a(\delta w_n, \delta w_n)\epsilon^2 \\
&\leq \sum_{n=1}^N a(w_n, \delta w_n)\epsilon.
\end{aligned}
$$

The terms involving $j$ are handled in a trivial way; this leaves the term involving $l_n$ which becomes, after some manipulation,

$$
\begin{aligned}
-\sum_{n=1}^N \langle l_n, z - \delta w_n\rangle\epsilon &= -\int_0^T \langle l_\epsilon(t), z - \dot{w}_\epsilon(t)\rangle\, dt \\
& \quad -\tfrac{1}{2}\langle l_N, z\rangle\epsilon + \tfrac{1}{2}\sum_{n=1}^N \langle \Delta l_n, \Delta w_n\rangle.
\end{aligned}
$$

But from (3.2), (2.21) and the Schwarz inequality we have

$$\begin{aligned}\sum_{n=1}^{N}\langle \Delta l_n, \Delta w_n\rangle &\leq \sum_{n=1}^{N}||\Delta l_n||_{Z'}||\Delta w_n||_Z\\ &\leq c\sum_{n=1}^{N}||\Delta l_n||_{Z'}^2\\ &= c\epsilon\sum_{n=1}^{N}\int_{t_{n-1}}^{t_n}||\dot{l}(\tau)||_{Z'}^2\, d\tau\\ &= c\epsilon\int_0^T ||\dot{l}(\tau)||_{Z'}^2\, d\tau.\end{aligned}$$

Combining all of the above results, we obtain (3.6).

From (3.4), (3.5) and the definition of $w_\epsilon$ we see by direct evaluation that

$$||w_\epsilon||_{L^\infty(0,T;Z)} \leq C_1 \quad \text{and} \quad ||\dot{w}_\epsilon||_{L^2(0,T;Z)} \leq C_2\ .$$

It follows that there exists a subsequence, denoted also by $\{w_\epsilon\}$, and a member $w$ such that

$$w_\epsilon \overset{*}{\rightharpoonup} w \ \text{ in } \ L^\infty(0,T;Z)$$

and

$$\dot{w}_\epsilon \rightharpoonup \dot{w} \ \text{ in } \ L^2(0,T;Z)$$

as $\epsilon \to 0$ .

It remains to show that $w$ satisfies the variational inequality (2.24). We return to (3.6) and consider each of the terms appearing there. First, integrating by parts and using the fact that $w_\epsilon(0) = 0$, we obtain

$$\begin{aligned}\limsup_{\epsilon\to 0} -\int_0^T a(w_\epsilon(t), \dot{w}_\epsilon(t))\, dt &= -\liminf_{\epsilon\to 0}\ a(w_\epsilon(T), w_\epsilon(T))\\ &\leq -a(w(T), w(T)) = -\int_0^T a(w(t), \dot{w}(t))\, dt.\end{aligned}$$

Next,

$$\limsup_{\epsilon\to 0}\int_0^T a(w_\epsilon(t), z)\, dt = \int_0^T a(w(t), z)\, dt$$

and

$$\begin{aligned}\limsup_{\epsilon\to 0} -\int_0^T j(\dot{w}_\epsilon(t))\, dt &= -\liminf_{\epsilon\to 0}\int_0^T j(w_\epsilon(t))\, dt\\ &\leq -\int_0^T j(w(t))\, dt\end{aligned}$$

by the weak lower semicontinuity of $j$.

The three terms in $J_\epsilon$ which are coefficients of $\epsilon$ vanish in the limit as $\epsilon \to 0$ by virtue of the estimate (3.4) and the boundedness of $l$ (recall that $l \in C(0,T;Z')$).

This leaves the terms involving the approximation $l_\epsilon(t)$ to the linear functional $l(t)$. By assumption and construction we have $l, l_\epsilon \in L^2(0,T;Z')$; furthermore, since for $t_{n-1} \le t \le t_n$ we have

$$||l(t) - l_\epsilon(t)||_{Z'} \le ||l(t) - l(t_{n-1})||_{Z'} + \frac{|t - t_{n-1}|}{\epsilon} ||\Delta l_n||_{Z'}$$

it follows that $l_\epsilon \to l$ in $L^2(0,T;Z')$ as $\epsilon \to 0$.

Thus

$$\int_0^T \langle l_\epsilon(t), \dot{w}_\epsilon(t)\rangle dt \to \int_0^T \langle l(t), \dot{w}(t)\rangle dt$$

as $\epsilon \to 0$.

The groundwork is now complete; using the above results we have

$$\begin{aligned} 0 &\le \limsup_{\epsilon\to 0} J_\epsilon \\ &\le \int_0^T [a(w(t), z - \dot{w}(t)) + j(z) - j(\dot{w}(t)) - \langle l(t), z - \dot{w}(t)\rangle]\, dt \ . \end{aligned}$$

By a standard procedure ([2], page 57) of passing to the pointwise inequality we find from (3.8) that $w$ satisfies the variational inequality (2.24) a.e. on [0,T].

### Uniqueness

Suppose that Problem P has two solutions, $w_1$ and $w_2$. Denote by $\Delta w$ the difference $w_1 - w_2$. From (2.22) we have, setting $z = \dot{w}_2$ and then $z = \dot{w}_1$,

$$\begin{aligned} -a(w_1, \Delta\dot{w}) + j(\dot{w}_2) - j(\dot{w}_1) &\le -\langle l, \Delta\dot{w}\rangle \ , \\ a(w_2, \Delta\dot{w}) + j(\dot{w}_1) - j(\dot{w}_2) &\le -\langle l, \Delta\dot{w}\rangle \ . \end{aligned}$$

Adding, we get

$$0 \le a(\Delta w, \Delta\dot{w}) = \tfrac{1}{2}\, \frac{d}{dt}\, a(\Delta w, \Delta w) \ .$$

Integration, the $Z$-ellipticity of a(.,.), and the initial conditions $w_1(0) = w_2(0) = 0$ together yield $w_2 = w_1$ , as desired.

We summarise the results of this Section in

THEOREM 1. For every $l \in W^1(0,T;Z')$ with $l(0)$ there exists a unique $w = (u,p) \in L^\infty(0,T;Z)$ with $w(0)$, and satisfying $\dot{w} \in L^2(0,T;Z)$ . □

## 4 Further remarks

There are various aspects of this problem which require further attention. For example, the linear kinematic hardening law is the simplest possible; suitable extensions of this assumption would be, firstly, a nonlinear kinematic hardening law in which hardening is in the form of an exponential decay superimposed on the linear law; this is treated in a recent contribution [10], in which the main theme is the formulation and analysis of various mixed variational problems for elastoplastic materials. A further extension would be to consider the possibility of isotropic hardening.

As mentioned in the Introduction, the perfectly plastic problem (that is, with $h \equiv 0$) requires separate treatment. The essential aspect of the corresponding theory for perfectly plastic materials would be that we would seek $u(t)$ in the space $BD(\Omega)$ for suitable $p$. Also, it is expected that the components of plastic strain $p$ would be at best bounded measures. This theory awaits attention, but a reasonable idea of its framework may be found in [13]. The mixed problems treated in [10] are steady problems; that is, they correspond to a situation in which the plastic strain rate in (2.3) is replaced simply by the plastic strain, or alternatively they could be viewed as a form of the time-discrete problem (3.1). A complete analysis of the quasistatic mixed problem still awaits attention. Likewise the dynamic problem, in which inertial effects are included, remains to be studied; this would of course take the form of a hyperbolic variational inequality, albeit not of standard form.

Finally, it would be useful to weaken somewhat the smoothness assumption on the force $f$, and hence on $l$, so that the results become valid for $l \in L^2(0, T; Z')$, for example.

## Acknowledgement

Support from the Foundation for Research Development is gratefully acknowledged.

## References

1. L-E Andersson, A quasistatic frictional problem with normal compliance. *Nonlinear Analysis* **16** (1991) 347-369.

2. G Duvaut and J L Lions, *Inequalities in Mechanics and Physics.* Springer, Berlin (1976).

3. R A Eve, B D Reddy and R T Rockafellar, An internal variable theory of plasticity based on the maximum plastic work inequality. *Quart Appl Math* **48** (1990) 59-84.

4. C Johnson, Existence theorems for plasticity problems. *Jour Math pures et appl.* **55** (1976) 431-444.

5. A Klarbring, A Mikelič and M Shillor, On friction problems with normal compliance. *Nonlinear Analysis* **13** (1990) 935-955.

6. J B Martin and B D Reddy, Variational principles and solution algorithms for internal variable formulations of problems in plasticity. In *Omaggio a Giulio Ceradini* (ed U Andreaus *et al*) Università di Roma, Roma (1988) 465-477.

7. J A C Martins and J T Oden, Existence and uniqueness results for dynamic contact problems with nonlinear normal and friction interface laws. *Nonlinear Analysis* **11** (1986) 407-428.

8. H Matthies, Existence theorems in thermo-plasticity. *Jour de Mécanique* **18** (1979) 695-712.

9. H Matthies, G Strang and E Christiansen, The saddle point of a differential program. In *Energy Methods in Finite Element Analysis.* (ed Glowinski, Rodin and Zienkiewicz). Wiley (London) (1979) 309-318.

10. B D Reddy, Mixed variational inequalities arising in elastoplasticity. (In review).

11. B D Reddy and T B Griffin, Variational principles and convergence of finite element approximations of a holonomic elastic-plastic problem. *Numer Math* **52** (1988) 101-117.

12. B D Reddy and J B Martin, Algorithms for the solution of internal variable problems in plasticity. *Comp Meths Appl Mech Engng* (to appear).

13. B D Reddy and F Tomarelli, The obstacle problem for an elastic-plastic body. *Appl Math Opt* **21** (1990) 89-110.

14. R Temam, *Mathematical Problems in Plasticity.* Gauthier- Villars (Paris) (1985).

15. E Zeidler, *Nonlinear Functional Analysis and Applications. IIA: Linear Monotone Operators.* Springer, Berlin (1990).

B D Reddy
Department of Applied Mathematics
University of Cape Town
7700 RONDEBOSCH
South Africa

T ROUBÍČEK

# A note about optimality conditions for variational problems with rapidly oscillating solutions

This brief note wants to draw an attention to a challenging observation that usual differential-equation apparatus is not appropriate for description of systems whose solutions admit "rapid oscillation" expressed in the limit in terms of Young measures [7], see also [1,6]. (This is parallel to that the classical differential equations are not appropriate when the solution is only weak, without sufficiently many continuous derivatives.) It is quite usual (see e.g. [2] or, for an evolution case [3]) that the Young-measure solution is merely put into a standard differential equation. This is surely a useful tool if one shows additionally that the Young-measure solution is a usual one, i.e. the Young measure is of a Dirac-mass type. Otherwise, this approach is not entirely correct, which we want to demonstrate on the following simple one-dimensional, scalar variational problem:

$$\Phi(u) \equiv \int_{-1}^{1} \varphi(x, u, u'(x))\,\mathrm{d}x \;\to \inf\;, \qquad u \in H_0^1(-1,1) \tag{1}$$

with $H_0^1$ the usual Sobolev space with zero traces. For simplicity, we will first investigate the concrete, rather trivial choice of $\varphi$:

$$\varphi(x,u,p) \equiv \varphi(x,p) = (1+\mathrm{sgn}(x.p)/2)p^2\;, \tag{2}$$

where $\mathrm{sgn}(\xi) = \xi/|\xi|$, with $\mathrm{sgn}(0) = 0$. In this example, $\varphi(x,u,.)$ is even convex and (1)-(2) apparently admits the only solution $u \equiv 0$. The corresponding Euler-Lagrange equation in the weak formulation looks as follows:

$$\langle \mathrm{D}\Phi(u), v\rangle \;=\; \int_{-1}^{1}(2+\mathrm{sgn}(x.u'(x)))u'(x)v'(x)\,\mathrm{d}x \;=\; 0 \quad \forall v \in H_0^1(-1,1)\,. \tag{3}$$

Of course, $\langle .,. \rangle$ denotes the duality pairing between $H^{-1}(-1,1)$ and $H_0^1(-1,1)$, and $\mathrm{D}\Phi(u) \in H^{-1}(-1,1)$ is the Gâteaux derivative of $\Phi$ at $u$.

We want to admit "rapid oscillations" of $u'$, which can actually occure when $\varphi(x,u,.)$ is not convex. Then, without going into details about the growth (cf. [1]), the Young-measure solution will be here understood as a couple $(u,\mu)$ with $u \in H_0^1(-1,1)$ and $\mu : [-1,1] \to \mathrm{rpm}(\mathsf{R})$ such that

$$\int_{\mathsf{R}} p\,\mu(x)(\mathrm{d}p) \;=\; u'(x) \qquad \text{for a.a. } x \in [-1,1]\;, \tag{4}$$

with "rpm" standing for regular probability measures. Of course, (4) ensures that $\mu$ plays actually the role of $u'$. Putting the Young-measure solution $(u,\mu)$ into (1) and (3) transforms them respectively to

$$\bar{\Phi}(u,\mu) \;\equiv\; \int_{-1}^{1}\int_{\mathsf{R}} \varphi(x,u,p)\mu(x)(\mathrm{d}p)\mathrm{d}x \;\to \min\;, \tag{5}$$

and, for all $v \in H_0^1(-1,1)$:

$$\langle \overline{\mathrm{D}\Phi}(u,\mu), v\rangle \;=\; \int_{-1}^{1}\left[\int_{\mathsf{R}}(2+\mathrm{sgn}(x.p))p\;\mu(x)(\mathrm{d}p)\right]v'(x)\;\mathrm{d}x \;=\; 0\;. \tag{6}$$

Obviously, (5)–(4) with $\varphi$ from (2) has again the only solution, namely $(u,\mu)$ with $u(x)=0$ and $\mu(x)=\delta_0$ for all $x\in[-1,1]$, where $\delta_p$ denotes the Dirac distribution at the point $p\in\mathsf{R}$. However, (6)–(4) admits a large variety of solutions that have nothing common with (5)! Indeed, every couple $(u,\mu)$ with $u$ an arbitrary Lipschitz function from $H_0^1(-1,1)$ nondecreasing in the interval [-1,0] and nonincreasing in [0,1] and with $\mu(x)=\frac{1}{2}\delta_{3u'(x)}+\frac{1}{2}\delta_{-u'(x)}$ will satisfy both (4) and (6). We can observe that (6)–(4) lost even the coercivity.

The explanation of this effect is the following. The Euler-Lagrange equation (3) represents the first-order necessary optimality condition, i.e. $\mathrm{D}\Phi$ vanishes, where the Gâteaux derivative $\mathrm{D}\Phi$ respects the geometry of the Sobolev space $H_0^1$. This condition was extended continuously onto a finer "compactification" (i.e. the space of Young-measure solutions), which gave (6) — the bar in (5) and (6) denotes the continuous extension. It can be shown by using the Ekeland $\varepsilon$-variational principle that every minimizer $(u,\mu)$ of (5) will actually satisfy (6). Indeed, by density and countability arguments, there always exists a sequence $\{u_\varepsilon\}_{\varepsilon>0}\subset H_0^1(-1,1)$ converging to $(u,\mu)$ for $\varepsilon\searrow 0$ in the sense that $u_\varepsilon\to u$ weakly in $H_0^1(-1,1)$ and $\delta_{u'_\varepsilon(.)}\to\mu$ in the sense of Young measures. Since $(u,\mu)$ is a minimizer, we may additionally suppose that $\Phi(u_\varepsilon)\le\inf_{v\in H_0^1(-1,1)}\Phi(v)+\varepsilon$. By Ekeland's principle, there is another sequence $\{\tilde u_\varepsilon\}_{\varepsilon>0}$ such that $\|u_\varepsilon-\tilde u_\varepsilon\|\le\sqrt{\varepsilon}$ and $\|\mathrm{D}\Phi(\tilde u_\varepsilon)\|_*\le\sqrt{\varepsilon}$, where $\|.\|$ and $\|.\|_*$ denote the norms in $H_0^1(-1,1)$ and $H^{-1}(-1,1)$, respectively. By continuity arguments, $\tilde u_\varepsilon$ will again converge to $(u,\mu)$ and $\mathrm{D}\Phi(\tilde u_\varepsilon)$ will converge weakly in $H^{-1}(-1,1)$ to the continuously extended Gâteaux derivative $\overline{\mathrm{D}\Phi}(u,\mu)$. It shows that $\overline{\mathrm{D}\Phi}(u,\mu)=0$, which is (6). In other words, (6) still represents necessary optimality conditions, but, as demonstrated above, only very little selective.

Realizing that Young measures form not only a compact, but also convex set with respect to a natural geometry, we can exploit theory of convex compactification developed in [4], and derive the correct first-order necessary condition (i.e. the Gâteaux derivative of the extended potential $\bar\Phi$ belongs to a negative normal cone) which uses actually the natural geometry of Young measures; cf. [5]. Supposing certain continuity of $\varphi$ and of its partial derivative $\varphi'_u$, this condition for $(u,\mu)$ to solve (5) takes the following, variational-inequality form; cf. also [5; (3.13)]:

$$\int_{-1}^{1}\left[\int_{\mathsf{R}}\varphi'_u(x,u(x),p)(v(x)-u(x))\;\mu(x)(\mathrm{d}p)\right. \tag{7}$$
$$\left.+\;\varphi(x,u(x),v'(x))-\int_{\mathsf{R}}\varphi(x,u(x),p)\mu(x)(\mathrm{d}p)\right]\;\mathrm{d}x\;\ge\;0\qquad\forall v\in H_0^1(-1,1)\,.$$

Such optimality conditions are as much selective as possible: supposing a coercivity of the problem, they are not only neccesary, but also sufficient provided the minimized potential $\bar\Phi$ is convex in the Young-measure geometry, which will happen for example if the integrand $\varphi$ takes the form

$$\varphi(x,u,p)=\varphi_0(x,u)+\varphi_1(x,p) \tag{8}$$

with $\varphi_0(x,.)$ convex; let us emphasize that $\varphi_1(x,.)$ need not be convex. On the other hand, (7)–(4) is unfortunately not much effective in the sense that it does not say much more than (5)–(4), which can be clearly seen when the potential $\bar{\Phi}$ is affine in the Young-measure geometry (it happens if and only if $\varphi$ is of the form (8) with $\varphi_0(x,.)$ affine). In this affine case, (7)–(4) is merely equivalent with (5)–(4). In other words, it can be also said that we did not (and probably even cannot) move too far from the extended variational problem (5)–(4), unlike we moved from (1) when wrote (3).

In problems from optimal control theory, the conditions of the type (7), being called the integral maximum principle there, can be localized in the variable $x$, which gives effective conditions of the Pontryagin type. Unfortunately, in variational problems this does not seem possible except very special cases.

Let us still remark that, if we do not insist on the Young-measure interpretation like in the above $L^\infty$-case, an analogical theory can be built also for the $L^p$-case, $p \geq 1$; cf. [5]. The difficulty with an escape of mass to infinity (see e.g. [6]) does not then appear at all.

*Acknowledgement.* This research was partly made while the author was supported by the Alexander von Humboldt Foundation, which also supported the presentation of this contribution on this conference.

## References.

1. J.Ball: *A version of the fundamental theorem for Young measures.* Preprint Heriot-Watt University, Edinburgh.

2. M.Chipot, D.Kinderlehrer: *Equilibrium configurations of crystals*, Archive Rat. Mech. Anal. **103** (1988), 237–277.

3. R.J. DiPerna, A.J.Majda: *Oscillations and Concentrations in Weak Solutions of the Incompressible Fluid Equations.* Commun. Math. Phys. **108** (1987), 667–689.

4. T.Roubíček: *Convex compactifications and special extensions of optimization problems*, Nonlinear Analysis, Th. Meth. Appl. **16** (1991) (in print)

5. T.Roubíček: *Minimization on convex compactifications and relaxation of nonconvex variational problems*, Report DFG No. 260, University of Augsburg, 1990. (to appear in: Advances in Math. Sciences and Appl.)

6. M. Valadier: *Young measures.* In: Methods of Nonconvex Analysis, Varena 1989 (A.Cellina, Ed.), Lecture Notes in Math. **1446**, Springer, Berlin, 1990, pp. 152–188.

7. L.C. Young: *Lectures on the Calculus of Variations and Optimal Control Theory.* W.B. Saunders Comp., Philadelphia, 1969.

*Author's address:*
Institute of Information Theory and Automation, Czechoslovak Academy of Sciences
Pod vodárenskou věží 4, CS-182 08 Praha 8, Czechoslovakia

*Presently on leave at:*
Institut für Mathematik der Universität Augsburg, Universitätsstraße 8, W-8900 Augsburg, Germany